Oxford IB Diploma Prog

PSYCHOLOGY

COURSE COMPANION

John Crane

Jette Hannibal

OXFORD
UNIVERSITY PRESS

OXFORD
UNIVERSITY PRESS

Great Clarendon Street, Oxford OX2 6DP

Oxford University Press is a department of the University of Oxford.
It furthers the University's objective of excellence in research,
scholarship, and education by publishing worldwide in

Oxford New York

Auckland Cape Town Dar es Salaam Hong Kong Karachi
Kuala Lumpur Madrid Melbourne Mexico City Nairobi
New Delhi Shanghai Taipei Toronto

With offices in

Argentina Austria Brazil Chile Czech Republic France Greece
Guatemala Hungary Italy Japan Poland Portugal Singapore
South Korea Switzerland Thailand Turkey Ukraine Vietnam

Oxford is a registered trade mark of Oxford University Press
in the UK and in certain other countries

© Oxford University Press 2012

British Library Cataloguing in Publication Data

Data available

ISBN: 978-0-19-838995-8

10 9 8

Printed in China

Acknowledgments

Suso Rodríguez-Blanco: I would like to dedicate this book to the loving memory of
The authors and publisher are grateful for permission to reproduce the following
copyright material:

Sir Frederic C Bartlett: extract from 'The War of the Ghosts' in Remembering: A
study in Experimental and Social Psychology (Cambridge University Press, 1932,
1995, 1997), reproduced by permission of the publisher.

Elizabeth Loftus and Katherine Ketcham: extract from Witness for the Defense: The
Accused, the Eyewitness, and the Expert Who Puts Memory on Trial (St Martin's
Press, 2001), reproduced by permission of Palgrave Macmillan.

Elizabeth F Loftus and John C Palmer: Table 1 and Table 2 from 'Reconstruction
of Automobile Destruction: An Example of Interaction Between Language and
Memory', Journal of Verbal Learning and Verbal Behaviour 13 (1974), copyright ©
1974, reproduced by permission of Elsevier.

Kay Randall: extract from 'Born to be a Bully? Study shows stress can change your
mind', reproduced by permission of Kay Randall, the University of Texas at Austin.

Marjorie Roberts: extracts from 'School yard menace: millions of bullies are making life miserable for millions of defenseless victims. What makes them mean?'
Psychology Today Vol. 22 Issue 2, February 1988, reproduced by permission of the
publishers.

Oliver Sachs: extract from Musicophilia, 'The Abyss: Music and Amnesia' first
published in The New Yorker, 24 September 2007, copyright © Oliver Sachs 2007,
reproduced by permission of The Wylie Agency.

Michael Shermer: adapted extract from 'The Doping Dilemma', Scientific American
Mind April 2008, reproduced by permission of the author.

Deborah Wearing: extract from Forever Today: A Memoir of Love and Amnesia
(Doubleday, 2005), reproduced by permission of The Random House Group Ltd and
Curtis Brown Ltd. London.

We are also grateful to the International Baccalaureate Organization for permission
to reproduce material from the IB Diploma Programme Psychology subject guide
and extended essay guide.

p. 7 Pidjoe/iStockphoto; p. 9 Karsten Schley/CartoonStock; p. 10 (top) Carnegie Mel-
lon; (bottom) Katya Monakhova/iStockphoto; p. 11 Bettmann/Corbis; p. 15 Evgenyb/
Dreamstime.com; p. 17 MadJack Photography/iStockphoto; p. 18 track5/iStockphoto;
p. 28 Sabrih/Dreamstime.com; p. 31 Michael De Leon/iStockphoto; p. 41 IMAGNO/
Austrian Archives; p. 42 Warren Anatomical Museum, Francis A. Countway Library
of Medicine; p. 44 Oak Ridge National Laboratory/US Department of Energy/Sci-
ence Photo Library; p. 45 Thomas Nixon, Karolinska Institute University Library;
p. 48 Neil Marchand/Liewig Media Sports/Corbis; p. 49 John Heseltine (c) Dorling
Kindersley, Courtesy of the Museo e Galleria Borghese, Rome; p. 52 pmphoto/
iStockphoto; p. 57 (top) Time Life Pictures/Stringer/Getty Images; (bottom) Tetsuro
Matsuzawa,Primate Research Institute, Current Biology, 2007;

p. 59 Proc Biol Sci. 2004 May 7; 271(Suppl 4): S131–S133/Val Curtis, London School
of Hygiene and Tropical Medicine; p. 61 Phartisan/Dreamstime.com; p. 63 Yuri
Panyukov/iStockphoto; p. 70 Bob Thomas/Contributor/Bob Thomas Sports Photog-
raphy/Getty Images; p. 73 Psychology Press; p. 76 Karl Schoendorfer/Rex Features;
p. 77 Scientific Learning Corporation (www.brainconnection.com); p. 89 The Brain
from Top to Bottom, Canadian Institutes of Health Research (http://thebrain.mcgill.
ca); p. 92 Walking Home, Floyd Honey Foundation (http://www.walkinghome.ca); p.
95 Brad C. Bower/Associated Press; p. 97 (top) Juda Ngwenya/Reuters; (bottom) map
created by Adrian White, University of Leicester (2006), data from UNESCO, the
WHO, the New Economics Foundation, the Veenhoven Database, the Latinbarom-
eter, the Afrobarometer, the CIA, and the UN Human Development Report; p. 104
Olaf Loose/iStockphoto; p. 107 Rich Legg/iStockphoto; p. 112 Jose Manuel Gelpi Diaz/
iStockphoto; p. 113 (top) Albert Bandura; (bottom) Jon Brenneis/Contributor/Time
& Life Pictures/Getty Images; p. 122 Andrew Toos/CartoonStock; p. 125 VCL/Chris
Ryan/Taxi/Getty Images; p. 129 Andrés Peiró Palmer/iStockphoto; p. 131 (top) Rapid
Eye Media/iStockphoto; (bottom) Ryan Klos Photography/iStockphoto; p. 132 from
Eye of the Storm, the very first documentary about Elliott's "blue eyes/brown eyes"
exercise, made by William Peters in 1970 for ABC News; p. 140 David Young-Wolff/
PhotoEdit; p. 158 http://flickr.com/photos/mrflip/94551489/; p. 164 (top) Promotional
photograph for the 1957 film The Prince and the Showgirl; (bottom) Fotovampir/
Dreamstime.com; p. 166 DoctorKan/Stockexpert; p. 168 Two Humans/iStockphoto;
p. 174 Will McIntyre/Science Photo Library; p. 183 (bottom) ktsdesign/Photolia; p.
186 Activa/Fotolia; p. 187 (top) Alexey Bannykh/Fotolia; (bottom) Jaimie Duplass/
Fotolia; p. 192 Digitalpress/SnapVillage; p. 198 Pawel Strykowski/Dreamstime; p. 200
Ivan Melenchon Serrano/MorgueFile; p. 201 Klaas Lingbeek-van Kranen/iStockphoto;
p. 202 Bettmann/Corbis; p. 207 Gary Sludden/iStockphoto; p. 208 Culver Pictures;
p. 213 Ecophoto/Dreamstime.com; p. 218 Scott Liddell/MorgueFile; p. 221 Tihis/
Dreamstime.com; p. 229 (top) Capital Pictures; p. 231 Floresco Productions/Corbis;
p. 236 morgueFile; p. 237 WHO http://www.who.int/tobacco/mpower/gtcr_download/
en/index.html; p. 239 (left) from OECD Health Statistics 2004, published in Maria
L. Loureiro, "Obesity: Economic Dimensions of a 'SuperSize' Problem", Choices,
fall 2004 (American Agricultural Economics Association), p. 36; (right) Jakubcejpek/
Dreamstime; p. 241, Drivers.com; p. 243 Natural History Museum, Vienna; p. 244
Wallenrock/Shutterstock; p. 245 (top) Food Standards Agency © Crown copyright
material is reproduced with the permission of the Controller of HMSO and Queen's
Printer for Scotland; (bottom) courtesy of "Go for your life" , a Victorian govern-
ment initiative managed by Cancer Council Victoria and Diabetes Australia, Vic.; p.
252 Christopher Dodge/Fotolia; p. 252 from The American Society on Aging and the
American Society of Consultant Pharmacists Foundation (www.adultmeducation.
com); p. 253 Dan Reynolds/CartoonStock; p. 256 Terry Lynch, talsgd.com; p. 257
Social Marketing Institute (www.social-marketing.org); p. 258 Nick Moir/Faixfax
Photos; p. 263 With kindly permission www.john-rabe.de; p. 264 John Darley; p.
267 Chambon Foundation; p. 268 clotilde hulin/iStockphoto; p. 273 Ivan Melenchon
Serrano/MorgueFile; p. 274 (top) from Edge Foundation (www.edge.org); (bottom)
Christina Murrey, The University of Texas at Austin; p. 278 from E Berscheid and H
Reis, "Attraction and close relationships" in DT Gilbert, ST Fiske & G Lindzey (eds),
Handbook of social psychology, 4th edn, vol. 2, McGraw Hill, Boston, 1998, p. 281
Linda Farwell, p. 293; p. 291 Mandy Godbehear/BigStockPhoto; p. 292 Bob Thomas/
Contributor/Bob Thomas Sports Photography/Getty Images; p. 294 CAM/Ottawa
citizen; p. 295 (top) Psychology Matters (http://psychologymatters.apa.org); (bottom)
http://www.coolsmartphone.com; p. 297 godfer/Fotolia; p. 298 from the Department
of Psychology, Institute of Neuroscience, University of Texas at Austin (http://www.
utexas.edu/features/archive/2002/bully.html); p. 304 Robert Cianflone/Getty Images;
p. 305 Anna Kirsten Dickie/MorgueFile; p. 306 morgueFile; p. 307 morgueFile; p.
311 from Robert S Weinberg and Daniel Gould, Foundations of Sport and Exercise
Psychology, Human Kinetics Europe, 2006; p. 312 morgueFile; p. 313 Poco_bw/
Dreamstime.com; p. 314 Mark Baker/Associated Press; p. 316 dtcreations/morgue-
File; p. 317 JUANPRESA/morgueFile; p. 318 roshibaba/morgueFile; p. 319 Andres
Kudacki/Corbis; p. 320 Alvimann/morgueFile; p. 324 CartoonStock; p. 325 taliesin/
morgueFile; p. 328 Digital Vision; p. 329 Mike Blake/Reuters; p. 330 Carrydream/
Dreamstime.com; p. 334 Michael Zagaris/Contributor/Getty Images Sport/Getty
Images North America/Getty Images; p. 336 Staff/Getty Images Sport/ Getty Images
North America/Getty Images; p. 340 With permission of Christina Maslach and CPP,
Inc., 2006; p. 358 Stephanie Colvey/IDRC CRDI

We have tried to trace and contact all copyright holders before publication. If notified, the publishers will be pleased to rectify any errors or omissions at the earliest
opportunity.

Cover photo: David Muir/Getty Images

Course Companion definition

The IB Diploma Programme Course Companions are resource materials designed to provide students with extra support through their two-year course of study. These books will help students gain an understanding of what is expected from the study of an IB Diploma Programme subject.

The Course Companions reflect the philosophy and approach of the IB Diploma Programme and present content in a way that illustrates the purpose and aims of the IB. They encourage a deep understanding of each subject by making connections to wider issues and providing opportunities for critical thinking.

These Course Companions, therefore, may or may not contain all of the curriculum content required in each IB Diploma Programme subject, and so are not designed to be complete and prescriptive textbooks. Each book will try to ensure that areas of curriculum that are unique to the IB or to a new course revision are thoroughly covered. These books mirror the IB philosophy of viewing the curriculum in terms of a whole-course approach; the use of a wide range of resources; international-mindedness; the IB learner profile and the IB Diploma Programme core requirements; theory of knowledge; the extended essay; and creativity, action, service (CAS).

In addition, the Course Companions provide advice and guidance on the specific course assessment requirements and also on academic honesty protocol.

The Course Companions are not designed to be:

- study/revision guides or a one-stop solution for students to pass the subjects
- prescriptive or essential subject textbooks.

IB mission statement

The International Baccalaureate aims to develop inquiring, knowledgable and caring young people who help to create a better and more peaceful world through intercultural understanding and respect.

To this end the IB works with schools, governments and international organizations to develop challenging programmes of international education and rigorous assessment.

These programmes encourage students across the world to become active, compassionate, and lifelong learners who understand that other people, with their differences, can also be right.

The IB learner profile

The aim of all IB programmes is to develop internationally minded people who, recognizing their common humanity and shared guardianship of the planet, help to create a better and more peaceful world. IB learners strive to be:

Inquirers They develop their natural curiosity. They acquire the skills necessary to conduct inquiry and research and show independence in learning. They actively enjoy learning and this love of learning will be sustained throughout their lives.

Knowledgable They explore concepts, ideas, and issues that have local and global significance. In so doing, they acquire in-depth knowledge and develop understanding across a broad and balanced range of disciplines.

Thinkers They exercise initiative in applying thinking skills critically and creatively to recognize and approach complex problems, and make reasoned, ethical decisions.

Communicators   They understand and express ideas and information confidently and creatively in more than one language and in a variety of modes of communication. They work effectively and willingly in collaboration with others.

Principled   They act with integrity and honesty, with a strong sense of fairness, justice, and respect for the dignity of the individual, groups, and communities. They take responsibility for their own actions and the consequences that accompany them.

Open-minded   They understand and appreciate their own cultures and personal histories, and are open to the perspectives, values, and traditions of other individuals and communities. They are accustomed to seeking and evaluating a range of points of view, and are willing to grow from the experience.

Caring   They show empathy, compassion, and respect towards the needs and feelings of others. They have a personal commitment to service, and act to make a positive difference to the lives of others and to the environment.

Risk-takers   They approach unfamiliar situations and uncertainty with courage and forethought, and have the independence of spirit to explore new roles, ideas, and strategies. They are brave and articulate in defending their beliefs.

Balanced   They understand the importance of intellectual, physical, and emotional balance to achieve personal well-being for themselves and others.

Reflective   They give thoughtful consideration to their own learning and experience. They are able to assess and understand their strengths and limitations in order to support their learning and personal development.

A note on academic honesty

It is of vital importance to acknowledge and appropriately credit the owners of information when that information is used in your work. After all, owners of ideas (intellectual property) have property rights. To have an authentic piece of work, it must be based on your individual and original ideas with the work of others fully acknowledged. Therefore, all assignments, written or oral, completed for assessment must use your own language and expression. Where sources are used or referred to, whether in the form of direct quotation or paraphrase, such sources must be appropriately acknowledged.

How do I acknowledge the work of others?
The way that you acknowledge that you have used the ideas of other people is through the use of footnotes and bibliographies.

Footnotes   (placed at the bottom of a page) or endnotes (placed at the end of a document) are to be provided when you quote or paraphrase from another document, or closely summarize the information provided in another document. You do not need to provide a footnote for information that is part of a 'body of knowledge'. That is, definitions do not need to be footnoted as they are part of the assumed knowledge.

Bibliographies   should include a formal list of the resources that you used in your work. 'Formal' means that you should use one of the several accepted forms of presentation. This usually involves separating the resources that you use into different categories (e.g. books, magazines, newspaper articles, Internet-based resources, CDs and works of art) and providing full information as to how a reader or viewer of your work can find the same information. A bibliography is compulsory in the extended essay.

What constitutes malpractice?
Malpractice is behaviour that results in, or may result in, you or any student gaining an unfair advantage in one or more assessment component. Malpractice includes plagiarism and collusion.

Plagiarism is defined as the representation of the ideas or work of another person as your own. The following are some of the ways to avoid plagiarism:

- Words and ideas of another person used to support one's arguments must be acknowledged.

- Passages that are quoted verbatim must be enclosed within quotation marks and acknowledged.

- CD-ROMs, email messages, web sites on the Internet, and any other electronic media must be treated in the same way as books and journals.

- The sources of all photographs, maps, illustrations, computer programs, data, graphs, audio-visual, and similar material must be acknowledged if they are not your own work.
- Works of art, whether music, film, dance, theatre arts, or visual arts, and where the creative use of a part of a work takes place, must be acknowledged.

Collusion is defined as supporting malpractice by another student. This includes:

- allowing your work to be copied or submitted for assessment by another student
- duplicating work for different assessment components and/or diploma requirements.

Other forms of malpractice include any action that gives you an unfair advantage or affects the results of another student. Examples include, taking unauthorized material into an examination room, misconduct during an examination, and falsifying a CAS record.

Contents

Introduction

This book has been written to be a companion to students of psychology in the International Baccalaureate Diploma Programme at higher and standard levels.

Psychology is a science that has developed tremendously within the last century. However, psychology is a highly academic discipline but one that is also part of our everyday life and affects us all at many levels. Psychology has an important role to play in understanding other people and oneself. Psychology is also a subject well suited for understanding cultural differences which is particularly important in an international programme.

A good psychology student is a critical thinker who is willing to ask questions and examine the evidence. This Course Companion encourages critical thinking, international mindedness, and the other goals of the IB learner profile both in its content and through workpoints. There are a number of workpoints in each chapter with thought-provoking questions and activities. Many of the questions are open-ended to which there are no "right" answers. The purpose of such questions is to apply your psychological knowledge and make you think critically about important issues and discuss them in an open-minded and knowledgeable way.

The workpoints cover a wide range of questions and activities. These include but are not excluded to

- *Knowledge questions* which are made to resemble those encountered in exam questions.

- *Critical thinking questions* to make you reflect on and evaluate psychological theories and empirical studies.

- *Research activities* which invite you to think about how research is conducted as well as potential problems in research. Some of these activities give you the opportunity to reflect on how to design research of your own in a given topic.

- Activities and questions related to *ethical issues* in research are found throughout the book.

The book also provides biographies of important persons related to psychological research. Many chapters include additional knowledge in "Did you know?" boxes which are meant to put the content of the chapters in perspective.

Throughout the book, psychology has been related to other disciplines such as history, anthropology, economics and biology. There are a number of questions related to the TOK programme. The IB learner profile is also addressed in workpoints asking you to integrate your psychological knowledge in thinking about CAS projects.

Sample examinations questions and sample answers are provided throughout the book and there is a special chapter devoted to strategies for writing exam papers including a brief introduction to how to create an argument in papers. This is more fully developed in the chapter on extended essay where you will also find important information on the research process. The chapter on internal assessment should guide you safely through your own experimental research.

We hope that this book will serve as a useful and thought provoking companion to your psychology course. Psychology is by its very nature a vast and dynamic subject and the demands of the syllabus can be addressed in a number of ways. This Course Companion should not be your only resource. It is a good idea to integrate resources from research in your own country as one of the supplements. The newspapers constantly write about new psychological research and we recommend that you to consider to integrate some of this new knowledge in your study of psychology as well.

John Crane and Jette Hannibal

1.1 What is psychology?

Learning outcomes

- Define psychology
- Describe psychology as a scientific discipline
- Outline how psychological knowledge is generated
- Explain what is understood by a theoretical explanation and an empirical investigation
- Describe the "levels of analysis"
- Explain what is understood by critical thinking and giving examples

Have you ever wondered why there are so many books and magazines on the market that deal with human behaviour? It seems that people have an enormous appetite for psychological information—they buy an increasing number of self-help books and subscribe to psychological magazines. Browse Amazon.com for self-help books and you will find titles like *Why Does He Do That? Inside the minds of angry and controlling men*, and *Who's Pulling Your Strings? How to break the cycle of manipulation and regain control over your life*. Some people prefer to go to psychics to get advice or seek information about the future. Others believe that they can find answers to big questions in astrology. In some cultures, you consult the elderly about important issues in your life. What do these people have in common with psychology students? They all want to understand why people behave the way they do. We humans share the belief that if we can discover the causes of behaviour, we will be able to explain them, and maybe also to control them.

People use psychology every day when they explain human actions in terms of beliefs, motives, love or childhood experiences. Around the world, humans explain other people's actions by attributing to them beliefs, motives, and plans which they infer from what they observe other people doing. This is termed "folk psychology" or "common-sense psychology", and it works well for us in our daily interactions with other people. Folk psychology is not the same as scientific psychology, even though the explanations sometimes seem to fit with scientific findings. People even use terms and ideas from psychologists, without knowing where they come from—for example, when they talk of "repressing" bad memories or say that somebody has a big "ego".

As a student of psychology, you now have the chance to get to know more about the fascinating human animal. Be aware, however, that psychology is complex and not always easy. There are no definite answers to explaining human behaviour, and there are no easy solutions, as suggested in much of the popular psychological literature. In the study of psychology, in addition to learning about

Psychics can predict the future—or can they?

research that explains behaviour, you will also develop useful critical thinking skills, so that in the future you will not be fooled by false claims and poorly conducted research.

Definition of psychology

There is no single definition of psychology that is universally acknowledged. A common definition is: *Psychology is the scientific study of mental processes and behaviour and how these are affected by internal processes and the environment.* The definition does not give a clear picture of what psychology is, however, and over the years psychologists have often disagreed about what should be studied in psychology and how it should be studied.

The first important part of the definition is the word "scientific". This means systematic and controlled study of human behaviour, with the hope of establishing cause-and-effect relationships or describing behaviour.

The terms "mental processes" and "behaviour" are the second significant aspect of the definition. Mental processes are covert behaviours—for example, attention, memory, emotion, and attitudes. Other behaviours are overt: they can be observed directly or measured with instruments. These include behaviours such as aggression, helping, and even sleeping.

The final component of the definition recognizes that behaviour is influenced by two sets of factors: internal processes—like hormones or genes—and the environment. For a century it was argued that it was one or the other—nature or nurture—that determined behaviour; today's approach acknowledges the contribution of both.

Pop psych and psychobabble

Pop psych, or popular psychology, is a term used for a wide range of popularized psychological theories and concepts that may or may not have a basis in psychology. Some serious psychologists write books that are intended for a wider public and these are considered to be valid, but pop psych books are often oversimplified accounts of psychological issues based on anecdotal evidence and popular beliefs. They are often full of what Rosen (1977) called **psychobabble**— that is, buzzwords taken from psychological terminology but used out of context. The difference between scientific psychology and pop psychology is primarily that the former is based on documented research evidence and the latter is mostly based on unsupported claims, beliefs, and popular opinion, as in the case of astrology.

Research in psychology

In 1987, the Australian researcher Geoffrey Dean conducted a study on astrology in order to test whether astrologers would be able to say something valid about people's personalities compared to the results of authorized psychological tests. He took 60 people who had high scores on introversion in a personality test (Eysenck Personality Inventory) and 60 people who had scored high on extraversion in the same test. He then gave astrologers the birth charts of the 120 participants and asked them to identify extroverts from introverts. The average success rate was only 50.2 per cent.

Nanninga (1996/97) conducted another scientific study to test the predictive value of astrology. He invited astrologers to participate in the Astrotest of the Skepsis Foundation. The astrologers who volunteered to participate received the birth chart (date, time, and place) of seven anonymous test participants, as well as seven questionnaires filled out by the same participants. The astrologers had to match each birth chart with a questionnaire.

The test was completed by 44 astrologers, many of whom were very experienced. Before the test results were revealed, the astrologers were asked to estimate how many correct matches they expected, and 36 astrologers did so. Half of these predicted that they had matched all the participants with the correct charts. Only 6 astrologers predicted fewer than four hits. The results did not entirely match the predictions. The most successful astrologer had three correct matches. Half of the astrologers (22) did not achieve a single hit. This was a very low score compared to the expectations. There was no evidence that the most experienced astrologers were any better than the less experienced. The astrologers themselves were surprised by the results, but only 4 concluded that the possibilities of astrology were more limited than they had thought; 7 concluded

that astrology only works in actual practice; and 16 still believed that science can prove astrology right.

Thanks to the horoscopes, I became pretty rich! I devise and sell that stuff!

The diversity of psychology

Psychology is a multidisciplinary science that includes knowledge from the natural and social sciences—for example, biology, sociology, and anthropology. Psychological researchers use a number of data collection methods—such as experiments, brain scanning, and interviews—to study a wide variety of topics, including group processes, conflict, love, body language, memory, emotions, social development, sex and gender, motivation, sport, stress, and adolescence.

There are many advantages in psychology's relationship to other sciences. Most of the time psychologists undertake research within their own field. This means that a social psychologist researches group processes; a neuropsychologist carries out brain scans to try to get a picture of memory in the brain; a cross-cultural psychologist compares gender roles in different cultures; and a cognitive psychologist investigates decision-making processes. Some developmental psychologists are interested in how factors like nutrition and stimulation affect children's health and learning capacity. This knowledge is used to create better conditions for children nationally and internationally, e.g. by international organisations like the UNICEF. But what could happen if knowledge from different fields were used to create entirely new areas of knowledge? The cognitive neuroscientist could combine knowledge from cognitive psychology on decision making with neurological evidence obtained through brain scanning.

One of the new areas of cognitive neuroscience is **neuroeconomics**. This may appear to be an odd coupling, but in fact there are several

TOK and ways of knowing

1 Why do you think people go to astrologers?

2 What role could astrologers serve in people's lives?

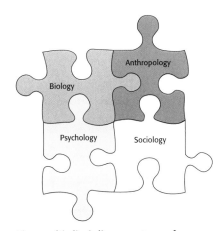

The multi-disciplinary nature of psychology

institutes of neuroeconomics, including the Center for Neuroeconomic Studies at Duke University and the Center for the Study of Neuroeconomics and Law at George Mason University in the USA. Neuroeconomics combines neuroscience, economics, and psychology to investigate how people make choices in economics. This includes looking at the brain when people evaluate decisions. In one study, researchers hypothesized that they would find activity in the brain's pain centre if people found that price of a product was too high. This is exactly what happened.

The question is how this knowledge can be used to provide a deeper understanding of human decision making in economics. This research, and the whole endeavour of neuroeconomics, is an example of the possibilities that exist for the integration of the various branches of science to study human behaviour.

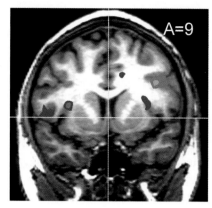
Brain scan neuromarketing

Be a thinker

1 Consider two possible advantages of being a multidisciplinary science.

2 List three topics that you think could be investigated using information and understanding from different areas of knowledge, and explain why.

Levels of analysis in psychology

The IB psychology course takes an integrative approach to studying human behaviour. This means that we will look at psychological issues on three levels of analysis:

● a biological level, which focuses on physiology and genetics
● a cognitive level, which focuses on mental processes like memory, thinking, perception, and attention
● a sociocultural level, which focuses on how environment and culture affect behaviour or thinking.

The notion that there are various levels of analysis can also be illustrated with the example of gender. Gender can be defined as what society and culture find appropriate for men and women to do. The biological level of analysis explains differences in gender behaviour with genetic make-up (XX and XY chromosomes) and hormones (testosterone and oestrogen).

The cognitive level of analysis could explain gender differences with gender schema theory—that is, people form mental representations of what it means to be either a boy or a girl, and these representations guide behaviour. The way we perceive a person is very much related to gender. This is called **social cognition**. At this level, therefore, it could be relevant to study how gender stereotypes may be formed and upheld, and to consider whether it is possible to change stereotypes.

The origin of gender is quite complex

At the sociocultural level of analysis, social learning theory explains that people learn gender behaviour by watching how other people of their own sex behave. This level also deals with how culture affects definitions of gender roles and may shape mental representations of gender.

It is not possible to come up with a single correct answer to the complex issue of why men and women are different and why they have different opportunities around the world. Is it because of biology? Or is it due to the way we come to think about what it means to be a woman or a man? Or is it because of the way culture shapes our way of thinking? Is it possible that it is related to all these things?

It could certainly be argued that all of the above factors may be relevant. This is why psychology has to take several levels of analysis into consideration when explaining the complexities of human behaviour. Each level contributes to an overall understanding of the phenomenon under investigation.

A brief history of psychology: from philosophy to scientific psychology

Psychology started, like many sciences, as part of philosophy, which also gave psychology much of its conceptual framework. The creation of psychology as an independent science took shape in the middle of the 19th century, with its roots in biology and a growing interest in the mind and the underlying processes of the brain. Since ancient Greece, philosophers have discussed the philosophy of the mind. The word "psychology" was not widely used until the 19th century. It comes from two Greek words—"psyche" (the mind or the soul) and "logos" (reason). Literally, psychology means "reasoning about the soul", and over the centuries philosophers have speculated on the nature of the soul—that is, the **philosophy of the mind**.

Philosophers have also asked questions about how human beings come to know the world. This is known as **epistemology**, from the Greek words "episteme" (knowledge) and "logos" (reasoning). In theory of knowledge, this is referred to as "ways of knowing". When we ask questions about how human beings know the world, we refer to processes such as sensation, perception, memory, language, and reason. Today, these areas are part of what is called **cognitive psychology**.

Ethics is also an integral part of philosophy and psychology. There have been numerous theoretical debates about human nature—for example, are people good or evil by nature? Are people inherently social? What motivates people? Such questions are psychological and can now be investigated scientifically. Today, ethical concerns are fundamental to psychological research and applied psychology.

In the mid 19th century, physiologists like Wilhelm Wundt began to study processes like neural transmission, reflexes, and perception. Wundt was particularly interested in the psychology of consciousness—the introspective study of the normal adult mind. His definition of psychology as the science of consciousness, however, soon met with criticism. In the USA, it was replaced by the psychology of behaviour. In Europe, Sigmund Freud's psychology of the unconscious had an enormous cultural impact, although the theory was controversial and certainly not accepted by everyone.

Profile

Wilhelm Wundt
In 1879, Wilhelm Wundt established an official institute at the University of Leipzig where graduate students could earn PhD degrees in experimental psychology. Wundt is often regarded as the father of modern academic and experimental psychology, but despite his support for experimental methods, he had a clear idea of their limitations. In Wundt's view, many important psychological problems could only be studied with non-experimental techniques such as introspection.

Modern scientific psychology is to a large extent based on "the psychology of adaptation"—that is, a psychology influenced by the ideas of Darwin on evolution, where the focus is on the biological study of the evolutionary utility of mind and behaviour.

Building blocks of scientific psychology: theories and empirical studies

When psychologists publish their work, psychologists refer to **theories** and make reference to **empirical studies**. These are some of the building blocks of scientific psychology.

A theory is an explanation for a psychological phenomenon. It is a statement used to summarize, organize, and explain observations. A theory can also be used to make predictions about observed events. Most theories are built on **concepts**—that is, hypothetical constructs that must be carefully defined so that they can be tested. In order to test a concept, psychologists need to develop tools to measure it.

An example of a concept is Bandura's **self-efficacy**. As a concept, self-efficacy is defined as one's own belief as to whether one will succeed in something, based on previous experiences.

Bandura's theory predicts that one's self-efficacy will determine if and how hard one will try to do a certain thing. For example, a researcher might be interested in the role of self-efficacy in predicting if people will engage in regular exercise to improve health. The researcher wants to find out if people who score high on a self-efficacy scale are more likely to engage in health-preserving behaviour than those who score low on the scale. On the basis of the findings, the researcher can either support self-efficacy theory or question its usefulness in people's health behaviours.

Theories in psychology are not like laws in the natural sciences. Psychological theories are merely dealing with principles—that is, *the theoretical explanations are probable rather than certain, and therefore they are always open to some degree of doubt.* It is often the case that one theory cannot explain all aspects of a psychological phenomenon. Since this doubt is part of scientific psychology, it is necessary to evaluate theories, examining their strengths and limitations.

Psychological theory in practice

Do you believe in hard work or talent? Professor Carol Dweck from Stanford University in the USA has formulated a theory of the importance of people's **mindset** in explaining success. Through systematic research, Dweck discovered that many talented people do not achieve their potential. She concluded that it is not talent or intelligence, as such, which is the key to understanding success. Rather, it is the way people explain things. She found that people tended to look at intelligence or talent as something that is either fixed or changeable.

According to Dweck, people with a **fixed mindset** believe that intelligence is static: because they want to appear smart, they avoid challenges, give up easily, and consider effort to be a waste of time. (If they have to work hard, they are not smart, are they?) They tend to ignore useful negative feedback and feel threatened by the success of others. The consequence for these people is that often they do not achieve their full potential.

In contrast, people with a **growth mindset** believe that intelligence is not fixed: they think that it can be developed and therefore they do not mind challenges. They persist when they experience setbacks; they consider effort to be part of the process of mastering something; they learn from criticism; and they find inspiration in the success of others. This approach reflects the belief that you can change things if you want to.

Be a thinker

Dweck's theory of motivation predicts that people who attribute their failures to lack of ability become discouraged even in areas where they are capable. Those who think they simply have not tried hard enough are encouraged to try harder when they experience setbacks.

1 Does this theory correspond to real life? Try to evaluate the theory using some of your own experiences.

2 To what extent does this theory offer insight into possible differences in terms of what people achieve in education, sport, or the arts?

Usefulness of research in real life

When a researcher collects and analyses data in order to investigate a psychological phenomenon, it is called an empirical investigation or study. It is research that can be observed and measured. Researchers in all areas of psychology constantly gather information using different methods, such as experiments, observations, surveys, and interviews. As with theories, it is necessary to evaluate empirical studies.

Some researchers want to explore a given topic and perhaps formulate a theory afterwards. Others want to test an existing theory. Some studies just want to describe a certain phenomenon. Many studies result in something useful that can be applied to real-life situations. One of the key goals of psychology is to improve the world we live in.

An example of empirical research is Carol Dweck's study of people's motivation to learn. Dweck demonstrated through numerous empirical studies that students who believe that intelligence is fixed are at risk for academic underachievement. She also found evidence that praising students for their intelligence can limit their intellectual growth because it reinforces the idea that intelligence is fixed. Dweck and Blackwell (2007) carried out an experiment with low-achieving students aged 12–13 years (seventh-graders). All students were given an introduction to the brain and study skills. Half of them also attended a neutral session on memory, while the other half attended a lecture on how intelligence can be developed through exercise—just as you can train your physical body. The result was that the students who were trained to adopt a growth mindset about intelligence were much more motivated, and this was demonstrated in their maths grades. Students in the group that did not attend the intelligence lecture showed no improvement, despite all the other interventions. According to Dweck, telling students that intelligence can be developed can have an incredible impact on their motivation to learn.

Be a thinker

How can you use research to improve real-life situations? The British Psychological Society's Research Digest contains many brief descriptions of empirical studies in the psychology of education. You can find these studies at http://bps-research-digest.blogspot.com/search/label/Educational

- Find an empirical study on this site that interests you.

- Write a brief summary of the study. State what the researcher was looking for, how the research was carried out, and what the findings were.

- If you were the headmaster or principal of a school, what would research like this mean to you? Would you make any changes to improve the school you work in?

Critical thinking

When you read an article in a newspaper or a story on an Internet site, you probably decide whether or not to believe it. The same is true when you hear a story or listen to gossip. We are not very conscious of this in our daily lives, even though we often evaluate the source of the information or consider if it sounds plausible. The ability to think critically is important if we are to function effectively in today's globalized world where everything changes so quickly. But we are not born critical thinkers. We need to learn it through practice.

Scientists are trained to be skeptical and critical. When they carry out peer review on scientific articles, they need to be able to find out how their colleague arrived at his or her conclusions in order to judge if the interpretation of the results is supported by the data. To be critical does not mean to be negative. It simply means that we apply critical thinking skills. IB students learn these skills in their subjects and in theory of knowledge.

What is critical thinking? It can be defined as the ability and willingness to assess claims and make objective judgments on the basis of well-supported reasons and evidence, rather than emotions, beliefs, myths, and anecdotes. King and Kitchener (1994) outlined in their book *Reflective Judgement* some of the important foundations of critical thinking, which have also been adopted in IB psychology.

"what's the evidence?"
"what're the perspectives?"

Critical thinker profile

- Questions assumptions and biases
- Evaluates available evidence and relates it to a theory or opinion
- Considers alternative interpretations
- Avoids emotional reasoning
- Does not jump to oversimplified conclusions
- Knows that plausible conclusions are based on evidence
- Is willing to reassess conclusions if new information appears
- Is able to tolerate some uncertainty

How can you demonstrate critical thinking skills in psychology? In evaluating a theory, you can ask what sort of evidence it is based on; if it is possible to test the theory; if there is evidence to support or contradict it; and if it is useful in explaining things in real life. In evaluating an empirical study, you can ask if it is based on a representative group of people; if it was conducted in a laboratory or a natural setting; if the participants were asked to do things they would do in real life; if it was conducted in an ethical manner; and if the findings are supported or questioned by the findings of other studies. Throughout this book you will be introduced to strategies for evaluating research, and this is useful not only in psychology, but in any evaluation of scientific study.

Research in psychology

If you saw a commercial promising that by taking a pill you could "think clearly, maintain focus, and increase memory", would you buy it?

Jorm, Rodgers, and Christensen (2003) found that 2.8 per cent of an Australian sample of 2551 adults, aged 60–64 years, said that they used medication such as Ginko Biloba to enhance memory, in spite of strong evidence of its ineffectiveness. The people who used it said they took the medication to enhance memory or to prevent memory loss, but in fact none of them showed any objective signs of memory impairment when they started taking the medication.

Danielle Turner, from the Department of Psychiatry at Cambridge University, has apparently found a drug that may enhance not only memory, but also concentration. She conducted research with a drug used to prevent people with narcolepsy from falling asleep all the time. She found that the healthy volunteers who received a drug called Modafinil scored higher on computer games designed to test their mental function than those given a placebo (dummy pill).

Which one is the memory pill?

Be a thinker

Discuss the findings of these studies. Would you buy a pill promising you a better memory? Give reasons for your answer.

We have now looked at psychological theories, concepts, and empirical studies. If you want to develop a better understanding about scientific psychology, you need to understand how psychological knowledge is generated, including the methods psychologists use to collect data.

Today, psychology uses a number of different research methods in order to achieve a more complete understanding of human behaviour. Like any science, psychology is constantly evolving in search of the "truth" that is never really found. Even when many studies generate evidence supporting a specific idea, there will invariably be other studies that challenge the findings. This can be hard to tolerate for a student of psychology—especially if you expect to find hard evidence that cannot be contradicted. On the other hand, the fact that evidence is often contested or inconclusive is one of the interesting and challenging things about psychology. Thinking critically is part of the psychology course, and if you can tolerate some degree of uncertainty, you will find that psychology has a lot to offer.

TOK and ways of knowing

- What ways of knowing is scientific psychology based on? How do you know this?
- What ways of knowing is common-sense psychology based on? How do you know this?

Understanding the research process

Learning outcomes

- Define the aim and target population of a study
- Discuss sampling techniques appropriate to research
- Discuss ethical considerations when carrying out research
- Explain the concept of generalizability
- Discuss the concepts of validity and reliability
- Explain what is meant by an application of findings
- Evaluate research studies

In 2007 a newspaper article in the Danish newspaper *Politiken* described a study which was carried out in Denmark to investigate if young people's attitudes towards health—for example, diet and exercise—will influence their behaviour. What would researchers need to do to carry out this type of study effectively? Researchers need to have a plan; people who are willing to participate in the study; and a method for collecting and analysing data. These are all important parts of the research process that must be carefully considered by the researcher. The process of thinking critically about research is very similar: when we read the conclusions of a study, we need to ask appropriate questions in order to assess the significance of the research in the best way. In this chapter, we are going to look at research in psychology and learn some simple questions that we should consider when presented with a study.

Aim, procedure, findings

The **aim** is the purpose of a study. An aim indicates which behaviour or mental process will be studied. The group whose behaviour the researcher wishes to investigate is called the **target population**. For example, we may want to know if bilingual students are better able to recall items on a list than monolingual students.

After identifying the aim, the researcher will plan a **procedure**. This is the step-by-step process used by the researcher to carry out the study. In research articles, the procedure is always written in a way that makes it possible for others to understand how the data were collected. It is important that the research carefully defines the actual behaviour being studied.

The **findings** state how the researcher interpreted the data that were collected. Research findings are always open to discussion and debate. Maybe the researcher has interpreted the results in a way that is biased, or perhaps there were flaws in the procedure. If other research studies confirm the findings, the study is more credible. However, findings say something only about the target group and

Careful investigation of something may require specific tools or measurements

may not be relevant to other groups or cultures. It is important to interpret findings in terms of the culture in which the research has been conducted, and always to be aware of potential cultural bias.

This classic study provides an idea of what to look for in research.

Research in psychology

The Pygmalion effect (Rosenthal and Jacobson 1968)

Professor Robert Rosenthal, of Harvard University in the USA, and Leonore Jacobson, a principal of an elementary school in San Francisco, carried out an interesting field experiment to determine whether teachers' expectations of students' performance actually had any effect on how well the students learned throughout the year. In other words, when teachers expect students to excel or fail, is that what is going to happen?

To begin their study, Rosenthal and Jacobson gave 18 classes of students (from kindergarten to sixth grade) an intelligence test so that the researchers could see if there was a development during the year in which they carried out the study. Then they chose 20 per cent of the students at random and told the teachers that these children showed "unusual potential for intellectual growth", and that they could be expected to "bloom"

during the year. However, because they were randomly selected, there was no relationship whatsoever between the score they achieved on the test and this claim made by the psychologists.

At the end of the school year, the students were retested. Those labelled as intelligent showed a significantly greater increase in test scores than the other children who were not singled out for the teacher's attention. The researchers explained this by the "self-fulfilling prophecy"—that is, the teachers' expectations influenced the performance of the students.

You can read more about the study on the following websites.

● http://fcis.oise.utoronto.ca/~daniel_sc/ assignment1/1968rosenjacob.html

● www.ntlf.com/html/pi/9902/pygm_1.htm

Apply your knowledge

1 State the aim, procedure, and findings of the study undertaken by Rosenthal and Jacobson.

2 Do you think the teachers were informed about the aim of the study? Comment on this.

Participants—who should be in the study?

Participants are those who participate in a study

People who take part in a psychological study are called **participants**. Normally, psychologists define a target population—that is, a specific group of people whom they are interested in for their study. For example, this could be adolescents who live with one parent; women who have given birth to twins; or people who have moved from one country to another. The nature of the group of participants, what psychologists call the **sample**, is very important in determining the usefulness of a piece of research.

The goal in sampling is to obtain a sample that is representative of the target population. If the researcher is interested in teenage drinking habits, for example, the population would be teenagers. In psychological research it is not possible to test the whole population. Researchers often try to obtain a sample that represents a population—that is, a **representative sample**.

The *size* of the sample matters if it is to be representative. Small groups are more open to distortions than large ones. In a small group, each individual has quite a lot of influence on the overall result.

Public Announcement

WE WILL PAY YOU $4.00 FOR ONE HOUR OF YOUR TIME

Persons Needed for a Study of Memory

*We will pay five hundred New Haven men to help us complete a scientific study of memory and learning. The study is being done at Yale University.

*Each person who participates will be paid $4.00 (plus 50c carfare) for approximately 1 hour's time. We need you for only one hour: there are no further obligations. You may choose the time you would like to come (evenings, weekdays, or weekends).

*No special training, education, or experience is needed. We want:

Factory workers	Businessmen	Construction workers
City employees	Clerks	Salespeople
Laborers	Professional people	White-collar workers
Barbers	Telephone workers	Others

All persons must be between the ages of 20 and 50. High school and college students cannot be used.

*If you meet these qualifications, fill out the coupon below and mail it now to Professor Stanley Milgram, Department of Psychology, Yale University, New Haven. You will be notified later of the specific time and place of the study. We reserve the right to decline any appllication.

*You will be paid $4.00 (plus 50c carfare) as soon as you arrive at the laboratory.

Researchers may advertise to get participants for their studies

How does a psychologist get people to participate in a study? Perhaps you have already experienced what it is like to become part of a sample. When you were getting off a bus or walking into a shopping centre, you might have seen people carrying clipboards with surveys that only require a few minutes of your time. Or you might have seen those undertaking marketing research by setting up a table in the middle of the supermarket and trying to convince you to take part in their study by offering free food or drink. These are examples of **opportunity sampling** (also called convenience sampling). This is a sample of whoever happens to be there and agrees to participate. It is an easy way for the researcher to get participants, but one has to question the nature of an opportunity sample. For example, what type of people shop at that supermarket? Is there a gender imbalance in who does the shopping in this community? Opportunity sampling is commonly used in university-based research. Psychology students are often told that they have to take part in a number of studies during the semester in order to get credits for their course. Opportunity sampling can lead to rather biased results, and it is problematic to generalize from studies that use opportunity sampling.

One example of **sampling bias** was discussed by Sears (1986). He found that over two-thirds of research performed at universities exclusively used students as participants. This brings into question whether the researcher can make the claim that these findings can be generalized to the larger population. Sears argues that samples of opportunity made up of university students have the following problems.

● Students have a strong need for peer approval.
● They were pre-selected for competence in cognitive skills.
● They are more egocentric than adults.

Another commonly used sampling method is the **self-selected sample**, which is made up of volunteers. One advantage of the self-selected sample is that it is relatively easy to obtain, and it is almost guaranteed that the sample will be highly motivated. The problem is that volunteer samples rarely reflect the more general population, which means that it is difficult to make generalizations—that is, it is not clear whether these results can apply to people outside of the group that took part in the study.

When participants recruit other participants from among their friends and acquaintances, this is called **snowball sampling**—the sample grows like a snowball rolling downhill. This is often used in social psychology research, where it may be difficult to access research participants—for example, where the target population is drug users, or students who do volunteer work in the local community.

Whenever a researcher chooses a sample, it is important to consider **participant variability**—that is, the extent to which the participants may share a common set of traits that can bias the outcome of the study. Think of the kind of people who would volunteer for an advertised study about attitudes towards homosexuality, how to improve spatial reasoning, or anxiety about mathematics.

In order to obtain a representative sample, psychologists may use **random sampling**. A random sample is defined as one in which every member of the target population has an equal chance of being selected. If a researcher were going to carry out a study at a school

Be a researcher

You want to make a study of people's motivation to engage in exercise. You decide to go to the local fitness centre and conduct some interviews. Discuss the following.

● If you use an opportunity sample at a local fitness centre, which group of people would be overrepresented? Which group would be underrepresented?

● Would you get a more representative sample if you advertised for participants in your school?

to find out how anxiety affects test performance, s/he could put all the names of the students into a hat, and then draw out 30 names. In some research, random sampling is considered to be the most desirable sampling method because it is assumed that if the sample is large enough, it is most likely to contain all the characteristics of the population. From a random sample, it is easier to **generalize** our findings to the larger population—that is, the behaviours observed in the random sample are assumed to be representative of those in the larger population.

A random sample aims at getting rid of selection bias, but it is not always successful. If the researcher conducted a study in a school with a very diverse student body, and one particular group was overrepresented in the randomly chosen sample, the findings might not be representative. In order to have a sample that takes into consideration the diversity of a target population, a researcher may choose a **stratified sample**. A stratified sample attempts to overcome this problem by drawing random samples from each subpopulation within the target population. For example, if the school had 20 per cent Indian students, then for a sample of 30 students the researcher would randomly select 6 students from the Indian population. In this way, the sample is a more accurate reflection of the actual distribution of the school population.

Considering ethics in research

Another important consideration in research is that participants should be treated in an ethical manner. Psychologists now agree to follow certain ethical standards in order to avoid harming participants.

In 1999, a study undertaken by a US sociology department was reported in the *New York Times*. The aim of the study was to determine how restaurants would respond to customer complaints. Over 240 restaurants in New York received a letter that was supposedly written by a Columbia University professor who had taken ill after celebrating his wedding anniversary at the restaurant. The letter read:

> *[I suffered from] extended nausea, vomiting, diarrhoea and abdominal cramps—all which point to one thing: food poisoning.*

Our special romantic evening became reduced to my wife watching me curl up in a fetal position on the tiled floor of our bathroom between rounds of throwing up…

Although it is not my intent to file any reports, I want you, Mr. X [he named each restaurant owner here] to understand what I went through in anticipation that you will respond accordingly.

I await your response.

What was the outcome of this study? As a result of this letter, untold hours were lost checking records for reservations or credit card stubs; food stocks were controlled; and kitchen workers were questioned. It also created an incredible amount of stress for the restaurants.

This is an example of a study that does not meet ethical standards. The professor who was in charge of the study apologized to the restaurants involved and promised never to use the data, but he caused a lot of harm. This is not allowed in psychological research.

When designing a study, it is necessary to determine if the procedure is ethical. All research needs to be conducted in a way that respects the dignity of the participants—whether they are animals or human participants. Psychological associations around the world have come up with sets of guidelines that psychologists must use in carrying out psychological research. These ethical guidelines also apply to research done within the IB psychology programme.

- **Informed consent:** Participants must be informed about the nature of the study and agree to participate.

- **Deception:** Sometimes the researcher does not want the participants to know the exact aim of a study because it could affect the results. Deception should generally not be used; however, slight deception—which does not cause any stress to the participant—may be used in some cases. At the end of the study, any deception must be explained to the participants.

- **Debriefing:** At the end of all studies, the true aims and purpose of the research must be revealed to the participants. Any deception must be revealed and justified. All participants should leave the study without undue stress.

- **Withdrawal from a study:** At the beginning of any study, participants should be told that they have the right to leave the study at any time, and that they can withdraw their data at the end of the study if they wish.

- **Confidentiality:** All the information that is obtained in a study must be confidential.

- **Protection from physical or mental harm:** It is important to make sure that no harm is done to participants. It is not permitted to humiliate a participant or force them to reveal private information.

Be a thinker
Reread the research carried out by Rosenthal and Jacobson, as explained at the beginning of this chapter. Discuss whether you think the study was ethical. State your reasons.

Evaluating findings
Once the study is complete, we need to present our findings. Interpreting findings is an essential skill for a psychologist. One way

that a study can be evaluated is to assess whether it has any practical applications. An **application** is how a theory or empirical study is used. For example, several studies of the role of chemicals in the brain (neurotransmitters) have led to the development of drugs which have successfully treated disorders such as depression and schizophrenia. People often think of applications in terms of therapy, but applications can also be made in education, crime, the workplace, or sport. Some examples of applications are:

● the use of memory research to improve how we take evidence from eyewitness testimonies (an application of cognitive theory in forensic psychology)

● the use of research on the effect of light on mood in order to improve working conditions in office spaces in Denmark (an application of biological theory in occupational psychology)

● applying findings from decision-making research to improve a football team's performance on the pitch (an application of cognitive theory in sport psychology).

Validity and reliability

Another way to discuss findings is to consider whether the research does what it claims to do. This is the most basic definition of what we call **validity**.

One way to look at validity in research is **ecological validity**, which simply means that the study represents what happens in real life. If an experiment has been carried out in a laboratory and the participants have done things that they would never do in real life, the experiment is said to lack ecological validity. It can also be the case that the situation in which the experiment took place was so well controlled that normal influences on behaviour were eliminated. If a study lacks ecological validity, it means that what was observed in the laboratory does not necessarily predict what will happen outside the laboratory.

Another consideration is **cross-cultural validity**. In other words, is the research relevant to other cultures or is it **ethnocentric**—that is, based on the values and beliefs of one culture? For example, in a US study of children's behaviour, psychologists developed a checklist of behaviours that were the norm among American children. When the checklist was used with Native American children, the children's parents did not feel that the behaviours listed were healthy normal behaviours for children in their society. In other words, the psychologists had been ethnocentric in their approach to assessing what is normal childhood behaviour, because their checklist was based only on their own culture.

If a study is **reliable**, it means that the results can be replicated. Usually, reliability is used in reference to experimental study, because the procedure is standardized and, theoretically, if another researcher uses exactly the same procedure, it should give the same results.

TOK and ways of knowing

A group of researchers want to explore students' stress levels during exams. In order to carry out the study, they used the following procedure.

● Researchers took blood samples from the students one month before the exam, one week before the exam, and on the day of the exam, in order to measure the level of cortisol (a stress hormone) in their blood.

● Each time a blood sample was taken, students were interviewed about how stressed they felt.

The first part of the procedure is related to the natural sciences, which is more objective. The second part of the procedure is related to the human sciences, which is more subjective. Is one way of knowing better than the other?

Some points to consider when looking at empirical studies

When we look at a piece of research, we have to ask a lot of questions. Being a critical thinker means that we do not accept research as "true" just because it was carried out by professional researchers. We should consider the questions introduced in this chapter—for example, what was the aim of the research? Who made up the sample of participants? Was the research valid and ethical? Can the findings be applied successfully to real-life situations? This is the beginning of evaluating psychological research based on critical thinking.

Researchers try to conduct their research in such a way that other researchers will not accuse them of methodological or ethical flaws. When we work with research, we should use critical thinking skills, which includes asking yourself some of the following questions.[1]

Is the study based on a representative group of people (sample)?

- If the participants are psychology students, they may not be representative of the population.
- Is there a bias in the sample? Is one group overrepresented? (e.g. gender, ethnicity, culture)

Was the study conducted in a laboratory or in a natural setting?

- A laboratory study is an artificial environment, so it is not possible to be certain that participants act as they would in real life.

Were the participants asked to do things that are far from real life?

- If participants are asked to do things they would not normally do (e.g. remember nonsense syllables), the study is said to lack ecological validity.

Are the findings of the study supported/questioned by the findings of other studies?

- Consider in what ways the findings are different and try to explain how and why. Maybe you can suggest which study was better designed, and show which results seem to be more valid.

Do the findings have practical relevance?

- Consider ways in which the findings have been applied to real-life issues.

Ethical considerations

- For example, were participants harmed? Look at the IB psychology code of ethics for psychologists to check if participants have been treated ethically. You could also check ethical guidelines on the homepages of The British Psychological Society and the American Psychological Association.

---

[1] Based on M. Jarvis, J. Russel, and P. Gorman. 2004. *Angels on Psychology*. Oxford, UK. Nelson Thornes. Pp 6–7.

Research in psychology: experimental methods

Learning outcomes

- Explain the purpose of a null and experimental hypothesis
- State the independent and dependent variables in an experiment
- State operational definitions of variables
- Explain confounding variables and how they may be controlled
- Outline different experimental methods (laboratory, field, natural)
- Discuss the strengths and limitations of the experimental method

The use of experiments in psychology

One of the most widely used methods in the study of behaviour has been the experiment. The goal of an experiment is to establish a cause-and-effect relationship between two variables. In order to do this, experiments are performed under highly controlled conditions. The experiment is an example of quantitative research, which generates numerical data. These can be statistically tested for significance in order to rule out the role of chance in the results.

Let us say that a researcher wants to find out if noise affects one's ability to recall information. The **aim** of the study is to see if one variable—noise—has an effect on another variable—recall of information. The variable that causes a change in the other variable is called the **independent variable** (IV). This is the variable that the researcher deliberately manipulates, while trying to keep all other variables constant. The variable that is measured after the manipulation of the independent variable is called the **dependent variable** (DV).

Overview of the experimental variables

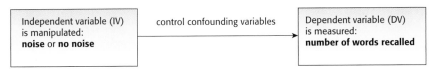

Experimental variables

It is important to remember that variables need to be **operationalized**. In other words, they need to be written in such a way that it is clear *what* is being measured. In the example used above, noise is the independent variable. This could be operationalized as high music at volume 35. A dependent variable simply identified as results does not say anything about what is actually being measured. An operationalized dependent variable could be the number of words remembered from a list of 20 words. Now we know exactly what the IV is expected to change.

Apply your knowledge

Operationalize your variables by considering each of the following descriptions and deciding whether it is an example of aggression or not. When you have finished working through the list with a partner, write a well-worded definition of aggression.

- Two men fight over a parking space.
- A football player kicks the ball into the goal.
- Two girls give a boy the "silent treatment" on the playground.
- A man kicks the back of his car when it will not start.
- Three students have a heated debate about whether global warming is happening.

In order to formalize the aim, the researcher formulates a hypothesis. The hypothesis is a prediction of how the independent variable affects the dependent variable.

An **experimental** (or alternative) **hypothesis** predicts the relationship between the IV and the DV—that is, what we expect will come out of the manipulation of the independent variable. In this case, we will have two conditions: one condition where participants have to recall words with very loud music, and one where the participants recall words with no music. In the second condition, there is no noise. This is called a **control condition**, because we compare the two conditions—that is, one with noise and one with no noise—in order to see if there is a difference.

An example of an experimental hypothesis could be: *Noise will decrease the number of words that an individual is able to recall from a list of words.*

In this example, the IV (noise) is predicted to have an effect on the DV (recall).

In experimental research, it is conventional to formulate both a null hypothesis and an experimental hypothesis. The null hypothesis states that the IV will have no effect on the DV, or that any change in the IV will be due to chance.

An example of a null hypothesis could be: *Noise has no effect on an individual's ability to recall a list of words; or, any change in the individual's ability to recall a list of words is due to chance.*

You may find it strange to make a null hypothesis, but in fact it makes sense. The researcher wants to *refute* the null hypothesis to show that the predicted cause-and-effect relationship between the IV and the DV actually exists. Sometimes, however, we have to accept the null hypothesis. This would happen if the results showed that there was no relationship between noise and recall of words. It is important to recognize that we can never *prove* anything—we can only *disprove*. Our goal is either to accept the null hypothesis, which means that we have to accept that there is no relationship between the two variables, or to *refute* the null hypothesis. We can accept the

> **Experimental hypothesis:**
> predicts the exact result of the manipulation of the IV on the DV.
>
> **Null hypothesis:**
> predicts that there will be no results or that the result will be due to chance.

experimental hypothesis only if we have demonstrated that the effect was due to the manipulation of the IV.

Be a thinker

Identify the *independent variable* and *dependent variable* in each of the following experimental hypotheses.

- People are more likely to make a risky decision when they are in a group than when they are alone.
- An increase in carbohydrates decreases one's ability to concentrate.
- People will react more quickly to an auditory stimulus than to a visual stimulus.
- Lack of sleep will affect learning new words negatively.
- Children who have watched a film with a model hitting a blow-up doll will exhibit more aggressive acts towards a blow-up doll than children who have not watched the film.

Different kinds of experiments

Many experiments are **laboratory experiments**. Researchers are able to have strict control of variables in a laboratory experiment, and this means that such experiments are easier to replicate. The limitation of the laboratory study is that the environment is artificial and therefore participants may react differently to how they would in real life. One way to evaluate the results of laboratory experiments is to look at ecological validity—that is, the extent to which the results predict behaviour outside the laboratory.

In social psychology, researchers have used what is called the **field experiment**—that is, the experiment takes place in a natural environment, but the researchers still manipulate variables.

In a well-known field experiment, Piliavin and Rodin (1969) investigated helping behaviour in the New York subway. They used a confederate (i.e. an accomplice of the experimenter) who collapsed in front of people on the subway. The researchers wanted to study people's willingness to help the person. The confederate was either sober and held a cane (the lame condition), or appeared drunk and held a bottle (the drunk condition). The researchers found that people were much more likely to help the person in the lame condition (90 per cent) than in the drunk condition (20 per cent). This was in line with their predictions. A strength of the field experiment is that it has ecological validity; but a limitation is that the researchers cannot control all the variables.

A **natural experiment** is an experiment where the researchers have no control over the variables. They are naturally occurring—that is, they are already there to study. An example of this could be research on children who have been kept in isolation by their parents, or research on stroke victims.

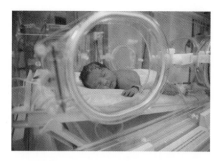

Research in psychology

Researcher Tiffany Field carried out research in the US to investigate the effect of touch on infants who were born prematurely. Eighty premature infants were allocated to either a "standard care" group or a group in which they were given a daily massage. The infants who received massages gained 47 per cent more weight, became more socially responsive, and were discharged six days earlier than those who received standard care. In addition to the beneficial effects for the infants, there were savings of about $10,000 per infant—or $4.7 billion if all of the 470,000 premature babies born each year were to be massaged. Touch therapy is becoming more widely practised across the US.

More information on Tiffany Field's work can be found at www6.miami.edu/touch-research

Apply your knowledge

- Identify the independent and dependent variables in this field experiment.

- Are there any ethical concerns with this study?

Points to consider with experiments

In an experiment, researchers attempt to control as many variables as possible. However, this is not always easy. **Confounding variables** are undesirable variables that influence the relationship between the independent and dependent variables. Here are three of the most common confounding variables. The experiment is an example of quantitative research, which generates numerical data. These can be statistically tested for significance in order to rule out the role of chance in the results.

- **Demand characteristics:** This is when participants act differently simply because they know that they are in an experiment. They may try to guess the aims of the study and act accordingly. This is also known as the **Hawthorne effect**. To counteract demand characteristics, a researcher can use a **single blind control**, which means that the participants do not know what the study is about.

- **Researcher bias:** Also known as observer bias, this is when the experimenter sees what he or she is looking for. In other words, the expectations of the researcher consciously or unconsciously affect the findings of the study. Using a **double blind control** can help to avoid this. In this design, not only do the participants not know whether they are in the treatment or control group, but the person carrying out the experiment does not know the aim of the study, nor whether each group is the treatment or control group.

- **Participant variability:** This is when characteristics of the sample affect the dependent variable. This can be controlled for by selecting a random sample—or randomly allocating the participants to the treatment and control groups.

One other consideration is **artificiality**. This is when the situation created is so unlikely to occur that one has to wonder if there is any validity in the findings. This refers to the question of ecological validity mentioned earlier in this chapter.

Research in psychology

Demand characteristics (Orne 1962)

Demand characteristics were first identified and illustrated by a study conducted by Martin Orne. Orne was trying to see whether he could discover any differences in behaviour between people who had been *hypnotized*—that is, people who believed that they had been hypnotized—and those who were simply pretending to be hypnotized. Orne asked them to perform a variety of tasks, and found that it was not possible to distinguish between the two groups in any way. The most important thing he discovered was that people who believed they were taking part in a psychological experiment acted in ways that were entirely different from how they would act in everyday life.

In one part of the study, participants were asked to add up columns of numbers presented to them on a sheet of paper. When they had finished the sum, they then had to tear up the paper, throw it away, and add the numbers on a second sheet. When they had finished that, they were told to tear it up and do a third, and so on. Orne found that normally people would do one or two of these sheets and then refuse to do any more. But if they believed that they were taking part in a psychological experiment, they would go on indefinitely. One participant continued for over six hours, and eventually had to be stopped by the experimenter, who wanted to go home.

What this study did was to raise a number of questions concerning experiments in psychology. People who are taking part in an experiment do so in a spirit of cooperation, and they want their results to be helpful to the experimenter. As a result of this, they are overly cooperative, and this can mean that a psychology researcher ends up with data which are nothing at all like the data that would be obtained from people acting more normally.

Correlational studies

Very often, an experiment cannot be carried out, but data are collected which show a relationship between two variables—these are correlational data. The principle in correlational studies is that some variables co-vary—that is, when one variable changes, the other variable changes as well. A **positive correlation** is when both variables are affected in the same way. As x increases, y increases. For example, the more hours you spend studying, the better you do on exams; or the fewer hours you spend studying, the less well you do on exams. A **negative correlation** means that as one variable increases, the other decreases. For example, as the number of hours watching television increases, exam scores decrease.

Because no independent variable is manipulated, no cause-and-effect relationship can be determined. For example, a researcher could study the average number of hours that a child watches television and the child's level of aggression. This would be difficult to do as an experiment, because it would be unethical. When the data are gathered, the researcher might find that as the number of hours of television viewing increased, so did the level of aggression in the child. This would be a positive correlation. However, it would not be possible to say whether the television viewing caused the aggression, or if it was the aggression which led the child to watch more television. This is called **bidirectional ambiguity**.

It could also be that there is no cause-and-effect relationship at all, but that another variable might be responsible for the behaviour. For example, a study in Hong Kong quoted by Zimbardo (1999) found a positive correlation between appliance ownership (dishwashers, washing machines, tumble dryers) and the practice of safe sex. Though mathematically this correlation may exist, it is rather doubtful that there is a cause-and-effect relationship.

Non-experimental methods: qualitative research

Learning outcomes

- Describe non-experimental methods
- Outline important differences between experimental and non-experimental methods
- Explain ethical issues related to interviews, observations, and case studies

The experimental method emphasizes reliability, validity, replicability, and generalizability. For a long time, the experiment was the most frequently used method in psychology, and there was little interest in the study of unique and personal human experiences. Eventually, a growing concern about artificiality and lack of ecological validity in research began to emerge, and today, non-experimental methods are seen as a valuable part of modern psychology. Some of the non-experimental methods gather data that are quantitative (e.g. survey), but many researchers now prefer qualitative research methods. Some researchers even combine different research methods in a study in order to collect richer data—**triangulation**. Researchers carefully consider which methods are most appropriate for the topic under investigation.

Qualitative researchers are interested in how people explain their everyday experiences, and therefore the research takes place in natural settings. The aim of qualitative research is to get insight into psychological processes such as: How do people work in teams in the workplace? How do people experience major life events, such as the transition to motherhood? How do IB students experience voluntary work in CAS?

Qualitative research projects are normally guided by one or more research questions, such as those just mentioned. A research question is different from a hypothesis. As mentioned earlier when we considered experiments (Chapter 1.3), a hypothesis is a claim—often derived from theory—that is tested against empirical evidence so that it can be either accepted or rejected. This is called a **deductive approach**. A research question, on the other hand, is open-ended, and invites detailed descriptions and, if possible, explanations. Qualitative researchers are interested in how people experience situations, so they adopt an **inductive approach**. The researcher does not normally define variables in advance because they think that these are more likely to express the researcher's ideas than the participant's. Instead, they first gather the data and then see what these could mean.

The goal of qualitative research is *not* to identify cause-and-effect relationships, but rather to describe the meanings attributed to events by the research participants themselves. In qualitative research, it is acknowledged that participants' and researchers' interpretations of events should be taken into account in the research process; therefore, prediction of outcomes is not a meaningful goal for qualitative researchers. Since the role of the qualitative researcher involves an active engagement in the research process, s/he also acknowledges a **subjective** element to the research process, whereas the experimental method is based on the assumption of **objectivity** in the research process.

In experimental research, description and analysis of data involves calculation of statistics and referring the results to the formulated hypothesis. The qualitative researcher will instead try to **interpret** and analyse the data in order to find the "meaning", knowing that there are no definite answers. The analysis of qualitative data is often very time-consuming.

Interviews

Since the beginning of psychology as a science, researchers have used interviewing as a way of collecting data. Freud, the father of psychotherapy, used clinical interviews to gather data to support his theories. Today, the research interview is one of the most common ways of gathering qualitative data. Interviews can take many forms, and they can vary in time, from a few brief questions to an in-depth interview that takes an hour or more. It is also important to have an **interview schedule**, which is a plan for conducting the interview. The structure of the interview may follow a tight interview schedule with structured questions, or take the form of an informal conversational interview with open-ended questions. According to Hayes (2000), interviewing is a social situation, and the interviewer needs certain skills because of its interpersonal nature—in other words, interviewers need training.

It is necessary for the interviewer to have people skills, because it is important to establish a positive relationship with the interviewee (the person who answers the interviewer's questions). The interviewer must also possess the necessary verbal skills. People are very good at reading non-verbal behaviour and they react to unconscious signs. Therefore, the interviewer should act professionally so that **interviewer effects** do not interfere with the process. Interviewer effects could be responses to the sex, age, or ethnicity of the interviewer. A well-planned research interview will take factors such as these into account, and the researchers will also keep in mind that people often adjust their responses to what they *think* is appropriate for the interviewer. This is called **participant bias**. The researcher also needs to be aware that most people want to present a positive picture of themselves, so they may not always tell the truth when asked personal questions. This effect is termed the **social desirability bias**.

TOK and ways of knowing

Look at the list of characteristics of experimental methods in the table and write down the equivalent in non-experimental research.

Experimental methods	Non-experimental methods
Hypothesis	
Variables	
Cause-and-effect relationship	
Deductive	
Objectivity	
Quantitative data	
Statistics	

The interviewer must establish a good rapport with the interviewee

31

Surveys

A survey is a way of collecting information from a large and dispersed group of people rather than from the very small number, which can be dealt with in a case study or in interviews. It may combine quantitative data with qualitative data or only use quantitative. Surveys often use questionnaires with closed questions to collect data because it is easier to do statistical analysis of such data. Sometimes more open ended questions or even interviews are used for data collection – either alone or as a supplement to questionnaires. The face-to-face approach allows for clarifications if the respondent does not understand questions; this may yield more reliable answers but it takes time.

One advantage of a survey is that it is a relatively simple and straightforward approach to the study of e.g. attitudes, values, beliefs and motives, and it can be extremely efficient at providing large amounts of data at a relatively low cost, in a short period of time. Sometimes interviews can supplement survey data to provide a more in-depth understanding of certain questions.

Many empirical studies use questionnaires to collect data, as do some of the studies mentioned in this book. Surveys use self-report data like the interview. Self-reporting may be biased because people do not always tell the truth. Questionnaires may also be vulnerable to response bias just like the interview – that is people adjust their responses so as to give the "right answer" to the researcher. Therefore, questionnaires need to be carefully planned and designed. If they are, they may reveal useful information.

Types of interviews

In a **structured interview**, the interview schedule may state exactly what questions should be asked, as well as the order of the questions. The interview procedure is thus highly controlled. In fact, this approach is quite similar to questionnaires, but the difference is that the interviewer asks the questions and may provide some guidance to the respondent. The data gathered in a structured interview are easy to analyse and compare with the data from other interviewees who have been asked the same questions. On the other hand, structured interviews may appear somewhat artificial in that the interviewer is bound to the interview schedule.

In an **unstructured interview**, the interview schedule only specifies the topic and the available time. One advantage of this approach is that it is open to the interests and motivation of the interviewee, so they can reveal more about themselves than in a structured interview. However, the data may be more difficult to analyse.

Semi-structured interviews are often preferred in modern psychology. A semi-structured interview could look like an informal conversation, but the interview does follow a schedule. The semi-structured interview schedule involves a set of questions that permits the respondent to answer more freely, while maintaining the focus of the interview. There will be a number of closed questions and a number of questions where the respondent can answer more freely and in their own words.

Ethics in interviews

The interviewer needs to observe carefully general ethical rules in research—for example, informed consent and confidentiality. This is particularly important if the interview deals with personal issues about the interviewee. One of the major strengths of the interview is that it allows a researcher to investigate personal experience, but

Be a researcher

You have been commissioned to carry out research using interviews on one of the following issues:

- positive and negative experiences in CAS projects
- what it is like to live in a foreign country
- teenagers and drug use and abuse
- prejudice in the classroom.

Choose one from this list and consider the following questions.

1 How would you carry out the research?

2 How would you obtain your sample?

3 What potential difficulties do you anticipate in carrying out the interview?

this may be sensitive and distressing in some cases. It is therefore very important that the interviewer has the professional competence required. If respondents reveal very sensitive information during the interview, they may suddenly feel uncomfortable about having done this, and they have the right to withdraw their information. It requires an ethical researcher not to abuse such information.

Observation

Observation is a data collection method which aims to describe behaviour without trying to establish cause-and-effect relationships. Most observations take place in a natural setting and are called **naturalistic observations**. The method was originally developed by researchers who studied animals in their natural environment. However, researchers also perform observations in laboratories—for example, observing mother-and-child interaction through a one-way mirror. The raw data collected during an observation may be visual (e.g. video), audio (tape recording of conversations), or written (e.g. notes, ratings made on the spot).

Observations may appear easy, but there are a number of challenges involved. First, it is not possible to record everything in the observational field. Second, it is important to try to avoid **researcher bias**—that is, the observation should not be affected by what the researcher expects to find. In order to counteract this problem, several observers can observe the same behaviour and then compare the results of their observations to ensure **inter-observer reliability**— that is, to make sure that what they observed actually happened.

A researcher can choose to carry out a **participant observation**, where he of she is part of the group that is being observed, or a **non-participant observation**, where he or she is not part of the group. The researcher wants the participants to act as they would normally. This can be very difficult, because people—and animals— often change their behaviour when they are observed—this is called **reactivity**. Sometimes researchers choose to perform a **covert observation**, where the participants do not know that they are being observed, in order to ensure that the participants behave in natural ways. In an **overt observation**, the participants know that the observer is a researcher.

Non-participant observation

In non-participant observation, the researcher is not part of the group being observed. This always raises the problem that participants might demonstrate reactivity. Demand characteristics could also influence the observation, as the participants try to guess what the research is about and what they think the researcher wants them to do. It is also possible that researcher bias may occur. An example of research using non-participant observation could be a study on interactions between students and teachers in a classroom, where the researchers sit and make notes in different classrooms for a number of hours over a period of six months. The researchers could choose to supplement this with video recordings.

Be a researcher

Work in groups of three. Decide on an event to observe for about five minutes. It can be students in the canteen, people on the bus, a video clip from the news, or even a clip from your favourite film. Each member of the group should take notes during the observation.

1 When you have observed the event, compare your notes. To what extent are your observations similar? Discuss this.

2 Are there any ethical considerations in what you did?

3 Discuss how you could make sense of the data.

Participant observation

In this method, the researcher becomes part of the target group. He or she attempts to feel what it is like to be in a particular social situation, rather than just looking at it from the outside. The process includes participation as well as documentation, interviewing, and reflection. For example, a researcher could observe a training session for teachers on how to use a new computer program in order to find out how educators respond to changes in technology in the workplace.

Sometimes a researcher finds it appropriate to carry out an overt observation, and sometimes it is more appropriate to perform a covert observation. Some researchers engage in covert observations that may be somewhat dangerous—for example, if they want to know what it is like to be part of a street gang or a group like Hell's Angels.

In both cases, the researcher needs to maintain a balance between participation and observation. This can be quite difficult, especially when the research deals with emotionally charged subjects, such as understanding how patients deal with serious illness or dying. The researcher needs to make detailed notes of all observations as soon as possible. It cannot always be done at the time, since participating in social situations sometimes requires the researcher's full attention.

Ethics of observational research

As in all psychological research, for observational studies a researcher needs to obtain the informed consent of the people being observed. Typically, the researcher tells the participants about the observation and shows them the location where the observation will take place. After completing the study, the researcher debriefs the participants about the findings.

In order to protect participants, researchers must make research proposals to ethics committees if they wish to carry out covert research. Ethical considerations in covert research include whether the research will provide important information that could not be obtained otherwise—for example, if the research could be used to the benefit of the participants.

It could be argued that observation of people in public places, such as in a café, do not violate the rights of the person. It is a public situation and people in a café could expect to be observed by others. But what if a researcher observes private behaviour—for example, if he or she attends an Alcoholics Anonymous meeting, where people reveal personal secrets?

> **Points to consider in observational research**
> 1 Is the observation structured (systematic or standardized) or unstructured?
> 2 Is the observation covert (researcher is incognito) or overt (researcher is known to be a researcher)?
> 3 Does the observation take place in a natural or an artificial setting?

Research in psychology

Covert participant observation (Rosenhan 1973)

Rosenhan conducted his famous participant observation in psychiatric wards. The aim was to show that psychiatric diagnosis was not based on an objective set of symptoms, but instead was related to the stereotypes of medical staff about what a mental disorder should look like, and if the behaviour of a patient matched such stereotypes. Rosenhan wanted to see if it was possible for anyone to fake insanity and convince the medical staff that they had a serious mental disorder, when in fact no disorder was present. This would indicate that the diagnosis of such disorders is not reliable.

Rosenhan and seven other individuals attempted to gain admission to psychiatric clinics across the US. They told the hospital staff that they had heard a voice saying, "One, two, three, thud." This was not true, but it was the only sort of deception used in interactions with the hospital staff. The pseudo-patients answered all other questions truthfully. They were all admitted to hospital for observation, and they stayed there for an average of 19 days before being released. Once inside the hospital, they all acted normally, but seven of the pseudo-patients were diagnosed with schizophrenia.

Seen from a patient's point of view, Rosenhan's report paints a disturbing picture of life in a large psychiatric hospital. One of the most telling findings was that while the medical staff could not distinguish the pseudo-patients from the real ones, the genuine patients were able to tell the difference. Rosenhan claims that the staff were biased and interpreted the behaviour of the pseudo-patients in line with the diagnosis. They did not seem to question the diagnosis, even though none of the pseudo-patients exhibited any symptoms that would support it. The researchers made notes while they were in the hospital, and the staff interpreted this as something abnormal and a symptom of schizophrenia.

The research project revealed something about the hidden processes at work within a psychiatric hospital. Rosenhan's research showed that it was possible that the diagnosis and treatment of the mentally ill was determined more by the preconceptions of the medical staff about the nature of mental illness than by the objective presence or absence of symptoms.

Be a critical thinker

1 Discuss ethical issues in Rosenhan's participant observation.

2 Was the use of covert observation justified?

Case studies

The case study method originated in clinical medicine, where it involved taking a patient's personal history in order to make a diagnosis. The case study approach is grounded in real life, and generally produces rich data that can provide insight into unique phenomena or an individual's behaviour.

In a case study, the researcher observes the behaviour of an individual or a group of individuals, such as a school class or social group. The case study is often concerned with descriptions of people's experiences, feelings, or thoughts about a topic under investigation (qualitative data), but it may also include measurements, such as blood testing, IQ scores, or survey data (quantitative data). Often the case study focuses on a limited aspect of behaviour, such as the individual experience of becoming a parent, memory problems after brain damage, conflicts in a school, or implementation of new management procedures in a company.

Case studies allow researchers to investigate a topic in far more detail than if they were dealing with a large number of research participants with the aim of averaging. The case study allows for in-depth investigations of human experience that cannot be investigated using other types of research methods. Examples of famous case studies include Corkin (1987), who studied the relationship between brain damage and memory functioning, and Koluchova (1976), who reported the consequences of childhood deprivation on later emotional and cognitive development in a set of twin boys.

The case study is not a research method itself, but rather an approach to the study of something unique—the case. Researchers use a number of data collection methods to generate material suitable for analysis—for example, qualitative techniques (semi-structured interviews, participant observation), personal artefacts (e.g. letters, diaries, photographs, notes), or official documents (e.g. case notes, clinical notes, appraisal reports). For example, researchers might use interviews where they rely on a person's own memories, as well as written material and careful observation of behaviour. Using multiple methods of investigation to explore the same phenomenon is called triangulation. The combination of different forms of subjective data (feelings, beliefs, impressions, or interpretations) with objective data (description of behaviour and the context in which it occurred, or even blood tests) allows the researcher to adopt different perspectives in looking at case studies, so that psychological phenomena can be explored from a biological, sociocultural, and cognitive level of analysis.

The case study method is important because it may highlight extraordinary behaviour and therefore stimulate new research. It can also contradict existing beliefs. Koluchova's case study of the severely deprived Czechoslovak twins, who made remarkable intellectual and emotional recovery when they were placed in a caring social environment, is an example of such a case study. The findings challenged the established theory that the early years of life are a critical period for human social development, which, if not properly developed, would produce irreversible results. It would be unethical or impossible to recreate such cases in a laboratory setting.

It is not possible to replicate the findings of a case study because of the uniqueness of the case being studied. Since the study cannot be replicated, the reliability of the data is said to be low. Generally, it is not possible to generalize the results of a unique case to the general population, since the individual studied is not representative. However, if the findings of one case study are corroborated by the findings of other case studies, it could be argued that it is possible to make some generalization.

Ethical aspects of the case study method

In a case study, the researcher often obtains deeply personal information which is not usually shared with other people. Eventually, some of this information may be published, or at least written up as a research report. Any researcher conducting a case study must be very protective of the identities of research participants. The researcher should try to obscure details that could lead others to work out an individual's identity. The researcher should also have the professional competence to deal with the focus of the case study—for example, in instances of sexual abuse, anorexia nervosa, or childhood deprivation. Ethical guidelines for psychologists, including informed consent, no deception, right to withdraw, debriefing, and confidentiality, should also be observed in case studies.

> **Data collection methods in a case study**
> - Interviews
> - Observations
> - Questionnaires or psychometric tests
> - Experimental tasks
> - Physiological data (e.g. blood sample to measure level of cortisol)

Research in psychology

Money (1974)

Not all researchers have lived up to the ethical standards for case studies that are now the norm. In the 1960s, Dr John Money was one of the world's leading sex researchers; he argued that children were born gender neutral. According to Money, biological sex did not have to correspond to psychological sex (gender), and therefore children could be raised successfully in whatever sex was assigned to them. He had done quite a lot of research on intersex children—that is, children born with ambiguous genitalia—but he believed that his theory of gender neutrality could be applied to all children.

The Reimer family in Canada had identical twin boys. Due to an accident during circumcision, one of the boys lost his penis. A psychiatrist announced that the boy would forever be physically defective, and the parents were devastated. They contacted Dr Money, who saw an opportunity to find support for his theory of gender neutrality with this boy who had been born with normal genitals. On his advice, the boy was castrated and raised as a girl.

However, things did not go according to plan. The little "girl" (Brenda) did not behave like a girl, and she experienced many problems in school with her peers, due to her masculine behaviour. Dr Money ignored the evidence that everything was not as he had predicted. He published scientific articles that used the case study as evidence that nurture is more important than nature. Feminists also supported the claim that biological differences could not explain gender differences. As a result of Money's articles, scientific textbooks were rewritten, and it became normal practice that children born with ambiguous genitals were assigned a new sex and had genital surgery.

One scientist, however, was not convinced that Money was right. Milton Diamond had examined the role of hormones on the developing fetus, and he argued that gender-specific behaviour was pre-programmed in the womb. After a number of animal studies, Diamond declared that if pregnant females were treated with testosterone, their female offspring would exhibit masculine behaviour in spite of their biological sex. This contradicted Money's claims, but he continued to put pressure on the Reimer family to continue treatment. Eventually, Brenda had a nervous breakdown and refused to see Money any longer. Finally, the family told "her" the truth, and "she" decided to become a boy again and took the name David.

Until the 1980s, Money continued to use the case as evidence for his theory of gender neutrality and the success of gender reassignment surgery. He spoke publicly against Diamond's theory of hormones as a major factor in gender development.

In 1997, Diamond published an article in *Archives of Pediatric & Adolescent Medicine*, where he presented important evidence that individuals are not gender neutral at birth, and that psychosexual development is not determined by genitalia or upbringing, but rather by chromosomes and hormones. He also argued that chromosomal males should be raised as males, and that any necessary surgery should maintain the individual's sex; he claimed that attempting to raise the child as a female was unlikely to be a happy solution in the long term. He is supported in this by the Intersex Society of North America, which advocates the abandonment of genital reassignment surgery for infants.

The story has a sad ending for the Reimer family. Both of the twin boys eventually committed suicide.

1　Outline two ethical problems in this case study.

2　What could be the reason that Money continued to use this case as evidence of his theory of gender neutrality?

TOK and ways of knowing

1　How do you know that the experimental method is a valid method of gaining knowledge?

2　How do you know that non-experimental methods, like the interview, observation, or case study, are valid methods of gaining knowledge?

3　Is it possible to decide whether some ways of knowing are better than others?

Biological level of analysis: physiology and behaviour

Learning outcomes

- Outline principles that define the biological level of analysis
- Explain how principles that define the biological level of analysis may be demonstrated in research (through theories and/or studies)
- Discuss how and why particular research methods are used at the biological level of analysis
- Discuss ethical considerations related to research studies at the biological level of analysis
- Explain one study of localization of function of the brain
- Explain, using examples, the effects of neurotransmission on human behaviour
- Explain, using examples, functions of two hormones in human behaviour
- Discuss two effects of the environment on physiological processes
- Examine one interaction between cognition and physiology in terms of behaviour
- Discuss the use of brain-imaging technologies in investigating the relationship between biological factors and behaviour

Principles of the biological level of analysis

The biological level of analysis argues that there are physiological origins of many behaviours, and that human beings should be studied as biological systems. This is not to say that behaviour is the result of biological systems alone, but that we should also consider how the environment and cognition may interact with biological systems and affect physiology. This relationship is **bidirectional** i.e. biology can affect cognition and cognition can affect biology.

Many physiological factors can play a role in behaviour: brain processes, neurotransmitters, hormones, and genes. However, physiology does not work on its own; it responds to environmental stimuli, such as a stressful experience, an attractive person walking by, or something as extreme as brain damage caused by an accident. One of the major controversies in the history of psychology is the so-called **nature versus nurture debate**, in which researchers debate whether human behaviour is the result of biological or environmental factors. The **interactionist approach** used by modern psychologists does not rely solely on either nature (biological) or nurture (environment), but adopts a more holistic picture of human behaviour. This is also the goal of IB psychology.

The biological level of analysis is based on certain principles about human behaviour. One of these principles is that behaviour can be innate because it is genetically based. If this principle is accepted it is logical to believe that evolution may play a key role in behaviour. Another principle is that animal research can provide insight into human behaviour; as a result, a significant amount of research is undertaken using animals. A third principle is that there are biological correlates of behaviour. The implication of this is that it should be possible to find a link between a specific biological factor (e.g. a hormone) and a specific behaviour, and this is the aim of researchers working at the biological level of analysis.

Biological researchers often adopt a **reductionist** approach to the study of human behaviour. This is a micro-level of research, which breaks down complex human behaviour into its smallest parts—for example, focusing on the role of a gene, a neurotransmitter, or a protein. This micro approach is sometimes criticized for being overly simplistic in explaining behaviour. However, it is important to have detailed knowledge of the components of human behaviour in order to understand how several factors may interact to cause certain behaviours. The key is that there are no easy answers to complex questions.

Mechanisms of neurotransmission and their effects on human behaviour

Nerve cells, called **neurons**, are one of the building blocks of behaviour. It is estimated that there are between 10 and 100 billion neurons in the nervous system, and that neurons make 13 trillion connections with each other. The neurons send electrochemical messages to the brain so that people can respond to stimuli—either from the environment or from internal changes in the body.

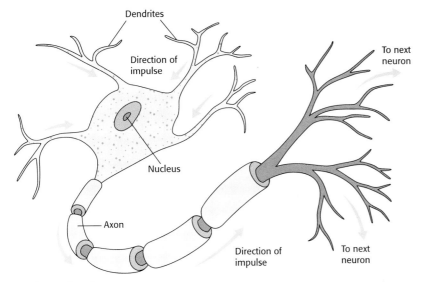

Neural impulses in a neuron

The method by which these messages are sent is called **neurotransmission**. When an electrical impulse travels down the body, or **axon**, of the neuron, it releases **neurotransmitters** which then cross the gap between two neurons. This gap is called a **synapse**. Neurotransmitters are the body's natural chemical messengers which transmit information from one neuron to another. The neurotransmitters are stored in the neurons' **terminal buttons**. After crossing the synapse, the neurotransmitters fit into receptor sites on the post-synaptic membrane, like a key in a lock. Once the message is passed on, the neurotransmitters are either broken down or reabsorbed by the terminal buttons. This is known as **reuptake**.

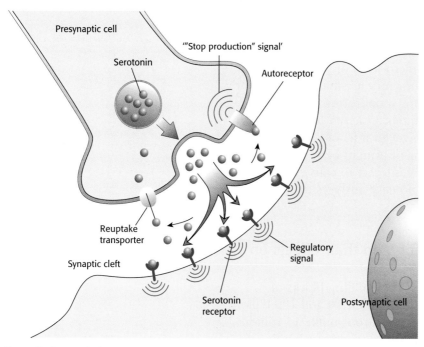

Synaptic transmission

Neurotransmitters have been shown to have a range of different effects on human behaviour. In fact, neurotransmission underlies behaviour as varied as mood, memory, sexual arousal, and mental illness. The table below, which highlights just a few neurotransmitters, gives an idea of the variety of behaviours which are influenced by these neurochemicals.

Neurotransmitter	Effect
Acetylcholine	Muscle contraction, and a role in the development of memory in the hippocampus
Dopamine	Voluntary movement, learning, and feelings of pleasure
Norepinephrine (noradrenaline)	Arousal, alertness, and stimulation of the sympathetic nervous system
Serotonin	Sleep, arousal levels, and emotion

One example of how the neurotransmitter serotonin can affect behaviour was seen by researchers at Tokyo University (Kasamatsu and Hirai, 1999). The aim of the study was to see how sensory deprivation affects the brain. In order to do this, the researchers studied a group of Buddhist monks who went on a 72-hour pilgrimage to a holy mountain in Japan. During their stay on the mountain, the monks did not consume food or water, they did not speak, and they were exposed to the cold, late autumn weather. After about 48 hours, they began to have hallucinations, often seeing ancient ancestors or feeling a presence by their sides. The researchers took blood samples before the monks ascended the mountain, and then again immediately after the monks reported having hallucinations. They found that serotonin levels had increased in the monks' brains. These higher levels of serotonin activated the parts of the brain called the **hypothalamus** and the **frontal cortex**, resulting in the hallucinations. From this study, researchers concluded that sensory deprivation triggered the release of serotonin, which actually altered the way that the monks experienced the world.

Because neurotransmitters fit tightly into receptor sites, like a key in a lock, drugs have been developed to either simulate the neurotransmitter if there is not enough of a specific neurotransmitter, or to block the site if it is excessive. The application of such research has improved the lives of many people.

There has been criticism of reducing the explanation of behaviour to the workings of neuroneurotransmitters alone. It is said to be reductionist. Can a complex human behaviour like attraction to a potential partner be attributed to a simple "love cocktail" of dopamine, norepinephrine, and oxytocin? Can mood be attributed simply to serotonin levels? Once again, most psychologists consider that neurotransmitters play a role, but do not rely solely on neurotransmission to explain behaviour.

Profile

Otto Loewi (1873-1961)

The pharmacologist and physiologist Otto Loewi was one of the first people to discover the role of the neurotransmitter acetylcholine. In 1921 he devised an imaginative experimental set-up using frog hearts and discovered that nerve impulses affect the heart using electrochemical transmission, though he did not know at the time that the substance he had identified was acetylcholine. Otto Loewi shared the Nobel Price in medicine with the British researcher Henry Dale in 1936 for their findings on neurotransmission.

Research in psychology

Martinez and Kesner on the role of neurotransmitters in learning and memory (1991)

The researchers carried out an experiment with the aim of determining the role of the neurotransmitter acetylcholine on memory. Acetylcholine is believed to play a role in memory formation. Rats were trained to go through a maze and get to the end, where they received food. Once the rats were able to do this, he injected one group of rats with scopolamine, which blocks acetylcholine receptor sites thus decreasing available acetylcholine. He then injected a second group of rats with physostigmine, which blocks the production of cholinesterase. Cholinesterase does the "clean-up" of acetylcholine from the synapse and returns the neuron to its "resting state". The third group, the control group, were not given any injections.

The results showed that those rats that were injected with scopolamine were slower at finding their way round the maze and made more errors than either the control group or the physostigmine group. The physostigmine group, on the other hand, ran through the maze and found the food even more quickly than the control group, and took fewer wrong turns.

The researchers concluded that acetylcholine played an important role in creating a memory of the maze.

The strengths of this research lie in its design and its application. The use of an experimental method with a control group made it possible to establish a cause-and-effect relationship between levels of acetylcholine and memory.

The limitation of the research is that it is questionable to what extent these findings can be generalized to humans. Is it possible to apply research on rats to human beings? At this level, it is assumed that memory processes are the same for all animals. This may be true to some extent. In fact, research has shown that acetylcholine-producing cells in the basal forebrain are damaged in the early stages of Alzheimer's disease. See more on biological factors in memory research in the profile box on Eric Kandel page 76.

The brain and behaviour

Over the past hundred years, few areas of psychology have developed quite so rapidly as brain research. As technology has progressed, so has our ability to monitor and map out the brain's activity. The brain is seen as the command centre of human activity, and psychologists continue to develop a deeper understanding of its role, and how it matures over a lifetime and adapts to the environment.

Prior to the development of modern scanning technology, one of the most common ways to study the brain was through the use of case studies of brain damage. Often such studies provide researchers with a situation that they could never ethically reproduce in a laboratory. Case studies of brain-damaged patients are often carried out **longitudinally**—that is, over a long period of time—in order to observe both the short-term and long-term effects of damage.

Research in psychology

Case study: Phineas Gage

Perhaps the most famous case study of how brain damage can affect behaviour is that of Phineas Gage, studied by Dr John Harlow. In 1848, Phineas Gage, a 25-year-old railroad foreman, was in a serious accident. While trying to blast through a rocky cliff, an explosion sent a metal pole through his skull. The iron entered Gage's left cheek, pierced the base of the skull, went through the front of his brain, and exited at high speed through the top of his head. The pole landed more than a hundred feet away, covered in blood and brains.

Amazingly, Phineas was awake and alert. His men carried him to the road and put him into an ox cart, in which he rode, sitting up, all the way to the local hotel, where he waited for the arrival of Dr Harlow. Phineas had lost vision in his left eye, but his vision was perfect in the right eye. He did not suffer any paralysis and had no noticeable difficulty with speech or language. However, Dr Harlow noted that the balance between his intellectual abilities and his emotional control had been destroyed. The changes became apparent as soon as his wound had healed. He had become highly agitated and irreverent, indulging at times in the grossest profanity that had not previously been his custom. He was impatient and indulgent. Though he could make plans for his future, he could never follow through on them. Dr Harlow described him as "a child in his intellectual capacity, but with the animal passions of a strong man". His use of pornographic language was so shocking that women were advised not to stay long in his presence.

What had happened to Phineas Gage? The longitudinal study of the damage to his frontal lobe provided evidence that the brain affects personality and social behaviours. However, at the time, it was believed that the injury had occurred in the best part of the brain in which to sustain damage—that is, a part of the brain that did not do much and was thus expendable. It would be some time before psychologists had developed the knowledge and technology to understand that the frontal lobe has a specific function, and that many behaviours are localized in this area.

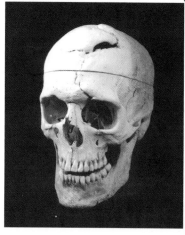

The skull of Phineas Gage

1 To what extent is this case study useful? Support your argument.

2 It has been argued that this case is important because it is among the first to indicate that damage to the frontal lobes can affect personality and behaviour. Does this ethically justify the use of a case study like this one?

Be a communicator

Case studies of brain-damaged patients have led to important findings about the brain. Write a newspaper article to inform the general public about the case study of Phineas Gage and what can be learned from it.

Further research

● Vilayanur S. Ramachandran has carried out several case studies that have given us insight into the workings of the brain.

● Oliver Sacks has written up many of his case studies in several highly readable books, and he has a great website www.oliversacks.com

Localization of brain function

Not long after the case of Phineas Gage, two psychologists made some interesting discoveries when looking at stroke victims. **Paul Broca** (1861) found that people suffering from damage in the left frontal lobe of the brain—an area that eventually came to be called Broca's area— were unable to understand and make grammatically complex sentences. Broca's patients had problems producing speech, but were able to understand it. This condition is now known as Broca's **aphasia**. Like Harlow, Broca used a case study in order to support his claims. His most famous patient was a young man named Tan. He was called Tan because that was the only word he could say. After his death, an autopsy revealed the source of his brain damage and led to the idea that the disability was the result of a specific brain trauma.

A decade later, **Carl Wernicke** (1874) first described the area that appears to be crucial for language comprehension—the left posterior superior temporal gyrus. Wernicke's patients could produce speech, but could not understand it. This condition is known as Wernicke's aphasia. The research undertaken by Broca and Wernicke provides us with a clear understanding of some of the factors involved in language processing.

By carrying out **post-mortem studies** of people who had suffered from strokes, Broca and Wernicke came to the conclusion that language processing is **localized**. When a behaviour is localized in the brain, it is possible to trace the origin of the behaviour to a specific part of the brain. Auditory and speech information is transported from the auditory area (the temporal lobe) to Wernicke's area for evaluation of significance of content words, and then to Broca's area for analysis of syntax. In speech production, content words are selected by neural systems in Wernicke's area; grammatical refinements are added by neural systems in Broca's area; then the information is sent to the motor cortex, which sets up the muscle movements for speaking. Studies in localization of function led to the desire to map out the brain's functions. Though localization does not explain all human behaviour, the mapping out of the brain was an important step forward in brain research.

Be an enquirer

Karl Kim and Joy Hirsch (1997) used fMRI (functional magnetic resonance imaging) to research how the brain processes language in bilingual individuals. One group consisted of those who had learned a second language as children; the other was made up of people who had learned their second language later in life. People in both groups were asked to think about something they had done the day before—first in one language, then in the other.

What the researchers found was very interesting. Both groups used the same part of Wernicke's area, regardless of which language they were thinking in; but their use of Broca's area differed. People who were bilingual from birth used the same region in Broca's area for both languages. However, those who had learned their second language later in life used a larger area of the brain, with the second language activating an area adjacent to the area activated by the first language.

- What conclusions could be reached from this study in terms of localization of function?

- What could be the advantage of using fMRI in this study?

In Chapter 3.1 you can read more on localization of function in relation to memory processes.

Localization of brain function and ethics in research

Modern research has focused on the role of the nucleus accumbens, the so-called "pleasure centre" of the brain.

In the 1950s, **Robert Heath** found that by electrically stimulating specific parts of the brain of depressed patients, they would experience pleasure. He let the patients press the buttons themselves to receive pleasure. In one example, during a three-hour session, a participant referred to as B-19 electrically stimulated himself 1500 times. According to a 1972 study published in the *Journal of Behaviour Therapy and Experimental Psychiatry*, "during these sessions, B-19 stimulated himself to a point that he was experiencing an almost overwhelming euphoria and elation, and had to be disconnected, despite his vigorous protests".

At around the same time, **James Olds** carried out research on rats to see what would happen if their pleasure centres were stimulated. He devised an experiment in which the rat would receive electrical stimulation of the nucleus accumbens by pressing a lever. It was found that the rats were willing to walk across electrified grids in order to get to the "pleasure lever". In fact, they even preferred the stimulation to eating and drinking.

So how does the discovery that pleasure may be localized help psychologists to understand human behaviour? It appears that the electrical activation of the nucleus accumbens is based chiefly on dopamine—a neurotransmitter that promotes desire—and serotonin—a neurotransmitter that promotes satiety and inhibition.

Animal studies show that all drugs increase the production of dopamine in the nucleus accumbens and reduce the production of serotonin. Both neurotransmitters play a central role in the feelings produced by such drugs as cocaine and nicotine. It is also known that frequent consumption of the drugs increases the amount of dopamine in the nucleus accumbens. Psychologists now believe that this could help to explain and treat drug addicts' obsessive drive to seek more of a drug, even though they know it is bad for them.

The use of technology in brain research

Modern technology is now extensively used in neuropsychology because it provides an opportunity to study the active brain. This allows researchers to see where specific brain processes take place and enables them to study localization of function in the living human brain. However, experiments with animals are still extensively used in brain research because they allow psychologists to study specific biological correlates of behaviour using invasive techniques. Many early experiments on the brain involved **invasive techniques**—for example, removing (ablation) or scarring (lesioning) brain tissue in order to study behavioural changes. Behaviour before and after lesioning was compared. In a classic study, Hetherington and Ranson (1942) lesioned a part of the brain called the ventromedial hypothalamus in rats. The rats increased their food intake dramatically, and often doubled their weight. This led researchers to believe that the hypothalamus acted as a brake on

A lesioned hypothalamus affects appetite regulation, which has doubled the weight of the rat on the left

> ### Be an enquirer
> **Consider ethics in animal research**
>
> Through research on the nucleus accumbens, psychologists have gained insight into the nature of addiction. In order to carry out these studies, animals suffered and were killed. Find arguments on both sides of the debate about whether it is ethical to use animal research for the betterment of human beings.
>
> A place to start is www.bbc.co.uk/science/hottopics/animalexperimnts

eating. More recent research, however, has argued that although the hypothalamus does play a role in the regulation of hunger, its exact role is not yet well understood.

Invasive techniques, however, raise serious ethical concerns. In cases of lesioning and ablation, the potential harm to the animal cannot be determined. In addition, any damage that is caused cannot be reversed. Finally, there is the question of causing pain to animals.

Modern researchers use techniques like the **EEG** (electroencephalogram) to study the brain. The EEG printout is often thought of as "brainwaves". When neurons transport information through the brain, they have an electrical charge. The EEG registers patterns of voltage change in the brain. Through EEGs, psychologists have been able to gain a better understanding of behaviours as diverse as sleep, emotions, and epilepsy. However, the EEG provides the researcher with limited information—it cannot reveal what is happening in deeper brain regions; nor can it show the actual functioning of the brain.

A **PET** (positron emission topography) scan monitors glucose metabolism in the brain. The patient is injected with a harmless dose of radioactive glucose, and the radioactive particles emitted by the glucose are detected by the PET scanner. The scans produce coloured maps of brain activity. The PET scan has been used to diagnose abnormalities like tumours, or changes as in Alzheimer's; to compare brain differences in normal individuals and in those with psychological disorders (neural activity is different in people with schizophrenia); and to compare sex differences—for example, Gur et al. (1995) found more active metabolism in primitive brain centres controlling violence in men than in women. The greatest advantage of PET (compared to MRI) is that it can record ongoing activity in the brain, such as thinking.

Finally, an **fMRI** (functional magnetic resonance imaging) provides three-dimensional pictures of the brain structures, using magnetic fields and radio waves. The fMRI shows actual brain activity and indicates which areas of the brain are active when engaged in a behaviour. These scans have a higher resolution than PET scans, and they are easier to carry out. This is one of the most frequently used technologies in biopsychological research today.

TOK: ethics

The use of PET and fMRI scans has helped psychologists to identify brain patterns for dysfunctional behaviours. In fact, some scientists say that these scanning images are like fingerprints. There is a certain pattern for people with schizophrenia, alcoholism, and depression, among other disorders. These patterns are present, even if the person does not show any symptoms of the disorder.

1 Do you think that doctors should scan patients to let them know if they have a predisposition for a mental illness? What effect do you think this would have on the individual?

2 Could this technology be misused? Does the potential abuse of technology and knowledge mean that it should not be pursued?

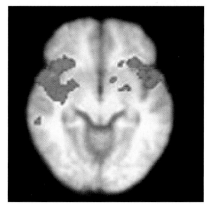

An fMRI scan of the brain

Evaluating brain scanning techniques
Though psychologists can learn a lot from brain imaging techniques, the technique is not without limitations.
- The MRI scanner is not a natural environment for cognition. There is a question of ecological validity.
- The use of colors may exaggerate the different activities of the brain
- Brain areas activate for various reasons – just because the amygdala lights up, doesn't mean that fear is necessarily part of the response being observed.

How the environment affects the brain

The brain is a dynamic system that interacts with the environment. In a sense, the brain is physically sculpted by experience. Not only can the brain determine and change behaviour, but behaviour and environment can change the brain.

Brain plasticity

Before the 1960s, the brain was thought to be influenced only by genetics, and therefore it was considered unchangeable. However, researchers such as Hubel and Wiesel (1965) demonstrated that the brain could change as a response to environmental input. These results were based on laboratory experiments with rats, but it has now become generally accepted that environmental enrichment can modify the brain, especially the cerebral cortex, which is the area of higher cognitive functioning. It seems that the brain is constantly changing as a result of experience throughout the lifespan.

Brain plasticity refers to the brain's ability to rearrange the connections between its neurons—that is, the changes that occur in the structure of the brain as a result of learning or experience. The changes that take place are related to the challenges of the environment and therefore represent an adaptation to it. Plasticity can change the functional qualities of various brain structures, depending on the regularity and type of new tasks that neurons are asked to perform. High levels of stimulation and numerous learning opportunities at the appropriate times lead to an increase in the density of neural connections. This means that the brain of an expert musician should have a thicker area in the cortex related to mastery of music, when compared to the brain of a non-musician. The same can be said about students who spend a lot of time studying, compared to students who do not. Every time we learn something new, the neurons connect to create a new trace in the brain. This is called **dendritic branching** because the dendrites of the neurons grow in numbers and connect with other neurons.

A series of studies of brain plasticity was carried out by Rosenzweig and Bennett (1972). The researchers placed rats into one of two environments to measure the effect of either enrichment or deprivation on the development of neurons in the cerebral cortex. The enriched, stimulating environment was characterized by interesting toys to play with. The deprived environment was characterized by no toys. The rats spent 30 or 60 days in their respective environments and then they were sacrificed. Post-mortem studies of their brains showed that those that had been in the stimulating environment had an increased thickness in the cortex. The frontal lobe, which is associated with thinking, planning, and decision making, was heavier in the rats that had been in the stimulating environment. Similar research studies have constantly demonstrated that cortical thickness increases even further if the rats are placed with other rats. The combination of having company and many interesting toys created the best conditions for developing cerebral thickness.

> **Possible exam question**
>
> With reference to one empirical study explain how environmental factors can affect one physiological process.
>
> Advice: The command term "explain" invites you to give a detailed account including reasons or causes. In this question you need to include a relevant empirical study to show a possible link between environmental factors and a physiological process. Use the research by Rosenzweig and Bennett to write a short answer response to this question. You can refer to one of the studies done by the researchers.

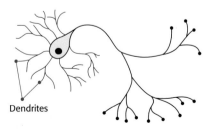

Dendrites

Dentritic branching

What does this mean? Can these findings be generalized to humans? The answer is: only to some extent. Psychologists cannot carry out controlled experiments to test this with humans, and human brains differ in terms of genetic make-up and the environmental inputs that they receive. Because of these differences, it may also be difficult to decide what is considered to be an enriched environment for a specific person. This raises the question of the importance of education in the growth of new synapses. If learning always results in an increase of dendritic branchings, then the findings from animal studies which show brain plasticity in response to environmental stimulation are important for the human cortex as well.

The effect of cognition on physiology

It seems that humans are able to influence the way the brain functions. Could meditation, for example, change brain activity? An experiment carried out by Richard Davidson (2004) attempted to answer that question. The experiment involved eight Buddhist monks who were highly experienced in meditation, and 10 volunteers who had been trained in meditation for one week. All the participants were told to meditate on love and compassion. Using a PET scan, Davidson observed that two of the controls and all of the monks experienced an increase in the number of **gamma waves** in their brain during meditation. Gamma waves have been linked to higher reasoning faculties. As soon as they stopped meditating, the volunteers' gamma-wave production returned to normal, while the monks, who had meditated on compassion for more than 10,000 hours in order to attain the rank of adept, did not experience a decrease to normal in their gamma-wave production after they stopped meditating. The synchronized gamma-wave area of the monks' brains during meditation on love and compassion was found to be larger than the corresponding activation of the volunteers' brains. This led Davidson to argue that meditation could have significant long-term effects on the brain and the way it processes emotions. These findings indicate that the brain adapts to stimulation—whether from the environment or as a result of our own thinking.

You can read about another effect of the environment on a physiological process on page 50: how light might affect hormonal levels and cause a depressive condition called Seasonal Affective Disorder (SAD).

One of the most well-known claims of brain plasticity is the **Mozart effect** (Rauscher et al. 1993). This is the reported phenomenon that listening to Mozart will temporarily increase spatial reasoning ability. The theory suggests that exposure to musical compositions that are structurally complex excites the same brain-firing pattern as when physically completing spatial tasks. The idea behind this theory is that simply by listening to the music, the brain will develop a more sophisticated ability to solve spatial problems.

More recent research has shown that the Mozart effect has little to do with Mozart and more to do with arousal. As people do something that they like—whether it is listening to Mozart, Madonna, or simply enjoying silence—they improve their spatial abilities. Thompson et al. (2001) found that when participants' moods were elevated, they had improved spatial skills; those whose mood did not change as a result of the music did not show any improvement. In the end, the Mozart effect may not be an example of plasticity, but rather a heightened sense of attention that increases learning in some people.

The majority of Mozart effect research suffers from problems with ecological validity. Most of the experiments were carried out in laboratory settings where participants were asked to complete tasks that were not something that they would do in the "real world". This leads to questionable results that are not likely to predict an individual's behaviour in a real-life situation.

Mirror neurons

Another way in which brains interact with the environment has to do with how people learn. One of the ways that people learn is by observing others and then imitating their behaviour. Recent research has shown that special neurons, called **mirror neurons**, may play a vital role in the ability to learn from—as well as empathize with—another person. A mirror neuron is a neuron that fires when an animal (or a person) performs an action or when the animal observes somebody else perform the same action. The mirror neuron is so called because it "mirrors" the behaviour of another.

Mirror neurons enable football supporters to experience the same feelings as the other individuals in their support group

Like many great discoveries in science, mirror neurons were discovered by accident. Gallese et al. (1996), at the University of Parma in Italy, were carrying out research on motor neurons. Because neural messages are electrical in nature, they were able to hear the crackle of the electrical signal when a neuron was activated. Through their research, they had isolated the neural response in rhesus monkeys reaching for food—in this case, a peanut. Every time the monkey reached for a peanut, the telltale crackling noise was heard. One day, one of the researchers reached for a peanut, and then he heard the noise of the electrical signal from the electrodes connected to the neurons in the monkey's brain. In other words, just by watching someone else reach for the peanut, the monkey's brain acted as though the monkey were carrying out the behaviour.

Having observed this in animals, psychologists wondered if it also occurs in humans. Marco Iacoboni (2004) asked participants to look at human faces while undergoing an fMRI. The aim of his study was to see if simply looking at the emotion expressed on someone's face would cause the brain of the observer to be stimulated. First, the participants had to imitate the faces they were shown, and then they had to simply watch as they were shown the faces again. The findings supported the research conducted with animals. Not only were the same areas of the brain activated in both cases, but it became clear that the limbic system was also stimulated—observing a happy face activated pleasure centres in the brain.

Researchers like Ramachandran have been looking at mirror neurons as a way to explain empathy for others. Mirror neurons appear to play a role in how people react to sports, theatre, and video games. It appears that when we see a football player crushed by an opponent, we "feel" the contact of the hit thanks to our mirror neurons. Researchers believe that mirror neurons have evolved to make us capable of understanding and interacting with fellow human beings. The study of mirror neurons is still in its infancy, but initial research appears very promising.

Functions of hormones in human behaviour

Hormones are another class of chemicals that affect behaviour. They are produced by the glands that make up the endocrine system.

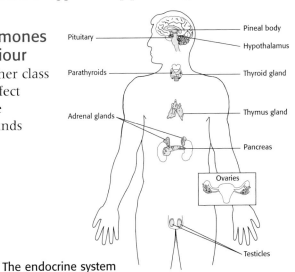

The endocrine system

Hormone	Glands	Function
Adrenaline	Adrenals	Flight or fight response, arousal
Cortisol	Adrenals	Arousal, stress hormone, memory
Melatonin	Pineal	Regulation of sleep
Oxytocin	Pituitary and hypothalamus	Mother–child attachment
Testosterone and oestrogen	Gonads	Development, emotion

Some hormones and their functions

Hormones enter directly into the bloodstream, so they take longer to produce changes in behaviour than neurotransmitters. Some chemicals serve as both hormones and neurochemicals. **Oxytocin** is a hormone that is produced by the hypothalamus after being stimulated by the pituitary gland. As a hormone, it plays a role in inducing labour contractions and lactation. Oxytocin is released with touches and hugs. It is associated with bonding between a mother and her child as well as between lovers. Oxytocin appears to change the brain signals related to social recognition via facial expression, perhaps by changing the firing of the neurons of the amygdala. This is the part of the brain that plays an important role in processing emotional stimuli. Oxytocin has been called "the love hormone" because it seems to be such an effective mediator of human social behaviour. If oxytocin is given to healthy individuals it seems that brain circuits involved in fear regulation are affected, and there is an increase in trust and generosity. Research is being carried out to see whether people suffering from social anxiety may benefit from doses of oxytocin.

TOK and ways of knowing

Bernini's *David*

Freedberg and Gallese (2007) have proposed that mirror neurons are the basis for our appreciation—or lack thereof—of art. When we see Bernini's *David* grimacing in his effort, or we see pain inflicted on another in a painting, it is our mirror neurons that help us to identify with the painting and see it as having aesthetic value.

If Freedberg and Gallese are correct in their assumption that mirror neurons play an important role in art appreciation, what knowledge of art can be gained by focusing on the individual's response?

To what extent is appreciation of the arts "feeling"—as seen in mirror neuron response—and to what extent is it a learned, cognitive response?

Through the study of the hormone **melatonin**, researchers hope to find a solution for those who suffer from insomnia (the inability to fall asleep) and jet lag. The production of melatonin by the pineal gland is stimulated by darkness and inhibited by light. Melatonin levels in the bloodstream peak in the middle of the night, and gradually decrease towards morning. As the days get shorter and winter approaches, the earlier onset of darkness means that we can become tired earlier. Until recent history, humans in temperate climates had up to 18 hours of darkness in the winter months. The use of artificial lighting has increased the "awake time" dramatically.

Melatonin release correlates with the circadian rhythm—the biological clock that is based on a 24-hour day/night cycle. It is suggested that taking melatonin in the early evening may improve one's ability to fall asleep. However, there is some evidence (Rosenthal 1987) that higher levels of melatonin contribute to **seasonal affective disorder (SAD)**—a subcategory of depression that is characterized by sleepiness and lethargy—as well as cravings for carbohydrates. Reduced levels of sunlight in autumn and winter are believed to disrupt the circadian rhythm in certain people, leading to this form of depression. This is perhaps why we see higher levels of SAD in Scandinavia. As increased sunlight improves the symptoms, phototherapy is often the main treatment for people with SAD. In phototherapy, people are exposed to bright light for several hours each day. Despite claims of some success with this treatment, there is a lack of definitive evidence of its effectiveness. Whether it is light therapy to combat depression or melatonin pills to aid sleep, one has to be careful about seeking quick solutions to complex questions.

See Chapter 7.1 for information about stress hormones.

Be a thinker

Until recently, as a species we used to go to sleep when the sun set and wake up when it rose. With the development of electricity and the ability to have lighting on demand, we have changed our environment in a way that is "unnatural" with regard to our physiology.

1 How do you think that the changes in our daily rhythms affect our lives?

2 Are we meant to sleep more in winter? If so, what does our manipulation of light mean for us as human beings?

2.2 Biological level of analysis: genetics and behaviour

Learning outcomes

- Outline principles that define the biological level of analysis
- Explain how principles that define the biological level of analysis may be demonstrated in research
- Discuss how and why particular research methods are used at the biological level of analysis
- Discuss ethical considerations related to research studies at the biological level of analysis
- Discuss the extent to which genetics influence behaviour
- Examine one evolutionary explanation of behaviour
- Discuss ethical considerations in research into genetic influences on behaviour

Behavioural genetics

Behavioural genetics deals with understanding how both genetics and the environment contribute to individual variations in human behaviour. It is interesting to note that humans share 93 per cent of genes with the rhesus macaque monkeys, even though humans do not look like these animals and do not behave like them. Although comparative psychology has revealed similarities between humans and monkeys, it is obvious that the 7 per cent difference in the genetic material accounts for a significant amount. This example demonstrates the complexity of genetics; although the basic premise of this field is that inheritance of DNA plays a role in behaviour, it is important not to misunderstand this. What is inherited are the genes that give rise to the development of specific physiological processes that contribute to specific characteristics and behaviour. It is not probable that a single gene is responsible for such complex behaviours as intelligence, criminal behaviour, altruism, or attachment. Instead, what is inherited may be one of the building blocks for such complex behaviours.

Psychologists argue that an individual may have a genetic predisposition towards a certain behaviour; however, without the appropriate environmental stimuli, this behaviour will not be manifested. For example, in the study of abnormal behaviour, the **diathesis-stress model** is used to explain the origin of depression. This model argues that depression may be the result of the interaction of a "genetic vulnerability" and traumatic environmental stimuli in early childhood. It is also known that not all people develop depression following a traumatic childhood, even if they have a sibling who becomes depressed. This illustrates the complexity of the problem and that there is no single cause-and-effect relationship between genes and behaviour.

Genetic arguments of behaviour are based on the principle of **inheritance**. Genes and their DNA are passed down from parents to their offspring. Humans have 23 pairs of chromosomes, with approximately 20 000–25 000 genes. In 1990, James D. Watson pioneered the Human Genome Project, with the goal of mapping the genetic make-up of the human species by identifying those 25 000 genes. This incredible project was completed in 2003. The mapping of human genes could be an important step in explaining human behaviour, as well as developing treatments. In spite of this spectacular accomplishment, however, the role of specific genes in specific behaviours remains unknown.

Genetic research

Genetic research in humans is to a large extent based on **correlational studies**. Researchers look at how different variables may co-vary. This means that a correlational study establishes that there is a relationship between variables, but the researcher does not manipulate an independent variable as in an experiment. Therefore, no cause and effect can be determined.

Twin studies, family studies and adoption studies

One of the most common ways to study the possible correlation of genetic inheritance and behaviour is through twin research. Researchers study twins because they share common genetic material.

There are two types of twins: **monozygotic** (MZ) and **dizygotic** (DZ). Monozygotic twins are genetically identical because they are formed from one fertilized egg that splits into two. These twins are of the same sex and should look very much alike. Dizygotic means from two eggs. DZ twins will not be any closer genetically than brothers and sisters—they will have about 50 per cent of their genes in common. They are formed from two separate fertilized eggs. These twins are not necessarily of the same sex. This is important, because psychologists use these different degrees of genetic relationship as a basis for their hypotheses. It should be the case that the higher the genetic relationship, the more similar individuals will be if the particular characteristic being investigated is inherited. In twin research, the correlation found is called the **concordance rate**.

Twins are often used in genetic research

Another way that behavioural genetics is studied is through **family studies**. Unlike twin research, this is a more representative sample of the general population. A child inherits half its genes from the mother and half from the father. It follows that ordinary brothers and sisters will share 50 per cent of their genes with each other; grandparents will share 25 per cent of their genes with their grandchildren; and first cousins will have 12.5 per cent of their genes in common. In family studies, these different degrees of genetic relatedness are compared with behaviour. The notion is that concordance rates will increase if heridability is high and vice versa. For example, if the heritability of IQ Iintelligence quotient) is high, there should be a strong correlation in IQ between children and their mothers, but a weak correlation in IQ between second cousins, and very little, if any, between strangers.

A final method used for genetic research is **adoption studies**. In principle, these allow the most direct comparison of genetic and environmental influences of behaviour. Adopted or foster children generally share none of their genes with their adoptive parents, but they do share 50 per cent of their genes with their natural mother. It would be reasonable to suppose, therefore, that if the heritability of a behaviour is high and environment has little part to play, then the behaviour of adopted children should correlate more strongly with the behaviour of their natural mother than their adoptive mother. If, on the other hand, the environment has the strongest role to play, the reverse pattern should be found.

Adoption studies are often criticized as these children are not representative of the general population. In addition, adoption agencies tend to use **selective placement** when finding homes for children, trying to place children with families who are similar in as many ways as possible to the natural parents. Consequently, the effects of genetic inheritance may be difficult to separate from the influences of the environment.

Overall, these approaches to the study of the relative influence of genetic make-up and the environment allow researchers to determine the extent of genetic influence. In spite of the weaknesses outlined here, it is clear that there is a correlation between several behaviours and genetic inheritance.

Intelligence

At the beginning of the 20th century, there was a great interest in the role of genetics in behaviour. Governments and schools sought to design tests that could indicate one's genetically endowed intellectual potential—or IQ. Alfred Binet, a pioneer in intelligence research at the beginning of the 20th century, developed an intelligence test in order to improve the French education system. One of the main controversies regarding intelligence is whether it is inherited or is the result of environmental stimuli. At this point in time, no serious researcher would argue that genetics does not play a role or that the environment has no importance. Research has shown, for example, that poverty seems to have an important influence on the development of children's intelligence.

Some intelligence research is controversial. In 1994, Harvard professor Richard J. Herrnstein published *The Bell Curve*. He claimed that the debate about whether and how much genes and the environment have to do with ethnic differences remains unresolved. The media furore over the idea that there may be intergroup differences in intelligence demonstrates the highly political nature of the topic.

Give me a dozen healthy infants and my own specific world to bring them up in, and I'll guarantee to take any one at random and train him to become any type of specialist I might select—doctor, lawyer, artist, merchant, chef and yes, even beggar and thief, regardless of his talents, penchants, tendencies, abilities, vocations, and race of his ancestors.

This quote from John B. Watson (1924) illustrates the purely "nurture" side of the debate. It is only recently that the interaction of biological and environmental factors has been considered.

One of the difficulties in determining the origin of intelligence is that there has been—and continues to be—much debate about the nature of intelligence. What is it, and how can it be measured? Charles Spearman, an early intelligence theorist, found that student performance across different subjects was positively correlated. As a result of this, he argued that there is a general intelligence factor that is the basis for all intelligence—something that he called the "g" factor. Modern intelligence testing attempts to assess this g, rather than looking at specific school subjects. Instead of testing a student's skill in history, mathematics, or art history, the test focuses on spatial ability, reasoning, divergent thinking, and verbal fluency. The question then is: where does g come from?

Research on intelligence

Bouchard and McGue (1981) reviewed 111 studies of IQ correlations between siblings from research studies on intelligence from around the world. This is what is called a **meta-analysis**—the statistical synthesis of the data from a set of comparable studies of a problem that yields a quantitative summary of the pooled results. They found that the closer the kinship, the higher the correlation for IQ. In order to investigate the role of genetics in intelligence, researchers have used identical twins who have been brought up separately from birth. This provides researchers with participants who have a 100 per cent genetic relationship, but have grown up in different environments. This is based on the assumption that any similarity between their IQs—beyond that expected by chance—must be due to genetics rather than the environment.

The **Minnesota Twin Study** (Bouchard et al. 1990) is a longitudinal study that has been going on since 1979. In this study, MZAs (identical twins raised apart) are compared to MZTs (identical twins raised together). This is the most cross-cultural study to date, with participants from all over the world. Another advantage of this study is that the mean age of the MZAs was 41 years old (at the start of the study). Until this point, almost all intelligence research on twins was carried out with adolescents.

Each twin completed approximately 50 hours of testing and interviews. The concordance rates of intelligence from the study are shown in the table below.

Same person tested twice	87%
Identical twins reared together	86%
Identical twins reared apart	76%
Fraternal twins reared together	55%
Biological siblings reared together	47%

Bouchard et al. determined a heritability estimate of 70 per cent— that is, that 70 per cent of intelligence can be attributed to genetic inheritance. This means that 30 per cent of intelligence may be attributed to other factors.

Much research has supported the findings of the Minnesota Twin Study. In addition, the size and nature of the sample has made it one of the most impressive twin studies ever carried out. In spite of this, there are some criticisms of the study.

● Bouchard relied on media coverage to recruit participants.
● There are some ethical concerns about the way he reunited the twins.
● There was no adequate control to establish the frequency of contact between the twins prior to the study.
● We cannot assume that twins who are raised together experience the same environment—this is called the "equal environment assumption".

One of the ways in which the final criticism has been challenged is by looking at adoption studies.

In adoption studies, the intelligence of the adopted child is correlated with the intelligence of the adoptive parent. Since there is no biological link between the adoptive parent and the child, the environmental influence should be evident.

Scarr and Weinberg (1977) and Horn et al. (1979) focused on parents who had raised both adopted and natural children. The assumption is that all the children had the same upbringing, in the same environment, with the same parents. Any significant differences between parent–child IQ correlations for adopted and natural children should be attributable to genes. The researchers found no significant difference in IQ correlations. This was very interesting, because in almost all the families in these studies, the adoptive parents were wealthy, white, and middle class, with high IQs, and the adopted children were from poor, lower-class backgrounds, with lower-IQ parents.

In other research, Wahlsten (1997) claims that well-controlled adoption studies conducted in France have found that transferring an infant from a family with a low socio-economic status to a home where parents have a high socio-economic status improved childhood IQ scores by 12–16 points, or about one standard deviation. This seems to suggest that intelligence has a lot to do with the environment as well as genetics. An enriched environment may raise IQ in children. It is likely that there is a strong interaction between genes and the environment to produce intelligence level.

Some concluding thoughts on intelligence

There are some other things to consider when examining the genetic explanation of intelligence. One problem, as discussed earlier, is the definition of intelligence. Is intelligence only based on knowledge, or is it related to our ability to solve problems? Hainer et al. (1988) carried out a PET scan study which indicated that when solving a reasoning problem, individuals with a high IQ had lower metabolic rates than those with a low IQ. This difference was seen only in problem solving, and not in data recall. This may mean that those with higher IQs use less energy to think than those with lower IQs. This is known as the **less effort hypothesis**.

Plomin and Petrill (1997) found that correlations between parent and child IQs change over time. Between the ages of 4 and 6 years, they found a 40 per cent correlation; in early adulthood it rose to 60 per cent; and in older adults it was 80 per cent. They concluded that it is possible that our genetic disposition pushes us towards environments that accentuate that disposition, thus leading to increased heritability throughout the lifespan. Socio-economic class appears to be one of the most important environmental factors in the development of intelligence. Poverty—not genetic inferiority—is key to understanding differences in intelligence.

The Flynn effect refers to the rise of average scores on intelligence tests in most parts of the world over the last century. James R. Flynn tried to document this in order to create awareness of its implications. According to Ulric Neisser, who wrote an article on the phenomenon in *The American Scientist* in 1997, the average mean scores on standard IQ tests have been going up by about three points every 10 years, and the increase is even higher in measures of abstract-reasoning ability. The cause of these gains is unknown, but experts discuss whether they reflect a real increase in intelligence or an increasing ability to crack intelligence tests. Other possible factors include better nutrition, improved schooling, different child-rearing practices, and the increased use of technology in modern life. In fact, Neisser thinks that living in a highly visual environment may play an important role in the rise in IQ scores.

Did you know?

As part of the early research on intelligence, the US and other western countries began a branch of science called **eugenics**. This was the attempt to find "good genes" and to encourage "better" breeding in order to produce healthier, more intelligent offspring. The eugenics movement led to immigration restrictions and racial discrimination, founded on the theory that intelligence was based on genetics alone. It attempted to rate entire groups of people as "fitter" or "inferior". In the US, eugenics led to the sterilization of women who were considered "feeble-minded". The centre for eugenics research was in Cold Springs Harbor, New York. What the movement failed to recognize was that it was poverty which played a key role in poor school performance, not membership of a particular ethnic group.

To read more about eugenics, go to www.eugenicsarchive.org/eugenics/

CAS

With the knowledge you have acquired in this chapter on how to improve intelligence, suggest how a CAS project could enhance learning possibilities for impoverished children in your community.

Evolution

Another principle which underpins the biological level of analysis is that the environment presents challenges to each individual. This means that those who adapt best to the environment will have a greater chance of surviving, having children, and passing on their genes to their offspring. This is the principle of Charles Darwin's theory of evolution.

Darwin's theory of natural selection explains how species acquire adaptive characteristics to survive in an ever-changing environment. According to the **theory of natural selection**, those members of a species who have characteristics which are better suited to the environment will be more likely to breed, and thus to pass on these traits. One example of this was seen by Darwin when he travelled the Galapagos Islands. Finches on different islands had different types of beaks. He found that the birds on each island had the beak that was most advantageous for the food available in that particular habitat. Over several generations, the result of natural selection is that the species develops characteristics that make it more competitive in its environment. This process is called **adaptation**. When Darwin presented his theory in the book *On the Origin of Species*, he was not aware of the biological processes through which traits are inherited.

In addition to arguing that traits may be handed down, Darwin also laid the foundation for psychologists and biologists to study animals with the hope of gaining insight into human behaviour. In *The Descent of Man* (1871), Darwin noted that humans have a number of behaviours in common with other animals. These include mate selection, love of mother for offspring, and self-preservation. He also went on to catalogue a number of facial expressions that people share with the apes. He argued that humans also share many of the same feelings as animals.

A key way in which evolution is studied is by looking at the behaviour of our closest relatives in the animal kingdom—primates. The aim of a recent study by Professor Tetsuro Matsuzawa (2007), of Kyoto University in Japan, was to examine spatial memory in young chimps. The researchers took three pairs of chimps and taught them to recognize the numerals from 1 to 9 on a computer monitor. Both the chimps and the human participants were later seated at a computer terminal, where the numerals flashed up very briefly on a touch-screen monitor in a random sequence. The numbers were then replaced with blank squares, and the participant had to remember which numeral appeared in which location, and touch the squares in the appropriate sequence.

The human participants made many errors, and their accuracy decreased as the numbers were replaced with blank squares more quickly. The chimpanzees showed remarkable memory for the spatial distribution of the numbers, with no difference when numbers were shown for shorter durations. Psychologists argue that it is a necessary adaptation for chimpanzees to have this type of memory so that they can remember where food resources—as well as dangers—are in the rainforest. Perhaps as agriculture developed,

Charles Darwin — the father of evolutionary theory

Chimpanzee testing her memory skills

this skill was no longer so essential for human survival. Humans may have surrendered this ability in order to use their brains to develop language. In other words, it appears that the memory skills of both chimpanzees and humans have adapted to become most suitable for the respective environments in which they each live.

Evolutionary psychology

Evolutionary psychology is grounded on the principle that as genes mutate, those that are advantageous are passed down through a process of natural selection. Evolutionary psychologists attempt to explain how certain human behaviours are testimony to the development of our species over time. It is important to remember that natural selection cannot select for a behaviour; it can only select for mechanisms that produce behaviour.

One example of evolutionary research is the study of emotions. Dan Fessler of the University of California at Los Angeles has carried out research on disgust. He argues that the emotion of disgust allowed our ancestors to survive long enough to produce offspring, who in turn passed the same sensitivities on to us. Fessler (2006) investigated the nausea experienced by women in their first trimester of pregnancy. During this period, an infusion of hormones lowers the expectant mother's immune system so as not to fight the new foreign genetic material in her womb. Fessler hypothesized that the nausea response helps to compensate for the suppressed immune system. To test the theory, Fessler gathered 496 healthy pregnant women between the ages of 18 and 50 years, and asked them to consider 32 potentially stomach-turning scenarios— including walking barefoot and stepping on an earthworm, someone accidentally sticking a fish hook through their finger, and maggots on a piece of meat in an outdoor waste bin. Before asking the pregnant women to rank how disgusting they found these scenarios, Fessler posed a series of questions, designed to determine whether they were experiencing morning sickness. In keeping with Fessler's theory, women in their first trimester scored much higher across the board in disgust sensitivity than their counterparts in the second and third trimesters. But when Fessler controlled the study for morning sickness, the response only held for disgusting scenarios involving food, such as the maggot example.

According to Fessler, many of the diseases that are most dangerous are food-borne, but our ancestors could not afford to be picky about what they ate all the time. Natural selection may have helped compensate for the increased susceptibility to disease during this risky period in pregnancy, by increasing the urge to be picky about food, however much additional foraging this may have required. That the sensitivity seems to diminish as the risk of disease and infection decreases is consistent with the view of disgust as a form of protection against disease.

In another study, Curtis et al. (2004) carried out research on the Internet to test whether there were patterns in people's disgust responses. They used an online survey in which participants were shown 20 images. For each image, they were asked to rank their level of disgust. Among the 20 images were seven pairs in which one was infectious or potentially harmful to the immune system, and the other was visually similar but non-infectious—for example, one pair was a plate of bodily fluids and a plate of blue viscous liquid. There were 77 000 participants from 165 countries. The findings confirmed that the disgust reaction was most strongly elicited for those images which threaten one's immune system. Interestingly, the disgust reaction also decreased with age. As the graph shows, disgust reactions were higher in young people than in older people. In addition, women had higher disgust reactions than men. Once again, this supports the idea of disgust as a key to successful reproduction.

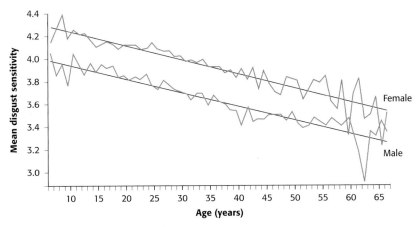

Level of disgust sensitivity in relation to age

The original survey can be found at www.bbc.co.uk/science/ humanbody/mind/surveys/disgust

In spite of such evidence, there are some things to consider when examining an evolutionary argument.

- Since it may be difficult to test empirically some evolution-based theories, researchers may be susceptible to confirmation bias— that is, they see what they expect to see.
- Little is known about the behaviour of early *Homo sapiens*, so statements about how humans "used to be" are hypothetical.
- Evolutionary arguments often underestimate the role of cultural influences in shaping behaviour.

Ethical considerations in research into genetic influences of behaviour

Research in human genetics aims to identify particular genes involved in hereditary diseases. This kind of research may pose risks to participants because of the link between genetic heritage and people's life. Genetic information obtained from such research can also be problematic for the participant's family. If misused, genetic information can be stigmatizing and may affect people's ability to get jobs or insurance.

In any study, participants should always know how their privacy and confidentiality will be protected, and what will happen to any genetic material or information obtained as part of the study. The aims and procedure of the study must be explained in plain

---

Possible exam question: Essay question (paper 1 section B)

Discuss the extent to which genetic inheritance influences behaviour with reference to relevant research studies.

This question uses the command term "discuss" which means that you should present a balanced view that includes a number of arguments that address the way in which genetic factors influence behaviour. You should present evidence from research and you should arrive at a conclusion based on the arguments presented.

language and participants must sign an informed consent paper to show that they have a clear understanding of the study they are participating in, and the implications, including any potential harm.

Confidentiality and privacy can be protected by coding information (where a code is assigned and only a small number of researchers have access to the codes) or by fully anonymizing the sample (where researchers cannot link samples or information to particular people). Anonymization protects confidentiality from insurance companies, employers, police, and others, but it also can limit the scientific value of the study by preventing follow up and further investigation.

Genetic research can reveal unexpected information that may harm research participants. Examples include evidence of misattributed paternity or unrevealed adoptions within a family. Another example occurs when a person discovers from the study that he or she carries the gene for a particular genetic disorder. This may cause undue stress as the participant then fears the potential onset of the disorder.

Some groups, including Aboriginal people, may have objections to genetic study as a cultural principle. Given the existence of other forms of discrimination against such groups, and the history of the eugenics movement, this is no surprise. In such cases it is very important to consult with relevant community leaders and organizations. Consent is a community matter for many Aboriginal and ethnic groups as well as an individual concern.

2.3 An integrative look at criminal behaviour

When we turn on the television for an evening of entertainment, what do we see? A good number of shows are dedicated to solving crime. Some programmes, like *CSI*, have become highly popular because they integrate medical and psychological information into the episodes. We appear to be both fascinated and appalled by the nature of crime. That aside, there is no doubt that crime is an important social question that psychologists need to address.

Early theorists believed that there were "criminal types". They came from certain ethnic groups and had certain physical characteristics, such as a strong jawline, high cheekbones, large ears, and extra fingers or toes. Today, psychologists recognize that the origins of criminal behaviour are complex, resulting from a combination of **risk factors**—among them both biological and environmental factors—which interact and aggravate one another. The more of these risk factors that are present, the more likely the individual is to engage in criminal behaviour. In this section, we are going to examine the nature of criminal behaviour from the three levels of analysis: biological, cognitive, and sociocultural.

Psychology can be applied to help prevent and solve crime

The biological level of analysis

Are some people born to be criminals? Modern researchers would argue that no one is born to be a criminal, but that various biological factors can *contribute* to criminality. There are several theories regarding the biological nature of criminality: these include genetics, brain abnormalities, and neurochemical imbalances.

Genetics

The argument that criminality runs in families does not mean that it is biological. Other family-related factors could also be influential. In order to determine the extent to which genetics may play a role in criminal activity, psychologists have carried out twin studies. Christiansen (1977) studied 3586 sets of Danish twins. He found a concordance rate of 35 per cent in MZ (monozygotic) male twins, and 13 per cent in DZ (dizygotic) male twins. The rate among female twins was significantly lower, with 21 per cent in MZ twins and 8 per cent in DZ twins. Studies like this indicate that there may be some genetic factors in criminal behaviour, but since the concordance rates are so low, it appears that other factors may play a more important role. A limitation of twin studies on crime is that MZ twins not only share a very common environment, but also, because they are identical, they are often treated more similarly than DZ twins are. This may help to account for the different concordance rates.

Further research on the genetic basis of criminality was carried out through adoption studies by Hutchings and Mednick (1975). They found that if both the biological and adoptive fathers had criminal records, 36.2 per cent of sons also had a criminal record; if only the biological father had a criminal record, it dropped to 21.4 per cent;

and if only the adoptive father had a criminal record, it fell to 11.5 per cent. When neither father had a record, 10.5 per cent of sons had one. This study clearly shows the importance of environmental factors, in combination with genetic factors, in determining behaviour. Once again, however, we have to remember the limitations of adoption studies. Children are often placed in an environment that is similar to the one from which they were adopted. Also, some children are adopted years after birth, raising the possibility that early experience with the birth-family may have contributed to later behaviour.

Overall, there are two significant limitations of genetic arguments for criminal behaviour. First, there is a problem with the term "criminal behaviour" itself. To think that we are going to find a gene for "crime" is very unlikely. Crimes can range from first-degree murder to tax evasion. Second, genetic theorists have a difficult time explaining why criminal behaviour tends to change over the lifespan, reaching its peak when individuals are in their 20s and declining in most people after the age of 30.

The brain

Brain research has looked primarily at the interrelationship between emotions and decision making. Emotions are controlled by the limbic system in the brain, and decision making takes place in the frontal lobe. It is the interaction of these two parts of the brain which may provide insight into the nature of criminal behaviour. Blair et al. (1999) looked at the brains of convicted psychopaths. PET scans revealed impairment of the pathways between the amygdala (responsible for emotional responses) and the frontal lobe. Blair argues that this impairment makes it difficult for the individual to moderate his or her emotional reactions. This in turn has a significant effect on how the individual interacts with others. Because social relationships are difficult, he or she never appropriately develops empathy or feelings of guilt, and thus acts more impulsively, without regard for the consequences.

The theory that a malfunctioning relationship between the frontal cortex and the limbic system may cause criminal behaviour is called the **frontal brain hypothesis**. As well as studying convicted criminals, much of the research has been carried out on patients with brain damage. Antonio Damasio has looked at the effect of brain trauma in children on their later development. In one case, a 3-month-old infant had a tumour removed from his frontal cortex. By the age of 9, the boy had behavioural problems in school—he was inattentive and socially isolated from his peers. His free time was spent alone in front of the television, and at times he would lose control of his emotions and physically threaten others. Such case studies lend support to the frontal brain hypothesis by showing a relationship between brain damage and antisocial behaviour. However, the hypothesis does not explain all criminal behaviour.

Neurotransmitters and hormones

Other biological research has focused on the role of neurotransmitters and hormones on criminal behaviour. These arguments seem to best explain the significant gender difference with regard to crime. In a 2004 US Federal Bureau of Investigation report on crime, 90.1 per cent of apprehended murderers were male, as were 82.1 per cent of those arrested for violent crime. How do biologists account for this difference?

Low levels of the neurotransmitter serotonin have been linked to antisocial and impulsive behaviour. Interestingly, men—who are reponsible for the vast majority of crimes committed—generally have lower levels of serotonin. In addition, James Dabbs has demonstrated that violent criminals have higher testosterone levels than non-aggressive criminals. Once again, these are correlational studies, and they do not establish cause and effect. Psychologists are also unsure of whether these chemical imbalances are genetic or the result of environmental factors.

The most important thing to remember about biological factors is that, except for the most severe cases of brain damage, these factors alone are not enough to cause violence. It is only when they are combined with cognitive and social risk factors that criminal behaviour will occur.

The cognitive level of analysis

Yochelson and Samenow (1976) have looked at how criminals think. The way we process information is a key component of the cognitive level of analysis (see Chapter 3.1). They have argued that criminal behaviour is a result of **cognitive distortions**—that is, errors in thinking. Some examples of these cognitive distortions are:

- blaming others for your own failures
- super-optimism: extremely wishful or magical thinking; establishing unrealistic, unobtainable goals
- "I think, therefore it is": not being able to accept mistakes in the face of incontrovertible evidence
- minimizing: to reduce or limit the true significance of a behaviour and avoid labelling it as "hurtful" or "wrong", thereby eliminating the responsibility for changing it
- build-up: exaggerating accomplishments and abilities to make ourselves look better in the eyes of others.

Yochelson and Samenow's research has sparked interest in the role of cognition in criminal behaviour, but their own research is rather limited. They only studied convicted criminals, and they did not look at the role these cognitive distortions play in the non-criminal population.

Cornish and Clark (1987) have proposed the **rational choice theory**. They argue that criminal behaviour is the outcome of a reasoned decision-making process. The theory is based on the assumption that criminals seek to benefit from the crimes they commit. If the benefits of the act outweigh the costs, they will go ahead. Support for this was found in research by Bennett and Wright (1984); they interviewed convicted burglars and asked them which factors would most influence their decision to rob a home. They found three factors that influenced the decision: risk (the chance of getting caught), financial reward, and ease of entry.

TOK: ethics

What if psychologists can determine that criminals have a biological predisposition towards their behaviour? Should the courts be more lenient if they are presented with medical evidence that an individual has a neurochemical imbalance or genetic predisposition? Would that force governments to rethink policies of punishment as a deterrent to crime?

Though this study seems to support the theory that there is a clear decision-making process which underlies criminal activity, one does have to question the research, since it is based on "unsuccessful" burglars—that is, those who were caught. In addition, some researchers argue that many violent crimes are not rationally planned out, but are the result of impulse and emotion.

Though cognitive factors may play a role, it appears that these thinking patterns alone do not explain the nature of criminal behaviour.

The sociocultural level of analysis

The sociocultural level of analysis considers how the society and culture we belong to affects our behaviour (see Chapter 4.1). The factors that affect our behaviour at this level of analysis include the social and cultural expectations people have of us, as well as the economic and political realities that exist where we live.

Poverty

The question of the role of poverty on criminal behaviour is rather complex. Many people would automatically assume that those who earn less money would be more likely to commit crimes. However, the research has been somewhat inconclusive on this point. Messner (1988) has recommended that instead of focusing on differences in income, we need to look at **structural poverty**—a more holistic approach to the issue. Structural poverty is characterized by single-parent families, low levels of education, high infant mortality rates, and low social mobility—that is, the chance to improve your situation. Messner found a much higher correlation between structural poverty and crime rates than between income levels and crime.

Another societal factor that is often connected to crime is unemployment. Many studies have clearly indicated a correlation between rates of unemployment and crime. However, these data are often misinterpreted as simply the result of loss of income. Unemployment, like poverty, is a very complex phenomenon. Unemployment can damage an individual's self-esteem and can provoke the feeling that life is meaningless. The change in status, as well as the subsequent boredom, may have more to do with rising crime rates than simply the loss of income.

Another theory is that these social factors may interact with biological factors and lead to criminal behaviour. Poverty is associated with a higher degree of stress on the mother of a developing child. This stress may affect the fetus and lead to impairments of brain functioning, which could eventually lead to criminal behaviour. More research is needed to determine the extent of the effect of poverty on brain development, but the studies already undertaken show the need for countries to address the issues of poverty and unemployment.

CAS: changing behaviour through social action

The Canadian Council on Social Development is a non-profit research organization that looks at the effect of poverty on criminal behaviour (among other issues). Research has shown that the effectiveness of social intervention is impressive.

- In the UK (2002), a programme which provided 10 hours of activities per week to the 50 youths most at risk in 70 of the most difficult neighbourhoods helped to reduce youth arrests by 65 per cent, and brought down school expulsions by 30 per cent.

- In Canada (2003), home visits to assist "at-risk" mothers with parenting skills helped to decrease the percentage of children who were later handed over to child protection authorities, from 25 per cent to just 2.3 per cent. In addition, a parent training programme produced a 67 per cent reduction in the number of teen arrests.

- US research (1999) found that incentives for youths to complete high school decreased arrests by 72 per cent.

Carry out some research on crime in your community. What are the most pressing social issues that may be affecting individual behaviour? What could your community do to lower crime rates in these neighbourhoods?

Labelling and self-fulfilling prophecies

Another way that society can affect our behaviour is by labelling individuals. Research has shown that when we are given a label— for example, that we are incompetent—we often live up to that expectation. This is called a **self-fulfilling prophecy**. So, to be labelled a "troublemaker" by the family, school, or society may actually result in criminal behaviour. A striking example of this was seen in Jahoda's (1954) research on the Ashanti people of Ghana. The Ashanti people have the custom of naming boys according to the day of the week when they are born. It is believed that the day of the week predicts a child's future temperament. Children born on Mondays are supposed to be calm, reserved, and peaceful. Children born on Wednesdays are supposed to be aggressive and problematic. Jahoda looked at local police records and found a high number of arrests for boys born on Wednesday, and a very low number of arrests for boys born on Monday. It appears that the naming of children has resulted in a self-fulfilling prophecy.

It is clear that the origins of criminal behaviour are quite complex. The three levels of analysis—biological, cognitive, and sociocultural—work together to explain why people commit crimes. These three levels of analysis interact—for example, biological factors may affect an individual's thought processes; thought processes may affect his or her social development; socio-economic status could have an effect on the health of an expectant mother, and thus on the development of the child. All the risk factors discussed above contribute to a potential behaviour. In attempting to solve the problem of crime, governments will find that there are no easy answers to these complex questions.

Biological factors
- Genetic predisposition
- Frontal brain hypothesis
- Levels of serotonin (neurotransmitter)
- Levels of testosterone (hormone)

Cognitive factors
- Cognitive distortions (faulty thinking)

Sociocultural factors
- Labelling and self-fulfilling prophecy
- Poverty and socio-economic class
- Early trauma or abuse

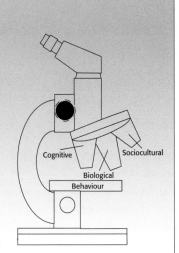

Possible extended essay questions

1 Is criminal behaviour primarily biologically based?

2 To what extent do biological and sociocultural factors determine criminal behaviour?

3 Which factors contribute most to criminal behaviour – biological, sociocultural or cognitive?

Cognitive level of analysis: cognitive processes

Learning outcomes

- Outline principles that define the cognitive level of analysis
- Explain how principles that define the cognitive level of analysis may be demonstrated in research
- Discuss how and why particular research methods are used by cognitive researchers
- Discuss ethical considerations related to research studies at the cognitive level of analysis
- Evaluate schema theory with reference to research studies
- Evaluate two models or theories of one cognitive process with reference to research studies
- Explain how biological factors may affect one cognitive process
- Discuss how social or cultural factors affect one cognitive process
- Evaluate the extent to which a cognitive process is reliable
- Explain the use of technology in investigating cognitive processes

Principles that define the cognitive level of analysis

When people are thinking about how best to solve a mathematical problem, trying to remember the title of a book, observing a beautiful sunset, retelling a joke they have heard, or thinking about what to do tomorrow, they are involved in cognitive processing. **Cognitive psychology** concerns itself with the structure and functions of the mind. Cognitive psychologists are involved in finding out how the human mind comes to know things about the world and how it uses this knowledge. **Cognitive neuroscience** combines knowledge about the brain with knowledge about cognitive processes.

The mind can be conceptualized as a set of mental processes that are carried out by the brain. Cognitive processes include perception, thinking, problem solving, memory, language, and attention. The concept of **cognition** refers to such processes. Cognition is based on one's **mental representations** of the world, such as images, words, and concepts. People have different experiences and therefore they have different mental representations—for example, of what is right or wrong, or about what boys and girls can and cannot do. This will influence the way they think about the world.

One of the most fundamental principles of cognitive psychology is that human beings are information processors and that *mental processes guide behaviour*. One goal of cognitive research is to discover possible principles underlying cognitive processes. Psychologists see the mind as a complex machine—rather like an intelligent, information-processing machine using hardware (the brain) and

> **Definition of cognition**
> Cognition comes from the Latin word *cognoscere*, which means "to know".
>
> Ulric Neisser (1967) has defined cognition as "all the processes by which the sensory input is transformed, reduced, elaborated, stored, recovered, and used".

software (mental images or representations). According to this line of thinking, information input to the mind comes via **bottom-up processing**—that is, from the sensory system. This information is processed in the mind by **top-down processing** via pre-stored information in the memory. Finally, there is some output in the form of behaviour.

Psychologists recognize the importance of cognition in understanding the complexity of human behaviour. Cognitive theories and models are applied to real-world scenarios. Health and sports psychologists have demonstrated that there is a subtle relationship between how people *think* about themselves and how they *behave*—for example, how they manage to deal with challenges. Remember the research by Dweck outlined in Chapter 1.1? Her research revealed that a person's mindset is important in predicting his or her behaviour. From social psychology we know that people who have fixed ideas about other people—this is called **stereotyping**—may be more prone to discriminate.

Another finding from cognitive research is that people's memories may not be as infallible as they think because of the **reconstructive nature** of memory. Researchers have discovered that people do not store exact copies of their experiences, but rather an outline which is filled out with information when it is recalled. It seems that people may sometimes have what are called **false memories**, because individuals cannot distinguish between what they have experienced and what they have heard after the event. Apparently, the brain is able to fabricate illusions which are so realistic that we believe they are true.

This is very clearly demonstrated in **perception**, defined as the cognitive process that interprets and organizes information from the senses to produce some meaningful experience of the world. Factors such as context, frequency, or recency seem to influence the way people interpret an ambiguous object or event. This means that what people think is *objectively* experienced may instead be the result of the brain's interpretation of the object or event.

A second principle of cognitive psychology is that *the mind can be studied scientifically* by developing theories and using a number of scientific research methods. This is demonstrated in theories and models of cognition which are discussed and continuously tested. Sometimes new findings result in amendments to original models, or a model or theory is simply rejected because the empirical evidence no longer supports it. Cognitive psychologists have to a large extent used the experimental method because it was assumed to be the most scientific method. However, the experimental tasks did not always resemble what people did in their daily lives. Even in the 1960s, Ulric Neisser said that cognitive psychology had become too artificial and that researchers should not forget that cognition cannot be isolated from our everyday experience. This is why cognitive psychologists now study cognition in the laboratory as well as in a daily context.

TOK and ways of knowing: perception

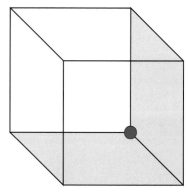

Visual illusion

Look closely at this object—called the **Necker cube**—for a few seconds. Is the blue dot on the near or the far corner? What happens if you stare at the blue dot for a long time?

At first, it appears that the cube is lying down and you see the blue dot at the end of the cube. If you stare for long enough, it appears that the cube is standing on its end and you are seeing the blue dot below you. The image has two equally meaningful interpretations and the brain simply switches back and forth between them. The brain interprets the picture the way it wants to, searching for some meaning because it does not have enough information to know exactly which face of the cube is in front. This ambiguous cube shows us that what we see is probably just the "best guess" of our visual system, and it is the brain that decides which one is favoured.

Discuss the following quote from the psychologist Daniel Gilbert: "Our experience of the world— how we see it, remember it and imagine it—is a mixture of stark reality and comforting illusion."

Be a thinker

Will it ever be possible to develop robots that can think like humans?

1 Work in groups of four and compare the human mind and the computer. Make a list of what the human mind can do and what the computer can do. Discuss your list. Does it make sense to you to compare the human mind to a computer?

2 What do you consider to be the major difference between the computer and a human being?

3 Discuss how computers are pictured in one science-fiction film that you have seen.

4 Discuss whether you think it will ever be possible to construct a robot that can be exactly like a human.

You may find this website helpful:
http://news.bbc.co.uk/2/hi/uk_news/wales/mid_/4495257.stm

A third principle that defines the cognitive level of analysis is that *cognitive processes are influenced by social and cultural factors*. One of the first to say this was the British psychologist Frederic Bartlett, who coined the term **schema**, which is defined as a mental representation of knowledge. Bartlett was particularly interested in how cultural schemas influence remembering. He found that people had problems remembering a story from another culture, and that they reconstructed the story to fit in with their own cultural schemas. In his research, he demonstrated that memory is not like a tape recorder, but rather that people remember in terms of meaning and what makes sense to them. This is also why memory is subject to **distortions**, according to Bartlett, who showed how this principle could be investigated scientifically.

Studying the mind

Traditionally, cognitive researchers have favoured the controlled experiment that takes place in the laboratory. The strength of this method is that all variables can be controlled, but the problem is that experimental research may suffer from artificiality. Today, researchers use a variety of other methods, including case studies. This might be a person with an extraordinary memory, or people with brain damage who have lost the ability to understand language. Since cognitive processes are localized in the brain, modern neuro-imaging technologies (e.g. CAT and fMRI) offer possibilities to look into brain processes that no researcher could even dream of 100 years ago. Neuroscientists can now study which brain areas are active when people make decisions, and how cognitive processes can be disrupted by brain damage—for example, amnesia or Alzheimer's disease. Researchers then use their data to support or refute cognitive models—or to propose new models.

Cognitive processes

The human mind is quite sophisticated. It can manipulate abstract symbols like words and images. These mental representations can refer to objects, ideas, and people in the real world; people use them when they think, make plans, imagine, or daydream. You have an idea of who you are and how you look somewhere in your mind—a self-representation. You also have ideas about how other people are. Mental representations are organized in categories, and the mind contains all sorts of mental representations stored in memory.

The human capacity to manipulate mental representations enables us to think about situations and imagine what might happen. People make plans, calculate risks, or create wonderful pieces of art. When authors write exciting stories, they rely on their imagination to construct imaginary universes and characters. The readers form mental images of the characters as they read the book, and sometimes they may even find that a book which has been made into a movie is not as good as their own "film". When reading books, people also imagine what will happen to the characters. Generally, the good guys and the bad guys do not fare the same. We have *expectations* as to what will happen to them because of pre-stored mental representations called **cognitive schemas**. "Mental representations" are how we store images and ideas in memory. Memory researchers believe that what we already know affects the way we interpret events and store knowledge in our memory.

Chicken and representation of chicken

Be a thinker

The way we represent objects in the world can be illustrated by this cartoon. The chicken may indeed be represented in different ways. Can you imagine a few other ways to represent the chicken?

A theory of a cognitive process: schema theory

When expert football players like Danish Michael Laudrup kick the ball directly into the goal during a penalty, it may look like any other goal to some of us. However, this particular kick is the result of many hours of practice, combined with an adjustment that matches the challenges of the particular situation. Laudrup needs to take into consideration the position of the goalkeeper and predict possible reactions, as well as determining how he should kick the ball. All this is done based on his previous experience, which is stored in his memory as knowledge—but there is even more to it. Players like Laudrup have learned the behaviour to perfection, but need to modify it to fit the particular challenge at hand. His kick must be manufactured out of the visual and postural information of the movement and its possible consequences. A lot of this is based on recognition of patterns. This "how-to-score knowledge" will help him decide what aspects of the situation he needs to pay attention to in order to place the football accurately between the goalposts. Specialists in a certain field have expert knowledge that comes from hours of practice, which means that to some extent they can do the right things at the right time more or less automatically, but they always need to be able to analyse each individual situation.

Cognitive psychologists would call "how-to-score knowledge" a **schema**, and **schema theory** is a cognitive theory about information processing. A **cognitive schema** can be defined as networks of knowledge, beliefs, and expectations about particular aspects of the world.

Schemas can describe how specific knowledge is organized and stored in memory so that it can be accessed and used when it is needed—as in the example of Michael Laudrup. It is not possible to

Michael Laudrup

see a schema inside someone's head, but using concepts like schemas help psychologists—and the rest of us—to understand and discuss what it would otherwise not be possible to do.

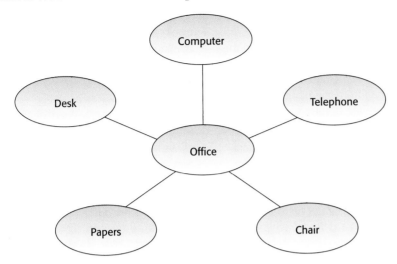

Office schema

Schema theory suggests that what we already know will influence the outcome of information processing. This idea is based on the assumption that *humans are active processors of information*. People do not passively respond to information. They interpret and integrate it to make sense of their experiences, but they are not always aware of it. If information is missing, the brain fills in the blanks based on existing schemas, or it simply invents something that seems to fit in. Obviously this can result in mistakes—called **distortions**.

Schema theory and memory processes

Schema theory has been used to explain memory processes. Cognitive psychologists divide memory processes into three main stages:

- **encoding**: transforming sensory information into a meaningful memory
- **storage**: creating a biological trace of the encoded information in memory, which is either consolidated or lost
- **retrieval**: using the stored information.

Memory processes

It is now believed that schema processing can affect memory at all stages. This is shown in the following research study on the next page.

Cognitive schemas:
- organize information about the world with fixed and variable slots; if a slot is left out or unspecified, it is filled by a "default value"—that is, a best guess
- can be related to form systems
- are active recognition devices (pattern recognition)
- help to predict future events based on what happened before
- represent general knowledge rather than definitions.

Research in psychology

Anderson and Pichert (1978)

The aim of the experiment was to investigate if schema processing influences both encoding and retrieval. The participants were given one schema at the encoding stage and another at the retrieval stage, to see if they were influenced by the last schema when they had to recall the information.

First, the participants heard a story about two boys who decided to stay away from school one day; instead, they went to the home of one of them because the house was always empty on Thursdays. The house was described as being isolated and located in an attractive neighbourhood, but also having a leaky roof and a damp basement. The story also mentioned various objects in the house, such as a 10-speed bike, a colour TV, and a rare coin collection.

The participants heard a story that was based on 72 points. These had previously been rated by a group of people for their importance to either a potential *house-buyer* (e.g. leaking roof, attractive grounds) or a *burglar* (e.g. coin collection, nobody home on Thursdays). Half of the participants were asked to read the story from the point of view of a house-buyer (the buyer schema) and half from the point of view of a burglar (the burglar schema).

Once the participants had read the story, they performed a distracting task for 12 minutes before their recall was tested. Then there was another 5-minute delay in the experiment. Half of the participants were given a different schema, so that those who used the burglar schema in the first trial were switched to the buyer schema and vice versa. The other half of the participants were asked to retain their original schema, and their recall was tested once again.

The researchers found that participants in the changed schema group recalled 7 per cent more points on the second recall test compared to the first trial. Recall of points that were directly linked to the new schema increased by 10 per cent, whereas recall of points that were important to the previous schema declined. The researchers also found that the group which continued with the first schema actually remembered fewer ideas at the second trial.

The results of the experiment indicate that schema processing must have some effect at retrieval as well as at encoding, because the new schema could only have influenced recall at the retrieval stage. The research also showed that people encoded information which was irrelevant to their prevailing schema, since those who had the buyer schema at encoding were able to recall burglar information when the schema was changed, and vice versa.

This experiment was highly controlled and conducted in a laboratory, so there may be issues of ecological validity. However, a strength of this experiment was the variable control, which enabled the researchers to establish a cause-and-effect relationship on how schemas affect different memory processes.

Evaluation of schema theory

Lots of research has supported the idea that schemas affect cognitive processes such as memory. The theory seems quite useful for understanding how people categorize information, interpret stories, and make inferences, among other things. Schema theory has contributed to an understanding of memory distortions as well as social cognition. Social psychologists often refer to "social schemas" when they are trying to explain stereotyping and prejudice.

Some of the limitations of schema theory are that it is not entirely clear *how* schemas are acquired in the first place and *how* they actually influence cognitive processes. Cohen (1993) has criticized schema theory, saying that the concept of schemas is too vague to be useful. However, many researchers use schema theory to explain cognitive processing. The US psychologist Daniel Gilbert has said that the brain is a wonderful magician but a lousy scientist—the brain searches for meaningful patterns but does not check whether they are correct.

A model of memory: the working memory model

Atkinson and Shiffrin (1968) were among the first to suggest a basic structure (or architecture) of memory, with their **multi-store**

model. Although this seems rather simplistic today, it certainly sparked research based on the idea of information processing, and it has been one of the most influential models to date. The working memory model, which is the focus here, builds on the multi-store model of memory. What is called short-term memory in the original model is changed to a more sophisticated version in the working memory model.

Models are attempts to describe complex phenomena; they are changed and developed based on research findings. Although models may clarify how memory might work, it is important to realize that even though evidence brings support to some of the ideas in a model, it can never be more than a model.

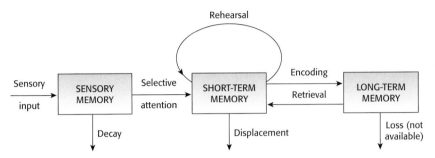

Multi-store model of memory

The multi-store model was suggested in the 1960s when the cognitive revolution began, and the model is clearly inspired by computer science, with the idea of humans as information processors. The model is based on two assumptions: first, that memory consists of a number of separate stores; and second, that memory processes are sequential. The memory stores are seen as components that operate in conjunction with the permanent memory store through processes such as **attention**, **coding**, and **rehearsal**. You need to pay attention to something in order to remember it, and you need to give the material a form which enables you to remember it. Rehearsal simply means keeping material active in memory by repeating it until it can be stored.

The model contains several stores. Information from the world enters **sensory memory**, which is **modality specific**—that is, related to different senses, such as hearing and vision. Information stays here for a few seconds, and only a very small part of the information attended to will continue into the **short-term memory (STM) store**. The capacity of STM is limited to around seven items and its duration is normally about 6–12 seconds. Material in STM is quickly lost if not given attention. Rehearsal plays a key role in determining what is stored in long-term memory.

The **long-term memory (LTM) store** is conceptualized as a vast storehouse of information. This storehouse is believed to be of indefinite duration and of potentially unlimited capacity, although psychologists do not know exactly how much information can be stored there. The material is not an exact replica of events or facts, but is stored in some outline form. Memories may be distorted when they are retrieved, because we fill in the gaps to create a meaningful memory as predicted by schema theory. This model is very simplistic and reflects the knowledge available in the 1960s.

Baddeley and Hitch (1974) suggested the **working memory model**, based on the multi-store model. However, they challenged the view that STM is a *single* store. Working memory is a model of

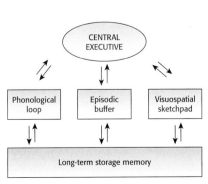

The working memory model

STM and it includes several components, whereas the multi-store model of memory only includes one. Now we will look at each of the hypothesized components of working memory.

The central executive

The central executive is a kind of *controlling system* that monitors and coordinates the operations of the other components, which are called **slave systems**. It is the most important part of the model because it is seen as a kind of CEO of the memory system. The central executive has limited capacity and it is modality free, which means that it can process any sensory information.

Baddeley has worked on the model since it was devised in 1974 and now suggests that the most important job of the central executive is **attentional control**. This happens in two ways.

- The **automatic level** is based on habit and controlled more or less automatically by stimuli from the environment. This includes routine procedures like cycling to school.

- The **supervisory attentional level** deals with emergencies or creates new strategies when the old ones are no longer sufficient—for example, when a car is suddenly coming at you when you are cycling.

It seems intuitively correct that people rely a great deal on automatic processing in their daily lives. Think about a situation in which you suddenly find yourself outside your front door, but you cannot really remember how you got there because you were talking to somebody on your mobile phone. You probably also know that if something had happened on the way—such as another person talking on a mobile bumping into you—you would become attentive to make a quick evaluation of the situation.

The episodic buffer

Imagine yourself consciously trying to recall the details of a landscape or the sound of your favourite band. According to Baddeley, they will appear via the episodic buffer. The role of the buffer is to act as a temporary and passive display store until the information is needed—much like a television screen. The processing of information takes place in other parts of the system.

The phonological loop

The phonological loop is divided into two components. The first component is the **articulatory control system**, or inner voice, which can hold information in a verbal form. This happens when you try to remember a telephone number and repeat it to yourself. The articulatory loop is also believed to hold words ready as you prepare to speak. The second component is the **phonological store**, or inner ear. It holds speech-based material in a phonological form. Research shows that a memory trace can only last from 1.5 to 2 seconds if it is not refreshed by the articulatory control system. The phonological store can receive information directly from sensory memory in the form of auditory material, from LTM in the form of verbal information, and from the articulatory control system.

The visuospatial sketchpad

The visuospatial sketchpad is also called the inner eye. It deals with visual and spatial information from either sensory memory or LTM.

Evidence of working memory

Most researchers today accept the idea of working memory. Experiments using **dual-task techniques**—also called interference tasks—seem to provide support for the model. In dual-task experiments, a participant is asked to carry out a cognitive task that uses most of the capacity of working memory—this might be telling a story to another person while at the same time performing a second cognitive task, such as trying to learn a list of numbers. If the two tasks interfere with each other so that one or both are impaired, it is believed that both tasks use the same component in STM.

Baddeley and Hitch (1974) performed an experiment in which they asked participants to read prose and understand it, while at the same time remembering sequences of numbers. They found that in dual-task experiments there was a clear and systematic increase in reasoning time if people had to undertake a memory-dependent task at the same time. They also found that the task was significantly impaired if the participants had to learn sequences of six numbers, but that they could manage to learn sequences of three numbers. The prediction of the working memory model is that there will be impairment in the concurrent task. However, the findings of the study showed that even though there was impairment, it was not catastrophic. The researchers take this as evidence that STM has more than one unitary store, and that a total breakdown of working memory demands much more pressure than the concurrent task in this experiment.

Evaluation of the model

Working memory provides a much more satisfactory explanation of storage and processing than the STM component of the multi-store model of memory. It includes active storage and processing, which makes it very useful for understanding all sorts of cognitive tasks, such as reading comprehension and mental arithmetic. The multi-store model assumes that mental processes are passive. The working memory model can explain why people are able to perform different cognitive tasks at the same time without disruption—known as **multi-tasking**.

There is substantial evidence that working memory plays an important role in learning, especially during the childhood years. Pickering and Gathercole (2001) used the **Working Memory Test Battery for Children** and found that there is an improvement in performance in working memory capacity from the age of 5 years until about 15 years. They also found that the capacity of working memory during childhood varies widely across individuals of the same age. Their work provides evidence that problems with working memory are associated with problems in academic performance. For example, deficits with the phonological loop have been linked to problems in mathematics and reading.

Holmes et al. (2008) studied the association between visuospatial sketchpad capacity and children's mathematics attainment in relation to age. Based on a sample of children in age groups of 7–8 and 9–10 years, they studied age-related differences in the relationship between the visual and spatial memory subcomponents of the visuospatial sketchpad and a range of mathematical skills. They found that in older children, mathematical performance could be significantly predicted by performance on the visual patterns test. According to Eysenck (1988), there is reasonable evidence that individual differences in intelligence may depend partly on differences in working memory capacity.

Memory and the brain

Memory is the job of the brain. Science is continuously exploring the way memory is organized in the human brain, but there are still many mysteries about the biological correlates of memory. Cognitive researchers and neuroscientists cooperate to find out how brain structures are involved in memory processes. As science progresses, it becomes clear that memory is quite complex and sophisticated.

Profile

Eric Kandel

Eric Kandel was a Nobel Prize winner in 2000. He studied learning and memory at a cellular level in the sea snail aplysia, a very simple organism. He found that STM as well as LTM result in synaptic changes in the neural network. The snail's memory is located in the synapses, and changes in these synapses are important in memory formation. In the 1990s, Kandel studied memory functioning in relation to synaptic changes in the brain structure called the hippocampus.

Some biological factors in memory

It is not yet possible to have a full picture of the complexity of the biological foundations of memory, but brain research has provided some major insights into the nature of memory. Kandel's research shows that learning, means formation of a memory—that is, growing new connections or strengthening existing connections between neurons to form **neural networks**. Over the years, researchers have used animals to study how areas of the brain are related to memory. Typically, animals learn to perform a specific task—for example, running through a maze—and a memory is formed. To find out what areas of the brain are involved in such a task, researchers cut away brain tissue and the animal has to run through the maze again. The procedure, called **lesioning**, is repeated a number of times until the animal can no longer perform the task.

Obviously, scientists cannot do this to human beings, so researchers study people who already have brain damage. Such case studies show that LTM must consist of several stores. Damage to different parts of the brain affects factual knowledge, for example, or knowledge about how to drive a car. It is clear that brain damage can affect one type of memory but leave others intact. It is relevant

Possible essay question

Evaluate a model or a theory of one cognitive process (e.g. memory, perception, language, decision making), with reference to research studies.

Assessment advice

In this essay question, "or" is in italics. Be aware that you should evaluate either a model or a theory, not both.

to know how scientists map the structures of long-term memory because they refer to them when they explain how specific areas in the brain affect certain kinds of memory.

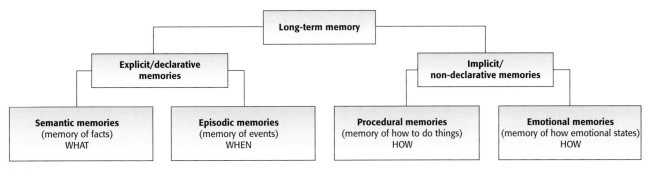

The long-term memory system

At the first level, LTM is divided into two systems: the first is **explicit memory**—also known as declarative—which consists of fact-based information that can be consciously retrieved. This type of memory focuses on "knowing what".

Explicit memory has been divided into two subsystems. The first is **semantic memory**, which is memory for general knowledge—for example, Mick Jagger is a singer in the Rolling Stones. The second is **episodic memory**, which is memory for personal experiences and events—for example, I saw Mick Jagger last year in New York.

The second unit of LTM is **implicit memory**, which contains memories that we are not consciously aware of. Implicit memory is also divided into several subsystems. One of these is **procedural memory**, which is the non-conscious memory for skills, habits, and actions—"knowing how". Implicit memory also includes **emotional memory**, which is not yet well understood. It seems that emotional memories may be formed via the limbic system and that they may persist even when brain damage has destroyed other memories.

Researchers like Kandel have pointed to the very important role of the **hippocampus** in the formation of explicit memories. Case studies of people with hippocampal damage have shown that they can no longer form new explicit memories, but apparently they can still form new implicit memories.

There is evidence that the **amygdala** plays a role in the storage of emotional memories—perhaps because emotions are used to evaluate experience. According to neuroscientist LeDoux, certain memories have emotional significance and this might explain why memories based on emotional events are remembered better. It may also be why people suffering from post-traumatic stress disorder (PTSD) have problems forgetting, because emotional memories are quite difficult to get rid of. Researchers are now beginning to find out how the brain regulates emotional expressions, and they have observed that when part of the prefrontal cortex is damaged, emotional memory is very hard to eliminate, and it is difficult to control emotional outbursts.

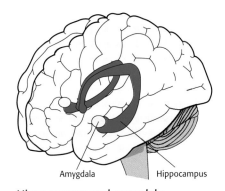

Hippocampus and amygdala

Clive Wearing—how brain damage affects memory processing

Can you imagine what it would be like if you were caught in the present and unable to remember anything from your past or to learn anything new? What if you were lost in time, with no sense of the past or the future?

This is exactly what happened to Clive Wearing. If you find it difficult to imagine, it may help you to read what the famous neurologist Oliver Sacks wrote about him in this article from the New Yorker (2007).

In March of 1985, Clive Wearing, an eminent English musician and musicologist in his mid-forties, was struck by a brain infection—a herpes encephalitis—affecting especially the parts of his brain concerned with memory. He was left with a memory span of only seconds—the most devastating case of amnesia ever recorded. New events and experiences were effaced almost instantly. As his wife, Deborah, wrote in her 2005 memoir, "Forever Today":

His ability to perceive what he saw and heard was unimpaired. But he did not seem to be able to retain any impression of anything for more than a blink. Indeed, if he did blink, his eyelids parted to reveal a new scene. The view before the blink was utterly forgotten.

[…]

It was as if every waking moment was the first waking moment. Clive was under the constant impression that he had just emerged from unconsciousness because he had no evidence in his own mind of ever being awake before… "I haven't heard anything, seen anything, touched anything, smelled anything," he would say. "It's like being dead."

Desperate to hold on to something, to gain some purchase, Clive started to keep a journal, first on scraps of paper, then in a notebook. But his journal entries consisted, essentially, of the statements "I am awake" or "I am conscious," entered again and again every few minutes. He would write: "2:10 P.M: This time properly awake…2:14 P.M: this time finally awake… 2:35 P.M: this time completely awake," along with negations of these statements: "At 9:40 P.M. I awoke for the first time, despite my previous claims." This in turn was crossed out, followed by "I was fully conscious at 10:35 P.M., and awake for the first time in many, many weeks." This in turn was cancelled out by the next entry.

Clive Wearing suffers from the most extensive amnesia ever seen; he suffers from both anterograde and retrograde amnesia. The transcript of his diary gives a heartbreaking insight into what it is like to lose one's memory. MRI scanning of Clive Wearing's brain shows damage to the hippocampus and some of the frontal regions. This indicates that retrograde amnesia could be explained as "trauma that disrupts consolidation of memory".

The case of Clive Wearing provides insight into the biological foundation of different memory systems. Wearing's episodic memory and some of his semantic memory are lost. He cannot transfer new information into long-term memory either.

Did you know?

Amnesia can be defined as the inability to learn new information or retrieve information that has already been stored in memory.

Neuroscientists distinguish between two key types of amnesia. **Anterograde amnesia** is the failure to store memories *after* a trauma. **Retrograde amnesia** is the failure to recall memories that have been stored *before* a trauma. Amnesia can be caused by brain injury or infection. In the case of prolonged misuse of alcohol, a special kind of amnesia called Korsakoff's syndrome may result.

Wearing can still play the piano and conduct the music that he knew before his illness. These skills are part of implicit memory. The fact that he can do this is evidence of a distributed memory system, since implicit memory is linked to a brain structure other than the hippocampus. His emotional memory is also intact, which is clearly demonstrated in the affection he constantly shows for his wife.

Normally, we do not know the identity of participants in case studies. Researchers are obliged to keep personal information confidential. However, the case of Clive Wearing is different because his wife has decided to come forward with his story.

Understanding research

1 What is a case study?

2 Discuss how a case study like this can be helpful for neuroscientists.

3 How would neuroscientists determine if this case study could be generalized to explain human memory?

Research in psychology

The case study of HM

One of the most famous case studies of amnesia in the history of psychology is HM, who was first studied by Milner and Scoville (1957). Over the years, many scientific studies have been conducted on HM and his identity has not been revealed. As a result of a head injury that HM sustained when he was 9 years old, he suffered from epileptic seizures. Since there was no drug treatment for his severe epilepsy at the time, the doctors decided to perform surgery to stop the seizures. They removed tissue from the temporal lobe, including the hippocampus. Following the operation, HM could recall information acquired in early life, but was unable to form new memories.

HM suffers mainly from anterograde amnesia and, just like Clive Wearing, he is unable to remember the faces of people he meets. He can carry on a normal conversation, but he does not recognize people who visit him regularly. He can read and reread the same magazines without knowing that he has already seen them.

It was a breakthrough in understanding the damage to HM's brain when researchers could use the MRI scanner in 1997. HM had been studied for 44 years before he was put into the scanner. Then it became clear exactly which areas were affected by the operation and that the damage was not as extensive as estimated by Scoville. The damage was pervasive, however, and included the hippocampus, the amygdala, and other areas close to the hippocampus. With the scanners, the researchers have a much better chance of testing which areas of the brain are related to which areas of memory and skill learning—something they could only speculate about beforehand.

Ethics in research

HM and Clive Wearing are famous case studies in cognitive psychology. HM has been studied extensively, with all kinds of tests, ever since his operation in 1953. He has even donated his brain to science when he dies. We do not know his identity. Clive Wearing's identity is known to us due to his wife's book.

1 Discuss why participants in case studies are normally anonymous.

2 Discuss the ethical considerations in studying an individual with an interesting disorder or brain damage, such as HM and Clive Wearing.

Cultural factors in cognition

It will probably be no surprise that the development of cognitive abilities, such as memory, thinking, and problem-solving, is influenced by the social and cultural context in which people live. Humans face different challenges around the world in order to survive. This was particularly true, of course, before the so-called modern era. After industrialization—and now with globalization and the development of modern technology—there has been a growing need for people with specialized education. The education systems reflect this. Just recall how much you need to learn, understand, and memorize, whether it be in mathematics, languages, or psychology. You also need to learn how to organize information in your memory, and how to retrieve the appropriate knowledge from your memory when you need it.

According to the US psychologist Jerome Bruner, children of any culture learn the basics of culture through schooling and daily interaction with members of the culture in which they live. Parents, grandparents, friends, peers, siblings, and teachers are among the most important in the transmission of knowledge—be it informal or formal.

Cross-cultural research—the role of schooling on remembering

Cognitive psychologists have traditionally conducted research in western countries. If one assumes that cognitive processes follow universal laws, then all humans all over the world, regardless of culture, would perform the same cognitive tasks with the same results. Following this logic, the same memory test could be applied globally. However, this is not the case. When researchers from the West performed tests with participants in non-western countries, they found that they did poorly on many memory tests. This was not always interpreted correctly—that is, there was a western bias in the test and it was therefore not valid when applied in another culture.

Cross-cultural psychologists are now aware that if you want to test memory in a group of people, it is necessary to have an insight into the language and culture of the group.

Cole and Scribner (1974) wanted to investigate *memory strategies* in different cultures. They compared recall of a series of words in the US and among the Kpelle people of rural Liberia. The researchers were aware that they could not use the same list of words in the two countries, so they started by observing everyday cognitive activities in Liberia. This helped them to develop memory experiments with relevant tasks, in close collaboration with the local college-educated people who spoke the language and acted as experimenters. They also made sure that the words used in the memory experiments were familiar to the participants. In spite of these precautions, Cole and Scribner found some striking cultural differences in the way the Kpelle people went about remembering and solving the problems presented in the experiments.

The researchers asked Liberian children from different age groups to recall as many items as possible from four categories: utensils, clothes, tools, and vegetables. Normally, one would expect that the older children would recall more items after practice, but the researchers found that this was not the case unless the children had attended school for several years. The non-schooled children did not improve their performance on free-recall tasks after the age of 10. They remembered around 10 items the first time. After 15 practice trials they remembered only two more items. Children who had attended school learned the lists just as rapidly as children in the US, and they used the same strategy to recall—that is, based on categorical similarity of the objects.

When the researchers analysed the data, they found that illiterate children did not use strategies like **chunking**—grouping bits of information into larger units—to help them remember. They also found that the Kpelle did not appear to apply rehearsal, as the position of a word in the list did not have an effect on the rate of recall.

In a later trial, the researchers varied the recall task so that the objects were now presented in a meaningful way as part of a story. This is called a **narrative**. The illiterate children recalled the objects easily and actually chunked them according to the roles they played in the story. The results have been supported in other cross-cultural studies on children's memorization skills. Rogoff and Wadell (1982) found that Mayan children could easily recall objects if they were related in a meaningful way to the local scenery.

Memory studies like these invite reflection. It seems that even though the ability to remember is universal, strategies for remembering are not universal. It is therefore a problem that many traditional memory studies are associated with formal schooling. Generally, schooling presents children with a number of specialized information-processing tasks, such as organizing large amounts of information in memory, and learning to use logic and abstract symbols in problem solving. It is questionable whether such ways of remembering have parallels in traditional societies like the Kpelle studied by Cole and Scribner. The conclusion is that people learn to remember in ways that are relevant for their everyday lives, and these do not always mirror the activities that cognitive psychologists use to investigate mental processes.

Reliability of one cognitive process: memory
How reliable is memory? The legal system uses eyewitness testimony, which relies on the accuracy of human memory to decide whether a person is guilty or not. Normally, juries in courts of law take eyewitness testimony very seriously but, recently, the use of DNA technology has demonstrated what some psychologists have claimed for years: eyewitnesses can be wrong. Researchers have demonstrated that memory may not be as reliable as we think. Memories may be influenced by other factors than what was recorded in the first place, due to the **reconstructive nature** of memory. The term "reconstructive" refers to the brain's active processing of information to make sense of the world.

Are recovered memories accurate?
Sigmund Freud (1875–1935) was convinced that forgetting was caused by **repression**. According to Freud, people who experience

> **Possible essay question**
> Discuss how social *or* cultural factors affect one cognitive process.

Assessment advice
Remember that "or" means that you should choose one of the factors, either cultural *or* social.

The command term "discuss" requires that you present a balanced argument that includes a review of hypotheses about how cultural factors affect a cognitive process.

intense emotional and anxiety-provoking events may use defence mechanisms, such as repression, to protect their conscious self from knowing things that they cannot cope with. They send the dangerous memories to the unconscious, which means that they will deny it ever happened. However, the memory will continue to haunt them in symbolic forms in their dreams until a therapist is able to retrieve the memory using specific techniques. Some researchers claim that these techniques can create false memories, which people consequently believe to be true.

Victims of child abuse may not want to remember the traumatic experiences, but is it possible to totally forget these things? This is exactly what the controversy of recovered or false memories is about. The newspapers have described cases where people say they have retrieved memories of child sexual abuse during therapy. The psychotherapist would not be surprised, because the aim of therapy is to gain access to the unconscious. The False Memory Syndrome Foundation was founded in the US in 1992 by parents and professionals to provide support to families that had been shattered by accusations of childhood abuse by their children after the latter had been through therapy. The US cognitive psychologist Elizabeth Loftus does not deny that childhood abuse happens, but she has argued that some of the recovered memories may simply be created by post-event information during therapy. Her laboratory research has supported the case that it is possible to manipulate people's memories.

In 2002, Loftus wrote an article on the case of the Washington sniper, who killed a number of people. The police asked people to come forward with information on the murderer and many reported having seen a white van in the vicinity of the shootings. In fact, the sniper's van was a blue Chevrolet Caprice. Loftus tried to find out where the myth of the white van came from. She discovered that a bystander had mentioned a white van in an interview. After this, other people reported that they had seen a white van. According to Loftus, a false memory had been created by the post-event information.

Empirical testing of reliability of memory

In his book *Remembering* (1932), Frederic Bartlett argued that memory is reconstructive and that schemas influence recall. He also demonstrated the role of culture in schema processing.

One of the methods used by Bartlett was **serial reproduction**, where one person reproduces the original story, a second person has to reproduce the first reproduction, and so on, until six or seven reproductions have been created. The method is meant to duplicate the process by which rumours and gossip are spread, or legends are passed from generation to generation.

The story in Bartlett's now classic study is based on a Native American legend. Bartlett asked the participants to read through the story twice. None of the participants knew the purpose or the aim of the experiment. After 15 minutes, Bartlett asked the participants to reproduce the story from memory. He asked them to reproduce the story a couple of times more when they had the opportunity to

---

TOK: is reasoning based on attitudes?

Which of these statements best reflects your view of how human memory works?

1 Everything we learn is permanently stored in the mind, although sometimes particular details are not accessible. With hypnosis, or other special techniques, these inaccessible details could eventually be recovered.

2 Some details that we learn may be permanently lost from memory. Such details would never be able to be recovered by hypnosis, or any other special technique, because these details are simply no longer there.

(Loftus and Ketcham 1991)

These questions were asked to 169 individuals in a survey conducted by Elizabeth Loftus. Of this sample, 75 had formal graduate training in psychology. They found that 84 per cent of the psychologists and 69 per cent of the non-psychologists believed that all information in long-term memory is there, and that what is not accessible can be recovered using hypnosis or special techniques.

Discuss how reliable you would find accounts of restored memories if you believed in statement 1 or statement 2. Explain why this is so. Support your argument with knowledge from TOK and psychology.

come into his laboratory, and he noticed how each participant's memory of an experience changed with each reproduction.

It appeared that *The War of the Ghosts* was difficult for people from western cultures to reproduce because of its unfamiliar style and content. Bartlett found some characteristic changes in the reproduction of the story.

- The story became shorter—for example, Bartlett found that after six or seven reproductions, it was reduced to 180 words.
- The story remained a coherent story no matter how distorted it was compared to the original. Bartlett said this was because people interpreted the story as a whole, both when they were listening to it and later when they were retelling it.
- The story became more conventional—that is, it retained only those details that could be assimilated to the shared past experience and cultural background of the participants.

According to Bartlett, people reconstruct the past by trying to fit it into existing schemas. The more complicated the story, the more likely it is that elements will be forgotten or distorted. Bartlett explained this as people's *efforts after meaning*—that is, people try to find a familiar pattern in experiences—past or new ones. According to Bartlett, memory is an *imaginative reconstruction of experience*, which is exactly what modern research supports.

Be an enquirer

Ask two people to make up a story. They must write it down on a piece of paper. Then place 10 people in a line and ask each of them to whisper the story to the person standing behind them. The last person in the line has to say the story out loud.

1 Compare the final version of the story with what was written down originally.

2 Discuss the changes. What kind of changes were made? Is there a consistent pattern?

Research in psychology

The War of the Ghosts (Bartlett, 1932)

One night two young men from Egulac went down to the river to hunt seals, and while they were there it became foggy and calm. Then they heard war-cries, and they thought: "Maybe this is a war party". They escaped to the shore, and hid behind a log. Now canoes came up, and they heard the noise of paddles, and saw one canoe coming up to them. There were five men in the canoe and they said:

"What do you think? We wish to take you along. We are going up the river to make war on the people."

One of the young men said: "I have no arrows".

"Arrows are in the canoe", they said.

"I will not go along. I might be killed. My relatives do not know where I have gone. But you", he said, turning to the other, "may go with them."

So one of the young men went, but the other returned home.

And the warriors went on up the river to a town on the other side of Kalama. The people came down to the water, and they began to fight and many were killed. But presently the young man heard one of the warriors say: "Quick, let us go home: that Indian has been hit". Now he thought: "Oh, they are ghosts". He did not feel sick, but they said he had been shot.

So the canoes went back to Egulac, and the young man went ashore to his house and made a fire. And he told everybody and said: "Behold I accompanied the ghosts, and we went to fight.

Many of our fellows were killed and many of those who attacked us were killed. They said I was hit, and I did not feel sick".

He told it all, and then he became quiet. When the sun rose he fell down. Something black came out of his mouth. His face became contorted. The people jumped up and cried.

He was dead.

(329 words)

Loftus's research on reliability of eyewitness testimony

One of the leading researchers in eyewitness testimony, Loftus, supports Bartlett's idea of memory as *reconstructive*. Loftus claims that the nature of questions can influence witnesses' memory. Leading questions—that is, questions that are suggestive in some way—and post-event information facilitate schema processing which may influence accuracy of recall.

Loftus designed an experimental procedure in which she manipulated questions after showing participants a film, in order to see how this affected what they remembered. In one such experiment, Loftus and Palmer (1974) investigated the role of leading questions in recall. The aim of the experiment was to see if changing *one* word in certain critical questions would influence speed estimates. The experiment used 45 students, who first saw films of traffic accidents and then had to estimate the speed of the car in the film.

The critical question (independent variable) in the experiment was: *About how fast were the cars going when they hit each other?* "Hit" was replaced by "smashed", "collided", "bumped", and "contacted" in separate trials. The dependent variable in this experiment was the estimation of speed (in miles/hour). The researchers found that the mean speed estimate was in fact affected by the words, so that "smashed" and "collided" increased the estimated speed.

The interpretation of the results was that the use of different verbs activates different schemas in memory, so that the participant hearing the word "smashed" may actually imagine the accident as more severe than a participant hearing the word "contacted".

Verb used	Mean speed estimate
Smashed	40.8
Collided	39.3
Bumped	38.1
Hit	34.0
Contacted	31.8

Speed estimates for the verbs used in experiment 1

A second experiment used 150 students as participants. They were divided into three groups and they all saw a film of a car accident. Then they were asked questions about the accident, including the question on estimation of speed, but this time only including "hit" or "smashed" in two of the groups. The last group—the control group—did not have questions on speed estimates.

A week later, the participants were tested again. The researchers wanted to see if memory was changed when it was retrieved. This time, the participants were asked a number of questions, but the critical question was whether or not they had seen broken glass in the film they had watched a week before. This time, they simply had to answer yes or no. In fact, there was no broken glass in the film, but 32 per cent of the "smashed" group said they had seen broken glass, compared to 14 per cent of the "hit" group. In the control group, only 6 per cent said they had seen broken glass.

Response	Verb condition		
	Smashed	Hit	Control
Yes	16	7	6
No	34	43	44

Distribution of yes and no responses to the question, *Did you see any broken glass?*

The researchers concluded that the different words had an effect on the estimation of speed as well as the perception of consequences. They explained that "smashed" provides the participants with verbal information that activates schemas for a severe accident. Broken glass is in line with this, so the participant is more likely to think that there was broken glass involved. Loftus's research indicates that it is possible to create a *false memory* using post-event information. These results indicate that memory is *not* reliable but can we conclude this without question?

This was a controlled laboratory experiment, so you may ask whether there are problems with ecological validity. There may also be a problem in using closed questions, where people have to answer yes or no. All the research participants were US students, which means that the sample is culturally biased. The research also begs the question of how well people are able to estimate speed. This too may have had an influence on the results.

Yuille and Cutshall (1986) have criticized Loftus's research for lack of ecological validity. Performing research on memory in a laboratory does not reflect how and what people remember in real life, they argue. They used Loftus's technique in interviewing people who had witnessed a real robbery and found that misleading questions did not seem to distort people's memory. Instead, they found that the memory for details in this real-life situation was quite amazing. This was seen particularly in witnesses who had been close to the event. In fact, it seemed that the wording of the question had no effect on recall, and those who were most distressed by the situation had the most accurate memories.

Be a researcher

Carry out a simple replication of Loftus and Palmer's (1974) research.

- State the hypothesis.
- What is the independent variable?
- What is the dependent variable?
- Describe the procedure.
- What type of data would you collect, and how could you analyse the data?

You can find more on Loftus's research and articles on her home page, if you would like to use this experiment as a basis for your IA:
http://faculty.washington.edu/eloftus

Be a communicator

A person in your country has been convicted for assault based on eyewitness testimony, but there is conflicting evidence. Write a brief article to the local newspaper in which you point out some of the problems with eyewitness testimony. Some factors to consider are set out below, but you can search the Internet for more information on some of the cases—for example, on the Innocence Project's home page:
www.innocenceproject.org

- Ronald Cotton was convicted of rape and imprisoned from 1984 to 1995, when he was released due to a DNA test that showed he could not have been the rapist. On the Innocence Project's home page you can find a long list of people who have been falsely convicted and subsequently freed due to modern DNA technology.

- Apparently, people have problems identifying individuals from other ethnic groups. This is a source of error that could have played a role in the Cotton case. Richard Rosen, a law professor at the University of North Carolina, says that there is plenty of evidence that people make mistakes when they have to make identifications across ethnic lines. Psychologists like Elizabeth Loftus say that this is because we are more able to distinguish the features of those we are most familiar with. She thinks that it could have something to do with the way we scan faces when we are looking at a face from a different ethnic group to our own.

Use of modern technology to investigate the relationship between cognitive factors and behaviour

Neuro-imaging techniques allow researchers to obtain images of brain functioning and structures. The knowledge gathered is used to understand the relationship between cognitive processes and behaviour. There are a number of techniques, and these are continually being developed to perform even more advanced research.

PET

PET (positron emission tomography) is a scanning method that can measure important functions in the brain, such as glucose consumption and blood flow. A PET scan is used to detect brain tumours or memory disorders due to Alzheimer's disease, because it can identify cellular-level metabolic changes in an organ or tissue.

The use of new technology has helped neuroscientists to develop methods to detect the signs of Alzheimer's disease so early that patients may not even have detected that something is wrong themselves. Researchers from the New York University School of Medicine have developed a brain-scan-based computer program that quickly and accurately measures metabolic activity in the hippocampus—an important brain structure involved in memory processes. Using PET scans and the computer program, the researchers showed that in the early stages of Alzheimer's disease, there is a reduction in brain metabolism in the hippocampus.

In a longitudinal study, they followed a sample of 53 normal and healthy participants—some for 9 years and others for as long as 24 years. They found that individuals who showed early signs of reduced metabolism in the hippocampus were associated with later development of Alzheimer's disease. One of the researchers in the team, Lisa Mosconi (2005), says that the results need to be replicated, but she thinks this new technique could be a useful tool in screening for Alzheimer's in people who do not yet show any symptoms of the disease.

MRI

MRI (magnetic resonance imaging) provides a three-dimensional picture of brain structures. The MRI and fMRI (functional magnetic resonance imaging) work by detecting changes in the use of oxygen in the blood. When an area in the brain is more active, it uses more oxygen. This is used to see what areas are active when people perform cognitive tasks such as reading or problem solving. The scanners can even be used in marketing research, to detect which areas are active when you look at a picture of your favourite brand.

Possible essay question

Discuss the reliability of **one** cognitive process (e.g. remembering, forgetting, attention).

Assessment advice

Notice that "one" is in italics in this essay question. That simply means that you should only deal with *one* process—for example, memory.

In this question, the command term "discuss" requires that you present a balanced view on whether the cognitive process you choose is reliable or not. In order to do this, you should argue in favour of a particular conclusion and present evidence to support it. This can be theories and/or empirical studies.

In questions like these, there are three possibilities to consider as a line of argument:

1 The cognitive process—for example, memory—is reliable.

2 The cognitive process is not reliable.

3 The cognitive process is sometimes reliable and sometimes not.

Choose your line of argument and find evidence to support it.

The scanners can detect the blood flow and produce maps showing which parts of the brain are involved in particular mental processes. In 2003, brain researcher Clinton Kilts, from Atlanta's Emory University in the US, conducted a series of experiments using MRI scanners to investigate the role of the brain in product preferences. He used a self-selected sample of volunteers. First, the participants were asked to rate a number of consumer goods in terms of preference, giving them points according to level of attractiveness. Then each of the participants was put into the MRI scanner, where they were shown pictures of the items and again asked to rate them, while the scanner registered brain activity. The researcher found that every time a person rated a product as particularly attractive, there was activity in a small area in the medial prefrontal cortex. This is an area that is known to be related to our sense of self and our personality. Kilts explained that if we are attracted to a product, we somehow identify with it, and that is why this area shows activity.

Kilts started to use MRI technology to understand what happens in consumers' heads when they make decisions about consumer brands—for example, why a person who said they preferred the taste of Pepsi during a blind taste-test still buys Coca-Cola. An experiment using an MRI scanner was carried out by Read Montague, from Houston's Baylor College of Medicine in the US. He invited 70 participants to a blind taste-test of Pepsi and Coca-Cola. Pepsi was by far the most preferred. Montague found activity in a brain area called the ventral putamen, which is part of the pleasure centre in the brain.

Kilts now works with the US marketing consultant company BrightHouse Institute, which founded a department for neurostrategy in order to explore the possibilities in this new research area. According to Kilt, you can use the knowledge from neuromarketing to make tools for testing the efficiency of marketing campaigns and brands. A bond between a product and the consumer is just what any company would love to create, so if they can get a consumer to identify with a brand, it becomes part of his or her self-image. Think about it: Are you a Stimorol guy? Are you a Gucci girl?

Not everyone is happy about this development. Some talk about Orwellian approaches and ask what will happen if marketing firms and political consultants can actually look inside the brain and see what triggers people to choose one brand over another, or one politician over another. Is the next step the ability to actually manipulate people to serve your own ends?

One important issue to discuss in the use of scanners is what these studies can actually show us. There is no doubt that it is possible to observe brain damage as in the case of HM (see page 79) and it is also possible to relate this to cognitive functioning such as memory. The scanners may also be useful to detect early signs of Alzheimer's disease. However, the brain is a very complex structure not yet totally understood and it is clear that activity in one area of the brain – or in several – does not mean that researchers at this point can establish cause-effect relationships between specific brain structures and preference for brands.

Extended essay question

Consider an extended essay on memory, based on neurological evidence and the use of the case study.

● To what extent can case studies of patients with brain damage provide insight into memory processes?

You should include more than one case study. Look in textbooks and online databases to find these.

Discuss how you could structure an argument that addresses this question based on the evidence. Here are some sites to get you started:

● http://scienceblogs.com/ neurophilosophy/2007/07/ remembering_henry_m.php

● http://homepage.mac.com/ sanagnos/corkin2002.pdf

Possible SAQ question

Discuss the use of technology in investigating the relationship between cognitive factors and behaviour (e.g. EEG, fMRI, computer simulations).

Assessment advice

The command term "explain" requires you to provide a detailed account, including reasons or causes for something. Here, you should describe how and why technology is used to study the relationship between cognitive factors and behaviour. This means that you do not have to evaluate the method. Remember that you should always include empirical studies to illustrate your argument.

3.2 Cognitive level of analysis: cognition and emotion

Learning outcomes

- Outline principles that define the cognitive level of analysis
- Explain how principles that define the cognitive level of analysis may be demonstrated in research
- Discuss how and why particular research methods are used by cognitive researchers
- Discuss ethical considerations related to research studies at the cognitive level of analysis
- Discuss the extent to which cognitive and biological factors interact in emotion
- Evaluate one theory of how emotions may affect one cognitive process

Where were you when Princess Diana died, or when you first heard about the attack on the Twin Towers on 9/11? Do you remember your first school day? Or your first date? You will probably remember events like these, while others, no matter how significant, may be forgotten. Some events, on the other hand, are not easily forgotten. Why do we clearly remember some events and forget others? The key appears to be that we remember better those experiences that involve emotions. Emotions are rich and diverse, and they are often what make the experience something special. The famous brain researcher Antonio Damasio explains that emotions are purely physical signals of the body which react to external stimuli. Feelings arise when the brain interprets these emotions.

Emotions consist of three components:

- **physiological changes**, such as arousal of the autonomic nervous system and the endocrine system that are not conscious
- the person's own **subjective feeling** of an emotion (e.g. happiness)
- **associated behaviour**, such as smiling or running away.

According to brain researchers, emotions serve as a guide to evaluate how important situations are, and it is not necessarily a conscious process. Cognitive psychologists like Lazarus and Folkman have suggested that it is not the emotion as such that is important, but rather how people appraise the situation and cope with it. Cognitive appraisal is simply an *interpretation*. A perceived dangerous event or stimulus (stressor) will result in a physiological response known as **fight or flight**, which prepares the individual for direct action to confront the danger or avoid it, *and* a cognitive appraisal of the arousal—that is, a decision about what to do, based on previous experience.

Biological factors in emotion

The amygdala is the small structure in the temporal lobe that appears to be critical in the brain's emotional circuit; it is believed to play a critical role in emotional memories. Studies of animals and humans indicate that stress hormones such as adrenaline are released when strong emotions are evoked.

In *The Emotional Brain* (1999), LeDoux describes two biological pathways of emotions in the brain. The first is a *short route* that goes from thalamus to amygdala; the second is a *long route* that passes via the neocortex and hippocampus before it results in an emotional response. The amygdala receives input from sensory processing areas in the neocortex and thalamus, and projects these to areas in the brainstem that control response systems such as fight or flight. It is the connections between the different brain structures that allow the amygdala to transform sensory information into emotional signals, and to initiate and control emotional responses.

Let us consider an example. Imagine a woman walking home, late in the evening. At the next corner, she sees a man waiting. She has just read in the newspaper a story about a woman being raped, so she is afraid, and her heart begins to race. She walks slowly, as if to prepare for what may come. This is the physiological arousal—the fight-or-flight response—which prepares the body for a reaction to a stressful experience. When the woman is just about to pass the man, he comes towards her, saying, "Excuse me, I am lost. Could you tell me where Lonner Street is?" The woman realizes that she has misjudged the situation and relaxes. She tells the man where the street is and continues walking calmly to her home.

How can this be explained? The emotional stimulus (a man who could be a potential aggressor) is first processed in the thalamus, which sends a signal to the amygdala. The perception of the potential stressor enables the brain to send signals to the body so that it can prepare for action. At the same time, the thalamus sends the information via the indirect pathway to the cortex and hippocampus for closer inspection. This results in a more detailed evaluation of the stimulus—an appraisal—and the outcome of this is sent to the amygdala. In the example above, the woman becomes aware that there is no danger, so she relaxes. Most of these processes are non-conscious.

According to LeDoux, the advantage of having direct and indirect pathways to the amygdala is *flexibility* in responses. In the case of danger, the fast and direct pathway is useful because it saves time. This could be important in matters of life and death. On the other hand, the long pathway allows for a more thorough evaluation of a situation, which can help people—and animals—to avoid inappropriate responses to situations.

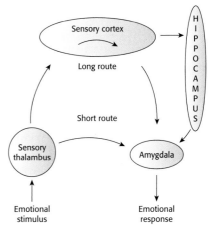

LeDoux's model of biological pathways of emotion in the brain

CAS

- Discuss, in a group, experiences you have had when emotions made a difference to what you did.

- Could it be that feelings such as empathy are important in deciding what to do for your CAS projects, or is this merely a result of deliberate evaluation of what is important?

Cognitive factors in emotion: appraisal

According to Lazarus, appraisals are evaluations related to how the situation will impact on one's personal well-being. Positive emotions emerge if the appraisal assesses potential benefit; negative emotions emerge if the appraisal assesses potential harm. Lazarus (1975) claimed that cognitive appraisal is an important part of people's reaction to emotional stress, and that stress experiences are not only physiological. People are psychological beings who are not simply passively responding to the world—they actively interpret and evaluate what is happening to them.

Lazarus and Folkman (1984) suggested that an individual's experience of stress can be moderated by a number of factors, which include appraisal of threat and appraisal of one's own resources for dealing with stress. These are influenced by personal characteristics such as motivation, beliefs about one's self and the world, and environmental variables such as the nature of the danger and social networks.

Folkman and Lazarus (1988) found that people use different strategies in stressful situations. One of them they called **problem-focused coping**, which aimed to change the problematic situation that causes emotional stress. They called the other **emotion-focused coping**, where the purpose is to handle the emotions rather than changing the problematic situation. Some of the methods used here are escape, self-control over expression of emotions, seeking social support, or attempting to provide a positive reappraisal of the situation.

Several studies have supported the suggestion that appraisal can have an effect on the way people cope with emotional arousal. In a classic experiment, Speisman et al. (1964) showed participants a film about an initiation ceremony involving unpleasant genital surgery. The aim of the study was to investigate if people's emotional reaction to the unpleasant film could be manipulated. This was done by showing the film with three different soundtracks. Condition one, the *trauma condition*, included a soundtrack which emphasized the pain and mutilation. In the second condition, the *denial condition*, the soundtrack showed the participants as willing and happy. In condition three, *the intellectualization condition*, the soundtrack gave the anthropological interpretation of the ceremony. The experiment deliberately manipulated the participants' appraisal of the situation and evaluated the effect of the type of appraisal on their emotional response. The results showed that participants reacted more emotionally to the trauma condition. This seems to support Lazarus's theory. Maybe it is not the events themselves that elicit emotional stress, but rather the individual's interpretation or appraisal of those events. This could also be seen as support to LeDoux's model of two biological pathways in the brain in that cognitive appraisal involves the hippocampus.

You might ask if a study like this can say anything about real life. It was a laboratory study with manipulation of variables, which always raises the issue of artificiality. There were also ethical issues involved here, because the researchers deliberately used deception and put participants in unpleasant situations. Cognitive appraisal then seems to influence the emotional reaction so this study could then illustrate how cognitive and biological factors interact in emotion.

Emotion and a cognitive process: the flashbulb theory

According to LeDoux, the arousal of emotion can facilitate the memory of events that occur during the aroused state. However, even though emotional memories may be indelible in terms of the emotions evoked by the event, the memories may not always be accurate.

The theory of **flashbulb memory** was suggested by Brown and Kulik (1977). Flashbulb memory is a special kind of emotional memory, which refers to vivid and detailed memories of highly emotional events that appear to be recorded in the brain as though with the help of a camera's flash.

Brown and Kulik found that people said that they had very clear memories of where they were, what they did, and what they felt when they first learned about an important public occurrence such as the assassination of John F. Kennedy, Martin Luther King, or Robert Kennedy. The participants recalled the assassination of John F. Kennedy most vividly. People in the study were also asked if they had flashbulb memories of personal events. Of 80 participants, 73 said that they had flashbulb memories associated with a personal shock such as the sudden death of a close relative.

Brown and Kulik suggested that there may be a special neural mechanism which triggers an emotional arousal because the event is unexpected or extremely important. At the time, it was only a hypothesis, but it is supported by modern neuroscience: emotional events are better remembered than less emotional events—perhaps because of the critical role of the amygdala.

Neisser (1982) has questioned the idea of flashbulb memories. People do not always know that an event is important until later. He suggests that the memories are so vivid because the event itself is rehearsed and reconsidered after the event. According to Neisser, what is called a flashbulb memory may simply be a narrative convention. The flashbulb memories are governed by a storytelling schema following a specific structure, such as *place* (where were we?), *activity* (what were we doing?), *informant* (who told us?), and *affect* (how do we feel about it?).

On 28 January 1986, the seven astronauts aboard the Space Shuttle *Challenger* were killed in a tragic accident. It was a shocking experience for those who watched the shuttle launch in person or on television. Neisser and Harsch (1992) investigated people's memory accuracy of the incident 24 hours after the accident, and then again two years later. The participants were very confident that their memories were correct, but the researchers found that 40 per cent of the participants had distorted memories in the final reports they made. Possibly, post-event information had influenced their memories. The researchers concluded that inaccuracy of emotional memories is common. Talarico and Rubin (2003) found that emotional intensity was often associated with greater memory confidence, but not with accuracy.

It has been suggested that not only post-event information, but also current attitudes and emotions may influence people's memories.

This means that past emotional memories are partly reconstructed based on people's current appraisal of events. This bias in memory was demonstrated in a study by Breckler (1994), who found that people's current attitudes towards blood donation impacted their memories about how they felt when they donated blood in the past. Holmberg and Holmes (1994) found that men whose marriages had become less happy over time tended to recall early interactions in the marriage as being more negative than they had originally reported. The data were correlational, so it is not possible to say that changes in appraisal actually cause changes in memory for emotions.

TOK and ways of knowing: emotions

1 What do you feel when you look at the homeless person? Why do you think you are feeling this way? How do you know what you are feeling?

2 Discuss in your group how you identify your own emotions, and how we know what other people are feeling.

3 Read the following passage and then discuss how science can add new dimensions to our own intuitive knowledge of emotions.

For years, psychologists, philosophers, and neuroscientists have wondered why we seem instinctively to understand other people's feelings and intentions. Some researchers now believe that this is due to a special kind of brain cells, called mirror neurons. It seems that mirror neurons respond in the same way when we actually perform an action ourselves and when we witness somebody else performing the same action. Researchers think that mirror neurons can explain why humans are capable of empathy, and also why people with autism are not able to show empathy—their mirror neurons are not functioning.

Possible essay question

Explain the interaction between cognitive and biological factors in emotion

Assessment advice

"Explain" is a command term that requires you to give a detailed account, including reasons or causes.

You could explain LeDoux's model and briefly refer to the study of Speisman et al. (1964)

Are rich people happier? Psychological research has found that this is not necessarily the case. Common beliefs about what contributes to happiness are not confirmed by psychological research. Winning a lot of money in the lottery may increase happiness in the short term, but after a while we tend to return to our usual level of happiness. One reason is that people get used to the situation.

According to Lyubomirsky (2001), our inborn genetic set-point for happiness probably accounts for 50 per cent of our happiness, whereas 10 per cent is due to circumstances, and 40 per cent is something that can be influenced by each individual. Happiness may also be culturally constructed, according to the journalist Eric Weiner, who visited 10 different countries—among them Bhutan, Thailand, Moldova, Qatar, the US, and Switzerland—and found that happiness is not so much a concrete state of mind as a cultural construction.

Did you know?

Happiness and economics
The philosopher Jeremy Bentham (1748–1832) defined happiness as the sum of positive emotions minus the sum of negative emotions. In his book, *Introduction to the Principles of Morals and Legislation* (1780), he wrote that any action that promoted happiness—defined as "pleasure and the absence of pain"—was morally right. He even suggested a way to calculate happiness. Economists such as Carl Menger (1849–1921) were interested in how people's economic choices reflected what they found to be important in striving for happiness. John Maynard Keynes (1883–1946), who was a founder of macroeconomics, claimed that the state should play an active role in creating better living conditions for the citizens; since then, economists have focused on material wealth and welfare systems as measures of happiness. Modern happiness research is based on the assumption that it is possible to measure people's individual experience of happiness.

Cognitive factors in happiness: beliefs about happiness

Modern happiness researchers face the dilemma that although people in the western world become richer, they are not happier. Psychologists have two explanations for this. One is that people compare themselves to others. This is based on a cognitive theory related to social psychology suggested by Leon Festinger. The **social comparison theory** is based on the idea that people learn about and assess themselves by comparison with others. According to this theory, people are happy if they have more than those they normally compare themselves to. The consequence is that one may be very happy with a new car—until a neighbour buys one just like it.

The second explanation is that people link happiness to reaching certain goals, but they tend to set higher goals once they have achieved the first ones; therefore they end up never really feeling happy. Julian Rotter proposed the **level of aspiration theory**, according to which people examine what they can gain and how likely it is that they will achieve it before making decisions about what to do. Expectations are influenced by previous experience as well as a desire to reach the goal. People come to formulate *general expectancy*—that is, general ideas about what to expect in different situations. If people link happiness to wealth and status—that is, if they expect to be happy when they buy a new house or earn more money, they are motivated to work hard to achieve this. The problem is that people only experience happiness for a brief time—if at all—once they reach their goal.

Myers and Dieners (1995) have shown that there is a discrepancy between wealth and happiness. They found that although the buying power of the average American had tripled since 1950, the proportion of Americans who described themselves as "very happy" remained stable at about one-third. This indicates that there is no direct link between an increase in wealth and happiness.

Hagerty (2003) studied the relationship between happiness and the distribution of wealth. He compared data from the US and seven other countries, and found that happiness was positively correlated with equality of distribution of wealth in the country. The average level of life satisfaction increased within a particular country as the inequality of income decreased. This could be explained by social comparison theory. We tend to compare ourselves to others, and it is well known to psychologists that comparing yourself to those who are more fortunate—**upward comparison**—leads to dissatisfaction. Competing for wealth with others is apparently *not* a recipe for happiness. But what if you compete with yourself and set goals believing that they will make you happier?

Happiness researchers do not recommend this strategy. In line with level of aspiration theory, they claim that people who link happiness to specific goals are less likely to be happy. It is like saying: "If only I had that Ferrari, I would be happy", or "If I can get promoted, I will be much happier". If people link happiness to these goals and then find that their happiness has not changed markedly when they achieve them, they believe that they have to set new goals. Psychological research has found that it is normal that people believe they will be happier in the future than they are right now. This is partly due to the media, which feature articles about successful famous people living in big houses and driving nice cars. They say they are happy and *look* happy on the photos. People tend to believe them because they think that success and money equal happiness. The media project a continuous stream of advertising where seemingly happy people purchase products. It is not strange that consumers come to believe that there is an association between happiness and certain products.

Johnson and Kruger (2006) found that although many people believe there is a relationship between happiness and money, it is rather satisfaction with one's salary that brings happiness. The actual size of the salary does not seem to matter much, as long as the person is satisfied with it, and it is enough to provide for his or her family. It seems, however, that some people become less satisfied with their salary because they think they should earn more, or that other people unjustly earn more than they do. By comparing themselves to others, they become less happy and want more and more.

Conway, di Fazio, and Mayman (1999) from Canada investigated the widespread illusion that money brings happiness in a group of

159 young men and women. The researchers used questionnaires to ask the participants to judge emotional reactions of high-status individuals with a lot of money and low-status people with no money. The researchers found that there was a widespread belief among the young people in the investigation that a high-status person, compared to a low-status person, was generally happier, less angry, less depressed, and experienced less fear in daily life. Making faulty associations between variables is called **illusory correlation**, and this is part of the way people think. The participants in the study did not believe, however, that status made a difference in love. The results of the study demonstrated that people have a firm belief that there is a positive relationship between wealth and happiness, even though this is not supported by psychological research.

Be a thinker and a communicator

Based on your knowledge of happiness, write an article on why having more money does not make us happier, and discuss factors that are more likely to provide happiness in people's lives. Think about how to support your arguments.

Case study

Challenging established beliefs of happiness

Conjoined twins Lori and Reba Schappel have been attached at the side of the skull for 40 years. They share a blood supply, part of the skull, and some brain tissue.

The sisters say they are very happy and optimistic. They have a good life and would never dream of being separated because that would ruin both their lives, since the likelihood is that they would both die. If one of them does die, however, they want doctors to perform surgery so that the other one can go on living. This is a procedure that has never been successful.

Lori used to work in a hospital, but since Reba is a country singer who has recorded an award-winning album, Lori has now given up her job to support her sister's career as a singer. Lori says that she does not think about being a conjoined twin every day because it is not the biggest thing in her life.

Their story is unusual and presents a genuine challenge to our beliefs about what it means to be happy. Psychological research shows that once people have established beliefs, no matter how they have acquired them, it is very difficult to change them. If their beliefs are challenged by evidence, they are likely to disregard it, and instead look for information that confirms their beliefs. People's claims about happiness come from their own unique perspective, and this is the lens for evaluation of experiences here and now.

Schappel sisters

Be reflective

1 Do Reba and Lori really know what happiness is?
2 Formulate a claim about what happiness is to you. Is it based on emotion or reason?

Sociocultural factors in happiness

According to the Dalai Lama, the head of Tibetan Buddhism, the key to happiness is in our own hands. Happiness can be achieved through systematic training of the mind and heart, and through reshaping attitudes and outlook. The whole purpose of life is happiness, and happiness is determined more by the state of one's mind than by external conditions, as long as basic survival needs are met.

The Dalai Lama maintains that *compassion* for other people is an important part of one's spiritual development, as well as being the basis for individual happiness. True compassion is a state of mind, which is non-aggressive and rests on the desire to help other people. A happy human being feels responsibility towards humanity and respects individual integrity. Such individuals accept that all human beings have an innate desire to be happy and want to avoid suffering. Acknowledging all people's right to happiness will help one feel connected to them, which is the true basis of compassion, says the Dalai Lama in an interview with Howard Cutler in *The Art of Happiness* (1998).

He says that if people base their happiness on wealth, they will lose their happiness if they lose their money. If they base their happiness on connectedness to other people, they will still have something valuable if they lose their money. Having empathy—that is, being truly able to understand other people, trusting them and enjoying their company—are important steps towards true happiness.

It is obvious that the Dalai Lama does not think that money is the road to happiness. The journalist Eric Weiner, who travelled to many different countries to search for the roots of happiness, declares that happiness is *not* money, because if it were, then people in Quatar, which is one of the richest countries in the world, should be very happy, and they are not. Bhutan is very poor, but people are happy. Life in Bhutan is imbued with spirituality, and meditation is part of everyday life for many. The Bhutanese are happy to spend their time doing nothing, and they find it acceptable that lamas—Buddhist priests—devote themselves to contemplation and the pursuit of wisdom, which in many western eyes is not productive.

The government in Bhutan is not focused on productivity, efficiency, and money, which is why it has regulated the amount of tourists who are allowed to enter the country. They want to preserve the unique nature of Bhutanese culture, which they consider to be of value. And then there is *happiness*.

The King of Bhutan has introduced the term **gross national happiness**—a measure of growth in happiness—as a contrast to the western gross national product (GNP), which is a measure of economic growth. Being a Buddhist, he thinks that the ultimate purpose of life is inner happiness, and that he—as the king of a Buddhist country—is committed to developing Bhutan in such a way that the development of the country is connected with the pursuit of happiness. One of the inhabitants defines happiness like this: *Knowing your limitations; knowing how much is enough.*

Eric Weiner's conclusion in his book *The Geography of Bliss* (2008), after his worldwide travel, is that there are many ways to happiness, and that each country defines what it understands as happiness, which could indicate that happiness is a cultural construction.

The happiest people in the world?

It seems that Danes are the happiest people on earth. According to surveys, more than two-thirds of Danes are "very satisfied" with their lives. Why is this? Christensen, Herskind, and Vaupel (2006) claim in their article, "Why Danes are smug: comparative study of life satisfaction in the European Union", that the Danes are probably happy for a number of reasons. The researchers rule out the climate—which is colder and cloudier than in many other countries—but point to the welfare state and the fact that Denmark has the highest level of income equality as a good explanation. Denmark has a prosperous economy and a well-functioning democracy. These factors are associated with contentment. Winning the 1992 European Championship in football by beating Germany 2-0 is probably another major contribution to Danish satisfaction, according to the researchers. The third important factor is probably that Danes do not have particularly high expectations about the future. The researchers suggest that the Danes are happy because they have low—but realistic—expectations about the future.

Danish football supporters

The British social psychologist Adrian White, from the University of Leicester, has created the first *Map of World Happiness*, based on data published by UNESCO, the CIA, the New Economics Foundation, the World Health Organization, and other official sources from around the world.

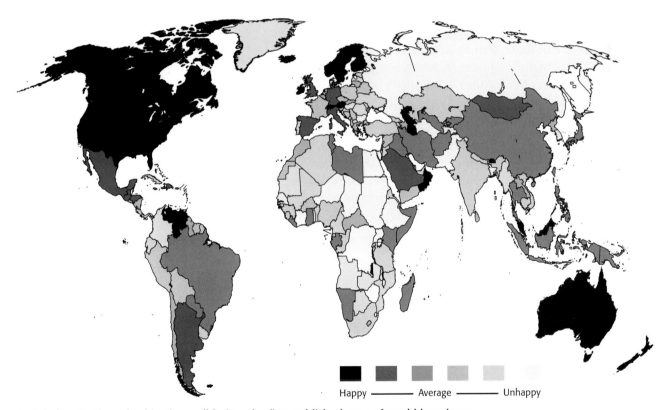

Happy ——— Average ——— Unhappy

A global projection of subjective well-being: the first published map of world happiness

The map is based on a **meta-analysis** of 100 different studies around the world, with responses from 80 000 people, who answered questions related to happiness and satisfaction with life. (A meta-analysis is a study that uses data from a number of studies.) Denmark came in first, followed by Switzerland. Other happy countries were Austria, Iceland, the Bahamas, Finland, and Sweden. The US was number 23 on the list; the UK 41; France 61; China 82; Japan 90; India 125; and Russia 167. The three least happy countries were the Democratic Republic of the Congo, Zimbabwe, and Burundi.

White said in a press release that "The concept of happiness, or satisfaction with life, is currently a major area of research in economics and psychology, most closely associated with new developments in **positive psychology**.

There is increasing political interest in using measures of happiness as a national indicator, in conjunction with measures of wealth. A recent BBC survey found that 81 per cent of the population think the government should focus on making us happier rather than wealthier. Further analysis showed that a nation's level of happiness was most closely associated with health levels (correlation of 0.62), followed by wealth (0.52), and then provision of education (0.51). These three predictor variables of health, wealth, and education were also very closely associated with each other, illustrating the interdependence of these factors. There is a belief that capitalism leads to unhappy people. However, when people are asked if they are happy with their lives, those in countries with good health care, a higher GDP per capita, and access to education were much more likely to report being happy according to the survey.

White says that happiness research is to a large extent related to positive psychology, a term first coined by the US psychologist Martin Seligman. One of the main goals of positive psychology is to conduct research that promotes human happiness and well-being. According to Seligman, his own research has demonstrated that it is possible to be happier—that is, more satisfied and engaged with life—as well as finding more meaning. People can learn to think positively and smile, in spite of life's adversities. Feeling positive emotions is important to Seligman because it seems to be related not only to mental, but also to physical health.

However, most positive psychology research is done in the West, and it is a challenge to the academic field to conduct research in countries where levels of happiness are low.

According to the happiness researchers Ed Diener and Joseph Smiley, it is true that the average life satisfaction of nations is highly related to income, because this is associated with fulfillment of basic needs and living longer. Experiencing positive emotions is also associated with social variables such as trust, safety, and lack of corruption. Happiness is thus not merely an individual affair, according to Diener, since it seems to be dependent on social institutions as well as the economy.

TOK: reflections

1 How does your culture define happiness? Do you think that people in your culture are happy?

2 How does your culture compare to the two studies above (Tibetan Buddhism and the Danes)?

Apply your knowledge

● Outline two problems that could be related to happiness research in psychology today as you see it.

● What could be done to counteract these problems?

Biological factors in happiness

Evolutionary psychologists have noted that people tend to adapt to their environment. We simply become used to the ways things are— this is called **habituation**. Humans have inherited a capacity to habituate to life's circumstances. They can adapt to negative factors such as noise or disability, but they also adapt to more positive experiences, so that no matter how nice an experience may be, they become used to it and it loses its primary thrill. According to evolutionary psychologists, humans have also inherited the tendency to notice trouble, so that we take positive things for granted, but focus on the more troublesome aspects of life. The reason for this is probably because our ancestors who noticed changes in the environment that could signal danger were more likely to survive and pass on their genes. Finally, humans seem to have an inner voice of dissatisfaction that prompts them—as it did our ancestors— to strive for more.

Genetics

The US researcher David Lykken has suggested that we have an innate baseline, or **set-point**, of happiness which is an aspect of our personality. In 1996, Lykken and his colleagues published the results of the **Happiness Twin Study**, which compared happiness scores among sets of identical and fraternal twins who grew up together or were reared apart. The twins were mostly white and born in Minnesota.

It is difficult to compare twins who are raised together and twins who are raised apart because it is a small sample. Identical twins are genetically identical. If they are separated and score the same on a variable like happiness, it is possible to rule out the role of the environment, since they have been brought up in different environments. The reasoning goes that if the twins show similarity in happiness levels, it must be due to genetic factors. In fact, researchers have found that identical twins are very similar in their happiness scores; it does not matter if they have been brought up together or reared apart. Fraternal twins do not show the same pattern at all. This is because fraternal twins do not resemble each other any more than other siblings. The researchers concluded that each individual has a genetically influenced set-point for his or her general feeling of happiness, and that 50 per cent of the differences in people's happiness levels are genetically determined. However, there are problems with twin studies like these. In order to make valid conclusions about the role of genes, the researchers have to assume that the twins share the same family environments. This is perhaps true for identical twins to a large extent, but less so for fraternal twins, who may be of different sexes.

The researchers also suggested that only 10 per cent of the variance in happiness levels can be explained by situational factors—for example, whether people are rich or poor, healthy or unhealthy, married or single. This is supported by research, which shows that rich or beautiful individuals are not happier than most people. According to the researchers, this is intriguing and goes against what most people believe. It also leaves room for people to actively pursue happiness for themselves, since 40 per cent seems to be within people's own control, according to Sonja Lyubomirsky, who wrote *The How of Happiness* (2007). She writes that there are opportunities to increase or decrease happiness levels through what people do and how they *think*. Her own research is based on systematic observations, comparisons, and experiments with very happy and very unhappy people.

In her book she provides an overview of typical characteristics of happy people.

- They devote a lot of time to family and friends.
- They can easily express gratitude for what they have.
- They are often the first to offer a helping hand to people who need it.
- They have an optimistic outlook on the future.
- They enjoy the pleasures of life and live in the present.
- They spend time doing physical exercise.
- They are committed to lifelong goals and ambitions such as fighting fraud.
- They cope well in times of crisis.

Lyubomirsky suggests strategies to increase happiness, such as expressing gratitude, avoiding overthinking and social comparison, investigating social connections, and practising acts of kindness.

It seems that being helpful to other people has a very positive influence on one's sense of self. Swartz et al. (1999) followed five women who had multiple sclerosis. They were trained to act as peer supporters for 67 patients who also suffered from multiple sclerosis. The training consisted of active and compassionate listening techniques. They were asked to call each patient for 15 minutes each month. The result showed that the peer supporters were happier and reported increased levels of satisfaction and self-efficacy. They participated in more social activities and experienced fewer episodes of depression. When they were interviewed about their experience, they said that the voluntary work had resulted in dramatic changes in their lives. They were now thinking of other people's problems instead of their own; they had become more tolerant and more open to other people, and their confidence in coping with life's ups and downs had increased. Overall, they concluded that the experience had improved their own lives considerably. Since this is a very small sample, it is not possible to generalize, but it illustrates the rewards of volunteering for community service.

CAS

Suggest a CAS project in your school, and discuss how other people could profit from it.

Discuss how you would develop yourself through this activity, taking into account the performance criteria from the CAS guide.

Extended essay questions

1 Why is there a difference between people's beliefs about happiness and what psychological research shows?

2 To what extent is it possible to increase one's happiness level?

3 Does culture matter in happiness?

4 Is it possible to use research about happiness to increase happiness?

Sociocultural level of analysis: sociocultural cognition

Learning outcomes

- Outline principles that define the sociocultural level of analysis
- Explain how principles that define the sociocultural level of analysis may be demonstrated in research through theories and/or studies
- Discuss how and why particular research methods are used at the sociocultural level of analysis
- Discuss ethical considerations related to research studies at the sociocultural level of analysis
- Describe the role of situational and dispositional factors in explaining behaviour
- Discuss two errors in attributions
- Evaluate social identity theory making reference to specific studies
- Explain the formation of stereotypes and their effect on behaviour

Principles of the sociocultural level of analysis

Early psychology focused solely on the role of the individual. Today, psychologists recognize that human behaviour can only be fully understood if the social context in which behaviour occurred is taken into account. One principle that defines the sociocultural level of analysis is that human beings are social animals and we have a basic need to "belong". The biological and cognitive systems that make up the individual are embedded in an even larger system of interrelationships with other individuals. The relationship between the individual and the group is bidirectional: as the individual is affected by being part of a group, the individual can also effect behaviour in the group.

A second principle that defines the sociocultural level of analysis is that **culture** influences behaviour. Culture can be defined as the norms and values that define a society. In an ever more multicultural society, there is a need to understand the effect of culture on a person's behaviour, because the study of culture may help us to better understand and appreciate cultural differences.

A third principle that defines the sociocultural level of analysis is that, because humans are social animals, they have a *social self*. People do not only have an individual identity, but also a collective or social one. For example, when Princess Diana died, people across the UK mourned as if she were part of their family. In the Czech Republic, when the national hockey team won the gold medal in the 1998 winter Olympics, one would have thought that every Czech had a brother on the team! Social identities are very important to the definition of who we are, and many behaviours are determined by membership of groups such as family, community, club, or nationality.

One last principle which is important at this level of analysis is that people's views of the world are resistant to change. A world view can be defined as the way the world is understood: how it is supposed to work, why it works the way it does, and what values are essential in the world community. Clearly, culture helps to shape our world view and our communities instill in us values which have been passed down from generation to generation. According to social and cultural psychologists, the sense of self is developed within social and cultural contexts.

Be reflective

As social animals, we belong to many different groups. As individuals, we help to shape the character of the group, and the group also shapes our character.

Brainstorm a list of the groups to which you belong. How important are these groups in your personal identity? What needs do these different groups fill in your life?

Research methods at the sociocultural level of analysis

In sociocultural research, the goal is to see how people interact with each other. Though experiments are sometimes used, the majority of research today is more qualitative in nature. It is important that the behaviour of the participants is as realistic as possible, to avoid studies that lack ecological validity. Therefore, a significant amount of research is **naturalistic**—that is, "as it really is". Much of the research is done in the environments in which the behaviour is most likely to take place. Early social psychologists mostly carried out laboratory experiments because that was considered to be the most scientific way of obtaining data. Modern sociocultural researchers tend to use participant observation, interviews, and focus groups in order to collect data to develop and support a theory. In spite of its "realism", however, it should be noted that the methods mentioned here result in descriptive data so they cannot be used for explaining cause-and-effect relationships.

Today, social psychologists frequently attempt to "see the world through the eyes of the people being studied". In order to do this, participant observation is often used. Participant observation is when researchers immerses themselves in a social setting for an extended period of time and observe behaviour. When the participants in the group know that they are being observed, this is an overt observation. If the researcher does not inform the participants that they are being observed, it is a covert observation.

Overt observations require the researcher to gain the trust of the group that is to be observed. For example, O'Reilly (2000) studied British expatriates on the Costa del Sol. Contrary to the prevailing belief at the time, she did not find that they were unhappy with their life in Spain—nor did they long to return home. In order to find this out, she had to spend a significant amount of time among the expatriates. She carried out several interviews, and she observed their behaviour in many different situations. In order to guarantee that they would discuss their lives openly with her, she had to develop a trusting relationship, in which she was non-judgmental of her participants. She needed to try to see the world through their eyes.

Covert observations are sometimes used with groups that would be hostile to an outsider observing their behaviour, or who would not be open and honest, perhaps because of the illegal nature of their activities—for example, drug users. Though the researcher must gain the trust of the members of the group, this is done through deceit. The researcher does not disclose his or her her intentions to the members of the group, and then records the participants' behaviour without obtaining informed consent. In addition to these ethical concerns, covert observers have difficulties taking notes and often have to rely on memory, meaning that their data are open to distortion. Finally, unlike overt observations, interviews cannot be carried out, for fear of being "discovered".

Research in psychology

Leon Festinger et al.'s *When Prophecy Fails* (1956)

Perhaps the most well-known covert observation was carried out by Leon Festinger and his colleagues. In Chicago, there was a religious cult that believed the world would end on 21 December. They believed that when the natural catastrophes began, they would be rescued by flying saucers, as long as they followed the prescribed rituals and read the sacred texts. They were also to remain isolated from all non-believers. This made it very difficult for psychologists to study them.

Festinger and his team decided to become cult members in order to carry out a participant observation. They remained with the cult up to the fateful day of 21 December—when nothing happened. Festinger monitored the group members' doubt, debate, and rationalization of what had taken place. The members of the cult, as part of maintaining their self-esteem, decided that God had not destroyed the world because of their prayers.

Be a thinker

- If you were a reporter covering the study, what questions would you ask Festinger and his team?
- Discuss the ethical concerns you would have with this research.

Attribution theory

Attribution is defined as how people interpret and explain causal relationships in the social world. Humans have a need to understand *why* things happen. For example, imagine you are sitting in a restaurant, waiting for your date to show up. He or she is late. Most of us would start to look for explanations as to why he or she has not yet arrived—for example, he is always late, or she has missed her bus. To take another example, anthropologist E.E. Evans-Pritchard was among the Azande people of central Africa when he came across the following situation. Several people in the village were killed when a granary doorway collapsed. The Azande attributed their deaths to witchcraft. Evans-Pritchard noted that the doorway had been eaten through by termites. "We understand that", he was told, "but why did those particular people happen to be sitting in the doorway at just the moment it collapsed? That's the witchcraft!" This study shows how people may have different ways of attributing causes to events.

Possible SAQ

Explain the use of one research method at the sociocultural level of analysis.

Assessment advice

This question asks you to explain, which means you have to give a detailed account including reasons or causes. You should give the main features of the method you choose, and then explain why this particular method is used at the sociocultural level of analyis. It is a good idea to have one example of a research study using this method to illustrate your points.

The origin of attribution theory can be traced to the influential writings of Fritz Heider in *The Psychology of Interpersonal Relations* (1958). When people try to understand behaviour, they are acting like naive psychologists. From observing other people's actions, people make inferences about intention and responsibility. People tend to make an attribution about behaviour depending on whether they are *performing* it themselves or *observing* somebody else doing it. This is known as the **actor–observer effect**. When people discuss their own behaviour, they tend to attribute it to **situational factors**—that is, something to do with external factors; when people observe someone else's behaviour, they are more likely to attribute it to **dispositional factors**—that is, something to do with personal (internal) factors. For example, in the case of the late date, the behaviour could be attributed to dispositional factors: "He's so insensitive", or "She's so forgetful". In the case of the Azande, it might be that the individuals who were killed were "unforgiving" or "out of line with their ancestors". The behaviour could also be attributed to situational factors. Once again, in the case of the late date, one might think, "I bet he missed his train", or "I hope she hasn't had an accident". In Evans-Pritchard's story, the termites destroying the doorframe would be a situational factor.

When a date doesn't show up, we try to attribute a cause for his or her late arrival

Errors in attributions

Attribution theory argues that people are more likely to explain another person's actions by pointing to dispositional factors, rather than to the situation. When people overestimate the role of dispositional factors in an individual's behaviour—and underestimate the situational factors—it is called the **fundamental attribution error**. Since people gather information by observing others, this often leads to illogical conclusions. For example, after watching George Clooney play several roles as a kind, loving male, when asked to describe him, people may say that he is kind and loving. One attributes these characteristics to his personality (dispositional) and not to the fact that he auditioned for and was given these roles in the films (situational).

Why is this error so common? Some psychologists argue that it is because people tend to think of themselves as adaptable, flexible, and ever-changing human beings. They do not like to think of themselves as a "type" of person. However, when they look at others, they do not have enough information about them to make a balanced decision, so they attribute behaviour to disposition. When they consider their own behaviour, they tend to think that they would have acted differently under different circumstances.

Placing the blame on the individual is common practice in western culture. People are held responsible for their actions. Some areas of psychology use specific theories to explain behaviour by referring to internal processes. People are more likely to say that a murderer is evil than to refer to environmental factors as explanations. In the western judicial system, juries look for a satisfactory motive if they are to convict someone of murder.

Research in psychology

Fundamental attribution error: Ross et al. (1977)

The aim of this ingenious study was to see if student participants would make the fundamental attribution error even when they knew that all the actors were simply playing a role. In their study, participants were randomly assigned to one of three roles: a game show host, contestants on the game show, or members of the audience. The game show hosts were instructed to design their own questions. The audience then watched the game show through the series of questions.

When the game show was over, the observers were asked to rank the intelligence of the people who had taken part. They consistently ranked the game show host as the most intelligent, even though they knew that this person was randomly assigned to this position, and—more significantly—he or she had written the questions. They failed to attribute the role to the person's situation—that is, being allowed to ask the questions—and instead attributed the person's performance to dispositional factors—in this case, intelligence.

There are some concerns about the experiment. First, the sample is somewhat problematic. The researchers made use of student participants. University students spend their days listening to professors who are seen as authorities. Therefore, one cannot be sure that this response to authority figures who ask questions and give answers is not a learned response rather than an attribution error. Second, student samples are not representative of the greater population, and therefore it is questionable whether the findings can be generalized.

This study reflects what we see in everyday life. People with social power usually initiate and control conversations; their knowledge concerning a particular topic can give others the impression that they are knowledgeable on a large range of other topics as well. Medical doctors and teachers are often seen as experts on topics that are not within their area of expertise. When they publish something outside of their field, their work is rarely challenged.

Another error in attribution is the **self-serving bias** (SSB). This is seen when people take credit for their successes, attributing them to dispositional factors, and dissociate themselves from their failures, attributing them to situational factors. Lau and Russel (1980) found that American football coaches and players tend to credit their wins to internal factors—for example, being in good shape, the hard work they have put in, the natural talent of the team—and their failures to external factors—for example, injuries, weather, fouls committed by the other team.

Why do we tend to employ the SSB? Greenberg et al. (1982) argue that the reason we do this is to protect our self-esteem. If we can attribute our success to dispositional factors, it boosts our self-esteem, and if we can attribute our failures to factors beyond our control, we can protect our self-esteem. In other words, the SSB serves as a means of self-protection.

It can also be argued that cognitive factors play a role in SSB. According to Miller and Ross (1975), we usually expect to succeed at a task. If we expect to succeed, and we do succeed, we attribute it to our skill and ability. If we expect to succeed and do not succeed, then we feel that it is bad luck or external factors that brought about this unexpected outcome. This also explains why it is not always one way or the other. If we expect not to do well, and in fact we do not do well, then we attribute it to dispositional factors; if we expect to fail, and we are successful instead, we tend to attribute our success to external factors—and luck. What has been described so far is commonly observed in people in the western world. There is, however, an exception. It has been found that people who are severely depressed tend to make more dispositional attributions thus blaming themselves for feeling miserable.

It also seems that there are cultural differences in SSB. In studies carried out by Kashima and Triandis (1986), significant cultural differences were found between US and Japanese students. In their experiment, Kashima and Triandis asked participants to remember details of slides of scenes from unfamiliar countries. When asked to explain their performance, the Americans tended to attribute their *success* to ability while the Japanese tended to explain their *failures* in terms of their lack of ability. This is called a **modesty bias**. Chandler et al. (1990) also observed this bias in Japanese students, and Watkins and Regmi (1990) found the same in Nepalese students. Why should this be the case?

The role of culture is pivotal in understanding the modesty bias. Bond, Leung, and Wan (1982) found that Chinese students who exhibited the modesty bias instead of the SSB were more popular with their peers. Kashima and Triandis argue that it is because of the more collective nature of many Asian societies: if people derive their self-esteem not from individual accomplishment but from group identity, they are less likely to use the SSB.

Social identity theory

Henri Tajfel's **social identity theory** assumes that individuals strive to improve their self-image by trying to enhance their self-esteem, based on either personal identity or various social identities. This means that people can boost their self-esteem through personal achievement or through affiliation with successful groups, and it indicates the importance of social belonging. Social identity theory is based on the cognitive process of **social categorization**. The theory has been used to explain social phenomena such as ethnocentrism, in-group favouritism, stereotyping, and conformity to in-group norms. Social identification may in fact underpin some of these behaviours because social categorization can produce competitive intergroup behaviour.

Tajfel argues that people who belong to a group—or, even more interestingly, when people are randomly assigned to a group—they automatically think of that group as their **in-group** (us) and all others as an **out-group** (them). What is more, they will exhibit in-group favouritism, and a pattern of discrimination against the out-group. The individual's self-esteem is maintained by **social comparison**—that is, the benefits of belonging to the in-group versus the out-group. The outcome of these comparisons is critical because it influences our own self-esteem. Cialdini et al. (1976) demonstrated this phenomenon among college football supporters. After a successful football match, the supporters were more likely to be seen wearing college insignia and clothing than after defeats. It is assumed that our need for a positive self-concept will result in a bias in these intergroup comparisons, so that you are more positive towards anything that your own group represents. Tajfel (1978) calls this "the establishment of positive distinctiveness".

Tajfel found that when people are casually assigned to a group—either by the flip of a coin, the drawing of a number from a hat, or by preference for a previously unknown artist—they see themselves

---

Possible SAQ

Describe **one** error in attribution.

Assessment advice

The command term "describe" requires that you give a detailed account of one error of attribution. In other words, you outline the theory and show how the error may happen. It is a good idea to include a study to make your points.

Possible essay question

With reference to research discuss two errors in attributions.

Assessment advice

The essay is longer than the SAQ and requires in-depth analysis. The command term "discuss" requires that you offer a balanced review of the explanations of two errors in attribution. You must include empirical research as evidence in your argument, which should be based on discussing the power of the explanation.

as being similar in attitude and behaviour, and a bond is formed among group members, even if they did not know each other before their assignment to the group. In the famous Kandinsky versus Klee experiment, Tajfel et al. (1971) observed that boys who were assigned randomly to a group, based on their supposed preference for the art of either Kandinsky or Klee, were more likely to identify with the boys in their group, and were willing to give higher awards to members of their own group. Asked for ratings of in-group and out-group on traits such as likeability, psychologists found that the out-group was rated as less likeable, but was never actually disliked. As later research would show, group identity alone appears not to be responsible for intergroup conflict. In the absence of competition, social comparison does not necessarily produce a negative outcome.

Social identity theory appears to be a good way of understanding human behaviour. However, there are some limitations to the theory. First, it describes but does not accurately predict human behaviour. Why is it that in some cases our personal identity is stronger than the group identity? Second, using the theory in isolation is reductionist—it fails to address the environment that interacts with the "self." Cultural expectations, rewards as motivators, and societal constraints such as poverty may play more of a role in behaviour than one's own sense of in-group identity.

Social representations

Moscovici (1973) developed the ideas of group theory with his concept of **social representations**. He defined social representations as the shared beliefs and explanations held by the society in which we live or the group to which we belong. He argues that social representations are the foundation of **social cognition**—they help us to make sense of our world and to master it; they also enable communication to take place among members of a community, by providing them with a code for social exchange and a code for naming and classifying unambiguously the various aspects of their world and their individual and group history. Social representations are, in a sense, cultural schemas that are fundamental to the identity of the group, and they provide a common understanding for communication within the group—for example, a group may have its own social representation of success, beauty, or intelligence. Adler (1990) found that if you ask a Russian mother to describe what it means for her child to *share* something, she will describe her children playing together with a toy at the same time; an American mother, however, will describe her children taking turns to play with the same toy.

Caroline Howarth (2002) carried out focus-group interviews with adolescents living in Brixton in London. She wanted to see how social representations of Brixton affected the identity of adolescent girls. Her focus groups used groups of friends, so that controversial, and sometimes personally upsetting, topics could be discussed with empathy and respect. She found that the very negative representation of "being from Brixton" by those from outside the area was not shared by the people living there. People from Brixton found that the people who lived there were "a diverse, creative, and vibrant"

Being part of a social group of friends is an important part of one's social identity

Profile

Serge Moscovici

Serge Moscovici is a Romanian-born French social psychologist, currently the director of the European Laboratory of Social Psychology, which he co-founded in 1975 in Paris. He was born into a Jewish family and from an early age Moscovici suffered the effects of anti-Semitic discrimination: in 1938, he was expelled from a Bucharest high school.

His research focus has been on group psychology and his theory of social representations is now widely used. He criticized US research on conformity to the majority and instead did research that showed how the opinions of a minority may influence those of a larger group.

community. This representation had an influence on the identity of those in Brixton—it influenced how the girls made friends and joined sports teams, their relations with the police, and their employment opportunities. This case shows how social representations may become the basis for stereotyping—both negative and positive—and how this can contribute to social identity.

Stereotyping

A **stereotype** is defined as a social perception of an individual in terms of group membership or physical attributes. It is a generalization that is made about a group and then attributed to members of that group. Such a generalization may be either positive or negative. For example, *women are talented speakers* or *women are bad drivers*. Stereotyping is a form of social categorization that affects the behaviour of those who hold the stereotype, and those who are labelled by a stereotype. Researchers now explain stereotyping as a result of schema processing.

Stereotype threat: the effect of stereotypes on an individual's performance

Stereotype threat occurs when one is in a situation where there is a threat of being judged or treated stereotypically, or a fear of doing something that would inadvertently confirm that stereotype. Steele and Aronson (1995) carried out an experiment to see the effect of stereotype threat on performance. They gave a 30-minute verbal test, made up of very difficult multiple-choice questions. When one group was told it was a *genuine test of their verbal abilities*, African American participants scored significantly lower than European American participants. In another group which was presented with the same test as *a laboratory task that was used to study how certain problems are generally solved*, African American students scored higher than the first group, and their performance on the test rose to match that of the European American students. In subsequent studies, the researchers found similar results in studies with females (in mathematics) and lower social class. This led them to conclude that stereotype threat can affect the members of just about any social or cultural group, if the members believe in the stereotype. Aronson argues that this could explain why some racial and social groups believe that they are more or less intelligent than others. Believing in such stereotypes can harm the performance of these groups.

According to Steele (1997), stereotype threat turns on **spotlight anxiety**, which causes emotional distress and pressure that may undermine performance. Students under the stereotype threat often underperform and this can naturally limit their educational prospects. Spencer et al. (1977) tested the effect of the stereotype threat on intellectual performance. The researchers gave a difficult mathematics test to students who were strong in mathematics. They predicted that women under the stereotype threat would underperform compared to the men taking the test. The stereotype threat that women experience in mathematics-performance settings originates from a negative stereotype about women's mathematics ability, which is quite common in society. For women who are good

A focus group is a type of interview in which several people are interviewed at the same time on a specific theme. One of the goals of a focus group is for the members of the group to feel comfortable in sharing their thoughts and for individuals to feel inspired and empowered by the comments of other interviewees. For more information about focus groups, see Chapter 10.2.

at mathematics and see mathematics as an important part of their self-definition, such a stereotype threat may result in an interfering pressure in test situations. Spencer et al. found that this was true: women in the experiment significantly underperformed compared with equally qualified men on the difficult mathematics tests. However, when the researchers tested literature skills, the two groups performed equally well. This was because women are not stereotype threatened in this area.

● ● ● ● ● ● ● ● ●

Be empathetic

In 1994, a controversial book, *The Bell Curve* (by Richard J. Herrnstein), was published, discussing the IQs of different ethnic groups. One of the stereotypes it perpetuated was that all Asians are very intelligent. In spite of this being a rather "positive" stereotype, how could this also be an example of stereotype threat? What are the negative effects of such a stereotype?

The formation of stereotypes

How is it that stereotypes develop? Though Tajfel argues that this is a natural cognitive process of **social categorization**, that does not explain how it actually happens. Campbell (1967) maintains that there are two key sources of stereotypes: personal experience with individuals and groups, and **gatekeepers**—the media, parents, and other members of our culture. He goes on to argue that stereotypes thus have a basis in some reality. His **grain of truth hypothesis** argues that an experience with an individual from a group will then be generalized to the group. This theory has been criticized, however, since errors in attribution are common.

Hamilton and Gifford (1976) argue, instead, that stereotypes are the result of an **illusory correlation**—that is, people see a relationship between two variables even when there is none. An example of this is when people form false associations between membership of a social group and specific behaviours such as women's inferior ability in mathematics. The illusory correlation phenomenon cause people to overestimate a link between the two variables, here "women" and "ability in mathematics". Illusory correlations can come in many forms and culturally-based prejudice about social groups can to some extent be classified as illusory correlations. Illusory correlation is an example of what researchers call "cognitive bias", that is, a person's tendency to make errors in judgment based on cognitive factors. Attribution errors are also examples of cognitive bias.

Once illusory correlations are made, people tend to seek out or remember information that supports this relationship. This is an example of **confirmation bias**. Generally, this means that people tend to overlook information that contradicts what they already believe. In a social context, they pay attention to behaviours that confirm what they believe about a group and ignore those behaviours contrary to their beliefs. Confirmation bias makes stereotypical thinking resistant to change. Snyder and Swann (1978) conducted a study in which they told female college students that they would meet a person who was either introverted (reserved, cool) or extroverted (outgoing, warm). They were then asked to prepare a set of questions for the person they were going to meet. In general, participants came up with questions that confirmed their perceptions of introverts and extroverts. Those who thought they were going to meet an introvert asked, "What do you dislike about parties?" or "Are there times you wish you could be more outgoing?" and extroverts were asked, "What do you do to liven up a party?" The researchers concluded that the questions asked confirmed participants' stereotypes of each personality type.

Stereotypes can also be formed as a means of taking on the in-group's social representation of the out-group. In other words, individuals may conform to the group norms with regard to the "other". Rogers and Frantz (1962) found that white immigrants to Rhodesia (today's Zimbabwe) developed more stereotypes—and prejudice—against the local people the longer they stayed there. They argue that this is because they adopted the social representations that were dominant in the group they were joining.

Research on stereotyping, prejudice, and discrimination is difficult to carry out. Often, **social desirability effect** is a confounding variable in such research. Although some research on stereotyping and prejudice indicates a decrease in the frequency of such behaviours, it is difficult to know if this is truly the case, or whether it is simply "politically incorrect" to make such statements. This has meant that in today's research on stereotyping and prejudice, researchers are moving away from self-report methods and looking at other ways to study this behaviour.

Apply your knowledge

Find two examples of stereotypes in the media—newspapers, magazines, books, packaging, products, posters, or films. Bring the image to class, and explain why the image represents a stereotype and why you think this image persists.

4.2 Sociocultural level of analysis: social and cultural norms

Learning outcomes

- Explain social learning theory, making reference to two relevant studies
- Discuss the use of compliance techniques
- Evaluate research on conformity to group norms
- Discuss factors influencing conformity
- Define the term *culture* and *cultural norms*
- Examine the role of two cultural dimensions on behaviour
- Using examples, explain *emic* and *etic* concepts

Introduction

A **norm** is a set of rules based on socially or culturally shared beliefs of how an individual ought to behave. The norms thus regulate behaviour within a group. When individuals deviate from social or cultural norms, they may be punished, marginalized, stigmatized, or—more positively—seen as creative and affecting change in the society. Being social animals, the need to belong plays a strong role in the desire to conform to group norms.

Social learning theory

How does a society or culture pass on its norms to individuals within the group? One of the most predominant theories is Albert Bandura's **social learning theory**. This theory assumes that humans learn behaviour through **observational learning**—in other words, people can learn by watching models and imitating their behaviour. Sometimes the model is trying to have a direct effect on the learner—for example, when a teacher instructs children how to solve a problem—but often models serve as indirect models, in that they are not trying to influence behaviour.

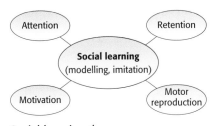

Social learning theory

According to Bandura, social learning involves the following factors.

- **Attention**: The person must first pay attention to the model.
- **Retention**: The observer must be able to remember the behaviour that has been observed.
- **Motor reproduction**: The observer has to be able to replicate the action.
- **Motivation**: Learners must want to demonstrate what they have learned.

Motivation to imitate the behaviour of the model is quite complex. There are several factors which may influence whether or not the observer decides to imitate and learn.

- **Consistency**: If the model behaves in a way that is consistent across situations—for example, always being brave—then the observer will be more likely to imitate than if the model behaves in different ways depending on the situation.
- **Identification with the model**: There is a tendency to imitate models who are like ourselves—for example, in terms of age and gender.
- **Rewards/punishment**: Bandura argues that people can learn from observing what happens to others; they don't have to experience the consequences themselves. This is called **vicarious reinforcement** in Bandura's theory and happens when we watch people around us – whether in reality or in movies. This is called observational learning.
- **Liking the model**: Warm and friendly models are more likely to be imitated than cold, uncaring models. A study by Yarrow et al. (1970) showed that children learn altruistic behaviour (helping others for no personal gain) better from people with whom they have already developed a friendly relationship than from people they do not know.

Younger children look to older siblings as models of behaviour

Social learning theory has been used to explain many things but particularly the role of violence in the media on aggression in children.

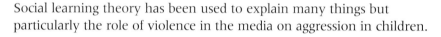

Research in psychology

Bandura et al. (1961)

Bandura's team had two aims in this study. First, they wished to see if children would imitate aggression modelled by an adult; and second, they wanted to know if children were more likely to imitate same-sex models.

Children aged 3 to 6 years (36 boys and 36 girls) were divided into groups. The groups were matched with regard to aggression based on an evaluation by their parents and teachers. One group was exposed to adult models who showed aggression by bashing an inflatable "Bobo" doll; a second group observed a non-aggressive adult who assembled toys for 10 minutes; and a third group served as a control and did not see any model. In the first and second groups, some children watched same-sex models and some watched opposite-sex models.

After watching the models, the children were placed in a room with toys. Very soon, they were taken out of the room, being told that those toys were for other children, and then they were put into the room with the Bobo doll. Bandura's group found that the children who had observed the aggressive models were significantly more aggressive—both physically and verbally. According to Bandura, the theory of social learning was demonstrated in the study, since the children showed signs of observational learning. With regard to the second aim, Bandura observed that girls were more likely to imitate verbal aggression, whereas boys were more likely to

imitate physical aggression. When boys observed women bashing the Bobo doll, they often made comments like "Ladies shouldn't do that!" In other words, the children were more likely to imitate the same-sex adult.

In spite of the fact that this study supports social learning theory, it is important to critically evaluate the study with regard to both its method and its ethics. First, the experiment has been criticized for low ecological validity. Not only was it carried out in a laboratory, but there are also other factors which make the situation less than natural. There is only a very brief encounter with the model, and the children are intentionally frustrated after they begin to play with a toy. This situation does little to predict what happens if a child is repeatedly exposed to aggressive parents or violence on television. One also has to question the actual aggression that was observed. Does the aggression against a Bobo doll indicate learned aggression in general, or it is highly specific to this situation?

In addition to questionable ecological validity, there are other methodological considerations. The aggression modelled by the adult was not completely standardized, meaning that the children may have observed slight differences in the aggression displayed. Also, in spite of the attempt to match the participants with regard to aggression, it was based on observations from teachers and parents, and this may not have been completely accurate. Finally, there is the question of demand characteristics: the children may have acted aggressively because they thought it would please the researcher.

One also has to consider the ethics of using young children in such an experiment. Observing adult strangers act in such a violent manner might be frightening to children. Also, it is questionable whether it is appropriate to teach children violent behaviour. There was no guarantee that once violent behaviour was learned, it would not become a permanent feature of the child's behaviour, or be generalized to other situations.

Different situations in the experiment on aggression

Profile

Albert Bandura
Albert Bandura (1925–present) joined the Department of Psychology at Stanford University in 1953 and stayed there until he retired. He initially suggested social learning theory as a reaction against the passive conception of humans in behaviourism. He pointed at the role of modelling in learning based on his famous experiment with the Bobo doll. Social learning theory, and later social cognitive theory with the important theory of self-efficacy, changed the direction of psychology. Social cognitive theory sees people as self-reflecting and self-regulating and the theory is now very influential in all areas of psychology.

Application of social learning theory in real life

According to social learning theory, there is a chance that violence on television will lead to more violent children. But is this so? The results of studies on the effects of televised violence are consistent. By watching aggression, children learn how to be aggressive in new ways and they also draw conclusions about whether being aggressive to others will bring them rewards or punishment. Huesmann and Eron (1986) carried out a longitudinal study, monitoring children's behaviour over a 15-year period. They found a positive correlation between the number of hours of violence watched on television by elementary school children and the level of aggression demonstrated when they were teenagers. They also found that those who watched a lot of television violence when they were 8 years old were more likely to be arrested and prosecuted for criminal acts as adults.

In an important study carried out in Canada, children were found to have become significantly more aggressive two years after television was introduced to their town (Kimball and Zabrack 1986). The results of two studies here indicate a link between watching violent television and aggressive behaviour, but we should critically consider the findings: could there be another explanation? For example, children who watched violent television may have lived in families which facilitated violent behaviour.

Be a critical thinker: the other side of the argument

The island of St Helena in the Atlantic Ocean has been the site of an interesting natural experiment. Television was first introduced on St Helena in 1995. Psychologists from the UK used this unique opportunity to investigate the effect of the introduction of television on aggression in children. Cameras were set up in the playgrounds of two primary schools on the island, and the behaviour of children (between the ages of 3 and 8 years) was observed *before* and

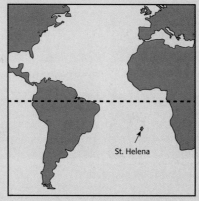

St Helena

after the introduction of television. A content analysis of the television programmes showed little difference in the quantity or level of violence watched, when compared with children in the UK, so children on St Helena were exposed to exactly the same level of violence.

Analysis of hundreds of hours of videotape, backed up by interview data from teachers, parents, and some of the older children, showed no increase in antisocial behaviour among the children of St Helena. The good behaviour evident before the arrival of television had been maintained even after five years of exposure to violent television. From: Charlton, T., Gunter, B. and Hannan, A. (eds.) (2002) *Broadcast Television Effects in a Remote Community*, Lawrence Erlbaum Associates.

1 Find information about the people and culture of St Helena. What are the major differences between this community and communities in the UK?

2 Discuss possible reasons why the results of this study are so different from the results of the studies conducted by Bandura et al. and by Kimball and Zabrack.

Television is not always a negative influence. There is strong evidence that children's shows such as *Sesame Street*—developed to teach academic and social skills—can help children learn positive behaviours such as sharing, empathy, and academic curiosity. A vast number of soap operas have made use of social learning theory in order to effect change in society. Bandura's social learning theory is the basis for television and radio dramas which aim to prevent unwanted pregnancies, reduce the spread of HIV, promote literacy, and empower women in developing countries. As a result of broadcasting the serial *Twende na Wakati* (Let's Go with the Times) in Tanzania between 1993 and 1996, researchers found increases in safe sex, women's status, and family planning.

The Sabido method

The Sabido method, named after Miguel Sabido, is a method for designing and producing radio and television drama that aims to change people's behaviour. Sabido applied social learning theory to soap operas in order to influence viewers' attitudes towards literacy. His method has been widely used all over the world to promote safe sex, family planning, and gender equality. The basic idea of social learning theory is that we can learn from role models, especially if they are people who we can identify with.

Be a communicator

1 Run an Internet search on the Sabido method. A good place to start is www.populationmedia.org/what/sabido-method

2 Find examples of the application of the method and discuss its effectiveness. Notice how it has been applied cross-culturally.

3 Describe the structure and the key people in a television drama based on the Sabido method. Then, in a group, try to identify a problem that is relevant in your own community (e.g. binge drinking or bullying) and create a show aimed at bringing about social change. After your performance, debrief the class on why you made the choices you did for your performance.

Evaluation of social learning theory

Social learning theory helps explain why behaviours may be passed down in a family or within a culture. It also explains why children can acquire some behaviours without trial-and-error learning. However, though a behaviour may be acquired, it is not always demonstrated. The child might learn something from watching a model, but may not exhibit that behaviour for some time. Some see this as a criticism of the theory. Because this gap exists between when one observes the model and when one may demonstrate the behaviour, it is difficult to establish 100 per cent that the behaviour is the result of observing the model. Neither does social learning theory explain why some people never learn a behaviour, in spite of the above criteria being met.

Social learning theory has developed into social cognitive theory and self-efficacy theory. Both are based on social learning theory but the focus is on beliefs and how self-beliefs influence behaviour. This is an important elaboration of social learning theory to include how

---

Possible SAQ

With reference to **one** research study explain social learning theory.

Assessment advice

The command term is "explain" which requires you to give a detailed account including causes. Here you should briefly outline predictions of the theory and include relevant concepts and then refer to one empirical study that illustrates or is based on social learning theory.

people are motivated not only by role models but also their own beliefs and previous experiences.

Social influence: compliance

Compliance is another important aspect of behaviour within a group. Conformity occurs when the situation does not exert direct pressure to follow the majority, but the pressure is often perceived by individuals as influencing their behaviour. Compliance can be defined as the result of direct pressure to respond to a request—for example, when people comply to buy certain products, even though the direct pressure may not always be apparent to the individual.

One of the leading researchers in the psychology of persuasion, Robert Cialdini, has outlined **compliance techniques**, or ways in which individuals are influenced to comply with the demands or desires of others. This is the cornerstone of advertising and marketing, where sales tactics are always carefully examined on the basis of what would most likely persuade consumers to buy specific products. Cialdini outlines six factors that influence the likelihood that people will comply with a request:

- **Authority**: People comply more often with those in positions of some authority. Advertisers use famous people to brand their product so that people associate the brand with the famous person. For example, *If that famous basketball player buys those shoes, then I should too!*
- **Commitment**: Once people have agreed to something, either by their behaviour or by a statement of belief, they are likely to comply with similar requests.
- **Liking**: People comply with requests from people they like.
- **Reciprocity**: People often feel they need to "return a favour".
- **Scarcity**: Opportunities seem more valuable to people when they are less readily available. This is why there are so many "last chance" and "limited time only" sales.
- **Social proof**: People view a behaviour as correct if they see others performing it.

Reciprocity

Travelling in the Middle East, tourists are often exposed to the compliance technique of reciprocity. Walking into a shop in the bazaar in Istanbul, you are greeted by the kind owner who invites you in, asks you where you are from, and then offers you a cup of coffee and some lovely Turkish pastries. As you sit there, the hospitality of the owner makes you feel a bit guilty about just walking out without buying anything. If you were already thinking of buying a carpet, you might decide to have him show you his collection. As he displays more and more carpets, taking them down from the rack, unrolling them, and then talking to you about their quality, you recognize that he is doing more and more work for you. You are more likely to feel that you need to purchase one of these carpets. If you were not thinking of buying a carpet—or do not have enough money even if you wanted to—you may find yourself looking around the shop for something small that you *could* buy, and maybe give as a gift to someone when you return home.

> **Be a critical thinker**
> How does our knowledge of mirror neurons potentially help to explain social learning theory?

> **Possible essay question**
> With reference to two studies, evaluate research on conformity to group norms.

Assessment advice
The command term "evaluate" asks you to discuss the strengths and the limitations of the conformity research in relation to the theory. There are many things that you may include in such an evaluation, e.g. methodological, ethical, cultural, and gender considerations.

What happens here is explained by the **reciprocity principle**—that is, the social norm that we should treat others the way they treat us. Anthropologists and sociologists claim that reciprocity is one of the most widespread and basic norms of human culture. This rule says that a person must try to repay what another person has provided. This is a way of creating confidence among people in that what is given to another is not lost but rather a sign of a future obligation that enables development of various kinds of relationships and exchanges. In fact, nearly everyone is trained from childhood to abide by this rule. Since this rule is so powerful it can be used to one's advantage as in the case of the carpet seller who offers a small gift because he knows that if a person accepts it, he or she is likely to buy something because of the rule of reciprocity.

Arousal of feelings of guilt plays a key role, as seen from the example above. The strategy of reciprocity is not limited to Middle Eastern cultures. It is common practice in many cultures to offer gifts, free travel, or free time in hotels to potential customers—for example, when they subscribe to a magazine, sign up for a trip, or plan to buy a property. Lynn and McCall (1998) even found that when restaurant customers are given a mint or sweet with their bill, the size of the tip they leave increases.

However, reciprocity does not always involve giving gifts. It can also be because one feels that the other person has already compromised on what he or she wanted, and that this compromise should therefore be acknowledged with some behaviour. One example of this is called the **door-in-the-face technique**. In this case, a request is made which will surely be turned down. Then a second request is made which asks less of someone. People are more likely to accept the second request because they feel that the person has already lowered the request in order to accommodate them. An example of this is a study by Cialdini et al. (1975). Posing as representatives of the "County Youth Counselling Program", he and his team stopped university students on campus and asked them if they would be willing to chaperone a group of juvenile delinquents on a day trip to the zoo—83 per cent refused to volunteer. Another time they stopped students and first asked if they would be willing to sign up to work for two hours per week as counsellors for a minimum of two years—no one agreed to volunteer. But when they followed up the students' refusal with the request to take the juvenile delinquents to the zoo, approximately 50 per cent of students agreed to serve as chaperones.

This behaviour can be seen in many contexts of daily life—for example, when the salesperson lowers the price of a product or service because the customer thinks it is too expensive. Once that compromise is made, the customer is more likely to make a purchase. So what can be done? The best defence against manipulation is perhaps not to reject totally what is offered by others but rather to accept initial favours in good faith—and in some cases be prepared to view them as tricks. If offers are seen in this way, there is no need to feel the necessity to respond with a favour unless you really want to.

Commitment

Commitment is characterized as being consistent with previous behaviour. Cialdini argues that once people make a choice or take a stand, they will encounter personal and interpersonal pressures to behave consistently with that commitment. Often, this occurs even when it appears illogical to the outsider. Kurt Lewin (1951) argued that behaviour is motivated by **goal gradients**. The longer people commit themselves to something, the less likely they are to abandon the goal. For example, have you ever waited in a queue that is not moving? The longer you stand in line, the less likely you are to change to another queue or simply give up waiting—even though it is illogical to think, "Since I have already waited two hours in this queue, it has to start moving soon!"

Getting people to make a commitment to something small, with the hope of persuading them to agree to something larger often employs the **foot-in-the-door technique**. For example, it is not uncommon nowadays to be stopped on a street corner and asked to sign a petition. These petitions may be for or against a law that may be passed, in support of a political party, or as part of a referendum. Often, such petitions are simply discarded but the simple act of having signed the petition may influence a person's later behaviour with regard to the issue. By getting people to agree to sign their name, it is hoped that they will then support that cause in upcoming elections. An example of a study that supports this view was carried out by Dickerson et al. (1992). The team wanted to see if they could get university students to conserve water in the dormitory showers. To do so, they asked students in Santa Cruz, California to do two things: first, they asked them to sign a poster that said, "Take shorter showers. If I can do it, so can you!" Then they asked them take a survey designed to make them think about their own water wastage. Their shower times were then monitored. Students who had signed the poster and then been forced to think about their own water usage had average shower times of about 3.5 minutes. This was significantly shorter than the average shower time across the dormitories as a whole. You could argue, of course, that it may be the other way round: they sign because they already have a commitment to the cause.

Cialdini et al. (1974) demonstrated the technique of **low-balling** in a university setting. They asked a class of first-year psychology students to volunteer to be part of a study on cognition that would meet at 7 a.m. Though enthusiastic about psychology, these were college students. Only 24 per cent were willing to leave the warm comfort of their beds that early in the morning to support research in psychology. In a second group they were asked the same favour, but this time they were not told a time. Of these, 56 per cent agreed to take part. When they were then told that they would have to meet at 7 a.m.—and that they could back out if they wished—no one backed out of their commitment. On the day of the actual meeting, 95 per cent of the students who had promised to come showed up for their 7 a.m. appointment.

A final example of the power of compliance techniques can be seen in the controversial practice of **hazing**. Hazing is a series of initiation rites in order to join an exclusive group, such as a sports team, or a college or university fraternity. Many US universities have barred the practice, after students have died while being exposed to extreme temperatures, drinking themselves into a coma, or literally digging their own graves. In spite of the many horror stories about hazing—and the efforts by universities to stop it—the practice continues. Hazing is a form of initiation that is similar to many of the initiation rites seen in other cultures. In many African societies, there are initiation rites for young men in order to indicate that they have reached adulthood. Also, military training involves "boot camps", which are not just about teaching recruits how to do their job, but also about humiliation and overcoming difficulty.

Why does this behaviour continue, even if it is potentially dangerous and humiliating for those involved? The individual must first choose to join the group, recognizing that there will be some initiation rite which he or she will have to endure. During the hazing, the participant must rationalize that this is "worth it" in order to be part of the group. Having completed the hazing, the individual has a sense of accomplishment, having proven his or her loyalty to the group. Young's 1963 study of 54 tribal cultures found that those with the most dramatic and stringent ceremonies were those with the greatest group solidarity. But can this be created in a group without any tradition of such practice?

Aronson and Mills (1959) carried out an experiment to see if someone who has had to endure trouble or pain to join a group will value it more highly than someone who was able to join the group with no effort. In their study, they asked female college students to join a sex discussion group. Some had to go through a severely embarrassing initiation in order to join, while others joined with no initiation ceremony. When the women were finally allowed to take part in the group, the meeting was made up of confederates who were trained to be as boring and uninteresting as possible. The women who went through the initiation ceremony reported that they found the meeting extremely valuable, whereas those who did not have any initiation recognized that the meetings were "worthless and uninteresting". Gerard and Mathewson (1966) carried out further research where women received electric shocks. Those who endured pain as part of their initiation were more likely to find their group interesting, intelligent, and desirable.

Social influence: conformity

One of the key ways that a society or culture passes down its values and behaviours to its members is through an indirect form of social influence called **conformity**. Conformity is the tendency to adjust one's thoughts, feelings, or behaviour in ways that are in agreement with those of a particular individual or group, or with accepted standards about how a person should behave in specific situations (social norms). Often, the term "peer pressure" is used to describe the conformity seen in schools, but conformity occurs at all levels of society and is not always simply about the need to fit in with a group of friends at school.

Initiation rites are used in some cultures to mark the passage into adulthood

Apply your knowledge
Using either of the compliance techniques discussed in this chapter, think about how you could reasonably (and ethically) increase participation in CAS activities in your school.

A classic study of conformity was carried out by Asch (1951). In his study, he wanted to find out to what extent a person would conform to an incorrect answer on a test if the response from the other members of the group was unanimous. The participant entered a room where there were six people and the researcher. The men in the room were dressed like businessmen, in suits and ties. These men were part of the study, and they were playing a role unknown to the participant. They were **confederates**, which helped the researcher to deceive the participant. After the participant took his seat, the group was told that they were going to take part in "a psychological experiment on visual judgement". They were then shown cards similar to the ones depicted here.

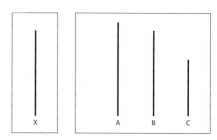

Asch's line test

The participant was asked to select the line from the second card that matched the length of the line on the first card. There were 18 trials in total. In some of the trials, the difference in the lines was hardly noticeable, while in others it was very clear. The confederates had been instructed to answer correctly for some of the trials, but to answer incorrectly for the majority of the trials. The goal was to see if the participant would conform to the wrong answers given by the confederates, even when it was very clear that this response was incorrect.

About 75 per cent of the participants agreed with the confederates' incorrect responses at least once during the trials. Asch found that a mean of 32 per cent of the participants agreed with incorrect responses in half or more of the trials. However, 24 per cent of the participants did not conform to any of the incorrect responses given by the confederates.

During the debriefing after the experiment, Asch asked the participants how they felt about the experiment. All reported experiencing some degree of self-doubt about their answers. Those participants who conformed said that they knew their responses were incorrect, but they went along with the group because they did not want to ruin the experimenter's results, and they did not want to appear to be against the group. Some argue that this could also be explained in terms of "the need to belong"—the need to be part of the group is stronger than the desire to give the correct answer.

This study is referred to as the **Asch paradigm**, and it has been replicated many times. Out of those replications and variations, psychologists have found that the following factors influence the likelihood to conform to the group.

- **Group size**: Asch (1955) found that with only one confederate, just 3 per cent of the participants conformed; with two confederates, the rate rose to 14 per cent; and with three confederates, it rose to 32 per cent. Larger groups did not increase the rate of conformity. In some cases, very large groups even decreased the level of conformity.
- **Unanimity**: Conformity was most likely when all the confederates agreed (Asch 1956). If one of the confederates disagreed, even if it was also an incorrect answer, the participant was significantly less likely to conform.

- **Confidence**: When individuals feel that they are more competent to make decisions with regard to a field of expertise, they are less likely to conform. Perrin and Spencer (1988) found that when they replicated Asch's study with engineers and medical students, conformity rates were almost nil.
- **Self-esteem**: Stang (1973) found that participants with high self-esteem were less likely to conform to incorrect responses.

Though the Asch paradigm has been successfully replicated in many variations, it is still important to take a critical look at the methodology of the study. First, there is the question of artificiality and ecological validity. Do these experiments accurately predict how people will react in real-life situations? In the original experiment, both the task and the use of strangers make this situation somewhat atypical. Asch, however, argued that experiments *are* social situations in which participants feel like an outsider if they dissent. In addition, as with most experiments, there is a concern for demand characteristics—that is, participants may act in a way that they feel is required by the features of the experiment.

In the original study, culture could also have limited the validity of the study. Since only one culture was studied, and the group was not multicultural, the study is limited in its application. Since culture is dynamic, it is possible that the Asch paradigm is no longer valid today, even if it were to be studied in the same cultural groups as the original study.

Ethical considerations also need to be addressed. The participants were deceived, and they were made to feel anxiety about their performance. Today this would not be regarded as acceptable.

Finally, Friend et al. (1990) argue that there is a bias in the interpretation of the findings. In fact, Friend claims that it should be striking to us that in the face of unanimity so many people *did not conform*. Perhaps the question should be which factors allow people to dissent, rather than which factors influence conformity.

A different way of looking at the Asch paradigm

Can a minority opinion sway the majority to change its views? Moscovici argues that when a minority maintains a consistent view, it is able to influence the majority. In a study carried out by Moscovici and Lage (1976), involving four participants and two confederates, the minority of two confederates described a blue-green colour as green. They found that the minority was able to influence about 32 per cent of the participants to make at least one incorrect judgment about the colour of slides they were shown. In addition, the participants continued to give their incorrect responses even after the two confederates had left the experiment.

How can minority opinions have such influence on the majority? Hogg and Vaughan (1995) argue that some of the reasons for the influence of a minorty group could be as follows.

- Dissenting opinions produce uncertainty and doubt.
- Such opinions show that alternatives exist.
- Consistency shows that there is a commitment to the alternative view.

Throughout the 20th century, there have been several examples of minority commitment to a view not held by the majority—from women's right to vote to civil rights movements. It is through such consistency, for example, that the environmental movement has gradually moved majority opinion more towards conservation and protection of the environment.

Research has shown that minority opinions are essential in a group's decision-making process; otherwise, a group may experience what Irving Janis called **groupthink**. Groupthink is characterized by group members having a unanimous opinion on an issue, and they do not seek out alternative or dissenting opinions. Often, the group is blinded by optimism that their decisions will be successful. Members of the group come to doubt their own reservations and refrain from voicing any dissenting opinions.

A study group is an effective way to prepare for an exam, but only if the members take care to avoid groupthink. Groupthink is what happens when someone in a group suggests an idea, and everyone accepts the idea without considering other possible options. For example, when the group is unsure what the reasons for the First World War were, one individual may come up with what seems at the time to be a plausible answer. If no one takes the time to verify the answer with outside sources, and the group fails to brainstorm alternative answers, groupthink may occur. Teachers can tell when groupthink has happened because several students have the same incorrect answer on an exam, often with exactly the same wording.

Why do people conform?

Deutsch and Gerard (1955) argue that conformity is a result of **informational social influence** and **normative social influence**. Informational social influence is based on the way people cognitively process information about a situation. Festinger (1954) said that people evaluate their own opinions and ideas through **social comparison**—that is, by looking at what others do. When one

"Louise, everyone is wearing that this year ...
don't be such a sheep to fashion."

notices that others are not behaving in the same way, or that they think differently, it causes anxiety. Festinger called this **cognitive dissonance**. If all of your friends like a certain type of music, and you do not, you may experience the odd feeling that you are not "with it". In order to get rid of this feeling, you may do one of two things. First, you may begin to listen to the music and conform to the group's opinion about it. Second, you may *rationalize* your opinion, and develop confidence that your opinion is acceptable, even if it is not what the majority of the group thinks.

The second reason people conform is because of normative social influence. This is based on our nature as social animals. People have a need to be accepted by others and to belong. They may conform to avoid rejection and gain social approval. If being opposed to a certain kind of music means never being invited to social gatherings by friends, the choice to learn to like this music is based on the need for their friendship, and the need to belong to that group.

Cultural aspects of conformity

One of the most significant cultural differences is how people react to the word "conformity". Studies show that not only do Asian cultures engage in more conforming behaviours than Americans do, but that they also value it to a greater degree. Americans, on the other hand, often see conformity as a negative trait, even though conformity is still part of being an American. One has to be careful not to divide the world's cultures into an East versus West dichotomy. A study by Cashmore and Goodnow (1986) found that there was a high level of conformity among Italians. In a study by Burgos and Dias-Perez (1986), the researchers found that with regard to childrearing, Puerto Ricans valued conformity and obedience in their children.

Do cultural norms affect conformity? Smith and Bond (1993) carried out a review of 31 conformity studies and found that levels of conformity—that is, the percentage of incorrect responses—ranged from 14 per cent among Belgian students to 58 per cent among Indian teachers in Fiji, with an average of 31.2 per cent. Conformity was lower among participants from individualist cultures—that is, North America and north-west Europe (25.3 per cent)—than from collectivist cultures—that is, Africa, Asia, Oceania, and South America (37.1 per cent). Bond and Smith (1996) found that people who score high on Hoefstede's collectivism scale conform more than people who score lower.

Berry (1967) used a variation of Asch's conformity paradigm and found that the Temne people of Sierra Leone conformed significantly more than the Inuit people of Canada. He explained this in terms of differences in economic practices. The Temne people have to survive on a single crop that is harvested by all the people in the community. This requires cooperation and coordination of effort, and this is why Temne culture focuses strongly on consensus and agreement. Berry found that consensus is less strongly focused in Inuit culture because the Inuit economy is based on continual hunting and gathering on a relatively individual basis.

Cultural norms

There are many different definitions of culture. Matsumoto (2004) mentions a book from 1998 that analysed 128 different definitions of culture. Culture is a complex concept that is used in many different ways (e.g. to describe food and eating habits, clothing, rituals, communication patterns, religion, and status behaviour). It is often used to describe what could be called "surface culture" because it is so visible. For example, people notice that food is different when they travel to another country and they say that this is due to cultural differences. Or they notice that in some countries women are covered and in others they are not. According to Kuschel (2004) culture cannot be seen but we can see the manifestations of culture. However, there is "deep culture" which is related to beliefs, attitudes, and values that underpin cultural manifestations. Kuschel claims that culture should not be used as an explanation of behaviour. Instead, descriptions of cultural factors can be used to understand how people have survived in their environment, how they have organized life in social groups, and what beliefs, attitudes, and norms influence behaviour in the social and cultural groups. These cultural factors may lead to specific kinds of behaviour. According to Kuschel you should ask questions related to how specific factors in the culture result in behaviours such as, for example, infanticide, initiation rites, rain dance, or honour killing. If culture is simply used as an explanation of behaviour, it will lead to circular arguments according to Kuschel, who also warns against generalizations. Since the concept of culture is so vague and includes so many variables, it should never be used as an explanation in itself.

According to Lonner (1995) culture can be defined as common rules that regulate interactions and behaviour in a group as well as a number of shared values and attitudes in the group. Hofstede (2002) described culture as "mental software", that is, cultural schemas that have been internalized so that they influence thinking, emotions, and behaviour. According to Hofstede, the mental software is shared by members of a sociocultural group. It is learned through daily interactions and by the feedback from other members of the group.

Understanding the role of culture in human behaviour is essential in a diverse, multicultural world. Many of the founding theorists of psychology took a solely western view. They attempted to find universal behaviours—that is, they were looking for "rules" of human behaviour that could be applied to all cultures around the world. This is an **etic** approach to psychology. Etic approaches are typically taken within cross-cultural psychology where behaviour is compared across specific cultures. Etic study involves drawing on the notion of universal properties of cultures, which share common perceptual, cognitive, and emotional structures. The **emic** approach looks at behaviours that are culturally specific. Emics have challenged psychologists to re-examine their ideas of "truth" with regard to culture. In most cases, truth may be relative, based on the culture in which one is raised. In that case, it is important for psychologists to recognize these cultural variations in order to best understand members of other cultural groups.

TOK: ethics

1 Which of the arguments regarding female genital mutilation do you find most persuasive, and why?

- It is moral because it is a cultural practice and different cultural practices should be respected.

- It is immoral because it is known how it inflicts pain on girls and removes their potential for pleasure. I disagree with this cultural norm.

- It is immoral and there is a need for social action to change this practice.

2 Can the values of one society ever be judged with any validity by applying the values of another culture?

The anthropologist Mead (1935) documented many instances of cultural variations in gender in her study of three different cultures living close to each other in New Guinea. The Arapesh people were characterized by women and men having the same sensitive and non-aggressive behaviour, as well as "feminine" personalities; among the Mundugamor, both men and women were ruthless, unpleasant, and "masculine"; in the Tchambuli community, women were dominant and men were more emotional and concerned about personal appearance—an apparent reversal of western norms. Mead's demonstration of cultural differences—while perhaps exaggerated—is in many respects a valid indication of how society can powerfully influence gender-role development, which has been shown in many other studies. Studies like these, by anthropologists, inspired psychologists to consider the role of culture in human behaviour.

Culture is defined by Matsumoto (2004) as "a dynamic system of rules, explicit and implicit, established by groups in order to ensure their survival, involving attitudes, values, beliefs, norms, and behaviours". This is a complex definition, so we will look at it piece by piece. Culture is *dynamic*—it changes over time in response to environmental and social changes. It also exists on many levels. One could talk about US culture, but also the culture of an individual school. A school or other large institution can have a set of guidelines that it works by—some of which are written (*explicit*) and some of which are simply understood (*implicit*). Though anthropologists often study the *objects* which make up a culture—for example, the foods, religious buildings, and grave sites—psychologists mainly focus on the subjective elements of culture. The group's attitudes, beliefs, values, and norms are the social representation which has been internalized by its members.

Cultural norms are behaviour patterns that are typical of specific groups. They are often passed down from generation to generation by observational learning by the group's gatekeepers—parents, teachers, religious leaders, and peers. Cultural norms include such things as how marriage partners are chosen, attitudes towards alcohol consumption, and acceptance (or rejection) of spanking children.

Cultural dimensions of behaviour

In addition to cultural norms, another component of culture is **dimensions**—the perspectives of a culture based on values and cultural norms. Hoefstede's classic study (1973) involved asking employees of the multinational company IBM to fill in surveys about morale in the workplace. He then carried out a content analysis on the responses he received, focusing on the key differences submitted by employees in different countries. His research looked at the 40 most represented countries in the surveys. The trends he noticed he called "dimensions".

Hoefstede argues that understanding cultural dimensions will help facilitate communication between cultures. This is important in international diplomacy as well as international business. Hoefstede gives the example of cultural differences in business in Middle

Understanding and respect of cultural norms can promote successful interactions

125

Eastern countries and western countries like the US. When negotiating in western countries, the objective is to work towards a target of mutual understanding and agreement, and shake hands when that agreement is reached—a cultural signal of the end of negotiations and the start of working together. In Middle Eastern countries, much negotiation takes place leading into the agreement, signified by shaking hands. However, this does not signal that the deal is complete. In fact, in Middle Eastern culture it is a sign that serious negotiations are just beginning.

Imagine the problems this creates when each party in a negotiation is operating under diametrically opposed cultural norms. This is just one example of why it is critical to understand other cultures you may be doing business with, whether you are on a vacation in a foreign country, or negotiating a multimillion-dollar business deal.

One dimension is **individualism**; another one is **collectivism**. In individualist societies, the ties between individuals are loose: everyone is expected to look after himself or herself and his or her immediate family. In collectivist societies, from birth onwards people are integrated into strong, cohesive in-groups, often extended families (with uncles, aunts, and grandparents), which provides them with support and protection. However, if an individual does not live up to the norms of the family or the larger social group, the result can sometimes be severe. Markus and Kitayama (1991) characterized the difference between US and Japanese culture by citing two of their proverbs: "In America, the squeaky wheel gets the grease; in Japan, the nail that stands out gets pounded down." Markus and Kitayama argue that perceiving a boundary between the individual and the social environment is distinctly western in its cultural orientation, and that non-western cultures tend towards *connectedness*.

A second dimension is **uncertainty** versus **avoidance**, which deals with a society's tolerance for uncertainty and ambiguity. It indicates to what extent a culture programmes its members to feel either uncomfortable or comfortable in unstructured situations. Unstructured situations are novel, unknown, surprising. Uncertainty-avoiding cultures try to minimize the possibility of such situations by strict laws and rules, safety and security measures, and, on the philosophical and religious level, by a belief in absolute Truth—*there can only be one Truth and we have it.*

Bond (1988) argues that Chinese culture replaces the uncertainty-avoidance dimension with **Confucian work dynamism**: instead of focusing on truth, some cultures focus on virtue. China and other Asian countries have a *long-term orientation*. These cultures value persistence, loyalty, and trustworthiness. Relationships are based on status. They have a need to protect the collective identity and respect tradition—what is often called "saving face".

Hoefstede found that Finland, France, Germany, and the US have a *short-term orientation*. In contrast to Confucian work dynamism, these cultures value personal steadiness and stability. There is a focus on the future instead of the past, and innovation is highly valued.

Possible essay question

Examine the role of two cultural dimensions on human behaviour.

Assessment advice

The command term "examine" asks you to take an in-depth look at the topic, uncovering basic assumptions. In this case, you might look at the cultural dimension of individualism versus collectivism, or the dimension of uncertainty versus avoidance. For each dimension, you should give clear examples of how the dimension affects behaviour. As part of your response, you may also use information on these topics that can be found in the different options.

● ● ● ● ●

Be reflective

Discuss how the role of marriage may be different in an individualistic culture and in a collectivist culture. How does culture affect the way we date, choose a partner, and potentially start a family?

● ● ● ● ●

Think internationally

Often, when people in western cultures talk about eastern cultures, the role of "saving face" is seen as a key difference between the two cultures. The importance is placed on not lowering one's status, and not being embarrassed by failure.

1 Is the fear of "losing face" exclusively an eastern trait? Does it ever appear in western culture?

2 How could the need not to lose face affect an individual's behaviour?

One does have to be careful, however, with applying the idea of dimensions too casually. Hoefstede warns against the **ecological fallacy**—that is, when one looks at two different cultures, it should not be assumed that two members from two different cultures must be different from one another, or that a single member of a culture will always demonstrate the dimensions which are the norm of that culture. These concepts simply give psychologists a way to generalize about cultures in order to better discuss the role that culture plays in behaviour.

There are also other ways to talk about the norms that define a culture. Anthropologist Edward T. Hall presents two other norms to consider.

Hall's **proxemic theory** (1966) is based on a culture's need for "personal space". In his book, *The Hidden Dimension*, he shows that different cultures have different perceptions of the amount of personal space that is required to be comfortable. People only allow their closest, most intimate friends into this bubble of space. In the US, for instance, people engaged in conversation will assume a social distance of roughly 10–15 cm/ 4–7 inches, but in many parts of Europe the expected social distance is roughly half that, with the result that Americans travelling overseas often experience the urgent need to back away from a conversation partner who seems to be getting too close.

Hall also described the norm of *time consciousness*. He distinguished between monochronic cultures and polychronic cultures. Monochronic cultures focus on one thing at a time. There is a high degree of scheduling, and punctuality and meeting deadlines are highly valued. In polychronic cultures, many things happen at once. The focus is more on relationships and interactions. Interruptions are expected as part of life, and there is little frustration experienced when things are postponed or late.

Be a critical thinker

1 Consider how Hall's two cultural norms would affect doing business cross-culturally.

2 With regard to time consciousness, is one of these cultures *healthier* than the other?

Be an enquirer

Check *www.Geert-hofslede.com* for more cultural dimensions on human behaviour and compare your culture with that of others.

An integrative approach to prejudice and discrimination

In spite of the efforts of schools to teach the history of anti-Semitism, racism, xenophobia (dislike or fear of foreigners), and homophobia, prejudice and discrimination continue to plague society. Clearly, these behaviours are complex, so they require complex solutions. Prejudice and discrimination can be considered the result of a complex interaction of different factors that can be addressed by different levels of analysis. Only by understanding the complexity of issues of prejudice and discrimination can they potentially be reduced.

Stereotyping is a *cognitive process* whereby people categorize others for example, in terms of belonging to a social group or simply just on the basis of their looks – think about the many jokes about blondes. Once a set of characteristics is used to describe a group of people, those characteristics are often attributed to all members of the group. **Prejudice**, however, is an *attitude*. An attitude can be defined as the combination of emotion and cognition. Not only does a person judge an individual based on a set of characteristics that is attributed to him or her because of the group to which he or she belongs, but contact elicits an emotional response. Prejudices may or may not be based on stereotyping. **Discrimination** is a *behaviour*. Discrimination is when a person treats someone differently based on his or her membership of a group, rather than on individual merit. This type of behaviour can range from denying the person a job (e.g. because they are overweight, old or suffer from a physical disability), to segregation, to violent hate crimes.

Biological research on the origins of prejudice

Recently, psychologists have looked more closely at the biological factors that contribute to prejudiced reactions. In one study, Hart (2000) found that when white and black participants were given brief subliminal glimpses of faces of individuals from other ethnic groups, both showed increased activity in the amygdala, the part of the brain that is responsible for processing emotional responses to stimuli. The participants, however, reported having no noticeable change in their emotional state during the study. In another study, Phelps (2000) found a correlation between those individuals whose amygdala was most strongly activated after being exposed to these subliminal stimuli and scores on a standardized test for ethnic prejudice. In addition to these subliminal studies, similar reactions in the amygdala have been observed when participants were asked to look at school yearbook photos of students belonging to different ethnic groups.

Studies of this nature have been used to support the findings of the Implicit Association Test (www.understandingprejudice.org/iat). Banaji and Greenwald (1998), the developers of this test, asked participants to respond to words by labelling them as either "good" (sunny, love, joy) or "bad" (vomit, garbage, evil). They did this in some cases by tapping their right foot for "good" and their left foot for "bad"; in the computer version, participants had to press specific keys. To test deeply subconscious prejudice, they added one more task. In the first round, they were also told to tap their right foot when they saw a picture of a young person, and their left foot when they saw a picture of an old person. In other words, tap the same foot when they saw a young person as when they saw a "good word". In the second round, the directions were reversed: participants were asked to tap their right foot when they saw an old person or a good word. Regardless of which condition was first, participants hesitated more when asked to pair "old" with "good" than when asked to pair "old" with "bad". This trend has also been demonstrated in cases of ethnicity, religion, and sexuality.

Perhaps the most intriguing study, however, was carried out by Fiske (2007). In her study, participants were placed into an MRI scanner and then shown a series of photos. These photos included people with disabilities, rich businessmen, older people, US Olympic athletes, and homeless people. Fiske was surprised at what happened when participants viewed the photo of the homeless person: their brains set off a series of reactions associated with disgust. An area in the brain called the *insula* was activated, which is usually a response to non-human objects such as garbage and human waste. Perhaps even more surprising, the part of the brain that is activated when we think about other people or ourselves—the dorsomedial prefrontal cortex— was *not* activated. In other words, in the case of the homeless, the participants' brains did not react to them as people.

Evolution-based arguments would explain this reaction to out-groups as a means of protecting the gene pool of a community and increasing the chance that genes will be handed down within a group. Being able to detect a potential threat from strangers could have an evolutionary advantage. Such a reaction may be useful in evolutionary terms because it helps to distinguish friends from enemies but what about today? Is it useful in a modern urbanized society where some people are marginalized and need protection? Fortunately, many people do care about less fortunate citizens but the interesting question is of course if this is against the way evolution shaped us.

There is interesting information on the implicit personality test if you search the Internet for "implicit personality test" and Banaji. You can also find information about this test (and a lot more about prejudice) on the UnderstandingPrejudice.org website.

Being homeless is the fate of people all over the world

Be a communicator: link to CAS

Fiske's research appears to support the idea that the dehumanization of a group leads to changes in the way the brain works. Dehumanization is a psychological process whereby opponents view each other as less than human and thus not deserving of moral consideration. If the homeless are seen as "less than human", this may explain why the dorsomedial prefrontal cortex was not activated in the participants.

One of the ways to potentially change this prejudice is to try to better understand the plight of homeless people.

Helping our communities understand the homeless is the first step in overcoming dehumanization. Prepare a presentation based on the following questions.

→

- What are the reasons that people become homeless?
- What problems do the homeless face in your community?
- How have some communities decreased their homeless problem and helped homeless people to reintegrate into society?

Evaluation of biological research

It is very tempting to attribute prejudice to automatic brain functions, but one has to be cautious. First, since prejudice has an emotional component, it means that cognitive factors play a strong role in determining whether one actually acts in accordance with these immediate brain responses. Bettelheim and Janowitz (1964) showed that one's stereotypes do not predict one's feelings of prejudice or acts of discrimination. As a follow-up on the research done by Hart and Phelps mentioned earlier, Cunningham (2004) did a study using brain scans and showed that when participants have longer exposure to images, it is not simply the amygdala, but also the frontal lobe that is activated. It is clear that though out-groups may trigger an immediate response from the amygdala, cognitive control of emotional reactions is exerted by the frontal lobe.

Another concern is the use of correlational research. Remember that correlational studies do not demonstrate causality, and can lead to bidirectional ambiguity. In Phelps's research, it is unknown if some participants were more prejudiced as a *result* of a more active amygdala, or if their prejudices had *led* to a stronger response from the amygdala. Since the research has been carried out on adults who would have been highly influenced by the values and attitudes of the cultures in which they grew up, one cannot easily determine the level to which their response is innate or learned. A heightened emotional response to a different ethnic group does not necessarily equate to racism. It could just mean, "Clearly this person does not look like me." Though there is evidently a biological component to prejudice, this level alone is not enough to explain the origin of prejudice.

Cognitive research on the origins of prejudice

Arguing that stereotypes alone cause prejudice is not sufficient. Allport (1954) argued that *hostility* is a key emotional component of prejudice. If this is so, how does it become connected to the stereotypes that develop in a culture?

One important factor in the development of prejudice is the way people make decisions. Shortcuts or tricks to making easy decisions, called **heuristics**, may influence how people interpret the behaviour of others. Tversky and Kahnemann (1982) argue that people make many judgments based on the **availability heuristic**—that is, they base decisions on the information that is most readily available. In the Czech Republic, if the discussions in the media and in social settings focus on the stereotypical poverty and crime rate among the Roma (gypsy) population, even without any personal experience, a businessperson may decide that a Roma would not be right for a job at their company.

You can read more on how cognition and emotions interact on pages 90–92 in Chapter 3.2 in this book.

The heuristics that Tversky and Kahneman suggested could be due to schema processing. It is accepted by many social psychologists that people use schemas to process social information. This is part of what is called **social cognition**. Since humans are social animals and dependent on other people they need to be able to form impressions of people and understand what they are doing. Social schemas give the individual the opportunity to process the enormous amount of information in the social world in an economic way. Fiske and Taylor (1991) suggested the term "cognitive miser" to describe the fact that people have limited capacity to process social information and therefore use shortcuts or develop simple rules (heuristics) in order to make complex issues more simple. An experiment by Darley and Gross (1983) showed how people used information from a previous video recording of a girl to make judgment about her in a situation that was ambiguous. The researchers wanted to test the hypothesis that schematic processing result in distorted perceptions of people when they have to make judgments about their ability. The participants first saw a video of a young girl in her everyday surroundings. In one of the videos, she appeared to be poor (e.g. dilapidated school and run-down neighbourhood); in the other video, the girl appeared to be from a middle-class family (e.g. good school and nice home). The researchers assumed that the participants would associate the status of girl with the surroundings because of schema processing.

When the participants were asked to predict the academic prospects of the two girls in the future, they all said that they would do fine and have an education. The researchers interpreted this as normal in that in the USA there is a fundamental belief that people should have the same opportunities.

In a follow-up of the first experiment, a new group of participants saw either one or the other of the two videos from the first experiment followed by a second video where the girl was seen from behind as she was responding in an ambiguous way to what appeared to be some kind of intelligence test. There was no mentioning of an intelligence test or any comment at all in this direction. In fact, it was not really clear from the video what happened in the scene.

After seeing the two videos, the participants were again asked to rate the girl's academic abilities. This time the answers showed a different picture. The "rich girl" was judged to be better across all domains than the poor girl. The researchers analysed the comments of the participants, and it was clear that they had a very different opinion on the girl and this was associated with the information from the video that they first saw. The participants even added things so that their account became more coherent and in line with how they saw the girl. For example, some said that it seemed as if the intelligence test for the "rich girl" was more difficult. The results of this experiment were interpreted in terms of social cognition. The researchers argued that due to ambiguous information about the girl in the second video, the participants used information from the first video to form an impression of Hannah subsequently to seeing the second video.

The study clearly shows how cognitive factors such as schema processing influence the way people judge others. The pre-stored schemas that poor people are less smart popped up when the situation was ambiguous and determined their response. You could say that their prejudice about disfavoured groups — in this case poor people — became active and led them to conclude that one of the girls did not have many chances. This is unfortunately sometimes true because of a self-fulfilling prophecy and stereotype threats.

In order to overcome prejudice, one has to be able to *decategorize*, but this is no easy task because stereotypes are resistant to change — partly due to the phenomenon called "confirmation bias", that is, people tend to look for information that confirms their stereotypes or prejudices — not the opposite. In order to challenge stereotypes and maybe change them, members of the group who do not fit the stereotype need to be presented to those who hold the stereotype— for example, Dr Mae Jemison, an African American nuclear physicist who was one of the first women in space. However, just presenting one member of a minority group who does not match the prevalent stereotypes is not enough to change stereotypes. Dr Jemison could be considered "an exception". This is what Allport called "fencing off from the group". Rothbart and John (1985) argue that whereas unfavourable traits need few examples to confirm and strengthen stereotypes, more examples are needed to disconfirm them.

Impression management theory (Tedeschi and Rosenfield 1981) argues that much attitude change is seen as an attempt to avoid social anxiety and embarrassment, or to protect the positive view of one's own identity. Devine (1989) found that even when a person considers himself or herself to be low in prejudice, when put into contact with a member of a stereotyped group, the person will immediately react according to the cultural norms—for example, clutching his or her wallet when a person from the minority group approaches. However, what is interesting is what happens afterwards. People who identify themselves as low in prejudice experience shame and/or guilt for their reaction, because this is not how they want to be seen by society—or how they want to see themselves. So, in order to reduce prejudice, perhaps helping people to identify themselves as not being prejudiced would help.

A striking study conducted on the role of cognition took place in a teacher's classroom. In the 1960s, Jane Elliott carried out a simulation with her elementary school students to explore the power of perception in one's willingness to discriminate. In the famous "blue-eyed/brown-eyed" study, she told the students that one group was superior, more talented, and better-looking than the members of the other group. Within a very short period of time, discriminatory acts took place by the superior group: name-calling, ostracism, and bullying were witnessed in the playground.

Jane Elliott taught students what discrimination feels like

Be a thinker: ethics in research

Elliott's work in the classroom is similar to a research method called *action research*, which aims to promote change. Though Elliott may have had good intentions, teaching young people the meaning of prejudice and discrimination, the results of the informal study bring into question the ethics of what she did.

1 Is it ever acceptable for teachers to carry out research on their students?

2 What ethical considerations must be made in order to guarantee the highest ethical standards?

3 The students were reunited several years after the experience, and they expressed that it was a hard but important experience in their lives. Comment on this.

The film *A Class Divided* shows the original footage of the Elliott study.
You can view it at
www.pbs.org/wgbh/pages/frontline/shows/divided/etc/view.html

Sociocultural research on the origins of prejudice

To argue that one's behaviour is the result of gender, sexuality, or ethnicity is an example of the fundamental attribution error. The **actor–observer bias** confirms the belief in a group that the in-group members are successful because of who they are, whereas the out-group is not successful because of who they are. It also makes it difficult to break the cycle of stereotyping and prejudice, because any success achieved by the out-group is seen as the result of luck, outside assistance, or circumstances.

Tajfel's social identity theory is fundamental to understanding the roots of prejudice and discrimination. Sherif (1961) carried out a famous field experiment on the role of group identity on intergroup conflict. In the **Robbers' Cave experiment**, Sherif wanted to see if the creation of groups alone would lead to conflict between two groups of boys aged 11 and 12 years. The groups were carefully chosen to make the participants as homogeneous as possible: they were all healthy, slightly above-average intelligence, European American, Protestant, and socially well-adjusted. In addition, they were from stable, middle-class families. None of them knew each other prior to the experiment.

The boys were unaware that they were part of an experiment. They were sent off to a summer camp, where the researchers were posing as the camp staff. They did this in order to achieve ecological validity. After a few days at the camp, the boys were divided into two teams. The researchers took care to make sure that any of the boys who had already become good friends were separated. The groups then engaged in a series of activities in order for them to "bond". The two groups were called the Eagles and the Rattlers.

Sherif hypothesized that when two groups have conflicting aims, their members will become hostile to each other. In order to test this hypothesis, he had the boys' teams compete against each other in a series of games. As the games continued, the boys began to freely insult members of the other group, and there were acts of aggression (fighting and raiding of tents) against the other team. Sherif wondered how to diminish the hostility between the groups that was the result of their newly formed group identities.

In order to diminish the hostility between the groups, the researchers established **superordinate goals**—that is, they created an urgent situation which affected both groups, and which needed all of them to participate in order for the problem to be solved. On one occasion, the water supply for the camp was disrupted; and on another afternoon, the truck broke down on an outing. By having to work together, the individual group identities were broken down, and a new, more inclusive group identity was created, and the boys now began to cooperate peacefully. The same can be observed where superordinate goals in response to natural disasters have been able to break down intergroup prejudice. In 1999, the press noted the "earthquake diplomacy" between Greece and Turkey which resulted when Turks helped Greeks after a level 5.9 earthquake struck, just six months after Greeks had helped Turks after an earthquake of similar magnitude had struck their own country.

The reduction of prejudice seen at the end of Sherif's field experiment is an illustration of Allport's **contact hypothesis**. Allport (1956) wrote: "It has sometimes been held that merely by assembling people without regard for race, color, religion, or national origin, we can thereby destroy stereotypes and develop friendly attitudes." More recent researchers, like Amir (2000), have added more detail to Allport's very simple hypothesis. Amir argues that prejudice is strengthened or increased if contact between two groups produces competition and is unpleasant. It is also a problem if the status of one group is lowered as a result of contact, or when one group is left frustrated. Prejudice can be reduced, however, when the contact is cooperative and the groups are seen as equals. There should be superordinate goals and the contact between the groups should be pleasant and rewarding.

Evaluation of the contact hypothesis

Pettigrew and Tropp (2000, 2003) carried out a meta-analysis of 516 empirical studies and found an inverse relationship between contact and prejudice. They also found that the inverse relationship was strongest when the contact was natural and not forced. Bowen and Bourgeois (2001) found that university students' attitudes about gays and lesbians were directly influenced by the part of the campus they lived on: those who lived closest to dorms where some gays and lesbians lived had fewer stereotypes and less prejudice against them.

The contrary can be said, however, when contact between groups is not natural, but forced. One of the limitations of Sherif's study is that all the participants came to the camp voluntarily. In addition, the group was homogeneous, and there was no long history of oppression. As a result, the groups had equal status contact. Ma'oz (2002) found that when Israeli and Palestinian students are brought together to reduce prejudice, equal status contact took place only 65 per cent of the time or less. Contact in which one group is seen as lower in status is likely to be rather ineffective.

Be a thinker

Can the media reduce intergroup prejudice and conflict?

Elizabeth Levy Paluck of Harvard University carried out a year-long field experiment in Rwanda to test the impact of a radio soap opera about two Rwandan communities in conflict, which featured messages about reducing intergroup prejudice, violence, and trauma. Compared to communities who listened to a control radio soap opera, listeners' perceptions of social norms and their behaviours changed concerning some of the most critical issues for Rwanda's post-conflict society, namely intermarriage, trust, empathy, cooperation, and discussion of personal trauma. However, the radio programme did little to influence listeners' personal beliefs. The results suggest that radio can communicate social norms and influence behaviours that contribute to intergroup tolerance and reconciliation.

● To what extent do you think that psychology can be used to promote peaceful cooperation in the world?

Summary

It is clear that no one factor completely explains the origin of prejudice or how to reduce it. The origins of prejudice are **multi-factorial**. The interaction of the three levels of analysis demonstrates the problems of looking at any one factor in isolation. Society and culture may teach certain stereotypes and prejudices, which influence the way people perceive or think about minorities or "outsiders". These learned perceptions may induce physiological arousal that may lead to hostile emotions against the out-group. Reducing prejudice, then, means looking at the complexities of the origins of prejudice at all levels, and attempting to affect change on each of these levels.

Extended essay questions

● To what extent can psychology contribute to the reduction of prejudice?

● Does prejudice always lead to discrimination?

● Is prejudice mostly biologically based or learned?

An interactionist approach to racism

Biological factors

● Response from the amygdala
● Evolutionarily advantageous, to protect our genes from the out-group

Cognitive factors

● Availability heuristics
● The role of perception
● Cognitive dissonance

Sociocultural factors

● Stereotyping (social cognition)
● Fundamental attribution error
● Contact hypothesis

5.1 Abnormal psychology: concepts of normality

Learning outcomes

- Discuss the extent to which biological, cognitive, and sociocultural factors influence abnormal behaviour
- Evaluate psychological research relevant to the study of abnormal behaviour
- Examine the concepts of normality and abnormality
- Discuss validity and reliability of diagnosis
- Discuss cultural and ethical considerations in diagnosis

Concepts of normality and abnormality

The area of psychological disorders is called "abnormal behaviour". Abnormal behaviour presents psychologists with a difficult task: it is difficult to define and therefore it is difficult to diagnose because it is, to a large extent, based on the symptoms people exhibit or report. Making a correct diagnosis is extremely important because this dictates the treatment people receive. Psychiatrists and psychologists use a standardized system called a diagnostic manual to help them, but such a system is not without faults. Since there is no clear definition of normality—or abnormality—and symptoms of the same psychological disorders may vary not only between individuals but also between social and cultural groups, it is clear that a psychiatric diagnosis may be biased or even wrong. Definitions of normality and abnormality can also change over time.

Often, a decision about whether or not an individual's behaviour is abnormal depends on a series of value judgments based on subjective impressions. Definitions of "normality" are part of the diagnostic process, which is why it is considered important to establish some objective criteria. At present, there is a tendency to rely on the *subjective* assessments of clinicians, in combination with the diagnostic tools of classification systems.

It is not an easy task to define what is normal and what is abnormal. Behavioural measures, such as intelligence and short-term memory, tend to be normally distributed—that is, the distribution from a sample of people tends to fall within a bell-shaped curve. Being normal falls within this bell curve. There are problems in using statistics in this way when we are dealing with abnormal behaviour because some things that are statistically normal—such as obesity— are not desirable or healthy behaviours—and some that are statistically rare—such as a high IQ—are not dysfunctional.

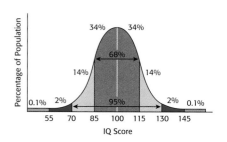

The bell curve of distribution of IQ scores in a population

Abnormality is sometimes defined as the subjective experience of feeling "not normal"—for example, feeling intense anxiety, unhappiness, or distress. This is often enough to seek help. However, the subjective experience of distress is not always a reliable indicator

136

of serious psychiatric problems, since patients with schizophrenia may be indifferent or unaware of their condition.

One way to define abnormality is to consider when behaviour violates social norms or makes others anxious. This definition is problematic. Cultural diversity affects how people view social norms: what is seen as normal in one culture may be seen as abnormal in another.

The difficulties outlined here illustrate the problems in diagnosing "abnormal behaviour". Rosenhan and Seligman (1984) suggested that there are seven criteria that could be used to decide whether a person or a behaviour is normal or not.

- *Suffering*—does the person experience distress and discomfort?
- *Maladaptiveness*—does the person engage in behaviours that make life difficult for him or her rather than being helpful?
- *Irrationality*—is the person incomprehensible or unable to communicate in a reasonable manner?
- *Unpredictability*—does the person act in ways that are unexpected by himself or herself or by other people?
- *Vividness* and *unconventionality*—does the person experience things that are different from most people?
- *Observer discomfort*—is the person acting in a way that is difficult to watch or that makes other people embarrassed?
- *Violation of moral or ideal standards*—does the person habitually break the accepted ethical and moral standards of the culture?

These criteria demonstrate the fine line between defining abnormality in ways that focus on distress to the individual, and defining it in terms of what is or is not acceptable to society. The first four deal with how the person is living life; the fifth represents a social judgment because it deals with what is seen as conventional or not; the remaining criteria clearly represent *social norms*. The danger of social judgments is that they often fail to consider the diversity in how people live their lives. There is an increasing awareness of how psychiatric diagnosis of ethnic minorities has been misapplied because doctors do not understand the cultural norms of the groups people come from. Defining abnormality is not easy, and it has a lot to do with the implicit theories people have about what is normal and what is abnormal.

The mental health criteria

Jahoda (1958) attempted to establish what is abnormal by identifying the characteristics of people who are normal. She identified six characteristics of mental health:

- efficient self-perception
- realistic self-esteem and acceptance
- voluntary control of behaviour
- true perception of the world
- sustaining relationships and giving affection
- self-direction and productivity

It is difficult to define these criteria precisely, so the question is what they actually mean. Jahoda, for example, stated that the unemployed were deprived of many of these characteristics, and that

Be a thinker

Discuss whether you would consider each of the following an example of "abnormal behaviour". What could be the possible criteria for your decision?

- Transvestitism
- Nail biting
- Maths anxiety
- Talking to oneself

this might account for much of the reported mental ill-health among unemployed people.

Evaluation of the mental health criteria

Jahoda's list seems intuitively appealing, but if the criteria were applied, most of us would seem somehow abnormal. In addition, they are to a large extent *value judgments*. Most people can agree on what constitutes physical health. However, this is not the case with psychological disorders.

It seems pretty clear that what is considered psychologically normal depends on the society and culture in which a person lives. There is an ongoing debate among psychiatrists involved in making diagnostic tools about how to define abnormality, and the criteria are changing—sometimes because norms change. An illustrative example of this can be seen in the change in views on homosexuality from Gross's *Psychology: The Science of Mind and Behaviour* (1996: 787).

An example of changing views on abnormal behaviour: homosexuality

The orthodox view was that homosexuality was abnormal. The story of the famous writer Oscar Wilde shows that society did not accept homosexuality—he was imprisoned for being homosexual. The older versions of the diagnostic system reflected that view, but DSM-III (*Diagnostic and Statistical Manual of Mental Disorders*, 3rd edn, 1980) declared that homosexuality is only abnormal if the individual has negative feelings about his or her sexual orientation. The same is seen in DSM-IV (1994), under "Sexual disorders not otherwise specified", where it is noted as "persistent and marked distress about one's sexual orientation". In the UK, homosexuality between consenting adults was illegal until the 1960s.

What has happened in the meantime is that people's attitudes to homosexuality have changed. Consequently, the conclusion must be that homosexuality in itself cannot be considered abnormal, and it is no longer classified as such. However, this example illustrates the inherent problem in classifying what is normal and what is abnormal.

Be a thinker

The DSM has classified transsexualism as a disorder. It is called "gender identity disorder" when people feel deep within themselves that they are the opposite sex. Many recent films, such as *Boys Don't Cry*, have portrayed the lives of people who are transsexual.

- Should this be declassified as a disorder, as homosexuality was?
- What are the arguments for and against declassification?

Possible essay question

With reference to research, examine the concepts of normality and abnormality

---

Assessment advice

"Examine" means that you should consider the concepts of normality and abnormality in order to reveal the problems in defining them (for example cultural variations) as well as implications of the definition in abnormal psychology.

The mental illness criterion

The mental illness criterion is rooted in a view from the medical world that abnormal behaviour is of physiological origin, for example the result of disordered neurotransmission. This is called the **medical model**. Consequently, treatment addresses the physiological problems, primarily through drug treatment. Abnormal behaviour is referred to as **psychopathology**—that is, psychological (or mental) illness that is based on the observed symptoms of a patient.

The term "mental disorder" is used in the *Diagnostic and Statistical Manual of Mental Disorders* published by the American Psychiatric Association (called DSM-IV); a handbook used by psychiatrists in the US to identify and classify symptoms of psychiatric disorders. This is a standardized system for diagnosis based on factors such as the person's clinical and medical conditions, psychosocial stressors and the extent to which a person's mental state interferes with his or her daily life.

There are several ethical concerns about the use of the medical model to define abnormal behaviour. This model argues that it is better to regard someone suffering from a mental disorder as sick rather than morally defective because responsibility is removed from the patient. According to Gross (2002), there have been examples of misuse of the medical model, since the criteria used for diagnosis are not objective and can be influenced by culture and politics. In the former Soviet Union political dissidents were diagnosed as schizophrenic, implying that they were not responsible for their deviant political beliefs. In the UK in the last century, women who were pregnant without being married could be admitted to an asylum.

Today, psychiatrists diagnose using a **classification system** that is supposed to be objective. The traditional medical model in psychiatry is now assumed to be reductionist, and most psychiatrists use a biopsychosocial approach to diagnosis and treatment. However, this does not prevent a psychiatric diagnosis resulting in the patient being labelled as different, or "not normal".

One of the most radical critics of the concept "mental illness" was the US psychiatrist Tomasz Szasz, who argued against the concept of "mental illness". In *The Myth of Mental Illness* (1962), he argued that while some neurophysiological disorders were diseases of the brain, most of the so-called "mental disorders" should be considered as *problems in living*. By saying this, Szasz went against the idea of organic pathology in psychological disorders.

In Szasz's view, even though people behave strangely and this is classified as mental illness by psychiatrists, such behaviours are not a symptom of an underlying brain disease. Consequently, the concept of mental illness is not used correctly by psychiatrists. According to Frude (1998) there are relatively few psychological disorders that can be associated with identifiable organic pathology.

However, is Szasz's argument still valid today? Neuropsychologists have, in some cases, revealed possible chemical abnormality in the brain (in the temporal cortex) in people suffering from schizophrenia (Pilowsky, 2006) but brain scans haven't yet provided an ultimate answer to the questions raised by Szasz.

Are you too shy?

A recent trend in schools is to diagnose very shy children with "social anxiety disorder". Not only are young students being diagnosed, but they are being treated too. Shyness is so common among US children that 42 per cent exhibit it. By the time they reach college, up to 51 per cent of men and 43 per cent of women describe themselves as shy or introverted. Psychiatrists say that at least one in eight of these people needs medical attention.

Yet it is debatable whether medical attention is necessary. According to Julie Turner-Cobb at the University of Bath, the stress hormone cortisol is consistently lower in shy children than in their more extroverted peers. The discovery challenges the belief that shyness causes youngsters extreme stress.

GlaxoSmithKline, the maker of Paxil, declared in the late 1990s that its antidepressant could also treat social anxiety and, presumably, self-consciousness in restaurants. Nudged along by a public awareness campaign ("Imagine being allergic to people") which cost the drug maker more than US $92 million in one year, social anxiety quickly became the third most diagnosed mental illness in the US, behind only depression and alcoholism. Studies put the total number of children affected at 15 per cent—higher than the one in eight whom psychiatrists had suggested were shy enough to need medical help.

Diagnosing psychological disorders

When an individual seeks help for a potential psychological disorder, how do psychiatrists go about making a diagnosis? While a doctor looks for signs of disease using X-rays, scanners, or blood tests, as well as observable symptoms, the psychiatrist will often have to rely primarily on the patient's *subjective* description of the problem. Diagnosis is accomplished through a formal standardized clinical interview—a checklist of questions to ask each patient. After the interview, a mental health status examination is completed, based on the clinician's evaluation of the patient's responses. Today the clinician—often a psychiatrist—uses a standardized diagnostic system. Kleinmutz (1967) has noted that there are limitations to this interview process.

- Information exchange may be blocked if either the patient or the clinician fails to respect the other, or if the other is not feeling well.
- Intense anxiety or preoccupation on the part of the patient may affect the process.
- A clinician's unique style, degree of experience, and the theoretical orientation will definitely affect the interview.

In addition to interviews, other methods can be used to assist with diagnosis. These include:

- direct observation of the individual's behaviour
- brain-scanning techniques such as CAT and PET (especially in cases such as schizophrenia or Alzheimer's disease)
- psychological testing, including personality tests (e.g. MMPI-2) and IQ tests (e.g. WAIS-R).

Be a critical thinker

1 Why could it be a problem to diagnose shy children with "social anxiety disorder"? Remember to provide evidence to support your answer.

2 Do you think this is a condition that should be treated with medication? Why or why not?

Psychologists refer to the ABCS when describing symptoms of a disorder.

- **A**ffective symptoms: emotional elements, including fear, sadness, anger

- **B**ehavioural symptoms: observational behaviours, such as crying, physical withdrawal from others, and pacing

- **C**ognitive symptoms: ways of thinking, including pessimism, personalization, and self-image

- **S**omatic symptoms: physical symptoms, including facial twitching, stomach cramping, and amenorrhoea—that is, the absence of menstruation.

The two major classification systems used by western psychiatrists today, the DSM and the ICD (*International Classification of Diseases*), are based largely on abnormal experiences and beliefs reported by patients, as well as agreement among a number of professionals as to what criteria should be used. This can explain why the criteria change in revisions of the diagnostic manuals as we saw earlier in the example of homosexuality.

Some argue that the difficulties met in trying to identify characteristics of "abnormality" reflect the fact that abnormal psychology is a social construction that has evolved over time without prescriptive and regulating definitions. It is also argued by some that the DSM-IV is gender and culturally biased.

Validity and reliability of diagnosis
The difficulty arises over whether classification can indeed be made effectively using classification systems. For a classification system to be reliable, it should be possible for different clinicians, using the same system, to arrive at the same diagnosis for the same individual. Although diagnostic systems now use more standardized assessment techniques and more specific diagnostic criteria, the classification systems are far from perfect.

For a classification system to be valid, it should be able to classify a real pattern of symptoms which can then lead to an effective treatment. However, the classification system is *descriptive* and does not identify any specific causes for disorders. It is difficult to make a valid diagnosis for psychiatric disorders because there are no objective physical signs of such disorders.

Appropriate identification of diagnostic criteria is, to a large extent, influenced by psychiatrists. In some cases, psychiatrists have suggested alternative systems for diagnosis because they found that the existing ones were not reliable. For example, The Great Ormond Street Children's Hospital in London has developed its own diagnostic system for children. Reliability of diagnosis using the DSM-IV system was 0.64 (64% agreement between raters), but this figure was artificially increased by the fact that most raters couldn't make a diagnosis. When they used another system—the ICD-10—there was 0.36 reliability. With the Great Ormond Street System, raters achieved a reliability of 0.88.

Be reflective and caring
Abnormal behaviour? Mental illness? Psychological disorder?

- Discuss possible reasons for the difficulty of finding terms that all can agree on as appropriate in abnormal psychology.

- Why can a diagnosis of a psychological disorder often be a problem for the individual?

Diagnosis means identifying a disease on the basis of symptoms and other signs. Diagnostic systems provide a set of templates which the clinician can use to compare information about disorders to the condition of a particular client. In this way, clinicians can use the same models for diagnosis.

The effectiveness of diagnosis can be measured in terms of two variables.

- Reliability: this is high when different psychiatrists agree on a patient's diagnosis when using the same diagnostic system. This is also known as inter-rater reliability.

- Validity: this is the extent to which the diagnosis is accurate. This is much more difficult to assess in psycholocial disorders, for example because some symptoms may appear in different disorders.

Some of the problems mentioned here are illustrated in Rosenhan's classic study.

Research in psychology

Rosenhan (1973)

Rosenhan wanted to test the reliability of psychiatric diagnoses. He conducted a field experiment where eight healthy people—five men and three women, all researchers—tried to gain admission to 12 different psychiatric hospitals. They complained that they had been hearing voices. The voices were unclear, unfamiliar, of the same sex and said single words like "empty" or "thud". These were the only symptoms they reported. Seven of them were diagnosed as suffering from schizophrenia. After the individuals had been admitted to psychiatric wards, they all said they felt fine, and that they were no longer experiencing the symptoms.

It took an average of 19 days before they were discharged. For seven of them, the psychiatric classification of the time of discharge was "schizophrenia in remission", implying that the schizophrenia might come back.

Rosenhan was not content with the findings that normal people could be classified as abnormal, so he decided to investigate if abnormal individuals could be classified as normal. He told the staff at a psychiatric hospital that pseudo-patients would try to gain admittance. No pseudo-patients actually appeared, but 41 real patients were judged with great confidence to be pseudo-patients by at least one member of staff. Of these genuine patients, 19 were suspected of being frauds by one psychiatrist and another member of staff.

Rosenhan concluded that it was not possible to distinguish between sane and insane in psychiatric hospitals. His study demonstrates the lack of scientific evidence on which medical diagnoses can be made. It also raises the issue of treatments—that is, if they are always properly justified.

The Rosenhan study illustrates the concerns about reliability in diagnosis of psychiatric illness. The diagnostic classification systems have been accused of being unreliable. Using the same diagnostic manual, two psychiatrists could easily diagnose the same patient with two different disorders. Beck et al. (1962) found that agreement on diagnosis for 153 patients between two psychiatrists was only 54 per cent. Cooper et al. (1972) found that New York psychiatrists were twice as likely to diagnose schizophrenia than London psychiatrists, who in turn were twice as likely to diagnose mania or depression when shown the same videotaped clinical interviews.

Di Nardo et al. (1993) studied the reliability of DSM-III for anxiety disorders. Two clinicians separately diagnosed 267 individuals seeking treatment for anxiety and stress disorders. They found high reliability for obsessive-compulsive disorder (.80), but very low reliability for assessing generalized anxiety disorder (.57), mainly due to problems with interpreting how excessive a person's worries were.

Lipton and Simon (1985) randomly selected 131 patients in a hospital in New York and conducted various assessment procedures to arrive at a diagnosis for each person. This diagnosis was then compared with the original diagnosis. Of the original 89 diagnoses of schizophrenia, only 16 received the same diagnosis on re-evaluation; 50 were diagnosed with a mood disorder, even though only 15 had been diagnosed with such a disorder initially.

If the same diagnosis has a 50:50 chance of leading to the same or different treatment, this suggests a serious *lack of validity*, probably due to bias in diagnosis. Since diagnostic classification systems are not 100 per cent objective, the diagnosis may be influenced by the attitudes and prejudices of the psychiatrist. Clinicians may expect

Be a critical thinker

1   What are the ethical concerns with Rosenhan's study?

2   In what ways did this study illustrate the problem of reliability and validity of diagnosis at the time?

certain groups of patients to be more prone to depression, and therefore more likely to interpret symptoms as related to depression even though the same symptoms would be interpreted as something else if they were presented by a different person. When this occurs consistently to a specific group it is called **overpathologization**.

Ethical considerations in diagnosis

Szasz (see page 138) also pointed at serious ethical issues in diagnosis. In *Ideology and Insanity* (1974), Szasz argued that people use labels such as mentally ill, criminal, or foreigner in order to socially exclude people. People who are different are **stigmatized**. The psychiatric diagnosis provides the patient with a new identity—for example, "schizophrenic". The criticism raised by Szasz, and the ethical implications in diagnosis, have eventually influenced the classification systems: in DSM-IV it is recommended to refer to *an individual with schizophrenia*. There remain, of course, considerable ethical concerns about labelling which result from identifying someone's behaviour as abnormal, since a psychiatric diagnosis may be a label for life. Even if a patient no longer shows any symptoms, the label "disorder in remission" still remains.

Scheff (1966) argued that one of the adverse effects of labels is the **self-fulfilling prophecy**—people may begin to act as they think they are expected to. They may internalize the role of "mentally ill patient" and this could lead to an increase in symptoms. Doherty (1975) points out that those who reject the mental illness label tend to improve more quickly than those who accept it.

In addition, those who are labelled as mentally ill often endure prejudice and discrimination. In a study carried out by Langer and Abelson (1974), testing social perception, they showed a videotape of a younger man telling an older man about his job experience. If the viewers were told beforehand that the man was a job applicant, he was judged to be attractive and conventional-looking, whereas if they were told that he was a patient he was described as tight, defensive, dependent, and frightened of his own aggressive impulses. This clearly demonstrates the power of schema processing.

There are several types of bias that may affect the validity of a diagnosis:

● **Racial/ethnic:** The study of the "Effect of client race and depression on evaluations by European American therapists" by Jenkins-Hall and Sacco (1991) involved European American therapists being asked to watch a video of a clinical interview and to evaluate the female patient. There were four conditions representing the possible combinations of race and depression: African American and non-depressed; European American and non-depressed; African American and depressed; and European American and depressed. Although the therapists rated the non-depressed African American and European American in much the same way, their ratings of the depressed women differed, in that they rated the African American woman with more negative terms and saw her as less socially competent than the European American woman.

- **Confirmation bias:** Clinicians tend to have expectations about the person who consults them, assuming that if the patient is there in the first place, there must be some disorder to diagnose. Since their job is to diagnose abnormality, they may overreact and see abnormality wherever they look. This was clearly demonstrated by Rosenhan's (1973) study.

Clinicians often believe that the more assessment techniques they use, the more valid their interpretation will be. Kahneman and Tversky (1973) point out that this is not the case. There is no positive correlation between the number of assessment techniques used and the accuracy of an eventual diagnosis.

Another ethical issue in diagnosis also refers to confirmation bias. When patients have been admitted to a hospital, *institutionalization* can also be a confounding variable when trying to establish the validity of a diagnosis. Once the pseudo-patients in Rosenhan's (1973) study were admitted to mental wards, it was very difficult for them to get out; one participant took 52 days to convince medical staff that he was well and the whole thing was an experiment. The problem is that once admitted, all behaviour is perceived as being a symptom of the illness. The behaviours exhibited by Rosenhan's participants were all regarded as being symptomatic of schizophrenia—for example, pseudo-patients were never asked why they were taking notes, but this was recorded by nurses as "patient engages in writing behaviour", implying paranoid behaviour; pacing the corridors out of boredom was seen as nervousness and agitated behaviour; waiting outside the cafeteria before lunchtime was interpreted by a psychiatrist as showing the "oral acquisitive nature of the syndrome".

Other aspects of institutionalization also contribute to the difficulty in assessing patients accurately.

- **Powerlessness and depersonalization:** This is produced in institutions through a lack of rights, constructive activity, choice, and privacy, as well as frequent verbal and even physical abuse from attendants. All these examples of powerlessness and depersonalization are illustrated brilliantly in the film *One Flew Over the Cuckoo's Nest*.

Cultural considerations in diagnosis

Conceptions of abnormality differ between cultures, and this can have a significant influence on the validity of diagnosis of mental disorders. Though many disorders appear to be universal—that is, present in all cultures—some abnormalities, or disorders, are thought to be culturally specific. These disorders are called **culture-bound syndromes**. For example, the disorder *shenjing shuairuo* (neurasthenia) accounts for more than half of psychiatric outpatients in China. It is listed in the second edition of the *Chinese Classification of Mental Disorders* (CCMD-2), but it is not included in the DSM-IV used in the western world. Many of the symptoms of neurasthenia listed in CCMD-2 are similar to the symptoms that would meet the criteria for a combination of a mood disorder and an anxiety disorder under DSM-IV.

> **Possible exam question**
> Discuss the validity and reliability of diagnosis.

Assessment advice
The command term "discuss" requires that you that you present a balanced review of the issues involved in making reliable and valid diagnosis and you must include a range of arguments. This means considering the extent to which diagnosis is or is not reliable and valid and why this could be so. Start by deciding what your main claim could be and then construct an argument supporting this. For this you need to include appropriate evidence.

The American Psychiatric Association (APA) has now formally recognized culture-bound syndromes by including a separate listing in the appendix of DSM-IV (1994). However, as Fernando (1988) points out, many of these "exotic" conditions actually occur quite frequently, but as long as they are limited to other cultures they will not be admitted into mainstream western classification, and the potential remains for misdiagnosis and improper treatment.

Depression, which is common in western culture, appears to be absent in Asian cultures. In trying to understand the reason for this, it has been observed that Asian people tend to live within an extended family, which means that they have ready access to social support. However, as Rack (1982) points out, Asian doctors report that depression is equally common among Asians, but that Asians only consult their doctor for *physical* problems, and rarely report emotional distress. They do not see this as the responsibility of the doctor, and instead tend to sort it out within the family. They might seek help for the physical symptoms of depression, such as tiredness, sleep disturbance, and appetite disturbance, but would probably not mention their mood state.

Hence, **reporting bias** may actually make cross-cultural comparison difficult. One of the major difficulties with studies using diagnostic data is that figures are based on hospital admissions, which may not reflect the true prevalence rates for particular ethnic groups or particular disorders. Low admission rates found in many minority ethnic groups may reflect cultural beliefs about mental health. Cohen (1988) explains that in India, mentally ill people are cursed and looked down on. Rack (1982) points out that in China mental illness also carries a great stigma, and therefore the Chinese are careful to label only those whose behaviour is indisputably psychotic—that is, where thinking and emotion are so impaired that the individual is out of contact with reality. In addition to cultural attitudes, low admission rates can also reflect a minority group's lack of access to mental health care.

Some psychologists, however, argue that it is not just a misinterpretation of diagnostic data, but that real differences exist between cultures in the symptomology of disorders. For example, Marsella (2003) argues that depression takes a primarily **affective** (emotional) form in individualistic cultures. In these cultures, feelings of loneliness and isolation dominate. In more collectivist societies, **somatic** (physiological) symptoms such as headaches are dominant. Depressive symptom patterns differ across cultures because of cultural variation in sources of stress, as well as resources for coping with stress. Kleinman (1984) has studied the **somatization** of symptoms in Chinese depressive patients—that is, the bodily symptoms of psychological dysfunction. He argues that it is impossible to compare depression cross-culturally because it may be experienced with substantially different symptoms or behaviours—for example, either as lower back pain (in China) or as feelings of guilt and existential anxiety (in western cultures). This makes it difficult for clinicians accurately to diagnose and suggest treatments. According to Kleinman, it is perhaps difficult to classify such different behaviours and symptoms as belonging to the same psychological disorder.

Be a researcher

Find two different psychological disorders on www.mentalhealth.com/p20.html and read the descriptions of them and suggestions for treatment.

1 Why do you think that there are both a US and a European description of the disorders? Compare and contrast the descriptions.

2 Now search the Internet for the same disorders in another culture, for example Chinese, and compare the descriptions to the other ones. Discuss your findings.

3 Compare and contrast treatments for the disorders you have chosen.

Another cultural consideration in diagnosis is **culture blindness**, that is the problem of identifying symptoms of a psychological disorder if they are not the norm in the clinician's own culture. Cochrane and Sashidharan (1995) point out that it is commonly assumed that the behaviours of the white population are normative, and that any deviation from this by another ethnic group reveals some racial or cultural pathology. Conversely, as Rack (1982) points out, if a member of a minority ethnic group exhibits a set of symptoms that is similar to that of a white British-born patient, then they are assumed to be suffering from the same disorder, which may not actually be the case. For example, within the culture of one ethnic group it might be regarded as normal to "see or hear" a deceased relative during the bereavement period. Under DSM-IV criteria, this behaviour might be misdiagnosed as a symptom of a psychotic disorder.

How can psychologists avoid cultural bias influencing a diagnosis?

● Clinicians should make efforts to learn about the culture of the person being assessed. This knowledge can come from professional development, consultation with colleagues, or direct discussion with the individual (Sattler 1982).

● Evaluation of bilingual patients should really be undertaken in both languages, preferably by a bilingual clinician or with the help of a trained mental health interpreter. Research suggests that patients may use their second language as a form of resistance, to avoid intense emotional responses.

● Diagnostic procedures should be modified to ensure that the person understands the requirements of the task. Symptoms of disorders should be discussed with local practitioners. Often, symptoms are described differently in different cultures. In the psychiatric survey of the Yoruba in Nigeria, it was decided to include culture-specific complaints such as feeling an "expanded head" or "goose flesh". When assessing post-traumatic stress disorder (PTSD) among Rwandans after the genocide, researchers worked with local healers to determine what was a normal Rwandan grief process, and which responses the community considered to be abnormal.

Apply your knowledge

Read the following description of Anne and answer the questions below.

Anne is a 16-year-old girl living in the Midwest United States. She is currently in the IB programme at her local school. Her appearance is strikingly different from the other girls in her class. She wears blouses which she has made out of various scraps of material, and these are accompanied by the same pair of trousers every day. She is a talented artist, and she draws constantly, even when told by the teacher that she will lose marks for not paying attention in class. She has no friends at school, but seems undisturbed by the fact that she eats lunch by herself and walks alone around the campus. Her grades are inconsistent; if she likes a class she gets top marks, but will do no work at all in those she dislikes. Anne often talks to herself. She refuses to watch television, calling it a "wasteland". She even refuses to watch videos/DVDs in class, saying that they are poor excuses for teaching. Her parents say that they do not understand her; she isn't like anyone in their family. Anne seems unaware of her social isolation, but occasionally can be very critical of her classmates. Her brother is embarrassed by her behaviour and distances himself from her at school.

1 Do you think this person's behaviour is normal?
2 Do you think it is dysfunctional?
3 Why or why not?

Abnormal psychology: psychological disorders

Learning outcomes

- Evaluate psychological research (through theories and studies) relevant to the study of abnormal behaviour
- Discuss the interaction of biological, cognitive, and sociocultural factors in abnormal behaviour
- Describe symptoms and prevalence of one disorder from two of the following groups: anxiety disorders, affective disorders, eating disorders
- Analyse etiologies (in terms of biological, cognitive, and sociocultural factors) of one disorder from two of the following groups: anxiety disorders, affective disorders, eating disorders
- Discuss cultural and gender variations in disorders

Introduction to psychological disorders

When discussing abnormal behaviour, psychiatrists and psychologists use a common vocabulary. An important thing to consider is what symptoms an individual exhibits. These are important in making a diagnosis—that is, finding out *what* the person suffers from. As stated in Chapter 5.1, clinicians often use a diagnostic manual (e.g. DSM-IV) when they diagnose psychological disorders. These manuals do not deal with causes of psychological disorders but only describe clusters of symptoms that are characteristic of specific psychological disorders. **Symptomology** refers to identification of the symptoms. It is also important to find out *why* people suffer from a disorder—that is, the **etiology**—but this is much more difficult to establish for a psychological disorder than for physical illness in general. In order to understand etiology, the IB focuses on the biological, cognitive, and sociocultural factors that may contribute to the onset of the disorder.

When discussing a disorder, there are data which assist in the diagnosis. First, it is important to consider the **prevalence rate**, which is the measure of the total number of cases of the disorder in a given population. **Lifetime prevalence** (LTP) is the percentage of the population that will experience the disorder at some time in their life. **Onset age** is the average age at which the disorder is likely to appear. Knowing the average onset age can help to determine how likely it is that a person who begins to show specific symptoms at a specific age can be diagnosed reliably.

Abnormal psychology is a very broad field of psychology. In order to focus your study, you need to look at two disorders, selecting one disorder from **two** of the following classifications of abnormal behaviour: anxiety disorders, affective disorders, and eating disorders.

- **Anxiety disorders** have a form of irrational fear as the central disturbance. In this book we will focus on post-traumatic stress disorder (PTSD).

- **Affective disorders** are characterized by dysfunctional moods. In this book we will focus on the major depressive disorder.

- **Eating disorders** are characterized by eating patterns which lead to insufficient or excessive intake of food. In this book we will focus on bulimia.

Depression

Depression is one of the most common psychological disorders. People who are depressed have very low moods and low levels of self-esteem. They lack motivation, and think everything is black and that they will never be happy again. We do not really know what causes depression, but current research suggests that there are biological, cognitive, and social factors involved. Treatments include drugs and different kinds of therapy. In order to find out why people suffer from depression, different levels of analysis are used.

- Biological factors may include people's genetic make-up and biochemical factors.
- Cognitive factors may include thoughts of hopelessness, pessimistic thinking patterns, or feelings of low self-esteem.
- Social factors may include the stress of poverty, loneliness, or troubled personal relationships.

Jane is a young mother of three children. She lives with her husband in a nice area outside a small town. She studied economics and had a good job as a consultant before she had her first child. She had to give up work because the family could not find appropriate care for the children. When she visits her doctor for a health check with one of the children, she tells the doctor that she feels very tired and that she is worried she is not a good mother. She finds it difficult to take proper care of the house and she feels lonely. Her husband comes home late, and sometimes he is away for days because of his job. They often quarrel about money and he does not help her with the children.

Be a thinker

1   Is Jane depressed? Support your claim.

2   What could be contributing to her state of mind?

3   If you were Jane's doctor, what questions could you ask her in order to identify possible causes of her condition?

4   What could you suggest to help Jane? State your reasons.

Affective disorders: major depressive disorder

Major depressive disorder can be diagnosed when an individual experiences two weeks of either a depressed mood or a loss of

Symptoms of major depressive disorder

- **Affective:** feelings of guilt and sadness; lack of enjoyment or pleasure in familiar activities or company

- **Behavioural:** passivity; lack of initiative

- **Cognitive:** frequent negative thoughts; faulty attribution of blame; low self-esteem; suicidal thoughts; irrational hopelessness; may also experience difficulties in concentration and inability to make decisions

- **Somatic:** loss of energy, insomnia, or hypersomnia; weight loss/gain; diminished libido

In major depression, symptoms such as the ones outlined here interfere with normal life activities such as work and relationships.

interest and pleasure. In addition, the diagnosis requires the presence of at least four additional symptoms, such as insomnia, appetite disturbances, loss of energy, feelings of worthlessness, thoughts of suicide, or difficulty concentrating.

Major depressive disorder is relatively common, affecting around 15 per cent of people at some time in their life (Charney and Weismann 1988). According to the Department of Health (1990), during the 1980s, depression accounted for about one-quarter of all psychiatric hospital admissions in the UK. Depression is two to three times more common in women than in men; it occurs frequently among members of lower socio-economic groups; and most frequently among young adults. Levav (1997) has found the prevalence rate to be above average in Jewish males—and there is no difference in prevalence between Jewish men and Jewish women. The difference could suggest that some groups are more vulnerable to depression, but it could also indicate a problem in making a reliable diagnosis: it can sometimes be difficult for a clinician to find out if a person is suffering from a major depressive disorder or perhaps just a form of what has been called "the blues".

Depression tends to be a recurrent disorder, with about 80 per cent experiencing a subsequent episode, with an episode typically lasting for three to four months. The average number of episodes is four. In approximately 12 per cent of cases, depression becomes a chronic disorder with a duration of about two years.

Etiology of major depressive disorder

While some cases appear to be primarily biological in origin, others seem to be triggered by an adverse social or environmental change. In the majority of cases, however, the development and course of the disorder will reflect complex interactions between several biological and psychological factors. There is now some evidence that changes in the level of certain neurotransmitters and hormones can precipitate a depressive episode. It is also likely that many cases of clinical depression are triggered by negative events in a person's life. Divorce, the death of a partner or a child, a serious accident, or being fired from work are associated with depression. Sometimes depression appears to be a response not to a particular event, but to long-term circumstances, which are a continuing source of stress and disappointment.

There may be an association between stress and depression, but it is important to point out that many people who are subjected to high stress do *not* develop a depressive disorder. There are important individual differences in vulnerability. The risk of becoming depressed is related to a number of factors, which can include genetic predisposition, personality and early history, cognitive style, coping skills, and the level of social support available.

It is important to remember that major depression is not caused by a single factor, but stems from a combination of factors. These may include genetic vulnerability, neurotransmitter malfunctioning, psychological problems, or particular life events or lifestyle factors, such as misuse of alcohol or drugs. The main message is that it is not possible for any doctor or psychologist to find *the* cause of depression in any individual. Treatment of depression aims to alleviate the symptoms and consider possible psychosocial factors which might be involved in a person's depression in order to help the individual to cope.

The biological level of analysis: genetic and biochemical factors in depression

Genetic researchers argue that genetic predisposition can partly explain depression. One of the main ways to investigate this is twin studies. Nurnberger and Gershon (1982) reviewed the results of seven twin studies and found that the concordance rate for major depressive disorder was consistently higher for MZ twins than for DZ twins. This is seen as support for the hypothesis that genetic factors might predispose people to depression. Across the seven studies reviewed, the average concordance rate for MZ twins was 65 per cent, while for DZ twins it was 14 per cent. The fact that the concordance rate for MZ twins is far below 100 per cent indicates that depression may be the result of a genetic predisposition—also called genetic vulnerability. The evidence from twin studies does not contradict the view that environmental events and acquired psychological characteristics play a role. In fact, long-term stress may result in depression in some individuals because they have a predisposition which makes them more vulnerable and therefore they are more likely to develop depression compared with people who do not have this genetic predisposition.

In fact, genetic researchers such as Duenwald (2003) have recently suggested that a short variant of the 5-HTT gene may be associated with a higher risk of depression. This gene plays a role in the serotonin pathways which scientists think are involved in controlling mood, emotions, aggression, sleep, and anxiety.

The finding of a possible correlation between the gene and depression does not indicate a cause since the data are correlational. According to Caspi et al. (2003), the results could indicate that genetic factors moderate responses to environmental factors, and they also warn that speculation about clinical implications of these findings is premature.

Neurobiological researchers have suggested that depression may be caused by a deficiency in neurobiological systems such as neurotransmitters and hormones.

One explanation is known as the **catecholamine hypothesis** suggested by Joseph Schildkraut in 1965. According to this theory, depression is associated with low levels of noradrenaline. The theory was further developed into "the serotonin hypothesis"—the idea that serotonin is the neurotransmitter responsible. Researchers have attempted to identify how biochemical changes could induce depression. There is evidence that drugs which decrease the level of noradrenaline tend to produce depression-like symptoms. Janowsky et al. (1972) demonstrated this in an experiment in which participants who were given a drug called physostigmine became profoundly depressed and experienced feelings of self-hate and suicidal wishes within minutes of having taken the drug. The fact that a depressed mood can be artificially induced by certain drugs suggests that some cases of depression might stem from a disturbance in neurotransmission. Furthermore, drugs that increase the available noradrenaline tend to be effective in reducing the symptoms of depression.

Delgado and Moreno (2000) found abnormal levels of noradrenaline and serotonin in patients suffering from major depression. However, abnormal levels of these neurotransmitters might not *cause* depression, but merely indicate that depression may influence the production of neurotransmitters.

Rampello et al. (2000) found that patients with major depressive disorder have an imbalance of several neurotransmitters, including noradrenaline, serotonin, dopamine, and acetylcholine. However, Burns (2003) says that although he has spent many years of his career researching brain serotonin metabolism, he has never seen any convincing evidence that depression results from a deficiency of brain serotonin. Since it is not possible to measure brain serotonin levels in living humans, there is no way to test the theory. This is supported by Lacasse and Leo (2005) who argue that contemporary neuroscience research has failed to provide evidence that depression is caused by a simple neurotransmitter deficiency. According to them, modern neuroscience has instead demonstrated that the brain is very complex and poorly understood. The reason that researchers such as Burns, Lacasse and Leo feel the need to criticize the serotonin theory publicly is that drugs affecting serotonin levels (for example Prozac) are heavily advertised and are among the most often prescribed drugs for depression and other psychological disorders.

The serotonin hypothesis is only one of the theories of depression that suggest that the cause of the psychological disorder is due to a chemical imbalance. However, it has not been possible to identify precisely the factors involved in such an imbalance. Research has been contradictory and, at present the focus is less on the neurotransmitters and more on the process of neurotransmission.

Another important biological theory of depression is the *cortisol hypothesis*. Cortisol is a major hormone of the stress system and the reason for focusing on this is that it has always been obvious to clinicians that stress can predispose an individual to psychological as well as physical disorders. In addition, patients with major depressive disorder have high levels of the hormone cortisol, which is present in large amounts when individuals are stressed. This indicates a possible link between long-term stress and depression. This has been supported in findings from studies on victims of child abuse.

Recent research seems to indicate that the over-secretion of cortisol may be linked to other neurotransmitters. High levels of cortisol may lower the density of serotonin receptors and impair the function of receptors for noradrenaline. This demonstrates how complex the brain's chemistry is, and why the treatment for depression remains problematic.

The relationship between stress and depression is not yet well understood but it is clear that it is not a one-to-one relationship. People develop depression without previously being stressed, and people who have experienced terrible stress do not necessarily develop depression. Cortisol belongs to a group of stress hormones called glucocorticoids that play a role in fear and anxiety reactions, and high levels of cortisol are associated with depressive symptoms.

Stress hormones affect behaviour by regulating the efficiency of certain neural pathways, for example those related to serotonin, noradrenaline, and dopamine. Long-term depression may result in structural changes in the brain, for example in the hippocampus, which loses many neurons if depression persists for a long time. Researchers have also found that there is often a decrease of glucorticoid receptors in the hippocampus and prefrontal cortex of suicide victims, but it is not possible to say whether this is caused by depression. There is a high prevalence of depression among people with Cushing's syndrome—a disease which results in excessive production of cortisol. When given a drug that normalizes cortisol levels, these people's depression disappears. This is seen as evidence of a link between cortisol and depression although researchers do not fully understand this link at present.

Research in psychology

The impact of poverty on child depression

A recent study by Fernald and Gunnar (2008) may help us to understand how poverty can affect children's mental health by altering their cortisol levels. The researchers surveyed 639 Mexican mothers and their children. They found that children of depressed mothers living in extreme poverty produced less cortisol, an important hormone which helps us to cope with everyday stress. These low levels of cortisol indicate that the stress system is "worn out", leaving the children susceptible not only to depression, but also to autoimmune diseases such as multiple sclerosis.

According to Fernald, there are a lot of data that show that socio-economic status has a significant effect on health—both physical and psychological. Gunnar says that since mothers in poor economic conditions are more at risk of being depressed, their children's health is likely to be affected by a combination of poor living conditions and their mother's depression.

1 Analyse the role of cortisol in depression suggested in this study.

2 Explain how this study shows possible psychosocial factors in depression. How could these be linked to cortisol levels?

Cognitive level of analysis: cognitive factors in depression

It has long been recognized that people who feel depressed tend to think depressed thoughts. It is commonly assumed that a depressed mood somehow leads to the cognitive symptoms. Cognitive theories of depression suggest that depressed cognitions, cognitive distortions, and irrational beliefs produce the disturbances of mood.

Ellis (1962) proposed the cognitive style theory, suggesting that psychological disturbances often come from irrational and illogical thinking. On the basis of dubious evidence or faulty inferences about the meaning of an event, people draw false conclusions, which then lead to feelings of anger, anxiety, or depression. Ellis contends that irrational beliefs—such as "My work must be perfect"—together with certain observations—"My last essay did not receive the top grade"—can easily lead to self-defeating conclusions—"Since I did not receive the highest grade I am stupid".

Be empathetic

1 Produce a list of the stressors which you think poverty causes for individuals.

2 If you were in public office, what would you propose in order to alleviate some of these stressors?

Beck (1976) suggested a theory of depression based on cognitive distortions and biases in information processing. Beck's cognitive distortion theory of depression is based on schema processing where stored schemas about the self interfere with information processing. Schemas are known to influence the way people make sense of experiences. He observed that depressive patients exhibited a negative cognitive triad characterized by:

- *Overgeneralization* based on negative events
- *Non-logical inference* about the self
- *Dichotomous thinking*—that is, black-and-white thinking—and selective recall of negative consequences.

According to Beck, negative cognitive schemas are activated by stressful events. The depressed person tends to overreact. This has to do with the way a person appraises situations—that is, their attributional style. If a person has negative expectations about the future, and a tendency to explain these in terms of internal, stable, and global factors, the depression may be maintained in a vicious circle, Beck suggests.

Research has confirmed a possible link between negative cognitions and depression. Most people who suffer from depression exhibit irrational beliefs and cognitive biases such as extreme self-criticism and pessimism. Blackburn (1988) also reported that depressed people experienced a number of disturbances in thought processes. According to Frude (1998) there is evidence that cognitive explanations of depression have received support from prospective studies of the outcomes of a depressive thinking style. A **prospective study** is a study in which participants are chosen on a basis of a variable (e.g. negative thinking style) and then followed to see what happens long term. A longitudinal prospective study by Alloy et al. (1999) followed a sample of young Americans in their twenties for six years. Their thinking style was tested and they were placed in either the "positive thinking group" or "the negative thinking group". After six years, the researchers found that only 1 per cent of those in the positive thinking group had developed depression compared to 17 per cent in the negative thinking group. The results indicate that there may be a link between cognitive style and development of depression. Researchers think that identification of negative thinking patterns may eventually help prevent depression.

Overall, it is not clear if depression is caused by depressive thinking patterns or if these patterns are merely the consequence of having a depression. If a negative cognitive style causes depression then replacing negative cognitions with positive thinking patterns could improve the patient's condition. This is exactly what CBT (cognitive-behavioural therapy) tries to do.

Sociocultural level of analysis: social and cultural factors in depression

Brown and Harris (1978) carried out a study concerning the *social origins* of depression in women. The researchers found that 29 out of 32 women who became depressed had experienced a severe life event, but 78 per cent of those who did experience a severe life event did not become depressed. They discovered that life events which resembled previous experiences were more likely to lead to

Be a critical thinker

1 Is it possible that depression is mostly related to cognitive factors? Present two claims and support them with appropriate evidence.

2 Consider alternative explanations to the ones you have just presented. Include evidence.

depression. On the basis of this, Brown suggested a **vulnerability model** of depression, based on a number of factors that could increase the likelihood of depression. One out of five women reported that a similar severe life event had previously resulted in depression. Such life events were, for example:

- lacking employment away from home
- absence of social support
- having several young children at home
- loss of mother at an early age
- history of childhood abuse.

The study is in line with the widely accepted **diathesis–stress model**, which is an interactionist approach to explaining psychological disorders. The model claims that depression may be the result of a hereditary predisposition, with precipitating events in the environment.

The World Health Organization (1983) has looked at cultural considerations linked to depression and identified common symptoms of depression in four different countries: Iran, Japan, Canada, and Switzerland. The symptoms were sad affect, loss of enjoyment, anxiety, tension, lack of energy, loss of interest, inability to concentrate, and ideas of insufficiency, inadequacy, and worthlessness. These findings are compatible with an earlier study, covering 30 countries, which was conducted by the psychiatrists Murphy et al. (1967). This study also found loss of sexual interest, loss of appetite, weight reduction, fatigue, and self-accusatory ideas, but it did not come up with a clear-cut pattern of universals.

Early research by Prince (1968) claimed that there was no depression in Africa and various regions of Asia, but found that rates of reported depression rose with westernization in the former colonial countries. However, modern researchers argue that depression in non-modernized settings tends to be expressed differently and may escape the attention of a person from another culture (see Chapter 5.1 for more about problems in diagnosis).

Kleinman (1982) showed that in China somatization served as a typical channel of expression and as a basic component of depressive experience. The Chinese rarely complain of feeling sad or depressed; instead, they refer these feelings to the body as the medium of their distress.

Marsella (1979) argues that affective symptoms (sadness, loneliness, isolation) are typical of individualistic cultures. In cultures which are more collectivist, i.e. have larger and more stable social networks to support the individual—and where one's identity is more linked to the group—somatic symptoms such as headaches are more common.

Cross-cultural research has demonstrated that there is a virtually identical core of symptoms present in depression in many different cultures. However, in addition to this core set of symptoms, there are manifestations which are culturally specific because *depression is not exactly the same the world over*. Each culture does not create its own distinct patterns of abnormal behaviour, but the clinician working with a culturally diverse clientele needs to combine personal

---

Possible essay question

Discuss the interaction of biological, cognitive, and sociocultural factors in abnormal behaviour.

Assessment advice

The command term "discuss" requires you to consider a number of explanations and provide appropriate evidence to support your argument. This includes relevant empirical research and theories.

This question is rather broad, so you could take a general approach to abnormal psychology or you could choose to focus on one example of a psychological disorder and use this as a starting point for your discussion.

sensitivity with cross-cultural competence, and to develop the ability to adapt quickly and realistically to different cultural settings.

Gender considerations in major depressive disorder

According to statistical evidence, women are two to three times more likely to become clinically depressed than men (Williams and Hargreaves 1995), and they are more likely to experience several episodes of depression. It is a widely held belief that women are naturally more emotional than men, and therefore more vulnerable to emotional upsets because of hormonal fluctuations. But is there any validity to this argument? Many researchers argue that the reasons for depression are rooted more in social causes than in biological ones.

Research in psychology

The theory of social factors in depression (Brown and Harris, 1978)

As mentioned above, a study of the social origins of depression was carried out by Brown and Harris, who examined the relationship between social factors and depression in a group of women from Camberwell in London. They studied women who had received hospital treatment for depression and women who had visited their doctor seeking help for depression. They also studied a general population sample of 458 women aged between 18 and 65 years.

They found that, on average, 82 per cent of those who became depressed had recently experienced at least one severe life event or major difficulty, compared to only 33 per cent of those in non-depressed comparison groups. They also found evidence of a *pronounced social class effect*—at least for married women. Here are some of the other findings of the study.

- Of the working-class women in the general population, 23 per cent had been depressed within the past year, compared with only 3 per cent of the middle-class women. Among the working-class women, those who had one or more young children were at higher risk of becoming depressed than those who were childless or whose children were older. Women who were currently caring for three young children were particularly likely to have experienced a recent depressive period.

- There was a strong association between risk and marital status, which held across all social classes. Women who were widowed, divorced, or separated had relatively high rates of depression.

- Although there was a strong overall association between depression and the experience of stressful life events, only a minority (about 20 per cent) of the women who had experienced severe difficulties became seriously depressed. This suggested that people differ in their vulnerability, and a number of "vulnerability factors" were identified in the study: lack of confidante, early loss of mother (before the age of 11), and being unemployed. One of the most protecting factors against depression was found to be the presence of a partner.

This study (and others along the same lines) has established that *social stress* plays a decisive role in triggering many depressive episodes, but it has also demonstrated that social factors may increase an individual's vulnerability to depression. It also confirms that social support may offer protection against the effects of potentially stressful events. The work described here focuses on objective social events and lifestyle characteristics, but it is clear that the affective impact of life events is mediated by cognitions (including the person's evaluation of events) and how the individual tries to cope with stress. The cognitive account may help to explain how various vulnerability factors actually operate to increase the risk of depression. This study did not include any consideration in terms of previous life history of the depressed women. It may very well be the case that some of these women had a previous history of childhood stress which might have resulted in a vulnerability in the brain's stress circuits.

Anxiety disorders: post-traumatic stress disorder (PTSD)

PTSD lasts for more than 30 days and develops in response to a specific stressor; it is characterized by intrusive memories of the traumatic event, emotional withdrawal, and heightened autonomic arousal, which may result in insomnia, hypervigilance, or loss of control over anger and aggressive behaviour. Often, PTSD patients experience a decreased interest in others and a sense of estrangement. They may also exhibit an inability to feel positive emotions—called **anhedonia**.

In the US, PTSD has a prevalence rate of 1–3 per cent and an estimated lifetime prevalence of 5 per cent in men and 10 per cent in women. Davidson et al. (2007) and Breslau et al. (1998) estimate that PTSD affects 15–24 per cent of indiviudals who are exposed to traumatic events. However, it is important to say that not all individuals exposed to traumatic events develop PTSD symptoms. In communities that have experienced traumatic events, average prevalence increases to 9 per cent. After the September 11 attacks in New York in 2001, PTSD rates were positively correlated with proximity to the site of the attack. The type of trauma appears to be a key factor: 3 per cent of those who experience a personal attack, 20 per cent of wounded veterans, and 50 per cent of rape victims develop PTSD. The most frequent trauma that triggers PTSD is the loss of a loved one, accounting for one-third of all cases.

Careful research and documentation of PTSD began after the Vietnam War. The National Vietnam Veterans Readjustment Study estimated in 1988 that the prevalence of PTSD among veterans was 15.2 per cent at that time, and that 30 per cent had experienced the disorder at some point since returning from Vietnam.

PTSD has subsequently been observed in all US veteran populations that have been studied, including those from the Second World War, the Korean conflict, the Gulf Wars, and in United Nations peacekeeping forces deployed to other war zones around the world. There are remarkably similar findings of PTSD in military veterans in other countries—for example, Australian Vietnam veterans experience many of the same symptoms as US Vietnam veterans.

PTSD is complicated by the fact that it frequently occurs in conjunction with related disorders such as depression, substance abuse, problems of memory and cognition, and other problems of physical and mental health. The disorder is also associated with impairment of the person's ability to function in social or family life, including occupational instability, marital problems and divorce, family discord, and difficulties in parenting.

Symptoms of PTSD

- **Affective:** anhedonia; emotional numbing

- **Behavioural:** hypervigilance; passivity; nightmares; flashbacks; exaggerated startle response

- **Cognitive:** intrusive memories; inability to concentrate; hyperarousal

- **Somatic:** lower back pain; headaches; stomach ache and digestion problems; insomnia; regression in some children, losing already acquired developmental skills, such as speech or toilet training.

Research in psychology

PTSD in post-genocidal societies: the case of Rwanda

The study of PTSD in survivors of the Rwandan genocide is an exceptional case. Unlike studies of Holocaust survivors, the research was conducted soon after the genocide had occurred. Unlike studies with Bosnians, the participants were not refugees to western countries, but continued to live in the communities where the atrocities had taken place.

In 1995, UNICEF conducted a survey of 3000 Rwandan children, aged 8–19 years. Of these:

- 95 per cent had witnessed violence

- 80 per cent had suffered a death in their immediate family

- 62 per cent had been threatened with death.

Des Forges (1999) has argued that eliminating Tutsi children was seen as a critical dimension in eliminating the Tutsi presence in Rwanda. Perhaps because of this direct assault on the children, one of the key symptoms in Rwandan adolescents is diminished expectations. Geltman and Stover (1997) have argued that trauma occurs when a child cannot give meaning to dangerous experiences in the presence of overwhelming arousal. According to a UNICEF survey (1999), 60 per cent of children surveyed did not care if they grew up. Dyregrov (2000) argues that the extent of loss and trauma which affected all levels of society throughout Rwanda may have rendered the traditional coping mechanisms and collective support less viable, and the whole adult community less receptive to children's needs, as adults coped with their own traumas and grief.

According to UNICEF, in 1997 there were 65,000 families headed by children aged 12 years or younger. Over 300,000 children were growing up in households without adults.

Dyregrov found that living in the community (rather than in centres) was associated with higher rates of intrusive

In Rwanda many children suffer from PTSD as a result of war and genocide

memories. In addition to the fact that living in the community where atrocities took place could expose children to stimuli which triggered memories of the genocide, this finding may be explained by the fact that the UNICEF Trauma Recovery Programme initially targeted the centres for training caregivers who worked with children. The centres facilitated a great deal of camaraderie among children who had lost both parents and other family members during the genocide, whereby they felt accepted and that their losses were not unique.

Lastly, Dyregrov argues that the notion of resiliency—the ability to recover from traumatic events—in children may lead political systems to evade responsibility for helping war-traumatized children. Resiliency in children is intimately tied to the availability of family and community resources—resources that may be severely restricted in some war-torn countries.

1 To what extent do the symptoms exhibited by Rwandan children correspond to what you have read in this chapter about PTSD?

2 Which factors could promote resilience in these children?

3 What surprised you most when you read about this case?

Etiology of PTSD

Biological level of analysis

Twin research has shown a possible genetic predisposition for PTSD (Hauff and Vaglum 1994), but most biological research focuses on the role of noradrenaline, a neurotransmitter which plays an important part in emotional arousal. High levels of noradrenaline cause people to express emotions more openly than is normal. Geracioti (2001) found that PTSD patients had higher levels of noradrenaline than the average. In addition, stimulating the adrenal system in PTSD patients induced a panic attack in 70 per cent of patients, and flashbacks in 40 per cent of patients. No control group members experienced these symptoms. Finally, there is evidence for increased sensitivity of noradrenaline receptors in patients with PTSD (Bremner 1998).

Cognitive level of analysis

This level of analysis focuses on how individual cognitions could make a difference to people who develop PTSD. There may be differences in the way individuals cognitively process experiences and there may be a difference in attributional styles.

Cognitive therapists have noted that PTSD patients tend to feel that they have a lack of control over their lives and that the world is unpredictable. They often experience guilt regarding the trauma—for example, as a victim of rape or as the sole survivor of a car accident.

Intrusive memories are memories that come to consciousness seemingly at random. They often appear to be triggered by sounds, sights, or smells related to the traumatic event. For example, a war veteran may begin to experience flashbacks while watching a fireworks display, or may experience extreme anxiety at the sound of a whistle. Brewin et al. (1996) argue that these flashbacks occur as a result of cue-dependent memory, where stimuli similar to the original traumatic event may trigger sensory and emotional aspects of the memory, thus causing panic.

This theory was used by Albert Rizzo, a professor at the University of Southern California, who developed a therapeutic tool using virtual reality to treat PTSD in veterans. In *Virtual Iraq* the traumatized soldiers can re-experience the horrors of the war and the therapist can manipulate variables that are relevant for each individual. This therapy is based on the concept of **flooding (i.**e. over-exposure to stressful events), because it is well-known that the stress reactions will eventually fade out due to what is called **habituation**. In this way, the power of the cues that trigger traumatic memories gradually diminishes.

Development of PTSD is associated with a tendency to take personal responsibility for failures and to cope with stress by focusing on the emotion, rather than the problem. Sutker et al. (1995) found that Gulf War veterans who had a sense of purpose and commitment to the military had less chance of suffering from PTSD than other veterans. Cognitive theorists have also found that victims of child abuse who are able to see that the abuse was not their fault, but a problem with the perpetrator, are able to overcome the symptoms of PTSD.

Be a researcher

If you were asked to go to a country that had experienced war or genocide, what issues do you think you would have to address in carrying out your research?

For more information on PTSD and Rwanda, go to http://cranepsych.com/Travel/Rwanda/index.html

This is a cognitive explanation because it deals with attributional style, which may well be linked to the same schema processing suggested in depression by Aaron Beck. Research by Suedfeld (2003) examined the attributional patterns in Holocaust survivors. Suedfeld found that the attributional style of Holocaust survivors tends to be much more external—that is, luck, God, fate. Interestingly, when asked why someone survived the Holocaust, survivors were more likely than a Jewish control group to mention help from others—including help from Gentiles, which was not mentioned by any members of the comparison group. Although help from others was prominent in the study, survivors nevertheless have low trust in others and demonstrate a skeptical view of the world.

This study shows that a specific attribution may be linked to Holocaust survivors. However, it is relevant to ask if this attributional style was the result of the Holocaust or particular to the Jewish community; this could perhaps be more about sociocultural factors than cognitive ones.

Sociocultural level of analysis

The majority of research on PTSD focuses on sociocultural explanations. Research suggests that experiences with racism and oppression are predisposing factors for PTSD. In meta-analysis of the literature, Roysircar (2000) cites research that among Vietnam War veterans, 20.6 per cent of black and 27.6 per cent of Hispanic veterans met the criteria for a current diagnosis of PTSD, compared to 13 per cent of white veterans. In his research on PTSD in Rwandan children, Dyregrov goes a step further, arguing that threat of death was the factor evidencing the strongest influence on intrusive thoughts and avoidance of behaviour, which simply means avoiding situations that can trigger anxiety and panic. This appears to have support from research in Bosnia, where in 1998 close to 73 per cent of girls and 35 per cent of boys in Sarajevo suffered from symptoms of PTSD. Kaminer et al. (2000) credited the higher rate of PTSD in girls to fear of rape.

Finally, there is also evidence that social learning may play a role in PTSD. Studies by Silva (2000) have indicated that children may develop PTSD by observing domestic violence.

Cultural considerations in PTSD

In many cultures it is common for survivors to initiate treatment with someone due to somatic complaints. According to the DSM, somatic symptoms of PTSD are atypical. Kleinman (1987) argues that it is irrational and ethnocentric to assume that non-western forms of this disorder are atypical—the form commonly seen in the West being assumed to be the norm. Often, non-western survivors exhibit what are called **body memory symptoms**. One example is the dizziness experienced by a woman which was found to be a body memory of her repeated experience of being forced to drink large amounts of alcohol and then being raped (Hanscom 2001).

Gender considerations in PTSD

Research has found that there is a significant gender difference in the prevalence of PTSD. Breslau et al. (1991) did a longitudinal study of 1007 young adults who had been exposed to community violence and found a prevalence rate of 11.3 per cent in women and 6 per cent in men. Horowitz et al. (1995) reviewed a number of studies and found that women have a risk up to 5 times greater than males to develop PTSD after a violent or traumatic event.

Symptoms of PTSD also seem to differ in men and women. Men are more likely to suffer from irritability and impulsiveness whereas women are more likely to have symptoms of numbing and avoidance. Men with PTSD are also more likely to suffer from substance abuse disorders whereas women are more likely to suffer from anxiety and affective disorders.

It could be that types of traumas carry different risks for the development of PTSD. This is perhaps one of the reasons why men and women differ in prevalence rates. Rape is experienced more often by women and rape carries one of the highest risks for producing PTSD. Other forms of sexual abuse and interpersonal violence are also more often followed by PTSD than, for example, accidents or natural disasters.

Another reason could be socialization differences which may lead girls to internalize their problems and boys to externalize them (Nolen-Hoeksema, 1994). PTSD research has found gender differences in symptoms. Males are more likely to externalize symptoms (e.g. delinquency, aggression) and girls are more likely to internalize symptoms (e.g. depression, anxiety) according to Achenbach (1991).

Eating disorders: bulimia

According to the National Institute of Mental Health (NIMH), between 2 and 3 per cent of women and 0.02–0.03 per cent of men in the US have been diagnosed with bulimia. According to Frude (1998) the female:male ratio of bulimia sufferers is approximately 10:1. Binge eating is the most common eating disorder and it affects around 2 per cent of all adults. Similar prevalence rates have been found in Japan and some European countries (e.g. Norway).

More than 5 million individuals are believed to experience an eating disorder (bulimia nervosa or anorexia nervosa) in the USA alone. Symptoms of bulimia, such as isolated episodes of binge eating and purging, have been reported in up to 40 per cent of college women according to Keel et al. (2006). Bulimia involves a preoccupation with eating, an idealization of thinness, and a fear of becoming fat. The onset of bulimia typically occurs in the late teens or early twenties.

The incidence of anorexia nervosa and bulimia nervosa may be increasing, although greater medical and public awareness of eating disorders has perhaps resulted in increased reporting of eating disorder cases.

Eating disorders are believed to be more common in industrialized countries, but appropriate studies have not been conducted in developing countries. The lifetime prevalence of bulimia in women living in Tehran, Iran, has been reported as 3.2 per cent. Body dissatisfaction and a desire to be thin are common in this culture.

A prevalence of 5.79 per cent for bulimia has been reported in Japan for women aged 15–29 years.

Individuals with **bulimia nervosa** undertake binge eating and then use compensatory methods to prevent weight gain, such as induced vomiting, excessive exercise, or laxative abuse. In order for a diagnosis of bulimia nervosa to be made, the binge eating and compensatory behaviours must occur, on average, at least twice a week for three months.

Bulimic patients may consume more in a binge than an average person eats in a day. Patients report that when they begin to binge they have feelings of disgust and guilt. Psychologists call this **ego-dystonic behaviour**—that is, the patient experiences the symptoms as something distressing that he or she is unable to control. For a person who is obsessed with the idea of not becoming fat, a binge episode is likely to produce panic and intense regret. Some argue that vomiting can be effective in reversing these feelings.

Bulimic patients are afraid of weight gain, and their self-esteem depends on maintaining a certain weight. They tend to be highly dissatisfied and have a distorted sense of their own body. Often, because the patients recognize that their behaviour causes stress for those they love, they feel a sense of shame. They may also experience shame regarding the waste of food. This combination of low self-esteem and guilt leads many bulimic patients to suffer from depression.

Most bulimics have an average body mass index (BMI), so there are no easily identifiable symptoms of the disorder. As a result of repeated vomiting, patients may have swollen salivary glands or erosion of tooth enamel, with or without cavities. The loss of stomach acid (which is high in potassium) through vomiting causes electrolyte imbalances that can cause problems for the heart, kidneys, and intestines. Extreme loss of potassium can eventually lead to heart failure.

Symptoms of bulimia nervosa

- **Affective:** feelings of inadequacy, guilt, or shame.

- **Behavioural:** recurrent episodes of binge eating; use of vomiting, laxatives, exercise, or dieting to control weight.

- **Cognitive:** negative self-image; poor body image; tendency to perceive events as more stressful than most people would (Vanderlinden et al. 1992); perfectionism.

- **Somatic:** swollen salivary glands; erosion of tooth enamel; stomach or intestinal problems and, in extreme cases, heart problems.

Etiology of bulimia nervosa

Biological level of analysis
Twin research shows some support for a genetic diathesis for eating disorders, though this research is still in its early stages. Kendler et al. (1991) studied 2000 female twins and found a concordance rate of

23 per cent in MZ twins and 9 per cent in DZ twins. In all studies there is a higher concordance rate in MZ than in DZ twins, but the rates vary from 23 to 83 per cent. The differences can be attributed to both the method in which the data were gathered and varying definitions of the disorder. Because of the highly secretive nature of bulimia, self-reporting has not always led to reliable data. Strober (2000) has found that first-degree relatives of women with bulimia nervosa are 10 times more likely than average to develop the disorder.

Serotonin also appears to play a role in bulimia. Increased serotonin levels stimulate the medial hypothalamus and decrease food intake. Carraso (2000) found lower levels of serotonin in bulimic patients. Smith et al. (1990) found that when serotonin levels were reduced in recovered bulimic patients, they engaged in cognitive patterns related to eating disorders, such as feeling fat.

Cognitive explanations

According to **the body-image distortion hypothesis** (Bruch 1962), many eating disorder patients suffer from the delusion that they are fat. Research has confirmed that they overestimate their body size. However, the studies have also shown that the degree of distortion varies considerably with contextual factors, including the precise nature of the instructions given to subjects. It appears that at least some of the reports given by patients reflect their *emotional appraisal* rather than their perceptual experience. In their reformulation of the body-image distortion hypothesis, Slade and Brodie (1994) suggest that those who suffer from an eating disorder are in fact *uncertain* about the size and shape of their own body, and that when they are compelled to make a judgment they err on the side of reporting an overestimation of their body size.

There seems to be a *gender difference* in the perception of body images. US undergraduates were shown figures of their own sex and asked to indicate the figure that looked most like their own shape, their ideal figure, and the figure they thought would be most attractive to the opposite sex. Men selected very similar figures for all three body shapes. Women chose ideal and attractive body shapes that were much thinner than the shape they indicated as representing their own shape. Women tended to choose thinner body shapes for all three choices (ideal, attractive, and current) compared to the men (Fallon and Rozin 1985).

In addition to perceptual distortions, Polivy and Herman have looked at the role of **cognitive disinhibition**. This occurs because of dichotomous thinking—an all-or-nothing approach to judging oneself. Bulimics follow very strict dieting rules in order to reach the weight that they feel is ideal. When they break their own rules, they tend to binge eat. Thoughts about eating (cognitions) act to release all dietary restrictions (disinhibition).

To study this, Polivy and Herman (1985) carried out a study where dieters and non-dieters were asked to take part in a taste test. Before taking part in the test, they were given a chocolate milkshake. After drinking the milkshake, they were given three types of ice cream to sample. They were told they could eat as much as they liked. Dieters ate significantly more than the non-dieters.

Polivy and Herman's study raises an interesting question: if 3 out of 4 women diet at some point in their lives, but only 1 in 33 women suffers from bulimia, why do we not see more bulimia?

The cognitive explanation that people with eating disorders suffer from perceptual distortion and maladaptive cognitive patterns is more *descriptive* than explanatory, as it does not explain how these distortions arise. It is difficult to establish cause and effect, since distorted eating patterns may result in distorted thinking, rather than vice versa.

Sociocultural level of analysis

The perfect body figure has changed over the years in the West. In the 1950s, female sex symbols had much larger bodies compared with those of the present day. Film stars represent an ideal that people compare themselves to, so they establish standards for how we should look, whether they intend to do so or not. The fact that at other times, and in other cultures, a more rounded figure has been considered ideal suggests that the current position might be open to change.

People constantly compare themselves to other people and their self-esteem is affected by this. Thanks to the media, we have become accustomed to extremely rigid and uniform standards of beauty. Televison, billboards, and magazines expose us to "beautiful people" all the time, making exceptional good looks seem real, normal, and attainable. Standards of beauty have in fact become increasingly difficult to attain, particularly for women. The current media ideal of thinness for women is achievable by less than 5 per cent of the female population.

Many eating disorders begin when a young woman who is not substantially overweight comes to believe that she *needs* to go on a diet. Aspects of the woman's personal history may contribute to her dissatisfaction with her own body shape, but the desire to be thin is often powerfully influenced by media images and messages. The media both reflects and helps to shape a strong cultural pressure towards thinness. The rise in the incidence of eating disorders which has become evident in recent years throughout Europe, and in the US and Japan, is frequently attributed to an increase in this cultural emphasis on thinness as an ideal body shape.

The body ideal of a model in 2007 is being underweight but the body ideal of film stars in the 1950s was curvy

Apparently, women are much more likely than men or children to be the target for the media propaganda that promotes thinness. However, the representation of the ideal female as thin is also apparent in the media coverage of children's fashion, and in the design of dolls, so that even very young girls are subjected to distorted models of the ideal body shape. Sanders and Bazalgette (1993) analysed the body shape of three of the most popular dolls available for young girls (Barbie, Sindy, and Little Mermaid), measuring their height, hips, waist, and bust. They then transformed these measurements to apply to a woman of average height and found that, relative to real women, the dolls all had tiny hips and waists, and greatly exaggerated inside leg measurements.

Distorted ideas about what is normal and acceptable mean that many children become dissatisfied with their own shape, even

Be a thinker

If psychologists were able to show that Barbie produces a distorted body image for young girls, should society ban the production of the doll?

though it is within the healthy range. Studies indicate that by the age of 12, body shape can be a major criterion in self-evaluation and the evaluation of others. There are numerous sources of social pressure—including from parents—that push even young children towards being thin.

Men, too, are now beginning to come under pressure. The ideal "worked-out" male figure that appears in many commercials produces a strong demand to mirror the ideal. In 1993, a MORI survey of adult males in the UK showed that one-third of men had been on a diet, and that nearly two-thirds believed a change in shape would make them more sexually attractive. It remains to be seen whether the growing emphasis on an ideal male shape will lead to an increase in the number of men who suffer from eating disorders.

Apply your knowledge

How could social learning theory be used to explain the etiology of bulimia, according to what you have learned from the information in this section?

Research in psychology

Cross-cultural differences in body dissatisfaction (Jaeger et al. 2002)

Jaeger et al. aimed to investigate body dissatisfaction, because it had been identified in past research as a risk factor for bulimia and as dependent on cultural factors. It was suggested that eating disorders are in fact western culture-bound syndromes. However, few past studies have compared cultures using rigorous methodology. This research aimed to gather reliable information about body dissatisfaction and interrelated factors (self-esteem and dieting behaviour), and consequent cultural differences in vulnerability to bulimia.

In total, 1751 medical and nursing students were sampled across 12 nations, including western and non-western countries. This was a natural experiment, as the independent variable (culture) could not be controlled by the experimenter. A self-report method was used to obtain data on body dissatisfaction, self-esteem, and dieting behaviour. A series of 10 body silhouettes, designed to be as culture-free as possible, were shown to the participants in order to assess body dissatisfaction. Body mass index (BMI), which takes account of height and weight, was also measured.

Significant differences between cultures were obtained. The most extreme body dissatisfaction was found in Mediterranean countries, followed by northern European countries. Countries in the process of westernization showed an intermediate amount of body dissatisfaction, while non-western countries showed the lowest levels. Body dissatisfaction was the most important influence on dieting behaviour in most countries, and it was found to be independent of self-esteem and BMI.

The significant differences between cultures support the explanation that bulimia is due to the "idealized" body images portrayed in the media, which encourage distorted views and, consequently, body dissatisfaction and dieting behaviour. Western countries are more exposed to these images, and they show higher body dissatisfaction than non-western cultures. Perhaps even more significant is the increase in body dissatisfaction in cultures undergoing westernization, where exposure to idealized images is increasing. The implications are that explanations of the disorder must be considered at a macro-level (society), rather than as originating solely within the individual (micro-level).

However, the study raises some concerns. First, it ignores the role of genetic factors in causing bulimia, even though heredity certainly plays a part in the development of the disorder. It is not easy to separate the influence of nature and nurture, but it is oversimplified and reductionist to consider only *one* explanation as a basis for eating disorders when there are many other possible explanations. Second, this is a natural rather than a true experiment, because the independent variable (culture) was not under the control of the experimenter. Causation cannot be inferred if the independent variable was not directly manipulated. As a result, it cannot be said that culture causes differences in body dissatisfaction and the subsequent risk for bulimia. Third, the participants in the study were all medical or nursing students. Such relatively well-educated groups do not form representative samples, and it is not at all clear that other groups in each country would have similar levels of body dissatisfaction.

Abnormal psychology: implementing treatment

Learning outcomes

- Discuss the extent to which biological, cognitive, and sociocultural factors influence abnormal behaviour
- Evaluate psychological research relevant to the study of abnormal behaviour
- Examine biomedical, individual, and group treatment approaches to treatment
- Evaluate the use of biomedical, individual, and group approaches to the treatment of one disorder
- Discuss the use of eclectic approaches to treatment
- Discuss the relationship between etiology and therapeutic approach in relation to one disorder

Introduction

The purpose of diagnosis is to implement treatment. From the very early days of human history people have suffered from psychological disorders. Although we cannot know for sure, it is believed that in ancient times people attributed "madness" to supernatural forces or possession by evil spirits. This is documented in numerous sources as varied as the Neolithic culture, Ancient Egypt, the Incas, and the Chinese culture. Historians believe that one way to treat madness (or epilepsy) was to drill a hole in the skull so that the evil spirit could leave the head. Evidence of this practice—which is called trepanation—comes from numerous findings of skulls with such holes. Since the hole in the skull had healed, the person who had been treated must have survived. The evidence from these skulls shows a possible link between diagnosis and treatment. This link still exists in that treatments of psychological disorders are mostly linked to theories about the causes of the psychological disorders.

The skull of a young girl who was trepanated with a silex around 3500 BCE

Possible relationship between etiology and treatment

Historically, there have been different views on causes of psychological disorders and these have all been influenced by knowledge and beliefs at the time. Some reflected the view that psychological disorders were caused by biological factors. Others said that they were rooted in the mind and yet others adopted an interactionist approach saying that it was a combination of biological factors and the mind. No matter the approach to abnormal psychology, the treatment of psychological disorders has generally linked what was thought to be the etiology — which simply means the cause of the disorder.

Sigmund Freud (1856–1939)
Freud was an Austrian psychiatrist trained as a neurologist. He was a pioneer of psychotherapy in the early 1900s and he founded the very influential psychoanalytic school which totally changed the view of psychological disorders at the time. His theory of the human mind focused among other things on the unconscious, sexual, and aggressive drives and how these forces determine human behaviour. Psychoanalysis included a therapeutic approach to cure psychological disorders by getting access to the unconscious through dreams and free associations. Freud has undoubtedly been one of the most influential people in psychology. Although his influence is now markedly less, his ideas still influence art and literature.

Contemporary abnormal psychology adopts a number of approaches to treatment (e.g. biomedical, individual, or group therapy) depending on the disorder. There is now a general belief that a multifaceted approach to treatment is the most efficient. This is called the *biopsychosocial* approach to treatment and it may include drug treatment, individual therapy (e.g. cognitive therapy), or group therapy (e.g. family therapy) as well as help to handle risk factors in the environment such as a stressful relationship. Today there is a tendency to consider the individual not as a patient (that is, a sick person) but rather a person who suffers from certain problems. This is why the term "client" from humanistic psychology has sometimes replaced the term "patient" in relation to therapy outside clinical settings.

Biomedical approaches to treatment are based on the assumption that biological factors are involved in the psychological disorder. This does not necessarily mean that biological factors cause the psychological disorder but rather that they are associated with changes in brain chemistry (neurotransmitters and hormones). A number of drugs are used to treat various disorders based on theories of the brain chemistry involved, but this does not mean that there is a full understanding of how neurotransmitters and symptoms are linked. Neither is it fully known why drugs work in some cases but not in others. The fact is that drugs are used because they can help to change a person's mood in a positive direction even though side-effects of the drugs are sometimes so strong that one drug is replaced by another. Not all individuals respond in the same way to a drug and it is not known why. Clinicians must find an appropriate drug and dosage for each individual, and they must be prepared to replace the drug if the patient does not benefit from it.

Individual therapies are those in which a therapist works one on one with a client. Most individual therapy today includes some kind of cognitive therapy, where a therapist helps a client to change negative thought patterns. Individual therapy is often seen as more personal than drug therapy, in which a person may feel more like a patient. It can also be more highly individualized to meet the need of the client. Individual therapy is the most commonly used and research has shown that it generally has a positive effect.

In *group therapy*, a group of clients meet with one or more therapists. This could be a group of women who have experienced sexual abuse in childhood and now suffer from depressive episodes. It has proven useful for specific groups to come together and share their experiences in group sessions. It allows them to talk about very private matters that they have kept secret and this can be part of the healing process. It also gives the therapist—or faciliator—the opportunity to counsel several clients at the same time. There are some advantages to group therapy. First, it is less expensive than individual therapy. Second, it provides a support group for the client and diminishes the role of the therapist, allowing the client to be less dependent on the therapist. Third, it helps clients to realize that "they are not alone." One of the great stresses for clients with many psychological disorders is the feeling that they are outside the norm or that their problems are unique and insurmountable. Finally, since many disorders are either caused by or promote poor social skills, group therapy allows clients to role-play and develop social skills in a safe, supportive environment.

Group therapy is often more economical than individual therapy

As with all forms of therapy, there are also disadvantages to group therapy. Some individuals may not want to disclose their problems in a group. Confidentiality may be an issue in the group, in spite of the requirements set by the therapist. Group dynamics may also play a role, with one individual feeling that he or she is not being heard in the group, or that others are getting priority from the therapist.

Cultural considerations in treatment

Psychologists must recognize that the culture of the client also plays a significant role in the success of therapy. Sometimes the therapeutic approach may not be appropriate. For example, Al Mutlaq and Chaleby (1995) have identified several problems with group therapy when applied in Arab cultures. These include strict gender roles, deference to members in the group based on age or tribal status, and the misperception that the therapy session is simply another social activity.

Sometimes therapists use a combination of western psychotherapy and **indigenous healing practices** to treat a client successfully. Indigenous healing encompasses therapeutic beliefs and practices that are rooted within a given culture. Research dealing with indigenous healing in non-western countries has identified several commonalities among indigenous practices. One is the heavy reliance on family and community networks. Another is the incorporation of traditional, spiritual, and religious beliefs as part of the treatment.

In Malaysia, *religion* has been incorporated into psychotherapy. Integrating religious beliefs and behaviours such as prayer and focusing on verses of the Koran that address "worry," are some techniques that have made psychotherapy culturally relevant. Sometimes, in therapy with Chinese clients, verses from Taoist writings that highlight main principles, such as restricting selfish desires, learning how to be content, and learning to let go, are read and reflected on by the client. Research has found that this approach, called, **Chinese Taoist cognitive psychotherapy**, was more effective in the long-term reduction of anxiety disorders than treating the patients with medications.

Community psychologists go beyond the traditional focus of responding to a person's distress on an individual level to include an analysis of psychological health at the community level. Miller (2000) proposes a community-based treatment to complement traditional therapy; her **ecological model** emphasizes the relationships between people and the settings they live in; the identification of naturally occurring resources within the community that can promote healing and healthy adaptation; the enhancement of coping strategies that enable an individual and community to respond effectively to stressful events and circumstances; and the development of collaborative, culturally grounded community interventions that actively involve community members in the process of solving their own problems.

Be a critical thinker

● Explain how explanations of disorders may be used in the choice of therapeutic approaches.

● Why would a psychologist from the West reisiding in another culture have to include cultural considerations in the choice of therapeutic approach?

The use of eclectic approaches

It is very common for many approaches to treatment to be tried at the same time. Research evaluating treatment has demonstrated that there is most often a positive effect if people take action to cope with or change behaviour. Taking drugs, participating in group sessions in a support group, and taking part in a number of therapy sessions may all positively contribute to increase mental health in suffering individuals.

Although it is possible that a client will go to a Freudian, a cognitive, or any other therapist, it is more likely that he or she will go to a therapist who practises **an eclectic approach to therapy**—that is, an approach that incorporates principles or techniques from various systems or theories. Eclectic therapy recognizes the strengths and limitations of the various therapies, and tailors sessions to the needs of the individual client or group. For example, in the case of a depressive patient who is suicidal, cognitive-behavioural therapy (CBT) may take too long to take effect, or the individual may not be in a state that would allow for discussions about his or her cognitive processes. Drug therapy may be used in order to lessen the symptomology of the disorder; then, once the individual is stabilized, CBT might be used. Also, as the individual becomes more self-reliant, group therapy may be recommended in order to help him or her develop strategies to avoid future relapse, as well as a support system.

The argument for an eclectic approach comes from research demonstrating that drug therapies alone often have significant relapse rates, that is the client begins to show symptoms of the disorder after having been symptom-free. Rush et al. (1977) suggest the higher relapse rate for those treated with drugs arises because patients in a cognitive therapy programme learn skills to cope with depression that the patients given drugs do not. A growing number of studies is showing that cognitive therapies are more effective than drug treatment alone at preventing relapse or recurrence except when drug treatment is continued long-term (Hollon and Beck 1994). Furthermore, a combination of psychotherapy (cognitive or interpersonal) and drugs appears to be moderately more successful than either psychotherapy or drugs alone (Klerman et al., 1994).

In this chapter, the different approaches to treatment will be examined and evaluated in depth in relation to one specific disorder—depression. This book will also outline possible treatments for the disorders mentioned in Chapter 5.2 to give you an opportunity to focus on the one that has captured your interest.

Measuring the effectiveness of therapy

In 1961, Eysenck criticized the effectiveness of psychotherapies, arguing that *spontaneous remission* alone was responsible for the individual's improved condition—in other words, even if the individual did not have therapy, he or she would have improved, simply through a natural process of recovery, just as with a common cold. This may still be a valuable argument.

Evaluating the effectiveness of therapy is problematic. How does one assess whether a therapy has worked? Here is a list of criteria to consider.

- For how long must a person show a relief from his or her symptoms to be categorized as a treatment success?
- Is a total absence of symptoms the only criterion that should be used?
- Should only observable behavioural change be used to assess success?
- Is it possible to gather quantitative data on the effectiveness of therapy, or only qualitative data?

Another key question is who decides whether the therapy was successful. Therapists are unlikely to state that their therapy was ineffective, especially if the client has spent a lot of time and money on the sessions. Another issue is self-reporting by the client. This assumes that the client is in a position to judge his or her own progress and actually understands the techniques used by the therapist. Family and friends could report on progress made by the client, but sometimes they may be part of the problem and not really objective observers.

In order to study effectiveness, psychologists make use of **outcome studies**, which focus on the result—did patients show improvement or not? Outcome studies, however, have some major shortcomings. It is simple to say that all of the participants in an outcome study suffered from depression, but it is highly unlikely that they all experienced the disorder to the same degree. Although the therapists all practised the same type of therapy, this was not a standardized procedure. Therapy is highly individualized and personal. It is not a linear sequence of techniques—assessment of the client is ongoing, and treatment techniques are continually adapted to meet needs as they surface. There is support for the claim that most treatments seem to have some positive effect. One meta-analysis of 475 studies (Smith et al. 1980) found that overall most therapeutic approaches seemed to produce improvement; however, when these results were broken down into types of disorders, there were significant differences between the efficiency of treatment. The researchers concluded that all methods are to some extent effective and that it may not be the specific kind of therapy that makes a difference but that non-specific factors may play a role. This is perhaps the same effect that is observed in the placebo effect, that is the fact that a person has a treatment is beneficial in itself.

One thing to conclude on the basis of the study is, however, that some approaches work better for some problems. This could be because it is not possible to find *the* cause of abnormal behaviour. Instead, genetic predisposition, prior experiences, and current circumstances all probably contribute to a psychological disorder. This reality of complex causation could also explain why people seem to the benefit from diverse treatments. This is one of the reasons why an eclectic approach is often adopted by psychologists and psychiatrists, According to Glassman (2000) around 30–40% of Canadian and US psychologists describe themselves as eclectic in orientation.

It could be that there is no difference in the effectiveness of therapies because the therapies have certain factors in common. For example, all therapies involve a warm interpersonal relationship, reassurance, and support, and the opportunity for the individual to gain insight into his or her experience. Bennun and Schindler (1988) found that the best indicator of success in therapy is how favourably clients rated their therapist during the initial session. Those who liked their therapist reported more improvement.

Biomedical approaches to the treatment of depression

The biomedical approach to treatment is based on the assumption that if the problem is based on biological malfunctioning, drugs should be used to restore the biological system. Since depression is known to involve imbalance in neurotransmission, drugs are used to restore an appropriate chemical balance in the brain, although it is not well known why not all patients respond in the same way to a drug.

Apply what you know
Choosing the right treatment is an important step on the road to improved psychological health. As a psychologist, what do you need to consider when deciding which treatment is appropriate for your client?

Drugs were first used to treat psychological disorders in the 19th century. Since the 1950s their use has become widespread, and psychoactive drugs account for a large proportion of prescriptions. The drugs typically operate by affecting transmission in the nervous system of neurotransmitters such as dopamine, serotonin, noradrenalin, or GABA. Basically, the outcome is to increase or decrease the levels of available neurotransmitters in the synaptic gap. Depending on which neurotransmitter they affect, and whether they enhance or diminish its effectiveness, they can have calming or energizing effects on different kinds of behaviour. The different methods of action of different drugs also mean that they produce different side-effects.

Antidepressant drugs are used to elevate the mood of people suffering from depression. The most common group of drugs used today is **selective serotonin re-uptake inhibitors** (SSRIs), which increase the level of available serotonin by preventing its re-uptake in the synaptic gap. The most common SSRI is fluoxetine, better known by its brand name—Prozac. This is now one of the most widely used anti-depressive drugs. (Costello et al. 1995). SSRIs are effective, and they are relatively safe. There are some side effects, though, such as vomiting, nausea, insomnia, sexual dysfunction, or headaches. Some researchers, such as Lacasse and Lee (2005) and Kirsch et al. (2008) are very critical towards what they call the "over-prescription" of SSRIs such as Prozac.

Evaluation of drug therapy

Generally, antidepressant drugs are an effective way to treat depression in the short term, significantly helping 60–80 per cent of people, according to some reports (Bernstein et al. 1994). However, they are not equally effective in all cases and may not be better than psychotherapy in the long term, according to some researchers. A controversial study by Kirsch and Sapirstein (1998) analysed the results from 19 studies, covering 2318 patients who had been treated with the antidepressant Prozac. They found that antidepressants were only 25 per cent more effective than placebos, and no more effective than other kinds of drugs, such as tranquillizers.

However, most psychiatrists agree that modern drugs provide effective long-term control for mood disorders, and may help to prevent suicide in depressive patients. Drugs have been extremely effective in reducing the number of hospital inpatients who are being treated for psychological disorders, but it is important to note that such reductions in numbers also reflect changing policies towards hospitalization.

The side-effects observed represent a major drawback and raise important ethical issues. Unless treatment is regarded as an emergency, it cannot be given without the patient's consent, except where the patient may not be capable of giving consent. This consent should be given on the basis of full information about the potential benefits and drawbacks of the drugs concerned, in which case it fulfils the ethical criterion of informed consent. Apart from the side-effects, the main criticism of drug treatments is that although they are effective in reducing the symptoms of a psychological disorder, they do not constitute a cure.

There is an enormous market for antidepressant drugs. In the UK for example, £291 million is spent annually on antidepressants (£120 million on SSRIs). SSRIs account for 16 million prescriptions a year in the UK according to an article from *The Times* (February 26, 2008). But are the drugs effective? Or could patients be helped in other ways? Kirsch et al. (2008) reviewed 47 clinical trials published by the US Food and Drug Administration on effectiveness of antidepressants. On the basis of their review, they claimed that medical treatment was not more effective than a placebo. According to Kirsch, antidepressant medication should generally only be prescribed to the most depressed patients or if alternative methods have failed. The review showed that depressed patients can improve without biochemical treatment.

This is supported by Blumenthal et al. (1999) who found that exercise was just as effective as SSRIs in treating depression in an elderly group of patients. Likewise, Leuchter and Witte (2002) found that depressive patients receiving drug treatments improved just as well as patients receiving a placebo. The researchers scanned the patients and found changes in brain functioning in both cases but the changes were different. Patients who got a placebo showed increased activity in the prefrontal cortex, whereas patients who received the antidepressant showed decreased activity in the same brain area. The researchers could see that brain changes happened within 48 hours of starting treatment in the drug group, whereas changes began after one to two weeks in the placebo group. It is not known why a placebo works but the results of this study clearly showed that the placebo worked and was better than no treatment. The researchers argue that the brain does not respond in the same way to a placebo and drugs but people's mental health improved in both groups. This indicates that although medication is effective, there may be other ways to help people who suffer from depression.

Elkin et al. (1989) carried out one of the best controlled outcome studies in depression, conducted by the National Institute of Mental Health. This study included 28 clinicians who worked with 280 patients diagnosed as having major depression. Individuals were randomly assigned to treatment using either an antidepressant drug (imipramine), interpersonal therapy (IPT), or cognitive-behavioural therapy (CBT) or another form of therapy. In addition, a control group was given a placebo pill, together with weekly therapy sessions. The placebo/drug group was conducted as a double-blind design, so that neither the patients nor the doctors knew which was which. All patients were assessed at the start, after 16 weeks of treatment, and after 18 months.

The results showed that just over 50 per cent of patients recovered in each of the CBT and IPT groups, as well as in the drug group. Only 29 per cent recovered in the placebo group. The drug treatment produced faster results, but the NIMH study shows that there is no difference in the effectiveness of CBT, IPT, and drug treatment. In other words, the study showed that it does not matter which treatment patients received, all the treatments had the same result.

Be a critical and ethical thinker

Would it be acceptable to give patients placebo pills instead of antidepressants? What arguments could be made for and against using a placebo? Support your answers with knowledge from this chapter.

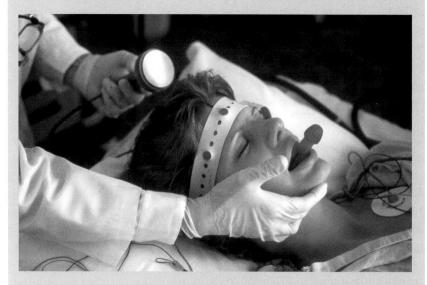

Be a researcher

One biomedical treatment for depression is electro-convulsive therapy (ECT).

1 Carry out some research on what ECT is, and how and when it is used today.

2 What are the advantages and disadvantages of this treatment? Compare this to the treatments for depression that you have read about here.

Individual approaches to the treatment of depression

One of the symptoms of depression is distorted cognitions (e.g. self-defeating thoughts). This has led cognitive psychologists to suggest that replacing negative cognitions by more realistic and positive ones can help the depressed person. Aaron Beck is a pioneer in cognitive therapy. He developed his theory in the early 1960s based on the idea of **cognitive restructuring** and his theory is still the core of many cognitive therapies (e.g. CBT). The principles of this approach are to:

- identify negative, self-critical thoughts that occur automatically
- note the connection between negative thought and depression
- examine each negative thought and decide whether it can be supported
- replace distorted negative thoughts with realistic interpretations of each situation.

According to Beck, a person's beliefs contribute to "automatic thoughts" based on schemas. In depression, negative self-schemas bias a person's thinking.

Cognitive-behavioural therapy (CBT)

CBT is a brief form of psychotherapy used in the treatment of adults and children with depression. In contrast to traditional forms of psychotherapy, which are concerned with a person's past history, CBT focuses on current issues and symptoms. Typically, there are around 12–20 weekly sessions, combined with daily practice exercises specifically designed to help the client to use new skills on a day-to-day basis. CBT is based on cognitive therapy (Beck) and includes behaviour modification.

The first aim of the therapy is to identify and correct faulty cognitions and unhealthy behaviours. The client is encouraged to find out which thoughts are associated with depressed feelings, and to correct them – this is called cognitive restructuring. This is based on the assumption that people's interpretations and inferences about the things that happen to them affect their thinking and behaviour. These cognitive processes may become distorted, but since they are accessible to consciousness, the individual has the power to change them. For example, people suffering from depression can be seen as focusing too much on their failures. The therapist will try to refocus the client's attention on what he or she does well and to take note of daily successes.

Beck argues that there are six patterns of **faulty thinking** which lead one to dysfunctional behaviour.

- **Arbitrary inference:** drawing wrong conclusions about oneself by making invalid connections—for example, when it rains on the day that you have organized a picnic, you think that only you have bad luck and that the world is against you.
- **Selective abstraction:** drawing conclusions by focusing a single part of a whole—for example, focusing on a single bad grade and ignoring the fact that you actually have an A in the class; or thinking that because you have fat thighs, you are a fat person, as is often the case with bulimics.
- **Overgeneralization:** applying a single incident to all similar incidents—for example, assuming that a relationship problem with a friend means that you are unsuccessful in relationships and have no true friends.
- **Exaggeration:** overestimating the significance of negative events—for example, when shortness of breath while exercising is seen as a sign of major illness and imminent death.
- **Personalization:** assuming that others' behaviour is done with the intention of hurting or humiliating you—for example, when someone does not greet you when he or she passes by, and you assume that person is angry with you or hates you.
- **Dichotomous thinking:** an all-or-nothing approach to viewing the world—for example, you either love me or you hate me.

Research has found that people with psychological problems are often prone to negative automatic thinking which they cannot control— for example, "I never do anything right." Underlying the cognitive distortions is a cognitive schema, which processes incoming information so that it fits with the biased self-perception— for example, positive events or successes may be filtered out to fit in with the view of the self as a failure.

The second aim of CBT is to encourage people to increase gradually any activities that could be rewarding, such as sport, going to a concert, or meeting other people. This is the behavioural component of CBT. A problem in depression is that depressed people typically stop doing things that may potentially be enjoyable because they think that it is not worth doing them. The CBT therapist can also help the client to find new ways to deal with what seem to be insurmountable problems, by breaking them down into small steps.

Aims of CBT

- Help the client to change faulty thinking patterns and underlying schemas.
- Help the client to develop coping strategies and problem solving skills, and to engage in behavioural activation.

According to Teasdale (1997), the important feature in cognitive therapy may be to teach the client meta-awareness—that is, the ability to think about their own thoughts. Thoughts and feelings are seen as mental events that can be examined objectively and changed if necessary. The aim of the therapy is to teach clients to monitor thought processes and then to test them against reality, so that they can eventually change their behaviour.

How effective is cognitive therapy in treating depression?

As we have already outlined, a number of studies and meta-analyses have demonstrated that cognitive therapy, including CBT, effectively treats patients with depression (e.g. Rush et al. 1977). It has also been found that cognitive therapy is superior to no treatment or to a placebo (e.g. Dobson 1989). In the 1989 study of 280 people with major depression carried out by Elkin et al. (see page 173) no significant difference was found in the effectiveness of individual therapy (CBT and another form of therapy) in comparison with a tricyclic drug and a placebo. The two therapies were slightly less effective than the drug but more effective than placebo.

A study by Riggs et al. (2007) studied effectiveness of CBT in combination with either a placebo or an SSRI. The study was a randomized double-blind study with 126 adolescents, aged 13–19, who suffered from depression as well as a substance use disorder and conduct disorder. Many of the participants were recruited from the social service and juvenile justice systems. The researchers wanted to include adolescents with substance misuse as well as depression because this group are at risk on many levels and not much research focuses on them. Clinicians are often less willing to prescribe antidepressants to them because they think that the adolescents should first and foremost stop abusing drugs.

The researchers found that the adolescents in the study complied with the treatment to a large extent. It was not possible to follow up six of the participants, two withdrew consent and 12 could not complete because they either went to jail or relocated. After the study the participants were rated by a physician who found that 67 per cent of the patients in the CBT group + placebo group and 76 per cent of the patients in the SSRI drug + CBT were judged as "very much improved" or "much improved" after being treated for four months. The researchers concluded that treatment with drugs and CBT is effective but that treatment with a placebo and CBT is almost as effective. The participants' self-reports after the study showed that depression had decreased and so had the other behavioural problems. The researchers argued that teaching the adolescents cognitive and behavioural techniques helped them to manage negative thoughts and feelings that could trigger substance use. They also say that it is important to treat adolescent depression—especially if a person suffers from another psychological disorder as well. Treatment could start with CBT alone, and if the patient does not respond to that, a drug from the SSRI group should be added.

Cognitive therapies are cost-effective because they do not usually involve prolonged treatment. They have also been found to be quite effective, especially for milder depressions. No negative effects have been found. Nemeroff et al. (2003) found that CBT in combination with drugs was the most effective in cases of chronic depression in people suffering from traumatic childhood experiences. This group was better helped with either therapy alone or a combination of therapy and drugs, rather than with drugs alone. Although the results are interesting and make sense, more studies are needed to confirm the findings.

Cognitive therapies have been criticized for focusing on symptoms rather than causes. It has also been argued that by providing clients with strategies for self-help, they are less manipulative than other treatments. Nevertheless, it is clear that the therapist is still making judgments concerning which thoughts are acceptable, so ethical considerations cannot be dismissed entirely.

Group approaches to the treatment of depression

In the treatment of depression, most group therapy is actually "couples' therapy", due to the strong link between depression and marital problems. Marital therapies for depression focus on teaching couples to communicate and problem-solve more effectively, while increasing positive, pleasurable interactions and reducing negative interchanges. Jacobsen et al. (1989) have found that this form of group therapy has shown to be just as effective as other forms in treating the symptoms of depression, but is more effective in improving the quality of the marital relationship. Couples therapy has been most successful in women suffering from depression related to marital distress.

The beneficial effects that a therapy group can have on an individual have long been recognized, but until recently there was a lack of high-quality studies comparing the effectiveness of individual and group therapy for patients with similar characteristics. Toseland and Siporin (1986) reviewed 74 studies comparing individual and group treatment. Group treatment was found to be as effective as individual treatment in 75 per cent of these studies, and more effective in the remaining 25 per cent. In no case was individual treatment found to be more effective than group treatment. Group treatment was more cost-effective than individual therapy in 31 per cent of the studies.

McDermut et al. (2001) provide a meta-analytic review of the effectiveness of group psychotherapy in the treatment of depression. Of the 48 studies examined, 43 showed statistically significant reductions in depressive symptoms following group psychotherapy; nine showed no difference in effectiveness between group and individual therapy; and eight showed CBT to be more effective than psychodynamic group therapy. Why is there a difference in these two meta-analyses? Yalom (2005), one of the fathers of group therapy, argues that obtaining scientific data to assess the effectiveness of group therapy is highly problematic since a group dynamic presents so many more variables than individual therapy. Some important factors to consider in group therapy are set out in the table below.

Factors to consider in group therapy
Group cohesion. No one person should be different from the rest. There needs to be a sense that all people "belong" in the group. For example, there should not be five males and one female.
Exclusion. Are there any characteristics that should be excluded from the group? For example, current substance abusers, married men, or people with a certain health condition?
Confidentiality. People must trust that they can speak freely in the group.
Relationship with therapist. Group therapy compensates for the fact that the therapist is not "one of us." The therapist must show empathy for the members of the group and attempt to understand their reality.

> **Possible essay question**
>
> Describe symptoms and prevalence of **one** psychological disorder.
>
> Evaluate the use of **one** approach to the treatment of the disorder (22 marks).

Biomedical, individual and group approaches to the treatment of PTSD

Antidepressants and tranquilizers are prescribed to treat people suffering from PTSD. The most commonly prescribed tranquillizers are Valium and Xanax, drugs from the benzodiazepine group which modulate the neurotransmitter GABA that is involved in regulating anxiety levels. Antidepressants are often prescribed because many PTSD patients suffer from depression; improvements in depression contribute to improvement in PTSD, regardless of how the PTSD itself is treated (Marshall, 1994).

Foa (1986) is an expert on PTSD. She works on the basis of CBT which includes exposure therapy and psycho-education. The idea is to give information about PTSD and then expose PTSD sufferers to the traumatic events by asking them to search their memory and describe the event again and again. This is to make them understand that "talking about the trauma" is not the same as experiencing the trauma. Foa argues that people suffering from chronic PTSD constantly try to avoid situations where they can be reminded about the trauma and some of them end up very reluctant to leave their home. According to Foa there are four goals of CBT when treating people with PTSD.

1 Create a safe environment that shows that the trauma cannot hurt them.

2 Show that remembering the trauma is not equivalent to experiencing it again.

Assessment advice

The exam question is divided into two parts. The first thing you have to do is to choose one psychological disorder that you will use for this question. It can be any from the three prescribed areas (anxiety disorders, affective disorders, eating disorders).

The command term is "describe" which just requires you to describe (1) symptoms of the disorder—at least two since the question says "symptoms" and then (2) prevalence, which simply consists of giving an estimation of how many people suffer from the disorder. It is a good idea to include data on gender and cultural differences in prevalence if this is relevant.

The command term in the second part of the question is "evaluate" which means that you should make an appraisal of one approach to treatment for the disorder mentioned in the first part of the question. You can choose any relevant approach and evaluate it in terms of strengths and limitations.

3 Show that anxiety is alleviated over time.
4 Acknowledge that experiencing PTSD symptoms does not lead to a loss of control.

Though CBT has yielded positive results, Keane (1992) has pointed out that patients may become initially worse in the initial stages of therapy, and therapists themselves may become upset when they hear about the patient's experiences.

As a result of traumatic events such as school shootings, a field of psychology called **traumatology** has developed. This is a line of intervention based on knowledge from how people react in traumatizing situations. Crisis intervention (sometimes called debriefing) is now common practice with the goal of preventing the onset of PTSD. Teams of psychologists arrive at the scene to help the survivors and witnesses of a traumatic event. The effectiveness of this intervention, however, is open to debate; the majority of people who experience trauma never develop PTSD. Mayou et al. (2000) argue that crisis intervention may do more harm than good. Immediately following a disaster, people are best served by the social support usually available to them in their families and communities; the coercion to be treated by strangers, even if well-intentioned, is not helpful and may even be intrusive and harmful. The argument goes that the procedures used in crisis intervention may help to lay more concrete memories of the event, rather than remove them.

In his work with Bosnian refugees, Weine (1998) has employed **testimonial psychotherapy** as a means of helping patients overcome their PTSD. According to Weine, traditional treatment is said to work by deactivating "networks of fear" in the psyche. Testimony is based on theories that consider collective traumatization to be at least as significant as individual traumatization. Bosnians approach matters of traumatization as a matter of collective as well as individual experience. What was targeted in the genocide was not only their individual lives, but also their collective way of life.

An essential component of testimonial therapy is the creation of an oral history archive to collect, study, and disseminate the survivors' memories. This gives meaning and purpose to the experience of the survivor. Testimony provides a time for an individual to look back over and reconsider his or her previous attitudes concerning ethnic identity, forgiveness, and violence. It also allows survivors to consider how their experience has affected how they feel about their lives today. For the survivor, the process of testimony permits the "entry into meaning."

In Weine's study, all patients were diagnosed by using the PTSD symptom scale, which had been translated into Bosnian. All testimonies were conducted in Bosnian, translated into English, and then translated back into Bosnian so that the interpreter and the survivor together could correct mistakes and add possible new recollections and details. This process of **back translation** is necessary for the researchers in order to study the data but on the other hand such translations also raises problems of reliability because there may be translation errors. This is also a well-known problem in cross-cultural psychology. The final document in Weine's study was given back to the survivor at the final session, and the survivor signed the document, verifying its accuracy. There are many survivors who do not like to seek or accept psychiatric treatment from a clinician. They will, however, participate in testimony psychotherapy in the community. Weine found that the rate of PTSD decreased from 100 per cent at pre-testimony to 75 per cent post-testimony, 70 per cent at two-month follow up, and 53 per cent at 6-month follow-up. This indicates that this therapeutic approach was rather effective.

As with group therapy for depressive patients, there is not yet a significant amount of empirical research to evaluate group therapy's effectiveness in the treatment of PTSD. In one of the largest studies, Friedman and Schnurr (1996) looked at the role of group therapy on Vietnam War veterans. The sample was made up of 325 veterans. They found that *psychoeducational groups* that worked on psychosocial deficits, such as anger management, social anxiety, and conflict resolution, helped veterans in later, more intensive group therapy. This was followed by *trauma-focused therapy*, which has three components: exposure to the traumatic memories, cognitive restructuring, and coping skills development. This group was compared to a control group that discussed only current life issues without addressing the trauma. Though there was a higher attrition rate among those in the trauma-focused therapy group (27 per cent compared to 17 per cent), those who worked through the trauma had a higher rate of improvement.

Biomedical, individual, and group approaches to treatment of bulimia

Researchers have tried to identify the most effective biomedical treatments for bulimia nervosa. Since people suffering from bulimia often suffer from depression, different drugs such as tricyclic antidepressants and SSRIs have been investigated.

According to McGilley and Pryor (1998) some of the most promising results have been found in controlled trials of SSRI (Prozac). A study with 382 patients conducted by a collaborative study group and published in 1992 found reduction of vomiting in 29 per cent of those receiving the drug compared to 5 per cent in those given a placebo. Higher dosages of the drug also resulted in a considerable reduction of binge eating (67 per cent) and vomiting (56 per cent). The results were replicated by Goldstein et al. (1995) who found that Prozac reduced binge eating 51 per cent compared with 17 per cent in patients given a placebo. The US Food and Drug Administration has approved the use of Prozac for the treatment of bulimia nervosa based on such studies.

Because most bulimics are in denial about their problem, it is estimated that 90 per cent of those who suffer from eating disorders do not receive treatment. Those who seek help and receive therapy are mostly treated with CBT—this is the most widely used individual therapy in relation to bulima nervosa. The therapy addresses the cognitive aspects of bulima, such as obsession with body weight, dichotomous thinking and negative self-image in combination with behavioural components of the disease such as binge eating and vomiting.

Be a researcher: virtual treatment

One of the more interesting uses of technology in psychology is the use of computers to create "virtual realities" to help patients with PTSD to overcome their anxiety. You can read more about this at:

http://www.newyorker.com/reporting/2008/05/19/080519fa_fact_halpern

The aim of the therapy is to restore some control of eating but avoid dieting because this is known as a trigger for binge eating. The patients typically have to record what they eat and how they feel about this, and they are also asked to tell what triggers binge eating and purging. The patients receive extensive feedback during therapy, and they are to taught to identify and deal with symptom triggers. They also learn cognitive techniques for improving self-esteem, developing adequate expressions of feelings and avoiding damaging thought patterns. Wilson (1996) found that CBT was superior to medication alone and that the combination of CBT and medication was superior to medication alone. However, CBT is not 100 per cent effective. Wilson (1996) found that 50 per cent of the patients who receive this therapy stop binge eating and purging. The remaining patients show only partial improvement, and some do not benefit from CBT at all.

The use of group therapy in the treatment of eating disorders is growing. McKisack et al. (1997) reviewed research on effectiveness of therapy in the treatment for bulimia nervosa. They found that group therapy was widely used and that it was relatively effective, especially if the therapy consisted of individuals who have been matched on certain characteristics, if the therapy was long and involved intensive scheduled sessions combined with additional treatment components.

A psychoanalytically based approach to group therapy was promoted by Minuchin in his *family systems model*. This model works on the basic assumption that an individual's dysfunctional behaviour is part of a larger dysfunction within the family. Minuchin's goal of family therapy is to promote a *restructuring* of the family system along more healthy lines. This idea has been widely used in family therapy.

Schmidt et al. (2007) did a randomized controlled test of CBT and compated it to family therapy in a a group of 85 adolescents suffering from bulimia nervosa. Both approaches resulted in significant reduction of bingeing and purging behaviours over a period of 12 months. The study also found that CBT was slightly more effective in that it reduced bingeing behaviours more rapidly.

In spite of the gains made by patients through group therapy, there are concerns.

- Patients may get negative ideas from each other. Ways to hide weight loss or induce vomiting may be learned from other group members.
- The group may adopt a pessimistic attitude toward improvement, and this may be resistant to change.
- The group may reinforce that such eating behaviours are normal.
- Competition in the group may lead members to engage in behaviour to gain the attention of the therapist.
- Well-meaning group members often become co-therapists of a group, to the point of insisting on change or judging others who don't comply with suggestions. Group members feeling judged or pressured may not attribute it to other group members, and may feel it is their own inadequacy or weakness that is the problem.

Possible research questions in extended essay

- Why are there gender differences in depression?
- To what extent are eating disorders a western phenomenon?
- Is it possible to effectively treat PTSD in veterans with a virtual reality approach?
- Why is it so difficult to make a reliable diagnosis for depression?

Developmental psychology: cognitive development

Learning outcomes

- Discuss the extent to which biological, cognitive, and sociocultural factors influence human development
- Evaluate psychological research (through theories and/or studies) relevant to developmental psychology
- Evaluate theories of cognitive development
- Discuss how social and environmental variables may affect cognitive development

If you have ever been able to witness the development of a newborn baby over the first twelve months, you will know that amazing things happen. This is partly due to a process called **maturation**—the unfolding of behaviours that are genetically programmed for all humans—or in other words they are "hard-wired". Another factor in development is **learning**. This is sometimes defined as the systematic changes in behaviour, thoughts, and feelings as a result of experience. Over the years, there have been some pretty heated discussions about whether *genetic predisposition* or the *environment* is the most important factor in development. This debate on the relative roles of "nature" (genetic inheritance) and "nurture" (environmental factors) is still going on to some extent. Researchers agree that a child's genetic make-up determines his or her developmental *potential*, but also that development of this potential is very much dependent on the environment in which the child grows up. Many developmental psychologists adopt an interactionist approach to development, by taking biological, cognitive, and sociocultural factors into consideration.

Research methodologies in developmental psychology

Researchers who study development use a number of methods and designs. Observations and interviews in naturalistic settings are now used extensively, but these methods do not lend themselves to control. The laboratory experiment is still widely used, but researchers are aware of the problem of ecological validity. Sometimes, combinations of experimental data are corroborated by findings from naturalistic studies, which provides a greater possibility for findings to be applied to real life. The case study method can offer insight into developmental factors, although there are ethical issues to consider in sensitive case studies—for example, cases of children who have suffered abuse or extreme deprivation. The balance between collecting scientific data and still respecting a child's integrity is important in developmental research.

Psychologists are interested in the environment in which the child grows up—the child's ecology or **developmental niche**. This includes the physical and social context, as well as cultural factors such as child-rearing practices and customs.

Longitudinal research is often used in developmental psychology, because researchers are interested in a group of participants over a given period in order to measure change. A researcher who wants to study how gender identity develops in young children might visit the same children a number of times over the first four years. A strength of a longitudinal study is that it provides the richest data as to the possible kinds of experience that might foster gender identity development in an individual child. Since the same children are studied, there are no participant variables. Two limitations of the longitudinal design are that such studies are time-consuming, and participants may leave the study if the research runs for a long time. When data are lost in this way, it affects the possibility of generalizing from the findings of the study.

In order to address some of the limitations of a longitudinal study, researchers may use a **cross-sectional design**, comparing two or more groups on a particular variable. The cross-sectional design may be used to compare changes of a variable or behaviour at different ages. Such comparisons may reveal age-related changes. A cross-sectional study uses different participants to represent the different age groups under investigation. This means that one cannot be absolutely sure that the differences found are not due to participant variables. The cross-sectional design is often used in spite of this, because it is not as time-consuming as the longitudinal design, and fewer participants are lost during the study.

From early on the baby participates in social interactions, stimulating not only cognitive but also social development

Cognitive development

Brain development

Newborn babies show some characteristics at birth that are universal in all human beings. They have inborn reflexes such as sucking and grasping, and they possess some basic visual and auditory abilities. They also seem to be prepared for social interaction with other humans. Modern research shows that a human baby responds to human faces from the very beginning. From early on, human babies can exchange sounds and non-verbal signals with the mother or primary caregiver, in a synchronized pattern of movements and sounds that is similar to a conversation. This may be due to the mirror neurons. The innate capacity for social responses in newborn babies enables them to interact with others long before language develops.

The brain of a newborn has more than a trillion nerve cells that communicate across many trillions of synapses. These are supported by a trillion glial cells, which account for around 90 per cent of the cells in the human brain. The central nervous system continues to grow in size and complexity after birth. Synaptic growth is most significant in the first year of life, but it continues during childhood and into late adolescence. However, neural connections can be formed through the entire life of an individual. Human brains are made for lifelong learning. The ability to develop and change in response to the environment is called **neuroplasticity**.

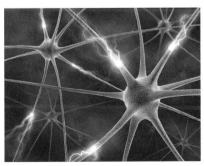

Neuroplasticity—growth of new connections due to maturation and learning

183

The brain's activity increases with synaptic growth. Modern technology makes it possible to investigate brain development by looking at the energy demands of various brain regions. Chugani (1999) performed a PET scan of glucose metabolism in newborn human babies and found that there was little activity in the cerebral cortex, which is associated with higher-level functioning. There was high activity in the brain stem and the thalamus, which are areas related to inborn reflexes. The research also established that the limbic system, with the amygdala, the hippocampus, and the cingulate cortex (associated with memory, emotional processing, and bonding), were active in the newborn. Chugani related this to the infant's capacity to observe and read the emotional content of human faces, and to communicate via facial expressions and eye contact. Bachevalier et al. (1999) found that if they lesioned these brain areas of a newborn monkey, it gradually lost the capacity for social behaviour. Eye contact decreased and the animal showed blank facial expressions. Such behaviour is also found in children who suffer from autism. The interpretation of observations like these is that reading facial expressions is to some extent an innate capacity, which can be lost due to brain damage.

From the age of six to nine months, the frontal lobes and the prefrontal areas of the cortex begin to function more fully, due to the growth and myelinization (development of the brain during adolescence) of neurons. There is also growth in lower-lying areas of the brain such as the hippocampus, which plays an important role in memory, and the cerebellum, which is the control centre for body movements. Psychologists believe that these changes in brain structure provide the physical basis for the child's ability to engage in more complex motor behaviour and an increased ability to learn. The research by Chugani shows that there is a steady increase in glucose metabolism in these areas, and that this continues until the infant is around one year old. This activity reflects the maturation of the frontal cortex, which appears to develop according to a fixed order, suggesting that it is genetically programmed.

PET scans have demonstrated that glucose metabolism steadily increases and reaches adult levels around the second year of life. After this, it exceeds adult levels, dropping to adult levels again during adolescence. This appears to be due to a surplus of synaptic connections, which allows the individual brain to learn and retain the synapses that are used, and eventually to eliminate those that are not. This is called **pruning**. Scientists believe that early exposure to diverse environmental influences creates the *unique* neural architecture of each individual, in line with the demands of the environment.

During middle childhood, growth in the area of the frontal lobes continues. Researchers like Case (1991) hypothesize that the pattern of brain changes taking place between five and seven years of age enables the frontal lobes to coordinate the activities of other brain centres, so that more complex behaviours become possible. These include attention control, forming explicit plans, and engaging in self-reflection. Evidence to support this theory comes from observations of humans with damage to the frontal lobes, as well as

Be a researcher and a communicator

Based on what you already know, and knowledge from this site on early brain development

www.sciencemuseum.org.uk/on-line/brain/238.asp

write a short article on the baby's brain development during the first two years.

Be an enquirer

Do some research on human brain development during the first 6 months of life. Find out what happens if the baby has been exposed to alcohol during the prenatal period.

1 How does the healthy baby brain develop in this period?

2 How does foetal alcohol syndrome (FAS) affect; the baby's brain in the first 6 months? What about later?

3 What are the consequences of FAS for the baby's life?

You can find useful pictures and explanations of how the brain develops if you search the Internet for pictures. Search for "brain baby" as well as "FAS brain".

Here are some sites to start with:

www.zerotothree.org/site/PageServer?pagename=ter_util_babybrainflash

www.come-over.to/FAS/FASbrain.htm

experimental research with animals. Individuals with frontal lobe damage are unable to plan ahead or stick to plans. They seem to have no self-control and they are easily distracted. These deficits are very similar to what we observe in young children.

Development of the brain during adolescence

When children reach their teenage years, they become able to think in more abstract ways. The brain changes taking place at this stage are less dramatic than those earlier in life, but they are no less important. Reorganization and myelinization of the higher brain centres like the prefrontal cortex continue at least until the age of 20. This enables teenagers to process information faster and to perform higher-level cognitive activities such as strategic planning. However, the area that controls impulses in the prefrontal cortex is among the latest brain regions to mature, at around 20 years, according to Giedd (2004). Giedd undertook a longitudinal study of normal children, carrying out MRI scans every second year. He found that 95 per cent of the structure of the brain is formed when the child is five or six, but he also concluded that areas in the prefrontal cortex appear to grow again just before puberty. Giedd hypothesized that the growth spurt in synapse formation just before puberty is a clear illustration that different parts of the brain mature at different times, and that the frontal cortex matures relatively late. However, this does not necessarily reveal anything specific about the relationship between behaviour and brain structures, although popular interpretations of neuroscientific findings have claimed that problem behaviour in adolescents is due to their immature brains.

Evaluation of brain development theories

Some brain researchers warn that it is not possible to establish a simplistic cause-and-effect relationship between the findings of neuroscientists in relation to maturation and interpretation of behaviour. There is growing controversy about how brain research can be used to understand development and possible education policies—for example, "enrichment strategies for babies" and large-scale early governmental intervention programmes for disadvantaged children. Many researchers agree that neuroscientific knowledge is still too limited to offer serious advice on public policy, and that it is wiser to use evidence from developmental psychology.

Piaget's theory of cognitive development

The way children think is different from the way adults think. This puzzled the Swiss psychologist Jean Piaget, who believed that maturation as well as the social environment is important in cognitive development. According to Piaget, interaction with the environment changes people, and cognitive development is dependent on how the individual child *interacts* with the social and physical world. This is known as the **constructionist approach**. The essence of knowing is *activity*, according to Piaget, who saw the child as "a little scientist" who comes to know about the world by physical or mental manipulation of objects. He suggested that children use strategies in thinking and problem solving that reflect different stages of cognitive development.

Be an enquirer and a communicator

Recently there has been a lot of debate about "the teenage brain". To learn more about the debate, watch PBS's Frontline show and study the extra material at www.pbs.org/wgbh/pages/frontline/shows/teenbrain/view/.

Now present the evidence based on this programme and what you have read in this chapter in the form of an oral presentation for your class.

Piaget started by observing his own four children, and producing baby diaries based on these careful observations and talks with them. He eventually developed a scientific method to study cognitive development in children. He used questions and observational strategies to develop a **clinical interview**. This is an open-ended, conversational technique that can provide insight into the child's own judgments and explanations of what happens. The method is not easy, and the researchers in Piaget's team were trained for a year before they could start collecting data.

Profile

Jean Piaget

Jean Piaget (1896–1980) started out as biologist, but specialized in psychology. He was interested in the nature of knowledge and how the child acquires knowledge. Piaget saw empirical studies of children and adolescents as the most important source of information about the nature of knowledge. He made a valuable contribution to understanding how thinking develops, and he inspired many child psychologists all over the world.

According to Piaget, knowledge consists of cognitive structures—schemas—which are mental representations of how to deal with the world. It is the *schemas* that develop or change. Piaget's theory of "genetic epistemology" focused on the way that new schemas emerge. The child's first experiences are based on a limited innate repertoire of schemas—for example, sucking, reaching, and grasping—which are modified as a result of experience. Piaget called this **adaptation**. He suggested that children actively *construct* knowledge themselves when they interact with and interpret new objects and events based on their existing knowledge. Adaptation has two forms according to Piaget: **assimilation** and **accommodation**.

Assimilation happens when new information can be integrated into existing cognitive schemas. Accommodation occurs when existing cognitive schemas have to be altered because they no longer match new experiences. Suppose a young boy learns a schema for "car" because he is driven in the family Volvo every day. Looking out of the window from his chair, he points at other cars and says "car". This is evidence that he has *assimilated* new information about cars into his existing car schema. He knows that cars come in different sizes, colours, and shapes, but they are still cars. Then the child goes to a farm and sees a tractor for the first time. He says "car". This is not a car, although it has four wheels and may look like a car. His parents tell him that this is a tractor, *not* a car. The boy will have to accommodate his schema for cars to exclude tractors. He will also have to create a new schema for tractors. Through the process of assimilation, the child consolidates cognitive schemas. Accommodation, on the other hand, results in change and new knowledge.

Piaget claimed that children's intelligence progresses through a series of cognitive stages, with each stage different in quality from the next. He saw the stages as a way to describe changes in the logic of thinking, and called them sensorimotor, pre-operational, concrete operational, and formal operational. These names come from the

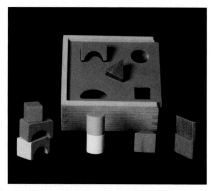

Toys can teach children about the physical world

way Piaget believed that children developed their knowledge. His view was that the sequence of stages was the same for all humans—that is, cognitive development is universal.

The sensorimotor stage (age 0–2 years)

According to Piaget, the newborn baby relies on innate reflexes and has limited knowledge. In this stage, the child learns through *movements* and *sensations*. Knowledge simply arises from looking, touching, hearing, sucking, grasping, and putting things in the mouth. The child gradually comes to have an idea of what different objects are like. To begin with, the child's movements are not at all purposeful because he or she has no control over them. However, when the child acquires more control over his or her body, he or she learns that a specific movement—like bashing a toy—will have specific consequences.

At around eight months old, children develop **object permanence**—that is, the idea that objects continue to exist even when they can no longer be seen. Piaget found that a 4-month-old will not look for an object if it is hidden. It is as if the rule "out of sight, out of mind" applies at this stage. However, an 8-month-old will look for the object if it is hidden. Between 8 and 12 months, the child will keep looking for the object in the place where he or she found it the last time. This happens even if the child watches someone hide it in a new place. It is not until they are around 18–24 months that toddlers possess fully developed object permanence.

The pre-operational stage (age 2–7 years)

At the beginning of this stage the child learns to speak. Children become capable of thinking in symbolic terms—that is, they can form ideas, but they can only focus on one aspect of an object or situation at a time, and they cannot transfer knowledge from one situation to another. Piaget argued that the child's understanding of the world is based on **egocentrism**. This means that the child can only see the world from his or her own viewpoint. The child does not understand that others might see things differently. Piaget saw egocentrism as a *cognitive limitation*—that is, children cannot understand that someone else's point of view might be different from their own.

The infant gradually comes to know that there are many different types of cars and tractors

Did you know?

In contrast to studies on egocentrism, much research is currently being undertaken into the development of children's **theory of mind**—that is, their ability to understand what other people think, believe, and know. This is a domain-specific approach to cognitive development, which is different from traditional cognitive developmental theories that aim to explain all aspects of cognitive development.

Crawling and exploring the environment is an important part of a child's development

Reseach in psychology

The three-mountain task (Piaget and Inhelder 1956)

Piaget's three-mountain task

The classic demonstration of egocentrism is Piaget and Inhelder's three-mountain problem. In this experiment, the child is asked to look at a model of three mountains— one big one and two smaller ones. The child can be seated in front of the model or at any other angle. The researcher then places a doll in various positions in the model. The child is shown different pictures and asked to choose the one that shows what the doll would see from its position. Children under six years consistently pick the photograph that shows what *they* see themselves. Piaget interpreted this as *egocentricity*. From around nine years, children can adopt the doll's perspective.

There has been criticism of this study. Some claim that young children are able to take another person's perspective if the material used is more familiar than that used for the three-mountain task. Donaldson (1984) argues that this task is not similar to what children experience in everyday life. She refers to a study by Hughes (1975), who carried out the three-mountain task in a different way. Hughes used an experimental set-up with a doll and a policeman. They were placed in an apparatus of two pieces of wood forming a cross. The experimenter then asked the child if the policeman could see the doll. After this, the child was asked to hide the doll so that the policeman could not see it.

Hughes's naughty boy task

Hughes found that nearly all children from the age of three and a half to five could perform the task. He explained that the reason for this was that the task was more meaningful and interesting to the children than Piaget's three mountain task.

A second limitation in children's thinking is that it is dominated by the *appearance* of things. According to Piaget, pre-operational children cannot understand the concept of **conservation**—that is, that physical properties remain the same even if the object's appearance is changed. This can be seen in Piaget's conservation experiment. The pre-operational child is presented with two similar glasses of water. When asked which glass contains the most water, the child will typically say that the amount of water in the glasses is the same. Then the experimenter pours the water from one of the glasses into a tall, narrow glass, while the child watches. The question is repeated. Now the child will say that there is more water in the tall, narrow glass. When asked why, the child typically argues that there is more water in the new glass because the glass is taller. Piaget explained that one reason for this perception is that children cannot mentally reverse the operation of pouring the water into the tall, narrow glass.

Piaget's conservation task

Piaget said that children at this age focus on the most visible change. They are not able to understand mentally that the amount of liquid must be the same, even though it has been poured into a different kind of glass. They cannot *conserve* the property of liquid by mentally reversing the pouring.

Li et al. (1999) tested 486 Chinese primary school children on the classic liquid conservation task. The researchers supported Piaget's theory that the percentage of children who get the answer right increases with age. They also found that children from schools with a good academic reputation generally achieved better results than those from less privileged schools. This indicates that differences in cognitive development are not only related to brain maturation, but also to factors such as education. Piaget did not include this in his theory.

The concrete operational stage (age 7–12 years)

For many children, this is the time when they begin formal schooling. They start to use some rules of logic in problem solving, but only when dealing with concrete tasks. If children at this stage are given the following problem: "House A is more expensive than House B. House C is more expensive than House A. Which is the most expensive?" they would be able to solve it, but they would need some images for support. Problem solving is generally random and not systematic.

Formal operational stage (from age 12)

By the end of this stage, adolescents—or adults—can use formal, abstract logic. They can mentally manipulate ideas, concepts or numbers, and they can think hypothetically. This means they can think about what could happen or what would never happen. They will also approach problem solving in a systematic way. Piaget believed that everybody reaches the formal operational stage when they are around 20, but this is not necessarily the case. Modern research has demonstrated that it depends on education to a large extent.

Be an enquirer

It is possible to find filmed replications of this experiment on the Internet (e.g. on YouTube). Try to find one to see how a study like this can be conducted.

Discuss how you could make a replication of the experiment yourself. What ethical issues would you need to take into consideration if you were to conduct such an experiment with young children?

Be a critical thinker

is there a cultural bias in Piaget's results?

1 Look critically at Piaget's three-mountain experiment. Can you imagine countries where such a task would be difficult to deal with? Why?

2 To what extent does a study like Li et al. (1999), using Chinese children in primary school, contradict the claim of cultural bias?

See pages 80–81 in Chapter 3.1 for more on the possible role of culture on cognitive processes.

Stage	Approximate age (years)	Characteristics
Sensorimotor	0–2	Knowledge develops as a result of sensations and actions
Pre-operational	2–7	Increase in use of symbolic thought and self-awareness, but dominated by the visual appearance of things; language development; egocentrism
Concrete operational	7–12	Logical reasoning based on real objects that can be manipulated; understanding of conservation
Formal operational	12+	Ability to use abstract reasoning and logic

Overview of Piaget's four stages of cognitive development

Evaluation of Piaget's theory

Piaget was the first to suggest a comprehensive account of cognitive development, and his theory has been very influential, especially in primary schools. Piaget's ideas suggest that children learn best when the teacher sets up situations where the child can discover ideas for themselves. This approach is called **child-centred learning** and it has been used extensively in education systems around the world.

It is generally accepted that there are fundamental differences in the ways that children and adults think. Piaget changed the traditional view of children as passive, suggesting instead that children are active in searching out knowledge and constructing mental representations of the world. He also suggested inventive research methods to investigate the way children think, and he gave a coherent theoretical account of the differences in thinking in the different stages, although he did not explain clearly why these changes take place. Many of his concepts have been tested empirically by others, and some research is still conducted on the basis of his ideas, so his theory is not simply historical.

As is usually the case in science, other researchers have pointed to limitations in his explanations. One objection concerns his methodology. Piaget's sample was very small, consisting mainly of his own children. It is questionable whether it is possible to generalize findings from such a small sample. There is also the problem of cultural bias in his research.

Many modern researchers have argued that Piaget underestimated children's cognitive capabilities, which led to a view of children as *deficient* rather than *competent* thinkers. These researchers have tried to demonstrate that cognitive capacities in children appear at earlier ages than Piaget suggested, and that his theory should therefore be modified. Baillargeon and DeVos (1991) argue that object permanence appears earlier than Piaget suggested. In a laboratory experiment, they showed three-month-old babies objects that moved behind a screen. One of these objects was either a small or a big carrot placed on a rolling car. There was a window in the upper half of the screen, so that it was possible to see the big carrot when it passed by in the rolling car. In one test, they had a small carrot move behind the screen so it was only visible before it went behind the screen and when it reappeared on the opposite side of the screen—it could not be seen through the window. In the second test, they moved the big carrot. Normally it would be possible to see the big carrot through the window when it passed behind the screen. However, the researchers created what they called "an impossible event", whereby the big carrot passed behind the screen but was not visible in the window.

Modern baby research uses methods that rely on children's *interest* in new objects. According to Baillargeon and DeVos, the infants looked longer at the "impossible event" with the big carrot than they did when the small carrot moved behind the screen. The researchers argued that this was because the children *expected* the big carrot to appear in the window. If their interpretation is correct, it provides evidence that infants are aware that objects they cannot see continue to exist. This means they have object permanence.

TOK

In many countries—for example, the Czech Republic, Korea, and Turkey—young students do much more advanced mathematics than in western countries. However, these students are actually memorizing model problems for advanced mathematical concepts. It is important that they "learn the maths", even if they are not cognitively able to understand it.

1 To what extent do these students "know mathematics"?

2 Do you think this approach to learning mathematics is valid?

This interpretation of the findings is based on the assumption that infants show more interest in new and unexpected events. It can be difficult to establish if this is actually true, but since other researchers have found similar results, it may be that this is a valid method by which to investigate object permanence.

An important limitation of Piaget's theory is that he underestimated the role of social learning—for example, instruction by adults or other children. He claimed that children acquire knowledge by exploring and acting on the world in a process of self-discovery. He studied individual children and did not pay much attention to the social and cultural context of cognitive development. It was Vygotsky who was to consider these issues.

Vygotsky's sociocultural approach to cognitive development

The Russian psychologist Vygotsky argued that it is not possible to describe the process by which children acquire knowledge without taking into account the child's social environment or culture. Culture provides knowledge, and it teaches children *what* to think and *how* to think. Vygotsky's sociocultural theory suggests that a child's cognitive development is based on *interaction* with other people, as well as the *cultural tools* to understand the world which are provided by the child's culture. Cultural tools should be understood as both the tools used in the culture (e.g. axes, computer), and the implicit and explicit rules or norms observed in the culture. Knowledge is transferred via imitation, instructions, or collaborative learning. Language is the primary form of interaction that adults use to transmit to the child the knowledge that exists in the culture, and as the child grows older, language comes to serve as the most important tool of learning.

An important element in sociocultural theory is the concept of **zone of proximal development**, which refers to the difference between what a child can do on his/her own and what he or she can accomplish with help. A child can increase in competence if he or she receives assistance to perform a task that is just slightly beyond his or her current ability. This is called **scaffolding**. Successful scaffolding can change the child's level of performance on a particular task. It implies that the adult must be sensitive to the child's abilities and signals, because children differ.

Vygotsky and Piaget both agreed that children actively construct knowledge and that they learn best if new knowledge is related to existing knowledge and abilities. Vygotsky claimed that most of what children learn comes from the culture in which they live. Since much of children's problem solving is mediated through others, it is wrong to focus on the child in isolation, as Piaget does. Vygotsky suggested **cooperative learning** instead of child-centred learning.

The effect of social and environmental variables on cognitive development

In February 2008, the economist Paul Krugman commented in the *New York Times* on findings from neuroscientists. Children growing up in very poor families, with low social status, experience high

TOK: ways of knowing

Piaget's theory deals with how children come to know about the world.

Discuss what ways of knowing a child uses at the different stages.

Be open-minded and reflective

Consider the following.

1   How could a culture influence what a child should learn?

2   Give some examples from your own culture of "tools" you need to learn to use. Why is that and what does this say about your culture?

3   Do people need to go to school to learn what is necessary in their culture? Why or why not?

levels of stress hormones that may impair brain development and cognitive functioning. He added that in 2006, 17.4 per cent of children in the US lived below the poverty line. Based on statistics, Krugman argued that children born to the poorest parents have an almost 50 per cent risk of remaining in that position. This is particularly true for children from ethnic minorities.

Cognitive researchers have found that poverty is one of the major risk factors in children's cognitive development. Factors such as poor nutrition, poverty-related health problems, home environment, parenting practices, and living in poor neighbourhoods, with high levels of crime and unemployment, are all factors that may impact cognitive development in children and influence the possibility of education. The effects of undernourishment may begin even before the child is born. Pregnant women who are undernourished are more likely to give birth to underweight babies, who are generally more at risk. Research in the US shows that poor children are more likely to experience stunted growth and problems with cognitive development than more privileged children.

Inadequate food intake limits children's ability to learn. Children who are chronically undernourished become less active and show less interest in their social environment, and exhibit less emotional expression. It is believed that it is not the malnutrition alone that results in cognitive malfunctioning, but rather the combined negative effects of exposure to undernourishment and other consequences of poverty. If children are given appropriate food and stimulation, it can modify cognitive impairment caused by earlier malnutrition. Nutrition and prenatal care for pregnant women, school breakfast programmes, and special food supplement programmes for women and children have positive effects on the cognitive development of children, according to Ernesto Pollitt, Professor of Paediatrics at the University of California.

One-third of children from low-income communities who enter kindergarten are behind their peers; in their fourth year of elementary school, 50 per cent of these children do not meet the standard for reading proficiency according to the National Center for Children in Poverty (2002).

Wertheimer (2003) found that children from poor families were less likely to be identified as academically gifted, more likely to repeat a year in school, less likely to participate in extracurricular activities, and more likely to suffer from learning disabilities and developmental delays, when compared to children who are not living in poverty.

Evidence like this indicates that children living in poverty suffer in a number of ways. Generally, their academic performance is worse than that of other children; they are less likely to enter university; and they are more likely to become teen parents and to be unemployed. In the US, a number of projects have been tried in order to counteract the most devastating effects of poverty. Pungello et al. (2006) described the benefits of the longitudinal Abecedarian Project. Between 1972 and 1977, this programme enrolled 111 infants. Around half the children were chosen at random to participate in early educational intervention, and the rest represented

Poverty has an adverse effect on a child's developmental opportunities

a control group. The programme was offered to children from poor families. The children received all-day, centre-based care throughout the year before entering kindergarten. The children in the programme are still being followed today.

The programme consisted of educational games that focused on developing cognitive and linguistic skills. Each child was offered adult–child interaction, such as talking with the child and showing him or her pictures or toys. The children also received general health care. The results showed that the programme had beneficial effects in terms of cognitive development and many other areas.

Schoon et al. (2002) investigated the long-term impact of poverty on academic achievement and attainment in adult life in a British sample. The researchers followed 30,000 individuals from birth to adulthood, from two cohorts of children. One cohort was born in 1958 and the other in 1970. The researchers adopted an *ecological* perspective of the life-course, looking at the interaction of individual and contextual factors. They found that children raised in socio-economically disadvantaged families have increased risk for poor academic performance, and that this seems to influence later success in life. Being born into a relatively disadvantaged family increases the probability of accumulated risk factors, which may set the child on a risk trajectory.

According to the researchers, the exact link between socio-economic background and individual development is not yet fully understood. It seems that there is a *cumulative effect* of positive or negative factors related to socio-economic factors. This means that individuals from more privileged homes have greater educational opportunities because of increased access to financial resources—for example, to pay for higher education—more role models, and greater parental expectations than children from less privileged backgrounds. However, early adverse experiences do not necessarily determine the life path of an individual. Werner and Smith (1992) carried out a longitudinal study of high-risk children and found that one-third had adjusted well to adult life.

Be a principled thinker

How could developmental psychologists (and politicians) use the evidence on the role of socio-economic factors to initiate programmes to create good conditions for cognitive development for all children, so that there would be equal opportunities in the education system?

Possible essay question

With reference to research, discuss how two social and environmental variables may affect cognitive development (22 marks)

Assessment advice

The command term is "discuss" which means that you have to present a considered and balanced review of factors that could affect cognitive development and say why this is so. You must include appropriate research to support your argument and evaluate the research before you arrive at a valid conclusion (criterion: critical thinking). Find the relevant knowledge in this chapter (criterion: knowledge and comprehension).

Be sure to consider what your main claim is before you outline the structure of your answer. In this essay, you need to present two factors only so structure your answer according to these two arguments (criterion: organization). Remember that you are assessed according to all three criteria (see Chapter 11).

6.2 Developmental psychology: social development

- Assess the extent to which biological, cognitive, and sociocultural factors influence human development
- Evaluate psychological research (through theories and/or studies) relevant to developmental psychology
- Examine attachment in childhood and its role in the subsequent formation of relationships
- Discuss potential effects of deprivation on trauma in childhood or later development
- Define resilience
- Discuss strategies to build resilience

Attachment and its role in the subsequent formation of relationships

Most babies of mammals exhibit the same patterns as human infants: they seek proximity to the mother and react with anxiety to separation from her, which is the essence of **attachment behaviour**. This supports the idea of an evolutionary basis of attachment. Bowlby believed that attachment was an innate pattern and that it helped infants to survive. According to Bowlby, a close relationship between the child and the mother is a basic biological need. He had observed how baby monkeys reacted with distress and screams when separated from their mother for a brief period. The mother and baby called for each other during the separation period, and the mother constantly tried to get her baby back.

Profile

John Bowlby
John Bowlby (1907–90) worked with children who had been separated from their parents during the Second World War. He observed that many of these children developed emotional problems, and he linked this to the fact of separation from the mother. He shared the psychoanalytic view that early influence (e.g. maternal deprivation) caused *permanent and irreversible damage* (Bowlby 1951). His attachment theory has been very influential.

Bowlby argued that behaviours such as smiling, babbling, grasping, and crying are genetically based social signals. These signals encourage parents to care for and interact with their baby, so that the infant will be fed, protected from danger, and provided with the affection necessary for healthy growth. According to Bowlby, attachment behaviour is characterized by a desire to be near the person the baby is attached to (proximity maintenance), returning to the attachment figure for comfort and safety in the face of distress (safe haven), reacting with distress when separated from the attachment figure (separation distress), and, finally, the attachment figure acting as a *secure base* for the child.

According to Shaffer (1996), attachment develops until around the age of seven months, when certain signs indicate the formation of specific attachment. At this age, the baby clearly shows separation anxiety when the primary attachment figure—often the mother—leaves the child. Research has shown that the infant can discriminate between a primary attachment figure and other people from around seven months. This is probably linked to brain maturation and general cognitive development. The visual system is becoming progressively more capable of making the fine distinctions necessary to recognize familiar faces and distinguish them from unfamiliar ones. It is believed that at this age the child has developed a mental representation of the attachment figure, which is what Piaget termed object permanence. This simply means that the child knows the mother exists, even when the child cannot see her. This could explain why the child protests when the mother leaves. The child also displays stranger anxiety, when unfamiliar people try to make contact with the child.

Interactional synchrony is important in formation of trust and attachment

A number of research studies have shown that maternal sensitivity is important in the development of attachment. If the caregiver does not respond to the child's signals, the child becomes very upset. Brazleton et al. (1975) carried out an observational study of mothers and babies during their interactions. The researchers found that both mothers and babies imitated each other's movements and emotional expressions, and took turns to initiate new movements. This is called **interactional synchrony**, and some of this is probably facilitated by mirror neurons. Showing interest in the baby and being responsive seem to be very important for the child psychologically. When the researchers asked the mothers to ignore their babies' signals, the babies became very upset. The study clearly shows that babies react strongly to the caregiver's signals, and that maternal responsiveness is important. Even though the mother is normally the main attachment figure, children have other attachment figures who also provide protection and comfort. In many cultures, childcare is shared. However, it is not important to attachment theory itself if there are one or more attachment figures. What is central to the theory is that attachment is not indiscriminate, but falls on specific individuals.

Internal working model

An important part of Bowlby's theory is that the developing child forms mental representations called an **internal working model** of his or her first attachment relationship. The motivation to form attachment is biologically based, but the process is based on experience. The internal working model is a cognitive schema of expectations concerning the attachment figures—for example, if they are likely to give support during times of stress.

195

The internal working model includes three important elements:

- ideas about attachment figures and what can be expected from them
- ideas about the self
- ideas about how the self and others relate.

If a child experiences love and affection, he or she come to see himself or herself as worthy of love and attention. This is the child's working model as Bowlby sees it. The working model will determine the child's relationship with other people and the way the child sees himself or herself in the future.

Working models are flexible, as they assimilate experiences. If the attachment figure occasionally provides less attention and sensitivity, it will not undermine the child's confidence, but if this continues, the working model may change. Children who have experienced neglect or rejection may develop a working model that is based not on reality, but on denial. In order for children to protect themselves from the idea that their parents do not love them, they may think that they *deserve* the neglect. Such a working model may eventually contribute negatively to mental health—for example, depression— and the quality of their relationships with others. Bowlby believed that humans tend to reproduce the internal working model in later relationships, and that inner working models like the one just described could explain "families of abuse".

Ainsworth and the strange situation paradigm

Bowlby's ideas had a major impact on the way researchers thought about children's emotional development. One of Bowlby's students, the US psychologist Ainsworth (1970), devised an experimental procedure called the **strange situation**, which resulted in a classification of attachment patterns. The strange situation is meant to measure the child's attachment behaviour, based on how the child reacts when the mother leaves and subsequently returns.

Mary Ainsworth
Mary Ainsworth (1913–99) was a US psychologist who operationalized Bowlby's concept of attachment so that it could be tested empirically. The strange situation paradigm is still widely used in research on attachment— including cross-culturally.

Ainsworth started her work on attachment patterns with the so-called Ganda project (1967) in Uganda. This was a longitudinal study using home visits, with naturalistic observations of mother–child interactions in the strange situation, and interviews with the mothers. The sample consisted of 28 unweaned babies from several villages in Uganda. When the study began, the babies ranged from 15 weeks to two years old. Ainsworth observed them every two weeks, for two hours at a time, over a nine-month period. The visits took place in the family living room, so it was a natural environment. Ainsworth used an interpreter when she interviewed the mothers.

Be a critical thinker

Is it really possible to compare animal and human behaviour when it comes to mother–child relationships? What would be in favour of such a comparison and what would be against it?

Ainsworth was particularly interested in the individual differences between mother–child pairs in terms of the quality of their attachment relationships. She made various rating scales to measure *maternal sensitivity* to the baby's signals. The babies were eventually classified into three attachment groups, based on their individual differences in relation to the strange situation. She found that the classifications correlated significantly with the ratings of the mother's sensitivity—this measure was based on interview data and observations of the amount of holding of the baby.

Ainsworth (1971) replicated the Uganda study in Baltimore, US, and she found the same distribution of attachment patterns. The sample consisted of 26 mother–infant pairs, who were each visited in their homes every three to four weeks for the first year of the baby's life.

Ainsworth's research resulted in a classification system—the Strange Situation Classification (SSC)—which had three groups of attachment types.

Types of attachment

- **Type A—avoidant** (20 per cent of the children): the child shows apparent indifference when the mother leaves the room, and avoids contact with her when she returns. The child is apparently not afraid of strangers. The mothers of type A children tend to be insensitive and do not seem interested in their child's play.

- **Type B—securely attached** (70 per cent of the children): the child is upset when the mother leaves and is happy to see her again. The child is easily comforted by the mother. The mothers of type B children are very interested in their child's play, and actively support play and communicate with their children during play.

- **Type C—ambivalent** (10 per cent of the children): the child is very upset when the mother leaves the room, and she has difficulty soothing the child when she returns. The child seeks comfort, but at the same time rejects it. The mothers of type C children tend to be inconsistent in their reactions to the children.

A supplementary attachment type suggested by Main and Solomon (1986) has now been included. Type D is characterized by **insecure-disorganised/disorientated attachment**. A child with this attachment type shows no particular reaction when the mother leaves or comes back. This attachment type has been associated with childhood abuse and chronically depressed mothers.

Factors to be considered in attachment

There seem to be a number of important factors involved in the development of attachment patterns. The first factor is *parental sensitivity*. Secure attachment is particularly dependent on emotionally responsive mothers, according to Ainsworth. Sensitive mothers tend to have securely attached babies, while insensitive mothers tend to have insecurely attached babies. This has been supported by other studies.

The strange situation is a research paradigm that explores the child's reaction to separation and reunion with the attachment figure. It includes the following episodes.

1 The parent and child are alone in a room.
2 The child explores the room without parental participation.
3 A stranger enters the room, talks to the parent, and approaches the child.
4 The parent quietly leaves the room.
5 The parent returns and comforts the child.

The second factor is the *infant's temperament*. Researchers such as Jerome Kagan (1982) suggest that innate differences in children's temperaments influence how the environment interacts with them. Kagan claims that it is more a matter of temperament than attachment that is measured in the strange situation paradigm, but not everyone is in agreement about this.

The third factor is *family circumstances*. Some families may not be capable of providing the necessary support to the child—for example, abusive families. A child's attachment type may also vary over time and setting, depending on the family's social conditions. If the family is hit by poverty or bereavement, the child may not receive the necessary support. A risk factor in the development of mental health seems to be a lack of formation of attachment to important people during childhood.

Attachment has been found to be dependent on child-rearing practices, and differences in attachment security seem to indicate differences in children's competence to regulate negative emotions and to establish positive relationships with others.

Cross-cultural studies of attachment using the strange situation

Bowlby and Ainsworth carried out most of their research in the western world. However, although attachment theory predicts that attachments will be formed, it does not claim that there is a *normative* pattern—that is, a cross-cultural, universal pattern. It only argues that attachment will be formed, regardless of the child-rearing practices used.

Maternal sensitivity is an important factor in development of secure attachment

Evolutionary psychology leaves room for globally adaptive patterns related to the culture in which children have to survive. If a culture requires the suppression of negative emotions, infants may develop avoidant attachment to meet this cultural demand. In such a culture, avoidant attachment may well be normative because it promotes general adaptation. Some researchers argue that secure attachment will be the norm where the social environment is generally supportive of the child, while insecure attachment is the norm in less supportive contexts (Main 1990).

Van Ijzendoorn and Kroonenberg (1988) carried out a major review of 32 worldwide studies, involving eight countries and over 2000 infants. They found that there are differences within cultures in the distribution of types A, B, and C. For example, Japanese studies showed a complete absence of type A, but a high proportion of type C. There seems to be a pattern of cross-cultural differences, so that type B is the most common cross-culturally. Type A is relatively more common in Western European countries, and type C is relatively more common in Japan. The difference has been associated with differences in child-rearing. The results of these studies indicate that if we want valid interpretations of the strange situation in a cross-cultural setting, we need to have good knowledge about child-rearing.

Evaluation of the strange situation paradigm

The strange situation paradigm is popular and still widely used. According to Goldberg (2000), the method is a unique combination of experimental and clinical methods. He finds it a well-standardized procedure which allows for natural interactions. Lamb (1985) claims that this widely used methodology is highly artificial and extremely limited in terms of the amount of information that is gathered, and that it fails to take into account the mother's behaviour. Marrone (1998) finds that although the strange situation has been criticized for being stressful—and therefore unethical—it is modelled on common, everyday experiences, where mothers leave their children for brief periods of time in different settings. However, it can be argued that exposing children to stress in an experimental setting is very different from what happens in everyday life.

The cross-cultural validity of the methods of assessing attachment and the meaning of the attachment classifications themselves has been questioned. The meaning of the strange situation has been challenged, in that it focuses on the measurement of attachment in terms of the infant's *reaction* to the separation and subsequent reunion with the mother. It does not take into account that the meaning of separation may differ according to culture. Japanese children are rarely separated from their mothers, so the separation during the strange situation may represent a highly unusual situation, which may mean something different for Japanese children and their mothers than for US children and their mothers.

Be a thinker: does culture influence maternal love and child-rearing?

The anthropologist Turnbull (1973) studied the Ik, a small tribe living in a remote mountain area of Uganda. He found that there was no sign of parental love towards children, such as would normally be expected. The parents were rather unhappy when a new child was born. Turnbull rarely saw signs of affection or tenderness, and the children were thrown out of the family hut at an early age and expected to take care of themselves. Seen from a western point of view, the Ik parents behaved in an "unnatural" way. However, Turnbull argues that the parents had reason to behave in this way. The living conditions of the Ik were very hard and they were often near starvation. This interfered with all social relationships and people adopted a very selfish attitude to life. Self-preservation was the most important thing, and even one's own child was seen as a competitor for food.

1 To what extent could the Ik tribe be seen as contradicting Bowlby's theory of attachment?

2 Why do most people not consider the Ik's attitude to infants as normal?

3 Is it possible to argue that culture overrides biology on the basis of this study?

The role of early attachment in the subsequent formation of relationships

Attachment theory assumes that internal working models continue throughout the lifespan, and longitudinal research indicates that they are relatively stable, although they can be modified. Research shows that there may be some relationship between the experience of attachment in childhood and adult love relationships, as predicted by Bowlby.

Hazan and Shaver (1987) were two of the first researchers to explore Bowlby's attachment theory in relation to adult romantic relationships. They found attachment theory a valuable perspective on adult love because it could explain positive emotions (caring, intimacy, trust) as well as negative ones (fear of intimacy, jealousy, emotional inconsistency).

Hazan and Shaver assumed that adult attachment behaviour is a reflection of the expectations and beliefs that people have formed about themselves and their close relationships, as a result of their experiences with early attachment figures—that is, inner working models. The researchers translated Ainsworth's three attachment styles to make them suitable for adult relationships. Then they devised a "love quiz" in a local newspaper, and asked respondents to indicate which of the three patterns best described their feelings about romantic relationships. The participants had to read the three statements shown in the box and indicate which paragraph best described their attitude to close relationships.

A self-selected sample of 620 people, aged 14–82 years, responded to the love quiz. The mean age was 36 years. There were 205 males and 415 females. A second study used a sample of 108 college students. The researchers found that about 60 per cent of respondents showed a secure attachment style, 20 per cent showed the anxious-avoidant pattern, and 20 per cent showed the anxious-ambivalent pattern. The researchers also asked participants to describe their parents' parenting style, using a simple adjective checklist. People who were securely attached said their parents had been readily available, attentive, and responsive. People who were anxious-avoidant said their parents were unresponsive, rejecting, and inattentive. People who were anxious-ambivalent said their parents were anxious, only sometimes responsive, and generally out of step with their needs.

In their article, "Romantic love conceptualized as an attachment process", Hazan and Shaver theorized that romantic love is a process that shares important similarities with early attachment relationships. They also found that differences in adult attachment were related to *beliefs* about the self and others, which could be explained by attachment theory. According to Hazan and Shaver, romantic attachment serves as a secure base against the challenges of life, and involves mutual attachment, care giving, and sex.

Although the researchers found some correlation between parenting style and adult attachment patterns, as predicted by their research hypothesis, they warned against drawing too many conclusions

Hazan and Shaver's love quiz

A I am somewhat uncomfortable being close to others; I find it difficult to trust them completely, difficult to allow myself to depend on them. I am nervous when anyone gets too close, and often, others want me to be more intimate than I feel comfortable being.

B I find it relatively easy to get close to others and am comfortable depending on them and having them depend on me. I don't worry about being abandoned or about someone getting too close to me.

C I find that others are reluctant to get as close as I would like. I often worry that my partner doesn't really love me or won't stay with me. I want to get very close to my partner and this sometimes scares people away.

about the continuity between early childhood experience and adult relationships. It would be overly deterministic to say that insecurely attached children would end up in insecure adult relationship patterns. In fact, it seems that the older people get, the more they are able to develop their own approach to life.

The study was based on a self-selected sample, which may not be representative. There was a sample bias in that more females than males participated in the study. Furthermore, self-report data may not always be reliable. Since the study was conducted in the western world, it is important to compare the results to cross-cultural research on attachment before drawing final conclusions, to see if a consistent pattern can be identified.

Potential effects of deprivation or trauma in childhood on later development

There can be many reasons for children growing up in circumstances that deprive them of the most essential care—for example, in orphanages around the world or in abusive families. But what are the consequences of deprivation or trauma in early life? Researchers agree that it may endanger healthy development, but a number of longitudinal studies have demonstrated that some children are **resilient**. Resilience refers to the ability to recover or bounce back from even very stressful events. Research shows that the consequences of early adversities are to a large extent dependent on the nature of *subsequent* life experiences.

Rutter et al. (2001) conducted a longitudinal follow-up on a group of Romanian, institution-reared children who were adopted into the UK, and they compared them to children who had been raised in UK institutions and subsequently adopted. He found that there was a significant difference in three areas. First, a substantial number of the Romanian adoptees had *attachment problems*. From parental interviews, it was clear that these children did not make a clear differentiation between adults, would go with a stranger easily, and did not check with their parents in anxiety-provoking situations. Second, there was a marked difference in measures of overactivity and cognitive impairment. Third, the Romanian children showed what the researchers called "near autistic features", which were not found in the British sample. It seems that the age of adoption was important, as there were significantly more problems in children who left Romania when they were older. Rutter argued that the chance of normal social functioning is substantially better if the child leaves the institution early. However, the researchers also found children who had endured the most long-lasting deprivation to be normally functioning by the age of six. According to Rutter, the degree of resilience in some children was remarkable. Overall, Rutter concluded that negative life events such as physical and sexual abuse have been associated with a wide range of psychiatric disorders, but that it need not end there. His study lends supports to other findings, showing that it is possible to recover from the adversities of a deprived childhood.

> ### Think about research and culture
>
> 1 Provide a brief description of the aim, procedure, and findings of Hazan and Shaver's (1987) research. Consider how methodological and cultural considerations could affect the interpretation of the results.
>
> 2 Would it be possible to conduct a study like this cross-culturally? What considerations would have to be taken into account before embarking on such research?

Children in a Romanian orphanage

Be a principled enquirer

According to the United Nations there are up to 150 million children worldwide living on the street. Do some research on street children and the life they lead.

You can start by searching for the World Street Children News website. Also try to find information on programmes and initiatives that target street children.

- Outline some risk factors which you think could potentially lead to problems later for these children.

- Which of the risk factors you have identified are included in the programmes you found? Which other factors are taken care of? Why could that be?

- Discuss with others: whose responsibility is it to help street children? Why?

Living on the streets has always been a threat to healthy development

Research in psychology

Koluchova (1971, 1991)

Clarke and Clarke (1998) claimed that deprived children can recover from even very adverse conditions if they are removed from such situations and given proper care and attention. This is supported in a classic case study of child abuse by Koluchova (1971, 1991). She undertook a longitudinal study of a pair of Czech twin boys born in 1960. The boys' mother had died when they were born and they spent their first 11 months in an institution, where they made normal progress. The father remarried and the twins lived with their father and his wife from around the age of 18 months to seven years. The stepmother kept them in conditions of severe deprivation. They spent their time in an unheated room, separated from the rest of the family, or in a cellar. They never came out, and they did not have adequate food, so they were suffering from vitamin deficiency when they were found. They had no access to exercise or stimulation of any kind, apart from the contact they had with each other. Apparently, nobody knew of their existence; but by the time they reached age seven, their situation came to the attention of the authorities. At that time, the boys could hardly walk, play, or speak. When they were found, they were sent to a preschool home for children, and eventually they were placed in foster care, and later adopted by two caring sisters.

When they were found, the twins' prognosis seemed very poor. However, after a year in a supportive environment, they were placed in a school for mentally retarded children. They made great progress and were moved to a normal school. The adoptive parents provided emotional security and intellectual stimulation. The boys' IQ scores were estimated to be around 40 at the time they were found, but by the age of 14, these had risen to around 100 for one, and 90 for the other. Their school performance was generally good and they were very motivated. They were functioning normally academically, they were socially well adjusted, and they had realistic ideas about further education. They are now married and live normal family lives.

Overall, this case study clearly indicates that if a child is removed from an extremely impoverished environment, it is possible to reverse the effects of deprivation. This was a case study with only two individuals and they had not been totally isolated, so they may have formed attachment to each other. The twins were found when they were relatively young, and their adoptive parents provided emotional and social stimulation. Other studies show that this could be a factor in facilitating successful development.

1 Based on your knowledge, explain the specific factors that influenced the boys' cognitive and social development (a) until they were found and (b) after they were found. Compare this to the findings from Rutter's study.

2 To what extent is it possible to use this case study to say something about development in general?

Resilience

The resilient child experiences the same stress as everybody else, but seems to recover so that he or she is not for ever marked by traumatic experiences. According to Schoon et al. (2002), resilience should be seen as positive adaptation, despite the experience of risk, and not as a personality attribute. Modern research in resilience acknowledges this and argues that it is important to differentiate between *specific risk factors* and *specific outcomes*—for example, how cognitive development relates to educational achievement, or how attachment problems relate to emotional development.

Generally, children are robust, but some children develop psychopathology or become criminals. Why is this? For each child who is born, development is about successful completion of a number of developmental tasks—for example, developing bonds with caregivers, being able to self-regulate, and showing initiative and pro-social behaviour. The individual child may have a difficult temperament, and there may be a number of risk factors in the child's environment that hinder normal development. Parental conflict, collapse of the family, poverty, parental drug abuse, social isolation, criminal family background, and belonging to a minority group are among the most common risk factors cited by developmental psychologists. Researchers also mention a number of potential **protective factors**, such as intelligence, sociability, special talents, close relationship to a parent or parental substitute, authoritative parents, socio-economic resources, good school, and relationships with pro-social adults.

Research shows that the consequences of early adversities are to a large extent dependent on the nature of *subsequent* life experiences. It seems that even severe deprivation may not have long-term effects if the subsequent rearing environment is good (Rutter 1981).

Resiliency research is inspired by several longitudinal studies on the relationship of life stressors in childhood to competence and adjustment in adolescence and adulthood. It seems that three factors are particularly important when it comes to protection from the damaging effects of stressful life events:

- the temperament of the child
- a close relationship with at least one parent
- social support in the community.

This is supported by Werner (2005), who studied resilience using a large-scale longitudinal design in the Kauai Longitudinal Study. According to Werner, even among children who have been exposed to multiple stressors, only a minority develop serious emotional disturbances or persistent behaviour problems. In the Kauai study, a multiracial cohort of 698 children, born in 1955 on the Hawaiian island of Kauai, were investigated at ages 1, 2, 10, 18, 32, and 40 years. Of the survivors in the sample, 30 per cent had experienced a cluster of risk factors. They had been born and raised in poverty, there were complications around birth, the family had many problems, and they were reared by mothers with hardly any education. Two-thirds of the children who had experienced four or

Profile

Emmy Werner
Emmy Werner is a US developmental psychologist whose longitudinal study of 698 infants (an entire birth cohort for the year 1955) on the Hawaiian island of Kauai has given developmental psychologists more insight into what can promote resilience. She and her colleagues found support for the link between risk factors and later problems but they also identified a number of protective factors that can balance out risk factors and help children become resilient.

more of these risk factors by the age of 2 years had developed learning or behaviour problems by the age of 10, or had delinquency records and/or mental problems by the age of 18. This is in line with earlier findings. However, one-third of the children did *not* show this pattern. They had developed into competent, confident, and caring adults, who succeeded in their school, home, and social lives. They had realistic goals and expectations for themselves, and by the age of 40, they were all working and had no specific problems. Werner linked this to the protective factors.

Strategies to build resilience

Researchers now work to find ways to protect children from the damaging effects of stressful life conditions. They want to understand how protective factors can counteract risk factors, because they can help to change or reverse expected negative outcomes. Research shows that resiliency can be cultivated by providing and promoting protective factors in the child's life. From this perspective, being resilient is to a large extent about **coping**— that is, finding appropriate ways to deal with the stressors of life. Children at risk are not able to do this by themselves.

A single risk factor does not normally affect healthy development, but it is well known that multiple risk factors often result in psychopathology. It seems that one of the most critical factors in healthy development is the relationship between parents and the child. This is why many resilience programmes include parent education. The New York Center for Children suggests the following strategies to promote resilience and prevent child abuse and neglect.

- *Home visit programmes* have proved effective, especially in high-risk families. It seems that this strategy can reduce child abuse, increase access to health care, and lower rates of maternal depression—thus enhancing the formation of attachment between mother and baby.

- *Teen mother parent education and parent groups.* Teenagers give birth to 8 per cent of babies in the US. Britner et al. (1997) found that a 12-week parenting education programme for unmarried teen mothers could prevent child abuse, improve the chance of high school graduation, and delay subsequent pregnancies. It was also found that groups for adolescent mothers were ideal for providing peer support and reducing social isolation and depression. The programme also involved the extended family in the baby's care.

- *Head Start and Early Head Start programmes* for all children and families. Love et al. (2005) found that parents who participated in Early Head Start became more emotionally supportive, better at stimulating language development, and used less corporal punishment.

- *After-school programmes* in all high-risk communities. Mahoney et al. (2005) carried out a longitudinal study of the effect of after-school programmes on the development of academic performance and motivation for disadvantaged children. They found that participants who participated in a full year's after-school programme achieved better test scores, reading achievement, and motivation.

Be a critical thinker
- Describe the findings of the study by Werner (2005). Can they be generalized?
- Which risk factors were identified?
- Why was a longitudinal design chosen?

Be a researcher
How does your community seek to promote resilience and prevent child abuse and neglect?

Lowenthal (2001) outlined strategies to teach resilience to maltreated children, suggesting that it was important to establish safe and predictable learning environments for these children. Lowenthal argues that children who experience a safe environment, learn to set realistic goals, work in small groups, participate in creative activities and to express their feelings in constructive ways. They also learn social skills (e.g. appropriate facial expressions, initiating contact), anger control, conflict management, and how to interpret the emotions and behaviours of other people. If children have the necessary support in their school work, they will eventually develop a sense of internal control, be able to cope with stress, and interact positively with other people.

Early interventions have a better rate of return than programmes introduced later in life. Engle et al. (2007) reviewed intervention programmes in developing countries (e.g. Guinea, Cape Verde, Bangladesh, Nepal). There were overall gains in skills such as sociability, self-confidence, and motivation. Some studies also found an increased rate of children entering school. The researchers found that parenting and parent–child programmes had positive effects on child development. In Jamaica, parenting practices improved when children and parents were involved in a home-visiting programme (Powel et al. 2004). In Turkey, Kagitcibasi et al. (2001) found positive short-term and long-term effects of teaching low-income mothers to play with their children.

Walker et al. (2007) studied risk factors in developing countries. In order to prevent what the researchers call the intergenerational transmission of poverty, and to build resilience in the children, they suggested food programmes and child development programmes for children with developmental problems. UNICEF has assisted governments to support parenting programmes in 60 countries, and at least 30 developing countries now have policies on early child development, according to Engle et al. (2007). The policies target improved nutrition to prevent stunting, as well as stimulation of cognitive and social-emotional skills, because these are known to provide the basis for later success in school and work. In developed countries, long-term benefits are derived from high-quality early interventions from centre-based programmes for disadvantaged children, in terms of better school achievement, better employment opportunities, better health outcomes, less welfare dependency, and lower crime rates (e.g. Currie 2001).

It seems that overall there are some strategies that are associated with success in preventing developmental problems and building resilience. First, it is more effective to provide services directly to children than simply providing information to parents. Second, it seems that demonstrations and opportunities for skill building and practice with parents increase effectiveness. It appears that early intervention can promote child development and prevent or ameliorate developmental loss, not only in developed countries, but also in developing countries.

Be reflective and caring

It is common policy in most countries to remove children at risk from their family and put them in foster care or institutions.

- Based on your knowledge from this chapter, discuss if this is to the benefit of the children.
- If you were a politician, what would you suggest to help children at risk?

Possible essay question

- Explain two potential effects of deprivation in childhood on later development.
- Discuss one strategy to build resilience. (22 marks)

Assessment advice

There are two parts in this question so be sure to address both. Take all the assessment criteria (see Chapter 11) into account. The examiner will look for relevant knowledge, evidence of critical thinking and organization. You need to structure the answer and argue clearly in favour of your claim.

The first question deals with two potential effects of deprivation on later development. Only mention two. The command term is "explain" which means that you should give a detailed account including reasons or causes. The answer should be supported by appropriate evidence.

The second part deals with strategies to build resilience. "Discuss" is a command term that requires you to offer a balanced review of one strategy. The strategy must be clearly presented and your argument should offer a range of factors and evidence in support.

Be a communicator

1 Based on your knowledge, outline three strategies that an organization would use to establish a centre to promote resilience in children in an impoverished community.

2 Write a letter to the magazine *IB World* where you argue in favour of a CAS project in such a centre, and outline how CAS students could contribute to making a positive difference.

6.3 Developmental psychology: identity development

Learning outcomes

- Assess the extent to which biological, cognitive, and sociocultural factors influence human development
- Evaluate psychological research (through theories and/or studies) relevant to developmental psychology
- Discuss the formation and development of gender roles
- Explain cultural variations of gender roles
- Describe adolescence
- Discuss the relationship between physical change and development of identity during adolescence
- Examine psychological research into adolescence

Formation and development of gender roles

When a child is born, the first thing that is noticed is the biological sex. Within a couple of years, the children themselves declare that they are a boy or a girl, and behave accordingly. Are there innate psychological differences between men and women, or are the differences due to socialization? Nearly all societies expect males and females to behave differently and to assume different gender roles. In order to live up to such expectations, the child must learn what it means to be a boy or a girl in the culture in which he or she is raised. All researchers agree that gender role socialization begins as soon as the newborn child has been identified as a boy or a girl. The child is given a name—a label—that will signal its sex to the rest of the world. After this, the world around them will treat them accordingly.

When children are around two years old, they can correctly label their own or another person's sex or gender. This is called **gender identity**. Development of gender identity is a step towards assuming a **gender role**, but it is only around the age of seven that children realize that no matter what clothes you wear or what you do, you still remain a male or a female. This is called **gender constancy**.

Men and women tend to occupy different social roles, and in most cultures there are ideas of what is typical or appropriate behaviour, according to biological sex. Children are socialized to assume appropriate gender roles through child-rearing practices. The anthropologists Whiting and Edwards (1973) studied children in Kenya, Japan, India, the Philippines, Mexico, and the US. In the majority of these societies, girls were more nurturing and made more physical contact. Boys were more aggressive, dominant, and engaged in more rough-and-tumble play. The researchers interpreted the gender differences in the six cultures as differences in socialization pressures—for example, the extent to which older girls were required to perform "nurturing tasks", such as looking after younger siblings.

Most toys are gender specific — could this be a preparation for adult life and gender roles?

There has long been controversy about the relative importance of either **nature** or **nurture** in the development of gender roles. It has been argued that basic biological and hormonal factors are important in the development of gender identity—that is, the psychological feeling of being either male or female is a result of biology (*nature*). The nature view holds that a child's gender identity is programmed before birth by genes and hormones, and is unchangeable. The *nurture* view claims that the way a child is dressed and treated is the most important factor in the development of gender identity. The child may have an innate sense of gender, but will learn to think and behave like either a girl or a boy. If this were true, theoretically it would be possible to override genetic sex and turn a boy into a girl, and make him think that he is a girl.

Biological explanations

Evolutionary psychologists claim that men and women have faced different evolutionary challenges, which have resulted in gender differences. The natural selection process has created fundamental biological as well as psychological differences that determine the gender division of labour. Men are competitive and aggressive because this increases their chance of attracting a partner and providing resources for their children. Women are nurturing because they need to raise the children and attract a partner who will provide for them and their children. Evolutionary explanations of gender roles are controversial. Critics of the theory argue that differences in gender roles are not the result of evolution, but rather a consequence of the different roles that cultures assign to men and women, as well as agreement on socialization practices that prepare children for these roles.

The biological difference between boys and girls is related to genetic sex, which is determined by chromosomes. For girls it is XX and for boys it is XY. During prenatal development, sex hormones are released, causing the external genitals and internal reproductive organs of the fetus to become male or female. It is the presence or absence of male hormones (androgens) that makes a difference

Profile

Karen Horney (1885–1952) was a German doctor trained as a psychoanalyst—a therapist using Sigmund Freud's methods. She moved to New York in 1934 where she established a private practice and trained new psychoanalysts at the New York Psychoanalytic Institute. She was forced to resign because her views differed too much from traditional Freudian ideas—especially in relation to women. She was totally against Freud's ideas that "anatomy is destiny", which means that biological sex determines your fate. According to Horney, personality traits are more determined by cultural factors than by biological factors. She was one of the first feminist psychologists and according to her, a masculine culture does not provide equal opportunities to men and women. She claimed that if women at her time wanted to appear like men it was because women were generally regarded as inferior to men.

The role of hormones—the theory of psychosexual differentiation

Some researchers argue that testosterone has a masculinization effect on the brain of the developing child, and that this can explain behavioural differences as well as gender identity in children. This is the **theory of psychosexual differentiation**. The theory holds that, like all animals, humans are born with innate predispositions to act and feel like females or males. The hormone testosterone is the key to developing the body as well as the mind. Prenatal exposure to testosterone establishes a male brain circuitry and inhibits the development of female brain circuits. According to this theory, prenatal exposure to hormones is the most important factor in the development of gender identity, and socialization plays a subsidiary role. This is supported to a certain extent by research with animals. If female rat fetuses are injected with testosterone, they behave like male rats. They do not exhibit normal female sexual behaviour in adulthood, even if they are given injections of the female hormone oestrogen at that time. This is taken as evidence that the testosterone has masculinized the developing brain of the female rat. However, is this enough to show that biological factors are the most important in determining gender role identity in humans?

The role of socialization—the biosocial theory of gender role development

The view that socialization is the most important factor in gender identity was addressed in the theory of "gender neutrality", or the **biosocial theory of gender development**, suggested by Money and Ehrhardt (1972). The theory sees the *interaction* between biological and social factors as important, rather than simply the direct influence of biology. Money and Ehrhardt claimed that biological factors such as hormones, in combination with how the child is labelled sexually, determine the way the child is socialized. Development of gender identity and adherence to gender role is primarily a consequence of socialization. According to Money, children are *gender neutral* at birth. Gender identity is the result of socialization—or nurture. This idea was welcomed by feminists, who had long claimed that there was no difference between men and women.

Money based his theory on case studies of individuals born with ambiguous genitals—termed **intersex** in the medical literature. This could be a baby girl, born with masculinized genitals, because she has been exposed to high levels of testosterone while in the womb. Or it could be a baby boy, born with a tiny penis that looks like a clitoris, because he was not exposed to enough testosterone. Money studied intersex children in the 1950s. He found that children who had been born as genetically female, but were raised as boys, thought of themselves as boys. Money then theorized that humans are not born with a gender identity, and that therefore it is possible to reassign sex within the first two years of life. The consequence of this was that any child with ambiguous genitals could be operated on and assigned whichever sex was most suitable. Psychologically, the child would adopt the assigned gender identity and grow up to be a perfectly happy man or woman. The theory has been extremely influential, and many doctors still perform operations on intersex children in line with Money's ideas. The question, of course, is whether individual cases can be used to say something more general about the development of gender identity. One of the most famous case studies in psychology indicates that this may be problematic.

209

Research in psychology

David Reimer

The case study of a boy who was turned into a girl at the age of 22 months was for many years used as "proof" that gender socialization is more important than biological sex. It was reproduced in all psychology textbooks, and nobody really questioned Money's evidence until the identity of the individual in the case study was suddenly revealed.

David Reimer was born in 1965 in Canada, the elder of twin boys. His parents named him Bruce. Eight months later, his penis was accidentally burnt off while he was undergoing a routine circumcision. The parents contacted Dr John Money, who worked at the prestigious Johns Hopkins University in Baltimore, US. They had seen him on television, in a programme about intersex children. Money declared that it was possible for an individual to change gender successfully through surgery, hormone replacement, and socialization. He claimed that the *assigned* sex determined gender identity—not the genetic sex. For David's parents, this meant hope. Money was thrilled because this was a unique case—a natural experiment—that could help him to apply his theory to *all* children. The evidence from a child who was born with normal genitals and had been brought up as a boy until the age of seven months would be powerful, especially since his identical twin was a perfectly matched control. This case might be seen as the ultimate test of the hypothesis that biological factors could be overcome by socialization.

Money advised the parents to let the boy grow up as a girl, since the child's gender identity was not yet developed. At the age of 22 months, the boy was surgically castrated, given oestrogen, and had a vaginal canal constructed. Bruce became Brenda, and was consequently raised as a girl. In Money's account of the case, the girl behaved as a typical girl and preferred dresses to trousers. He took this as evidence that his theory was correct. However, David Reimer later revealed that he never really felt like a girl. He hated dresses and preferred to play with his brother's toys. He was very lonely and felt different from other girls. He also felt intimidated by Money. In adolescence, he refused to have further surgery or to take any more oestrogen. When he was 15, his parents finally revealed the truth. He felt very relieved and decided to become a male again. He took the name David and underwent reconstructive surgery to have a penis. He even met a woman with three children, whom he married at the age of 21.

The journalist Colapinto (2000), who interviewed him when he was 31 and wrote a book called *As Nature Made Him*, further describes how David hated the visits to Money, who made him feel humiliated, confused, and unhappy. In Colapinto's view, David's case is living proof that Money's theory was not correct. There are also serious ethical issues in this case study, as it appears that Money misused David for the purposes of his own scientific career. He withheld information that went against his theory, and he did not treat David according to ethical guidelines that are now commonly accepted.

This case study seriously questions Money's theory that socialization can override biological factors. In fact, it lends support to the theory of hormonal psychosexual differentiation. Today, developmental psychologists tend to adopt an interactional approach. Psychosocial development is a *combination* of biology and the sociocultural environment. This makes sense if we consider the important changes in gender roles that have taken place over the last 50 years in the western world. Although many feminists support the view that gender roles are socially and culturally constructed, and therefore can be changed, the findings of the case study of David Reimer suggest that biology may be more important than some might wish to acknowledge.

Be a thinker

1 What reasons could Money have to suggest that socialization was more important than biology? Could such a theory be suggested today?

2 Explain the ethical issues involved in this case study and how these could affect the interpretation of the data.

3 Discuss the role of biological sex in gender identity.

Social learning theory and development of gender roles

According to social learning theory, one reason boys and girls behave differently is that they are treated differently by their parents and others. It is also known that boys and girls are often given different toys and have their rooms decorated differently. Generally, children learn to behave in ways that are rewarded by others, and to avoid behaviours that are punished or frowned on. This is known as **direct tuition**.

There are two important factors in social learning theory. The first is the presence or absence of *reward* for gender-appropriate behaviour, and *punishment* for gender-inappropriate behaviour. The second factor is *modelling* of behaviour demonstrated by same-sex models. The learning process is individual because the child learns through direct interaction with the physical environment. By observing others behaving in particular ways and then imitating that behaviour, children receive positive reinforcement from significant others for behaviour that is considered appropriate for their sex (Bandura 1977).

The children themselves act as "gender police". Fagot (1985) carried out an observational study of the behaviour of children aged between 21 and 25 months. She found that boys made fun of other boys who played with dolls or with girls. Neither did the girls like it when a girl started playing with a boy. It seems that there are similar pressures from peers among older children. The children in this study were very young, so it is unlikely that gender identity had been achieved. This could indicate that the observed behaviour might be based on a basic in-group/out-group identification. Sroufe et al. (1993) observed children around the age of 10–11 years, and found that those who did not behave in a gender-stereotyped way were the least popular. These studies indicate that children establish a kind of social control in relation to gender roles very early, and it may well be that peer socialization is an important factor in gender development.

A strength of social learning theory is that it takes into account the social and cultural context in which gender socialization occurs. It predicts that children acquire internal standards for behaviour through reward and punishment—either by personal or vicarious experience. A number of empirical studies support the notion of modelling. One weaknesses of social learning theory is that it cannot explain why there seems to be considerable variation in the degree to which individual boys and girls conform to gender role stereotypes. A second limitation is that the theory suggests that gender is more or less passively acquired. Research actually shows that this is not the case. Children are active participants in the socialization process, and they perceive and understand their experiences differently as they develop cognitively. Developing gender identity is a rather complex process that involves cognitive processes as well as environmental and biological factors.

Gender roles follow cultural norms

Gender schema theory and development of gender roles

Gender schemas are mental representations of the genders—for example, gender stereotypes. Gender schema theory is based on the

211

assumption that cognitive processes play a key role in the development of gender identity (Martin and Halvorson 1978), and that children actively construct gender identity based on their experiences. The theory argues that the most important factor in gender identity is children's ability to label themselves as boys or girls. Once they can do that, they have established a "gender schema" that guides subsequent information processing.

Children's tendency to categorize on the basis of gender leads them to perceive boys and girls as different. Once they have identified themselves as male or female, they are motivated to be like others in their group, and this leads them to observe same-sex role models more carefully. According to Martin and Halvorson, children have mental representations of what is suitable for boys and for girls. They have a gender schema for their own sex (the in-group) and for the opposite sex (the out-group). These schemas include information about attributes, activities, and objects that are gender consistent. Gender schemas determine what children pay attention to, what they interact with, and what they remember. A boy is generally more interested in toys or activities that conform to his gender schema, and he will be more likely to imitate same-sex models. This is because gender schemas serve as an internal, self-regulating standard. However, gender schemas may become a self-fulfilling prophecy or a stereotype threat. Cultural beliefs about females and males are incorporated in the gender schema, and this influences the way children think about themselves and their possibilities.

An experiment by Martin and Halvorson (1983) showed how information may be distorted to fit existing schemas. The researchers used a sample of boys and girls aged 5–6 years. They showed them pictures of males and females in activities that were either in line with gender role schemas—for example, a girl playing with a doll—or inconsistent with gender role schemas—for example, a girl playing with a gun. A week later, the children were asked to remember what they had seen on the pictures. The children had distorted memories of pictures that were not consistent with gender role schemas—they remembered the picture of a girl playing with a gun as a picture of a boy playing with a gun.

A strength of gender schema theory is that it can explain why children's gender roles do not change after middle childhood. The established gender schemas tend to be maintained because children pay attention to and remember information that is consistent with these schemas. This is in line with the findings of research on gender stereotyping. Another strength of gender schema theory is that it depicts children as actively trying to make sense of the world by using their current knowledge.

One limitation of gender schema theory is that there is too much focus on the individual child in gender development. Social and cultural factors are not taken into account. Another problem is that it is not really possible to explain how and why gender schemas develop and take the form that they do.

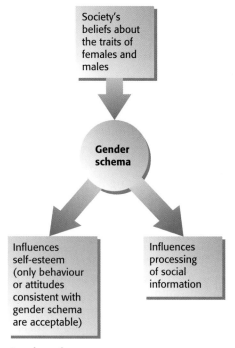

Gender schema

Sociocultural influences on development of gender roles

One major controversy in psychology is whether gender roles are universal. Cross-cultural studies of gender can help to determine to what extent culture plays a role in the creation and maintenance of gender roles.

Historically, females and males have had different jobs in almost every culture, and they still do. Gender-based divisions of labour probably came about as a consequence of childbearing and the nursing abilities of women, and the fact that men are generally bigger and stronger. Work that is compatible with child-rearing tends to be assigned to women. Eagly (1987) put forward the **social role theory**, which suggests that gender stereotypes arise from the differing roles men and women typically occupy. Women are seen as best suited for the roles they typically have, and men are seen as most suited to what they do normally. In many societies, there are gender ideologies that constrain the activities of men and women. Roles are allocated, consistent with societal beliefs about the nature of women and men. These beliefs are often expressed directly—for example, through religious teaching or through people's daily communications.

According to Williams and Best (1990), gender stereotypes arise out of gender roles. Once the stereotypes act as norms for men and women, they provide models for gender role socialization. The purpose of this is to teach children what is socially appropriate and to prepare them for adult roles. Research has demonstrated that children display gender stereotypes very early. Best et al. (1977) conducted a cross-cultural study on gender stereotypes with a sample of children in the UK, Ireland, and the US, aged five and eight years. They found that the majority of boys and girls in the two age groups agreed that females were soft-hearted, whereas males were strong, aggressive, cruel, and coarse. Many more characteristics were stereotyped in the group of eight-year-olds, and they were quite similar to stereotypes obtained in studies with adults.

The anthropologist Mead (1935) compared gender roles in three New Guinean tribes who lived within a radius of 100 miles, and published the results in her famous book, *Sex and Temperament*. Before she went to New Guinea, Mead already believed that what are called masculine and feminine traits are the result of culture (or ideology) rather than biological sex. The evidence she collected seemed to support this, since she found very different conceptions of gender roles in the three tribes. Although her research was carried out many years ago and has been criticized by other researchers, her observations are still thought-provoking

In the Arapesh tribe, men and women were cooperative, gentle, and loving—the western stereotype of female behaviour. Men and women shared the tasks relating to the crops and children. In the Mundugumor tribe, men and women were arrogant, competitive, and emotionally unresponsive. They were always quarrelling, and neither men nor women were interested in the children, so they quickly became self-reliant. This was a human trait that was highly

Be a critical thinker

- What is the evidence that gender roles are biologically based?

- What is the evidence that gender roles are learned in social and cultural contexts?

- In what ways can anthropological evidence contribute to an understanding of formation and development of gender roles? Support your argument.

Division of labour in a society has historically been based on gender

valued by the Mundugumor. The last tribe was the Tchambuli. The men here were the opposite of traditional western gender roles: they spent most of their time gossiping with other men, and discussing things like body adornments. The women were responsible for the production of food, and making tools and clothes.

Most traditional cultures distinguish between men's and women's work, but Mead's study shows that labour division is not the same in all cultures. If one can find cultures where gender roles are so different, this supports the view that such roles are not universal or uniquely based on biological differences. This was exactly Mead's point. She argued that human behaviour is not determined by genes alone, but that it is the product of the beliefs and values of a culture. Mead has been criticized for being biased in her research and ignoring the role of biological factors. However, her research does indicate that cultural demands could play a larger role in gender role development than biological factors. She also showed that cross-cultural research is important, because it provides knowledge that questions the assumption that gender roles are universal and therefore unchangeable.

This is clearly demonstrated throughout the 20th century in the western world, where gender roles have changed steadily. Women have entered the labour market, and in the Scandinavian countries around 76 per cent of women are now employed. Women are entering all kinds of professional fields, although there is still a gender difference in certain areas. There are more women than men working as nurses and midwives, for example, and there are more men than women working as plumbers and engineers. Of course, women still have children, but in the Scandinavian countries the children spend the day in kindergarten, so that the mothers can work; fathers participate in childcare and have the right to paternal leave. Research shows that being fathers is an important part of their identity. In Denmark, for example, there are several "father clubs" on the social networking website Facebook, where young fathers can discuss their roles and arrange meetings. A research study from Roskilde University by Reinicke (2006) has revealed that young fathers in Denmark say that it is important for them to have close contact with their baby and take part in caring for the child. This clearly indicates that Mead had a point when she said that gender role ideology has a crucial impact on what is expected from men and women, and that gender role differences reflect cultural expectations.

Possible essay question

Discuss two factors relevant to the formation and development of gender roles

Explain cultural variations of gender roles (22 marks)

Assessment advice

This is a parted question so be sure to answer both parts. Even though it is a parted question, take all the assessment criteria (see Chapter 11) into account, and also organization. You need to structure each part and argue clearly in favour of your claim.

The first part of the question deals with two factors that could be relevant to the formation and development of gender roles. Part a is worth more marks than part b so spend more time on this. "Discuss" is a command term that requires you to offer a balanced review of two strategies. The answer could focus on two psychological theories related to gender role development, for example a biological and a cognitive theory but it could be any relevant explanation. Each of them must be clearly presented and your argument should offer two factors and empirical evidence in support of your argument.

The second part of the question deals with cultural variations of gender roles. The command term is "explain" which means that you should give a detailed account which includes reasons or causes for your explanation. The answer should be supported by appropriate evidence, for example anthropological evidence or a psychological theory like social role theory.

Be reflective: nature or nurture?

1 Why are there differences in gender roles? Discuss this in light of your knowledge.

2 If gender roles are biologically based, is it possible to change them?

3 Find two examples of what is typical of gender roles in your culture. Discuss if it would be possible to change these roles.

Adolescence and the relationship between physical change and the development of identity

In the western world, adolescence is defined as the period of development between puberty—the age at which the young person becomes capable of sexual reproduction—and adulthood. The World Health Organization describes the period of life between 10 and 20 as adolescence, but there are cultural variations in the ages considered to represent adolescence. In western cultures, teenagers are generally not considered mature enough to assume the responsibilities and rights of adulthood, but in other cultures there is practically no time between sexual maturity and adulthood.

All individuals experience the same bodily changes during puberty, but the sequence of changes may vary. Young people experience a growth spurt, which means they change dramatically in size and shape. They also reach puberty, which means they reach sexual maturity and become capable of having children themselves. Until puberty, boys and girls produce roughly the same amount of "male hormones" (e.g. testosterone) and "female hormones" (e.g. oestrogen). At the start of puberty, the pituitary gland causes a surge of sex hormones, so that girls produce more oestrogen and boys more testosterone.

The physical growth spurt is accompanied by an increase in the distribution of body fat and muscle tissue, as well as the maturation of the reproductive organs. The young person has to become familiar with his or her new body, and hopefully establish a positive body image as he or she integrates a revised self-schema. It may well be that cognitions about the body are more important for self-esteem in adolescence than at any other time in life. The examples of eating disorders, especially in the western world, may indicate that adolescence is a sensitive time as regards body image.

Girls typically experience the growth spurt between the ages of 10 and 13. This is around two to three years before boys. The body grows taller and heavier, and gradually assumes an adultlike appearance. The most noticeable changes in girls are the development of breasts and a widening of the hips. For boys, the growth spurt is characterized by a broadening of the shoulders and an increase in muscle strength. This often brings boys closer to their body ideal. For girls, the gain in body fat and rapid weight gain is not always welcome, because it does not fit with the western ideal of thinness.

Sexual maturation, or puberty, normally takes place two years earlier in girls than in boys. Breasts develop during a period of three to four years, as fatty tissue accumulates around the nipples. Pubic hair appears and the sex organs begin to mature. The time of the first menstruation—called **menarche**—is about 12 years in the West. In the years following the onset of menstruation, girls complete their sexual maturation, as the breasts develop fully and hair appears on the arms, legs, and armpits.

For boys, sexual maturation starts with an enlargement of the testes around the age of 11–12, followed by a growth of the scrotum and the appearance of pubic hair. The penis grows, and sperm production begins at about 15 years. Boys also grow facial hair and body hair. A sign of sexual maturity is the lowering of the voice, which is due to growth of the larynx and a lengthening of the vocal cords. This is a period when the boy's voice may start "cracking", because he has to adjust to the larger size of the larynx.

Consequences of puberty on identity

The dramatic physical changes in the adolescent body are related to changes in identity, and adolescents become increasingly aware of their own sexuality at this time. It is not always possible for adolescents to explore this sexuality, as this is an area that is heavily influenced by social and cultural norms. While some cultures have a permissive attitude to adolescent sexuality and allow for experimentation, other cultures are very restrictive and do not accept premarital sex at all.

The changing body also affects body image. Some teenagers are quite happy about their new looks because they look more like adults. However, it seems that a significant group of young people suffer from **body image dissatisfaction**. This is the feeling that there is a discrepancy between the young person's body image and their ideas of what an ideal body should look like. Researchers have found body image dissatisfaction to be a strong predictor of teenage depression, eating disorders, exercise dependence, and steroid use among young people in the US, according to Stice and Withenton (2002).

Boys' body images are generally more positive than those of girls, and boys are much more likely than girls to welcome weight gain. According to the **cultural ideal hypothesis** suggested by Simmons and Blyth (1987), puberty brings boys closer to their ideal body, whereas girls move further away from theirs. Cultural demands on boys are that they should be big and strong. Boys are generally not dissatisfied with their body unless they become overweight, or if they are not as muscular and large as they would like to be. Early maturing boys tend to be satisfied with their bodies because they conform to cultural stereotypes of masculinity, whereas late maturing boys normally express dissatisfaction with their bodies until they have reached the same level as their peers.

The cultural ideal hypothesis predicts that since the cultural demand for female thinness is prevalent in the West, girls should be more likely to express body dissatisfaction and to diet than boys. This is indeed what research has found. In western cultures, girls show more concern about their appearance and express more worry about how other people will respond to them, according to Caufmann and Steinberg (1996). Teenage girls want to be seen as attractive. If their body appears to be far from the cultural ideal of slimness that dominates in the West, they develop a negative body image and low self-esteem. This is also likely to happen if the body develops at a pace that is very different from the other girls around them. Early maturers tend to have less positive body images. There are consistent findings that body dissatisfaction is the norm among girls in the West.

There are cultural differences in the way adolescents relate to bodily changes in puberty. Ferron (1997) conducted a small-scale survey in

The cultural ideal hypothesis predicts that adolescent males are happier with their new body than adolescent females

which she used semi-structured interviews to collect data in a cross-cultural sample, consisting of 60 US and 60 French adolescents. Boys and girls were equally represented. One of the themes in the interview was how bodily changes during puberty affected body image, and how the adolescents coped with it. Ferron found that the most important cultural differences between US and French adolescents were based on their beliefs about the possibility of reaching the ideal body image.

Ferron found that 75 per cent of the US adolescents did not accept any biological predisposition in terms of body shape. They were convinced that they could obtain a perfect body if they tried hard enough and adhered to specific rules. Of the Americans, 80 per cent believed in the effectiveness of specific diets or exercise programmes, but less than half the French adolescents believed this to be the case. The Americans were also more likely to suffer from self-blame and guilt, and to adopt unhealthy weight-regulating strategies, such as unbalanced diets or continuous physical exercise. The French sample had perceptions of ideal body image as well. However, 75 per cent of them acknowledged that physical appearance is predetermined and could not possibly be extensively modified through willpower or particular behaviour. The only thing they considered blameworthy was signs of physical carelessness. Ferron also found that 75 per cent of the American girls believed that their personal worth depended on the way they look. This is why they would do almost anything to get as close as possible to the ideal body image.

If adolescents internalize distorted schemas about what a normal and attractive body looks like, they may become unhappy with their own body shape, even if it is perfectly healthy. The fact that a growing number of teens are in fact overweight, or even obese, only adds to the number of psychological problems related to body image and self-esteem in puberty.

Psychological research into adolescence

Erikson (1902–1994) formulated a theory of lifelong development in his influential book *Childhood and Society* (1950). The fifth stage of his theory concerns adolescence. He saw this period as a time of *identity crisis*, and he termed the stage **identity versus role confusion**. According to Erikson, this stage of identity crisis is marked by the rapid physical growth and hormonal changes which take place between 12 and 18 years of age. The self-concept changes or develops as a result of the "developmental crisis". According to Erikson, issues of identity are particularly important in adolescence, because it is important to develop a strong sense of personal identity. The individual searches for a new sense of continuity and sameness, and is concerned with questions of sexuality, future occupation, and identity. Erikson called this a **moratorium**—that is, a time to experience different possibilities—which involves identity confusion and the search for an individual identity. If the identity crisis is resolved successfully, the adolescent will feel confident about his or her identity and possible occupation in the future. The danger at this stage is **role confusion**—that is, uncertainty about who one is and what one is to become. To counteract this uncertainty, the

Be a thinker

1 How may cultural ideals influence adolescents' body image?

2 Discuss how globalization could influence cultural ideals of body image.

217

adolescent may engage in subgroups and develop a negative or socially unacceptable identity. According to Erikson, a negative identity may be preferable to no identity at all for an adolescent. The young person may stick with an identity as addict, delinquent, or football hooligan, if more attractive alternatives seem unavailable. He claims that adolescents must establish an adult personality and develop a commitment to work and a role in life. They need to prepare for the next stage—**intimacy versus isolation**—when they have to commit themselves to another person. According to Erikson, one needs a strong sense of identity in order to become intimate with another person, but there is a risk. Some people are afraid of intimacy; they fear commitment because they are afraid of losing his or her own identity.

There is some support for the theory's description of the adolescent developmental crisis. Espin et al. (1990) undertook a longitudinal case study that tested Erikson's ideas. The researchers carried out a content analysis of 71 letters from a Latin American girl to her teacher over a period of nine years, between the ages of 13 and 22. It appeared to be a traumatic period in her life, because she and her parents were arrested for political reasons. When the researchers investigated changes of themes in the letters in relation to age, they found that themes of identity predominated in the earlier letters, and increased from 13 to 18 years, but then declined. This showed that issues of identity were prominent in the period predicted by Erikson. Themes of intimacy, which appear in early adult life according to Erikson's theory, increased steadily through the next period, but became predominant after the age of 19. This was a single case study, so the findings cannot be generalized, but it lends support to Erikson's theory. If this study could be corroborated with similar research, the results would be better supported.

There is also evidence that adolescents do not necessarily experience a developmental crisis. Rutter et al. (1976) conducted a study on the Isle of Wight, off the south coast of England, to investigate the concept of crisis. The adolescents of the entire island participated in the study, so it was a representative sample for a community (cohort). There were 2030 participants, aged 14–15 years. The researchers used questionnaires from parents and teachers, and interviews. There were two areas of interest in the study. The first was conflict between parents and children (generation gap), and the second was "inner turmoil", in terms of observed behavioural or psychiatric disorders.

The study found that the average adolescent is not in a state of crisis and conflict with their parents. A minority of the sample experienced this, most often when there were psychiatric problems of some sort. This is not in line with Erikson's predictions. The study also found that only one-fifth of the adolescents reported feeling miserable or depressed.

These results question the idea of adolescence as a time of crisis and turmoil. Some teenagers experience problems with identity and with their parents, but adolescent turmoil could be a myth. The fact that it was a **cohort study**—that is, all adolescents born in the same years on the island—increases the validity of the data. The combination

It takes a strong sense of identity to establish an intimate relationship with another person, according to Erikson. See also page 200 on the role of attachment in formation of relationships

of interviews and questionnaires, with adolescents as well as parents and teachers, gave credibility to the results, because the data could be corroborated. However, there are always problems concerning the reliability of self-report data.

Another problem is that Erikson's theory is western biased. Not all cultures have the equivalent of adolescence, because some young people go directly to adulthood. Condon (1987) reviewed anthropological evidence on the Inuit of the Canadian Arctic from the beginning of the 20th century. In that society, young women were regarded as adults at puberty, when they were usually married and began having children. Young men were treated as adults when they could build an igloo, hunt large animals on their own, and support themselves and their families. The difficult living conditions in the Arctic meant that there was no time for teenagers to spend several years thinking about what they were going to do with their lives, or developing their identity. This questions the universality of Erikson's theory.

Erikson's theory is a stage theory based on the assumption that development is *universal*, sequential, and characterized by specific developmental tasks at each stage, although there may be individual differences in terms of when and how it is experienced. Today, stage theories dealing with psychological development are being questioned. Due to growing cross-cultural evidence, such as that mentioned above, it is also clear that the stages described by Erikson are not applicable to other cultures. Erikson's theory is *descriptive* and not explanatory, which is seen as a weakness by some. In spite of these reservations, his theory is often cited in psychology textbooks, and one reason for this is that it is the only theory dealing with lifelong development.

In western cultures there may be room for a moratorium. This is not possible in all cultures. Erikson's idea of a moratorium was meant to make the transition easier, but this is not always so, because each individual faces the task of finding an identity on their own. There is no clear procedure to follow.

There is evidence that identity formation is not a project of adolescence alone. O'Connell (1976) conducted retrospective interviews with a sample of married women with children in school. The study showed that the women had experienced an increasingly strong sense of identity when moving from adolescence and further on, due to experiences such as marriage and having a child. The study indicates that identity formation is a lifelong project related to experiences. Another problem is that young people experience *gradual* rather than sudden changes in identity and self-esteem during normal development. Finally, crisis can occur throughout adult life. Identity formation may be very prominent in early adult years, but identity formation is not only a phenomenon of adolescence.

Be a critical thinker

Erikson's theory was developed in the 1950s in the USA. His ideas on adolescence were primarily based on his clinical work with adolescent boys, but he also did some research on Native American children (Sioux).

- Are his ideas on adolescence culturally biased? Why or why not?
- To what extent is his theory supported by empirical evidence?
- Is it possible to formulate a universal theory of development? Support your argument.

Be reflective and be an enquirer

1 What constitutes an individual's identity? Is it possible to come up with a complete description?

2 Design a small interview study with two or three adolescents. Ask them how they have experienced the transition from childhood to adolescence, in terms of changes in identity and their relationship with their parents.

7.1 Health psychology: stress

Learning outcomes

- Discuss the extent to which biological, cognitive, and sociocultural factors influence health-related behaviour
- Evaluate psychological research (through theories and/or studies) relevant to health psychology
- Describe stressors
- Discuss physiological, psychological and social aspects of stress
- Evaluate strategies for coping with stress

Introduction

Health psychology is a new discipline within the field of applied psychology. It can be defined as "the scientific study of psychological processes related to health and health care" (Friedman and Adler 2007).

Today, most of the serious infections that previously caused death have been eliminated in the western world. The focus on health is now, to a large extent, on prevention because it is now acknowledged that many health problems are related to lifestyle. It is believed that if people can change their lifestyle, their general health will improve. Therefore, the focus of prevention is a core concept in public health, as demonstrated by the foundation of the World Health Organization (WHO) in 1948. In the Declaration of Alma-Ata in 1978, the positive aspects of health were further reinforced, with a focus on complete physical, mental, and social well-being. Since 2001, the American Psychological Association (APA) has added "promoting health" as the key element of its mission statement.

> Health is a state of complete physical, mental and social well-being, and not merely the absence of disease and infirmity. (WHO)

Profile

Aaron Antonovsky

Aaron Antonovsky (1923–94) was a professor of medical sociology, who conducted research on the sociological and psychological aspects of health. He wondered why some people stay healthy, in spite of extreme stressors. It appeared to him that instead of focusing on why people become ill, it was perhaps more reasonable to focus on why some people stay healthy. These ideas came to him when he carried out research into problems among Israeli women during menopause. His target group was women who had been in Nazi concentration camps, some of whom were confident and happy, despite their traumatic experiences.

Health psychologists are concerned with understanding how different factors, such as biology, behaviour, and sociocultural contexts, influence health behaviour and the development of illness. Within this field, people are considered as "systems"—that is, health problems are caused by a combination of factors, such as genetic predisposition (biological), behaviours and beliefs (e.g. lifestyle and health beliefs), and sociocultural context (e.g. family, social support, and cultural influences).

This approach has led to the **biopsychosocial model** of health and illness, which is widely adopted within the field. The model takes into consideration the different systems that are linked together. This affects the explanation of health problems, as well as the strategies to deal with them. Many health psychologists are involved in research on how to prevent illness, as well as how to promote health and reduce health risks. The goal of health psychology is to find ways to help people to stay healthy, and to start and adhere to treatments—for example, in relation to alcoholism, stress, and obesity. The way to do this, according to the biopsychosocial model, is to address various factors within the system in order to prevent or treat health problems.

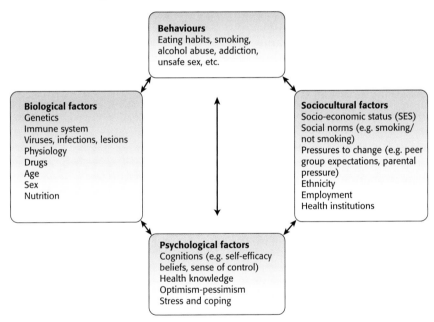

The system approach within the biopsychosocial model

Stress and stressors

When was the last time that you experienced a pounding heart, a rapid pulse, sweating hands, and "butterflies" in your stomach? No matter what the occasion was, you know what it feels like to be stressed. These symptoms are the body's response to a new or threatening situation.

Generally, stress is described as a negative emotional experience, accompanied by various physiological, cognitive, and behavioural changes. When dealing with stress, psychologists often consider the factors set out in the figure shown on the next page.

Being constantly accessible can be a stressor – for some it is very difficult to turn off the computer

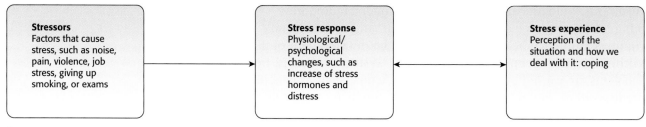

Stress concepts

Any adverse or challenging event—physiological or psychosocial—could be labelled a stressor. According to Professor of Neurology Robert Sapolsky of Stanford University, humans are the only species that can *imagine* stressors. People react in exactly the same way physiologically and psychologically if they think that their boss will fire them as if they were actually facing the stressful situation of losing their job. The word "stress experience" does not mean that it is necessarily a conscious experience. The body reacts to the stressors whether they are conscious or not. Beliefs and expectations also seem to play a role in the intensity and character of people's methods of coping with stressors.

Acute stressors appear suddenly, do not last long, and call for immediate attention. This is the case with physical injury or the attack of a predator. The body will move into a state of alert and deal with the stress, eventually returning to what is called **homeostasis**—that is, the balance between the external environment and the body's normal physiological state. **Chronic stressors** last for a long time and are a constant source of worry. This kind of stress is dangerous because it affects the body in many damaging ways, partly because of a rise in the stress hormone cortisol. In chronic stress, the body does not return to homeostasis because the stressor is constantly present—whether real or imagined.

There are many examples of stressors in life. People who work as air-traffic controllers or CEOs, for example, experience high levels of stress. The same is often true of those who work as nurses, doctors, counsellors, or teachers. People in jobs that require them constantly to meet deadlines, as is the case with journalists, are also vulnerable to stress; as are children who are bullied or who are the victims of physical and sexual abuse.

Work stressors

A healthy work environment is one in which work is organized in such a way that people can manage it. Research has demonstrated that work-related stress arises if there is a mismatch between the demands made on a person and their ability to cope with those demands—for example, because there is not enough time, they do not have the necessary support, or they have no control over how to handle their job.

Be reflective

Moving to another country can be exciting and gives you the opportunity to experience another culture, but is there a downside? Discuss whether such an experience could be a stressor and support your argument.

Some of the main work stressors that have been identified by the UK National Work-Stress Network are:

- monotonous, unpleasant, or meaningless tasks
- working under time pressure or working long hours
- lack of clear job description
- no recognition or reward for good job performance
- heavy responsibility, but lack of control or influence over the demands of the job
- job insecurity and lack of career prospects
- harassment or bullying
- new management techniques or new technology.
- Poor leadership and poor communication

Work stressors

Changes in daily routines can be stressful—even those which are pleasant, such as getting married or being promoted. This is because it requires the individual to adjust to a new situation. These **life events** may influence health in terms of increased physical illness following the stressful event. The Holmes-Rahe Scale (1967) assigned values to stressful events based on an opportunity sample of 394 people from the US, who were asked to look at a list of 43 life events and tick off those that had occurred to them in the previous 12 or 24 months. The participants were asked to rate the events in terms of how long they thought it would take to readjust and accommodate the stressor. The researchers compared the responses of the different groups and found surprising agreement. Further studies have shown that evaluation of stressors is fairly constant across the many groups tested by Holmes and Rahe in the US. They have also found a small correlation between high ratings and subsequent illness and accident.

SOCIAL READJUSTMENT RATING SCALE*	
LIFE EVENT	**LIFE-CHANGE UNIT**
Death of one's spouse	100
Divorce	73
Marital separation	65
Jail term	63
Death of a close family member	63
Personal injury or illness	53
Marriage	50
Being fired	47
Retirement	45
Pregnancy	40
Change in one's financial state	38
More arguments with one's spouse	35
Change in responsibilities at work	29
Son or daughter leaving home	29
Trouble with in-laws	29
Beginning or ending school	26
Change in living conditions	25
Trouble with one's boss	23
Change in work hours or conditions	20
Change in eating habits	15
Vacation	13
Christmas	12

Social readjustment rating scale

Be a thinker

1 List five stressors that you have encountered in the past year.

2 How did you react to each of these events, physiologically and psychologically?

3 Why did you experience these events as stressful?

4 How did you deal with the stressors? Did it work?

Physiological, psychological, and social aspects of stress

Stress and coping are two terms often used together. **Coping** is defined as efforts to deal with a threat in order to remove it or diminish its impact on the person. According to Sarafino (1994), stress arises when people perceive a discrepancy between the demands of a situation and their perception of their own resources. This perception may be realistic—but it may also be unrealistic. What matters is the individual's own evaluation of the situation, and this has an impact on the way that person confronts the stressful situation.

223

Research in psychology

Biopsychosocial aspects of the stress experience (Steptoe and Marmot 2003)

Steptoe and Marmot conducted a survey on the interaction of social, psychological, and physiological aspects of stress. The researchers used a sample of 227 British men and women, aged 47–59. The aim of the study was to look at differences in physiological stress responses to a number of stressors. They used seven questionnaires, each related to a different stressor. Blood samples were also taken, in order to have a physiological measure for stress (e.g. cholesterol) that could indicate an elevated risk for heart problems.

The seven stressors in this investigation were: job stress; environmental stress, in terms of neighbourhood and housing; economic problems; lack of social support from close relatives; loneliness; lack of feelings of control over one's own life; and lack of **self-efficacy** in relation to stressors. Self-efficacy is defined as a person's feeling of competence to deal with a specific task or problem. According to Steptoe, perception of control and

self-efficacy are important psychological measures in individual stress experience.

The researchers found that a person scoring high on one stressor did not necessarily have a high score on another. However, participants who had a high mean score on all seven stressors also had blood tests indicating that they were in the high-risk group for developing heart problems. The same relationship was seen in terms of psychological effects of stress—for example, depression, anxiety, and low quality of life. The researchers argue on the basis of these results that stress research must focus on specific stressors in isolation, as well as combinations of stressors, since the accumulated effect of several stressors may put individuals at increased risk. Since health research is, to a large extent, about prevention of illness, knowing which stress factors are implicated in heart disease, for example, can help to design interventions.

Physiological aspects of stress

The physiological changes of the sympathetic nervous system prepare the individual to either confront or escape from the source of stress—"fight or flight" (Cannon 1914). The body's stress response is arousal—for example, increased blood pressure and providing glucose to the muscles. The adrenal glands release stress hormones (e.g. adrenalin) to energize the body, so that the person can confront or avoid the threat.

Hans Selye (1956) suggested the **general adaptation syndrome (GAS)**. The model describes three stages in the stress process. The initial stage is called "the alarm stage", which is the equivalent of the fight-or-flight response. The second stage is called "the resistance stage", and involves coping, along with attempts to reverse the effects of the alarm stage. The third stage is called "exhaustion"; this is reached after the individual has been repeatedly exposed to stressors and is incapable of further coping. Selye based his theory on research with rats, which all showed the same *general* symptoms when they were exposed to different stressors.

Understanding research

1 What method was used in Steptoe and Marmot (2003) and how did the researchers collect the data?

2 What were the stressors identified in this study? Why do you think the researchers focused on these stressors in particular?

3 Which psychological factors had an effect on experienced stress? Why?

4 What did the researchers conclude about the relationship between the different aspects of stress?

5 Are there methodological, cultural, or ethical considerations to take into account in this study?

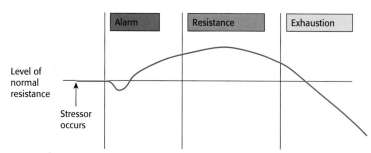

According to Hans Selye, the body reacts in three phases to a stressor. In the first phase, alarm, the body mobilizes to confront the threat, which temporarily expends resources and lowers resistance. In the resistance phase, the body is actively confronting the threat and resistance is high. If the threat continues, the body moves into exhaustion.

The general adaptation syndrome (GAS)

Early stress models emphasized physiological changes and described the individual as automatically responding to external stressors. The strength of GAS is that it can explain the extreme fatigue that people experience after long-term stress. One weakness is that psychological factors only play a minor role in the model. However, most of the focus on psychophysiological pathways in modern stress research is based on the stages that Selye called *alarm* and *resistance*.

Researchers are interested in how stress is related to health problems. They are now aware that long-term stress causes an increase in cortisol, which can lead to depression or memory problems. Cortisol also affects the immune system, thereby making the individual more susceptible to infection, because of a decrease in the number of natural killer cells (T-cells).

Kiecolt-Glaser et al. (1984) analysed blood samples from volunteer medical students one month before and on the first day of their final examination. Students also completed scales of life events, bodily symptoms, and satisfaction with interpersonal contacts. The researchers found that the second blood sample had a significant decrease in the amount of T-cell activity. This was seen as evidence that the high stress had diminished the effectiveness of the immune system. It was also found that students scoring high on stressful life events and loneliness had lower T-cell counts than low scorers. This indicates that psychological stress influences the immune system, and that factors such as loneliness may increase the effects of stress.

Cognitive aspects of stress

Cognitive appraisal, in terms of expecting either positive or negative outcomes of a disease, seems to predict health outcomes. Longitudinal studies show that HIV-positive people who have more pessimistic expectations develop HIV-related symptoms more quickly, and die of AIDS sooner (Reed et al. 1999). Expectations also seem to predict some of the immune changes associated with the disease, and they are particularly strong in those individuals with HIV who have lost a close friend to AIDS in the past year. Kemeny et al. (2006) explain this with the possibility that pessimistic expectations may simply lead to people giving up, and this influences the immune system.

Kamen and Seligman (1987) reported that attributional style—for example, having a pessimistic or optimistic approach to life—could predict poor health later in life. The researchers argued that pessimism may be related to health through a decrease in T-cells and suppression of the immune system. According to the researchers, this was a direct effect of attributional style and beliefs on the body. Greer et al. (1979) suggested that denial and a fighting spirit (not hopelessness) predicted longer survival for breast cancer, thereby indicating a link between beliefs and physiology. It is not the case that optimism can *cure* cancer, but it can help people cope with cancer in a way that may prolong life for optimistic patients.

Social self-preservation theory, suggested by Kemeny et al. (2005), suggests that threats to one's "social self", or to social esteem and status, are associated with specific negative cognitive and

Political instability and terror contribute to stress

affective responses, such as shame and humiliation. It seems that such threats can influence physical health—for example, via the immune system or through increased levels of cortisol. According to Kemeny, HIV infection often occurs in stigmatized groups (e.g. gay and bisexual men or drug abusers) and is a stigmatizing sexually transmitted disease itself. HIV-positive gay and bisexual men who are particularly sensitive to rejection related to their sexuality show more rapid progression of the disease than those who are less sensitive to such social-self threats. Social self-preservation theory predicts that biological responses to stress are mediated by self-conscious emotions such as shame and sensitivity to rejection.

All these examples of psychophysiological processes are part of what is called **psychoneuroimmunology** (PNI). PNI is based on the assumption that an individual's psychological state can influence the immune system via the nervous system. This perspective provides a scientific basis for "positive thinking" in health, but generalized conclusions remain problematic.

Social aspects of stress

Humans are dependent on other human beings. Group living is perhaps one of the most significant aspects of humanity, and our well-being may be threatened if social relationships are stressful. Experiencing abuse in the family or being bullied are social stressors. Living in a violent neighbourhood is another example.

On the other hand, stress can be alleviated via social support—for example, having good friends or a loving family. The early family environment, along with cultural norms, seems to provide the groundwork for social competence. Warm and nurturing families teach children how to manage stress effectively. By observing effective role models, they also develop the necessary social skills involved in positive social interactions. Smith et al. (1992) found that adults whose interpersonal interactions were marked by hostility and cynicism were less likely to report having social support. This negative style is associated with early experiences in a family environment that was unsupportive or conflict-ridden.

Coping and coping strategies

Most contemporary views of stress and coping are inspired by the work of Lazarus and Folkman (1975). Their stress model, called the **transactional model of stress**, is based on the assumption that stress involves a *transaction* between an individual and the external world. It is only if a potentially stressful event is *perceived* as stressful that a stress response is elicited.

The **transactional model of stress** introduced the importance of psychological factors in dealing with stress. The concept of "appraisal" refers to a cognitive and emotional evaluation. According to Lazarus, appraisal comes in two forms: (1) **primary appraisal**, which means that the event is judged to be either irrelevant, positive, or negative to one's well-being; and (2) **secondary appraisal**, which means that different relevant coping strategies are considered before choosing a way to deal effectively with the

---

TOK

1 How would you know if people living in a violent neighbourhood are stressed?

2 List different ways of knowing.

3 Is one way of knowing better than another? Support your argument.

Possible essay question

Describe two stressors

Discuss two physiological, psychological, or social aspects of stress. (22 marks)

Assessment advice

This is a parted question so be sure to address both parts. Even though it is a parted question, you need to structure each part and argue clearly in favour of your claim.

The first part asks you to describe two stressors. The command term "describe" means that you should give a detailed account of the two stressors that you choose to deal with in your answer. Examples of stressors may be work stress or becoming ill.

"Discuss" in the second part is a command term that requires you to offer a balanced review of two aspects of stress. The answer could focus on physiological and psychological aspects and how they interact. The important thing is to include two different aspects from two different levels of analysis. Each of them must be clearly presented and your argument should offer two factors and empirical evidence in support of your argument.

Overall, the argument should be supported by appropriate evidence, for example psychological research into different aspects of stress.

stressor. Issues such as confidence or doubt may be part of secondary appraisal. The two appraisal processes influence each other and should be seen as continuous and interdependent. People may also reappraise the situation and their coping strategies in order to choose a new and perhaps more efficient way of coping.

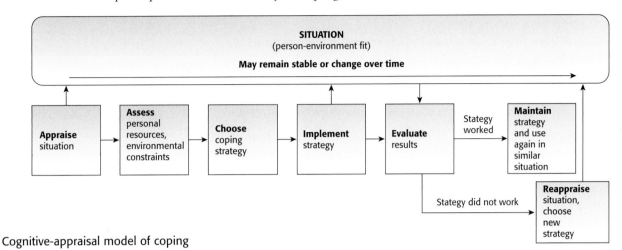

Cognitive-appraisal model of coping

Folkman and Lazarus (1988) suggested two main coping strategies. The first one is **problem-focused coping**, which is dealing with the stressor itself. The purpose is to change the problematic situation— for example, quitting an impossible job or leaving an abusive partner. The second strategy is called **emotion-focused coping**. The purpose is to *handle* the emotional aspects of stress rather than changing the problematic situation. There are several ways that people do this, such as going to the movies, relaxation exercises, seeking social support, or taking drugs to alleviate tension.

According to Carver (2007), it is difficult to make a clear distinction between the two ways of coping. Problem-focused coping is probably more likely to happen if the person feels they can control the stressor. Emotion-focused coping is more likely in cases where people feel they have little control over the stressor. Generally, a situation perceived as one that has to be endured—for example, in the case of the death of a loved one—is more likely to result in emotion-focused coping. However, it should be noted that the two kinds of strategies influence each other. Problem-focused coping may result in the reduction of unpleasant emotions. Likewise, emotion-focused coping (e.g. talking with close friends) may reduce tension and eventually result in more effective problem-focused coping.

Emotion-focused coping, like drowning your sorrows in alcohol, can be effective in the short term, but may turn out to be ineffective in the long run, since people may develop an addiction. This kind of emotion-focused coping is sometimes called *avoidance coping*, because the aim of it is to avoid the negative feelings associated with the stressor. Another way of coping is *proactive coping*, which is intended to avoid a stressful experience. Studying hard for an exam in order to avoid the stress of failing could be an example of proactive coping.

Ursin and Erison (2004) found that, generally, people benefit positively and experience lower levels of stress if they actively do things to reduce stress. If people *believe* they can manage stress, the stress is less intensive and of shorter duration. This has implications for reducing risk factors in health—for example, in terms of the relationship between stress and heart disease, and it can explain why taking yoga classes or being with friends can reduce stress.

Social support as a coping strategy

Psychologists have long known that having friends is important to mental well-being. A longitudinal study of ageing initiated in 1992 found that regular personal and telephone contact with friends and family increases life expectancy (Gilles et al. 2005). Social support also seems to be an important factor in the way people cope with stress.

Social support can be defined as the experience that one is part of a social network, with mutual assistance and obligations, and that one is cared for by others. Social support can come from a partner, relatives, friends, or various social support groups. The support may be in the form of **emotional support** (e.g. warmth and understanding), **informational support** (e.g. helping a person to understand and cope better with a stressful situation), or **practical support** (tangible help, e.g. financial assistance). Giving social support to others may strengthen a personal relationship and provide a sense of purpose, because it signifies that one is important to others. In fact, just *knowing* that you could get support from your network may be the most important factor in the beneficial effects of social support. This in itself can promote well-being.

Taylor (2002) carried out a meta-analysis of research of stress and coping, and found that there is a gender difference in relation to social support. Women tend to provide more social support to others, draw on socially supportive networks more consistently in times of stress, and may be more benefited by social support. This is formulated in her **theory of "tend and befriend"**, which suggests that due to evolution, males and females have different stress responses, which are adaptive for their sex. Males tend to exhibit the fight-or-flight response, which is triggered by the hormone testosterone. Females, on the other hand, tend to exhibit the tend-and-befriend response, which is triggered by the hormone oxytocin. "Tend" refers to nurturing activities, and "befriend" refers to seeking social support.

Thoits (1995) found that women were more involved than men in both giving and receiving social support. It seems that, across the lifespan, women are generally more likely to mobilize social support—especially from other women—in times of stress. Belle (1987) found that adult women maintained more same-sex close relationships than men and mobilized more social support in times of stress than men. They also reported more benefit from contacts with their female friends and relatives, and they provided more social support themselves than men do. These findings appear to generalize across a number of cultures as well (Whiting and Whiting 1975).

Be reflective

- Think back to the last situation that you experienced as stressful. What exactly was the stressor? Why did you find it stressful?

- How did you react (physiologically and psychologically) last time you felt stressed?

- What did you do to cope with the stress? Check the coping strategies outlined in this chapter to see if you used any of these.

- How would you help a friend who said he or she was stressed? Why?

According to Taylor (2008), the literature suggests that culture is a variable that may moderate how social support is perceived. One dimension of culture is independence (western cultures) versus interdependence (non-western cultures). In individualistic cultures, there is a strong emphasis on the self as *independent*, whereas collectivist cultures perceive the individual as part of a social group—the self is *interdependent*. This has implications for seeking social support. Taylor et al. (2004) explored cultural differences in the use of social support as a form of coping. European, US, and Korean students were asked about their ways of coping with stress, including individual and social coping strategies. They found that a significantly lower number of Korean students used social support as a way of coping. They hypothesized that the Asian concern about disruption of harmony in the group, social criticism, or losing face could be an explanation.

Is the social support provided by the *Sex and the City* girls to each other in times of stress typical for women?

A number of social support groups—for example, in the form of self-help groups for people with HIV, cancer, obesity, or alcoholism—have arisen over the years. Evans (1979) reported that in 1979, more than 15 million Americans were using social support groups as a primary vehicle for their mental health service. Kessler et al. (1997) estimate that in the US, about 25 million people participate in support groups at some point in their life. Davison et al. (2000) found that white people and women are more likely to participate in such groups than non-white people and men. The purpose of all these groups is to share experiences and help each other to face the problems and stress related to specific conditions.

The importance of Internet-based social support groups is rising. These groups can help people who do not have a network, or may offer an additional source of support; participating in such groups provides people with the sense that they are actually *doing* something. Since they are so popular, it would seem that such groups are quite efficient at helping people.

Klemm et al. (1999) conducted a content analysis of postings on various Internet-based cancer support groups, including breast cancer and prostate cancer. The researchers found that the most common postings on the webpages were seeking information, and giving information, encouragement and support. These categories accounted for 80 per cent of the postings across all Internet-based support groups in the study. Women were more than twice as likely to provide encouragement and support, and men were more than twice as likely to offer information.

Wenzelberg et al. (2003) carried out a randomized controlled experiment, which was aimed at evaluating the beneficial effects of online support groups. The participants were 72 women diagnosed with breast cancer. They were randomly assigned to a 12-week Web-based social support group. Before they joined the group, the

Be a critical thinker

- Is the empirical evidence that social support is a powerful coping strategy convincing? Why or why not?
- To what extent is the theory of Tend and Befriend supported by evidence?

The importance of Internet-based social support groups is rising

participants were told that the purpose of the intervention was psychoeducational, and that the group was not meant to serve as an alternative to psychotherapy. The researchers found that the Web-based programme was moderately effective in reducing participants' scores on perceived stress and depression.

The researchers argue that Web-based support groups offer advantages, but that there are ethical issues that need to be addressed. One is the privacy of the participants. According to the researchers, securing participant confidentiality is important in groups like these, and it is also important that participants understand the role of the facilitator.

CAS: online help

1 If you were to undertake a CAS project on how to establish an online support group for IB students suffering from exam stress, how would you go about it?

2 Use your knowledge on stress and suggest how you could provide informational and emotional support. Would it be possible to provide practical support online?

Mindfulness stress reduction as a coping strategy

One reason for stress is people worrying about the past or the future, doing too many things at the same time, and not being present in the moment because they are thinking about what they have to do next. Since the mind is related to the body in a complex way, relaxation and learning to relax and concentrate on one thing at a time could be a way to reduce stress. A large body of research has documented the beneficial effects of relaxation techniques in stress reduction. One such technique is **mindfulness-based stress reduction** (MBSR), developed by Kabat-Zinn at the University of Massachusetts Medical Center in 1979. Since it began, more than 16 000 individuals have completed the programme.

The origins of MBSR lie in Buddhist teachings, but these are applied within a behavioural medicine framework. The course involves training in meditation. The aim of the programme is to cultivate "mindfulness", defined as: "the awareness that emerges through paying attention, on purpose, in the present moment, and non-judgmentally to the unfolding of experience moment by moment" (Kabat-Zinn 2003). MBSR aims to teach people how to approach stressful situations "mindfully"—that is, to respond to the situation instead of reacting to it automatically. The idea is that, with repeated practice, the individual develops the ability to calmly step back from thoughts and feelings during stressful situations, instead of engaging in negative thinking patterns that may escalate various stress responses.

The core practices of MBSR

The body scan is the first meditation practice taught on the course, and it is set as a daily home practice for the first two weeks. It is usually performed lying down, with the eyes closed, and involves the person directing their attention to different parts of the body in turn, from the toes to the top of the head. People are instructed to stay awake, and to experience and accept whatever sensation comes to them. This often leads to a deep sense of relaxation, which is the purpose of this practice.

Working through the **yoga exercises** (hatha yoga), participants become aware of the body's different sensations, including those of tension and relaxation. This can help people to be able to identify physical signs of stress sooner—for example, tension in the back and shoulders. Regular yoga exercises also result in more strength and flexibility, so that people can become more "grounded" in their bodies. Kabat-Zinn uses the term "rebodying", and finds that this is a contrast to the focus on "the head"—that is, thoughts.

Sitting meditation is introduced gradually from the second class. People sit in an upright but relaxed posture, with their eyes closed. Attention is focused on the physical sensation associated with breathing. They are asked to focus on the breath and to let it flow freely, but to allow the mind to wander at will, moment by moment. The awareness may include attention on the body—for example, the sounds of breathing, the sensations of the skin, feelings, or thoughts. No condemning, no judging, only awareness of the here-and-now sensations of the body; and when the mind wanders, the participant learns to accept it, but then to pay attention to breathing once more.

The participants are provided with audiocassettes that guide them through the meditation exercises for informal practice at home. They are also encouraged to bring **mindfulness into their everyday lives** from the beginning of the course. This can be performed while carrying out a routine daily activity, such as taking a shower. The person is asked to focus on the present moment and to be aware of that, noticing the sensations experienced while doing it, just like in meditation.

The MBSR method is very popular, but is it efficient? Shapiro et al. (1998) carried out a controlled study with a group of premedical students who were offered the MBSR course at the University of Arizona. People who signed up for the course were offered course credits. They were randomly assigned to the course (37) or to a waiting list (36). There were equal numbers of men and women in the sample. Participants in the MBSR group and the waiting-list group filled out a self-report questionnaire assessing stress at the start of the term (before the course) and during exams at the end of the term (after the course). The study was designed to coincide with exams, since this is known to be a high-stress period. The participants also completed a questionnaire on empathy.

The researchers found no difference between the two groups at the beginning of the term, but they did identify differences around the time of the exams. People on the waiting list expressed more anxiety compared to those who had participated in the MBSR class, who were in fact less anxious than at the start. This suggests that the course had taught them to cope effectively with the stress of exams. They scored higher on the empathy questionnaire than the controls, and they were also less depressed and had fewer symptoms of psychological distress. The findings were replicated in a new controlled study with 130 medical students. Taken as a whole, this points to effectiveness in stress reduction.

Can these results be generalized to other people? The participants were medical students; they were a self-selected sample; and they were offered course credits to participate, which probably ensured the low drop-out numbers in this study. These are just some of the considerations that must be included in any evaluation of this research.

Speca et al. (2000) performed a controlled test with a sample of cancer patients. They recruited the participants by publishing the MBSR course in a cancer clinic in Calgary. Those who were interested were randomly allocated to the experimental group or to a waiting list (the latter group serving as a control). The effectiveness of MBSR was assessed using a stress symptoms questionnaire. The experimental group showed a reduction in total mood disturbance (anxiety, anger, depression) of an impressive 65 per cent, and a reduction of 35 per cent in stress symptoms. The time spent practising meditation correlated positively with improvements in mood. There were no changes in the average scores for the control group over the same period. The results provide evidence that MBSR had a therapeutic effect. However, it may be that some of the effect was due to social desirability effects, which could play a role in the patients' self-reports on mood and stress changes. Maybe they wanted to show that they had complied with the treatment and that it had had an effect? This cannot be ruled out.

Group-based psychosocial interventions, such as MBSR, that facilitate adaptation and adjustment to stress—for example, as a consequence of chronic illness—are both cost- and time-efficient. The controlled clinical trials in relation to cancer patients indicate that MBSR is a promising approach, but more research is needed.

Evaluating the evidence

1 Is one of the two coping strategies mentioned in this chapter preferable? Support your argument.

2 To what extent are the two coping strategies culturally biased?

3 To what extent are the two coping strategies gender biased?

Health psychology: substance abuse, addictive behaviour, and obesity

Learning outcomes

- Discuss the extent to which biological, cognitive, and sociocultural factors influence health-related behaviour
- Evaluate psychological research (through theories and/or studies) relevant to health psychology
- Explain factors related to the development of substance abuse or addictive behaviour
- Examine prevention strategies and treatments for substance abuse and addictive behaviour
- Discuss factors related to overeating and the development of obesity
- Discuss prevention strategies and treatments for overeating and obesity

Factors related to the development of substance abuse or addictive behaviour

A substance is anything people ingest to alter mood, cognition, or behaviour. People have always used a range of substances in the hope of an effect, such as inducing self-confidence, having fun, or relaxing. Most substances—even coffee—can produce dependence, as well as withdrawal symptoms after long-term use. In this chapter, the focus will be primarily on the substance nicotine.

The term **addiction** suggests that the individual cannot control his or her behaviour. An addiction is characterized by behavioural and other responses that always include a *compulsion* to use the substance continuously, in order to experience the psychological and physiological effects and to avoid discomfort in its absence. Addiction is not only related to drugs. People may be addicted to many different things, for example alcohol, sex, gambling, or shopping. Recently a new form of addiction has emerged—Internet addiction.

In the UK, the General Household Survey (GHS) found that in 2006, 23 per cent of all men and 21 per cent of all women were smokers. Of these British smokers, 59 per cent said it would be difficult to go without smoking for a whole day, and 16 per cent said they had their first cigarette within five minutes of waking up. This could indicate "addiction".

Definitions of terms

Substance use: consumption or use of any substance (e.g. alcohol, nicotine).

Substance addiction: characterized by continued use of the substance, despite knowing about problems associated with the substance; persistent desire and/or unsuccessful effort to control substance use. Addiction can be psychological and/or physiological:

● *Psychological addiction* relates to **craving**— that is, a strong desire to smoke. Situations associated with smoking, as well as the smoker's mood and psychological state, come to serve as "triggers" for the craving— for example, after a meal, when talking on the phone, during work or study breaks, and when feeling angry.

● *Physiological addiction* relates to symptoms such as **tolerance**—that is, a person needs more of the drug in order to achieve the same effect— and **withdrawal symptoms** if the substance is not taken—for example, nausea, irritability, anxiety, difficulty concentrating, and increased appetite.

The general increase in life expectancy over the past 150 years is considerably less for smokers than for non-smokers. Already in the 1950s, evidence indicated that smoking was predictive of lung cancer. Today, a substantial number of the adult population still smoke, even though most of them are aware of the related health risks.

In order to understand why people begin to smoke, why they continue, and why they experience difficulties giving up, researchers have investigated biological, psychological and social factors that may promote smoking.

Biological factors related to addictive behaviour: smoking

The biological level of analysis can explain why smokers continue to smoke once they have started. The active ingredient in tobacco is **nicotine**, a psychoactive drug. By inhaling tobacco smoke, the average smoker takes in 1–2mg of nicotine per cigarette. Some of the effects of nicotine are as follows.

● It stimulates the release of adrenaline, which increases heart rate and blood pressure.

● It stimulates the release of dopamine in the brain's reward circuits, which results in a brief feeling of pleasure. Within a few minutes, the acute effects of nicotine wear off. The pleasant feeling causes the smoker to continue smoking to maintain the pleasurable effects and prevent withdrawal symptoms.

● It acts on acetylcholine receptors in the brain, as if it were the natural neurotransmitter. With repeated smoking, the brain adapts to what it regards as normal levels of acetylcholine in order to restore balance. One way to do this is to grow more acetylcholine receptors.

Research suggests that nicotine may be as addictive as heroin and cocaine. Once smokers are addicted to nicotine, they will experience withdrawal symptoms when the level of nicotine is not constant in the body. A substantial number of smokers declare that they would like to quit smoking—up to 70 per cent of current smokers in the US, according to figures from the Centers for Disease Control and Prevention (CDC).

TOK

An "addict" is defined as an individual who has no control over his or her behaviour. A smoker who cannot quit, despite wishing to do so, is therefore an addict.

1 Can people be held responsible for smoking if they have no control over their behaviour?

2 Discuss whether the public should support treatments of tobacco-related diseases that follow addiction, such as lung cancer.

For WHO and national health boards around the world, a major concern is preventing children from starting smoking. According to the American Lung Association, around 6000 adolescents under the age of 18 start smoking *every day*. People who start smoking in childhood have an increased chance of lung cancer, compared to smokers who begin later in life. They are also more likely to become addicted, because the young brain is particularly vulnerable to the addictive effects of nicotine. This is a major reason why governments and health psychologists try to prevent young people from starting to smoke in the first place.

Research in psychology

Addicted after the first puff?
(DiFranza et al. 2006)

DiFranza et al. (2006) conducted a longitudinal study of 217 adolescents (mean age of 12) in Massachusetts (US). Most of the children were European American, and they all reported having inhaled a cigarette at least once. They completed psychological evaluations and reported their history of tobacco use, as well as answering questions relating to attitudes and beliefs, and to social environment, such as family and community. Eleven of them were interviewed. Tobacco dependence was assessed, based on reported cravings, changes in tolerance, time devoted to smoking, and inability to quit.

The results indicated that the adolescents who had an immediate experience of relaxation after the first puff were more likely to become addicted to cigarettes, with 67 per cent of those who recalled a relaxation effect after their first inhale becoming dependent, compared to 29 per cent of those who did not experience such an effect. According to the researchers, post-inhale relaxation was also the biggest risk factor for being unable to stop later. Of the participants who experienced the relaxation, 91 per cent said they were unable to quit, and 60 per cent of those said it was as if they had lost control. The conclusion of this study seems to be that it takes far less to become addicted than was previously thought—at least for some individuals. It is not known why some are more sensitive to nicotine than others.

Evaluating research

1   The data in the study were based on self-reports. Could this create a problem in the interpretation of the results?

2   Is it a problem that the study used an US sample? Why or why not?

3   What are the implications of the study?

Cognitive and sociocultural factors related to addictive behaviour: smoking

Charlton (1984) found that young smokers associated smoking with fun and pleasure.

Advertising agencies know that manipulating cognitions is a powerful tool, because people's self-image and beliefs are important. If you believe that smoking is cool, the probability that you will smoke is high. According to WHO Director General Margaret Chan, the tobacco industry spends billions of dollars in an effort to attract young people in developing countries to its addictive products.

Peer pressure is an important factor in beginning to smoke

Be reflective

1 What is the reason that young people start to smoke in spite of knowing that it is unhealthy?

2 Do you think advertisements can make young people take up smoking? Why or why not?

3 What is the main reason people start smoking, in your opinion? Support your argument.

Much research on smoking focuses on *individual factors*—for example, how attitudes or cognitions may predict smoking behaviour. According to Ogden (2004), this is a problem because it takes individuals out of their social context, and a person's behaviour and beliefs are developed through interaction with the social world. Social learning theory includes this aspect.

According to social learning theory, smoking is learned. One of the most important factors predicting smoking behaviour is *parental smoking*. Bauman et al. (1990) found that 80 per cent of a sample of US adolescents aged 12–14, whose parents did not smoke, had never tried to smoke themselves. If the parents smoked, half the children had tried smoking. This is confirmed by findings from a number of longitudinal studies in the UK. Children were twice as likely to smoke if their father smoked (Lader and Matheson 1991). In addition, *parental attitude* towards smoking is important. Murray et al. (1984) found that in families where the parents were strongly against smoking, the children were up to seven times less likely to smoke.

Another very important factor in smoking is *peer-group pressure*. For adolescents, the peer group is a source of social identity and learning social norms—and this may include smoking. Unger et al. (2001) carried out a cross-cultural survey on adolescent smoking in a representative US sample (n=5143) of Californian adolescents (mean age 13).

The study found that European American students who had close peers who smoked were more likely to smoke than other students (e.g. Asian American and Hispanic students). The researchers explained that in individualistic cultures, adolescents typically create their own youth culture, characterized by rebellion, in order to set themselves apart from their parents. In collectivist cultures, the bond between the teen and the parents is considered important. Rebellion is not tolerated, so adolescents are more likely to conform to the roles and norms that parents prescribe for them.

Social class has been found to predict smoking. In most countries, there is a strong association between socio-economic class and cigarette smoking. Estimates from 2007 from the Centre for National Disease Control and Prevention in the USA show that prevalence of smoking is related to socio-economic factors. Cigarette smoking is more common among adults who live below the poverty level (30.6 per cent) than among those living at or above the poverty level (20.4 per cent).

Be an enquirer

It is not possible to include contemporary cigarette advertisements here but it is possible to look at how cigarette advertising was done in the past.

Do some research in this collection of vintage cigarette advertisements and pick four from different periods: www.chickenhead.com/truth/

● What is the purpose of advertising?

● Explain how each of these advertisements tries to persuade people to buy the featured brand.

● What methods were used? Do you think that this was effective? Why or why not?

When you have done this, you can search this webpage to see international examples of tobacco advertisements.

www.tobaccofreekids.org/adgallery/

Pick a few of these and then answer the same questions as you did with the vintage ones.

Search the Internet for WHO and tobacco advertising in Asia.

This site contains information on tobacco promotion strategies in Asia. Consider ethical issues in these strategies. Also use the information from Chapter 4.2.

www.wpro.who.int/media_centre/fact_sheets/fs_20020523.htm

China is a huge market for tobacco. China has about 350 million smokers – nearly a quarter of its population. One third of the world's smokers are Chinese according to official records in China, which also state that there are 15 million young smokers in the country. Two-thirds of Chinese men smoke, according to an investigation published in the *British Medical Journal* in August 2001.

A Health Ministry report estimates that around 40 million of the country's 130 million teenagers aged between 13 and 18 have tried smoking. Of those who had tried smoking, most had smoked their first whole cigarette by the time they turned 13. This was an increase of 15 per cent from 1998. The report from the Health Ministry says that tobacco advertising is, to a large extent, responsible for the increase in cigarette smoking because advertisers target young people by associating smoking with independence and sex appeal.

The government is now taking measures to reduce smoking, such as banning smoking in public places.

WHO has outlined the **MPOWER** strategy to serve as a guide for national anti-tobacco strategies. According to WHO, only 15 countries mandate pictorial warnings; and only 5 per cent of the world's population lives in countries with national bans on advertising, smoke-free legislation, and access to services supporting cessation.

WHO REPORT ON THE GLOBAL TOBACCO EPIDEMIC, 2008
The MPOWER package

fresh and alive

mpower

World Health Organization

WHO campaign the tobacco industry's marketing strategies towards young people

- **M**onitor tobacco use and prevention policies (e.g. help to build strategies).

- **P**rotect people from tobacco smoke (e.g. smoke-free areas and smoke-free legislation).

- **O**ffer help to quit tobacco (e.g. counselling and national quit services).

- **W**arn about the dangers of tobacco use (e.g. information and pictures on billboards).

- **E**nforce bans on tobacco advertising, promotion, and sponsorships.

- **R**aise taxes on tobacco.

Prevention strategies

A number of strategies have been adopted by governments all over the world to prevent smoking and its devastating consequences on health. Since the 1990s, most European countries have put either a ban or restrictions on advertising, but most of the world's population is not protected by such restrictions. WHO wants a total ban on tobacco advertising, tobacco promotion, and tobacco sponsorship (e.g. of sports and music venues). Tobacco companies have always marketed their products where they can reach the youth audience, but they are now targeting adolescents in the developing world because it has become increasingly difficult to market their products in most western countries.

On No Tobacco Day, 31 May 2008, WHO targeted children and adolescents in an attempt to prevent smoking. According to WHO figures, two out of three countries have no information about tobacco use, so people do not even *know* the dangers of smoking.

Most smokers start as teenagers. Consumer research has shown that tobacco advertising has a powerful effect on the smoking attitudes and behaviour of young people. This is partly because of the use of imagery and positive association, and partly due to the fact that young people are more brand-conscious than adults, and are therefore more likely to smoke the most popular and well-advertised products. Tobacco sponsorship also promotes brand association, which makes it easier to begin smoking. Charlton et al. (1997) found that boys who showed a preference for Formula One motor racing that was sponsored by cigarette manufacturers were more likely to begin smoking.

WHO strategies are implemented in a number of countries. Public health interventions to prevent smoking and promote cessation target all individuals. In recent years, there has been an increase in health campaigns (e.g. work-site interventions and community-based programmes). Government strategies encompass restricting or banning tobacco advertising, raising taxes on tobacco, and banning smoking in public places. A number of countries have followed the prevention strategies outlined by WHO—for example, the Scandinavian countries, the UK, Ireland, and the US. Banning smoking in public places can motivate people to stop smoking and prevent relapse, according to research from Italy (Lemstra et al. 2008) and Canada (Gorini 2007).

Treatments

For those who smoke, there are treatments offering ways to reduce the individual's dependence on smoking. The hard part is dealing with withdrawal symptoms. **Nicotine replacement therapy** (NRT), such as nicotine chewing gum, patches, and spray, can help to some extent. Nicotine chewing gum is a useful addition to treatment programmes because it can prevent short-term **relapse**— that is, falling back into smoking.

In the late 1990s, a drug called **Zyban** came onto the market to help people give up smoking. It was originally an antidepressant, and it acts on the sites in the brain affected by nicotine. This drug can help people to quit, because it relieves the withdrawal symptoms and blocks the effects of nicotine if people resume smoking.

Research indicates that if treatment is tailored to the individual's situation, there is a greater chance of success. Research also shows that long-term cessation programmes are more successful in preventing relapse. Pisinger (2008) studied research on the effect of interventions at the individual level. She concludes that the most efficient methods are those that include consultations and participation in smoking cessation interventions, either alone or in groups. Nicotine replacement procedures, as well as the drug Zyban, are efficient, especially in combination with other interventions.

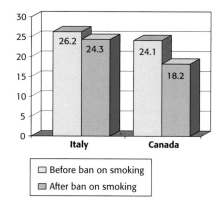

Lemstra M. Implications of a public smoking ban. Can J Public Health. Jan–Feb. 2008; 99(1): 62–65

Gorini G. What happened in Italy? A brief summary of studies conducted in Italy to evaluate the impact of the smoking ban. Annals of Oncology. 2007; 18: 1620–1622'

Smoking ban reduces prevalence

Method	Effect	Evidence
Written material (leaflets, brochures)	Small	Moderate
Internet	Small	Weak
Consultations with nurse	Small to moderate	Moderate
Consultations with doctor	Moderate	Moderate
Consultations with cessation instructor	Moderate to high	Moderate
Group-based cessation treatment	High	Strong
Nicotine replacement therapy (NRT)	High	Strong
Zyban	High	Weak to moderate
Alternative treatment	None	Weak

The effect of interventions on the individual (based on Pisinger 2008)

Multifaceted approaches to smoking cessation are efficient

Olsen et al. (2006) studied the effectiveness of standard smoking cessation interventions in real-life settings, run by nurses and staff who had received three days of training. The standard intervention is a multifaceted approach. The data came from the Danish National Smoking Cessation Database, which was established in 2001.

The standard interventions in Denmark were run by health staff who had received a three-

day training course. They were trained in interviewing and advising smokers to quit using a manual with guidelines. The cessation units were situated in various places, such as schools, workplaces, pharmacies, and hospitals, with 101 cessation units participating in the study.

Of the smokers registered on the database (n=2751), 76 per cent followed a standard group format, where 10–12 smokers met with the counsellor for five sessions of two hours each month. The first two sessions were spent preparing and planning the smoking cessation. Some of the major topics were readiness, ambivalence, and motivation. The participants also completed a test for nicotine addiction, and were introduced to nicotine replacement therapy and the drug Zyban. The participants themselves decided if they wanted to use the medical treatments. Physiological measures, such as exhaled carbon monoxide concentration, were taken at each session.

The last sessions took place 3 days, 10 days, and 3 weeks after the quitting date. The group members shared their experiences—for example, coping strategies and relapse prevention strategies. Issues such as weight problems and the importance of becoming free of nicotine were also discussed. The rate of continued abstinence

was calculated after six months, based on the completed follow-up forms, with 18 per cent of all the enrolled participants reporting that they continued to abstain from smoking.

After 12 months, 16 per cent reported that they were still abstinent. The researchers found that gender, age, and low nicotine addiction were the factors that determined abstinence at 12 months. The participants in group-based interventions and those in cessation interventions in pharmacies were the most likely to stay abstinent after a year. The researchers concluded that the interventions were successful and could be implemented at a relatively low cost.

Some of the strengths of the study were the large sample and the population-based real-life setting. The weaknesses were the lack of a control group and the loss of data, because there was a relatively large drop-out of participants during the programme.

Factors related to overeating and the development of obesity

According to WHO, obesity has reached epidemic proportions globally, with more than a billion overweight adults in the world. At least 300 million of these are clinically obese. Overweight is now affecting more people than malnutrition and hunger (WHO 2004). Obesity is not only found in affluent countries; it is also an increasing problem in developing countries, according to WHO.

The body mass index (BMI) is a measure used to determine obesity. Obesity is defined as an excess of body fat measured as BMI. It is calculated using a person's weight (in kilogrammes), divided by the square of their height (in metres). A person with a BMI of 30 or more is generally considered obese. A person with a BMI equal to or more than 25 is considered overweight.

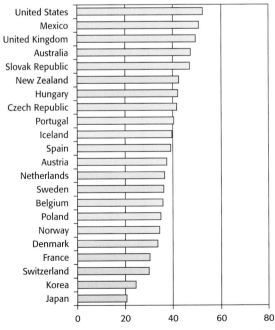

Percentage of obese and overweight population by country

Overweight and obesity are prevalent in developed and developing countries

239

The question is *why* we see this epidemic. The answers are not simple, but most researchers seem to agree that environmental factors—such as availability of food, proportion of fat in the diet, and lack of exercise—are among the major causes of obesity. Overweight and obesity are the result of an *imbalance* in stored fat and energy used for physical activity, and for various bodily functions such as respiration and blood pressure.

Physiological aspects of obesity

There are a number of physiological theories of obesity. One of them is linked to **genetic predisposition**. It seems that body size runs in families. Having one obese parent results in a 40 per cent chance of becoming obese, and having two obese parents increases the likelihood of becoming obese to 80 per cent. According to Garn et al. (1981), the chances of thin parents having an overweight child is about 7 per cent. Since parents and children generally share environment as well as genetic makeup, it could be that the former also plays a role.

In order to investigate the relative role of genes and the environment, researchers can carry out twin studies. Stunkard et al. (1990) studied 93 pairs of identical twins who were reared apart. The researchers compared the twins' BMI and found that genetic factors accounted for 66–70 per cent of the variance in their body weight. They concluded that there must be a strong genetic component in the development of obesity, but also that genetics played a greater role in those twins who were slim. Although results from twin studies indicate a genetic factor in obesity, the role of this factor is not really clear. One suggestion relates to metabolism, which may be genetically determined, but the evidence is still inconclusive. Another suggestion relates to the amount of fat cells in the individual, which may also be genetically determined.

There is evidence that genes determine individual susceptibility to weight gain. However, the obesity epidemic cannot be attributable to genetic factors alone, since the increase in prevalence of obesity has taken place over too short a period for the genetic make-up of the population to have changed substantially.

One explanation of obesity relates to evolution. According to this hypothesis, humans are genetically programmed to eat when food is available, in order to store fat for times when food is scarce. This genetically determined behavioural programme has worked well during evolutionary selection, but it is now inappropriate, because food is abundant and people are no longer as physically active.

Sociocultural aspects of obesity

According to Jeffery (2001), the current obesity epidemic is caused by environmental factors. There are two main factors: lack of physical activity and eating behaviour.

The body uses energy during physical activity, and if one eats more than is burned, fat will be stored. The increase in obese people has been linked to the **sedentary lifestyle** of modern people—that is, the lack of physical activity. In the past, people used much more energy on work and transportation than they do today. Television viewing has increased over the years, and so has the use of videos and computer games. Prentice and Jebb (1995) studied changes in physical activity in a UK sample. The researchers found a positive correlation between an increase in obesity, and car ownership and television viewing. However, the data were correlational, so a cause-and-effect relationship cannot be established.

Researchers have found a positive correlation between increased car ownership and obesity

The economists Lakdawalla and Philipson (2002) estimated, based on individual-level data from 1976–1994, that 60 per cent of the total growth in weight was due to a decrease in physical activity, with 40 per cent due to an increase in calorie intake.

Pacific Islanders are now among the fattest in the world, according to the International Obesity Taskforce: 55 per cent of Tongan women, 74 per cent of Samoan women, and nearly 80 per cent of men and women living in Nauru are obese. Traditionally, these Pacific cultures associated obesity with wealth, but obesity was not a health problem because people maintained traditional lifestyles.

It has been argued that *overeating* is causing obesity. In some cases, this might be so—for example, in compulsive eating disorders, but this is a psychiatric diagnosis. Generally, research has not been able to support that overeating is the main reason for growth in obesity rates in the population.

Did you know?

Binge-eating disorder (BED) is characterized by compulsive overeating. It is a psychiatric disorder, like anorexia and bulimia, but the condition seems to be more chronic than these other eating disorders. Binge eating is defined as repeated bouts of uncontrolled eating. Patients suffering from BED may or may not be obese, but most of them are. Some of them become morbidly obese, with a BMI of 40 or more. The prevalence of BED in the population is estimated at around 1–5 per cent. In patients seeking help for weight loss, the rate of BED is higher—around 25 per cent. Research has found a link between dieting and binge eating (Polivy and Herman 1989). Binges often take place in secret, when the person is alone. Binge eaters eat rapidly and stuff themselves to the point of feeling sick. It is believed that some binge eaters engage in *emotional eating*—that is, bingeing is used as a coping mechanism for stress or negative emotions. Treatments for BED often involve antidepressants, cognitive-behavioural therapy (CBT), and a programme of healthy eating and exercise.

It has also been suggested that compulsive eating should be seen as an *addiction*. Research with animals has demonstrated that the same dopamine-producing areas in the brain become active in craving for food as in craving for other substances.

As with any addiction, there may be specific personality factors that put individuals at risk for compulsive eating—for example, the inability to regulate tension and a fragile sense of self. Binge eaters try to conceal their abuse of food, as most addicts try to hide their addiction. According to Volkow (2002), who suggested the theory, most people's weight problems are not caused by food addiction. There are multiple causes of overweight and obesity, including unhealthy eating habits, lack of exercise, genetic vulnerability, and stress, but in some individuals, food addiction could be an explanation.

The UK National Food Survey has collected data on food intake in the home over the past 50 years. The population data from this UK database show that since 1970 there has been a distinct decrease in the amount of food eaten. Similar results were produced by Prentice and Jebb (1995), who found that the population data did not show an obvious relationship between the increase in obesity and changes in food intake. The British *Foresight Report on Tackling Obesities: Future Choices* (2007) concluded that obesity is an inevitable consequence of a society flooded with energy-dense, cheap foods, labour-saving devices, motorized transport, and sedentary work. The report argues that the notion that the current obesity epidemic is caused by individual indulgence or laziness alone must be changed.

Prentice and Jebb (1995) found that there has been a change in *what* people eat. According to the Organization for Economic Cooperation and Development (OECD), the daily calorie intake grew by 25 per cent in the US between 1973 and 1999. The same trend has been found in the Netherlands, New Zealand, and Spain. In Japan, calorie intake is low and stable, which corresponds to the lowest rate of obesity. However, the picture is not clear. In countries like Australia, the daily calorie intake has grown moderately, but the percentage of obesity has increased by 23.4 per cent. This indicates that increase in calorie intake alone cannot explain the increase in obesity.

The fat proportion theory of obesity argues that the obese may not eat more than the non-obese, but simply eat proportionally more fat content. Blundel et al. (1997) found that high fat eaters (more than 45 per cent of their energy came from fat) were 19 times more likely to be obese than those who got less than 35 per cent of their energy from fat. Similar findings have been found in other studies. Since fat is more likely to be stored—whereas carbohydrates are burned—eating a diet rich in fat could contribute to obesity.

According to Petersen (2006), the health gap between people in different socioeconomic groups is widening. People with higher education eat healthier foods and exercise more. They are also more likely to respond positively to recommendations from researchers on how to improve health.

This is in line with Chou et al. (2004), who found that wealthier and more educated individuals are less likely to have obesity problems compared to those of lower socio-economic status.

Research in psychology

Relationship between BMI, energy intake, and physical activity (Forslund et al. 2005)

Forslund et al. (2005) undertook a cross-sectional study in 22 medical centres in Sweden, to investigate how snacking may influence weight. They used self-reports (questionnaires) to compare the energy intake (estimated in kilocalories based on the answers) of 4259 obese men and women with 1095 controls. They were interested in how much of the energy came from meals and how much came from snacking. Snacking was defined as eating between the main meals. The participants had a physical exam and blood tests were taken.

The obese people ate on average six times a day, compared to five times in the non-obese group. The obese were also more likely to eat later in the day than the non-obese. The researchers noticed that, overall, obese participants reported a significantly higher energy intake than the control group. Snacking was more frequent in the obese group, and women were more frequent snackers than men. The proportion of energy from fat was more pronounced in the obese group. Generally, energy intake was more likely to come from sweet, fatty food choices in obese frequent snackers. The non-obese ate more healthy snacks. The researchers found that

→

obese participants exercised less than the non-obese. The obese also had lower education levels than the non-obese.

	Obese men (n=1891)	Non-obese men (n=505)	Obese women (n=2368)	Non-obese women (n=587)
mean BMI	37.1	25.8	38.7	24.7
total energy (kcal)	3234	2766	2683	2223
% no physical activity during leisure time	31.5	9.5	32.3	11.0

Energy intake and physical activity in obese versus non-obese (adapted from Forslund et al. 2005)

The researchers say that there may be the same under-reporting in this study as is often found in dietary research. The obese participants were volunteers for an intervention study, so they may not be representative of obese people in general, but rather of obese individuals who want to lose weight. They may have been more likely to make eating and exercise decisions that other obese people would not.

Be reflective

1 Do the results of this study correspond with other findings?
2 What are the implications of the study?
3 If you were a doctor, how would you use the results of this study to advise your obese patients?

Cognitive factors related to obesity

In the West, the cultural ideal is the thin body—especially among females. Since many women are dissatisfied with their body weight, a substantial number of females diet on a regular basis. Negative body image and low self-esteem are the norm in overweight and obese individuals. The West is characterized as an individualistic culture. It is believed that individuals are responsible for their own fate. Having a slim body demonstrates control, and the fat body thus becomes a sign of the opposite, according to Nylander and Soerensen (2004). Body shape attitudes are influenced by cultural norms, and dissatisfaction with body shape is an important incentive to diet.

People who diet replace physiological hunger sensations with "cognitive restraint"—that is, they put a limit on what they can eat. This is not enough to eliminate the body's hunger signals. According to **cognitive restraint theory**, dieting in itself could therefore lead to obesity. This is particularly true when there is extreme cognitive restraint, so that diets go below hunger levels, such as when people eat only 800 kcal per day.

Venus of Willendorf: this sculpture was created around 22 000–24 000 years ago; it is believed that it is an idealized female body, signifying fertility; in cultures where food was scarce, obesity was a sign of wealth

Many obese people are chronic dieters, and most of these have experienced breaking their diets. Restraint theory predicts that extreme cognitive restraint is likely to make an individual respond to external cues (e.g. smell of food) or emotional events (e.g. feeling down because weight loss is very small) with a "loss of control" and overeating. This is partly explained in terms of the **false hope syndrome** (Polivy 2001). It seems that obese dieters set unrealistic goals and are overly optimistic about how quickly they can reach their goal. They also believe that weight loss will produce more radical changes in their lives than can rationally be expected, and they forget to use past experiences. This cocktail of false hopes and unattainable criteria for success could be an explanation for the lack of success in dieting and maintenance of weight loss.

Weight loss is not quick, and this fact may result in negative emotions and giving in to eating more than allowed. Because many dieters are guided by an all-or-nothing way of thinking, they are more likely to fail. If people believe that *one* little transgression (e.g. eating an ice cream) has ruined the overall attempt to lose weight, there is an overwhelming chance that they will not only stop the diet, but also indulge in food. This is described as the "what-the-hell effect", and it has been demonstrated repeatedly in chronic dieters.

Supersize Me

The documentary *Supersize Me* was created by the film-maker Morgan Spurlock, who wanted to find out if there was any support for charges raised against McDonald's for causing health problems. He subjected himself to a diet based only on fast food from McDonald's for a month. At the same time, he carried out research in schools in the US, and found that many of them served fast food. Doctors found him perfectly healthy when he started his experiment, but after less than a month his health was seriously affected. You can find clips from the film on YouTube.

Supersize Me

Be a critical thinker

1 Can a documentary like *Supersize Me* count as evidence that fast food is seriously damaging health? Why or why not?

2 What would it take to conduct a scientific study with the same variables? Would there be ethical considerations?

Summing up

According to Ogden (2004), the evidence for the causes of obesity is complex and unclear, but overall there are three factors that are probably involved.

- Some individuals may have a genetic predisposition to become obese.
- Obesity is linked to a lack of exercise.
- Obesity is linked to consuming relatively more fat and relatively less carbohydrates.

Be a thinker

1 What is the evidence to support each of the three factors identified by Ogden (2004) as being involved in obesity?

2 Could you find other factors that could be included in explanations of obesity? Support your argument.

Prevention strategies

WHO has formulated a prevention strategy for obesity: the Global Strategy on Diet, Physical Activity and Health (DPSA 2004). A number of national programmes have been developed and implemented to promote lifestyles that include a healthy diet and physical activity. Childhood obesity is of particular concern. According to WHO estimates, around 22 million children under the age of five were overweight in 2007. Most of these live in low- and middle-income countries.

One important prevention strategy is concerned with *healthy eating*. A balanced diet requires a balanced intake of "macronutrients" (fats, carbohydrates, proteins) and "nutrients" (vitamins and minerals). In order to inform people about what healthy eating is, the British Nutrition Foundation (2007) has created "the eatwell plate". This is an overview of a healthy diet, showing the recommended proportions and types of food. The key message from the eatwell plate is the importance of a balanced diet, with a variety of foods.

In 2008, the British government launched a massive campaign to prevent obesity, based on the principles from WHO. A similar strategy to prevent childhood obesity has been initiated in Australia. (You can find out more about the evaluation of such prevention strategies in Chapter 7.3.)

The eatwell plate

Apply your knowledge

1 To what extent do the strategies from the UK and Australia correspond to knowledge from research?

2 How likely is it that they will help people to change their lifestyle? Support your answer.

The anti-obesity campaign for kids (ages 0–12 years) in Australia, "Go for your life", works with childcare services and primary schools to encourage and support children to enjoy healthy eating and physical activity. In particular the programme focuses on these healthy messages.

- **Tap into water every day**, and limit sweet drinks. The aim is to increase water consumption and reduce the consumption of sweet drinks.
- **Turn off, switch to play**. The aim is to decrease screen time (television, electronic games, computers) and increase active play.
- **Plant fruit and veg in your lunch box**. The aim is to increase consumption of fruit and vegetables.
- **Move, play and go** every day. The aim is to increase active play, physical activity and education.
- **Limit "sometimes" foods**. The aim is to decrease consumption of high-energy foods, such as soft drinks, chocolates, and lollies.
- **Stride and ride**. The aim is to increase active modes of transport.

Treatments

Modern approaches to the treatment of obesity are based on knowledge of obesity as a complex condition that has many causes. Obesity treatments typically take a psychosocial approach—for example, combining diet with information about healthy living, exercise, cognitive restructuring, and relapse prevention.

Blair-West (2007) suggested that successful dieting should be based on knowledge from research, such as restraint theory and stages of change theory (Prochaska and DiClemente 1983). The stages of change theory claim that the process of change can be divided into five stages: precontemplation, contemplation, preparation, action, and maintenance. Knowing where people are in the process is important for success in treatments. Blair-West has set up a new treatment programme in Australia that includes the following.

1 **Realistic goal-setting** (weight loss of about 8 per cent of body weight per year). The focus is on long-term weight loss and maintenance, rather than achieving short-term weight loss.

2 **Low-sacrifice diet**—people should eat less, but not necessarily sacrifice all the food they love the most. They should identify the more fattening foods they eat, as well as those they could sacrifice (low sacrifice) and those they would like to keep (high sacrifice). The latter should be eaten in smaller amounts through portion control (e.g. mindfulness and savouring). They are also advised to eat high-sacrifice foods early in the day. This is to prevent breaking a diet resulting in overeating. This strategy aims to achieve a healthy, sustainable eating lifestyle, with slow and gradual, long-term weight loss, and to avoid weight rebound.

3 **Physical activity** and exercise in some form.

4 **Information** about the dangers of being overweight and the health benefits of losing weight.

Cognitive-behavioural therapy (CBT)

CBT aims to change cognitions and eating behaviour. Judith Beck, from the Beck Institute of Cognitive Therapy and Research, has developed a new CBT-based programme for weight loss. She conducted a pilot study (Beck 2005) at the Institute to measure the effectiveness of CBT in obese women. The participants were 10 women who weighed between 90 and 136 kilogrammes. A year later, all the women had lost weight and have kept it off.

According to Beck, it is important to target those thoughts and beliefs that prevent the patient from losing weight when they have decided to do so. The important thing is not why the patient is overeating, but dealing with cognitions that lead directly to eating. CBT must focus on the patient's permission-giving beliefs that lead to overeating—for example, "It's okay to eat now because I am upset."

Stahre et al. (2007) conducted a randomized trial with a group of obese women in Sweden (mean age 48.5 years and mean BMI 36.5). Half of them participated in a programme that included elements of CBT, and the control group participated in a programme that included moderate-intensity physical activity. The treatment lasted for 10 weeks (two hours per week). The participants' weight was controlled periodically over an 18-month period. There was a small drop-out in both groups.

The CBT programme involves three stages.

1 Challenging eating behaviours (e.g. learn to recognize and adjust destructive eating patterns; monitor calorie intake; identify alternatives to social and emotional eating; start a manageable exercise programme).

2 Challenging cognitions (e.g. confront dysfunctional thinking that prevents healthy eating habits; improve body image and self-confidence; increase social support; adjust thinking to prevent shame and hopelessness).

3 Long-term maintenance of weight loss (e.g. maintain motivation and strengthen coping skills that can deal with challenging situations and setbacks).

In the cognitive programme, the weight loss was 8.6kg at the end of the treatment and 5.9kg after the 18-month follow-up. Participants in the control group had lost an average of 0.7kg, and after the 18-month follow-up, they had gained 0.3kg on average. The researchers concluded that CBT seems to be efficient, and it is also cost-effective.

Dieting

All obesity programmes involve dieting in one form or another. Wadden (1993) carried out a review of studies using randomized control trials to examine the effectiveness of moderate and severe caloric restriction on weight loss. He found that patients stay in treatment for 20 weeks and that 50 per cent will lose around 9kg or more. He concluded that modern methods show improved results in the short term, compared to previous methods, which mainly focused on weight loss alone. As for long-term effects, the picture was different. Wadden found that most obese patients treated in research trials tended to regain their lost weight. This is supported by findings from a meta-analysis of 92 studies of interventions for the treatment and prevention of obesity (NHS Centre for Reviews and Dissemination 1997). The conclusion was that weight gain after treatment was the norm.

Heatherton et al. (1991) reported that dieting in the non-obese predicts weight fluctuations. The same is seen in weight cycling—or "yo-yo" dieting—in obese people. Brownell et al. (1989) conducted research with rats, and found that repeated weight loss was followed by weight regain. The consequence is that weight loss becomes difficult due to an increase in the percentage of body fat and decreased metabolism. The researchers found the same result in human dieters and athletes who yo-yo dieted.

Drug treatments

According to a fact sheet published by the National Institute of Health in the US, obesity should be considered a chronic disease. The recommendation is to use weight-loss medication in combination with programmes of healthy eating and regular physical exercise. Few studies have evaluated the safety and long-term effectiveness of drugs, though, and some are concerned that they may be overprescribed. Most of the drugs approved by the US Food and Drug Administration (FDA) are meant to be used in the short term, but may be used for longer periods. There are two types of drugs: **appetite suppressants** and **lipase inhibitors** (reduction of fat absorption).

- Appetite-suppressant drugs promote weight loss by decreasing appetite or increasing the feeling of being full, because they increase the level of neurotransmitters that affect mood and appetite (e.g. serotonin and adrenalin levels). There is some evidence for the effectiveness of these drugs, although they have some side effects, such as nausea, constipation, and dry mouth.
- Lipase inhibitors act on the gastrointestinal system and reduce fat absorption. There may be a range of unpleasant side effects, especially after eating a meal with high fat content. This could probably have a preventive effect, since eating fat becomes associated with unpleasant consequences such as diarrhoea.

Be an enquirer

1 Which strategy or treatment of those mentioned here is most likely to be successful in helping an obese person? Why?

2 What is the obesity situation in your country? Find data on figures and prevention strategies. Are they in line with those suggested by WHO?

3 If you were invited to participate in a group that needed to produce an obesity prevention plan for children in your own country, what would you suggest?

Berkowitz et al. (2006) carried out a randomized trial with a sample of adolescent boys and girls (age range 12–16 years), to investigate if the appetite-suppressant drug sibutramine reduced weight more than a **placebo** (a sugar pill) in obese adolescents; 386 participants received the drug and 130 received the placebo. The study was longitudinal. The participants also received counselling about how to eat less food, increase physical activity, reduce stress, and keep track of how much they ate.

The average weight of the participants at the beginning of the study was 97.7kg. Adolescents who took sibutramine usually lost weight (6.4kg). Those who took the placebo usually gained weight (1.8kg). Participants who took sibutramine typically lost weight rapidly during the first eight months and then maintained their weight until the end of the study. The main side effect of the drug was rapid heart rate. About a quarter of the participants left the study, which ran for one year only. There was no follow-up study of the long-term benefits or harm of the drug. The researchers did not control weight changes after the study, which makes it difficult to determine whether the weight loss was permanent.

Surgical treatments

Surgical treatments can be used on patients with severe obesity. There are a number of surgical procedures, but the most common are the **gastric bypass** and **gastric banding**. Gastric bypass is a surgical procedure that cuts off part of the stomach—for example, using stapling—so that it can no longer be used to absorb food. Gastric banding involves putting a band around the upper part of the stomach so that only a small part of the stomach receives food. This helps the patient to feel full sooner. Maggard et al. (2005) performed a meta-analysis of effectiveness associated with surgical treatments of obesity, based on 147 studies. Surgery resulted in weight loss of 20–30kg, which was maintained for up to 10 years and was accompanied by a general improvement in health. They concluded that gastric bypass was more efficient overall than gastric banding.

> ### Possible extended essay questions
> - Why is there an "obesity epidemic"?
> - How could psychological factors prevent successful dieting in an overweight or obese person, and is it possible to do something about this?
> - To what extent do biological, psychological and sociocultural factors influence addictive behaviour?

Possible essay question
Outline two factors related to the development of obesity.

Discuss one prevention strategy or one treatment for obesity.

Assessment advice
In the first question, the command term is "outline". This requires you to give a brief account or summary of two factors that are considered important in the development of obesity.

The last part of the question requires you to discuss either a prevention strategy or a treatment for obesity. You should only answer one of them. "Discuss" is a command term that requires you to offer a balanced review of either a prevention strategy or a treatment. Your answer should include a range of arguments in support of why such a strategy or treatment is chosen, what it targets and why. It could also refer to some evaluation of the strategy but it is not required. As in all answers, you need to include research (theories and studies) as evidence to back up your line of argument.

Health psychology: health promotion

Learning outcomes

- Discuss the extent to which biological, cognitive, and sociocultural factors influence health-related behaviour
- Evaluate psychological research (through theories and/or studies) relevant to health psychology
- Examine models and theories of health promotion
- Discuss the effectiveness of health promotion strategies

An important part of health psychology is to put theory into practice in health promotion. This can be done by attempts to promote healthy behaviour, and some of these have already been dealt with in Chapter 7.2. Psychologists try to understand the role of *behaviour* and *beliefs* in health problems, because they assume that one way to change unhealthy behaviours is to change attitudes and beliefs. The main goal in prevention programmes is to encourage people to change their health-threatening behaviours, or to prevent people from developing health-threatening behaviours in the first place. This is not as easy as it sounds because the exact link between beliefs and behaviours is not known. Another problem is that at the time that health-threatening behaviours develop, people often have little immediate incentive to change their behaviours. For example, problems related to smoking occur many years after people have taken up smoking, not when they start the habit.

Models of health promotion

Health psychologists often base interventions on theories and empirical research related to decision making, in order to understand what factors contribute to people's decisions to change. Two important theories on decision making that have guided interventions are the health belief model (HBM) and the stages of change theory.

The health belief model (HBM)

The HBM was originally developed by Rosenstock (1974), and is one of the oldest social cognition models. It has been used to predict whether a person will choose to engage in healthy behaviours in order to reduce or prevent the chance of disease and premature death. The HBM predicts that individuals will take a health-related action if they think that a negative health problem—for example, developing lung cancer (smoking) or type 2 diabetes (obesity)—can be avoided by taking the recommended action, and that they will be successful in doing so.

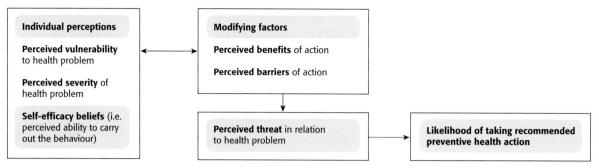

The modified health belief model

The HBM sees people as *rational* and suggests that the likelihood that a person will engage in healthy behaviour depends on a number of factors, such as the following.

1 **Evaluation of threat** (perceived vulnerability)—for example, overweight may result in developing a heart condition; smoking may result in lung cancer. The person will probably recognize this as a serious condition, but may also believe that it does not happen to people like them, for example people their age. The model claims that people only act if they perceive a threat—for example, a physical symptom like chest pains, death of somebody from heart disease or lung cancer, or information from a mass media campaign.

2 **Cost–benefit analysis** (outcome of changing behaviour): the person will evaluate whether the perceived benefits will be higher than the perceived barriers—for example, **financial** because you have to buy healthy food and this is more expensive than chips and burgers; or **difficult** because you have to engage in exercise and you are very heavy; or **social** because you like eating fast food with your friends, but you also want to live longer.

The HBM can identify some of the important cognitions involved in health behaviours. Research has supported the role of *perceived threat* in predicting health behaviour. External cues such as health information seem to be especially important. This could be information in the form of fear-arousing warnings, which is used in the prevention and cessation of smoking (e.g. Sutton 1981).

The HBM model includes self-efficacy beliefs—that is, the belief that you can perform adequately in a particular situation. This feeling of competence will influence perception, motivation, and performance. Bandura (1977) suggested that self-efficacy beliefs are important predictors of what people believe they are capable of. People make judgments of self-efficacy primarily on the basis of previous achievements. Other sources of judgment include:

● observations of the performance of others i.e. modelling ("If he can do it, so can I")

● social and self-persuasion ("You can do it")

● monitoring emotional states—for example, feeling anxious suggests low expectations of efficacy ("I don't feel up to it today").

Research in psychology

Quist-Paulsen et al. (2003)

Quist-Paulsen et al. (2003) conducted a field experiment in which they investigated patients who had been treated for heart problems in a Norwegian hospital. It is known that mortality is reduced by 50 per cent beyond three to five years if such patients stop smoking. Normally, 30–45 per cent of heart patients will stop spontaneously.

The researchers wanted to see if a longer intervention, including fear arousal, would promote smoking cessation and prevent relapse. They randomly assigned participants to a treatment group and a control group. All patients were offered group counselling sessions. Patients in the control group received no further counselling on how to stop smoking. Patients in the treatment group had personal advice from trained nurses, and received material that stressed the risks of continued smoking and the improved outcomes of cessation. Patients were advised to stop, and nicotine replacement was offered to those with cravings. Spouses were also advised to stop smoking.

The nurses contacted the patients nine times after they went home, to encourage cessation. They stressed the negative aspects of smoking on their condition (fear arousal). Patients also had two consultations in the year after leaving hospital. The researchers found that 57 per cent of the intervention group and 37 per cent of the control group had stopped smoking. They concluded that the programme based on fear arousal and relapse prevention was effective for this group of patients.

Ethical considerations in research

1 Do you think it was ethical to say to people that they were more likely to die if they did not give up smoking, or was it justified to say this? Support your answer.

2 How would you explain the results of the study?

A problem in the HBM is the focus on individual *cognitions*. It does not include emotional, social, and economic factors, which are known to influence health behaviours as well. It seems difficult to make standard measurements of many of the concepts—for example, perceived vulnerability. The HBM is also criticized for assuming that people are rational, which is not always the case. In fact, it seems that people are sometimes "unrealistically optimistic" about their health. This means that even though there is a threat, it is not always perceived as such.

Research has found that awareness of health risks does not necessarily inhibit people from engaging in potentially risky behaviour, Studies have found that people are quite optimistic about their health. Weinstein (1987) asked people to rate their risk of developing various disorders compared to people like them. Individuals usually rate their chances of illness as lower than for other people. This is the case in smokers, to a large extent. Weinstein suggested that the following factors affect "unrealistic optimism".

● People tend to believe that if a problem has not appeared yet, then it is unlikely to happen in the future.

● People tend to think that personal action can prevent the problem.

● People believe that the problem is rare.

● People have little or no experience of the problem.

Cognitive dissonance

The theory of cognitive dissonance (Festinger 1975) is based on the assumption that people try to appear rational to themselves and to others. The theory has proved successful for making explicit predictions about how people react when they are exposed to attitude-relevant information. In general, dissonance theory predicts that people are motivated to attend to information that supports their beliefs, and to avoid information that contradicts them, in order to avoid **cognitive dissonance**—an uncomfortable tension. For example, if someone really likes smoking cigarettes, he or she would be expected to avoid information that stressed the negative consequences of smoking (e.g. cancer), and instead attend to the positive aspects (e.g. "it makes me relax"). In order not to create tension or dissonance, people simply avoid attitude-dissonant information, according to the theory.

The effects of cognitive dissonance can perhaps be seen in the ways that people evaluate their level of personal risk. McMasters and Lee (1991) investigated the knowledge and beliefs of smokers. They compared smokers, non-smokers, and ex-smokers, and found that all the groups had a similar amount of factual knowledge about the effects of smoking; but when smokers were asked to estimate their personal risk, they rated it as lower than it would be for the average smoker.

Cognitive dissonance may be an important factor in understanding the role of cognition in changing attitudes (e.g. in anti-smoking campaigns.) Cognitive dissonance works in several ways. People can discredit the source of information, be selective about what information to notice, or analyse the information in alternative ways so that it has different implications. However, the theory has been criticized for not explicitly addressing the emotional or social aspects of decision making.

Stages of change model

It is not necessarily true that people need professional help to change their unhealthy behaviour. Quite often they give up smoking or start exercising through their own efforts. Prochaska et al. (1982) investigated 872 smokers who had given up smoking either by themselves or after a therapeutic intervention. The model identified five stages of change, which highlighted the processes involved in the transition from a smoker to a non-smoker (or from a non-exerciser to an exerciser). They found that cessation was not necessarily linear, but involved a shift across the five stages.

1 **Precontemplation:** The person is not seriously considering quitting.

2 **Contemplation:** The person is aware that there is a problem and that something should be done, but there is no commitment to quitting. Prochaska et al. (1982) found that some of the smokers in their study stayed in this stage throughout the study.

3 **Preparation:** The person is seriously considering quitting. Perhaps by reducing the number of cigarettes or postponing the first one.

Be reflective

- How would a smoker react to this warning according to cognitive dissonance theory?

- Under what circumstances would a smoker perhaps listen to the warning? Use the knowledge from this chapter to answer.

4 **Action:** The person has stopped smoking. Prochaska et al. (1982) found that smokers often make a number of action attempts before they reach the maintenance stage.

5 **Maintenance:** The person works to maintain non-smoking and prevent relapse.

The model is based on the assumption that cessation is a *dynamic process*. People may switch back and forth between stages— for example, from preparation to action, and then back again to preparation. Individual cognitions such as perceptions of vulnerability and self-efficacy, also influence smoking behaviour. In another study, Prochaska et al. (1991) wanted to find out if the stages of change model could be used to predict smoking cessation. There were 1466 individuals participating in a minimum intervention programme to stop smoking. They were mostly European American females who had started smoking at the age of 16 and now smoked, on average, 29 cigarettes a day. They completed assessment questionnaires at baseline and there were follow-ups at one and six months.

The questionnaires measured:

1 confidence that they would not smoke (smoking abstinence self-efficacy)
2 perceived stress
3 physical tolerance
4 perceptions of the pros and cons of smoking
5 smoking processes of change (referring to the model's stages).

Based on (5), the smokers were categorized as either precontemplators, contemplators, or in the preparation stage of change.

The results showed that participants in the preparation stage of change smoked less, were less addicted, had higher self-efficacy, rated the costs of smoking as higher, and had experienced more quitting attempts than the other two groups. This suggests that the model is a useful tool for predicting successful outcome of smoking cessation interventions, because it indicates that interventions must focus on when an individual is *ready* to change in order to be successful. The model has been used to develop a number of interventions and behaviour-change programmes.

Hawkins et al. (2001) used the stages of change model to investigate predictions of weight loss in a sample of 200 African American women living in two rural counties in central Virginia, US. Of the 200 women, 142 were overweight or obese (BMI over 25). They were classified into different stages of change. Those in the preparation stage (48 per cent) were more likely to view weight loss as positive than the other groups. The two most important predictors for change were what friends think about weight and positive attitude to weight loss. The researchers concluded that such knowledge can be useful in designing health education initiatives and encouraging social support in weight-loss interventions.

West and Sohal (2006) challenged the stages of change model. According to them, many ex-smokers report that they just decided to stop and then did so, without making any plans. They

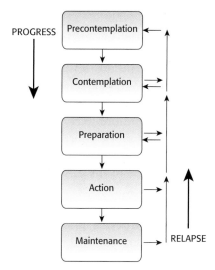

Stages of change model

Preparing for change may be the first step towards change

investigated whether smokers were more likely to be successful in smoking cessation if they had planned to stop, compared with smokers who had made no such plans but had just given up. The researchers did this on the basis of a large-scale cross-sectional survey of ex-smokers and smokers who said they had made at least one attempt to quit. The results indicated that unplanned attempts to quit were more likely to succeed for at least six months than planned attempts. Therefore, they suggested a process of change based on "catastrophe theory"—that is, smokers are more likely to react to a cue in the environment and decide to stop at once. This is because smokers have varying levels of motivational tension to stop, and environmental triggers (e.g. a media campaign or a friend quitting) can result in a change in the motivational state. This might lead to an immediate decision to give up smoking, and it seems to be a more complete transformation than one involving a plan to quit at some point in the future.

Health promotion strategies—are they effective?

The goal of health promotion strategies is to enhance good health and prevent illness. WHO (1986) defined health promotion as "the process of enabling people to increase control over, and to improve their health". This clearly indicates that health is something that can be promoted. However, it is not easy to get people to behave in healthy ways because of the many factors that control health habits. A woman who wants to stay slim may eat healthy food and exercise, but she may also smoke because she believes that it helps her to keep her weight down. People may decide to quit smoking and be successful for a year, but then start smoking again. Research has also shown that people who have no formal education are more likely to be obese and to smoke, and that they are also less likely to change their behaviour.

Psychologists know that one-to-one contact is an effective way to change behaviour in individuals or small groups, but this approach is not possible when whole populations have serious health problems. This has led psychologists and health workers to devise methods by which to reach large numbers of people. Modern health-promotion activities are typically concerned with some of the following issues in relation to health problems like obesity or smoking.

- Health education programmes to raise awareness in the public about health risks and encourage changes in behaviour (e.g. media campaigns of health risks of obesity and smoking)
- Public health campaigns that aim to change beliefs, attitudes, and motivations (e.g. informing smokers about the dangers of smoking and showing them how they can stop)
- Changing the wider determinants of health (e.g. changing the physical environment—more stairs and fewer escalators—and creating more exercise facilities)
- Public or private health services that can help people change their behaviour (e.g. family doctors, pharmacies, or smoking cessation clinics)

Be a researcher

- Interview two people who have tried to stop smoking or who have managed to stop. Ask them the same questions about their experience, e.g. if they cared about health messages in relation to smoking, details about stoping or attempts to stop, their evaluation of the process and so on.

- Based on your data, outline the two most important factors in stopping smoking.

- Do your findings confirm any of the theories mentioned in this chapter? If they do, what does this mean? And what if they don't?

● Political activities (e.g. legislation aimed at improving and increasing physical activity, and set standards for foods available in schools; raising tax or implementing bans on smoking; reducing tax on healthy food and raising tax on sugar and fat)

Yee et al. (2006) investigated how 20 states in the US had implemented evidence-based health-promotion strategies to change or influence behaviours related to obesity, nutrition, and physical activity. The interventions mainly targeted increasing physical activity (83 per cent), increasing fruit and vegetable consumption (55 per cent), balancing caloric intake and expenditure (38 per cent), and decreasing television viewing time (38 per cent). This study clearly supports that health promotion is now often based on research findings.

Health campaigns

Health campaigns are often criticized for being ineffective. Some people argue that they cannot make people change their habits and that they do not really help those who need to change the most. According to Holm (2002), who conducted a survey on the efficiency of health campaigns in relation to food habits in Denmark, health campaigns are useful, but they cannot stand alone. They must be seen as an integral part of the entire health promotion project. The campaign can establish a norm for what is considered to be healthy food. It can also create a general framework for an understanding of good practice in losing weight. Holm claims that a campaign needs to be based on people's daily life (e.g. food culture) in order to be effective. A successful health campaign in Denmark in the 1990s aimed to decrease the use of butter on the national rye bread sandwiches that constitute the Danes' lunch. From 1985 to 2001, the amount of people who said they did not use butter on the sandwich increased from 7 per cent to 40 per cent. The use of low-fat milk has also increased in Denmark after health campaigns. This shows that such campaigns can promote change.

It is difficult to make precise evaluations of the effect of a health campaign, but according to Holm, there is a long-term effect of all the campaigns in Denmark. Each of them contributes to increased knowledge and motivation to change unhealthy habits. The campaign to increase physical activity for adults—"30 minutes every day"—has probably contributed to the rise in memberships of fitness centres. According to Holm, successful campaigns in relation to obesity prevention must address three levels: what the individual can do, what can be done in the community, and what should be done by the government.

In the modern world, the *media* plays a decisive role in health promotion. According to Sepstrup (1999), media campaigns can only be used to convey *simple* messages. If the goal is to change attitudes and promote behavioural change, the media campaign should be combined with other measures. The media campaign is excellent in creating attention and communicating knowledge about a specific topic, but it is not enough on its own. People must have the necessary means to actually do something. The simple message—

Be reflective

Think about any health campaigns that you have recently seen or heard about in your country or community

● What was the campaign targeting? And who was the target group?

● What was the overall message of the campaign?

● Which methods did the campaign use?

● Would any of the messages have convinced you—or your friends—to change behaviour if you were in the target group? Why or why not?

such as "Smoking kills you" or "Exercise 30 minutes every day"—must be supported by activities targeting people in their local area, so they can get the necessary support to change their habits.

"VERB—It's what you do" was a national, multicultural campaign that ran from 2002 to 2006 in the US. The campaign was coordinated by the Department of Health and Human Services' Centers for Disease Control and Prevention. It used commercial marketing strategies to persuade the target audience—children aged 9–13 years—to be physically active every day. The campaign was also meant to reach parents and adults in professional charge of children—for example, coaches and teachers—and give them ideas about how to promote physical activity on a daily basis.

Huhman et al. (2005) conducted a large-scale survey of children and parents to investigate the campaign's effectiveness to create awareness and promote physical activity. They found that after one year, 74 per cent of the children were aware of the VERB campaign. There was an increase in sessions of free-time physical activity for children who were aware of the campaign compared to those who were unaware of it. The researchers concluded that commercial advertising in health promotion is promising.

> ### Be reflective
>
> 1 How can knowledge about persuasive communication be used to create a successful health campaign?
>
> 2 Is the "Smoking kills" more effective than the "Mom I love you" prevention strategy? Support your argument using your psychological knowledge (e.g. cognitive dissonance).

Persuasive communication

Psychologists have investigated what makes a communication persuasive. Some of the following characterize successful persuasion.

1 The source—that is, the person who communicates the message—must be credible (trustworthy or an expert).

2 The audience (target group) should determine how the message is framed. One-sided arguments are not well received by an informed audience.

3 The message should be short, clear, direct, and explicit. Fear appeals—for example, "smoking kills you"—are likely to backfire, but they may be effective if they are accompanied with specific information about *how* to change—for example, the address of a smoking cessation centre or information about how to increase self-efficacy in quitting. Indirect fear appeals—for example,

playing on the emotions you have for your loved ones—can be effective.

4 Attitude change is more likely to last if the target group has participated actively in the communication, rather than just receiving it passively.

Health warnings on cigarette packets

An emotional appeal

Overall, smoking has decreased since smoking-prevention campaigns have been introduced. An extraordinary campaign was the TRUTH anti-tobacco campaign in Florida (US) in 1998–99. One of the aims of this campaign was to prevent teen smoking by changing the attitudes of teenagers and encouraging them to form groups and spread the message in the community.

The campaign included a massive advertising drive, including 33 television commercials, billboards, posters, the Internet

Logo of the Florida campaign

(e.g. YouTube), programme sponsorship, merchandise, and local youth advocacy groups. The campaign also sponsored the YouCare video contest at YouTube, where teenagers uploaded their own films.

One of the core components of the campaign was young people confronting the tobacco industry and accusing them of manipulating young people to encourage them to smoke. The campaign leaders conducted focus-group interviews with teenagers to identify appropriate ways of running the campaign. They found that teenagers were well aware of the dangers of smoking, so this should not be the message of the campaign. Instead, the strategy of a youth movement against the tobacco industry was decided by teen delegates at the Teen Tobacco Summit in 1998: "Truth, a generation united against tobacco". The campaign included the formation of a new youth anti-tobacco advocacy group called SWAT (Students Working Against Tobacco), who worked at grass-roots levels.

The campaign carried out a number of telephone surveys of its target audience, to measure effect and awareness of the campaign, as well as changes in attitude among adolescents. One of the findings was that teenagers' negative attitude to smoking had risen. Follow-up surveys indicated that non-smoking teens who refrained from smoking through the campaign were more likely to say that they had been influenced by the campaign. The Florida Youth Tobacco Survey (FYTS), conducted in February 1999, found that the number of middle- and high-school teenagers defined as "current smokers" went down by 19.4 per cent and 8 per cent respectively. During this time period, 29 000 teenagers from Florida made the decision not to smoke, which is one of the largest annual declines observed in the US since 1980.

Sly et al. (2002) carried out a survey 22 months after the campaign to investigate if the anti-tobacco advertisements had had an effect on attitude changes such that the non-smokers would remain non-smokers. They found that amount of exposure to the ads with the key message theme—that is, that the tobacco industry manipulates teenagers' attitudes to smoking—during the campaign predicted that the person had remained a non-smoker.

The findings from this campaign indicate that it is possible to change people's attitudes and behaviour if the campaign is clear and focused on a target group.

The same was found in the UK, where McVey and Stapleton (2002) demonstrated that anti-smoking television advertising was successful in motivating people to give up smoking, and preventing those who had stopped from starting again.

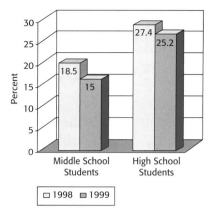

Cigarette use among Florida teens (1998 and 1999)

Possible essay question

Describe one model or one theory of health promotion.

With reference to research discuss the effectiveness of one health promotion strategy

Assessment advice

The command term "describe" requires you to give a detailed account of either one model or one theory of health promotion. This could be any of the ones you have studied in this chapter.

The second part of the question uses the command term "discuss" which requires you to give a balanced review of one particular health promotion strategy and evaluate its effectiveness. This could relate to the model or theory described in the first question so that this is included in the second part as a background of what could be effective. Your answer could link the effectiveness of a health promotion strategy to a specific campaign which would also give exact data to support your argument.

Make sure you look at the markbands in Chapter 11. These indicate that besides relevant knowledge, you also need to demonstrate critical thinking skills be able to structure your answer (organization). This is the same for all essays in paper 2.

Be a thinker

1 What do you think contributed to the success of the Florida campaign?

2 What do you think was the most important factor?

3 Can you use the results of this campaign to say something in general about what makes campaigns successful? Use your psychological knowledge to support your argument.

Human relationships: social responsibility

Learning outcomes

- Discuss the extent to which biological, cognitive and sociocultural factors influence human relationships
- Evaluate psychological research (that is theories and/or studies) relevant to the study of human relationships
- Distinguish between altruism and pro-social behaviour
- Contrast two theories explaining altruism in humans
- Explain cross-cultural differences in pro-social behaviour with reference to research studies
- Examine factors influencing bystanderism

Patrick Morgan

Patrick Morgan was a 16-year-old student when he made headlines in Australia. He and some friends were waiting for the train to Sydney when he saw an emergency situation. An elderly woman fell down the gap between the train and the platform when she tried to get off her train. Patrick ran over as fast as he could. He risked his life by jumping under the stationary train to give the woman first aid. Meanwhile, his friend ran to tell the train driver not to pull away from the station.

A police officer said: "I think it's particularly special—a young person of his age without looking for his own safety has gone to assist her."

But the teenager says he was just acting instinctively. Patrick said: "I thought I was just doing what anyone else would do."

Stories of people taking risks to help others always make a great impression on us. Heroes like the German Oskar Schindler, or Paul Rusesabagina from Hotel Rwanda, have been the focus of very successful Hollywood films. What is it that makes these people do what they do? Are these just special individuals, or are there reasons why these people were more likely to help than others?

Pro-social behaviour is defined as behaviour that benefits another person or has positive social consequences (Staub 1978). This definition is often considered too vague, because although it discusses the *outcome* of the behaviour, it does not consider the *motivation* of the behaviour.

Helping behaviour is behaviour that intentionally helps or benefits another person. In other words, it is planned with the goal of "making a difference". Going to a hospital to assist at a children's clinic is an example of helping behaviour. **Altruism** is when one helps another person for no reward, and even at some cost to oneself. This is the case in the story of Patrick Morgan.

Psychological research on altruism

Altruism is a rather puzzling behaviour. It does not appear to make much sense that an individual would risk his or her life for a stranger. There are biological arguments for the origins of altruism, but there are also arguments that altruism is a behaviour that results from cognitive processes. Psychologists argue that there are two types of altruism: *biological altruism*, which has its roots in evolutionary psychology, and *psychological altruism*, which is based more on cognitive psychology.

Evolutionary explanations of altruism

Darwin suggested that the evolution of altruism should be seen in relation to what could be advantageous to the group a person belongs to, rather than what could be advantageous to the individual alone.

Kin selection theory predicts that the degree of altruism depends on the number of genes shared by individuals. The closer the relationship between the helper and those being helped, the greater the chance for altruistic behaviour. This has been supported by a number of empirical studies with animals. Altruistic behaviour could appear to be unselfish but some argue that it should, in fact, be seen as selfish. Dawkins (1976) proposed "the selfish gene theory", arguing that there is an innate drive for the survival and propagation of one's own genes. It is not the individuals or the species, but rather the genes that compete. Those genes that are most fit for survival are characterized by ruthless selfishness, according to Dawkins. Any organism will try to maximize its "inclusive fitness"—that is, the number of copies of its genes passed on globally, not necessarily by a particular individual. Since animals living in social groups share many genes, altruistic behaviour is seen as a way to guarantee that one's own genes will be passed on to future generations. Seen from this perspective, it becomes clear why individuals are willing to sacrifice themselves to protect the lives of their kin.

Although this theory is supported by extensive observations and documentation of altruistic occurrences, it does not explain *why* a smaller number of people, like Patrick Morgan, help complete strangers. As with all evolutionary theory, it is difficult—if not impossible—to test under controlled conditions. Finally, Dawkins assumes that genes directly cause behaviour, a claim that is not yet adequately supported.

Another theory related to biological altruism is the **reciprocal altruism theory** suggested by Trivers (1971). The theory is an attempt to explain the evolution of altruism among individuals who are not related. The theory postulates that it may benefit an animal to behave altruistically if there is an expectation that the favour will be returned in the future. In other words, you scratch my back and I'll scratch yours. The basis of this theory is that, through mutual cooperation, both are more likely to increase their chance of survival. One example of this could be the small fish who clean larger fish by removing parasites from their mouths and gills. The small fish feed on the parasites, and the large fish are freed from parasites, so there is a mutual benefit. It has been observed that when the large fish is attacked by a predator, it waits for the cleaner to leave before fleeing from the predator. Trivers sees this as an example of reciprocal altruism. The large fish returns to the same small fish regularly to be cleaned, so it makes sense for the large fish to attend to the small fish's welfare by not swallowing it, so that the large fish can get cleaned again in the future.

Axelrod and Hamilton (1981) tested reciprocal altruism with humans, using a version of the game called the prisoner's dilemma, where players interact in pairs. Individuals A and B can choose either to "cooperate" or to "defect". If they both cooperate, both gain some reward. If they both defect, there is no pay-off to either of them. Each player's reward depends on his own strategy, as well as that of the other player. If the players only play against each other once, the best strategy, of course, is to defect, so that there is a chance that one's own gain is maximized. Viewed in evolutionary terms, there is no chance that cooperative behaviour can evolve, so natural selection will favour the defectors, and a cooperator will eventually be eliminated from the population. If two players meet each other many times, they can adjust their strategy so that it fits with their opponent's last move. This is called the "tit-for-tat" strategy, and a player following it will initially cooperate and then respond with the same move as their opponent's previous action. If the opponent was cooperative, then the player is cooperative. If the opponent was defective, the player is also defective. Axelrod and Hamilton argue that cooperation of this nature is an evolutionarily stable strategy.

It is called the prisoner's dilemma because it is based on a hypothetical story of two criminals who have been arrested for a serious crime. They are interrogated separately; they both know that if neither of them confesses, the evidence cannot give them more than one year in prison. However, if one confesses and testifies against the other, he will get parole and the other one a life sentence. Because of the options, there is a strong tendency to confess when the advantages and disadvantages are considered. The payoff can be seen in the table in the margin.

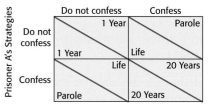

The prisoner's dilemma

The prisoner's dilemma shows how actions determined by self-interest (e.g. economic benefits in financial speculations) are not necessarily in the group's interest. Thomas Hobbes (1586–1679), a political theorist, whose "social contract theory" has inspired politics and economics, argued that it must be taken into account that people are motivated by self-interest. He believed that uncontrolled pursuit of self-interest would result in chaos and that governments have the responsibility of preventing this chaos.

In terms of evaluation of this theory, it is questionable whether animal behaviour can be generalized to that of humans. Human behaviour is influenced by culture to a far greater extent than that

Be a thinker

To what extent is "reciprocal altruism" part of politics? Think about different issues like the regulation of the economy during an economic crisis or protection of the environment.

of other animals, and is often the product of conscious beliefs and desires. In general, humans do behave more altruistically towards their close kin than towards non-relatives. Also, we tend to help those who have helped us in the past. There are behaviours, however, like adoption, that do not benefit kin and thus cannot be explained by a purely biological model.

Psychological explanations of altruism

Psychological altruism is witnessed in higher-level mammals, and appears to have some conscious cognitive component, rather than the instinctual nature of biological altruism. Lerner and Lichtman (1968) carried out an experiment where participants were assigned to work in pairs. For each pair, one of the participants was a confederate—that is, they were playing a role, working in conjunction with the researcher. Participants were told that one of them would be the learner—who would receive electrical shocks, and the other would be the control. Participants then drew from a hat what they thought was a random number, but in fact the confederate always received the role of "learner". When the confederate acted distressed, most of the true participants behaved altruistically and took over the role of learner. How can this be explained?

Schaller and Cialdini (1988) proposed the **negative-state relief model**. They argue that egoistic motives lead us to help others in bad circumstances in order to reduce the distress we experience from watching the bad situation. The negative-state relief model also explains why people walk away instead of helping: this is another way of reducing distress.

Though this theory appears to explain some behaviour, feelings of distress do not always lead people to take action. The model does not accurately predict how one will behave—either altruistically or selfishly—in any given situation.

The **empathy-altruism model** of Batson et al. (1981) suggests that people can experience two types of emotions when they see someone suffering. One is *personal distress* (e.g. anxiety and fear), which leads to egoistic helping. A second is *empathetic concern* (e.g. sympathy, compassion, tenderness), which leads to altruistic behaviour. If you feel empathy towards another person, you will help him or her, regardless of what you may gain from it. Relieving the person's suffering becomes the most important thing. When you do not feel empathy, you consider the costs and benefits of helping in making your decision.

In Batson's classic experiment, students were asked to listen to tapes of an interview with a student named Carol. She talked about her car accident in which both her legs were broken. She talked about her struggles, and how far she was falling behind at school. Students were each given a letter, asking them to meet with Carol and share lecture notes with her. The experimenters varied the level of empathy, telling one group to try to focus on how Carol was feeling (high empathy level), while members of the other group were told they did not need to be concerned with her feelings (low empathy level). The experimenters also varied the cost of not helping. The high-cost group was told that Carol would be in their psychology

Are you really caring?

● When you participate in CAS activities to help other people (for example, working in a soup kitchen or helping street children), what is your motivation? Include what you have learned here and discuss your reasons.

● Do your reasons make a difference to the ones you help? And to yourself?

class when she returned to school. The low-cost group believed Carol would finish the class at home. The results confirmed the empathy-altruism hypothesis. Those in the high-empathy group were almost equally likely to help Carol in either set of circumstances, while the low-empathy group helped out of self-interest. Thinking about seeing her in class every day probably made them feel guilty if they did not help (Aronson et al. 2005).

Batson's findings have been consistently replicated, so it appears that the theory of empathy-altruism is consistent with its predictions that helping behaviour based on empathy is unselfish. However, the research has only investigated short-term altruism, and the interpretation of the results has not taken personality factors into account. This could be seen as a weakness of the explanation.

Though Batson's model makes it easier to predict behaviour, it is difficult to measure one's level of empathy. Batson argues that empathy is an innate trait in all of us, but it is not clear why we do not experience a predictable level of empathy in a given situation. Could it be that there are biological differences which determine one's level of empathy? Or is empathy something that has been learned?

Research in psychology

Imitation promotes helping
(Van Baaren et al. 2004)

Van Baaren et al. (2004) showed that when a person is being imitated or mimicked, helping behaviour is increased. Their laboratory experiment involved a participant and a confederate. The participant was told that the confederate would imitate the participant's body language and gestures during a conversation. This is called non-verbal synchronization, and it is believed to play a role in establishing trust between people. It is also believed that nonverbal synchronization happens in daily interactions to a large extent without people's conscious knowledge. The researchers found that participants whose gestures were imitated helped the confederate to a greater extent when the confederate dropped some pens on the floor.

This study showed that people who are being imitated show an increase in helping behaviour. In addition, imitating (as well as being imitated) promotes pro-social behaviour. This can be explained by imitation causing an empathic mode in people who imitate and are being imitated. Stel and Vonk (2004) showed that participants become more empathic when imitating other people's facial expressions. Compared to participants who did not imitate, those who did became more emotionally attuned to the person who was being imitated. Could it be that mirror neurons play a role in our willingness to help others? If humans are hardwired to understand others, the mere act of imitating someone may perhaps activate emotional responses as well. This could explain why participants in this study felt sympathy towards the person they had imitated.

John Rabe: a good Nazi?

John Rabe was born in Hamburg in 1882. In 1908, he moved to China, where he worked in the Siemens office in Nanjing. Rabe became a staunch supporter of Nazism and the representative town leader for the Nazi Party in Nanjing. In 1938, he would tell German audiences: "I believe not only in the correctness of our political system, but I am behind it 100%."

When the Japanese army approached the city, he decided to stay. On 25 November 1937, he wired Adolf Hitler to request the Führer's intercession in asking that the Japanese government grant the factory the status of a neutral zone.

After the atrocities began, Rabe roamed the city, trying to prevent the atrocities himself. Rabe sheltered as many Chinese as he could, turning his house and office into a sanctuary, and allowed hundreds of Chinese women to live in straw huts in his backyard. In order to keep up the hope of the refugees, he hosted birthday celebrations for the children.

He explained his reasons for doing what he did in the following way: "…there is a question of morality here. I cannot bring myself for now to betray the trust these people have put in me, and it is touching to see how they believe in me."

(Adapted from Iris Chang, *The Rape of Nanking*)

John Rabe

Apply your knowledge

1 To what extent could Rabe's actions to save the Chinese workers be classified as "altruism"?

2 What other explanations can you think of for his behaviour?

Pro-social behaviour and the bystander effect

Altruism is seen as the ultimate act in terms of humans helping one another. But what about helping other people in less threatening situations? What are the chances that someone would stop to help if you dropped your books in the corridor between classes? What about offering your seat to another person when you are on a bus? Are there some people who are simply kinder than others? The following study considers whether there are dispositional factors that make some people more likely to help others.

Research in psychology

The good Samaritan (Bateson and Darley 1973)

Does religious devotion make a difference in terms of willingness to help fellow human beings? Darley conducted a field experiment in which 40 students at Princeton Theological Seminary were asked to participate in a study of religious education. In the first session, a personality questionnaire concerning religiosity was administered. In a second session, the participant received instruction in one campus building and was then sent to a second building to give a presentation. Some were told to talk about jobs in which seminary students would be effective, and others were asked to speak on the parable of the good Samaritan, a biblical parable about a person who stops to help a stranger. In addition, before they left to give the presentation, some were told that they did not have to hurry, some were told that they had sufficient time, but that they should go to the building directly, and others were told that they were already late and had to hurry. While they were walking to the other building, the participants passed a person who appeared to have passed out in an alleyway. The IV was whether they were told to hurry; the DV was to what extent the seminarians stopped to help.

The results were that overall 16 (40 per cent) helped: 63 per cent of those in the low-hurry condition, 45 per cent of those in the intermediate hurry condition, and only 10 per cent of those in the late condition. Participants in a hurry were likely to offer less help than those who were not in a hurry. Whether the participant was going to give a speech on the parable of the good Samaritan or not did not significantly affect helping behaviour. Neither did the researchers find any correlation between religiosity and likelihood to help. The decisive factor seemed to be whether they had been told to hurry or not. In other words, it appears that situational rather than dispositional factors played the more significant role in this study.

Research into helping behaviour began after an incident in 1964, when a young woman named Kitty Genovese was stabbed to death by a serial rapist and murderer. The murder took place over a period of about half an hour, during which the victim was screaming for help. The press reported that 38 of her neighbours watched from their windows as she attempted to escape her murderer, but they did not even call the police to assist her. How could this happen? The US researchers Latané and Darley carried out a number of experiments in order to find an answer.

Latané and Darley suggested a term for not helping someone in need of help: **bystanderism**. They suggested that the reason for not helping Kitty Genovese was that the witnesses had seen others watching the incident, so they all thought that other people would call for help. The presence of others seems to determine whether or not people will intervene.

It seems that when people assess a situation, certain factors influence whether they will help or not. Based on research, Latané and Darley found that the two most common factors are *diffusion of responsibility* and *pluralistic ignorance*.

Diffusion of responsibility: When several people watch an incident like the Kitty Genovese murder, they seem to reason that somebody else can, should, and probably will offer assistance. This could explain why people are generally more likely to help when they are the only person available to offer assistance. Latané and Darley (1968) did a laboratory experiment in which they told student participants that they were going to be interviewed about living in a high-pressure urban environment. They were told that in order to preserve anonymity they would be interviewed over an intercom. Some of the students were told there were five other people in the discussion

Be a critical thinker

Evaluate the method used in the Darley study (above).

1 What concerns do you have about how the study was conducted?

2 Do you think the results could be applied cross-culturally? Why or why not?

Profile

John Darley
John Darley is a professor of psychology at Princeton University. Much of his research in social psychology has focused on decisions and actions that have moral implications, including decisions about whether people help others as well as the effects of punishment on individuals. Related to this, he has studied how interpersonal power plays out in social interactions, and how this could affect management styles.

group; some that there were only two others; and some that there was only one other. All the comments they heard from other group members were actually pre-recorded. At a certain point, one of the voices cried for help and made sounds of severe choking, as if the person was having an epileptic seizure. When the students thought they were the only person there, 85 per cent rushed to help. When they thought there was one other person, this dropped to 65 per cent. And when they thought there were four other people, the figure dropped again, to 31 per cent. This study shows that believing somebody else will intervene lowers the probability of a person taking responsibility. The results could also be influenced by the fact that the participants could not see the victim.

Pluralistic ignorance: When in a group, people often look to others to know how to react—this is called *informational social influence*. This means that if people see that others do not react to what seems to be an emergency, then they will not react either—even though there may be a problem like in the Kitty Genovese case. This is termed pluralistic ignorance. This was tested by Latané and Darley (1969). They asked participants to sit in a waiting room before participating in an experiment. Here the participants heard the female experimenter fall and cry out in the next room. The participants reacted more often and more quickly when they were alone than when they were sitting with a confederate who showed no reaction to the noise and did not offer assistance. The researchers concluded that in order for people to help, they need to understand clearly that help is needed. During post-experimental interviews, the participants revealed that they had felt anxious when they heard the experimenter fall, but since the others in the waiting room appeared calm, they concluded that there was no emergency. In experiments, as well as in real life, there may be ambiguity about a situation. It might be difficult to interpret what is going on, and it seems that people are less likely to intervene if they think there is a relationship between people—for example, in cases of domestic violence.

The arousal–cost–reward model of pro-social behaviour

Psychologists argue that when it comes to deciding whether to help, we tend to weigh the costs (humiliation, pain, financial loss) against the benefits (financial reward, esteem, affection, avoidance of failure or humiliation). This is the basis for **social exchange theory**, which claims that human relationships are based on a subjective cost–benefit analysis—that is, it is rational. We are more likely to help when we feel that the benefits of helping outweigh the potential costs.

Piliavin and his colleagues have proposed the **arousal–cost–reward model** (1969, 1981), which is based on the Kitty Genovese case, but covers both emergency and non-emergency helping. The model emphasizes the interaction of mood and cognition in determining behaviour. It says that arousal is the emotional response to the need or distress of others. Arousal is seen as a motivational factor because it is unpleasant and the bystander is motivated to reduce it. This idea agrees with the negative-state relief model (Schallerand Cialdini 1988). The cost–reward factor should be seen in terms of assessing possible costs and rewards associated with helping, or not helping.

Ethics in research

1 Outline two ethical considerations in the experiments described here. Do these considerations affect the way that the results of the experiments were interpreted?

2 Do you think that the research can be justified? Why or why not? Support your argument.

Research in psychology

Piliavin et al. (1969)

Piliavin et al. carried out a field experiment in order to study how various situational factors may influence helping behaviour. They chose a field experiment rather than a laboratory experiment to guarantee a higher rate of ecological validity.

The participants in the study were an opportunity sample of New York subway travellers who were observed between 11a.m. and 3p.m. While they were on a non-stop 7.5 minute journey between stations, they would witness one of two scenarios: either a man with a cane who appeared ill or a man who appeared drunk would fall to the floor of the subway car. The "victims" were men, aged 25–35, who were dressed and acted identically. They collapsed to the floor 70 seconds after the train left the station, and remained on the floor until they were helped. A "model-helper" was instructed to help after 70 seconds if no one else offered assistance.

Two female researchers recorded the data. They noted the IVs: the type of victim (drunk or ill) and the size of the group. They measured the following DVs: frequency of help, speed of help, sex of helper, movement away from the victim, and verbal comments. In other words, they gathered both quantitative and qualitative data.

There were 103 trials, and of these, 38 involved a drunk victim who smelled of alcohol and carried a bottle in a bag, while the remaining 65 trials involved a sober victim with a cane.

Overall, 93 per cent of the time, someone helped spontaneously; 60 per cent of the time, more than one helper was involved. The cane victim received help 100 per cent of the time, with a median response time of 5 seconds; the drunk victim received help 81 per cent of the time, with a median response time of 109 seconds. Most importantly, diffusion of responsibility was not observed.

The study has high ecological validity because it was carried out in the field—that is, in a real-life situation. The researchers also obtained a lot of detailed data. However, a field experiment is always less controlled than a laboratory experiment. The study also had far fewer trials with drunk victims than with victims with canes. Finally, though the procedure was highly standardized, it is questionable how some of the DVs, such as moving away from or towards the victim, were measured accurately.

Piliavin et al. argue that observation of an emergency situation always creates an emotional arousal in bystanders. This arousal may be perceived as fear, disgust, or sympathy, depending on aspects of the situation. Arousal can be increased by a number of factors, including empathy with the victim, proximity to the emergency, and the length of time the emergency continues for. Arousal can be reduced by a number of factors, including helping, seeking help from another source, leaving the scene, or deciding the person does not need or deserve help.

According to this model, we are motivated to help people not by altruism (acting in the interest of others), but as a way of reducing unpleasant feelings of arousal. Piliavin et al. argue that the chosen response depends on a cost–reward analysis by the individual that includes:

- cost of helping, such as effort, embarrassment, and possible physical harm
- cost of not helping, such as self-blame and perceived censure from others
- rewards of helping, such as praise from self, onlookers, and the victim
- rewards of not helping, such as getting on with one's own business and not incurring the possible costs of helping.

According to Piliavin et al., the results of their field experiment in the New York subway can be explained using their arousal–cost–reward model, for example as follows.

Evaluating research

1 Discuss why Piliavin et al. obtained the results they did. Include theoretical considerations.

2 What are the ethical considerations with this study?

- The drunk is helped less often because the perceived cost is greater—helping a drunk is likely to cause disgust, embarrassment, or harm. The cost of not helping is less because nobody will blame someone else for not helping a drunk, because a drunk person is perceived as partly responsible for his own victimization.
- Diffusion of responsibility is not found in the cane-carrying situation because the cost of not helping is high and the cost of helping is low.

The role of social norms in pro-social behaviour

Social norms may play either a positive or a negative role in the likelihood of an individual to help. Studies of heroic helpers—such as committed civil-rights workers in the segregated Southern US in the 1960s, or Christians who sheltered Jews from the Nazis during the Third Reich—have found that they often identify strongly with a parent who exemplified norms of concern for others (Oliner and Oliner 1988). Religion may also make a difference. Among college students and the general public, religiously committed individuals are more likely than the less committed to give time and money to help those in need (Colasanto 1989).

Be a critical thinker

To what extent do the experiments by Piliavin et al. support the following theories?

- The arousal-cost reward model
- The negative-state relief model
- The empathy-altruism model

For each of the theories, state what the theory would predict and compare to this to the findings of the experiments.

Did you know?

André and Magda Trocmé

During the Holocaust in France, in a tiny mountain Huguenot village called Le Chambon-sur-Lignon, 350 miles from Paris, 5000 Jews, mostly children, found shelter with 5000 Christians, almost the entire population of the village. Defying the Vichy government, which was collaborating with the Nazis, the villagers of Le Chambon hid Jews in their homes for years. They provided the refugees with forged identification and ration cards, as well as education for the children, and then sent them to safety in Switzerland.

The Chambonnais were descendants of the Huguenots, the first Protestants in Catholic France. Having endured persecution in France, they were able to understand the plight of the Jews. Under the leadership of a young French pastor, Andre Trocmé, the people of Le Chambon felt it was their duty to help people in need, never considering their actions heroic or dangerous. Trocmé told a Vichy official who had threatened him about sheltering the Jews: "We do not know what a Jew is…we only know humans."

Be a critical thinker

The case study of the people of Le Chambon seems to contradict the good Samaritan study conducted by Darley. How could you explain the differences in the findings of these studies?

Social norms, however, can also be problematic. The norm of family privacy can make people reluctant to intervene in what they see as a "family affair". To test this, Shotland and Straw (1976) did a field experiment where they staged an attack by a man on a woman in front of male and female bystanders. Half the bystanders heard the victim say, "I don't know you!" while the other half heard, "I don't know why I ever married you!" Sixty-five per cent of the bystanders tried to prevent the stranger's assault, while only 19 per cent intervened when they thought it was a marital dispute.

If social norms determine helping behaviour, it might be argued that changing norms may decrease bystanderism. Beaman (1978) showed a group of students a film about helping. Two weeks later, each student was observed in an apparent emergency. Of those who helped, 43 per cent had seen the film, versus 25 per cent who had not. Staub (1983) also carried out a study to see if helping behaviour could be learned. He asked young children either to write letters to other children who were in hospital, to tutor a younger child, or to make toys for chronically ill children. He found that the children he asked were more likely to help when placed in a situation where help was desired than children who had engaged in similar activities—like making a toy for themselves or studying with friends—that were not helpful to others. The research here indicates that social norms play an important role in pro-social behaviour. Social norms can also explain why people do not always intervene in the case of domestic violence, for example: the social norm that you should not interfere in other's private affairs is perhaps stronger than the norm of helping.

Cross-cultural research on pro-social behaviour

Cross-cultural research on pro-social behaviour has shown that culture does play a role in one's likelihood to help in some situations. The structure of the family seems to play a significant part. Whiting (1979) reported data on nurturing and helping behaviour by children aged 3–11 in six countries. They found considerable differences in the level of helping displayed by children from these countries. Kenyan, Mexican, and Filipino children scored high, while US children scored the lowest. Cross-cultural differences in pro-social behaviour are correlated with the children's involvement in the responsibilities of family life. Helping was least likely in communities where the children completed school and were seldom assigned responsibilities for family farming or household chores. Graves and Graves (1985) found that caring for younger children provides a child with considerable opportunities to learn to behave in a pro-social manner. In other words, it appears that pro-social behaviour can be learned in an environment that both models the behaviour and has social norms that expect all members of the group to contribute to the common good.

It seems that *social identity theory* could explain how we determine whether to help someone or not. We tend to provide more help to those whom we perceive to be similar to ourselves—that is, a member of our in-group, than those who appear to be unlike us. Katz (1981) found that people were more likely to help members of

---

Be a thinker

In Denmark an instrument called a pillory was used in the 1600s to punish people if they had broken the social norms, stolen bread, cheated in business or become a prostitute. People passing by spat and cursed at them.

1 Do you think that bypassers felt empathy for the people in the pillory?

2 What could the example of the pillory suggest about the role of social norms in relation to pro-social behaviour?

their own rather than another ethnic group. Bond and Leung (1988) found that while Chinese and Japanese participants offered more help than did US participants to others whom they perceived to be from an in-group, they were less likely than Americans to help others perceived to be from an out-group. But is this difference unique between these cultures? More extensive research is necessary in order to find out.

In the 1990s, a series of studies was conducted by Levine et al., in which helpfulness towards strangers was assessed in 36 cities across the US and 23 large cities around the world. Independent field experiments in each city were conducted to measure helping behaviour in various situations. The experiments focused on simple acts of assistance that we encounter every day. Is a dropped pen retrieved by a passing pedestrian? Does a man with an injured leg receive assistance picking up a fallen magazine? Will a blind person be helped across a busy intersection? Will a person try to provide someone with change when asked? Do people take the time to mail a stamped, addressed letter that has apparently been lost?

The first studies were carried out in 36 cities of various sizes in different regions of the US. Overall, they found that people in small and medium-sized cities in the south-east were the most helpful, and that residents of large north-eastern and west coast cities were the least likely to help. The research indicated that the best predictor of helping behaviour was *population density*.

Using the US data for comparison, the research was then replicated in 23 international cities. In the blind-person experiment, for example, participants in five cities—Rio de Janeiro (Brazil), San José (Costa Rica), Lilongwe (Malawi), Madrid (Spain), and Prague (Czech Republic)—helped the pedestrian cross the street on every occasion, whereas in Kuala Lumpur (Malaysia) and Bangkok (Thailand), help was offered less than half the time. If you drop your pen in New York, you have less than one-third of the chance that you do in Rio of ever seeing it again. The two highest-ranking cities in terms of helping are in Latin America: Rio de Janeiro and San José.

Levine also found that helping rates tended to be high in countries with *low economic productivity*, characterized as low gross domestic product per capita—that is, less purchasing power for each citizen. Helping rates were also higher in cities with a slow pace of life (measured by walking speeds) and in cultures that emphasize the value of social harmony. The idea that a city's "personality" affects individual behaviour is known as the *simpatico hypothesis*—that is, people in communities where social obligations take priority over individual achievements tend to be less economically productive, but show more willingness to assist others. This trend did not hold for all the cities in the study, however. Pedestrians in the fast-paced, first-world cities of Copenhagen (Denmark) and Vienna (Austria), for example, were very kind to strangers, whereas their counterparts in slower-paced Kuala Lumpur were not helpful at all.

The evidence indicates that helping tends to be less dependent on the *nature* of the local people than it is on the characteristics of the local environment. It is noteworthy that studies show that where a person was raised has less effect on helping than the place where they currently live. In other words, Brazilians and Thais are both more likely to offer help in Ipanema than they are in Manhattan.

Though it is tempting to draw immediate conclusions from the Levine study, it is important to recognize the methodological limitations of this study on helping research. Here are some general problems to consider.

1 *How does a researcher measure pro-social behaviour?* It is important to identify which behaviours would be valid indicators of pro-social behaviour. Do all five of the tasks which Levine and his team set up really reflect pro-social behaviour?

2 *Can we translate behaviours across cultures?* Some of the behaviours that were tested were not easily tested in other cultures. For example, there might be reasons why a lost letter may not be returned—it could be considered a scam in some places; illiteracy might play a role; while in some countries mail boxes may be unattended or non-existent.

3 *Can we really generalize about an entire culture? And can we then see universal trends?* This is seen in Levine's conclusions regarding the simpatico hypothesis. In spite of a general trend, Vienna and Copenhagen appear not to follow the rule.

4 *Can we attribute meaning to a person's refusal to help?* Why do some people refuse to help? New Yorkers gave many good reasons for their reluctance to help strangers (e.g. it is likely that others do not expect it, might abuse you verbally, might be suspicious towards you).

5 *Ecological validity.* Finally, research in the field is more realistic, and thus provides ecological validity. However, there is a multiplicity of uncontrolled confounding variables, which means that it is not possible to establish cause-and-effect relationships.

Based on these considerations, it would be reasonable to conclude that pro-social behaviour is the result of a complex interaction of environmental and social factors, and that it is not possible to isolate individual variables to determine which play the most significant role in whether an individual helps or not. It is also clear that cross-cultural research on helping behaviour is difficult because of the bias of the researchers in defining, observing, and interpreting helping behaviour.

> **TOK**
>
> Can we ever come to understand pro-social behaviour?
>
> How could you include what you have learned in TOK about ways of knowing to what you have learned here on pro-social behaviour to find valid arguments?

Be an enquirer

1 You are asked to develop a study of helping behaviour in two different cultures. How would you go about it?

2 What would be an appropriate helping behaviour to consider? Justify your decision.

3 How would you overcome some of the problems listed above in your research?

Human relationships: interpersonal relationships

Learning outcomes

- Evaluate psychological research (through theories and studies) relevant to the study of human relationships
- Evaluate psychological research (that is theories and/or studies) relevant to the study of human relationships
- Examine biological, psychological, and social origins of attraction
- Discuss the role of communication in maintaining relationships
- Explain the role that culture plays in the formation and maintenance of relationships
- Analyse why relationships may change or end

The humanistic psychologist Abraham Maslow claims that there is a basic human need to belong and to be accepted by others. People live in groups and families and they define themselves in terms of important others. Relationships are one of the most significant sources of happiness and unhappiness in people's lives. Close relationships—whether with a family member, partner, or friend—influence not only our emotional state, but our health as well. Consider the following research findings, which all indicate the importance of social support on people's well-being.

- Married people report being happier and healthier than those who are single (Steinhauser 1995).
- Compared with people in troubled marriages, those who are happily married have immune systems that ward off infections more effectively (Kiecolt 1987).
- The chances of surviving for more than one year after a heart attack are more than twice as high among elderly men and women who can count on two or more people for emotional support than among those who do not have such support (Berkman et al. 1992).
- Steven Cole (2007) found that chronic loneliness increased gene activity linked to inflammation, and reduced gene activity associated with antibody production and antiviral responses. These patterns of gene expression were specific to loneliness, not to other negative feelings such as depression. Inflammation is associated with diseases such as arthritis and heart disease.

A **close relationship** is defined as a relationship involving strong and frequent *interdependence* in many domains of life. Interdependence means that each partner's thoughts, emotions, and behaviour influence the other's.

One of the difficulties of studying loving relationships is the very definition of "love". Berscheid and Hatfield (1972) have distinguished between *passionate* and *companionate* love, with passionate love being a complete absorption in another that includes sexual feelings and intense emotion. Companionate love is warm, trusting, tolerant affection for another whose life is deeply intertwined with one's own. These may coexist, but not necessarily. Passionate love is gradually replaced by companionate love. Research shows that passionate love tends to decrease over time; and while women are more satisfied with marriage if they continue to feel sparks of passionate love, male satisfaction does not seem to be affected by it (Aron and Henkemyer 1995).

Robert Sternberg suggested a **Triangular Theory of Love** (1988), arguing that passion, intimacy, and commitment work together to create a loving relationship. According to Sternberg, there are three ingredients in love: *passion* ("butterflies" in the stomach, euphoria, and sexual arousal), *intimacy* (warmth, closeness, and sharing), and *commitment* (intent to maintain a relationship in spite of the difficulties and costs).

With this theory, the type and strength of a couple's love is determined by both the individual strength of the three components and the interaction between them. Sternberg suggested a number of different love types. *Romantic love* is the combination of high intimacy and passion, but without commitment; *companionate love* is the combination of intimacy and commitment, without passion; *infatuation* is passion alone; and *consummate* love involves all three areas relatively equally. Using a group of 80 men and women aged 17–69 (mean age 31 years), Sternberg (1988) investigated how relationships developed over time. Applying his theory, Sternberg found that intimacy and commitment rise over time, while passion seems to diminish. Sternberg's theory is descriptive—that is, it characterizes possible forms of love, but does not explain why there are different forms of love or what the function of love is. The description of the ingredients of love corresponds to how people generally perceive love, according to Aron and Westbay (1996), and these features of love seem to be consistent across culture, age, and sexual orientation, according to a study by Fehr (1993).

Origin of attraction: biological level of analysis

All animals, including humans, display much of the same behaviour when they are attracted to each other. Evolutionary theories argue that the purpose of attraction is to procreate, that is to ensure that an individual's genes are passed onto the next generation. This can be seen in the animal world where the males fight to have access to the females, for example when stags compete to have all the females. The females usually take care of the next generation alone. However, in the animal kingdom there are examples of lifelong relationships, for example Canada geese or prairie voles. When it comes to understanding the nature of human relationships—for example why some relationships last and others don't—the different levels of analysis offer a variety of explanations.

A characteristic symptom of romantic love is the *obsession* with the loved one. Lovers are not able to turn off their thoughts, so most of their waking hours pass with thinking about their sweetheart. The

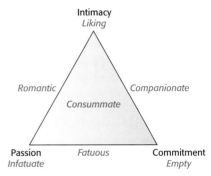

Sternberg's triangular theory of love

Be an enquirer

1 Find 10 participants of different age, gender, and culture, and ask them what constitutes love? Is there a difference between the answers given by men and women in your results?

2 Could you suggest some ideas why it might be difficult to agree on what love is cross-culturally?

3 What methodological considerations could you undertake to carry out a more complete study?

The winning male stag takes it all

biological level of analysis argues that the overwhelming sense of love which makes your head spin and your heart throb, is actually the result of a biochemical cocktail. The anthropologist Fischer (2004) argues that the "symptoms" exhibited in human romantic passion indicate that dopamine, adrenaline, and serotonin all play an important role. In her book, *Why We Love: The Nature and Chemistry of Romantic Love*, Fischer presents the thesis that romantic love is hardwired into our brains by millions of years of evolution. According to Fischer, romantic love is not an emotion, but rather a motivation system—a need or a craving—designed to enable lovers to mate. In this sense, humans are much like other animals.

It is adrenalin that makes your heart race, your palms become sweaty, and your mouth go dry when in the presence of that new special someone. Adrenaline is a stress hormone. Increased levels of this hormone result in high energy, less need for sleep and food, and more focused attention on the potential mate, according to Fischer.

Serotonin is another neurotransmitter that may be involved in love. It could perhaps explain the continuous focus on the beloved. A study in Pisa (Italy) showed that the early stage of love really changes the way people think. Marazziti et al. (1999) studied 60 individuals: 20 were men and women who had fallen in love in the previous six months; 20 others suffered from untreated obsessive–compulsive disorder; 20 more were normal, healthy individuals who were not in love—these were used as controls. By analysing blood samples from the lovers, Marazziti discovered that the serotonin levels of new lovers were equivalent to the low serotonin levels found in people with obsessive–compulsive disorder. The researchers analysed serotonin levels in the blood, not in the brain. Fischer (2004) argues that until scientists have documented the activity of serotonin in specific brain regions, it is not possible to document the exact role of serotonin in romantic love, but the study did establish a possible connection between romantic love and low levels of serotonin in the blood.

Fischer et al. (2003) used an fMRI (functional magnetic resonance imaging) to investigate blood flow in the brains of 20 men and women, who were madly in love, when they were asked to look at photographs of their beloved and of a neutral acquaintance. The nature of the photographs was the independent variable in this experiment. The participants first filled out a questionnaire—the Passionate Love Scale—with statements relating to how they felt about their relationship. This was done in order to compare the brain activity of each participant to what they reported on the questionnaires.

The participants first looked at the photograph of their beloved for 30 seconds while they were scanned. Then they had a filler task to distract them before they looked at the neutral photograph for 30 seconds while being scanned. This was repeated six times. The researchers got what Fischer calls "a beautiful picture of the brain in love", showing activity in the brain's reward system, which is activated by a pleasant stimulus.

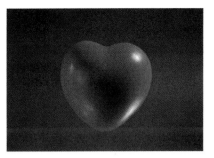

It is biological factors that make a lover's heart race – but it is not interpreted as such

The researchers found that the "brain's reward system" was particularly active when the lovers looked at pictures of the object of their love—and they also found that the more passionate they were, the more active the brain's reward circuitry was. This confirmed the pre-experimental self-reports, thus supporting a correlation between the attitudes towards the lover and brain activity.

The role of hormones in bonding

As a relationship develops over time a couple moves from passionate love, with the obsession and ecstasy, to a more intimate relationship with feelings of comfort, security and relatedness called *attachment*. The British psychiatrist Bowlby (1969) suggested that humans have an innate attachment system which consists of specific behaviours and physiological responses called *attachment behaviours*. He was mostly concerned with the attachment between a mother and child, but it is believed that the same processes are involved in romantic love.

Modern research has discovered that two hormones help to increase the bond between lovers. Adult attachment appears to be the result of the hormones oxytocin and vasopressin. **Oxytocin** is a powerful hormone, released in both men and women during touching and sex, that tends to deepen and intensify feelings of attachment. Thus, couples feel closer and more bonded. Oxytocin is also released during childbirth, and scientists believe that it helps to secure the bond between mother and infant. Experiments conducted on laboratory rats have shown that when oxytocin is inhibited, new mothers reject their young. Similarly, oxytocin injected into female rats that had never mated caused them to demonstrate nurturing behaviour towards other rats' young.

Another important hormone for long-term commitment is **vasopressin**, which is also released during sex. An experiment on the role of vasopressin was conducted using prairie voles (Winslow et al. 1993). These animals tend to form stable pair bonds and have more sex than is necessary for reproduction, just as humans do. When male prairie voles were given a drug that suppressed the effects of vasopressin, they lost their devotion to their mates and no longer protected them from potential suitors. This was taken as evidence that vasopressin plays an important role in males' attachment and mating behaviour.

Evolutionary explanations

Though research on biochemistry helps us to understand what is happening to an individual when falling in love and forming attachments, it does not explain *why* we find some people more attractive than others, or why some people stay together. Sociobiologists use evolution in order to propose an explanation.

Buss (1996) has suggested that jealousy may be biologically based. He found that women's patterns of jealousy vary through their menstrual cycle. When oestrogen levels are low (during menstruation), women appear to be more sexually jealous. When oestrogen levels are relatively high (during ovulation), women tend

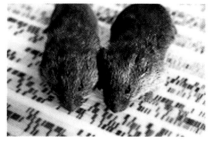

Prairie voles

Profile

David Buss

David Buss (1953–) is highly respected by the scientific community for his study of human mating strategies, but his interpretations are controversial, and often challenge the dominant beliefs in society. In fact, he has been threatened several times for his interpretations especially by feminist psychologists who claim his theories are biased towards males.

to be more emotionally jealous. This is the basis for Buss's argument that human sexual behaviour is grounded in the need to optimize the potential for reproduction, with the goal of the best genetic combination possible for the offspring, as well as maximizing parental care after birth. In the case of menstruation, the female worries that the male will seek out other females to mate with since she is unable to mate at the time; in the case of ovulation, since the potential for having a child is there, she fears the male will develop an emotional attachment to another female, and thus jeopardize the security of her child.

In another example, Low (1990) carried out an analysis of 186 cultures and found a strong correlation between the number of parasites the population is exposed to—or the degree of *pathogen stress*—and the degree of **polygyny**—that is, when males have more than one sexual partner or spouse. As the degree of pathogen stress increases, the number of unmarried men increases. Buss (1993) found that women and men in regions of the world with high levels of pathogen stress rated the importance of physical attractiveness of a prospective mate much more highly than individuals living in regions of the world with lower pathogen stress. For example, symmetrical facial features are considered more attractive in most cultures. In males, the development of prominent cheekbones and a masculine chin is related to androgen levels during puberty. Illness during adolescence can suppress androgen secretion, which affects the development of facial characteristics that are considered attractive. Good teeth may also be an indication of a lower parasite load. Schackelford and Watson (1987) found that men with fewer symmetrical facial features were less physically active, manifested more symptoms of depression and reported more minor physical problems (e.g. colds, headaches, gastrointestinal problems). Men with asymmetric faces and body features also have higher basal metabolic rates and sometimes even lower IQs.

Research in psychology

The dirty shirt study (Wedekind 1995)

Is it possible that our body odour plays an important role in attraction? Wedekind (1995) tested the role of genes related to the immune system (major histocompatability complex—MHC) in mate selection. MHC genes are co-dominant, meaning that both sets of inherited genes have an effect on the child's immune system; so the more diverse the MHC genes of the parents, the stronger the immune system of the offspring. It would obviously be beneficial, therefore, to have evolved systems of recognizing individuals with different MHC genes, and preferentially selecting them to breed with.

For his study, Wedekind recruited a group of 49 women and 44 men, with a wide range of MHC genes. Wedekind gave each man a clean T-shirt and asked him to wear it for two nights. To ensure a strong body odour,

he gave the men supplies of odour-free soap and aftershave, and asked them to remain as "odour neutral" as possible. They were also forbidden to eat spicy food.

After the men returned the shirts, Wedekind put each one in a plastic-lined cardboard box with a sniffing hole on top. The women were scheduled to return at the midpoint of their menstrual cycle, when women's sense of smell is at its best, and each was presented with a different set of seven boxes. Three of the seven boxes contained T-shirts from men with MHC similar to the woman's own; three contained T-shirts from MHC-dissimilar men; and one contained an unworn T-shirt as a control. The women were asked to rate each of the seven T-shirts as pleasant or unpleasant.

Overall, says Wedekind, the women he tested were more likely to prefer the scent of men with dissimilar

MHC. However, their preference was reversed if they were taking oral contraceptives.

When mice are pregnant, they prefer the familiar odour of MHC-similar males. By nesting with relatives, the mothers get help nursing the pups, as well as protection from strange and potentially dangerous males. This finding may help to explain the difference in women taking contraceptives—which raises oestrogen levels in the body—to those who were pregnant, who also preferred the odour of MHC-similar males.

Origins of attraction: the cognitive level of analysis

One of the psychological origins of attraction relates to perception and social cognition. Researchers argue that the extent to which people perceive another person as similar to themselves may be one explanation for attraction. Contrary to the adage that "opposites attract", it appears that those whom we perceive to be similar to ourselves are more attractive to us. Couples tend to be similar in age, religion, social class, cultural background, personality, education, intelligence, physical attractiveness, and attitudes. Maybe this is because over the course of history people tend to live in groups with people who are like themselves. Even though modern societies often consist of many different ethnic groups, there is a tendency for people to live in areas where people are like themselves. Also, people tend to assume that those who are similar to themselves will like them. Shared interests are also part of what attracts people to each other. Finally, Byrne (1971) argues that other people's support for one's own views and attitudes is rewarding because it validates one's opinions and boosts self-esteem.

Morry (2007) suggested the *attraction-similarity model*, which the researcher believes underpins people's perceptions of relationships. She claims that individuals have beliefs about relationships; generally, people tend to see friends and partners as similar to themselves. Attraction, therefore, predicts perceptions of similarity, and the two seem to combine so that people experience psychological benefits as a result.

Markey et al. (2007) investigated the extent to which similarity is a factor in the way people choose partners. Using questionnaires, the researchers asked a large sample of young people to describe the psychological characteristics, values, and attitudes of their ideal romantic partner, without thinking of anyone in particular. Afterwards, they were asked to describe themselves. The results showed that the way the young people described themselves was similar to what their ideal partner looked like. In a follow-up of the study, the researchers used 106 young couples who had been together for a year. The 212 participants filled out a questionnaire about their own as well as their partner's characteristics. The result was in line with the first investigation. The study confirmed that people want partners who are similar to themselves. This could explain why they perceive their partner to be similar; but perception and actual behaviour may not always be congruent at the end of the day. The study was based on questionnaires—that is, self-reports— which are liable to lack some reliability. However, the results are

TOK

Some sociobiologists argue that monogamy is not a natural human behaviour. Unfaithfulness may be beneficial to both sexes. The male increases his chances of passing on his genes; the female has the opportunity to have a better combination of genes, while still having the current loyal partner to raise the child.

Does the argument that this is a natural and logical behaviour mean that it is moral? Why or why not?

based on a relatively large sample, and this enhances the validity of the study. The sample consisted of young Americans, so it is not possible to generalize to other populations unless similar research were to be conducted in other cultures to confirm the results.

Davis and Rusbult (2001) have shown that attraction can also foster similarity, with dating partners experiencing attitude alignment. This may mean that similarity is the result, not the cause of attraction.

Research in psychology

The role of self-esteem in relationship formation (Kiesler and Baral 1970)

If people seek a partner whom they feel is similar to themselves, are there factors that could influence a person's perception of themselves, and thus whom they would choose as a partner?

In order to test whether self-esteem has an effect on partner selection, Kiesler and Baral (1970) carried out an experiment. They administered a fake IQ test to a group of men. They then gave them fictitious scores. One group was told that they had scored "off the charts"—the highest scores ever seen on the exam. The second group was told that there must have been a misunderstanding, because their scores were so low that the researchers could not account for the errors; these participants were asked to redo the test in the near future. Scores were given to each participant privately. After the scores were given, the individual men waited in a waiting room for their pay for taking part in the study. During that time, a very attractive female walked into the room. The experimenters wanted to see if the participants' self-esteem affected their willingness to engage in discussion with an attractive woman. They found that the men who had had a self-esteem boost (high scores) engaged in conversation with the woman more quickly, and that they were more engaged in discussion than the men who were given low test scores.

Evaluating research

1 What is the independent variable in this study?

2 What is the dependent variable in this study?

3 Identify one ethical concern about Kiesler and Baral's study.

4 What are two variables/factors that could have affected the results of this study?

Reciprocity

The theory of reciprocity is based on social exchange theory. It states that relationships are dependent on people's perception of rewards and costs. Reciprocity occurs when you like those who show that they like you. The reason why reciprocity occurs is that helping a partner makes one feel good about oneself—a phenomenon called *self-enhancement*. Studies suggest that people seek feedback that matches and supports their self-concepts as well—a process known as *self-verification*. In romantic relationships, him/herself often extends to idealizing one's partner: people view their partner more favourably than the partner views him/herself. Research on the degree to which a partner matches a person's romantic ideal indicates that evaluations according to ideal standards influence how relationships progress, as demonstrated in the study by Markey et al. (2007).

Origins of attraction: sociocultural level of analysis

The analysis of attraction in the previous section can also to some extent explain sociocultural factors in attraction. It seems that people prefer similarity in a partner, as well as a partner who can contribute positively to thier own self-esteem. People who live close to one another tend to be similar and so probably also have the same social and cultural norms of what is attractive in a partner. It is worth considering how such social and cultural norms can determine who can become a partner in the first place. It is also worth considering how contact and interaction may influence whom a person is attracted to. Western social psychologists have investigated this for many years. They found that people are attracted to those with whom they have a positive interaction. Several studies have found that frequency of interaction is a good prediction of liking. Festinger et al. (1950) found that friendships in a dormitory tended to form among those who lived near one another. Nahemow and Lawton (1975) found that in homes for the elderly and on college campuses, the distances between rooms predicted friendship and attraction.

Why does simple interaction with others increase liking? First, we compare our feelings and reactions to others so that we can better understand ourselves (Schachter 1959). We test the validity of our views and opinions by comparing them to the view held by others. Second, interaction provides us with a sense of connectedness and attachment. As social animals, this is a basic human need. Finally, the familiar is more likeable than the unfamiliar. This has been demonstrated in research by Zajonc et al. (1971), when researchers asked participants to evaluate photos of strangers. Some of the photos were shown repeatedly during the experiment. Those strangers who were shown more frequently were rated more positively. Zajonc argues that the *mere exposure effect* increases a sense of trust.

Role of culture in the formation and maintenance of relationships

While interpersonal attraction is at the basis of formation of relationships in western cultures, it is also clear that when attraction diminishes there is a risk of losing interest in a partner and thus ending the relationship. Cultural norms also play an important role in the formation and maintenance of relationships. Moghaddam (1993) has noted that much of the theory and research on the origins of relationships is a reflection of US culture, and not enough cross-cultural research has been carried out. Since our society has become more diverse, it is important that psychologists attempt to look more carefully at the role of culture in relationships.

Goodwin (1995) argues that passionate love is largely a western phenomenon. In the West, marriage is seen as the culmination of a loving relationship. In cultures where arranged marriages occur, the relationship between love and marriage is the other way round. In a conversation about the high US divorce rates with someone from a non-western culture, Matsumoto (2004) noted that he received the following response: *The reason for this difference is quite clear. You Americans marry the person you love; we love the person we marry.* Gupta & Singh (1992) found that couples in India who married for love

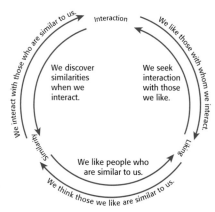

Interaction, similarity, and liking all tend to influence one another. Thus, if any one of these factors starts a relationship, the other two will tend to contribute to a self-sustaining spiral of friendship.

reported diminished feelings of love if they had been married for more than five years. Those who had arranged marriages reported higher levels of love. Yelsma and Athappilly (1990) compared people from Indian arranged marriages with people from Indian and American love marriages, and found the former to be more satisfied.

Simmons et al. (1986) found that romantic love was valued more in the US and in Germany than in Japan. They argue that romantic love is less valued in more traditional cultures with strong, extended family ties. Dion & Dion (1993) have noted that in traditional societies, marriage is often seen as more than just the union of two individuals; it is held to be a union and alliance between two families. Whereas Americans tend to view marriage as a lifetime companionship between two individuals in love, people of many other cultures view marriage more as a partnership formed in order to have children and for economic and social support.

Levine et al. (1995) found that individualistic countries were more likely to rate love as essential to the establishment of a marriage, and to agree that the disappearance of love is sufficient reason to end a marriage. Countries with a large GDP (Gross Domestic Product—a measure of the total market value of all goods and services produced in a country each year) also showed this tendency. They also found that divorce rates are highly correlated with the belief that the disappearance of love warranted the dissolution of marriage.

In one of the largest cross-cultural studies on relationships ever undertaken, Buss (1994) gave two questionnaires regarding mate selection to more than 10,000 respondents from 37 cultures. There were many striking similarities in the responses. In 36 out of 37 cultures, women ranked financial prospects as more important than males. In all 37, men preferred younger mates, while women preferred older mates. In 23 of the cultures, males rated chastity as being more important than women did. The degree of agreement in sex differences across cultures led Buss to view mate selection preferences as universal, arising from different evolutionary selection pressures on males and females. However, there were some interesting differences:

- **USA:** Love ranked first.
- **Iran:** Love ranked third. Ranked high: education, intelligence, ambition, chastity.
- **Nigeria:** Love ranked fourth. Ranked high: good health, neatness, desire for home and children.
- **China:** Love ranked sixth. Ranked high: good health, chastity, domestic skills.
- **South Africa (Zulu):** Love ranked seventh. Ranked high: emotional stability and maturity, dependability.

The role of communication in maintaining relationships

Another important factor in the maintenance of relationships seems to be attributional style. In happy relationships, attributions tend to be positively biased towards the partner—that is, positive behaviours are seen as dispositional, and negative behaviours are seen as situational.

Possible essay question

Examine two levels of analysis (for example biological and socio-cultural) with regard to the origins of attraction.

Assessment advice

The command term "examine" means that you must argue in a way that uncovers the assumptions and interrelationships of the origins of attraction. In this case, you need to address the principles on which the explanations (theories) are based, as well as discuss the strengths and limitations of them. You also need to include empirical studies to support your argument.

Be empathetic

1 Based on the research regarding the role of cultural norms on relationships, what do you think would be the difficulties of having a cross-cultural relationship?

2 How do you think these difficulties could be overcome?

Unhealthy relationships are the opposite: these relationships also employ a stable and global attribution to the partner's behaviour. In discussing problems in a relationship, this attribution style leads to phrases like "You always…" and "You never…"

It seems that communicating attributions for negative events or behaviour could determine whether a relationship will end. It is important, however, to consider if it is the quality of the relationship which leads to negative communication or the attributional style which leads to the breakdown of a relationship. Bradbury and Fincham (1990) did a meta-analysis of research studies on the attributions married couples made on each other's behaviour. They found that poor marital quality in a couple predicted dispositional attributions to negative behaviours and situational attributions to positive behaviours. Bradbury and Fincham (1992) argue that the attributions a married couple make will influence their behaviour towards each other. They found that wives who had the tendency to make dispositional attributions about their husbands in negative situations were also more likely to behave negatively towards their husband. The opposite was found in wives who made dispositional attributions about their husband in positive situations. According to the researchers, this might be because unhappy couples simply have negative attributions and behave negatively towards each other.

A study done by the same researchers in 1993 followed married couples in a 12-month longitudinal study and found that the kind of attributions made by the couple in the beginning of the study did predict marital satisfaction at the end of the study. Level of satisfaction with the relationship in the beginning of the study did not predict what kinds of attributions the couple made at the end of the study. This could indicate that it is the kinds of attributions which influence the behaviour of couples rather than the other way round.

The findings are in line with the theory of idealization and positive illusions of the partner mentioned earlier. It also supports the findings on the role of positive and negative emotions in the longitudinal study by Flora and Segrin (2003). The researchers found that the negative feelings of women towards their partner predicted marital problems. For men, it was merely their partners expressing negative feelings that predicted problems.

Generally, the attributions that partners make about each other are associated with levels of satisfaction with the relationship as well as their behaviour towards each other. Negative communication causes marital dissatisfaction and may eventually lead to the end of a relationship.

It seems, then, that communication plays an integral role in the maintenance of relationships. This is supported by Altman and Taylor's **social penetration theory**, which argues that close relationships are formed by a gradual process of self-disclosure. Closeness develops if the participants proceed in a gradual manner from superficial to intimate levels of communication and this is associated with attraction. **Self-disclosure** is the sharing of facts about one's life with a loved one, as well as inner thoughts, feelings, and emotions—for example, "I don't know if I am smart enough to get into the university I want to attend", or "I am afraid that I am going to have problems making friends when we move to our new location". Disclosing something about yourself makes both strangers and friends like you more (Collins and Miller 1994). Self-disclosure leads to self-validation—the feeling of being truly known and accepted by the listener. A deeper mutual understanding allows each partner to meet the needs of the other more easily. It is also a symbol of trust, which is a key factor in attachment.

Can self-disclosure be related to attraction? A meta-analysis of self-disclosure studies by Collins & Miller (1994) found that people who disclose intimate information about themselves are more liked than people who don't. The researchers also found that people tend to disclose more personal information to those that they like, and finally, if people disclose information to someone, they tend to like the person more. This clearly indicates that disclosure could be an important factor in establishing and maintaining a relationship.

There are some key differences in the ways that men and women communicate with one another. For example, women self-disclose more than men. Women also disclose more to other women than men do to other men (Reis 1986).

According to Deborah Tannen (1990), women are more likely than men to respond to someone's negative feelings with understanding and acceptance—to reassure that it is all right to feel bad, perhaps sharing an account of a time when they had similar feelings. Men are more likely than women to take the initial disclosure as a complaint about a problem, and to offer helpful advice on solving it. This leads to misunderstandings: a woman may feel that a problem-solving response belittles her feelings, by failing to deal with them directly. For example, a woman is upset that after her pregnancy, she does not appear to be able to lose the weight she has gained. Another woman might respond: "I know. It's as though you are not in control of your body." A man might reply: "You could always join a health club to get back into shape."

Men may be equally troubled by women's typical responses. When a woman says, "I know, sometimes I feel the same way," the man may feel that she is denying the uniqueness of his feelings and failing to support him in finding a solution to the problem.

Deborah Tannen also found that there are key differences in the ways that men and women have conversations:

- Women tend to use more language tags (yup, uh-huh, right, no kidding). This happens alongside the main speaker, serving as support. Tannen calls this **overlapping speech**.
- Men tend to interrupt and change the topic more frequently.
- Women tend to be more inclusive, asking the other person's opinion.

As you might imagine, this may lead to a situation in which, when a man says, "I think that it might be fun to go fishing all summer," and his wife says, "Uh-huh," she thinks that she has communicated "I hear you," but he hears, "I agree." Understanding gender differences in communication styles is an important part of successful problem resolution in heterosexual relationships.

Profile

Deborah Tannen
Although she has written numerous academic publications, Deborah Tannen is best known for her general-audience books on interpersonal communication. She became well-known after her book *You Just Don't Understand - Women and Men in Conversation* was published in 1990. It was on the New York Times best seller list for nearly four years and was translated into 29 languages. She has since made numerous appearances on major television and radio shows. *You're Wearing That? Understanding Mothers and Daughters in Conversation*, her latest book, was also on the best seller list.

Finally, the way we communicate our feelings may be framed in such a manner as to make it difficult for a partner to respond in a way that will alleviate conflict. An example of this is when we blame our partner for something rather than simply expressing our own feelings. For example, when getting ready to go to the theatre, your partner decides to change his/her outfit just as you are about to leave. If you say, "You always wait to the last minute to do things!" you are setting yourself up for an argument. Using the global and stable attribution here means that your partner will probably end up defending him/herself. A more healthy approach is to say, "I feel anxious when I think that we are going to be late."

Why do relationships change or end?

Some psychologists have taken a rather economic approach to relationships. **Social exchange theory** (Kelley and Thibaut 1959) argues that relationships are maintained through a cost–benefit analysis. In other words, the costs of the relationship must not outweigh the benefits. The more one invests in a relationship, the more one expects "greater returns". A relationship will endure only as long as it is profitable to both partners in appropriate equivalent degree. Though non-equivalence may be tolerated in the short-term, the balance must be restored if the relationship is to survive.

The American psychologist Elaine Walster argues that social exchange theory is too simplistic an explanation, and that there is no reliable way of determining costs and benefits. She argues instead that **equity theory**, or the *perception* of equality, is what determines whether a relationship will be maintained.

Equity theory has been used to explain infidelity. For example, a woman feels that she is putting more into the relationship than her husband. Though she loves him, he is currently not making a good salary, he is not doing his share of the housework, and he has not been showing her enough affection. In cheating on her husband, she feels guilt that she now "owes" him her loyalty, thus rebalancing the sense of equity. In a study of 2000 couples, Hatfield (1979) found that those who felt deprived or under-benefited had extramarital sex sooner after marriage and with more partners than those who felt either fairly treated or over-benefited.

Those who felt that their relationship was perfectly equitable were more likely than others to think that they would still be together in one year and in five years. Those who felt greatly under-benefited and those who felt greatly over-benefited were least likely to think that their relationship would be intact in the future. What is most interesting is that the over-benefited were just as doubtful about future prospects as were the under-benefited.

In spite of the empirical support, exchange theories are criticized for being too "cold", and for failing to take into account emotions which could override "profit motive". It is also culturally bound, rooted in a capitalistic interpretation of society. Finally, it is difficult to quantify costs and rewards in order to test the theory rigorously.

Equity theory of love predicts that people are happiest in relationships where benefits and costs are balanced so that both partners contribute and receive more or less the same.

- To what extent is the theory supported?

- Do you think it is a good idea to use theories from economics to explain human relationships? Why or why not?

Be reflective

1 What would be the costs and benefits of starting a relationship at this point in your life?

2 Do you think there would be differences if you were starting a relationship at age 30? And at age 50?

Rusbult et al. (1991) have shown that one's **patterns of accommodation**—that is, the processes of responding to a partner's negative behaviour, are integral to the maintenance of relationships. *Constructive accommodations* include discussing problems openly and honestly, waiting for the situation to improve naturally, and forgiving each other; *destructive accommodations* include silent treatment, recounting lists of past failures, and physical avoidance. Of course, it is not as simple as this—for example, in cases of domestic violence and spousal abuse, what might be considered constructive in a healthy relationship may prove to be destructive and keep an individual in an unhealthy and potentially dangerous relationship.

There appear to be several factors that influence whether one engages in constructive or destructive accommodations. *Idealization* of one's partner seems to lead to constructive accommodations. Murray and Holmes (1997) found that those with positive illusions about their partner reported less conflict and fewer destructive patterns of conflict resolution. Another factor is a person's feeling of commitment to his/her partner. Those who have a sense of commitment tend to overlook their partner's faults; engage in open communication of concerns and needs; and express willingness to change behaviour to help the relationship.

Finally, attachment styles also appear to play a key role in accommodation. Securely attached individuals are more likely to engage in constructive conflict resolution. In his research, Simpson (1996) tested the role of attachment style by how a sensitive topic was discussed by a dating couple. First, he administered questionnaires to identify an individual's attachment style. Then the dating couples discussed a major problem in their relationship. Insecurely attached individuals tended to be anxious and to employ negative strategies during the discussion—resulting in negative feelings during the discussion and harm to the relationship. The results indicate that attachment styles had a clear influence on how couples go about resolving conflict.

For more on attachment styles see page 194.

Flora and Segrin (2003) investigated well-being in relation to perception of the relationship in married and dating couples. The sample consisted of 66 young couples who had dated for at least six months, and 65 young couples who had been married for around four years. It was a longitudinal study, using self-report data based on questionnaires and interviews. The researchers wanted to find out if the amount of common interests and activities, as well as a desire to spend time together, was a predictor of the quality of the relationship. They interviewed 262 participants about the emotional aspects of their relationship—for example, the degree of positive and negative feelings, contentment, or disappointment with their partner. The interviews were recorded and transcribed for analysis. After one year, the couples were contacted again. None of the married couples had separated, but a quarter of the lovers had split up. Those who were still together were asked to fill out a new questionnaire to get an idea of their satisfaction with the relationship, as well as their personal well-being.

Feelings of commitment often increase when a couple expects their first child

Possible essay question

Examine **two** explanations of the origins of attraction (for example biological, psychological or sociocultural).

Assessment advice

The command term is "examine". This means that you should consider different arguments (for example theories) as well as which assumptions they are based on (for example the biological level of analysis). You must also consider the explanatory power of an explanation and this is best done by looking at empirical studies.

In this question you must address the "origins of attraction". This means that you should consider two explanations of origin of attraction related to different levels of analysis. The way the question is formulated, you can choose two explanations from the same level of analysis but you can also choose two from different levels of analysis.

The researchers were interested in finding possible factors that could predict the break-up of relationships, as well as factors influencing satisfaction. For those who dated, the most important factor was the common interests and activities, as well as a desire to spend time together. This was particularly true for men, and, overall, it was more important than the degree of negative and positive feelings. For the women, the best predictor of staying in the relationship was the quantity of their own negative feelings—for example, in relation to disappointment with their partner.

As for contentment with the relationship a year after the first investigation, there was a positive correlation between common interests, activities, and desire to spend time together in males. The amount of positive and negative feelings was also an important factor after a year, but it was particularly their partner's negative feelings that mattered. For the women, there was a positive correlation between common interests, activities, and desire to spend time together, but the most important factor in predicting satisfaction was the frequency of their own negative feelings due to disappointment in the first investigation. The more negative feelings, the less satisfied they were a year later. The research indicates that there may be a gender difference in men's and women's ideas of what constitutes a good relationship. Men seem to favour common interests and a desire to be together more than positive and negative feelings overall. However, if their partner expresses too many negative feelings towards them, this can result in the breakdown of the relationship. For women, satisfaction with the relationship was to a large extent dependent on the degree of their own negative feelings with their partner.

In spite of everyone's best intentions, relationships do not always survive the many changes that they experience over time. There are a number of trends, however, which have been noted by researchers.

- Women terminate relationships more often than men (Gray and Silver 1990).
- Marriages in which the partners are younger than average tend to be unstable (Duck 1988).
- There is a relationship between divorce and early parenthood. The arrival of a baby brings added financial problems and takes time away from a young couple who might not have established a stable, intimate relationship (Pringle 1986).
- Marriages between couples from lower economic groups and lower educational levels tend to be more unstable (Duck 1992).
- Marriages tend to be more unstable between people who had divorced parents or who had a greater number of sexual partners before marriage (Duck 1992).

Exchange theory helps to explain why some relationships end. For example, in the case of self-disclosure, unless the friend matches such behaviour, disclosure will cease. It could also be that what used to be considered a benefit is now a cost. Felmlee (1995) calls this the **fatal attraction theory**—the same trait that initially caused attraction ultimately leads to the dissolution of the relationship.

Can you predict the breakdown of a relationship?

Duck (1992) did a meta-analysis of longitudinal studies which tried to identify what factors could predict dissolution of a relationship. The following factors were identified.

- People who had parents that had divorced were more likely to break up their own marriage.
- Teenage marriages were less likely to last than marriages between older persons.
- Marriage between partners of different backgrounds (for example, socioeconomic, cultural or different education) was more likely to end early.
- Marriage between people from a lower socio-economic background were more likely to end in divorce.
- Marriage between partners who have had many sexual partners before the marriage is less likely to last a long time.

1 Consider how and why these factors may contribute to instable relationships.

2 If you were the researcher, how could you gather evidence to investigate this?

● ● ● ● ●

Be a thinker

How would you explain the trends listed here?

For example, a partner who travels a lot may bring the benefit of interesting conversation, cosmopolitan appeal, and a bit of time to be alone when s/he is travelling. Over time, however, the relationship may dissolve because s/he is never at home.

According to Duck (1992), relationships offer comfortable predictability. Crisis occurs when this predictability is disrupted. This could be the result of having a child, moving to a new city, or "breaking the rules". Argyle & Henderson (1984) have studied the *rules* that tend to govern relationships. They argue that rules function mostly to maintain relationships in order that the goals of the relationship may be obtained. This happens by minimizing the potential for conflict. Some rules that are typical in relationships are respecting your partner's privacy, not talking to others about what has been self-disclosed, and being emotionally supportive. Deception is probably the most important rule that should not be broken.

Could it be that people simply fall out of love? Sprecher (1999) carried out a longitudinal study to find out. Over a period of several years, couples self-reported their feelings about the relationship. In the relationships that eventually broke up, individuals reported higher levels of general dissatisfaction and frustration with the relationship, but there was no change in their feelings of love for one another. The research indicates that the frustration outweighed the positive feelings of love for the partner. This explains why breaking up is often such a painful process.

Apply your knowledge

Carry out a little more research on communication styles between the genders. Then produce a short skit in which you demonstrate a constructive and destructive communication pattern for the same situation.

Possible extended essay questions

- To what extent can attraction be explained by biological factors alone?
- Why are some relationships more stable than others?
- Do men and women have different expectations in relationships?
- What is the role of cultural factors in the formation of relationships?

Learning outcomes

- Evaluate psychological research relevant to the study of human relationships

- Discuss the interaction of biological, cognitive, and sociocultural factors in human relationships

- Evaluate research on sociocultural origins of violence

- Discuss psychological research on the reduction of violence

- Explain short-term and long-term effects that violence can have on individuals

In February 2007, the Danish newspaper *Politiken* reported an increase in aggression towards homeless people in Copenhagen. Sociologist Ole Gregersen from the Danish National Centre for Social Research argues that this is a new form of meaningless violence against innocent and defenceless people after an evening in town. The perpetrators are young men in groups, who attack and humiliate the homeless in the dark hours. They sometimes even film the aggression on their mobile phones. For most people, events like these are scary because they are meaningless and cruel.

According to Hogg (1995), aggression is part of the human condition, and virtually everyone is affected by it—indirectly or directly. **Aggression** is sometimes defined as any sequence of behaviour in which the goal is to dominate or harm another individual. **Violence** is understood as an aggressive act in which the actor or perpetrator abuses individuals directly or indirectly. Violence exists in a number of forms—for example, verbal, physical, and psychological—and it may be inflicted by individuals, groups, institutions, or nations. Violence threatens individuals in numerous and complex ways. Though there are random acts of violence, such as murder and school shootings, a large amount of violence is ongoing and routine—for example, bullying and domestic violence. War and genocide are institutionalized and systematic forms of violence between social groups.

In some environments, such as schools, violent behaviour is a *low base-rate behaviour*—that is, it is relatively rare. This means that it is difficult to observe and easy to miss. When observing behaviour in a naturalistic setting, it is possible not to observe any violent behaviour over a long period of time. This does not mean that it never happens, however, as the examples of school shootings show. The problem is that it is difficult to predict when violence will occur in such settings, and what form it will take. The British primatologist Jane Goodall's study of the chimpanzees in Gombé, Tanzania, is an illustration of this. Her observations have taken place over the past 40 years. She had always believed that although chimps were very similar to humans, they were our "peaceful relative". However, because the research went on for so long, she had the chance to observe something rare among chimps—the so-called raiding parties. Groups of chimps hunted down and brutally killed members of another community—an act of brutal aggression formerly believed to be unique to humans. She also reported cases of infanticide and rape among these animals who are usually very peaceful.

Like chimps, most humans are not aggressive, but at times violence occurs, apparently for no specific reason. Low base-rate behaviours are multifactorial in origin—that is, there is no single explanation as to the cause. This was the case in the Columbine High School shooting in the US, where many factors may have contributed to the violent behaviour of the perpetrators, including a long history of being bullied, social isolation, depression, and access to weapons.

Violence: the biological level of analysis

Evolutionary psychologists have observed violent behaviour in primates. This includes fighting between males, infanticide of other males' offspring (e.g. in chimps and gorillas), rape (an estimated 40 per cent of orangutan copulations are rape), and "raiding parties". Most violence is committed to obtain females for breeding or protect offspring. It is rather difficult to argue a link between the school shooting at Columbine, for example, and "breeding access". However, evolutionary psychologists have argued that male hormones have evolved to give males a reproductive advantage. The most important hormone in this respect is **testosterone**, the male hormone which is implicated in both sexual arousal and aggression. In most species, males tend to be more aggressive than females, and this is usually attributed to the higher levels of testosterone in males. It has been found that the level of aggression correlates positively with the amount of testosterone in the blood. Bernhardt (1997) found a positive correlation between high testosterone levels and antisocial behaviour in males of low socio-economic status. This illustrates that in humans the link is not straightforward, since there are complicating factors such as social roles and socio-economic status. Therefore, testosterone levels should be interpreted within a cognitive and sociocultural context.

Testosterone is thus not an "aggression hormone". Rather, it is related to dominance and status-seeking, according to Mazur and Booth (1998), who observed that in athletes testosterone rises before competitive matches. Level of testosterone can be measured in saliva. Men who win a competition (even a chess match) have higher levels of testosterone than those who lose. Cohen (1998) found that young US males who were part of an urban street culture where "honour" is an issue had high levels of testosterone. This was explained by their hyper-responsiveness to insults in order to maintain status and respect. The results suggest that testosterone biases towards holding status, and that the feedback effect helps to maintain the high level of the hormone. This is supported by findings from the US. Cohen reports that people from the Southern states who display more of an honour culture have a higher testosterone response to a challenge than people from the North, who are not part of an honour culture.

Archer (1994) claims that it is difficult in humans to distinguish cause and effect in the dynamic process of behaviour and testosterone level. Early experience and modelling can bias a male towards a competitive and aggressive style. High levels of testosterone will strengthen this, and continuous incidents of status fights—verbal or physical—elevate testosterone levels so that this becomes the normal situation.

Sapolsky (1998) argues that testosterone has a *permissive effect*—that is, the mere presence of the hormone is enough to allow for aggressive behaviour. When animals are castrated, aggression levels plummet. But when they are then injected with testosterone, from 20 per cent of the base rate to 200 per cent, there is a return to "normal aggressive levels". In other words, the level of testosterone alone is not responsible for the level of aggressive behaviour; there must be other factors involved.

Serotonin also plays a role in aggressive behaviour. People who have low levels of serotonin are highly irritable and aggressive, so there is a negative correlation between serotonin levels and aggression. People low in serotonin are easily frustrated and impulsive, demonstrating what psychologists refers to as *fast-track anger*—that is, they act first and think later. Bernhardt (1997) suggested that it is the interaction of low levels of serotonin (which causes irritability) and high levels of testosterone (which leads to dominance-seeking behaviour) that results in aggression. Environmental stimuli can make levels of testosterone rise; they can also make serotonin levels fall. Serotonin can be affected by extreme environments—for example, childhood physical abuse results in fewer serotonin receptor sites, and thus less serotonin activity in the brain.

There is also evidence that frontal-lobe abnormalities may play a part in aggressive behaviour. Grafman et al. (1996) examined the relationship between frontal-lobe lesions and the presence of aggressive and violent behaviour. They studied 57 normal controls and 279 veterans, matched for age, education, and time in Vietnam, who had suffered penetrating head injuries during their service in the war. Family observations and self-reports were collected, using scales and questionnaires that assessed a range of aggressive and violent attitudes and behaviour. The results indicated that patients with frontal-lobe lesions consistently demonstrated Violence Scale scores significantly higher than the controls.

Raine et al. (1997) performed a PET (positron emission tomography) study on a sample of murderers who had pleaded "not guilty by reason of insanity". Raine predicted dysfunction in localized brain areas such as the prefrontal cortex, amygdala, and hippocampus—areas involved in control based on cognition (hippocampus and prefrontal cortex), communication between the two hemispheres (corpus callosum), and emotion (amygdala). The researchers predicted no abnormality in other areas of the brain. They found lower activity, measured as glucose metabolism, in the prefrontal cortex compared with the controls. Asymmetry was found in the amygdala and the medial temporal lobe, including the hippocampus. Generally, the murderers showed increased right-hemisphere activity.

The lower activity in prefrontal cortex and corpus callosum indicates a problem in integrating the information necessary to modify behaviour and control impulses. Abnormalities in the hippocampus and amygdala suggest a problem in forming and using emotionally laden perceptions and memories. According to Raine, the findings cannot show that violence is determined by biology alone. He argues that social, psychological, cultural, and situational factors also play a role in predisposing an individual to violence.

Violence: the cognitive level of analysis

Antisocial behaviour and aggression have been linked to deficits in cognitive functioning such as attention, planning, organization, reasoning, cognitive flexibility, and self-regulation. Research suggests that social environmental factors—for example, growing up in a violent family—can affect the way the brain processes information. This could partly be due to stressors that affect the brain but it could also be due to learning, or a combination of the two. This research suggests that violent acts are perhaps caused by previous experiences which have resulted in biased cognitive processing, especially cognition related to social information. This is called social cognition, broadly defined as the way people make sense of and respond to their social world (Fiske and Taylor, 1991).

There are two ways that social cognitive processing may be affected by risk factors. Firstly, people's *general knowledge structures* (cognitive schemas) about the world are influenced by experience. This includes a person's self-schema and social schemas—that is, views of oneself, other people and how one should behave in social situations. It also includes what the developmental psychologist Bowlby (1973) called "inner working models", which are cognitive schemas of what people expect from others and the emotions which are linked to this. Overall, inner working models relate to the emotional bonds—called attachment—that a person forms with others. The self-schemas, social schemas, and inner working models are all theoretical explanations of how an individual's experience is stored in memory and used to deal with the world. *Information processing* is also affected by cognitive schemas. This includes the way a person interprets social situations and makes judgments about other people's motives (attribution) as well as how a person decides how to respond.

Research into aggression has found that cognitive processes may be involved in some aggressive and violent acts. An individual who has been subjected to abuse, social rejection, or violence by his or her peers seems to be at risk for developing antisocial behaviour. This is related to general knowledge structures and social information processing (Dodge et al. 1990). Researchers have argued that there is a link between negative views of the self and aggressive behaviour (Baumeister et al. 1996) but Bradshaw (2004) found in a study with 125 male and female adolescents (mean age 19.9) from New York that there was an even stronger link between aggression and an individual's negative view of others .This indicates that a negative attributional style could be involved in aggression and violent behaviour. According to Bradshaw, aggression is mediated by negatively socially biased information processing. Bradshaw also found that exposure to violence in childhood was closely related to biased social information processing, which is in line with social learning theory (Bandura, 1973). It seems that witnessing violence influences beliefs regarding the appropriateness of aggression. Overall, Bradshaw found that hostile attribution bias, self-reported aggressive response reaction, and justification of aggression was positively correlated to negative view of others but she did not find any relationship between view of self and aggression. However, the research was based on self-reports that may be unreliable.

Brain injury can also cause cognitive problems, as mentioned in the section on the biological level of analysis. This can lead to frustration and may result in violent verbal and physical outbursts of aggression. Most people with brain injury experience this. The aggression is often directed towards family members or other people close to the person.

Anger management training aims to identify trigger situations—for example,forgetting information or misplacing something—as well as the early signs of anger—for example, feeling hot. Once these are identified, the person is helped to reduce the level of arousal and apply an alternative solution to the problem. Cognitive therapy techniques are used to identify and deal with maladaptive thinking patterns. This is combined with specific behavioural techniques so that the person with brain damage can focus on building pro-social behaviour instead. Demark and Gemeinhardt (2002) found that cognitive-behavioural therapy (CBT) was an efficient method of anger management.

Social learning theory, suggested by Bandura (1965), has been applied in the study of violent behaviour. Gerbner et al.'s (1994) **cultivation theory** argues that media violence gives children a perception of a world that is more hostile than it is in reality; teaches them at some level that violence is acceptable, normal behaviour; and causes them to develop scripts that problems can be solved through violence. Merrill (1996) has used social learning theory to describe how scripts for domestic violence—that is, violence against a spouse or loved one—are learned. She argues that learning to resort to violence comes from three factors: direct instruction by others to act in violent or threatening ways; modelling of violent or controlling behaviour; and rewards for threatening, controlling, or abusive behaviour.

One of the common beliefs about bullies and others who engage in violent behaviour is that such behaviour is the result of poor self-esteem. Research by Baumeister and Bushman (1998) contradicts this idea. In their *Theory of Threatened Egotism*, they argue that when someone threatens, questions, or undermines one's self-concept, those with inflated, tenuous, or unstable forms of high self-esteem are more likely to act aggressively. The researchers define **egotism** as an inflated sense of one's own importance, and they relate this to **narcissism**. A **narcissist** is a personality type who cares passionately about being superior to others, while at the same time doubting that this is actually the case. It could be argued that the narcissist has a distorted self-schema and that social information processing is affected by this.

Research in psychology

Baumeister and Bushman (1998)

Based on the theory of threatened egotism, Baumeister and Bushman predicted that aggression should be high among narcissists if their self-esteem is threatened—for example, by criticism. The researchers first asked participants to fill out a questionnaire to measure self-esteem. One of the measures was extremely high levels of self-esteem—narcissism. Participants were then asked to write a brief essay expressing their opinions on abortion. Each received his or her essay back with comments that another participant had (supposedly) written. The essays were randomly selected for good and bad comments. The positive comment was: *No suggestions. This is a great essay!* The negative comment was: *This is one of the worst essays that I have ever read.*

Participants then took part in a reaction-time test. Whoever responded more slowly received a blast of noise—with the volume and duration set by his or her opponent. The results were that aggression (the blasting noise) was highest among narcissists who had received insulting criticism. Non-narcissists were significantly less aggressive, as were narcissists who had been praised.

The study was a laboratory experiment where the researchers deliberately manipulated a variable that was supposed to affect the participants' levels of self-esteem. There is a question of ecological validity here: whether the individual would respond in this way to any negative feedback, or whether the artificial nature of the situation created the irritability.

Be a researcher

1 What are some of the ethical considerations to take into account with this study?
2 What conclusions can you draw from the study?

Violence: sociocultural level of analysis

Sociocultural theory suggested by the Russian psychologist Vygotsky in the 1930s suggests that use of violence is the result of *power differences* between different social groups. Traditionally, differences between groups are determined by gender, social class, or ethnicity. The dominant group has always displayed dominance, as has been seen in the biased power relationship between men and women. This is reflected in research findings that men are more likely to be violent towards women than women are towards men. History has numerous examples of violence towards powerless social groups. The persecution of the Jewish population during the second world war or genocide in Rwanda and Bosnia illustrate that dominant social groups are prepared to use extreme violence against minority groups. The violence in these cases has even been publicly justified by the perpetrators. The important thing to remember here is that such violent behaviour was accepted by large groups in the community where it took place and some took part in the violent acts without feeling guilt or remorse. If social norms dictate that it is acceptable to be violent towards specific groups, it is likely that people will be violent. For example, if social norms dictate that people can spank their children, more children will be spanked.

Social norms within a society provide guidance for individuals as to how emotions may be expressed. Norms dictate how power is distributed within the society and define how males and females are supposed to behave. Hence, it could be argued that violent

Social norms may be part of the reason for violence towards children

communities breed violent behaviours, since it is a survival mechanism which is learned through modelling; in other words, social learning theory plays a role in handing down behaviours that are considered important for members of the society.

Although individuals are responsible for their own behaviour, it seems that there are situations in which this rule does not apply. According to **deindividuation theory**, the psychological state of deindividuation is aroused when individuals join crowds or large groups. The state is characterized by diminished awareness of self and individuality. Being in a large group provides a degree of anonymity, which allows an individual to avoid responsibility for his or her actions, thus shaking off the usual social controls and becoming more impulsive, irrational, aggressive, and even violent.

Football violence is a major problem when supporters of one team attack those from the other side after the match. When they are in a crowd, people do things they would not normally do when alone. This is also demonstrated in a classic experimental study by Zimbardo (1969).

Football hooliganism can be extremely violent

Research in psychology

Zimbardo (1969)

In a classic social psychology study, female undergraduates were asked to deliver electric shocks to another student to "aid learning". Half the participants wore bulky lab coats and hoods that hid their faces. They were spoken to in groups of four and never referred to by name. The other half wore their normal clothes, were given large name-tags to wear, and were introduced to each other by name. They could also see each other (dimly) when they were seated at the shock machines. Both sets of participants could see the student being shocked.

All the participants were told something about the learner prior to each experiment: either "she is honest, sincere, and warm", or "she is conceited and critical". Hooded participants delivered twice as many shocks, and the amount of shock did not vary depending on the description of the learner. Participants wearing name-tags related the amount of shock to the description given.

The results indicate that those whose identity had been obscured were more likely to deliver a harsher punishment. Deindividuation appears to have lowered their sense of self-consciousness and sense of accountability for their behaviour.

Though the experiment yielded interesting results, the study is problematic. First, there is a high level of artificiality in the procedure. It is questionable whether these results would be seen in routine, everyday experiences. There is some evidence that this reflects what happens in extreme political unrest, or in the case of torture (Haritos-Fatouros 2003). In addition, there is the ethical concern that the participants may have been subjected to undue stress, and that this stress may have had a long-term effect on the individuals.

In order to address issues of ecological validity, Diener et al. (1976) carried out a naturalistic observation of children on Halloween. The aim of the study was to establish if deindividuation had an effect on a child's behaviour—in this case, how many pieces of candy the child would take as a trick-or-treater.

Children in one group were asked for their names and addresses, whereas those in another group were not. Thus the independent variable was individuation—whether or not their identity was highlighted. The children were then encouraged to take a single sweet. Those who were individuated (by asking for their personal details) took more than the single sweet in 8 per cent of cases. Those who were deindividuated (by virtue of being dressed up in Halloween costumes and not being asked for details) took more than one sweet in 80 per cent of cases. This result indicates the importance of deindividuation on self-consciousness and feelings of responsibility.

Reicher (1987) argues that deindividuation increases an individual's sense of group identity. Thus, the norms of the group become the guiding force of one's behaviour. Johnson and Downing (1979) showed this in a variation of Zimbardo's experiment. When participants wore a Ku Klux Klan outfit, they were more likely to give stronger shocks; however, when wearing a nurse's outfit, they delivered lower levels of shock. In other words, group identity and its social norms determined the level of violent behaviour exhibited.

Reicher applies **social identity theory** to collective behaviour—that is, the behaviour of a group. The social identity of the group provides indications as to what is and is not acceptable—that is, social norms. For example, violent football hooligans might find destruction a legitimate and normal behaviour pattern. Crowd members will look to the members of the core group for guidance on how to behave. **Self-categorization theory** (Oakes et al. 1993) suggests that people look for other individuals in the group with whom they can identify. This would explain why police and rioters may act very differently in the same environment.

Violence: the case of bullying

Bullying is when a person is exposed repeatedly over time to negative actions on the part of one or more other people. A negative action is when someone intentionally inflicts, or attempts to inflict, injury or discomfort on another. Bullying may be direct (physical force or verbal threats/teasing) or indirect (characterized by social isolation or exclusion). Bullying is not only a phenomenon that concerns children. Unfortunately, the workplace is also the scene for many cases of bullying, and every year, people who are exposed to this fall ill through stress and depression. Some may never return to work again.

According to Nansel et al. (2001) who surveyed 15 000 US students between ages 12 and 17, around 17 per cent said that they had been bullied during a school year. Around 19 per cent reported that they had bullied others and 6 per cent said that they were bullying others and being bullied themselves. This study also found that boys are more likely to bully than girls. Around 50 per cent of the girls reported that they had mainly been bullied by boys. However, this does not mean that girls do not participate in bullying. Girls are less physically violent than boys but they bully in indirect ways such as excluding someone from the group, spreading rumours, and manipulating friendship relations. Indirect bullying is, however, just as harmful as direct bullying.

Bullying is found in many countries. Kim (2006) reported that a nationwide study in Japan found that 21.9 per cent of students in elementary school had been bullied and that 24.4 per cent of elementary school students reported that they had bullied others.

For bully victims school can be a tough experience

The figures were much lower for students in high school, however, which indicates that bullying in Japanese schools is primarily happening in elementary school. This is mirrored in findings from Korea. Kwak and Lee (1997) found that in Korea a total of 18.3 per cent of students in elementary and middle school reported that they had experienced bullying in the last semester and 26.8 per cent of the total participants in the survey had bullied others in the previous semester.

Norwegian psychologist Dan Olweus (1993), considered by many to be the "father" of research on bullying, found the following trends when surveying bullying in Norwegian and Swedish schools.

- 1 in 10 students has been the victim of bullying.
- The percentage of students who are bullied decreases with age.
- Girls were more exposed to indirect and more subtle forms of bullying than direct bullying.
- Boys carried out a large part of the bullying to which girls were subjected.
- Teachers and parents were often unaware of bullying.

In a US study of 15 686 students aged 10–15, Nansel et al. (2000) found that 17 per cent of students reported having been bullied "sometimes", or more frequently, during the school term. About 19 per cent reported bullying others "sometimes" or more often. And 6 per cent reported both bullying and having been bullied.

According to Olweus, bullying is a very complex phenomenon that is not easily understood. In a social group such as a school or a workplace, bullies and their victims have key positions in the problem, but the rest of the people play a role also. They may, for example, be bystanders and do nothing or they may dislike the bullying and try to help the victim. Group processes such as *social contagion* (imitation) and diffusion of responsibility due to deindividuation could also play a role, especially when there are several bullies. The bullying circle suggested by Olweus is an attempt to outline some of the factors involved in bullying.

Olweus's bullying circle

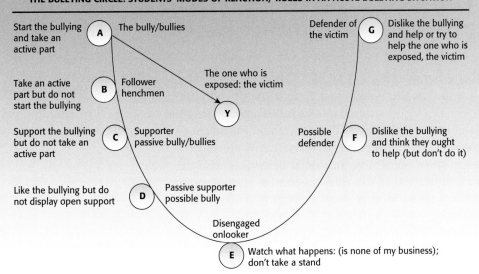

THE BULLYING CIRCLE: STUDENTS' MODES OF REACTION/ ROLES IN AN ACUTE BULLYING SITUATION

A — The bully/bullies — Start the bullying and take an active part

B — Follower henchmen — Take an active part but do not start the bullying

Y — The one who is exposed: the victim

C — Supporter passive bully/bullies — Support the bullying but do not take an active part

D — Passive supporter possible bully — Like the bullying but do not display open support

E — Disengaged onlooker — Watch what happens: (is none of my business); don't take a stand

F — Possible defender — Dislike the bullying and think they ought to help (but don't do it)

G — Defender of the victim — Dislike the bullying and help or try to help the one who is exposed, the victim

Olweus has argued that the dichotomy of bully and victim is too simplistic—there may be many people involved in bullying, either directly or indirectly. His model of the "bullying circle" illustrates the different roles that people may play.

Be reflective

1 What roles have you personally observed in the bullying circle?
2 Explain these different roles using your knowledge from this chapter.

Apply your knowledge

To what extent does research on deindividuation apply to the practice of "happy slapping"?

A modern twist to bullying is a behaviour called *cyber-bullying*. This involves the use of information and communication technologies such as email, mobile phones, pager text messages, instant messaging, defamatory personal websites, and defamatory online personal polling websites, to support deliberate, repeated, and hostile behaviour by an individual or group that is intended to harm others (Belsey 2004).

The perception of anonymity is what emboldens the cyber-bully. Their belief that they cannot be identified can remove social inhibitions and norms, allowing bullies to behave in ways that they would never do in person (Patchin and Hinojosa 2006). The cyber-bully may also believe that he or she will not be caught or punished (Brown et al. 2006), so the element of fear of discovery that may act as a behavioural control in an individual is absent in cyberspace.

Happy slapping is a particularly nasty form of cyber-bullying. The initial incident (2004) involved a target who was approached and lightly slapped on the face while a third person videotaped the event on a mobile phone. The video was then uploaded to a website. The "slapping" has escalated to increasingly violent events. Four teenagers were prosecuted in the UK in January 2006 for beating a man to death in such an incident (see www. guardian.co.uk/uk/2006/ jan/24/ukcrime.topstories3).

"Happy slapping"

Cyber-bullying differs from face-to-face bullying in that there is a lack of tangible feedback from the victim, which means that the bully does not have to witness the effect of his or her behaviour on the target (Belsey 2005; Brown et al. 2006). The absence of the experience of seeing the harm reduces the likelihood of an empathetic reaction (Willard 2006).

Origins of bullying behaviour

Research has found that there may be a genetic factor in bullying behaviour. Eley et al. (1999) studied antisocial behaviour in 1500 pairs of Swedish and British twins. The researchers found that identical (*monozygotic*) twins were more likely than fraternal (*dizygotic*) twins to show aggressive antisocial behaviour and this was interpreted as an indication of the role of genes in this behaviour. Male identical twins and fraternal twins were just as likely to exhibit symptoms of non-aggressive antisocial behaviour. This was taken as an indication that the environment plays a strong role. They also found that antisocial behaviour in girls was more likely to be genetically based. The study also found that play with peers greatly influences the behaviour of both boys and girls and that this influence could be different for each member of a twin pair. We cannot conclude that bullying is caused by genes, but this suggests that violent behaviour could, to some extent, be related to genetic make-up. Research also suggests that environment plays a role.

Lieu and Raine (2004) did a longitudinal study over 14 years following 1000 children living in Mauritius, an island in the Indian Ocean. The children had different ethnic backgrounds such as Indian, Creole, French, English, and Chinese. The research focused on nutrition at age three and then looked for vitamin, protein, and mineral deficiency. The children's cognitive level was also measured and potential risk factors such as income, health, occupation, and living conditions of parents were recorded at base rate. At age 8, 11 and 17 years the researchers investigated how the children were behaving in school and at home based on either teacher or parent evaluations. They also used a control group who did not suffer from malnutrion. The researchers found that overall there was a major increase in aggressive behaviour in the children suffering from malnutrition; for example, a 51 per cent increase in violent and antisocial behaviour at age 17. Poor nutrition could also influence intelligence and could lead to antisocial behaviour later. On the basis of the results the researchers suggested that malnutrition in the first years of life may be responsible for antisocial and aggressive behaviour throughout childhood and late adolescence. The researchers argued that malnutrion is a risk factor for developing children, not only for health but also for cognitive development and behaviour.

Olweus (1993) argues that the roots of bullying are a combination of parental influence, aspects of a child's home environment, and problems with anger management. It appears that too little love and too much freedom in childhood can contribute to the development of an aggressive personality. Studies by Eron (1987) found that parents of bullies are often authoritarian, using very strict, and often physical, methods of punishment. Living with parents who abuse them teaches children that aggression and violence are effective and normative ways to reach a goal. This is stored in social schemas and affects how they handle social situations in the future.

Aside from their often troublesome home lives, some aggressive children may have difficulty interpreting the intentions of their classmates. Dodge (1980) gave aggressive and non-aggressive boys a brief hypothetical story to read. Each boy imagined that a classmate spilled a lunch tray all over his back. Dodge asked them about the classmate's intentions, and how they would respond if this really happened to them. The aggressive boys read hostile intent into the story 50 per cent more frequently than the others, and the response was based more often on aggressive action. The negative attitudes towards others go hand in hand with a negative attributional style.

Other research by Dodge shows that such children are always ready to defend themselves, regardless of whether a classmate really means to harm them, and especially when they feel threatened. They make errors in presuming hostility where none exists. Consequently, other children grow to dislike their aggressive classmates, and their originally unfounded suspicions become a self-fulfilling prophecy. This indicates bias in information processing due to negatively based cognitive schemas.

Bullies often carry their aggression with them into a relatively unsuccessful adulthood, according to data Eron and his colleagues (1987) collected in a 22-year study. The study showed that they are more likely than their less aggressive classmates to abuse their spouses, and they tend to punish their children more severely, in effect raising a new generation of bullies. Eight-year-old bullies have a 1-in-4 chance of having a criminal record by their 30th birthday, compared to other boys' odds of 1 in 20. These data are correlational, so it is difficult to know the cause of these differences. It is also important to note that bullying may also be a *symptom* of antisocial behaviour, rather than the *cause* of it.

Did you know?

Some social psychologists now believe that gossip is an important part of human relationships. It can be used to harm others as in the case of bullying, but Foster (2004) suggests that gossip is important because it is the glue that binds social groups together and helps people with learn social norms. It also helps them to develop an identity and compare themselves to others. Foster defines gossip as a conversation between two or more people about another person who is not present and says that there is both good and bad gossip. Bad gossip consists of spreading rumours and lies to harm another person and is part of bullying.

CAS: be reflective

1   Make up a list of school norms in order to prevent or reduce bullying in your school community. Phrase things as: *Teachers should…*, *All of us should…*, *Students should not…*, *None of us should…*

2   Discuss your overall plan and how you would be able to evaluate its success in the future.

Effects of violence (bullying) on the individual

Olweus (1992) found a correlation between frequent victimization in middle school and low self-esteem and depression by the age of 23. Elliot and Kirkpatrick (1999) administered surveys to several thousand UK students and concluded that 20 per cent of those who had been bullied had attempted suicide, whereas only 3 per cent of participants who were not bullied had attempted suicide.

Bullying may have long-term consequences

297

The effect of bullying on its victims is complex. Because the mental health and academic abilities of victimized students are rarely measured before the bullying begins, it is difficult to determine the actual extent of harm caused by bullying. Most of the data gathered are through self-report, where the roles of cause and effect are attributed by the victim, but with no control for other variables. It is also usually retrospective, with the data gathered several years after the actual bullying has stopped.

The effects of bullying on its victims (Olweus 1992)

Short-term	Long-term
Anger	Lingering feelings of anger and bitterness
Depression	Difficulty trusting people
Higher rate of illness	Fear/avoidance of new social situations
Lower grades than non-bullied peers	Increased tendency to be a loner
Suicidal thoughts and feelings	Low self-esteem

Delville (2002) observed the effects of bullying on the health and brain development of adolescent hamsters. In his experiment, male pubescent hamsters were placed for an hour a day, for two weeks, into an adult hamster's cage. The older hamsters responded with hostility to the adolescent males, biting and chasing them.

A control group of adolescent male hamsters were simply placed in an empty, unfamiliar cage for one hour a day. Both environments elicited stress reactions in the young hamsters, but the long-term effects of the two different kinds of stress were surprisingly dissimilar.

Cortisol, a stress hormone secreted by the adrenal glands in hamsters and humans, was found to be high in both groups of adolescents during the first day of the experiment. However, the cortisol levels remained elevated for the entire two weeks only in the chased and threatened hamsters. The bullying was a stressor to which they could not seem to adapt. Research has found that chronic over-secretion of stress hormones adversely affects brain function, especially memory. Too much cortisol can prevent the brain from laying down a new memory, or from accessing already existing memories. Chronic bullying could then actually have an effect on the victim's brain development.

Hamsters bully intruders into their territory

The role of bullying on cortisol levels in humans has been supported by research by Carney and Hazler (2007). The researchers measured cortisol levels in the saliva of 94 sixth-grade students between the ages of 9 and 14. They also asked them to fill out a questionnaire on their experience of being bullied or watching someone being bullied, plus additional measures of anxiety and trauma. Cortisol levels were measured first thing in the morning and just before lunchtime. Lunchtime was chosen because it is one of the less supervised times of the day, when adolescents are more likely to be bullied or observe someone being bullied. Thus, anticipatory stress—the fear that something would happen during lunch—should affect cortisol levels.

Their findings demonstrate the limitation of the animal research carried out by Delville. Bullying does appear to cause a spike in cortisol levels, but it appears that in humans who experience long-term bullying—or the fear of witnessing someone being bullied—have low levels of cortisol—in other words, a cortisol deficiency—called hypocortisol. This condition is linked to chronic fatigue syndrome, chronic pain, and post-traumatic stress disorder (PTSD).

There seem to be several factors, however, which determine the extent of the negative impact that bullying has on its victims. Victims will often engage in downward comparison in order to understand and cope with their victimization. **Downward comparison** refers to comparing oneself to those who are worse off. Victims may find solace in the fact that their victimization did not leave major physical scars, or that it could have been worse. It is interesting that when such negative models are not immediately available, victims will create scenarios in which they received even greater physical, emotional, or personal damage (Greenberg and Ruback 1992). This internal "it-could-have-been-much-worse" exercise seems to help the victim to gain perspective, and may even relate to a focus on the positive aspects of being a survivor (Thompson 2000).

A 2004 study (Kliewer et al.) of a sample of Spanish college students suggests that there is a direct relationship between victims' perceptions of control over their bullying experience and the extent of long-term difficulties they experience as a result of bullying. Bullied students who believed they were able to influence and/or escape their bullies reported fewer negative long-term effects from having been bullied than did students who felt helpless to influence their situation while it was happening. Perception of control (and not reality of control) was key in this study, as no relationship was found between the various ways that students coped with being bullied and how they turned out.

Joseph (2003) studied the effects of bullying on mental health in a sample of 331 adolescent students in England. He found that victims of bullying often suffered from PTSD—a disorder characterized by high levels of anxiety and other psychological and behavioural problems. Joseph found that up to one-third of bullied children suffered from PTSD and that it did not matter what form the bullying took. This is contrary to common beliefs that physical bullying is the most serious type.

Snyder (2003) did a longitudinal study observing 266 children from kindergarten to elementary school interacting on the playground. The researchers recorded instances of aggression and victimization and found that boys who experienced bullying were more likely to become depressed and demonstrate antisocial behaviours. Being aggressive may be a way to avoid bullying for a while but in the long term it increases the risk of being victimized by peers. Snyder also found that antisocial behaviour made girls into a target for bullying in both the short and long term.

Having the support of family members and peers, who can be confided in when one has been bullied, tends to lessen the impact of bullying. When a bullying victim is surrounded by a supportive social network, that individual receives many positive messages about their worth from network members, and thus there are fewer opportunities for bullies' negative messages to be validated and take over self-esteem.

Possible essay question

Explain short-term and long-term effects that violence can have on individuals.

Discuss how violence can be reduced. (22 marks)

Assessment advice

In the first part of the question the command term is "explain" which means that you should give a detailed account of the issue (effects of violence on individuals) including causes and reasons. Here, you could include the case of bullying.

In the second part of the question the command term is "discuss" which means that you should offer a balanced review of possible ways to reduce violence and your arguments should be supported by evidence. Here, you could discuss effectiveness of anti-bullying measures.

The case of gay and lesbian students

The following data have been gathered from US schools in the Human Rights Watch report *Hatred in the Hallways* (2001).

- Gay and lesbian youths are two to three times more likely to attempt suicide than heterosexual young people. Of completed youth suicides, 30 per cent are committed by lesbian and gay youths annually, and suicide is the leading cause of death in this group.
- In a national study, 28 per cent of gay and lesbian high-school students were seen to have dropped out of school because of harassment resulting from their sexual orientation.

- 45 per cent of gay males and 20 per cent of lesbians report having experienced verbal harassment and/or physical violence during high school, as a result of their sexual orientation.
- 26 per cent of gay and lesbian youths are forced to leave home because of conflicts with their families over their sexual identities.
- 53 per cent of students report hearing homophobic comments made by school staff.

Reducing violence and bullying

Every time a school shooting makes the news, the public responds by demanding tougher gun laws and tighter controls for security in schools. There may be some justification for these demands. When Jamaica implemented strict gun-control and censored gun scenes from television, robbery and shooting rates dropped dramatically (Diner and Crandell 1979).

However, to focus solely on the use of firearms ignores the day-to-day bullying and exclusion which takes place in schools and has a long-term effect not just on its victims, but on society as a whole. Several strategies are now employed with the goal of reducing bullying in schools.

One of the strategies is the use of counselling in schools to teach all students appropriate anger management, as well as helping them to develop empathy. Efforts at reducing violence often involve altering people's immediate perceptions of others or the situational cues that may increase aggression. Dodge (1981) found that children who have problems processing social cues tend to display a bias in their reactions to ambiguous harmful actions. They tend to react to them automatically as hostile. But while the immediate reactions are of this nature, their more considered reactions are not. Teaching students to take time to process (like counting to 10) may make all the difference.

Feshbach and Feshbach (1982) trained junior school children to imagine how they would feel in other children's circumstances, to recognize the feelings of others, and to try to share their emotions. Compared with children in control groups, the children who engaged in this empathy training were much less aggressive in everyday playground activities. More recent research has used "virtual reality" in order to improve empathy. Figueiredo et al. (2007) are testing the long-term effects of a computer game in which each child takes the role of an invisible friend of the victimized character, discussing problems and exploring possible solutions and coping strategies. The advice given subsequently

Be empathetic

1 Why do you think this particular minority group has such a problem with bullying in schools?

2 What can schools do to improve the situation for gay, lesbian, bisexual, and transgender teenagers? You may want to consult www.glsen.org to find further information about improving schools for these students.

influences the actions of the victim. The goal is to encourage students to be more reflective about bullying, and to test out strategies for intervention in a non-threatening environment.

Those who lack social skills account for a high proportion of the violence occurring in any given society (Toch 1980). Schneider (1991) suggests that social-skills training can be effective in reducing the likelihood of a person being either the source or the target of aggressive behaviour.

Elliot Aronson (1979) has shown that the use of the "jigsaw classroom"—also known as cooperative learning—lowers the rate of bullying in schools and increases positive interaction between out-groups during play or free periods. Students must rely on each other for their learning. The classroom works on the idea that everyone has something to contribute to the learning process, and that by working together towards a common goal, everyone is valued. Limber (1992), however, argues that jigsaw classrooms and peer mediation may be appropriate in resolving conflict between students with equal power, but bullying is a form of victimization. It is not a "conflict", it is a form of abuse, and it should be addressed as such.

Many researchers, however, argue that the only way to reduce bullying in schools is to take a "whole-school" approach. Vreeman (2006) found that bullying can be curbed, but that many common methods of dealing with the problem, such as classroom discussions, role-playing or detention, are ineffective. Whole-school interventions, involving teachers, administrators, and social workers committed to culture change, are the most effective, and are especially effective throughout high school. Olweus (1972) developed a whole-school programme for schools in Norway. In this programme, teachers are trained to recognize and deal with bullying; cooperative learning is used; head teachers ensure that lunchrooms and playgrounds are adequately supervised; and counsellors conduct intensive therapy with bullies and their parents. An important part of the programme is for teachers and administrators to model non-aggressive conflict-resolution strategies in the classroom. It is also important that teachers are present in the school during break-times. The mere presence of adults in the corridors and at lunchtime significantly lowers bullying. The programme has reduced bullying by about 50 per cent.

A policy of "zero tolerance"

In an effort to stem this rising tide of school violence, many school districts have implemented zero-tolerance policies. These policies vary widely, but most are based on the principle that violence, or even the threat of violence, has no place whatsoever in schools, and will not be tolerated in any form. Under such policies, students who threaten or commit acts of violence have been punished, often suspended from school, and sometimes expelled—regardless of the actual harm done or the scale of the threat. In a small percentage of these cases, school-based sanctions have been followed by juvenile or criminal court prosecutions.

Be a researcher

1 What is the attitude towards bullying in your community? Find out how the problem is addressed (e.g. by public campaigns).

2 Carry out some research on the zero-tolerance debate. What are the advantages and disadvantages of a zero-tolerance approach to bullying in schools?

Sport psychology: emotion and motivation

Learning outcomes

- Discuss the extent to which biological, cognitive, and sociocultural factors influence behaviour in sport
- Evaluate psychological research (that is theories and/or studies) relevant to the study of sport psychology
- Evaluate theories of motivation in sport
- Discuss the role of goal setting on motivation of individuals
- Discuss theories on the effect of arousal and anxiety on performance

Sport and exercise psychology is a fast-growing field, no longer limited simply to helping athletes improve their performance. By studying sport and exercise behaviour, psychologists can acquire a deeper understanding of psychological aspects of motivation, efficient teamwork strategies, and how people cope with setbacks. In addition, sport psychologists can play an important role in increasing the public's awareness of the need to exercise, as well as helping public health promoters to find ways to encourage people to engage in regular exercise.

Currently, although almost anyone could tell you that exercise is important for a healthy life, statistics from Weinberg and Gould (2006) do not indicate that people are following the advice.

- Only 10–25 per cent of US adults are active enough to maintain or increase cardiovascular fitness.
- Among adults, 30 per cent do not participate in any physical activity.
- Among adults, only 10–15 per cent participate regularly in vigorous exercise three times a week for at least 20 minutes.
- Of those people who start an exercise programme, 50 per cent will drop out within six months.

How does one go about improving attitude and commitment to sport? One way is the setting of appropriate goals, according to sports psychologists.

Goal setting

Every year, more than 50 000 people run in the London Marathon. Most of them have no expectation of winning the race. The same can be said for any marathon. It is clear that the runners must have different goals for the same event, although this does not seem to influence their motivation to participate.

Psychologists identify three types of goals. **Outcome goals** focus on the competitive result of the game. If your goal is to win the bowling tournament, you may bowl your best night ever, and still not win—and thus not reach your goal. Since it is competitive, you do not have total control, since your success is based on your opponent's ability. **Performance goals** focus on achieving objectives independent of other competitors. Setting a better time for a 10km run, or improving the percentage of successful serves from 50 per cent to 70 per cent are performance goals. **Process goals** focus on the actions one must take to be successful in a sport and improve performance—for example, a basketball player releasing the ball at the peak of his or her jump. Studies have shown that using a combination of these three types of goals produces better performance than focusing on just one.

Much of today's research on goal setting is based on the original theory of goal setting established by Locke and Latham (1981). They argue that performance is regulated by the conscious goals that individuals attempt to achieve on a task.

To be effective, goals should be specific, measurable, and behavioural in terms. An ineffective goal is "to improve my golf game". An effective (and achievable) goal is "to lower my golf handicap from 14 over par to 11 by improving the accuracy of my short-iron approach shots to the green".

Locke explains why goal setting is effective with his **direct mechanistic view**. He argues that goals help athletes to concentrate on specific skill development; goals provide direction and focus for activity. Goals also help the athlete to persist by creating sub-goals.

Burton (1989) argues that goal setting also has a psychological effect in that setting goals may affect cognitive processes such as self-efficacy. This is known as the **indirect thought process view**. This argues that goals lead to changes in psychological factors that influence performance, like anxiety and levels of confidence. Unrealistic outcome goals can raise anxiety and harm performance, whereas attainable performance goals can lower anxiety and boost confidence. This clearly has an effect on one's level of motivation.

Effective goal setting: SMARTS (Smith 1994)

- **S**pecific: it is difficult to know whether vague goals have been achieved or how to obtain them.

- **M**easurable: if achievement cannot be measured, then your self-confidence will not benefit from goal setting, nor can you observe progress towards a greater goal.

- **A**ction-oriented: specify exactly what has to be done to reach the goal.

- **R**ealistic: when a goal is perceived to be unreachable, no effort will be made to achieve it; discouragement is bound to result.

- **T**imely: goals should be attainable in a reasonable amount of time.

- **S**elf-determined: goals should be set by, or have input from, the participant.

Research in psychology

Goal setting and performance in lacrosse (Weinberg et al. 1994)

Weinberg et al. (1994) carried out a season-long study on university-level lacrosse players. They used a matched-pairs design, where coaches rated players on their ability and then randomly assigned them to either a "goal-setting condition" or the control group. The coaches were not told which group was which.

The goal-setting group set both short-term goals and long-term, seasonal goals. Each week, players received feedback on the progress of their goals. Compared to players in the control group, players in the goal-setting condition had consistently higher levels of both offensive and defensive measures of performance throughout the season. This indicates that goal setting can not only potentially increase a team's scoring performance but also helps a team to better compete against their opponent.

Be a researcher

What methodological considerations should be made when evaluating this study?

Motivation in sport

The story of Jesse Martin

Jesse Martin

On 31 October 1999, Jesse Martin became the youngest person to circumnavigate the globe solo, non-stop, and unassisted. He was not yet 18 when he set out from Melbourne, Australia.

During Jesse's amazing voyage, he and his sailboat survived force 10 gales, a collision with a whale, and a near collision with a tanker in the middle of the night. Jesse's journal entries on his trip show that he found things even in the worst situations which kept his spirits up: dolphins accompanied him through a difficult patch while sailing through the Doldrums, and he noted in his journal that the stormy skies highlighted the beauty of a rainbow.

When asked what kept him going when things were tough, he replied:

Well, the dream of sailing is perfect weather with a nice breeze pushing you along. But obviously you've got the crappy weather in between that you get through and that you just have to deal with. You know that eventually the weather is going to change, so the thought in your head is, "I just get through this."

I really realized out there that after I went through bad weather, the next day was most often the best time I had because there was a sense of achievement, and relative to the bad weather you appreciated the sun coming out. So you kind of need the bad weather in a way.

From an interview in the *Herald Sun*, February 2007

Be a thinker

1 What do you think motivated Jesse Martin to sail round the world? Produce a list of possible motivators.

2 What would it take to motivate you to undertake such a trip—or to take on a similar challenge?

3 What is the role of having goals for motivation? Is it possible that goals can help you during tough times?

Do you try out for the school basketball team? What makes the marathon runner continue despite pain? Do you know someone who seeks the advice of a personal trainer? Why do football players continue despite injury? In other words, what motivates people to persist in activities that are sometimes painful, time-consuming, and even bring failure? Sport psychology deals with motivation a lot, although the term may seem a bit vague and is perhaps misused in daily language—when students are labelled as "unmotivated", for example. When a coach tells an athlete that he or she needs to show a bit more motivation, this is not helpful advice because it is too vague.

Motivation is defined as the direction and intensity of one's effort (Sage 1977). The *direction of one's effort* refers to whether an individual seeks out or is attracted to certain activities. The *intensity of one's effort* refers to how much effort a person puts into a task or situation. Going to the gym three times a week is not enough; one actually has to put in some effort to undertake a regime of exercise. Do you seek the lowest amount of exercise so that you can simply say, "I go to the gym"? Or do you work with a trainer and then follow the regime religiously? Or do you push yourself too hard, often resulting in fatigue and potential injury? Intensity also includes one's persistence in the face of failure or adversity.

One way of looking at motivation is to discuss intrinsic versus extrinsic motives. **Intrinsic motives** are those that come from within the individual. This could be the fun of being with the team, the satisfaction of a faster finishing time in a 100m race, enjoying the competition, or improved well-being after an hour in the gym. Intrinsic motivation depends on the individual's own attitudes and perceptions, and it involves cognitions and appraisal of situations. Intrinsic motivation does not have to be provided by others, and serves as a continuous drive towards satisfying individual needs. This means that intrinsic motivation can be very persistent.

Extrinsic motives are the external rewards that we can gain from taking part in sport or exercise. This could be praise from your coach, the chance to be with your friends, a major contract with a professional sports team, or the status that follows from being famous.

Both internal and extrinsic motives are important in sport and exercise. Psychologists can target both intrinsic and extrinsic motives to improve the performance of the individual.

Studies show that people tend to report intrinsic motives more than extrinsic motives for taking part in sport and exercise. Ashford et al. (1993) carried out a series of interviews at a local sports centre in the UK. Their content analysis of the interviews revealed key motives for participation at the centre: physical well-being, psychological well-being, improvement of performance, and achieving personal and competitive goals.

Smith et al. (1979) conducted a field study on children and their coaches. They found that the children whose coaches gave positive feedback when they corrected mistakes were more enthusiastic about the coming season, compared with children who did not receive positive feedback. They also found that children who started out with the lowest levels of self-esteem benefited dramatically from the positive approach in training. This study shows that extrinsic motivation (positive feedback) may influence intrinsic motivation (enthusiasm). It is believed that extrinsic motivation is most efficiently applied if it is given as a result of a particular behaviour and is appropriate to the individual. However, there is evidence that excessive motivation of this nature may also work the other way, so that it actually demotivates.

Intrinsic motivation could be the main reason for running a race

Research in psychology

The role of extrinsic rewards on motivation (Deci 1972)

Deci carried out a study to determine if extrinsic motivators would increase motivation in the workplace—in other words, would the rewards for people's work help them to find greater motivation to perform well?

The study was a laboratory experiment with 72 participants who were allocated to groups, and each was given a task to do. Each group had a different condition: they received either a flat payment for the work, performance-related pay, punishment if they failed to do well, or feedback on their performance. There was also a control group who received no treatment, and simply carried out the task.

Contrary to expectations, receiving performance-*related* pay, punishment, or negative feedback *reduced* intrinsic motivation. In the control group and in the flat payment group, there was no increase in motivation. However, in the positive feedback group, intrinsic motivation increased. It appears that positive feedback enhances self-esteem and the pleasure taken in performing the task—leading to increased intrinsic motivation.

The results of this study show that extrinsic motivation is related to intrinsic motivation. Positive feedback can increase people's sense of self-efficacy and motivate them to try harder next time. This is well known to sport coaches.

Be a researcher

1 What are some of the methodological considerations for this study?

2 What could be the implications of this study for coaches?

Theories of motivation in sport

Need achievement motivation theory

It seems obvious that there is a link between the wish to achieve and success. An athlete who strongly wishes to succeed will determine to a large extent how hard s/he will train before competition, as well as how much effort to invest in the competition itself. Some sport psychologists believe that the most important factor in motivation is the need to achieve, while others focus on the motive of avoiding failure.

Winning a race depends on a fine balance between situational and dispositional factors

McClelland and Atkinson (1961) argue that human motivation is the balance between the motivation to succeed and the fear of failure—or, in the case of sport, the enjoyment of the sport and competitive anxiety. They argue that when people approach a sport or exercise situation, they do so with an approach–avoidance conflict. On the one hand, they are motivated to participate because they *want to succeed*, but on the other hand, they are also motivated to avoid participating because they want to *avoid failure*. According to the theory, our motivation for achievement is the difference between intrinsic motivation for the sport and competitive anxiety. If our intrinsic motivation is moderate, but our anxiety is high, we will not be motivated to engage in sport or exercise.

According to McClelland et al. (1953), those with a high motivation to achieve are more likely to show high levels of performance, persist longer, and value feedback from coaches, as well as attributing failure to internal (dispositional) factors such as effort. In contrast, those with a high motive to avoid failure will tend to avoid tasks that involve evaluation or the risk to fail. These athletes tend to attribute failure to external (situational) factors such as luck. The

Be an enquirer

● What do you think motivates race-car drivers? Find some important race-car drivers on the Internet and see if you can get an idea of what motivates them—what could be their intrinsic or extrinsic motives?

● Is there a difference between what motivates a Formula-1 driver and an elite swimmer?

two motives are present in most athletes, but it is the difference between them which provides the personality factor called achievement motivation. The greater the difference between the two, the higher the achievement motivation.

The theory deals with how dispositional factors—for example, emotional reactions and persistence—as well as situational factors —for example, feedback from a coach or behaviour of team mates— influence achievement. It claims that the balance between desire to succeed and fear of failure can predict whether a person will engage in sport activities or not. It can thus predict motivation patterns rather than performance, although it is assumed that achievement motivation can also influence performance—for example, playing in a more competitive match will raise anxiety and thus lower one's ability to reach achievement goals. However, it is difficult to put the concepts to the test, and the model does not reliably predict performance. Fodero (1980) studied elite gymnasts and failed to find a relationship between achievement motivation and performance.

The role of goal setting on motivation of individuals

A contemporary framework for studying motivation in sports has been the **achievement goal perspective** approach. The theory of goal motivation was originally developed within the context of education, but it has been applied in various fields, including sport psychology. It is based on a social-cognitive approach to explain striving for competence. Goals should be seen as cognitive representations of the different purposes people may have in achievement situations, and they are assumed to guide behaviour and cognition, and affect sport situations as well as academic work.

Two goals in particular have received attention from achievement goal researchers: **task-oriented goals** (related to mastery) and **ego-oriented goals** (related to social comparison). Central to task-oriented goals is the belief that effort leads to success, and the focus is on the intrinsic value of progress. Ability is shown by developing new skills, improving level of competence, or achieving a sense of mastery. In contrast, ego-oriented goals focus on one's ability and sense of self-worth. Ability is shown by doing better than others, surpassing the norm, or achieving success with little effort.

According to Duda and Hall (2001), people's own interpretation of success and failure creates a framework for understanding their motivation. Achievement goal theory argues that motivation is the result of the interaction of achievement goals, perceived ability, and achievement behaviour. The theory predicts that athletes with a task orientation would tend to show greater persistence in the face of failure and a greater sense of control over their performance, and would tend to choose tasks that are moderately difficult, but realistic to achieve. Athletes with an ego orientation would tend to choose tasks that guarantee success. Elliot and Dweck (1988) have found that athletes with an ego orientation tend to have an **entity view** of their ability—that is, their ability is fixed and may not be changed by effort; individuals who are task-orientated tend to have an **incremental focus**—that is, the belief that hard work and effort will improve performance.

How much effort is put into the game could depend on achievement orientation

Duda et al. (1998) investigated goal perspectives in how children define sport success and judge their overall competence, in a sample of 192 youth sport participants with a mean age of 11.5 (males) and 11.2 (females). The children were engaged in a variety of organized sports, such as soccer, swimming, basketball, and ice skating.

The researchers used a questionnaire with two parts. The first measured individual differences in dispositional goal orientation via a Task and Ego Orientation in Sport Questionnaire. The questionnaire asked participants to respond to the statement: "I feel most successful in sport when…" on a five-point Likert-type scale, and to indicate their agreement with task-oriented answers (e.g. "when I do my very best"), or ego-oriented answers (e.g. "when others cannot do as well as me"). The second part of the questionnaire asked participants about their individual views on the goals of sport, using the Perceived Purposes of Sport Questionnaire.

The researchers found that there was a relationship between task orientation and the perceived purposes of sport involvement. Those who were strongly task-oriented thought that the purposes of sport were to increase self-esteem, encourage a physically active lifestyle, and promote cooperation and foster behaviour that made one a respectful and productive citizen in society. It appeared that task-oriented participants generally saw sport more as an "end in itself" than as a means to extrinsic outcomes. The researchers hypothesized that a task-oriented youth sport athlete would therefore be less likely to drop out because they enjoyed participation in sport. They also found that males were more likely to perceive sport participation as a way to increase status and popularity than females—that is, boys focused more on the extrinsic and personal gains. The boys were also more likely to say that sport should promote deceptive tactics and a superior attitude in order to win. The study indicates that the type of goals are important for achievement since they can influence how much effort a person is willing to invest, and can explain why people drop out of sport.

Achievement orientation can also explain the frustration that some college athletes experience. If they have been the stars of their local basketball league during their high-school years, but have faced very little true competition because no one has their skill level, their orientation may affect their motivation to continue playing at college level, where one might assume that the playing field would be more level. If they have a task orientation, then they will set goals for improvement and continue to strive to play better on court. If they have an outcome orientation, then the fact that they can no longer do what they always used to do and be the best could result in frustration and demotivation.

Achievement goal theory is important because it shows that not all athletes have the same motivations, and this may affect performance. It also shows how the **motivational climate** may have a long-term effect on how people respond to sport and exercise. If a physical education class is highly competitive, and the teacher befriends the best athletes and bullies those of low ability, this reinforces the "entity view" of sport.

Fontayne et al. (2001) claim that motivational theories such as the achievement goal theory have a western bias, and perhaps also a male bias. They also argue that the focus on only two goal structures is reductionist because it hinders the generation of information about other important goals.

Cognitive evaluation theory

A final motivation theory is the cognitive evaluation theory (CET) (Deci 1975). CET argues that events that affect one's feelings of competence and self-determination have an effect on the level of intrinsic motivation. Deci argues that there may be two different aspects to an event. First, the **controlling aspect** determines for whom one is doing the activity. Is it solely for internal reasons that the individual is doing it, or is it external? (e.g. Do I play baseball because I love it, or because if I don't play, my father will think that I am a loser?) The theory predicts that the less *control* individuals perceive about *why* they are doing the sport, the less motivation they will have. The second aspect is the **informational aspect**, which changes one's feelings of competence about the sport. An award which honours one's talent and skill on the field is high in informational aspect, and thus highly motivating, whereas if a coach is primarily negative and critical, motivation will decrease.

Ryan (1977) carried out a study to see if scholarships have an effect on collegiate football players' motivation. The original study found that those students who were on scholarships reported less intrinsic motivation and higher levels of dissatisfaction in the game. So, does this mean that winning a scholarship will deprive athletes of enjoying the sport? Further research by Amorose and Horn (2000) argues that scholarships are not the root of the problem. The majority of dissatisfied players reported coaches using the scholarships to control the players' behaviour—for example, "You'd better start scoring or you are going to lose that scholarship." In other words, here the controlling aspect was increased, and the athlete felt less control over the sport. It may actually be the type of coach, and not the scholarship, that is the deciding factor in motivation. Coaches who are more democratic and less authoritative generally give more positive and instructional feedback, and therefore increase intrinsic motivation in their players.

Be a critical thinker

Fontayne et al. (2001) argue that motivational theories have a western bias.

- Explain what is meant by a western bias.
- Can you find something that supports the argument of a western bias? What about something that goes against it?
- The head coach of China's gold medal-winning women's rowing team at the Olympics in 2008 said that a particular female rower, Zhang, was chosen to participate in the team because of her "daring spirit". The team actually won. Could you explain the coach's evaluation of Zhang in terms of motivational theories? Why or why not?

309

Culture and motivation for sport: playing football in the US and in Malawi

Guest (2007) carried out a participant-observation with two men's collegiate soccer teams, one in the US and the other in Malawi.

In the US, unlike most other countries, sport is integrated into formal education. Physical education emphasizes the intrinsic value of competition and self-improvement through effort and work. In contrast, sport is not a prominent part of the education system in Malawi. Malawi is a more collectivist society. This can be seen in the response to one of Guest's questions about the role of sport in daily life: "One thing, it gives, it is a source of, it is a pastime activity. At the same time it is for physical fitness, it helps one's health. I can also say, probably, uniting the nation too."

The overall findings from the content analysis of the interviews and observations were striking. Competition was the most frequently identified motivation for US players, at 70 per cent, while *no Malawi players talked about competition as a motivation*. The US players saw sport participation as an opportunity to test themselves and develop abilities through direct challenges. Conversely, Malawians more frequently identified status as motivating, and tended to talk about sport as a chance to demonstrate their worth through exhibition. The Malawi players saw sport participation as an opportunity to exhibit abilities, regardless of competitive success.

The most prominent Malawian response was that sport provides a pastime, allowing a person to avoid trouble. Players often stated that sport gave something to people who were not good in school, or who would otherwise not be productive members of society. They tended to talk extensively about how sport keeps people from drinking, crime, drug use, or prostitution. Although the US players did mention this, the cultural script was different. The US players argued that sport provokes self-improvement and gives people an expressive "outlet".

Be reflective and an enquirer

1 How could you explain the differences in motivation between the two soccer teams, using your knowledge of motivation?

2 Malawi has a national football team called the Flames. Search the Internet (e.g. Wikipedia) and find information about the team's winning record. To what extent could the difference in motivation shown in this study hurt Malawi's chances of ever winning an international football competition? What other factors could play a role?

3 Would a western coach be appropriate for this team? Why or why not?

The effect of arousal and anxiety on performance

The challenge is hitting good golf shots when you have to…to do it when the nerves are fluttering, the heart pounding, the palms sweating…that's the thrill!

Tiger Woods (2001)

This quote from one of the world's most famous sports people illustrates that being able to control the physiological and psychological arousal that is inevitably part of any competition may be an important factor in winning the game.

Arousal is described as a general physiological and psychological activation, varying on a continuum from deep sleep to intense excitement. While arousal simply denotes a level of energy, **anxiety** is an emotional label for a negatively interpreted arousal experience. Sport psychologists address three main dimensions of anxiety: *cognitive anxiety*, which involves worry and negative appraisal of oneself and the future; *somatic anxiety*, which is characterized by rapid heartbeat, increased perspiration, shortness of breath, and other stress symptoms; and *state anxiety*, which is characterized by tension, agitation, and restlessness.

The inverted-U hypothesis

Yerkes and Dodson (1908) argued that for every motor task we carry out, there is an optimum level of physiological arousal. Performance is best at this level, but drops off when arousal falls below or rises above the optimal level. This theory proposes a curvilinear relationship between arousal and performance. According to the theory, increases in arousal have a positive effect on performance up to a certain point but after this point, further increases in arousal will affect performance in a negative way.

It is important to remember that not all sports have the same optimal arousal level. Some sports, like darts or billiards, require low levels of arousal. This is why it is considered an unfair advantage to take beta blockers (which regulate heartbeat and blood pressure) during billiards or snooker.

Though the inverted-U theory seems to explain why some athletes do poorly at high levels of arousal, it does not account for cognitive factors. Today, the focus of much research is on cognitive anxiety and its role in performance. Fazey and Hardy (1988) argue that when cognitive anxiety increases beyond the optimal level, the drop-off in performance is not gradual, as is seen in the inverted-U hypothesis, but rather declines dramatically. This is what they called the **catastrophe model**. This model could give an idea of why missing an easy putt may affect golfers so that they make further poor shots—even if they are able to regulate physical anxiety.

The catastrophe model describes the factors that may be involved but cannot explain exactly how cognitive anxiety and physiological arousal are interrelated to affect performance. Another criticism is that it ignores the confidence and self-efficacy of the athlete. It is possible that an athlete's judgment of his or her ability to perform in a sport will affect anxiety and arousal levels.

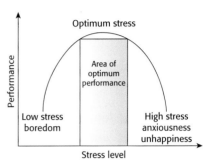

The relationship between stress and performance

How do sport psychologists explain choking?

The *Explicit Monitoring Theory* (Baumeister 1984) argues that anxiety causes athletes to become overly conscious of their movements; actions that have been learned to perfection so that the athlete does not normally think about them will suddenly become conscious and this distracts the athlete, who regresses to a novice standard.

Gucciardi and Dimmock (2002) tested 20 Australian golfers, with handicaps ranging from 0 to 12. They performed putts under three conditions—focusing either on three words that related to their technique (e.g. "arms", "weight", "head"); on three irrelevant words (e.g. three colours); or on just one word that summed up their putting action (e.g. "smooth").

They did all this in a low-anxiety context first, and then it was repeated with the pressure increased by the offer of cash rewards for the best performances. Would the anxiety of the high-pressure context cause the golfers' performance to deteriorate?

The added anxiety only caused the golfers' performance to deteriorate when they were focusing on three words that represented components of their putting action. These findings appear to support the idea that anxiety affects performance by causing people to think too much about their actions, not because it is distracting.

Individualized zone of optimal functioning

Hanin (1997) found that top athletes have a zone of optimal anxiety in which their best performance occurs. According to the **optimum arousal theory**, individual athletes will perform at their best if their level of arousal or competitive anxiety falls within their optimum functioning zone. Thus, some athletes perform best under conditions of high arousal, some when arousal is moderate, and some when it is low. The challenge for the coach is to determine the athlete's zone and identify the techniques that will place the athlete in this zone prior to competition.

Studies have confirmed that individual athletes have different preferred levels of anxiety, and that there is moderate support for the idea that they perform better when in the individualized zone. However, it is difficult for researchers to measure whether an athlete is in his or her zone during a competition. It is also a construct that cannot be reliably defined—is it primarily a cognitive state or a state of physiological arousal? The construct, however, has been very useful to coaches and athletes in mental preparation for competitions, as a metaphor for ways to individualize optimal functioning.

Self-efficacy increases with experiences of mastery

The role of self-efficacy in sport

Self-efficacy—people's belief in their capacity to succeed— also plays a key role in their ability to deal with arousal and anxiety in sport. According to the self-efficacy theory, four sources of information aid the construction of efficacious beliefs. The source of information with the largest effect on self-efficacy is *enactive mastery experience*. For athletes, this means that repetitious practice and experience from competitive games will tell them the most about their capabilities. Second, the theory suggests that athletes' self-efficacy will benefit from *observing models* achieving success, whereas failing models will harm their self-efficacy. *Verbal persuasion*—by coaches, team mates, the crowd, or in the form of self-talk—will also affect athletes' self-efficacy. Finally, the theory explores an individual's interpretation of physiological and affective states. A positive interpretation of physical arousal will increase one's sense of efficacy.

It is crucial that athletes cope with failure and stressful situations, since they often experience both (Bandura 1997). The affective processes regulate athletes' beliefs in their ability to cope with these stressors and failures. Athletes with strong efficacy beliefs tend to believe in their ability to cope with stressors and failures. This means that subsequent performance will not suffer from the athletes' distress or impairment (Bandura 1997). Athletes with weak efficacy beliefs will not believe in their ability to cope with failure and stress. They will dwell on their coping deficiencies, and focus on the things they did wrong and the errors they might make in the future. Such athletes will often be distressed, and this will severely impair their future performances.

Limiting beliefs are thoughts that hold an athlete back. Psychological barriers can have a major effect on performance. A classic example occurred when Roger Bannister became the first person to run the mile in less than four minutes. Although many athletes had been

Possible essay question

Discuss **two** theories of the effect of arousal and anxiety on performance.

Assessment advice

"Discuss" is a command term that asks you to offer a considered and balanced review of two theories of the effect of arousal and anxiety on performance. This question asks you to look at two theories in some depth. You should describe the theories and you should use relevant research and examples to back up your argument. This question also involves looking at the strengths and limitations of the theories.

consistently running the mile in around four minutes, the barrier was considered impossible to break. Within 18 months of Bannister breaking through this barrier, 16 athletes had managed to do the same.

Research in psychology

Self-efficacy among weightlifters (Fitzsimmons et al. 1991)

Fitzsimmons et al. (1991) used an experiment to test how expectations could affect performance among weightlifters. Participants were asked to perform a single maximum bench-press under differing conditions. A baseline measure for normal performance was thus established for each participant.

Then participants were asked to make further lifts, but were not told the real amount of weight they were lifting. The experimenters deceived participants, leading them to believe that they were lifting either more or less weight than they actually were. If a participant had lifted 70kg in their first lift, they were told they were lifting 70kg in the second lift, when they were actually lifting 75kg. Participants performed best when they believed they were lifting less weight than they were in reality. Although participants were being asked to lift more than their previously achieved maximum, the greater weight was lifted because of confidence gained from the previous lift.

However, Fitzsimmons found that there was a significant difference between novice and experienced weightlifters. When experienced weightlifters were deceived, the differences were relatively small. This study indicates that *beliefs* are indeed an important factor in achievement but also that beliefs are affected by previous experiences. The way people interpret situations influences their confidence levels and thus anxiety.

Be a thinker

What do you think accounts for the differences between novice and experienced weightlifters that Fitzsimmons observed in his experiment?

Sport psychology: skill development and performance

Learning outcomes

- Discuss the extent to which biological, cognitive, and sociocultural factors influence behaviour in sport
- Evaluate psychological research (that is theories and/or studies) relevant to the study of sport psychology
- Discuss the extent to which the role of coaches does affect individual or team behaviour in sport
- Explain relationships between team cohesion and performance
- Describe aids and barriers to team cohesion

Techniques for skill development

We all know the old saying, *practice makes perfect*. However, this may not be as accurate as we might like to believe. When athletes try to explain their poor performance, they often refer to lack of concentration or being nervous. Success is dependent on both mental and physical abilities, but it is important that the training includes correction of errors and building confidence. If an athlete repeats the same errors over and over, then performance will actually decrease. Also, high levels of repetition can lead to fatigue, which, in turn, can lead to demotivation or injury. If the athlete is well trained and motivated, it is possible to stay in control and even come back after some setbacks, as can be seen in the example of the junior tennis player Caroline Wozniacki, who became Junior Wimbledon Champion 2006.

Caroline Wozniacki

It was finally my turn to enter the court and I was a little excited after the last days with rain and so on.
I played well in the 1st set and won 6-0. In the 2nd set I got in the lead with 5-2 and started to try some different things. But Yakimova started to hit harder and go for the winners and won the next 2 games. But I was feeling confident all the time and I told myself to speed it up again in the next game. At 5-4 I broke her serve and won the match with 6-0 6-4. It was not my best match at this tournament but I'm very happy about my win.

From Caroline's website blog at www.carolinewozniacki.dk/

Sport psychologists have found that there are a number of ways to improve skill development and performance. These include

psychological skills training, which aims to enhance performance and increase enjoyment. Sport participants will inevitably experience setbacks, mistakes, and mental letdowns, so it is important to prepare for this in advance. Athletes also know the feeling of being "in the zone", where everything seems to work perfectly. Coaches and athletes all recognize the importance of mental skills in sport, expressed in the concept of "mental toughness". In fact, Scully and Hume (1995) found that mental toughness was perceived to be the most important determinant of success in sport. Caroline Wozniacki is an example of this. In the middle of an important match that she was losing, she was able to come back
and actually win the match. Mental toughness is mostly defined as the athlete's ability to focus and to rebound from failure, the ability to cope with pressure, determination to persist in the face of adversity, and mental resilience.

Research which has compared the psychological skills and characteristics of successful and less successful athletes—for example, Williams and Crane (2001)—has concluded that successful athletes are more confident and are better at regulating arousal; they have better concentration and focus, and are able to stay in control without forcing it; they have more positive thoughts and imagery, and show more determination and commitment. The conclusion was that successful athletes achieve peak performance by using mental goal setting, imagery, arousal control and management, coping strategies, and mental preparation routines.

According to Weinberg and Gold (2006), most coaches believe that sport is at least 50 per cent mental when competing against an opponent of similar ability. In certain sports, such as ice skating, tennis, and golf, coaches estimate that the mental part is up to 90 per cent. In fact, the famous tennis player Jimmy Connors claimed that professional tennis is 95 per cent mental. The golfer Tiger Woods is known for his ability to remain focused and come back even after poor performance at the beginning of a game; mental preparation is part of his overall training programme, which also includes serious physical training. It seems, however, that physical practice—no matter how hard—is not enough. Mental practice must be an important part of the training scheme.

Mental imagery

Athletes will often construct and rehearse scenarios in their heads concerning the outcome of their actions in order to gain insight into how best to execute their capabilities. According to Munroe (2000), there are four functions of mental imagery.

- *Cognitive specific imagery*: athletes use this function to help them to learn new skills by working on technique and making corrections (e.g. passing a ball, tackling to the line).

- *Cognitive general imagery*: the rehearsal of game plans, strategies of play, and routines; athletes use this function to learn strategies and rehearse how they will perform them in training or competition.

Be reflective

Could knowledge about "mental toughness" perhaps be applied outside sport?

Which areas do you think it could be applied to, and why? Support your point.

- *Motivational specific imagery*: imagining outcome goals and the activities necessary to achieve those goals.

- *Motivational general imagery*: a function related to physiological arousal. The motivational general arousal function of imagery is used by athletes to get "psyched up", maintain composure, or stay relaxed and calm.

While imagining the scenario, it is important to include as many senses as possible, not simply a visualization, but also the sense of body movement (kinaesthetic), the sounds of the stadium, and even the smell of the court. It is also important to evoke the effect or emotional state of competition in order to recognize and control the emotions connected to specific situations—for example, using the quick version of the progressive relaxation technique.

Baroga (1973) studied the imagery techniques of 446 weightlifters from 37 different countries at national and international competitions. He found that mediocre weightlifters displayed a short period of mental preparation with non-activity thought content—that is, they thought about friends, family, or nothing specific. The best lifters mentally rehearsed a positive performance of the exact skill. As with much early research on mental imagery in sport, this study was retrospective—that is, interviews were carried out after the competition, so it is difficult to determine the reliability of the data.

Rushall (1970) conducted a field experiment to determine the effect of mental rehearsal on performance on a 50-yard butterfly swim. Individuals were compared over six sessions: in one condition there was no mental rehearsal, and in the second condition, for 30 seconds participants rehearsed the 50-yard swim, thinking of the dive, the first few strokes, settling into a rhythm, the turn, clear thinking as fatigue set in, points of technique under stress, and a hard finish. The rehearsal was to be completed while looking at the part of the pool in which it would occur, from behind the block. The results were that performance was significantly better after the imagining techniques than without them.

Swimmers often use imagery to improve their performance

Isaac (1992) tested 78 participants on trampoline skill development. She divided the participants into an experimental and a control group. The coach did not know which group was which. Both groups were trained in three skills over a six-week period. The experimental group physically practised the skill for 2.5 minutes, which was then followed by 5 minutes of mental practice, then an additional 2.5 minutes of physical practice. Meanwhile, the control group physically worked on the skill for 2.5 minutes, which was then followed by 5 minutes of a session trying a mental task of an abstract nature, such as a mathematical problem or a logic puzzle. Then 2.5 minutes were spent physically working on the skill again. The results were that the experimental group showed significantly more improvement than the control group, regardless of the skill they had prior to training. These two studies certainly point at some very powerful effects of mental imagery on performance.

Not only does mental imagery seem to enhance athletic performance, but it has been shown to enhance intrinsic motivation

Be a thinker

- Why could it be that imagery is a powerful tool in skill development and performance? Mention at least two reasons and support your argument with evidence.

- Have you ever tried imagery yourself? Why or why not?

- If you have tried imagery, how did it work out? Can you explain why?

as well. In a study by Martin (1995), 39 beginner golfers were grouped into an imagery or control group. For three sessions, both groups were taught how to hit golf balls. The imagery group practised in an imagery training session designed for this specific golf skill. In addition to better performance, the participants in the imagery group had more realistic self-expectation, demonstrated a stronger sense of self-efficacy, and set higher goals to achieve.

Sports psychologists have attempted to understand the exact mechanisms that cause mental imagery to work. Numerous theories exist, but sports psychology lacks a single theory that completely explains the effectiveness of mental imagery. The earliest theory was proposed by Carpenter (1894), and is called **the psychoneuromuscular theory**. This theory maintains that imagery rehearsal stimulates the actual motor pattern that is being rehearsed. Thus, mental imaging strengthens the neural pathways that control the muscles related to skills.

Mental imagery can improve a golfer's capacity to hit the ball

Lang (1979) proposed the **information-processing model of imagery**, which assumes that an image is a functionally organized, definite set of propositions stored by the brain. This image has two main types of statements: *stimulus propositions*, which envision the scenario, and *response propositions*, which describe the individual's response to that scenario. Hence, the image is actually a script for athletic behaviour that can be reproduced, without conscious thinking, in actual practice or competition. Paivio (1985) suggested that imagery mediates behaviour through cognitive or motivational mechanisms that affect specific or general response systems. This refers to different ways of using imagery, for example cognitive specific imagery, which deals with development of specific skills, or motivation specific imagery, which deals with imagery that can motivate, such as visualizing oneself with a gold medal.

Evaluation of mental imagery

There is so much interest in imagery techniques in sport that a whole journal has been created: the *Journal of Imagery Research in Sport and Physical Activity*. There are a number of approaches to imagery but the essence in most models is that imagery content determines outcomes. The Sport Imagery Questionnaire (SIQ) model suggested by Hall et al. (2005) has proven useful in measuring the different aspects of imagery but there is no single model yet which can explain why imagery is effective. Callow and Hardy (2001) suggested that it is not the content of the image that is important but rather what it means to the athlete. Short et al. (2004) used SIQ and found that different athletes used the same image for different things. They also found that one image can have many different functions for the same athlete.

Athletes and coaches claim that imagery works, and there is some experimental evidence that appears to confirm the role of imagery in improving performance. However, since it is very difficult to isolate the use of mental imagery as a variable, it is possible that other factors may play as important a role, and that imagery techniques alone will not improve performance. For example, Bandura (1994) found that athletes with a strong sense of self-efficacy will imagine scenarios of success, which provide guidance and support for future performances. Athletes with low self-efficacy, on the other hand, tend to construct failure scenarios and focus on the many things that can go wrong, which may actually impede performance. For instance, a tennis player might rehearse making a difficult volley over and over again, and whether the volley is successful or not, in the constructed scenario, is dependent on the player's self-efficacy. Consequently, if athletes doubt their efficacy, they might spend most of their time rehearsing the negative scenarios, and this will affect performance negatively.

Hall (1985) argues that individual differences in imaging practice also make it difficult to support empirically the role of imagery. There is much contradictory research and poor control of imaging elements in the literature. Also, a large number of studies test individuals on novel tasks. This may mean that the inability to understand the task may be a confounding variable in this research. Finally, since many of the studies have been carried out in laboratories, one has to question the ecological validity of the findings. In spite of the inconclusive evidence on the effectiveness of imagery, it is a fact that this technique is widely used in sport and many athletes find it effective. The fact that scientific research has not yet been able to explain why it works does not make it less effective. It can, perhaps, be compared to the placebo effect. Nobody knows how it works—but it does.

Concentration training: self-talk

Another technique to develop skills and improve performance in sport is self-talk, which refers to the way in which athletes talk to themselves during competition or in practice. Positive self-talk lowers arousal and stress, and focuses attention. Psychologists have identified three types of self-talk.

- *Positive*: not focused on any specific task or skill (e.g. "Come on, you can do it!" or "Hang in there just a bit longer"). This increases energy and motivation.

- *Instructional*: focuses on the technical or skill level of the game (e.g. "Bend your knees" or "Pay attention to the defence").

- *Negative*: critical and self-defeating statements (e.g. "You are such an idiot. How did you miss that one?"). These statements lead to anxiety and self-doubt, and should be avoided.

Attention can be distracted by either internal distractors, such as fatigue or lack of motivation, or external distractors, such as visual or auditory stimuli from the audience. Self-talk helps the athlete to focus attention and improve performance. In one experiment, 90 per cent of female tennis players who were given specific self-talk strategies improved their volleying skills (Landin and Hebert 1999). In another study (Martin et al. 1995), long-distance runners who used positive self-talk were able to improve their running economy—that is, they were able to consume less oxygen while running a given distance.

Tennis players often use self-talk to stay focused during matches

Be a critical thinker

"Positive self-talk can increase self-efficacy in tennis or any sport—if you believe in it".

Critically evaluate this statement with reference to research.

Van Raalte et al. (1994) examined the effect of self-talk on the performance of 24 junior tennis players (mean age 15.4 years) during tournament matches. It was found that negative self-talk was associated with losing, and that players who reported believing in the usefulness of positive self-talk won more points than those who did not believe in its benefits. This study raises the question of whether it is the belief in the efficacy of self-talk, rather than the self-talk itself, which contributes to improved performance. Araki et al. (2006) tested this. Their results indicated that belief in self-talk was not significantly correlated with performance; however, those who used positive self-talk performed significantly better than those who used negative or mixed self-talk. Therefore, it appears to be the type of self-talk, and not belief in its efficacy, which has an effect on the athlete.

Tiger Woods: no shortcuts to success

Golf Digest from October 2000 has an article which explains the mental toughness of Tiger Woods, who was trained by his father, Earl Woods. Earl Woods had a degree in psychology and was trained in the military; he also played golf himself. According to Earl, there are no shortcuts to success, and that is what he taught his son.

Tiger Woods grew up on the golf course and spent most of his time playing. From early on he watched motivational videos. When he was 13, Tiger began to work with Dr Jay Brunza, a psychologist who coached him on techniques for relaxation, visualization, and focusing. He also taught Tiger to self-induce entry into what athletes call "the zone"—that is, the state where they are able to attain peak performance under pressure. According to Brunza, Tiger Woods worked hard to master these techniques at an early stage and to absorb them into his technical excellence.

Relationships between team cohesion and performance

Training individual athletes is one thing, but training a team requires some extra skills in terms of building team spirit. There are a number of group dynamics to take into consideration within a sporting team. One of the most important is **cohesion**. The way players interact and think about each other has a tremendous impact on the way a team performs. As Hall (1960) put it: "The fittest to survive and succeed are those able to find their strength in cooperation, able to build teams based upon mutual helpfulness, and responsibility for one's fellow teammates."

Carron (1982) defines **cohesion** as a dynamic process reflected in the tendency for a group to stick together and remain united in the pursuit of its goals and objectives. In other words, a team is cohesive if the members get along, are loyal, and are united in the pursuit of the team's goals. A cohesive team can be distinguished from a non-cohesive team by many characteristics. A cohesive team has well-defined roles and group norms, common goals, a positive team identity, shared responsibility, respect and trust, a willingness to cooperate, good communication, and pride in membership. Another indicator of the amount of cohesiveness in a team is the frequency of statements of "we" and "our", in contrast to statements of "I", "me", and "mine".

Be a critical thinker

1 Can you use the case of Tiger Woods to illustrate the usefulness of mental training in athletes? Why or why not?

2 Do you think it is possible to find out why mental training seems to be so effective?

A successful team: the Spanish national football team won 1-0 over Germany in Europe 2008

Carron also distinguishes between two types of cohesion. **Task cohesion** is the degree to which group members work together to achieve common goals and objectives; **social cohesion** reflects the degree to which members of a team like each other and enjoy each other's company. Research shows that both forms of cohesion have a major effect on performance in both interactive sports (like basketball or football) and co-active sports (like bowling or gymnastics). Carron's research also indicates that cohesion plays a significantly stronger role in the performance of female teams than male teams.

Gould et al. (1999) interviewed American Olympic teams representing eight different sports. The researchers wanted to see if cohesion had an effect on their performance when compared to past performance. They found that low-cohesion groups underperformed. Though this meets the expected outcome, the study is problematic because Gould's study was *retrospective*—that is, cohesiveness was assessed at the end of the season using self-reports. The fact that the data were retrospective may have influenced memory as well as interpretation of events.

Slater and Sewell (1994) studied three male and three female university hockey teams, measuring cohesion at the beginning, middle, and end of the season. They found that early cohesion is correlated to later performance. However, they also found that good performance is linked to increased cohesion. In other words, the relationship between cohesion and performance is bidirectional: *cohesion increases performance, and performance (i.e. success) increases cohesion*.

Grieve et al. (2000) carried out a field experiment with undergraduate male volunteers who were randomly assigned to receive either a cohesion-producing or a cohesion-reducing manipulation before competing in three-man basketball games. The findings were that the level of cohesion had no impact on team performance. Winning had an impact on increasing cohesion more than losing did. Grieve argued that team cohesion results from winning, and is not bidirectional, as others have claimed. However, this study has been criticized because the group size was only three players, and this may not have been enough to produce the effects seen in larger teams.

Boone et al. (1997) conducted a field study in the US with 64 members of four Division III head baseball teams (age 17–23 years) over a season. Two of the teams had winning records and two had losing records. The aim was to measure team cohesiveness. They used a specific questionnaire, the Group Environment Questionnaire (GEO). This measures individuals' perceptions of a team in terms of individual and collective factors, which can be related to development and maintenance of the group. The researchers found that there was no significant difference between the two groups. Throughout the season, the measures were unaffected by the win/loss record. The players' feelings about the attraction to the group for personal involvement, acceptance, and social interaction did not change. They concluded that the baseball players in the study were

Building team spirit before the match boosts team cohesion

Be reflective

Cohesion seems to play a role in exercise behaviour. Paskevich et al. (2001) found that when there is high cohesion in an exercise class, participants attend more regularly, are more like to arrive on time, are less likely to drop out, and have stronger efficacy beliefs related to exercise.

1 In your view, what is the difference between exercising alone or in a group?

2 Which factors could play a role in group exercise? Use your knowledge from psychology.

attracted to the group for social purposes and were therefore not affected by the outcome of the matches they participated in. This contradicts the experimental study by Grieve et al (2000). The overall evidence on the role of performance on group cohesion is inconclusive. It may make a difference if you are part of a professional or amateur team; and the potential for financial rewards may also have an impact.

The role of culture on cohesion

Do different cultures define cohesion in the same way? It appears that they may not. Kenow and Williams (1999) studied cohesion strategies in coaches from Australia and the US. In order to do this, the researchers conducted interviews with coaches and asked them to complete questionnaires.

When the two samples of coaches were compared, Australian coaches reported significantly greater instances than their US counterparts of accepting individual differences among team members, learning personal information about each athlete,

praising team cooperation despite defeat, disbanding cliques, and striving to maintain a tranquil team climate. US coaches reported a higher incidence of promoting team cooperation through team drills, a strategy rarely used by Australian coaches.

It is possible that there may be a cultural norm of behaviour for developing team cohesion. It appears that the US coaches stressed one strategy over all others, whereas the Australian approach involved multiple strategies.

Research on group cohesion is problematic for several reasons. It is difficult to manipulate team cohesion and maintain ecological validity in a study. It is also difficult to measure team cohesion because it is not so easy to operationalize. Psychologists use two key methods for measuring team cohesion: questionnaires and sociograms. First, they use questionnaires. This helps the researchers to see the team through the experience of its members. However, since questionnaires are self-reporting, a social-consensus effect may influence the responses—that is, team members may say what they think they are expected to say. It may also make a difference when the questionnaire is administered. Having lost a major tournament, or having completed the most successful season ever, might have an effect on the objectivity of the responses. Questionnaires also tend not to reveal cliques within a team, or identify if anyone is socially isolated or not actively contributing to the success of the team.

Psychologists also use **sociograms** to determine the level of group cohesion. Sociograms are diagrams that show the relationships that exist within a group. To generate information for the sociogram, individual team members are asked questions such as, "If you were on a road trip, which three members of the team would you most like to share a room with?" or "Which three team members would you least like to spend time with off the court?" Confidentiality is essential when gathering information. Based on the information, a sociogram is drawn. Sociograms give researchers a more complex look at the level of cohesion, rather than simply rating it "high" or "low".

Be a researcher

What methodological considerations would you take into account in evaluating this study?

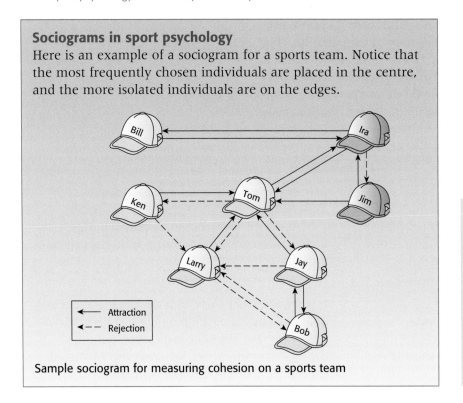

Sociograms in sport psychology
Here is an example of a sociogram for a sports team. Notice that the most frequently chosen individuals are placed in the centre, and the more isolated individuals are on the edges.

← Attraction
←-- Rejection

Sample sociogram for measuring cohesion on a sports team

Interpreting data

Discuss the level of cohesion on the team, based on the sociogram. If you were a coach, would you be concerned about the level of cohesion on the team? If so, what would you do to address it?

Common barriers to group cohesion

Research has shown that there are many factors which may decrease team cohesion. These include:

- clash of personalities in the group
- conflict of task or social roles among members of the group
- breakdown in communication among group members or between the group leader and members
- one or more members struggling for power
- frequent turnover of group members
- disagreement on group goals and objectives.

Goals are an important ingredient of success, and they play a major role in the development of individual athletes' skills and of task cohesion. Team goals should be developed by the athletes and coaches together. The coach should not be the sole decision-maker in the establishment of "team" goals. The coach and the team captains can provide leadership in goal setting, but, ultimately, goals should be determined by the whole team. Developing the goals together gives all athletes a sense of ownership and ensures commitment. In a study by Widmeyer et al. (1992), it was found that a stated team goal, along with its acceptance, was the most important contributor to task cohesion. If everyone owns the goal, everyone will work together to achieve it.

Outcome goals which state that the team will win every game in the season, or win the season championship, do not motivate throughout the season. Members may lose sight of goals and stray from the path necessary to accomplish the goals (Weinberg et al. 1991). **Process goals** seem to be more efficient in promoting team cohesion. Process goals describe what is to be done in practice, as well as competition, and are not focused on the outcome (Locke and

Latham 1985). Process goals enhance cohesion by providing daily successes that are accomplished by the team together. Process goals focus on the small steps that lead to the common goal—this could be greater team confidence or **collective efficacy**. Bandura (1997) defined this as a team's shared belief in its ability to reach a common goal. One step in the process could be to increase the time a basketball team is in possession of the ball. When the team examines previous performance, they should recognize that the information—not only about winning or losing but also about what worked and what did not work—influences team members in how they approach future competitions. Therefore, a process-oriented approach can help team members to develop a notion of team cohesion and ways to achieve success together.

Communication is important in team cohesion. There should be effective two-way communication that is clear and direct. Good communication skills result in an increase in self-esteem, respect, trust, and decision-making skills. Cohesion can decrease when communication is ambiguous or inconsistent. Sullivan (1993) developed a communication skills training programme for interactive sports teams and found that this led to more open and honest communication, as well as an increase in morale and team cohesion. Beauchamp et al. (2005) asked athletes to engage in role-playing exercises, during which they would simulate being in a critical situation to perform, or circumstances in which they felt pressured by the coach. This helped players to develop a sense of empathy for team members, and increased a sense of team spirit.

Role clarity—that is, making sure that players understand their role on the team—and *role acceptance*—that is, that members are willing to accept the responsibilities and conditions of that role—are also important in team cohesion. *Role ambiguity* is one of the key reasons for team member dissatisfaction (Bray et al. 2005). It is important for a member of a team to know if he or she is the one directing offence, otherwise competition within the team—or outright conflict—will result. Goal setting can help to avoid role ambiguity; it is also important that the coach communicates his or her expectations directly to team members.

In order for players to accept their roles, each has to feel that his or her role has meaning and contributes to the team's success. Players who are not in the starting line-up or do not get significant playing time can become discouraged. According to Weinberg (2007), role acceptance depends on four conditions: opportunity to use specialized skills; feedback and role recognition; role significance; and autonomy—that is, the opportunity to work independently. Coaches play a very important role in helping players understand and accept their roles. It is important that coaches minimize the status differences of the roles and emphasize the team goals.

The role of coaches

In several of the studies in this chapter, it is clear that the coach plays an important role in both individual and team performance. Horn (1985) found that a coach's feedback can have a positive effect

Apply your knowledge
According to Carron et al. (1985) task cohesion is defined as a group's orientation towards reaching the group's goal. Social cohesion is defined as the general orientation towards developing and maintaining social relationships within a group.

- Which of the two—task cohesion or social cohesion—is more important in professional sport? Support your argument.
- Would it be the same in your school's sports team?

on athletes' self-perceptions of competence and expectations of success. Chase et al. (1997) studied the effect of a coach's sense of self-efficacy on his or her players. In a study of four collegiate women's basketball teams, they found that the coaches' sense of self-efficacy had a major effect on the anxiety and concentration-dependent performance (e.g. free throws and turnovers) of the team. The higher the coach's sense of self-efficacy, the better the performance of the team players.

... So it is very important that you remember NOT to allow yourselves to be intimidated by the opposition, who-ever they are...

A coach's sense of self-efficacy has a major impact on the performance of the team

A coach's expectations regarding the ability of the individual athlete can determine the level of achievement each athlete will ultimately reach. In other words, if the coach thinks you cannot do it, you might not be able to—it becomes *a self-fulfilling prophecy*. To explain this process, Horn and Lox (1993) proposed the **expectation-performance model**. The model has four steps.

● **Step 1:** the coach develops an expectation for each athlete.

● **Step 2:** these expectations influence the coach's treatment of individual athletes.

● **Step 3:** the coach's treatment affects the athlete's performance, learning, self-concept, aspirations, and achievement motivation.

● **Step 4:** the athlete's behaviour and performance conform to the coach's expectations, thus reinforcing the coach's expectations.

Rosenthal (1974) identified the important role of feedback in self-fulfilling prophecies. **Feedback** refers to the verbal information a coach gives an athlete regarding ability or performance. Studies revealed that coaches provide athletes with different types and amounts of feedback, based on expectations of ability (Rejeski et al. 1979; Solomon et al. 1996).

Low expectations of coaches may have adverse effects on athletes. Athletes most often demonstrate poor performance when they are consistently given less effective and intensive instruction, and less active time in drills. The coach's behaviour can negatively affect an athlete's self-efficacy and intrinsic motivation so that the athlete experiences anxiety and self-doubt. Several studies have shown that athletes use a coach's feedback to determine how competent they are.

According to Duda and Pensgaard (2002), there are several ways in which coaches can improve intrinsic motivation. These include:

● focus on instruction and emphasize the importance of the link between improved technique and success

● facilitate group goal-setting

● give personal feedback

● acknowledge that athletes can make mistakes

● treat all participants as important.

However, as with much research in sport psychology, it is difficult to manipulate variables in an ecologically valid way. It is impossible to isolate the behaviour of the coach as the sole reason for an athlete's performance or motivation. García-Bengoechea (2003) carried out a study that indicates that peers may have just as strong an effect on an athlete's motivation and performance as the coach. Twelve athletes—six female and six male, aged 13 to 17 years, representing a variety of individual and team sports and competitive levels—took part in two in-depth, semi-structured, one-on-one interviews about their perceptions of the influence of others on their sport motivation. Through an inductive content analysis, the researchers found that the athletes felt that peers were just as important as coaches in their motivation.

Slavin (1995) argues that a key responsibility of coaches is to facilitate a "community of cooperative learners". Athletes not only benefit from the coach's expertise, but can also learn from and help each other. The results of García-Bengoechea's study also show that coaches need to consider the internal dynamics of the team in order to facilitate an environment where athletes engage in positive interaction and provide support for each other.

Research also suggests that it is important for coaches to deal efficiently with teammates who display a negative attitude towards their peers, themselves, and the activity. Wild and Enzle (2002) demonstrated the role of *social contagion* in affecting team motivation—in other words, motivational attitudes can spread from person to person during the social interaction of practice. It is important to note that although peers play a central role in the sport motivation of adolescent athletes, the motivational impact of parents and coaches is not necessarily decreased.

In order for athletes to maintain intrinsic motivation for sport, they must have access to an interrelated network of people who fulfil a number of motivational functions (e.g. providing support and competence-related information), and who play a variety of motivational roles (e.g. models to emulate and agents of socialization of achievement orientations).

A good coach can effectively increase individual and collective efficacy

Possible essay question

To what extent does the role of coaches affect individual or team behaviour in sport?

Assessment advice

This question requires that you examine the role of a coach in team sport so you must consider research that deals with the interrelationships between a coach and individual or team behaviour in sport.

You need to include evidence on how a coach's behaviour can affect an athlete or a group of athletes. This does not necessarily have to be in professional sport. One way to answer the question is to look into the role of the coach's expectations of performance, or in the case of a team, how the coach can influence team cohesion and team performance. You should also look at how the coach can counteract negative attitudes in the group. The answer could also, for example, include the role of peers in motivation, as compared to the coach. The answer must be focused and demonstrate critical thinking skills, for example demonstrated in how you use and evaluate the evidence. Take a look at the assessment criteria in Chapter 11.

Apply your knowledge

You are part of a new coaching team that has inherited a high-school soccer team that had a great deal of dissension and infighting during the previous season.

1 Discuss what you would do before and during the season to build both task and social cohesion in your team. Use your psychological knowledge to argue in favour of your ideas to the other members of the coaching team.

2 Search the Internet for ideas on how to coach from real life (e.g. ideas from famous football coaches). To what extent does their advice correspond to what you have learned in psychology? Comment on this.

Did you know?

Each year since 1993, the Best Coach/Manager ESPY Award has been presented to a head coach or manager of a team playing professionally in a US or collegiate sports league. The award is given based on balloting of fans over the Internet, from pre-selected choices produced by ESPY. The ESPY is an annual sport awards event created and broadcast by the US cable television network ESPN. The event is hosted by a contemporary celebrity.

1 Carry out some research in your own country on awards for coaches.

2 What is the purpose of awards for excellent coaching?

3 What could be the effect of this on the development of coaching?

Sport psychology: problems in sport

Learning outcomes

- Discuss the extent to which biological, cognitive, and sociocultural factors influence behaviour in sport
- Evaluate psychological research (that is theories and/or studies) relevant to the study of sport psychology
- Discuss athlete response to stress and chronic injury
- Examine reasons for using drugs in sport
- Discuss effects of drug use in sport
- Compare models of causes and prevention of burnout

Often people say that they play recreational sports or have joined an exercise class in order to alleviate stress. Though regular exercise does play a role in alleviating stress, it is undeniable that stress can be problematic for competitive athletes. Stress has been implicated as a reason for sport injury, the use of performance-enhancing drugs, and burnout. By understanding the role of different stressors on athletes' behaviour, psychologists will be able to prevent negative behaviours and help to rehabilitate athletes who have suffered from injury or substance abuse.

Stress and injury

According to Finch et al. (1998), 20–30 per cent of total injuries in a population are related to sport. This happens in spite of knowledge of the factors that influence the risk of injury. A substantial number of people practising exercise and sport are forced into a period of rehabilitation every year. It is estimated that annually, 3.5 million US children under the age of 14 are injured playing sports or participating in recreational activities (National Safe Kids Campaign 2004). The number of adults similarly injured ranges from 3 to 17 million, depending on the level of injury that is considered. In Australia, it is estimated that each year, 1 in 17 players suffers a sporting injury—this equates to nearly a million people who are directly affected in Australia alone, with 40 000 of these requiring hospitalization or surgery; the cost of sporting injuries to society has been placed as high as A$400 million per year.

In 2006, the National Electronic Injury Surveillance System (NEISS) looked at a sample of 96 US hospitals to document injury rates for different sports. The table shows a summary of their results.

Sport	Number of injuries
Basketball	529 837
Cycling	490 434
American football	460 210
ATV/moped/minibike	275 123
Baseball/softball	274 867
Exercise using equipment	269 249
Soccer	186 544
Swimming	164 607
Skiing/snowboarding	96 119
Lacrosse and rugby	85 580

Be an enquirer

1 What further questions would you have to raise about the data before you could draw any conclusions?

2 What could account for the different numbers of injuries in the data from the US? Try to find similar data for sport injuries for the country you live in, and compare them to the US data. Comment on your findings.

Sports psychologists study the role of stress on athlete performance. It has been found that athletes with higher stress levels experience more injuries than those with less stress in their lives. These stressors include high expectations from coaches and parents, financial problems, managing an academic schedule because of scholarship demands, and balancing family life with a heavy practice schedule. However, it has also been found that other factors play a role in sport injury. Smith et al. (1990) carried out a study of 452 male and female high-school athletes which addressed the relationship between a number of factors, such as stressful life events, social support, coping skills, and the number of days when the participants could not take part in their sport because of injury. The researchers found no correlation between the number or intensity of stressors and injury, but they did find a higher injury rate in participants with low levels of social support and low coping skills. Ford et al. (2000) found that individuals who have low self-esteem or are pessimistic have higher levels of injury, which indicates that personality factors may play a role.

A significant body of evidence supports the notion that stress can cause increased muscular tension, which disrupts coordination and increases the risk of injury. How do psychologists explain the relationship between stress and injury?

Ice skaters have a high rate of injury

Williams et al. (1991) argue that stress disrupts an athlete's attention by reducing peripheral attention. In other words, when athletes are stressed, they are less able to pay attention to what happens around them. A runner is under great stress leading up to a competition, and might be more prone to injury because she ignores irregularities in the terrain of the course. Or an athlete preparing for a competition in high jump fails to warm up properly because he is having problems with his girlfriend and this disrupts his concentration. This is particularly problematic in most team sports, in which athletes must have complete access to the full field of view, and focus their vision on this view to forestall unwanted collisions with other participants or equipment. Under high stress conditions, athletes pay too much attention to what is going on in their own heads, and not enough attention to what is happening on the field of play. They also show slowed reaction time. Andersen and Williams (1999) measured changes in anxiety, visual perception, and reaction time during stress among 196 collegiate athletes participating in 10 sports. The athletes also completed measures of life events and social support at the beginning of the season. Measures of life-events stress, social support, perceptual changes, and changes in reaction time during stress were used as predictors of the number of injuries. For the entire sample, the only significant predictor of injury was negative life-events stress. Correlations were performed for those with least social support (bottom 33 per cent, n=65). Among this group, those individuals with more negative life events and greater peripheral narrowing during stress incurred more injuries than those with the opposite profile.

Sport psychologists also examine physiological factors related to stress. Smith et al. (2000) argue that muscle tension can interfere with normal coordination and thus increase the chance of injury.

Be knowledgeable and empathetic

If you were a coach and trained the school's athletes, what advice would you give them to minimize injuries? Use the research on the relationship between injury and stress on these pages to support your answer.

The highly stressed figure skater who becomes stressed during a difficult movement may experience muscular tension and fall.

Stress may also have an effect on how an athlete recovers from an injury. Cramer et al. (2000) suggest that the body's natural healing process can be disrupted by high levels of depression and stress. Psychological stress increases glucocorticoids (stress hormones), which impair the movement of healing immune cells to the site of the injury and interfere with the removal of damaged tissue. Prolonged stress may also decrease the action of growth hormones, which are essential during the rebuilding process. Perna et al. (2003) found that stress causes sleep disturbances, which may interfere with the protein synthesis necessary for physiological recovery.

Athlete response to injury

It is important that rehabilitation personnel have an understanding of how athletes respond to injury and rehabilitation when they are treating injured athletes. Though stress may be part of the cause of injury, it is also a result. Athletes experience *physical stress* (e.g. pain or physical inactivity), *psychological stress* (e.g. fear that their dreams are shattered, anxiety about letting down the team), and *social stress* (e.g. social isolation because they are not able to take part in team activity). How an athlete copes with these stressors resulting from injury is crucial to their rehabilitation. There are two key models which describe how athletes respond to injury: the grief response and cognitive appraisal models.

An injured marathon runner

The grief response model (Hardy and Crace 1990)

The grief response model is based on a stage model created by Kübler-Ross (1969), which she applied to coping with terminal illness. The model argues that an athlete goes through a series of stages before reaching a stage of acceptance, which then allows rehabilitation to occur. The stages are:

1 denial
2 anger
3 bargaining
4 depression
5 acceptance and reorganization.

Denial is characterized as the individual's inability to accept that he or she is really injured. This may result in continued play and an underestimation of the seriousness of the injury. Once the injury is acknowledged, anger results, as the athlete realizes what this means for the season, or potentially for his or her career. Bargaining represents the deals that the athlete makes with himself or herself or a higher power—for example, "I will make sure I never do this again, as long as I get to play in the finals". Depression results when the athlete understands the limitations that the injury will put on his or her performance in the future. Finally, acceptance is the stage where coping with the injury begins.

The grief response model seems rather intuitive, and it is commonly accepted among coaches as an explanation of athletes' responses to injury. However, among academic psychologists it is criticized on many levels. It can be argued that it is flawed, considering that Kübler-Ross's model was not intended to be representative of athletes' experiences of athletic injury. In general, the model lacks empirical support; most evidence for the model is descriptive and anecdotal in nature. Many of the studies carried out are retrospective, asking athletes to discuss how they felt as they went from the incident that caused injury to the diagnosis and through rehabilitation. The reliability of these testimonies in light of the model is rather questionable.

Brewer (1994) argues that though many athletes show aspects of this model, they do not follow a set pattern. Not all stages are shown, and they do not always follow the same sequence. Udry et al. (1997) stated that they could only provide minimal support for the stage of denial, and no support for the bargaining stage as a response to athletic injury. It has been proposed that athletes do not deny the existence of an injury, but are more likely to be attempting to make sense of it and determine its severity.

Psychological reactions to injury include cognitive and emotional factors. Petitpas and Danish (1995) suggested that **identity loss** may be important—that is, if an athlete cannot participate because of an injury, it may be experienced as a loss of personal identity, especially if the athlete has invested a lot of his or her identity in the sport. This loss of identity may seriously affect the athlete's self-concept in a negative way. Since the injured person cannot participate in training and competitions, this may result in a general **lack of confidence**. Some athletes may feel this as a loss in personal status and lose confidence in themselves. The result is perhaps decreased motivation, bad performance, and sometimes additional injuries, if the athlete tries to compensate. Some athletes also have problems acknowledging that they cannot perform in the same way as before the injury. A general feeling of fear and anxiety may result from not knowing whether they will recover completely, or from seeing others taking their place.

Did you know?

Although ballet is considered a major division of the performing arts, ballet dancers and athletes experience similar levels of physical and mental stress during training and performances (Heil 1993). The leaps and lifts, the hip turnouts and grand pliés, plus the sheer repetition of steps and stretches, places ballet near the top of a list of physically demanding activities, according to a 1975 *Journal of Sports Medicine* survey. According to a recent study in the *Journal of Orthopaedic Sports Physical Therapy*, the annual injury rate at classical ballet companies ranges from 67 per cent to 95 per cent.

In an interview with a ballerina published by The Press of Atlantic City Media Group (June 2008), she revealed that she had sprained her left ankle nine times, and had Achilles tendinitis and flexor tendinitis in her left foot. When she was younger, she had Osgood-Schlatter disease in her knees. Other injuries included hamstring knots and pulled hamstrings—not major tears, just smaller ones; a labral (cartilage) tear in her right hip; numerous back spasms; a disc bulge behind L5 and S1 (in her lower back); plantar fasciitis and heel stones that made it hurt to stand; a stress fracture in her fibula, right leg; and she had sprained both her wrists.

Why do dancers continue in spite of the pain? One reason is that a dancer's career window is small—generally from the age of 18 to 35. Any rehabilitation would take a dancer off stage for at least six months, and in that time someone would take the individual's spot, and his or her career might be over.

A ballerina from the Royal Danish Ballet, Silja Schandorff said in an interview on Danish television in 2008, that she had many injuries and that she often danced with bleeding feet, but also that she totally forgot the pain once she was on stage. This indicates that the intrinsic motivation to perform is more important than pain, and that pain is something that all ballerinas—and all dancers—accept as part of their career.

Cognitive appraisal models

Udry et al. (1997) proposed an information-processing model of injury response. The model also takes emotional reactions into consideration. In the first stage, *information regarding the injury is processed*. The athlete focuses on information related to the pain of the injury, how it happened, the negative consequences of the injury, and what rehabilitation will entail. The second step is characterized by *emotional upheaval and reactive behaviour*. It is in this stage that expressions of anger and frustration may be exhibited. Wiese-Bjornstal et al. (1995) reported evidence that some athletes are said to have expressed relief from external pressures when injured (e.g. parents, coaches, teammates, perfectionism, and commitment). Some athletes also report an immense sense of loss when injured. Studies have revealed that a number of injured athletes, approximately 10–20 per cent, experience extreme responses to injury, particularly depression, which surpass levels usually recommended for clinical referral (Brewer 1995). The final stage is *developing a positive outlook and coping with the injury*.

Wiese-Bjornstal (1998) proposed an alternative model of *cognitive appraisal*. Cognitive appraisals are processes through which a potentially stressful situation is assessed as being stressful, along with the individual's evaluation of the extent of that stress. Appraisals influence the way in which an individual copes with a stressful situation. Coping is defined as an individual's ever-changing efforts to manage circumstances that are appraised as stressful. Coping varies between individuals, depending on the circumstances, individual differences, and the individual's cognitive appraisals.

Cognitive appraisals are said to occur in two forms, primary and secondary appraisals. Primary appraisals involve an assessment of what is at stake, taking into account challenge, benefit, threat, and harm or loss. Secondary appraisals mirror primary appraisals and involve an assessment of the coping options available to manage the demand. The appraisal process shapes the degree of perceived stress, and the content and strength of the emotional and behavioural responses. Wiese-Bjornstal's model suggests that dispositional and situational factors determine how an athlete appraises his or her injury. The appraisals subsequently affect emotional responses (e.g. anger, depression) and further influence behavioural responses (e.g. adherence to rehabilitation).

Be an enquirer

1 Do some research into the types of injuries that are common in two of your favourite sports.

2 To what extent could stress be a factor in injuries? Is it possible that factors other than stress play a role in these injuries?

3 What would you suggest to prevent injuries if you were a coach?

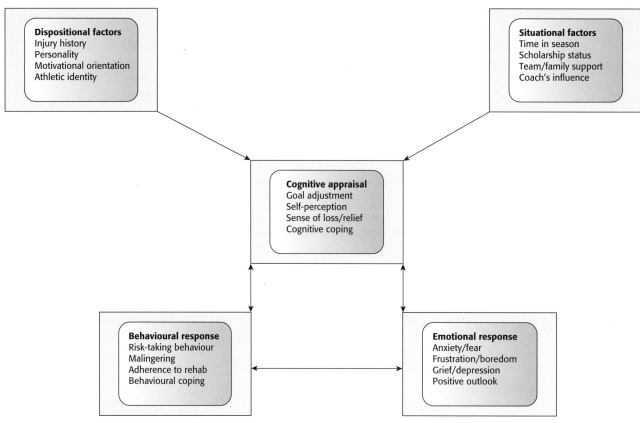

Wiese-Bjornstal's cognitive appraisal model of response to injury

Hardy (1992) reviewed the literature on psychological stress in sport. The researcher was interested in the effects of stress on performance, vulnerability to injury, and rehabilitation from injury. He found that the major sources of stress reported by sport performers themselves include fear of failure, concerns about social evaluation of others (especially the coach), lack of readiness to perform, and loss of internal control. He found that, overall, research on the link between psychological stress and injury was limited, but the available literature suggests that techniques such as goal setting, imagery, and relaxation skills, which are used to enhance performance, can be used to reduce the risk of injury and promote faster recovery from injury.

Reasons for using drugs in sport

Doping is prohibited by the International Olympic Committee and all other official sport associations; but all the same, newspapers all over the world continue to report stories of doping in professional sport. Being a high-performing athlete is a profession that requires dedication, long-term commitment, and sacrifice. Today, the athlete's body is seen as a highly specialized tool that can be manipulated to increase performance. Athletes are expected to seek all possible ways to improve their performance, including specialized training, hi-tech material, and scientific and medical support, including the use of nutritional supplements. In the past 20 years, international sport has seen an increase in the use of *performance-enhancing drugs*. Why has this continued to be a trend, in spite of all the negative publicity received by athletes who have been accused of using these drugs?

Many of the reasons cited by athletes for drug use are physical. They want to increase performance by increasing strength, endurance, alertness, and aggression, as well as decreasing fatigue and anxiety. It could also be that they want to look more attractive. In a study of male high-school students in the US (Whitehead et al. 1992), 48 per cent said that they used steroids to increase attractiveness. Drugs are also used to help gain or lose weight, commonly seen in sports like ice skating and gymnastics.

There are also psychological reasons for drug use. These include coping with stress and protecting self-esteem. Many athletes say that drug use is a response to the expectations of coaches, parents, and friends.

Finally, there are social reasons why drug use occurs. Anshel (1998) argues that social learning theory plays a role in the use of performance-enhancing drugs among young athletes. When young athletes see professional athlete role models using these drugs—and receiving rewards—they justify the risks as worth it. Newman and Newman (1991) observed that conformity played a significant role in the use of steroids among Canadian adolescent athletes.

One of the most recent theories as to why athletes engage in drug use is based on game theory. Among the many banned drugs in cycling, the most effective is erythropoietin (EPO), an artificial hormone that stimulates the production of red blood cells, thereby delivering more oxygen to the muscles. Game theory highlights why it is rational for professional cyclists to dope: the drugs are extremely effective, as well as difficult or impossible to detect; the pay-offs for success are high; and as more riders use them, a "clean" rider may become so non-competitive that s/he risks being cut from the team.

The game of prisoner's dilemma (Axelrod 1984) is the classic example of game theory. The situation is as follows: two men, partners in crime, are arrested and held in separate prison cells. Of course, neither man wants to confess or be disloyal to the other, but the police give each of them the following options.

1 If prisoner A confesses but his friend, prisoner B, does not, prisoner A goes free and prisoner B gets three years in jail.
2 If prisoner B confesses and prisoner A does not, prisoner A gets three years and prisoner B goes free.
3 If both confess, they each get two years in jail.
4 If both remain silent, they each get a year in jail.

PRISONER'S DILEMMA		My Opponent's Strategy	
		Cooperate (remain silent)	**Defect** (confess)
My Strategy	**Cooperate** (remain silent)	One year in jail (high pay-off)	Three years in jail (sucker pay-off)
	Defect (confess)	No jail time (temptation pay-off)	Two years in jail (low pay-off)

Prisoner's dilemma

Consider the choices from the point of view of prisoner A. He has no control over what his friend does. Suppose prisoner B remains silent. Then prisoner A earns the "temptation" pay-off (zero years in jail) by confessing, but gets a year in jail (the "high" pay-off) by remaining silent. The better outcome in this case for prisoner A to confess. But suppose, instead, that prisoner B confesses. Then, once again, prisoner A is better off confessing (the "low" pay-off, or two years in jail) than remaining silent (the "sucker" pay-off, or three years in jail). Each prisoner is better off confessing, no matter what the other prisoner decides to do.

So, how does this relate to the use of EPO in the Tour de France? The rules of cycling clearly prohibit the use of performance-enhancing drugs. The drugs are effective, difficult (if not impossible) to detect, and the pay-offs for success are great; therefore, the incentive to use banned substances is powerful. To not use the drug if others are using it means that you are not competitive. Once a few elite riders "defect" from the rules (cheat) by doping to gain an advantage, their rule-abiding competitors must defect as well. Shermer (2008) argues that these factors have led to an increase in doping in the sport.

In the case of the Tour de France, the winner takes home $10 million. If others are doping, and you are not, you have no hope of winning. The cost of getting caught cheating is approximately $1 million. The likelihood of getting caught doping is 10 per cent. So the rationale for using drugs could be based on the game theory matrix set out in figure here.

In other words, if I cooperate and do not take performance-enhancing drugs, I will lose. If I cheat and win, but get caught, I will still bring home $8.9 million—after paying the fine. In other words, game theory shows that there is a cognitive rationale created by the situation which encourages people to use drugs. Until the penalties for use are strict enough, or the drug-testing reliable and rigorous enough, the incentive will be there to cheat.

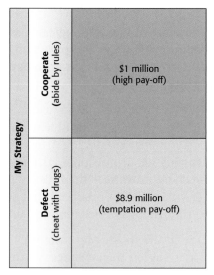

Game theory matrix

The story of Lyle Alzado

Lyle Alzado

Lyle Alzado was one of the first major US sports figures to admit to using steroids. In the last years of his life, as he battled against the brain tumour that eventually caused his death at the age of 43, Alzado recounted his steroid abuse in an article in the magazine *Sports Illustrated*.

I started taking anabolic steroids in 1969 and never stopped. It was addicting, mentally addicting. Now I'm sick, and I'm scared. Ninety percent of the athletes I know are on the stuff. We're not born to be 300lbs or jump 30ft. But all the time I was taking steroids, I knew they were making me play better. I became very violent on the field and off it. I did things only crazy people do. Once a guy sideswiped my car and I beat the hell out of him. Now look at me. My hair's gone, I wobble when I walk and have to hold on to someone for support, and I have trouble remembering things. My last wish? That no one else ever dies this way.

TOK

The story of Lyle Alzado brought steroid use into the mainstream media, but doctors argued that Lyle's death was not caused by his steroid use. Who should be held accountable for steroid use in athletes and the effects that they eventually have on their health?

Effects of drug use in sport

The long-term effects of drug use in sport are both physical and psychological. One of the most commonly used types of performance-enhancing drugs is anabolic steroids, the synthetic derivatives of the naturally occurring male hormone testosterone. Testosterone's natural effects trigger the maturing of the male reproductive system in puberty, including the growth of body hair and the deepening of the voice. The hormone's anabolic effect helps the body to retain dietary protein, which aids in the development of muscles.

With unsupervised steroid use, mega-dosing, or *stacking* (using a combination of different steroids), the effects can be irreversible or go undetected until it is too late. Also, if anabolic steroids are injected, transmitting or contracting HIV and hepatitis B through shared needle use is a very real concern. Unlike almost all other drugs, all steroid-based hormones have one unique characteristic—their dangers may not be manifest for months, years, or even decades. Therefore, long after giving them up, the athlete may develop side effects.

Although anabolic steroids are derived from a male sex hormone, men who take them may actually experience a "feminization" effect, along with a decrease in normal male sexual function. Some possible effects include: reduced sperm count, impotence, development of breasts, shrinking of the testicles, or difficulty or pain while urinating. On the other hand, women often experience a "masculinization" effect from anabolic steroids, including: facial hair growth, deepened voice, breast reduction, or menstrual cycle changes.

With continued use of anabolic steroids, both sexes can experience the following effects, which range from merely unattractive to life-endangering: acne, rapid weight gain, liver damage, heart attack or stroke, elevated cholesterol levels, and weakened tendons. Anabolic steroids can also halt growth prematurely in adolescents.

Steroids can cause severe mood swings. Individuals can go from bouts of depression or extreme irritability, to feelings of invincibility and outright aggression, commonly called 'roid rage. This is a dangerous state beyond mere assertiveness. Recent evidence suggests that long-time steroid users and steroid abusers may experience the classic characteristics of addiction, including cravings, difficulty in stopping steroid use, and withdrawal symptoms.

The table lists some of the other most commonly used performance-enhancing drugs and their effects.

Drug	Reason for taking it	Side effects
Beta blockers	Reduce anxiety	Low blood pressure, slow heart rate, depression
Diuretics	Weight loss	Dehydration, muscle cramps, kidney stones, increased cholesterol levels
EPO	Enhance oxygen transfer and stamina	Blood clots, heart attack, stroke
Narcotics	Mask pain	Increased pain threshold leading to failure to recognize injury, dependency, threat of overdose

The effect of drugs on gender

Heidi Krieger

During the cold war, the German Democratic Republic was renowned for the use of performance-enhancing drugs among its Olympic athletes. From 1972 to 1988, the GDR won 384 Olympic medals. The massive doping programme is reported to have involved tens of thousands of athletes—many of them children. Today, it is estimated that approximately 10 000 former athletes bear the physical and mental scars of years of drug abuse.

One of the most famous cases is that of Heidi Krieger, the former East German shot-put champion. Heidi Krieger was, by the time of her 1986 European Championships win, 95kg (209lbs), with a deep voice and facial hair. She was by then already confused about her true sexual identity.

The effects of the systematic doping finally led her to undergo a sex-change operation in 1997. It was the moment when *Heidi* died and *Andreas* was born. In an interview with the British newspaper *The Independent*, the former Heidi, now Andreas, said, "For me the tragedy is still that I had no choice in determining my sexual identity, the drugs decided my fate."

TOK: ethical reflections

"All high-performing athletes use drugs to enhance performance. If I don't use it, I cannot compete with them." Is this statement justified?

Models of causes and prevention of burnout

A final result of stress is a condition called burnout. *Burnout* is a psychological, emotional, and sometimes physical withdrawal from a formerly enjoyable activity, in response to excessive stress or dissatisfaction over time (Smith 1986). Some of the symptoms of burnout are exhaustion (loss of energy or interest), decreased performance, feelings of failure or depression, and lowered self-esteem. In addition, some people experience depersonalization—that is, a detachment from the sport and a feeling of "why am I doing this?" Others experience devaluation, when they no longer find any worth in the activity. Raedeke and Smith (2001) found that depersonalization is more common in coaches and teachers; athletes tend to devalue the activity.

It is important to note that not all athletes who drop out are burned out, and this is one of the problems of studying burnout. There are many other reasons why someone may discontinue sporting activities, and often athletes stay in a sport despite burnout, because of scholarships or the expectations of parents or a coach.

The cognitive-affective stress model

Smith (1986) proposed a model to explain the origins of burnout. The key to his model is the way in which an athlete interprets stress, failure, and/or setbacks. Both the personality of the athlete and their motivational orientation may affect their interpretation.

The first stage of the model is what Smith called *situation demands*— these are the high demands on an athlete which result in stress. Stress often occurs because demands exceed resources. The next stage is *cognitive appraisal*—the athlete's interpretation of the situation demands. In other words, do they see the stressor as a challenge that they are optimistic they will be able to meet, or are they anxious and fearful that failure will reflect poorly on their identity as an athlete? This leads to the third stage, *physiological responses*. In cases that lead to burnout, this includes muscle tension, irritability, fatigue, and sleep disruption. If the stress is not managed, the final stage exhibits behavioural responses—for example, decreased performance, problems with other team members, and eventual withdrawal from the team.

Research has revealed that some people have characteristics that act as buffers against stressors. Kobasa (1986) showed in one study that a personality characteristic known as **hardiness** was a key factor in whether or not highly stressed executives succumbed to illness. The hardy executives, who avoided illness, tended to perceive stressors as challenges rather than threats, so maintaining a sense of control over events. Kobasa suggested that hardiness incorporates three key elements:

- control—the perceived ability of the individual to exert influence rather than experience helplessness
- commitment—that is, a refusal to give up easily
- challenge—involving a person's ability to grow and develop, rather than remain static, and to view change rather than stability as the norm.

Clough and Earle (2001) have proposed a model of **mental toughness** in sport. They have developed a questionnaire to assess mental toughness which they have used in the following experiment.

The aim of the study was to show how mental toughness was related to performance and cognitive appraisal. Twenty-three volunteers were classified as having either high or low mental toughness, based on their responses to the questionnaire. The participants then performed 30-minute static cycling trials at three different intensities, of 30, 50, and 70 per cent of their maximum oxygen uptake, rating the physical demands of the trials at 5-minute intervals.

As predicted, those with higher levels of mental toughness reported significantly lower perceived exertion at 70 per cent of maximum than that reported by the "less tough" participants. As the researchers acknowledged, this is consistent with the cliché that "when the going gets tough, the tough get going". The observed

337

differences at higher levels of exertion could reflect a tendency of the more tough-minded to somehow reduce the perception of strain. Mentally tough exercisers might perceive themselves as having greater control during such conditions, or interpret the higher intensity as a challenge rather than a threat.

Coakley (1992) argues that stress is a symptom and not a cause of burnout. The cause is the hierarchical nature of high-performance sport, and its effect on the identity and sense of control in young athletes. He argues that young athletes do not develop a normal identity because they do not spend enough time with peers outside of the sport environment. Their identity is limited to success in sport, so experience of injury or lack of success can then lead to burnout. Athletes also feel a lack of control over decision making, since so much of their performance may be dictated by coaches or team captains. The inability to make decisions means that the athlete does not see alternatives, and thus may not be able to handle the stressors.

> ## Be an enquirer
>
> Search the Internet for evidence on how a famous athlete like David Beckham has coped with injury and how the public reacts to this (see for example the BBC website and the blog there).
>
> - What is the biggest problem for the athlete as he or she sees it?
> - And how does the public see it?
> - Do you think that the interest of the public could influence recovery? Why or why not?

Research in psychology

An examination of stress and burnout in Division I-A university football trainers

Hendrix et al. (2000) carried out a study with the aim of testing Smith's model, to examine the relationship of hardiness, social support, and situational factors to perceived stress—and the relationship of perceived stress to burnout.

The participants were 118 football trainers working in National Collegiate Athletic Association Division I-A in the US. Correlational analyses were performed to examine the impact of perceived stress on three burnout factors: emotional exhaustion, personal accomplishment, and depersonalization. The researchers used questionnaires regarding stress and social support, as well as the Maslach Burnout Inventory, to measure the three dimensions of burnout.

The results were in support of Smith's model of stress and burnout. Athletic trainers who scored lower on hardiness and social support and higher on situational demands tended to have higher levels of perceived stress. Furthermore, higher perceived stress scores were related to higher emotional exhaustion and depersonalization, and lower levels of personal accomplishment.

Much more research on the role of perceived stress and social support on burnout still needs to be done. Many studies, like this one, are cross-sectional, which means there are no data on how these factors may influence athletes over time, which a longitudinal study might reveal. In addition, the researchers are reliant on self-reported data. Once again, a longitudinal study might support the reliability of the coaches' responses. However, researchers need to be aware of possible confounding variables, such as social consensus effect.

Self-determination theory

Raedeke (1997) argued that burnout results because athletes have decided that they do not want to participate, but feel that they must. In other words, they lack intrinsic motivation to continue with the sport. The reasons that an athlete may stay with the sport in spite of the lack of motivation are varied. For example, the "self" is so tied to being an athlete that the person does not know alternatives that would preserve their sense of self. In some cases, they may lack real alternatives to sport. This may be the case of a student who has trained since a young age and did not receive a regular education. Some may also feel that they have invested too much time, energy, or money to stop—especially if the financial support has come from parents who have made great sacrifices to help their child, or from a university scholarship.

In another study, of 200 competitive swimmers, Raedeke (1998) found that those who felt they lacked control over their choice to swim were more prone to burnout and felt decreased commitment to the sport. Kjormo and Halvari (2002) also found support for this in a study of Norwegian Olympians. Interviews indicated that a lack of free time to spend with significant others was a key source of burnout. Creswell and Eklund (2000) found that athlete autonomy, competence, and social support—as well as money problems—all led to burnout in New Zealand rugby players.

The kid had it all, but just didn't like baseball

Ryan Jaroncyk was a first-round draft pick of the New York Mets in 1995. The Mets had awarded him an $850,000 signing bonus, as well as a $100,000 college scholarship fund, when he agreed to play. By the end of the 1996 season, Jaroncyk was no longer playing ball. In a letter to the Mets' general manager he explained that he did not like baseball, and that he found it "boring". He said that he felt ambivalent about baseball, and found the lifestyle "empty".

Jaroncyk had begun playing baseball at age five, with the encouragement of his father. He says that he felt a lot of pressure from his parents, especially his father, to continue playing, even though he tried to quit while in high school. With regard to his dad, Jaroncyk says: "He really wanted the best for me, but he went about it the wrong way."

Be reflective

1 Why do you think that parents put pressure on their children to excel in sports?

2 Do you think there was some way for Ryan to resolve this problem before he got all the way to the major leagues?

Measuring burnout

It is difficult to carry out empirical research on burnout. It is neither possible nor desirable to create an experimental situation that would result in the burnout of team players. It is also difficult to categorize burnout—is all burnout the same? Are there such things as "high" levels of burnout and "low" levels of burnout? Do they have the same causes? Gould et al. (1996, 1997) carried out a long-term study of competitive youth teams. They identified two strains of burnout: dominant strain and physically driven strain. *Dominant strain* is the more common of the two. This is the result of athletes' perfectionism and situational pressures; perfectionism predisposes athletes to a higher risk of burnout. Physically driven strain is less common. This is when athletes cannot meet the demands placed on them, and eventually are no longer able to set goals or be motivated for the sport.

Another problem with measuring burnout is that, originally, psychologists studied those who had dropped out because of self-identified burnout; but there is no guarantee that those who were still playing were not also burned out. A standardized test was needed to identify burnout. The most commonly used is *Maslach's Burnout Inventory,* which was originally used to measure burnout in the workplace. This test measures the perceived frequency and the intensity of feelings related to burnout. The three scales are emotional exhaustion, depersonalization, and a sense of personal accomplishment. This test is considered highly reliable and is used in other professions as well—especially with teachers. Raedeke (1997) defined burnout in sport as a syndrome of physical and emotional exhaustion, sport devaluation and reduced athletic achievement. This put a particular focus on sport devaluation, which is a reinterpretation of the concept of depersonalization in Maslach's model. According to Raedeke, it is necessary to look at what characterizes burnout in sport, and it is not exactly the same as burnout in a work context.

Preventing burnout

Sport psychologists investigate causes of burnout and ways to prevent it. However, coaches are involved in the daily training of athletes and their experiences also contribute to an overall understanding of a complex issue.

Profile

Christina Maslach

Christina Maslach received her PhD in psychology from Stanford University in 1971. She has researched a number of areas within social and health psychology but she is best known for her pioneering research on job burnout. She is the author of the Maslach Burnout Inventory (MBI), which is now widely used not only in relation to work but also in sport psychology.

Research in psychology

Raedeke et al (2002) swimming coaches' identification of burnout signs and possible prevention strategies

The researchers wanted to find out how coaches identified burnout signs and what they used as prevention strategies. They used a qualitative approach with semi-structured interviews and conducted content analysis of the transcripts. The researchers interviewed 13 US swimming coaches and argued that if coaches are able to identify early signs of burnout, they can prevent it. These are some of the signs of burnout identified by coaches.

1 *Withdrawal*, for example, not showing up for training and stopping interaction with teammates.

2 *Reduced sense of accomplishment*, for example feeling incongruence between physical ability and desired goals. Lack of improvement could be one of the first warning signs. This could be in general, or it may be seen in frustration where the swimmer is not able to make progress after the injury.

3 *Diminished sense of progress*, for example if the swimmers believe that they can not achieve beyond a certain point. This could be due to unrealistic expectations of performance, perceptions of

diminished rewards from swimming perhaps combined with unfavourable comparison with other swimmers on the team. It could also be because they are physically and psychologically exhausted.

4 *Devaluation of the sport* is a sure sign of possible burnout. Devaluation could range from hatred of general detachment from the sport.

5 *Exhaustion* is very critical to burnout because it reflects a state where physical and psychological resources have dried up, either because the athletes have pushed themselves too hard or because of external pressure.

6 *Pressure*—external and self-pressure—to succeed can lead to burnout, especially pressure from parents and coaches. The coaches in the investigation mentioned parental pressure as a key factor in burnout but self-pressure as seen in the overly motivated athletes who are very hard on themselves is also a source of burnout.

7 *Loss of control* is a feeling that athletes have when there is not a healthy balance between doing the sport and "having a life". It can lead to negative self-perception if there is only focus on the sport.

Being able to identify early signs of burnout in an athlete is the first step to prevent it. The most important strategy is to provide support structures that include support from the coach, the team, and the parents, as well as continued recognition of achievement. The coach should be empathetic and listen to the individual athletes and encourage team friendship, cohesion, and support. This is particularly important when the athletes are young. This can be done by keeping the young athletes with their age group and not pushing them ahead when they are talented. The coaches in the study also mentioned that goal-setting sessions with all the swimmers reinforced individual commitment and enhanced support within the group. For adolescent swimmers there were special problems because this is a time of finding an adult identity and focusing on relationships with peers. There is also the problem that some of the support structures tend to dry up (e.g. parental enthusiasm) when the child has been competing for many years. However, parental support and recognition are important to prevent burnout in young athletes. According to the coaches in this study, because serious competition demands greater time commitment from the swimmer. Lack of support can lead to a feeling of lack of accomplishment which could eventually result in burnout.

Raedeke et al (2002) found that the following coach strategies could prevent burnout.

- Create a supportive training environment – e.g., be empathetic and giving individualized feedback, and encouraging team cohesion and friendship in the group. It is also important to involve parents.

- Keep the training exciting and fun.

- Be flexible and give the athletes time off from swimming to prevent them feeling fed up with the sport.

- Help athletes set realistic but challenging goals and provide a number of training techniques, for example, emphasizing quality over quantity.

Sport psychologists make several recommendations to coaches to help athletes avoid burnout. These include: identifying symptoms of burnout early so that they can be addressed; encouraging open communication and the expression of feelings of frustration, anxiety, and disappointment; and setting short-term goals for competitions and practice.

However, perhaps the greatest area of study is the use of relaxation techniques to cope with stress. Use of relaxation techniques lowers the level of stress that an individual experiences. Since stress is believed to be one of the main causes of many problems for athletes, relaxation techniques may also lower one's risk for injury and decrease the chances of engaging in substance abuse.

Cognitive affective stress management

Smith (1980) proposed an integrated approach of mental and physical coping strategies to deal with stress. It parallels his cognitive-affective stress model of burnout. In this programme, there are four steps.

1 **Pre-treatment assessment:** A consultant conducts personal interviews to assess the situations that produce stress, the player's response to stress, and the effects of stress on performance.

2 **Treatment rationale:** The consultant helps the player understand his/her stress response by analysing stress reactions.

3 **Skill acquisition:** The athlete is trained in muscular relaxation, cognitive restructuring, and self-instruction. Muscular relaxation is *progressive relaxation*, in which muscle groups are first tensed, then relaxed. *Cognitive restructuring* identifies irrational or stress-inducing self-statements like, "I know I'll mess up", "I can't let

my coach down", or "If I am not successful, I am not worth anything". Self-instruction provides athletes with the means to improve concentration and problem-solving skills—for example, "Don't think about how far behind we are, just think about what you have to do", or "Take a deep breath and relax".

4 **Skill rehearsal:** The consultant induces high levels of arousal/ stress through film and imaginary rehearsals, in order to practise the coping strategies.

Stress inoculation theory (SIT)

Meichenbaum (1985) proposed an alternative approach called stress inoculation theory (SIT). The athlete is exposed to and learns to cope with stress in increasing amounts, thereby enhancing his/her immunity
to stress. There are three stages.

1 **The conceptualization stage:** The athlete is made aware of the effects of positive and negative thoughts, self-talk, and imagery.

2 **The rehearsal stage:** Athletes learn the use of such coping skills as imagery and positive self-statements.

3 **The application stage:** Athletes practise their coping skills in low-stress situations, gradually progressing to moderate- and high-stress situations.

The goal of SIT is to help athletes develop a sense of "learned resourcefulness". They learn to prepare for a stressor: "It is going to be rough; keep your cool." They learn to control and handle the stressor: "Keep your cool because he is losing it." They cope with feelings of being overwhelmed: "Keep focused—what next?" And then they evaluate their coping efforts: "Wow—you handled that well!"

For more about stress and how to cope with stress, see Chapter 7.1.

> **Possible essay question**
>
> Compare two models of causes of burnout.
>
> Describe one strategy to prevent burnout.

Assessment advice

The command term in the first question is "compare". This requires you to give an account of the similarities between two models of causes of burnout, for example two models related to cognitive-affective stress model such as hardiness and mental toughness. You should include empirical research and examples to support your answer. You need to look at how the two models are similar in the explanations throughout your answer.

The command term in the second question is "describe" which means that you should give a detailed account of a strategy. You could choose any relevant strategy and "describe" how it addresses some of the problems mentioned in the first question.

10.1 Qualitative research: theory and practice

Learning outcomes

- Distinguish between qualitative and quantitative data
- Explain strengths and limitations of a qualitative approach to research
- Discuss the extent to which findings can be generalized from qualitative studies
- Discuss ethical considerations in qualitative research
- Discuss sampling techniques appropriate to qualitative research (e.g. purposive sampling, snowball sampling)
- Explain effects of participant expectations and researcher bias in qualitative research
- Explain the importance of credibility in qualitative research
- Explain the effect of triangulation on the credibility/trustworthiness of qualitative research
- Explain reflexivity in qualitative research

Introduction to qualitative research

Academic psychology deals with a broad range of areas—from the action of single hormones to factors that may contribute to genocide and the role of human relationships on health. The diversity of psychology means that many different methods are used to gather and analyse data. The methods researchers choose to carry out research are dependent on a number of factors, such as the purpose of the research, the characteristics of the participants, and the researchers' beliefs about the nature of knowledge and how it can be acquired. The last part has to do with **epistemology**—that is, questions such as how can we know about the world? And what is the basis of our knowledge? Another part has to do with **ontology**—that is, does a social reality exist independently of human perceptions and interpretations?

There are three main questions in the debate in relation to epistemology, according to Ritchie and Lewis (2003). These questions are basic for understanding the differences between research in the natural sciences and the social sciences, although it is important to understand that social researchers adopt quantitative (e.g. surveys) as well as qualitative methods. The argument is that the two approaches should not be seen as competing, but as complementary to different types of research questions.

The discussion of the relative strengths and limitations of research methods is related to philosophical debates on the nature of knowledge and science, to which there are no definite answers, so the debate is likely to continue among researchers. The debate relates to different views of the world and how it can be studied. Some of these views are set out below.

1 *What is the relationship between the researcher and the researched?*
In the natural sciences, the object of research is considered to be
independent of and not affected by the researcher. The researcher
is seen as objective and the research is seen as value-free.
Qualitative researchers believe that being studied will affect
people so that they do not behave naturally. The relationship
between the researcher and the participants is not objective and
value-free because the researcher brings assumptions into the
research process and these influence the way data are collected
and analysed. Therefore, the researcher needs to reflect on his or
her own background and beliefs, and how these could play a role
in the research process (**reflexivity**).

2 *What can be held as truth?* This deals with how the natural and
social sciences regard what is "truth". In the natural sciences,
truth is based on the **correspondence theory of truth**, which
claims that the truth or falsity of knowledge is determined by
whether or not it accurately describes the world. There must be a
match between observations of the natural world and an
independent reality. A more appropriate view for the social
sciences is represented in the **coherence theory of truth**.
This theory claims that the truth or falsity of knowledge is not
absolute, but rather consensual. The truth is determined by
whether or not it can be supported by other observations or
statements. However, this is based on the assumption that "the
truth" is somehow lodged in the data, and that a researcher and
peer reviews could arrive at the same interpretation.

3 *How is knowledge gathered?* The natural sciences often rely on
deductive processes—that is, hypothesis testing where the
evidence is used to support a conclusion. The focus is on cause-
and-effect relationships, generalization, and prediction. The social
sciences often rely on inductive processes where the collected
evidence is used to reach a conclusion. The focus is on
understanding the complexity of social processes. It should be
remembered, however, that the natural and social sciences use
inductive as well as deductive processes in research.

It has been argued that qualitative research is not "scientific" because it
is not built on the scientific method of the natural sciences. However,
"science" as seen by some qualitative researchers should be defined in a
broad sense as a systematic, rigorous, empirical task that must be carried
out properly in order to produce trustworthy and reliable knowledge.
This could include imposing procedures to ensure the quality of
research. There is an ongoing debate among qualitative researchers as to
whether reliability (i.e. if the research methods and techniques used
produce accurate data) and validity (i.e. that the research explains what
it intended to) can be used in qualitative research. Some argue in favour
and attempt to reformulate the concepts to fit better with the nature of
qualitative research, while others claim that the very nature of
qualitative research does not invite reliability and validity checks. Yet
another position is introducing new concepts to describe validity and to
ensure transparency and consistency of conclusions in qualitative
research through alternative ways of checking results. The IB psychology
programme has adopted the last position.

According to Ritchie and Lewis (2003), the social world does not exist independently of individual subjective understanding, and researchers can only come to understand it through the participants' *interpretations*. This is the *interpretative approach* which is based on understanding things from the view of the people involved. According to Ritchie and Lewis, the external reality is diverse and multifaceted, and the goal of qualitative research is to get a picture of this multifaceted reality. The researcher should strive to be as objective and neutral as possible in the collection, interpretation, and presentation of qualitative data—for example, through reflexivity. They also argue that a combination of qualitative and quantitative methods may be necessary and helpful, but not all qualitative researchers agree with them.

According to Rolfe (2006), there is no unified qualitative paradigm, and it is only in qualitative research textbooks that it appears to be so. He claims that it makes little sense to talk about qualitative research as completely distinctive and separate from quantitative research.

Difference between qualitative and quantitative data

Psychological data come in many different forms, depending on the phenomenon the researcher is interested in. In quantitative research, the data are in the form of "numbers" that are easy to summarize and submit to statistical analysis. There are standard formats for data analysis, such as statistical tests. Quantitative data are meant for generalization beyond the sample from which the data were drawn.

Qualitative data are gathered through direct interaction with participants—for example, through one-to-one or group interviews, or by observations in the field. The data consist of text—for example, from transcripts or field notes. Textual data are open-ended and flexible—that is, they are open for interpretation. The term used is "rich data", which means that they are rich in their description of people, places, conversations, and so on. Because the data are rich (i.e. voluminous and open to interpretation), they are not easy to analyse, and there is no single way to approach analysis. Data may be analysed via theory or the data can generate theory. Qualitative researchers use what is called a "rich-thick" description of the data when they write their research reports to document their interpretation.

Strengths and limitations of a qualitative approach to research

Qualitative researchers are concerned with meaning—that is, they are interested in how people make sense of the world and how they experience events. They want to understand "what it is like" to experience particular conditions and how people deal with them. The objective of qualitative research is to describe and possibly explain events and experiences. This can lead to suggestions of how to overcome the problems that the research identifies. Qualitative researchers study people in their own environment, preferably in naturally occurring settings, such as schools, homes, hospitals, and streets.

Based on this brief account, we can outline some of the strengths and limitations of qualitative research.

Strengths

- Provide rich data—that is, in-depth descriptions of individual experiences based on concepts, meanings, and explanations emerging from the data.

- Particularly useful for investigating complex and sensitive issues, such as coping with illness, human sexuality, homelessness, or living in a violent relationship.

- Explain phenomena—that is, go beyond mere observation of phenomena to understand what lies behind them. (e.g. Why do people become homeless?)

- Identify and evaluate factors that contribute to solving a problem. (e.g. What initiatives are needed to successfully resettle people who are homeless?)

- Generate new ideas and theories to explain and overcome problems.

- People are studied in their own environment, which increases validity.

Limitations

- Can be very time-consuming and generate a huge amount of data.

- Data analysis can be difficult because of the amount of data and no clear strategy for analysis.

- Interpretation of data may be subjective (but reflexivity can help to minimize this).

Is it possible to generalize from qualitative studies?

Scientists normally want their findings to apply to other people than those who participate in a particular study. Generalizing findings from a study means that the results are relevant outside the context of the study itself. Some qualitative researchers do not find it relevant, but others argue that it is important that findings can be generalized. According to Lewis and Ritchie (2003), qualitative research could distinguish between the following forms of generalization.

- **Representational generalization**, which means that findings from qualitative research studies can be applied to populations outside the population of the study. A typical question could be if findings from interviews with people in a study on homeless people are representative of homeless people in general. This could have implications for the development of homeless programmes. Qualitative research normally involves small samples that are not selected to be statistically representative, and non-standardized interview methods may be used. This makes it difficult to generalize findings. However, if evidence from other studies confirms the findings, it is argued that generalization is possible (Hammersley 1992).

- **Inferential generalization**, which means that the findings of the study can be applied to settings outside the setting of the study. This is also called "transferability" or "external validity". If the study on homeless people is a pilot programme to test the effectiveness of a service to resettle homeless people, the question is whether the findings can be applied to other services that provide help to homeless people. Whether or not the findings can be transferred to another setting will depend on the depth of the description of the researched context and the phenomenon. This description may allow for inferences to be made, but it will rest as a hypothesis until it is supported or disproved by further evidence.

- **Theoretical generalization**, which means that theoretical concepts derived from the study can be used to develop further theory. The findings from a study might lead to inferences about what could be effective policies to help homeless people. In that way, the findings from the study may contribute to wider social theory.

Ethical considerations in qualitative research

There are, overall, the same ethical issues involved in qualitative research as in quantitative research. These include informed consent, protection of participants from psychological or physical harm, respect for the participants' integrity and privacy, and the right to withdraw from the research. However, there are special ethical considerations to be made due to the very nature of qualitative research. The characteristics of qualitative or field research usually include long-term and close personal contact with the participants—for example, during interviews and/or participant observation, which may have implications for what the participants disclose to the researcher. It could also be the case that researchers become too personally involved in the problem under investigation and thus lose their objectivity.

Ethical issues in terms of anonymity may arise in case studies or in research designs with a small number of participants, because of the risk that they may be identified in research reports. In case studies where covert observation is used, the participants have not signed informed consent and do not have the right to withdraw from the research, because they do not know that they are being studied.

Informed consent

The rule is that informed consent should always be obtained. This is stressed in all guidelines on ethical conduct in research. However, in some cases, where it would not otherwise be possible to study a phenomenon (e.g. use of violence in a street gang), ethics committees may offer dispensation from the rule because the goal of the research is to obtain knowledge that may eventually prevent violence.

The participants should know that participation is voluntary. This is particularly important if the research is conducted by people who have some kind of relation to members of the sample, since participation could then be motivated by feelings of obligation. The researcher must provide the participants with sufficient information about the study, such as who funded the study, who will conduct the study, how the data will be used, and what the research requires of the participants—for example, in terms of time and the topics the study will address. It should also be made clear that consent can always be renegotiated. In cases where children aged under 16 years are involved, consent must be obtained from parents or legal guardians.

Protecting participants from harm

The researchers should take preventive action in all research, to avoid harming the participants. This is particularly true in sensitive research topics, such as sexual abuse, domestic violence, or alcoholism in the family. Due to the nature of qualitative methods—for example, in-depth interviews—participants may disclose very private information that they have never shared with anyone before. This can happen because the interview situation seems like a friendly encounter, where the participant may feel comfortable and safe. However, the participant may regret such revelations and feel upset after the interview when the interviewer has gone. This situation should be avoided.

Prior to the interview, and before they agree to participate, the participants should have a clear understanding of the topics to be addressed. The researchers must approach sensitive issues through clear and direct questions, so that participants are not drawn into irrelevant and sensitive details by mistake. If the participants show signs of discomfort, the researcher should be empathetic and consider stopping the interview. If the interview has dealt with emotional and sensitive issues, the researcher should try to return to less sensitive topics towards the end. It is not advised that the researcher should provide advice or counsel the participant, but he or she might provide useful information about where to find help if this is necessary.

Anonymity and confidentiality

The participants should be informed about the issues surrounding anonymity and confidentiality. The identity of the participants should not be known outside the research team, but in cases where sampling has involved a third party (e.g. managers, friends, teachers), this cannot be done, and in this case the participants should be informed.

Confidentiality means that research data will not be known to anyone outside the study. The researcher may have to change minor details in the report to avoid the possibility of participants being recognized. Confidentiality also relates to the way data are stored after the research. If interviews or observations have been videotaped and archived, it can be difficult to guarantee total anonymity, so these should be destroyed when transcripts have been made. If the researcher finds it necessary to archive non-anonymized data, the participant should give written informed consent.

Sampling techniques appropriate to qualitative research

Sampling methods in qualitative research differ from those used in quantitative research, where the purpose of sampling is to generate samples that are representative through random selection of participants.

Sampling methods are classified as either **probability** (related to statistical probability and representativeness) or **non-probability**

sampling. Probability is generally believed to be the most rigorous approach to sampling for statistical research. Quantitative methods use inferential statistical tests based on samples that are randomly selected from a target population.

The sample numbers involved in qualitative research are much smaller than in quantitative research. The sample is not intended to be statistically representative. The researcher may still want to have a representative sample from a target population, but the focus is not on statistical representation. A sample in qualitative research is chosen because it represents *important characteristics* of a population, and it is these characteristics that are the main concern in evaluation of research.

The researcher can use a number of sampling procedures—for example, purposive sampling, convenience sampling, and snowball sampling. All the sampling methods presented here rely on prescribed selection criteria. They all use small samples, but the sample can be supplemented during the research process.

Purposive sampling

Purposive sampling targets a particular group of people. The researcher decides early on which criteria should be used for sampling. These are based on the aim of the study and existing knowledge in the field. The participants are chosen on the basis of particular characteristics that will help the researcher to explore the research topic. This could refer to socio-economic characteristics (e.g. living below the poverty line), specific experiences (e.g. childhood abuse), occupation (e.g. nurse), or social roles (e.g. mother). All the features of relevance must be present in the sample. It may also be important that there is diversity within the sample—for example, in relation to age and gender.

Purposive sampling is useful in situations where the researcher needs to obtain a sample quickly to investigate an urgent problem, such as the introduction of a new rehabilitation scheme for people who have had strokes. A study like that could allow for a detailed picture of particular issues that may arise when using the rehabilitation scheme, and it can help to change features of the scheme before it is implemented more generally.

Purposive sampling may be the only option, if the desired population for the study is rare or difficult to locate—for example, if the researcher wants to study elderly women who are homeless, or illegal immigrants.

A problem with purposive sampling is that the sample may be biased. However, even though purposive sampling involves deliberate choices, it is not necessarily biased. It is believed that if the sampling process is based on objective criteria, and these are clearly documented and explained, the bias is limited.

Snowball sampling

This is a way of sampling which is used to get hold of participants without investing a lot of time and energy. The researcher simply asks participants in the study if they know other potential participants.

Snowball sampling can be used to locate hidden populations—for example, when people with the required characteristics are rare or hard to find—by having existing participants refer to new participants. If a researcher is studying homeless people, it is not possible to have a list of all the homeless people in an area, but if the researcher finds one or two, they may help to locate others.

The advantage of snowball sampling is that it is cost-efficient, because the researcher does not have to use expensive and time-consuming techniques to locate participants. The major limitationof the method is that it is very difficult to avoid bias in the sample. There are also confidentiality concerns, because the participants know the identity of other participants.

Convenience sampling

This method of sampling has already been introduced in Chapter 1.2, so this account will concentrate on issues related to qualitative research.

Convenience sampling selects a particular group of people who happen to be available. They are simply asked if they would like to participate. The researchers may want to study the effectiveness of a programme for the prevention of antisocial behaviour in a youth group, using basketball training and coaching. The researchers follow the adolescents for a year, to see the impact the programme has on the young people. The sample represents the young people who are in the programme, but could also represent similar young people in similar programmes around the country. In order to see if this is the case, however, similar research must confirm it.

Effects of participant expectations and researcher bias in qualitative research

One of the more important factors to consider in psychological research is that humans are not responding passively to research. Researchers need to be aware that research is an active process that requires reflection and interrogation of the data, the participant, and the research context, in order to avoid **participant expectations** (also called reactivity) or researcher bias. Participant expectations can be explained as the participants' ideas of the research and the researcher which can affect the trustworthiness of the data. If the participant feels they have to behave in certain ways in order to please the researcher, this will affect the value of the data in a negative way.

Researcher bias can be explained as the researcher not paying enough attention to the participants, so that it is the researcher's own beliefs that determine the research process. It is imperative in qualitative research that participants' perceptions and beliefs in understanding social processes must be given priority over the researcher's own.

If it is assumed that "reality" in a research study is multiple and co-constructed, then we should be aware that participants who are asked to comment on the researcher's interpretation of the data will not necessarily arrive at the same conclusions as the researcher.

Be a researcher

You have been asked to conduct a qualitative research study on football fans' perception of their favourite team.

- What sampling method would be appropriate? Why?
- Could another sampling method be considered? Why?
- What should you consider overall when selecting your sample?

Some would argue that a "credibility check" could impose an artificial conformity on the analysis of the data. This would impact on the meaningfulness of the findings. However, being aware of sources of bias is important. One way to minimize the effect of participant expectations and researcher bias is reflexivity throughout the research process.

Importance of credibility in qualitative research

According to Rolfe (2006), **credibility** corresponds roughly to the concept of internal validity that is used in quantitative research. Credibility is linked to the concept of "trustworthiness". **Trustworthiness** (i.e. credibility or validity) of research is established when the findings of the research reflect the meanings as they are described by the participants.

Some qualitative researchers (e.g. Sandelowski 1993) argue that issues of validity in qualitative studies should not be linked to truth or value, but rather to trustworthiness, which can be obtained if the researchers try to make their reflections and decisions in the research process transparent, so that they can be scrutinized. According to Sandelowski (1986), it means "leaving a decision trail, so that the reader would be able to track and verify the research process". There are no objective criteria for trustworthiness. A study is trustworthy if, and only if, the reader of the research report judges it to be so, according to Rolfe (2006).

Qualitative researchers could check whether their accounts are credible by referring to others' (e.g. participants, other researchers) interpretation of the data, or by applying other methods of analysis in relation to the same subject matter. According to Guba and Lincoln (1989), such peer reviews—or checks—are the single most critical technique for establishing credibility within each individual study.

Effect of triangulation on the credibility/trustworthiness of qualitative research

Triangulation can be defined as a kind of cross-checking of information and conclusions in research, brought about by the use of multiple procedures or sources. If there is agreement between the procedures or sources, there is support (or corroboration) of the interpretation of the data.

Triangulation involves the use of different perspectives, methods, and sources to check if the interpretation of data can be supported. There are different forms of triangulation.

- *Method triangulation* involves comparing data that come from the use of different methods. This could involve qualitative and quantitative methods.

- *Data triangulation* involves comparing data that come from data gathered from other participants or other sources, for example collected by different qualitative methods (e.g. observations and interviews).

- *Researcher triangulation* involves the use of several observers, interviewers, or researchers to compare and check data collection and interpretation.

- *Theory triangulation* involves looking at the data using different theoretical perspectives.

Many qualitative researchers believe that triangulation can be useful in checking if the findings are trustworthy. Triangulation can provide a new way of looking at the same data, and it can add to credibility if it confirms the conclusions that have been drawn. However, Hammersley (1992) claims that it is not possible to know with certainty that an account is true, because there is no independent and completely reliable way to find "truth". The only way to get closer to the truth is to carefully examine all the evidence and see whether it supports the interpretation.

According to some researchers, it is important in qualitative research to establish a set of strategies, which can increase confidence that research findings actually represent the meanings presented by the participant—that is, increase trustworthiness. Triangulation can be one method used to do this. However, the most radical qualitative researchers argue that it is not possible to establish predetermined, distinct criteria for trustworthiness and credibility, because qualitative research is based on more or less subjective interpretations of the world.

Reflexivity in qualitative research

Reflexivity is a concept that has gained importance in qualitative research. Reflexivity is based on the assumption that it is important that the researcher is aware of his or her own contribution to the construction of meaning in the research process. Reflexivity is a process that occurs throughout the research. It allows the researcher to reflect on ways in which bias may occur, by acknowledging that his or her own background and beliefs can influence the way the research is conducted. This line of thinking argues that researchers should provide sufficient details about issues that may potentially bias the investigation—for example, revealing where they stand in terms of political ideology if this could be of importance.

According to Willig (2001), there are two types of reflexivity.

1 *Personal reflexivity*, which involves reflecting on the ways in which factors such as the researcher's values, beliefs, experiences, interests, and political commitment have influenced the research. It also involves thinking about how the research has affected the researcher personally and professionally.

2 *Epistemological reflexivity*, which has to do with thinking about the ways in which knowledge has been generated in the study. There are several ways to do this—for example, asking if the research question has limited what could possibly be found, if the design of the study and the way the data were analysed has biased the results, or if a different approach could have brought about a different understanding of the topic under investigation. Questions such as these encourage the researcher to think

critically about the knowledge that has been generated, as well as the assumptions which underpinned the research process.

However, qualitative researchers differ in the emphasis they place on reflexivity in their research, according to Willig (2001). Some consider both personal and epistemological reflexivity to be an integral part of the research report (e.g. Ritchie and Lewis 2003), while others acknowledge the importance of reflexivity, but do not include an in-depth discussion of it in their research reports.

Be a critical thinker

- Give two reasons for why reflexivity could be important in qualitative research.
- What is the main difference of this approach to the researcher's role in the natural sciences?

Qualitative research: interviews

HL

Learning outcomes

- Evaluate semi-structured, focus, group and narrative interviews
- Discuss considerations involved before, during, and after an interview (e.g. sampling method, data recording, traditional versus postmodern transcription, debriefing)
- Explain how researchers use inductive content analysis (thematic analysis) on interview transcripts

Semi-structured interviews

Semi-structured interviewing is the most widely used method of data collection in qualitative research in psychology, according to Willig (2001). One reason for this is that interview data from semi-structured interviews can be analysed using several theoretical approaches.

The semi-structured interview involves the preparation of an interview guide that lists themes that should be explored during the interview. This guide serves as a checklist during the interview, and helps to ensure that the same information is obtained from all the participants in the study. However, there is a great deal of flexibility in that the order of the questions and the actual wording of the questions are not determined in advance. Furthermore, the interview guide allows the interviewer to pursue questions on the list in more depth.

This kind of interview uses closed and open-ended questions. The closed questions trigger the participants to talk in a focused way, and the open-ended questions give the participant an opportunity to respond more freely. Most of the questions posed to the participants in the semi-structured interview are open-ended and non-directive, because the purpose of the interview is to get insight into people's personal experience of the phenomenon under investigation. The interview will often appear to be informal and rather conversational, because the semi-structured interview encourages two-way communication.

The interview may take place as a face-to-face interview, but there are many other ways to collect data—for example, via the telephone. Sometimes the data from the interview are supplemented with diaries or other pieces of writing that can be used in the analysis.

Strengths of the semi-structured interview

- On socially sensitive issues, it is better for acquiring data because the researcher can ask the interviewee to elaborate on his or her answers.
- Less biased by the researcher's preconceptions.

- Has the flexibility of open-ended approaches, as well as the advantages of a structural approach. It enables the researcher to make interventions, asking participants either to clarify or to expand on areas of interest.
- Allows for analysis in a variety of ways because it is compatible with many methods of data analysis.
- The interview guide sets out the themes to explore, but does not allow for pursuing themes that have not been prepared in advance.

Limitations of the semi-structured interview
- The focus on individual processes—the one-to-one situation is somewhat artificial and this could bring issues such as ecological validity into question.
- Data analysis is very time-consuming.

Focus groups

Focus groups were originally used within communication and market research. It is a popular method to assess health education messages and to examine public understanding of health behaviours. Focus groups are gaining in popularity in psychology, especially within health psychology, where it has become an alternative to semi-structured interviewing—for example, in research on people's experiences of disease and health services.

The idea behind a focus groups is that group processes can help people to explore and clarify their views in ways that would be difficult to achieve in one-to-one interviews. Group discussions are particularly suitable if the researcher uses open-ended questions that encourage the participants to explore the issues of importance to them. This enables the participants to talk freely and to generate their own questions.

A focus group normally consists of around 6 to 10 people. If there are more, it may be difficult for everyone to participate actively. The members of a focus group often have a common characteristic which is relevant for the topic of investigation, which is why purposive sampling is often used.

Participants in a focus group are supposed to interact with each other as they would do outside of the research context. This is more likely to happen if participants already know each other. The researcher has the role of facilitator—that is, someone in charge of making progress in the group. The facilitator introduces the group members to each other, establishes the topic of the research, and monitors the group discussion—for example, bringing the group back on track, asking group members to respond to issues raised by others, or identifying agreements and disagreements among group members. It is also the facilitator who sets the time limits for the discussion.

In the focus group, participants respond to and comment on each other's contribution to the discussion. Statements may be challenged or extended in ways that generate rich data for the researcher.

Focus groups may be:
- **homogeneous** (participants share key features) or **heterogeneous** (participants are different)
- pre-existing (e.g. a group of colleagues) or new
- concerned (where participants have a direct interest or commitment) or naive (they do not have a commitment).

In focus groups, the participants use everyday interpersonal communication patterns—that is, arguments and jokes. This has made focus groups an important data collection technique in cross-cultural research, because the method does not discriminate against people who cannot read or write. It is believed that everyday forms of communication may reveal more about what people know and experience than answers to questions in interviews.

Strengths of the focus group
- A quick and convenient way to collect data from several individuals simultaneously.
- Provides a setting that is natural, so it can be argued that it has higher ecological validity than the one-to-one interview.
- Particularly useful for exploring people's knowledge and experiences because it can be used to gain insight into *what* they think, *how* they think, and *why* they think that way. This includes the way people talk about the problem under investigation—for example, the words they use. It can also highlight cultural values or group norms.

Limitations of the focus group
- Not appropriate for all research questions. If the research deals with sensitive matters and the participants are supposed to talk about their personal experiences, it is not guaranteed that people will disclose information.
- The presence of other participants may result in group dynamics such as conformity.
- Focus groups can be a problem when the participants are not free—for example, in nursing homes or prisons. This raises ethical issues.

Narrative interviews
The narrative approach to psychology is based on the assumption that human beings are *storytellers*, and that the researcher's task is to explore the different stories being told (Murray 2003). Apparently, it is a universal human activity to tell stories about past events, and it can be seen as a way in which "knowing" is translated into "telling". For human beings, constructing narratives becomes a way of understanding the world and oneself. According to Parker (2005), a narrative is the way the self constructs a story of identity in relation to other people and the sociocultural context in which they live. However, narratives should not be seen as true representations of the world, but rather as individual *interpretations* of it.

According to Bruner (2006), the principal way in which people's minds—or "realities"—are shaped to the patterns of daily life is through the stories they tell, listen to, and read. These stories can be true or fictional, but it is through these stories—the narratives—that people make sense of what is happening around them. People construct their realities on these narratives and come to live in a world fashioned by them. The narratives are often constructed like real stories, with an opening, a middle, and an ending.

> **Example of interview questions in the narrative interview**
> - I would like you to tell me about yourself—where you were born, where you grew up, where you went to school, and so on. You should just tell me as much as possible about yourself.
> - I would like you to tell me what you thought when you received the diagnosis, and how you coped with it.

The purpose of narrative interviewing is to see how people impose a kind of order on their experiences so as to make sense of events in their lives. The narratives are representations of an individual's life—a mix of facts and interpretations—and they help to create identities and construct meanings in individual lives. Narrative interviewing can also help in understanding how individual lives relate to the historical and cultural context in which people live. One example of this could be the way feminist psychology in the western world has changed women's narratives about what women can and cannot do.

A narrative interview can take different forms. The life-story interview is the most extended form of a narrative interview. Another form focuses on how an individual experiences a particular situation, both personally and in relation to the social world. Overall, the researcher will always be interested in integrating the personal narrative into the broader cultural narrative.

Murray (2002) investigated how women who had been diagnosed with breast cancer integrated the disease into their everyday lives. The researcher wanted to find out what meaning they gave the illness, using the narrative interview. He found that there were striking similarities in the narratives. They were all constructed around a beginning (life before the cancer diagnosis), a middle (diagnosis, treatment, own reaction, and reaction of family and friends), and an end (looking back on how the disease disrupted life, and a redefinition of identity as a survivor of cancer, as well as a change in life expectancies).

Strengths of the narrative interview

- Valuable means of exploring the complexity of individual experiences, as well as how these relate to wider social and cultural contexts, because narratives provide an in-depth understanding of how people construct meaning in their lives.

- Narrative interviews can be used with all people because they can use everyday language and talk freely.

Limitations of the narrative interview

- Narrative interview results in an enormous amount of data and it can be time-consuming to transcribe and analyse.

Considerations before, during, and after an interview

There is quite a lot of planning involved in conducting an interview. The researchers should consider relevant *sampling methods*. In most qualitative research, small samples are used, and the sample will often have particular characteristics in common. In that case, a purposive sample will be adequate. You can read more about these considerations in Chapter 10.1.

Training of the interviewer is important in order to avoid **interviewer effects**—that is, effects caused by the presence of a particular interviewer. People are good at reading non-verbal signs, and this can have a profound effect on the way they respond. An

Be reflective

Do you think that the narrative approach would be appropriate if you were to conduct a study on what it is like to be a new student at an your school? Why or why not?

357

unconscious non-verbal sign, such as the interviewer frowning, could make participants change their answers, or upset them. Therefore, interviewers must be trained so that they do not react in ways that may intimidate the participants and jeopardize the interview.

Choice of interviewer may also be an issue. People are known to respond differently to male interviewers than to female interviewers. Generally, it is appropriate to consider how interviewer effects can be counterbalanced by varying age, gender, and ethnicity in interviewers conducting research.

The sex of the researcher is an important issue to consider in qualitative research; in some cultures, women are not allowed to talk to unknown males

The interviewer should plan the interview carefully and establish an *interview guide*. The interview guide is a kind of script for how to conduct the interview. It is based on previous literature in the field and the aims of the actual research. The interviewer must also carefully consider ethical issues that could arise from the interview. This is particularly relevant if the research is about sensitive topics. In qualitative research, the interview guide should be used flexibly, and should include a relatively small number of open-ended questions that allow the researcher to identify the respondent's own ideas and terms in the interview, so that questions become more relevant to the respondent.

Questions can be:

- **descriptive questions**, which invite the participant to give a general account of something ("What happened?" or "What does it feel like to be a mother?")

- **structural questions**, which invite the participant to identify structures and meanings to use to make sense of the world ("What does it mean to your life to suffer from AIDS?")

- **contrast questions**, which allow the participant to compare events and experiences ("Did you prefer being in that school or the other one?")

- **evaluative questions**, which ask about the respondent's feelings about someone or something ("Did you feel afraid when you had the HIV test?").

Data recording must be considered in the preparation of the interview. Taking notes during the interview interferes with eye contact and non-verbal communication, but in some situations it may be the only solution. Today, researchers often use tape or video recording. However, taping the interview may also affect the situation and the participant may feel uncomfortable about being recorded. It is therefore important to ask the participant in advance and explain why the recording is being made and how it is going to be used. It is also a good idea to offer the respondent a copy of the transcript of the interview, if possible. This information should be part of the briefing that takes place before the interview.

Transcription of the data—that is, how to change the interview into a written text that can be used for analysis—should be decided in advance. Researchers often use professional transcribers because transcription is a time-consuming job, but they will have to decide which method of transcription to use. Most qualitative methods of analysis require that the material is transcribed **verbatim** (i.e. word by word), and this is generally enough for thematic analysis. However, some researchers may find it important to include features such as pauses, interruptions, intonation, volume of speech, incomplete sentences, false starts, and laughter. It all depends on the research question and the method of analysis chosen. Transcriptions that include these features are called **postmodern transcripts**.

Finally, the researcher should inform the participant about the research and ask him or her to sign an informed consent before the research begins. This *briefing* should be extensive and should include the goal of the study, methods used, and any inconvenience that may occur.

During the interview, it is important to establish a **rapport** (i.e. a trusting and open relationship) between the interviewer and the participant. It is very important that the interviewer demonstrates ethical conduct. Even though there may be a relaxed atmosphere during the interview, the interviewer should never abuse the informal ambience to make the respondent reveal more than he or she is comfortable with after the interview.

If the interview is being recorded, the interviewer needs to make sure that the recorder is placed in a position where it will record clearly, and that the interviewer retains eye contact with the participant.

> **I:** So you're saying there's a difference between a crown court and a magistrates' court?
>
> **R:** Yeah. I mean the magistrates' court's sort of very just like skirty issues really, it just looks at getting things through quickly because it has such a build up of cases to get through.
>
> **I:** Do you think they're effective in the way they work?
>
> **R:** I think the magistrates' is the least effective. I think it's hard to expect sort of it to operate when it has somebody with not much legal training making decisions on law. I mean you wouldn't get that in the crown court say because they value the legal training of the judge in those places… so you have like a lesser court so it's just like an appointed position that anyone can have. There's obviously going to be less justice there.

Part of a transcription from an interview

The interviewer should use the interview guide flexibly, but ensure that all important themes are addressed. It is a good idea to use an **active listening technique**—that is, restate the participant's comments and integrate them in later questions in order to show that the interviewer is listening. Generally, the interviewer should be a good listener, empathic, and non-judgmental, and should encourage the participants to develop their viewpoints in their own words.

Most people like to be cooperative in a face-to-face situation. This can affect their answers—for example, if they think that the researcher is expecting a particular answer, or if they conform to the answers that other people give in focus groups. It is important to be aware that people may adjust their responses according to what they consider to be relevant. Participant expectancy effects of this kind need to be taken into consideration in any interview study.

After the interview, the participant must be debriefed. This includes information about the way the results are going to be used, and reassuring the participants that ethical considerations such as confidentiality and anonymity will be observed. It could also include the researcher asking the participant to read the transcripts of the interview and give feedback on them. The post-interview situation is an important part of the research process and should ensure that the participant is fully informed and feels confident. If the participant has revealed very sensitive information during the interview and feels uncomfortable about having done so when reading the transcript, the researcher must accept that the participant has the right to withdraw the information.

Use of inductive content analysis (thematic analysis) on interview transcripts

Data analysis: interpretative phenomenological analysis (IPA)

A common practice in analysis of qualitative data is the identification of key themes, concepts, and categories. There are several examples of thematic analysis—for example, grounded theory, which was invented for studying social processes in sociology. It involves **coding**—that is, finding specific categories in the data material. In the first stage of analysis, descriptive labels are given to discrete instances of phenomena. From here, new *low-level categories* emerge, and as the coding process continues, *higher-level categories* emerge where the lower-level categories are integrated into meaningful units. This way of analysing data identifies and integrates categories of meaning from the data, with the aim of generating new theory based on the data. It is not the same as traditional content analysis, where the categories are defined before the analysis begins, since the categories emerge from the data material in grounded theory.

According to Willig (2001), grounded theory enables the researcher to study social processes, but interpretative phenomenological analysis (IPA) allows the researcher to gain an insider's view of how individual participants make sense of the world. This is the reason why psychologists are now increasingly using this approach. IPA is based on the same principles of identification of themes and organizing them hierarchically as grounded theory. It is now used in health psychology—for example, in research investigating how people cope with serious illness.

The goal of IPA is to gain insight into how an individual perceives and explains a phenomenon. The data for analysis come from qualitative sources, such as semi-structured interviews, focus groups, diaries, or narrative interviews. The researcher works on the basis of texts—mostly transcripts—which are studied extensively in order to extract themes relevant to the research question. This means that data collection and analysis are not based on an existing theory or prior assumptions. The answer to the research question will emerge from the data themselves, so the IPA takes an inductive approach and supports the view that theory can emerge from the data. However, Grigoriou (2004) argues that it may sometimes be helpful to introduce theory in the analytic process.

Be a researcher

- What would you have to consider if you were to conduct research interviews in relation to coping with AIDS cross-culturally?

- How could you prepare for the interviews?

Thinking about knowledge and ways of knowing

The IPA approach is linked to philosophy—**phenomenology**—which is concerned with the way things appear to us via experience. In psychology, phenomenology refers to the conscious subjective experiences (e.g. perceptions, emotions, cognitions, behaviour) of individuals within their particular social, cultural, and historical contexts. These experiences are only accessible to the individual; they cannot be directly observed by other people, but they can be shared via language. The IPA acknowledges that it is impossible to gain direct access to a research participant's understanding of the world. It can only happen through texts (e.g. diaries) and transcripts of interviews.

This **idiographic approach** (related to the unique or particular) is central to IPA. The method is based on the assumption that cognitions are important in understanding people's subjective world. Smith (1996) argues that there is a relationship between what people think (cognition), say (account), and do (behaviour), and he has developed IPA based on these ideas.

IPA is also linked to **hermeneutics**—that is, the theory of interpretation and **symbolic interactionism**—which claims that the meanings individuals ascribe to events are of central concern, but these meanings are obtained through a process of social interaction and social interpretation.

Analysis is based on an *interpretation* of the participant's experience, but interpretation derives from paying close attention to the presented phenomenon rather than one imported from outside (Smith 2004). IPA is interested in the diversity of human experience, and looks for divergence and convergence in the themes which become apparent in the analysis of texts. The researcher can only make an *interpretation* of these texts in order to get insight into the lived experience of the participants, and it is not possible to determine whether this interpretation really reflects the lived experience of the participants.

Analysis involves a systematic search for themes in the first reading. Subsequent readings will try to connect the themes in meaningful ways in order to establish superordinate (or higher-order) themes and subthemes. In the research report, the researcher will use the elicited themes to draw conclusions, and these will be supported by verbatim extracts (quotations) from the participants—that is, rich-thick descriptions.

IPA works with transcripts of semi-structured interviews. Willig (2001) outlines the following stages as analytic strategy in IPA.

1 **Reading and rereading of the transcripts** in order to become familiar with each participant's account. The researcher produces notes about initial thoughts and observations that could be useful for analysis—for example, key phrases, preliminary interpretations, connections, contradictions, language use, summary statements. One way to do this is to note the comments in the left-hand margin of the text.

2 **Identification of emergent themes** that characterize each section of the text. The themes spring out of the text and are assumed to capture something essential about it. These themes can be noted in the right-hand margin. The researcher may or may not use psychological terminology at this point. The emerging themes from this first reading could be called "raw data themes".

3 **Structuring emergent themes.** The researcher will typically list all the emergent themes and see if they relate to each other in clusters and hierarchies. Clusters are then given labels that capture the essence of the theme. These could be *in vivo* terms used by the participants, brief quotations, or descriptive labels. One example

could be a "childhood cluster", which includes themes such as "relationship with friends" and "relationship with family". This childhood cluster could be termed "when I was a child" (*in vivo/* quote) or "early years" (descriptive). The themes can be organized in higher-order themes and subordinate themes. The clustering of themes should make sense in relation to the original data, so the researcher needs to check the source material again and again to be sure that the interpretation can be supported by the data.

4   **Summary table of the structured themes and relevant quotations that illustrate each theme.** This table should only include the themes that capture the essentials of the participant's experience in relation to the research question. Other themes should be excluded. The summary table includes cluster labels with their subordinate theme labels, brief quotations, and references to where relevant extracts may be found in the interview transcript, with reference to page and line numbers.

Qualitative researchers analyse the data until they reach a point where they can find no new information. This is called **data saturation**.

Research in psychology

A qualitative research study on relationships (Grigoriou 2004)

Grigoriou (2004) examined close friendships between gay men and heterosexual women. The participants were eight pairs of gay men and heterosexual women who were close friends. The sample consisted of British men and women. She used face-to-face semi-structured interviews to gather data. The interview schedule started with demographic questions, which were followed by questions regarding initiation, maintenance, and qualities of their friendships. Participants were then asked questions about the roles of their friends and families, as well as their feelings towards them. The schedule asked questions about the perception of others in their social network about their friendship. The participants who were single were asked to reflect on their previous partner's conception of this friendship. Finally, the participants were asked to compare friendships between gay men and heterosexual women with other forms of friendship they might have.

The transcripts were verbatim and were submitted to IPA analysis because this was considered to be the most appropriate way to gain an insight into the individual participant's own understanding of his or her friendship. The analytic strategy in this study followed the description outlined in the section on IPA in this chapter.

In terms of *reflexivity*, the researcher revealed that her interest in the topic came from being a heterosexual woman herself involved in a friendship with a gay man. She also considered whether she might have influenced the participants' accounts in that they were aware of her motivation to conduct the study—for example, the fact that the gay men described their female friends very positively.

The same could be the case for the heterosexual women, who did not report any negative feelings towards gay men or heterosexual women in any respect. The researcher reported that some gay men did report drawbacks and problems in relation to friendships with other gay men in a way that they probably would not have done if they had been interviewed by a gay man.

As for a credibility check, the researcher checked with other researchers to confirm that her analysis was grounded in the data.

Data analysis eventually revealed the following predominant themes and subthemes.

1   **Defining the friendship between gay men and heterosexual women** with the following subthemes:

   a   *a close friendship, a different friendship, a complete friendship, a friendship for sad and happy times, a friendship free from pressure, a friendship that is defined with kinship terms.*

2   **Friends as family**

   a   *subthemes for gay men*

      i   functions of family choice

         ● a fun family

         ● a supportive family

      ii   she is like a sister bud

      iii friends or family as friends?

   b   *subthemes for heterosexual women*

      i   different use of kinship terminology for gay men and heterosexual women.

3 **Valued characteristics of the friendship between gay men and heterosexual women**, with the following subthemes for both:

a openness

b trust

c social support

d having fun

e *subtheme for gay men*

  i feeling more rounded

f *subthemes for heterosexual women*

  i being valued for their personality and not their sexuality

  ii gay male friends as substitutes for heterosexual men.

4 **Comparing this friendship to other friendships**, with the following subthemes:

a gay men: compare this friendship with gay male friends and with heterosexual men.

b heterosexual women: compare this friendship with heterosexual women and with heterosexual men.

5 **Participants' understanding of their social network's perception of the friendship between them**, with the following subthemes:

a the family's perception of friends

b partner's perception of the friendship

The report consists of the analysis supported by quotes from the transcripts (e.g. page 14).

> *Similarly, when male participants were asked to draw similarities between their friendships with heterosexual women and other forms of friendship they had, their reaction was often a quite strong assertion that their friendship with heterosexual women was a different sort of friendship. For example, when Mike was asked if his friendship with Lucy was similar to his friendships with other gay men, he replied:*
>
> *"Erm, how is it similar? I think it is different because I would rather talk to Lucy and ask her advice on really very-very personal things that I wouldn't actually ask gay men for."*

(Grigoriou 2004: 14)

In conclusion, the research found that the participants were satisfied with their friendships for a number of reasons. For women, the lack of an underlying sexual agenda contributed to positive self-esteem, because they were valued for their personality and not their sexuality. The men expressed disappointment and lack of trust with the gay community and said that they trusted their female friends because they could rely on them. This last conclusion is contrary to previous research on the issue, but the researcher says her sample was small and only represents the people in the sample.

Methodological considerations

1 What could be the reason for choosing a thematic analysis of the interviews?

2 What is the advantage of making a verbatim transcript?

3 Why do you think the researcher revealed in the research report that she was a heterosexual woman who had a friendship with a gay man?

4 How did the researcher address issues of credibility?

5 How did the researcher address issues of trustworthiness?

6 Is it possible to generalize the findings from this study? Why or why not?

HL

Learning outcomes

- Evaluate participant, non-participant, naturalistic, overt, and covert observations
- Discuss considerations involved in setting up and carrying out an observation (e.g. audience effect, Hawthorne effect, disclosure)
- Discuss how researchers analyse data obtained in observational research

Introduction

In observations, the researcher enters a situation where some behaviour of interest is likely to take place and then make notes about it. The phenomenon of interest could be the nature and frequency of particular forms of behaviour, power relations in an organization, or the way people attribute meanings to gender roles.

If the researcher is to study power relations in a group of people, he or she makes systematic observations of the behaviour of the group in order to understand what it means to be a member of that particular group. The job of the researcher is to provide accounts of the observation on different levels of interaction, in order to identify and explain social structures within the study group. The observations are sometimes combined with other methods (e.g. interviews) to provide comparative results (triangulation).

Observation is an important method of gathering data. The aim is to gather first-hand information in a naturally occurring situation. There are two basic methods of observation:

- **participant observation**, where the observer takes part in the situation being studied while doing the research
- **non-participant observation**, where the observer is not part of the situation being studied.

Participant observation

In participant observation, the researcher becomes part of the group he or she observes. The aim of this research strategy is to gain a close and intimate familiarity with a given area of interest—for example, a religious group or a street gang—through personal involvement with people in their natural environment. The purpose is to develop a scientific understanding of the group.

In participant observational research, the researcher observes, listens, participates, and produces field notes. It is a very demanding task. Researchers must spend a great deal of time in surroundings that may not be familiar (e.g. prisons or hospitals); they must initiate and maintain relationships with people they may or may not like

Did you know?

The observational method is sometimes called **ethnography** because it uses the same method—fieldwork—as ethnographers and social anthropologists. This method originated in social anthropology. Fieldwork can be described as active participation in a group's life in order to gain information about how the group behaves and how social life is organized. By living with the people they were studying, anthropologists were able to give an inside account of their lives and generate new knowledge of the culture being studied. A famous example of fieldwork is Margaret Mead's work on adolescent girls on the island of Samoa in the 1930s.

(e.g. criminals); they must take a lot of notes on whatever happens (e.g. what people do, their body language, and their speech patterns); and they may run certain risks during the course of their work (e.g. injury at work if they are working in a factory). After the fieldwork is complete, the researchers spend many months analysing field notes and diaries before they write their research report.

Participant observation has been used in psychological research for some time—for example, in studies of urban communities, abused women in shelters, drug addicts, and professional thieves. It has proved to be a valuable method to gain insight into the lives and beliefs of subcultures. The researchers record their own experiences in the field in order to understand the universe of the participants in the study, and they use these experiences for scientific analysis by placing their field notes within a theoretical framework in order to explain the data. One example of participant observation is Festinger et al. (1956) on a cult. Festinger used participant observation to test an existing theory—cognitive dissonance.

Some researchers question whether traditional participant observations truly provide insight into people's minds. However, most qualitative researchers suggest that this can be done by active participation in a group's life over a period of time, without having any preconceived ideas. Some researchers believe that you can only truly understand people's world views if you base your work on the way people understand the world themselves. People's "theories of the world" are grounded in their daily interactions and communications. In order to discover these theories of the world, the researcher should look for regularities and patterns in the data to eventually discover the "rules" and "beliefs" that influence people.

The researcher is very important in that he or she is the *instrument* of data collection. The researcher enters the social world of other people, but they also affect the researcher in certain ways. It is important that the researcher is aware of this and that *continuous reflections* become part of the interpretation of the data. Critical thinking like this is always important, but particularly when the researcher chooses to study a group (e.g. an ethnic minority) in which he or she has a personal or political engagement. In the analysis, the researcher includes this and any other relevant biographical data because this is an important perspective in the interpretation of the data. This is an example of *reflexivity*.

Strengths of participant observation
- Combines the emic dimension (subjective participant perspective) with the etic dimension (objective observer perspective).
- Provides very detailed and in-depth knowledge of a topic, which cannot be gained by other methods.
- One of the best methods to avoid researcher bias because the researchers seek to understand how and why the social processes are the way they are, instead of imposing their own reality on the phenomenon.
- Provides a holistic interpretation of a topic, because the researcher takes into account as many aspects as possible of that

particular group of people, in order to synthesize observations into a whole. The researcher uses material from the participants themselves to generate "theory", and tries to explain one set of observations in terms of its relationship with others.

Limitations of participant observation

- Difficult to record data promptly and objectively.
- Time-consuming and demanding. The researcher needs to be physically present and try to live the life of the people he or she is studying. This takes time—as does data analysis—if the researcher is to arrive at an account that is reasonably objective and contextually sensitive. This is not possible in short-term projects.
- Risk that researchers lose objectivity. Researchers are supposed to immerse themselves, or "go native"—that is, be able to see the world from the point of the view of the participants. This may present problems in terms of objectivity. In participant observation there is a delicate balance between involvement and detachment.

Non-participant observation

Non-participant observation means that the researcher is not part of the group being studied. It is a research technique by which the researcher observes participants, with or without their knowledge. The researcher does *not* take an active part in the situation as in participant observation. One example of non-participant observation could be a researcher studying gender differences in teacher feedback in a school class. Critics of this method argue that people who are observed do not behave naturally. This is called "reactivity", and it is assumed that reactivity will invalidate the data. Some observational research takes place in psychological laboratories—for example, through one-way mirrors. It is believed that this kind of observation does not really reflect what people do in real life, but it may be useful to conduct research in this way all the same because it is easier and faster to gather data by this method.

Deception is sometimes used in non-participant observation, because some information cannot be obtained if participants know they are being studied. However, it is essential that the researcher always respects the individual's privacy and the rule of confidentiality in such research.

Naturalistic observation

Naturalistic observation simply means that the observation takes place in the participants' natural environment, and that the researchers avoid interfering with the behaviour they are observing. The most important thing in naturalistic observations is that the researcher should not interfere with the naturally occurring behaviour. If the researcher spends some time with the participants before the observation begins, they will get used to his or her presence. The researcher could also use cameras to film behaviour—for example, in a playground—and then use this for analysis. If cameras are present for a long period, they will probably not interfere with natural behaviour.

Be a researcher

Which of the following observational methods would be the best to study?

- How teachers use feedback to encourage students.
- How students interact with each other during class projects.
- How students use the Internet to search for information.

Give reasons for your answers.

If a psychologist wants to know how small children experience the world, he or she could spend time in a kindergarten observing the children. Kampman (1998) studied how children in kindergartens developed friendships with other children. He spent six months in an institution observing the children, and found that they show an interest in other children from a very early age. He argues, on the basis of his observation, that it is important that the institutions and parents help children to develop friendships because it strengthens social competency and trains them to resolve conflicts.

In *unstructured observations*, the researcher will record all relevant behaviour. There is no checklist. The behaviour to be studied is unpredictable. Data collection and analysis are difficult.

In *semi-structured observations*, data collection is not constrained by predetermined categories of analysis, but the researcher has decided what overall areas to look for. Data collection is easier and this approach allows for analysis at a greater level of depth and detail.

In *structured observations*, the researcher will record specific predetermined features of behaviour, using a checklist that has been developed before the observation. Data collection is easier, but data analysis is restricted to the preset categories. This may not reflect what really happens.

Strengths of naturalistic observation
- Ecological validity: the collection of data takes place in a natural environment and it is assumed that the participants behave in natural ways (in contrast to research in laboratories).
- Can be used to collect data in cases where it would be impossible or unethical to do so otherwise—for example, research on people with Alzheimer's disease.

Limitations of naturalistic observation
- There is the risk that people do react to being observed—that is, there may be *reactivity* involved.
- If the researcher collects the data alone, there may be problems in checking the data. However, multiple observers in the same field can compare data to ensure match of the data (sometimes called inter-observer reliability). The researcher can also document the fieldwork extensively and explain how he or she arrived at the conclusions reached, in order to promote credibility.
- Ethical considerations concerning the appropriateness of observing strangers without their knowledge. The researcher should also be aware not to violate the privacy of participants.

Overt and covert observation
Participant and non-participant observations can be overt or covert. The researcher decides in advance which technique is most appropriate for the research. There are strengths and limitations of both approaches.

Be a researcher

Plan a trip to a location (e.g. the zoo, a supermarket, a bus stop) and decide whom or what to observe. Then consider the following: should you make a detailed plan of what to observe before you start (structured observation) or would you prefer one of the other observational methods? Give a reasoned answer.

In an **overt observation**, the participants know they are being observed. This is the main strength in terms of ethical considerations. They may or may not have given formal consent, depending on the research. This depends on the degree of involvement of the researcher. Whatever the circumstances, the researcher will let the participants know that he or she is a researcher, but it is not always clear to them what the purpose of the study is. A researcher studying a group of women in a women's shelter might simply say that she is writing a book on domestic violence and how women cope with it. This may be enough to gain acceptance for the project. However, there will always be some kind of involvement because it is important that the researcher has a good relationship with the participants. The quality of the data depends on that. In overt participant observations where the psychologist actively participates in the group being studied, the participants are informed about the research and give informed consent.

In a **covert observation**, the participants are not aware of being studied, so they have not agreed to it. The participant has to "make up a story" to justify his or her presence in the setting in order to mask his or her real purpose in being there. This method has been used over the years in settings where it would otherwise be difficult to gain access, or when it is important that the presence of the researcher does not affect the behaviour of the people in the study. There are ethical issues involved in covert observations. First, is the fact that the participants have not been asked. Second, it can be dangerous for the researcher if he or she is investigating a group of people who are known to be violent, such as street gangs.

Ethics in research

1 Was the use of covert participant observation justified in Festinger's study? Why or why not?

2 Would it be possible for the public to recognize the participants in this study?

3 What ethical rules should the researcher always consider in covert observations?

Research in psychology

Festinger, Riecken, and Schachter (1956)

One famous case study using covert participant observation was the investigation of a cult by Festinger, Riecken, and Schachter. The researchers wanted to find out how people in a cult would cope with the situation when their prophecies failed. They joined a cult that believed the world was scheduled to end on a specific date, and they got to know the cult members. Because of this, they were able to talk with the members and see how their beliefs changed when the world did not end.

The social psychologist Leon Festinger read a newspaper article about a religious cult that claimed to be receiving messages from outer space, predicting that a great flood would end the world. Festinger and some co-workers joined the group and pretended they were converts to the beliefs of the cult. The members of the cult believed they were going to be rescued by a flying saucer when the rest of the world was destroyed. The cult members had publicized the prophecies, and some of the members had sold their houses and given up their jobs. The researchers wanted to see what happened to the cult members when the world did not go under. The theory of cognitive dissonance predicted that the cult members would either change their beliefs to restore balance in their cognitions, or that they would change their behaviour to fit their beliefs. When the date arrived and there was no flood, some of the group members coped with it by saying that their prayers had saved the city. In this way, they created meaning from what had happened and there was balance in their cognitions. Other members simply left the cult. This indicated that they had changed their beliefs. The study confirmed the theory of cognitive dissonance.

Considerations involved in setting up and carrying out an observation

An observation is not just about "hanging around". A researcher who decides to carry out an observation must prepare it carefully.

Preparation of observation

The researcher needs to find out about the problem under investigation and set up a plan for the observations—for example, contact people and make the necessary arrangements. The researcher should also decide whether to conduct a participant or a non-participant observation. It is also a good idea to decide exactly what to focus on in the field, while leaving space for flexibility. It may be a good idea that the researcher becomes familiar with the setting and the people before starting the observations. This could reduce some of the problems of having a stranger in the setting.

The researcher must take some initial decisions as to the purpose of the research and what kind of notes to make during observations.

- Descriptive? The researcher just observes what is happening and does not make any inferences.
- Inferential? The researcher makes inferences about what is observed, including comments on individual reactions and expressions of emotion.
- Evaluative? The researcher makes inferences and evaluates the behaviour—for example, if expressions of self-hate in a minority group are evidence of power relationships in the wider society.

Researchers should also be aware of their own position—for example, feminist or political in relation to the subject area—because this needs to be clear in relation to the reflections conducted during the research. The researcher's perspective may well influence his or her interpretation of the situation, and this is acceptable in qualitative research as long as it is declared openly.

> **Classroom research 1**
>
> If a researcher wants to undertake observations in a classroom, he or she could conduct pre-observational interviews with the participants (teachers and students). The participants should also be briefed about the purpose of the research and what is going to occur during the observations. The researcher could present the purpose of the research, but some of it may not be revealed—for example, the purpose could be said to be how teachers and students interact in the classroom, but not that the researcher is interested in how this affects the students' motivation and interest, or whether gender and ethnicity influence teacher feedback. The contacts with participants before the observation can reduce the risk that they will behave in ways that are not natural when the observation takes place. Participant expectancy (reactivity) is minimized.

Conducting the observation

The researcher meets with the participants and establishes a rapport. This may involve a "culture shock" and adjustment to the context, especially in cases of participant observation. The researcher must be aware of ethical rules of conduct.

In participant observations, it is important to be involved in the setting and with the people, while staying analytical. The goal is to preserve researcher "objectivity", so that the data collection is not influenced by selective perception. It may be an advantage that several observers work at the same time, or the researcher might use independent observers. The advantage is that one observer might notice what another has missed. Furthermore, it allows the researcher to become aware of the amount of agreement between the observers.

There is always the risk that participants do not behave naturally. This is called participant expectancy (or reactivity). It can be a problem whenever people are being observed. The researcher may come to the investigation with an in-built bias (researcher bias or the Rosenthal effect), which may result in selective perceptions and a biased interpretation of the data. Both factors may influence the credibility (validity) of the data, because the behaviour of the observed persons may be untypical of their normal behaviour—that is, it lacks ecological validity. This can be counterbalanced by credibility checks.

The field notes must be rich, thick, descriptive, and very detailed at all stages of the observation. The notes should include a variety of information from several perspectives.

Classroom research 2

While undertaking observations, the researcher should provide a highly detailed description of the interactions in the classroom in relation to each of the areas of interest. This might be how the teacher gives feedback to individual children (e.g. in relation to gender or minority groups); how the children react to the teacher (e.g. facial and verbal expressions); who is talking and who is not talking in the class; and if there is evidence that the students are learning anything. There should be notes for each focus area, and the notes should also include space to write reflections.

After the observations

After the observations, the researcher can conduct post-observational interviews, and the participants must be debriefed, unless the observations were covert. Data analysis is then carried out—for example, using grounded theory based on field notes.

Classroom research 3

The observation notes (and perhaps video recordings of a couple of classes) must be analysed and synthesized. The researcher will include the information from the interviews conducted prior to and after the observations. He or she will probably also include information that can place the observations in context—for example, racism or gender inequality in the wider society.

Be reflective

A researcher wants to conduct a research study in a shelter for abused women to find out how and if they support each other.

- Which observational method would you recommend, and why?
- Why might it be important for the researcher to establish a rapport with the participants?
- What ethical considerations should the researcher observe in a study like this?

Analysis of data obtained in observational research

Qualitative researchers are concerned with the process as well as the end product of the research. They take an *inductive* approach to data analysis—that is, they begin to create a picture as they collect the data and examine them. The analysis is based on the researcher's field notes, but these are often compared to data from other sources (e.g. interview transcripts, pictures, narratives), as it is common in participant observation to use a variety of sources.

One way to analyse the data from observations is grounded theory analysis. Researchers using this method prepare their data—that is, having "thick" field notes. The core of grounded theory analysis is based on three related processes: **description**, and **coding and connecting themes** to **produce an account**.

Description

The first step in observations is to provide a complete description of the phenomenon of interest. The description includes the context of the action, the intentions of the actor, and the process in which the action is embedded (Denzin 1978). A "thick" description provides rich data.

Coding and connecting themes

The coding of the data means that they are organized into categories. This is an important part of qualitative analysis. The purpose is to provide tools for analysis. Without categorization, it is not possible to know *what* is analysed and it is not possible to compare the data.

The classification process consists of reading and rereading the field notes in an interactive way. The researcher must be able to identify bits of data and create categories, by asking questions like who? what? when? where? why? The researcher can create graphical representations of the categories and their connections, and supply case examples. This approach can open different routes to examine the data and makes it easier to see how the categories and subcategories may be related by themes. The researcher should write a summary of the analysis so that independent readers can follow how and why the connections are reached. These notes about notes are called **memos**.

When the data have been classified into themes, the researcher can look for higher-order themes (main themes) and subthemes. The interpretation of the data is based on comparison of the collected data, and sometimes the researcher will include evidence from other sources—for example, interview data or information on the social context. It is important to think critically and not only look for data that *support* the interpretation. The researcher should also search for evidence that could contradict the interpretation. Critical thinking means looking for alternative explanations.

Producing an account

The end product is a written account based on all the elements of the analysis. The researcher produces a coherent explanation and an overall theoretical framework for understanding the phenomenon under investigation. The theoretical framework is "grounded"—that is, it is based on the categories identified during the observation. However, it may also be that researchers use theoretical triangulation—that is, including alternative theories to explain the phenomenon. (For more on triangulation, see Chapter 10.1.) The researcher continuously consults the data to see if they support the interpretation. He or she may also consult the participants, to ask them whether they can support the interpretation. Finally, he or she can ask other researchers to take a critical look at the account and the data to see whether they can support them. The important thing is that the researcher makes it possible for the reader to track and verify how the conclusion is reached.

There are issues of generalization from an observational study. According to some researchers, it is possible to make inferential and theoretical generalizations. (For more about this, see Chapter 10.1.)

Be a researcher

You have been asked to conduct observational research to study bullying in a school.

1   Describe how you could set up and execute such a project, using your knowledge.

2   How would you record the data and prepare them for analysis? Why?

3   What would be the ethical considerations to take into account?

Qualitative research: case studies

L

Learning outcomes

- Evaluate the use of case studies in research
- Explain how a case study could be used to investigate a problem in an organization or group (e.g. a football team, a school, a family)
- Discuss the extent to which findings can be generalized from a single case study

Use of case studies in research

The case study is defined as an in-depth investigation of human experience. A single case can be one person, but it could also be a family, a social group, an event, or an organization. The design of a case study can be a single case study, or multiple case studies where a series of cases are compared.

The case study often takes place in the participant's natural environment. For example, a single case study may involve interviewing staff in a small but growing computer company on the social psychological aspects of managing staff (Hayes and Lemon 1990). This information could eventually be used to compare cases with larger companies, in terms of how they had tackled staff management issues at a similar stage in their history.

According to Willig (2001), case studies can be **intrinsic** case studies and **instrumental** case studies. Intrinsic case studies represent nothing but themselves. The cases in intrinsic case studies are chosen because they are interesting in their own right. This could be a person who has been kept prisoner in a basement for many years by a perpetrator. The researcher simply wants to gain insight into one particular phenomenon by studying that case. Instrumental case studies represent more general phenomena of interest, such as losing a child, being homeless, or being diagnosed with cancer. In principle, any individual who has experienced the phenomenon under investigation is a useful case in instrumental case studies.

Willig (2002) also makes a distinction between **descriptive** and **explanatory** case studies. The purpose of descriptive case studies is to generate a detailed description of a phenomenon. It is believed that such a description will in itself generate new knowledge. The findings of the descriptive case study are not analysed in terms of existing theory. In explanatory case studies, the aim is to describe *and* find possible explanations for the phenomenon under investigation. This includes theoretical analysis based on existing theory, or generation of new theory based on the data (e.g. grounded theory).

According to Willig (2001), a case study should always be seen in *context*. The researcher should include psychological, sociocultural, historical, or biological dimensions that are relevant to the phenomenon under investigation. It is important to specify the context in which the case is explored—for example, a case study on resilience in street children could focus on early development, family relations, personality, and social support. Although a case study may be narrowly focused, modern researchers do not believe that individuals can be understood in isolation.

When a researcher has found a case to study, he or she must decide on the participants and how to collect the data. The participants can be found using the sampling methods described in Chapter 10.1.

As for data collection, the semi-structured interview is a widely used method, but it is not the only one. Case studies often include a certain amount of triangulation. Because they are complex, it is believed that using different perspectives will result in **rich data** (i.e. data which are open to a number of interpretations) and a better all-round understanding of the situation. Conclusions based on multiple sources are considered to be more trustworthy and accurate. Research on resilience in a group of street children, for example, might use focus groups, semi-structured interviews, and observations, as well as accounts from adults in the community and newspaper articles on street children.

The case study is not a research method itself, but rather a *research strategy*. Data for case studies can come from a number of methods, such as semi-structured interviews, participant observation, diaries, personal notes (e.g. letters, photographs, notes), or official documents (e.g. case notes, clinical notes, appraisal reports), as well as questionnaires.

Strengths of the case study method

- **Opportunity to investigate phenomena that could not be studied otherwise.** The case study gives researchers the possibility to investigate cases which could not be set up in research laboratories. The case studies of Clive Wearing in Chapter 3.1 and the Czech twins in Chapter 6.2 are examples of this. It would not be possible to create such situations for research purposes.

- **Permits insight into social processes in a group.** The case study method offers the possibility to study such processes using different methods—for example, looking at group culture, communication patterns, beliefs, and attributions, and how these influence behaviour and decisions.

- **Stimulates new research**, because the case can highlight phenomena which need further investigation. For example, case studies of people with brain damage have sparked off research in memory processes and biological correlates of memory, using animal research to test theories. Case study research on intervention programmes for youth at risk has resulted in more case studies to evaluate the effectiveness of interventions, in terms of how the users see them.

Be a critical thinker

What would be preferable in a case study on serial killers—a descriptive or an explanatory case study? Why?

Be a researcher

1 What data collection method would be the most appropriate if you were to conduct a case study with a street gang? Why?

2 Mention some ethical considerations in such a study.

- **Contradicts established theory and helps to develop new theories.** Case studies have sometimes contradicted established psychological theories. One example is the case study mentioned in Chapter 6.2 of the severely deprived Czech twins, who showed remarkable recovery when they were placed in a caring social environment. This challenged the established theory that the early years of life determined human social development. This case and similar studies of deprived children have shown that some (but not all) children are resilient, and this has sparked off research into factors that promote resilience.

Limitations of the case study method

- **Difficult to define a case study** according to Willig (2001). It can be difficult to determine whether a series of related studies constitute a proper case study or if they are just a collection of studies dealing with the same question.

- **Researcher bias**—that is, the researcher's own subjective feelings may influence the case study. There is a potential risk for researcher bias in case studies, in that the researcher's own beliefs can influence the way the data are collected and analysed, but this could be controlled via reflexivity and strategies to achieve trustworthiness. According to Flyvbjerg (2001), there is no greater researcher bias in case studies than in other methods of enquiry.

- **Memory distortions and effects of social desirability.** Qualitative data depend to a large extent on people's cognitions (perceptions, memory). The reliance on memory when reconstructing the case history (i.e. in narrative interview) could be subject to distortion. Participants in case studies may also change their accounts in order to appear more socially acceptable. However, this could be the case in most research studies.

Ethical aspects of the case study method

If there are only one or a few participants in a case study, there is the risk that they can be identified in the research report, so researchers have to be very careful and do their best to anonymize the participants.

Another ethical issue in relation to case study research is that it often requires the active involvement of the participants, who are asked to participate in interviews or write about their experiences in depth. This can be time-consuming and involve self-reflection that may affect the participants negatively in that they will have to deal with painful memories and emotions. The researcher is responsible for the consequences that the research process has on the participants and must deal with this in ethical ways. (Read more about this in Chapter 10.1.)

How could the case study be used to investigate a problem in an organization or group (e.g. a school)?

Many students who belong to minority groups and come from an impoverished background do not perform well academically. Some drop out before they finish school, while others barely make it to their exams, but have already lost the motivation to stay in the educational system. This is a problem since society focuses so much on education as the basis of professional life, and this means that many of these young people never get a job. In school classes the majority of the students are from minority groups. As is the case in some urban schools, the students do not learn what they are supposed to and many seem to give up. They are often hostile to the school and the teachers.

In the Danish school system (among others), young children have a class teacher who teaches them many subjects. Although a number of factors are at stake in a complicated case like this, a class teacher can have a significant influence on the children's attitudes to learning and on their development of self-efficacy. Pedagogical strategies and communication patterns in the class are important factors. However, minority students' membership of a minority group contributes to social identity and expectations about the future. Studying students' beliefs via the attributions they make about their own possibilities in the education system could be an important way to learn about how they experience school.

The case study approach is an ideal strategy to investigate a situation like this, because it provides an opportunity to combine different data collection methods (triangulation). The method can bring out important data from the viewpoint of the participants, using multiple sources of data. This provides the basis for a more in-depth and holistic analysis.

Aim

The aim of the study is to explore psychological and social processes that prevent children from learning and to find ways to promote student self-efficacy. The research will focus on one question: "Can specific teaching strategies used by a class teacher promote motivation and build self-efficacy in minority students in one class?"

Design

The design could be a single case explanatory case study, because the aim is to go beyond description and actually explore whether specific teaching strategies can promote change in students' motivation. Data collection should include participant observation, semi-structured interviews, focus groups and student writings, in order to have multiple sources of data. The study will include method and theory triangulation in the analysis.

A number of class sessions could be video taped for further analysis. Semi-structured interviews could be tape recorded and transcribed verbatim. Two focus group interviews—one after two months and another after eight months—could be previewed.

The participants might be a class with students aged 9–10 years, because it has previously been found that it is around this age when students seem to give up on their schooling. The sample should be purposive, because the class has to match two criteria: the majority of students belong to minority groups and they should perform below average in their academic work. A school in the inner city could be contacted to ask if it would participate in the study. The teacher should be known as an efficient teacher and should agree to participate in special teacher training sessions. The researcher should follow the class for one year (as a co-teacher in Danish, history, and mathematics in our example). The study thus takes place in the natural environment of the students.

Field research

While conducting the research in the field, working as a co-teacher for one year while collecting data enables the researcher to establish rapport with the students, and to get an idea of what it is like to be a student. During the year, the researcher will collect data using different methods. There is the problem, of course, that this situation could cause the researcher to lose objectivity.

The researcher could start with an unstructured participant observation while working as a co-teacher, in order to get a first impression of the students, the teacher, and the interactions between them. Field notes are taken after two classes. The teachers' and the students' interactions, as well as interactions between the students, are used as themes of interest. This provides the basis for a semi-structured observation later. It is important to get a view of how the students themselves experience the situation, so that obstacles to learning can be identified.

Other observations focus on the implementation of teaching strategies—for example, how the teacher discusses immediate goals with the students; how he or she arranges class projects in which students can explore topics that they have chosen themselves; how he or she makes them perform oral presentations to strengthen their use of language; and the teacher's use of feedback.

The researcher conducts two semi-structured interviews with the students in the class during the year, following an interview guide with a focus on the students' experience of the teaching. The interviews are transcribed verbatim. Student essays should be read and used for analysis as well. The researcher conducts semi-structured interviews with the teacher every month.

Data analysis

Analysis of the data should be an ongoing process and should help to generate themes that can be used to formulate questions for the interviews. The two interviews with each student should be analysed and compared to look for changes in relation to motivation and self-efficacy during the year. One method that could be used is IPA, described in Chapter 10.2, but grounded theory could also be used. The data may generate theory, but they could also be analysed using existing theory, such as self-efficacy theory.

Conclusion

The conclusion of such a case study could lead to recommendations for better teaching strategies in minority groups—for example, giving more focus to language development; involving students in goal setting; skills training that creates a bridge to the next level of

education; feedback to enhance the quality of the work; and incorporation of teaching projects chosen by the students themselves. These strategies were found to be important in this case study. The findings from the case study could be used to design further case studies like this one, in order to find out if the same pattern is found in similar studies. If this is found to be so, it could be argued that the findings can be generalized using inferential or theoretical generalization. They could also be used to generate theory about efficient teaching strategies that could be used in interventions in other case studies.

1 Give two reasons why the case study could be an appropriate method to use to study attitudes to learning in a minority group.

2 Give one weakness and one strength of the study in relation to what you know about the case study and data collection in general.

3 Discuss whether there could be cultural considerations in this example of a case study.

The extent to which findings can be generalized from a single case study

It has been argued by researchers within the quantitative tradition that a case study cannot be of any value outside the case because it cannot be replicated, it cannot be used for prediction, and the results cannot be generalized. Qualitative researchers do not agree.

However, the discussion among qualitative researchers shows some disagreement as to how generalization can be made. A single case study normally uses a small sample that has been purposively selected so that it is not statistically representative. This makes it difficult to generalize findings to other populations. However, if evidence from other studies confirms the findings, it is argued that it is possible to generalize to other people who are similar to those in the case study (Hammersley 1992).

A single case study may be used for inferential generalization—that is, the findings can be applicable to similar settings if the researcher has provided a "rich-thick" description of the phenomenon and the context. This is referred to as "transferability". The efficient teaching strategies of the teacher in the case study on the role of teaching strategies on minority children's motivation could be used as a hypothesis on a causal link between specific strategies and specific outcomes, but it will remain a hypothesis until it is supported or disproved by further evidence.

According to Yin (1994), the results of single case studies can be generalized to existing theory—that is, theoretical generalization—but not to populations. If the patterns found in a single case study can be found in multiple cases—that is, they replicate the pattern found in the single case study—the theory derived from the single case study gains in robustness.

10.5 Writing paper 3 questions

Learning outcomes
- Demonstrate knowledge and understanding of qualitative research methodology

The assessment objectives are related to assessment objectives 1, 2, and 3, but there is one assessment objective which is specific for paper 3. It is related to assessment objective 2—Application and analysis:

At HL only, analyse qualitative psychological research in terms of methodological, reflexive, and ethical issues involved in research.

The total mark for paper 3 is 30 marks. Paper 3 accounts for 20 per cent of the overall mark in psychology.

Paper 3 questions are short-answer questions (SAQs), so the information provided about SAQs in Chapter 11 also applies here. There are three questions in a paper and you have one hour to answer all of them.

The exam question presents you with a piece of stimulus material based on documentation of a piece of research. This can be a summary of a study, an abstract, or an extract from a study, interview, or observation, of approximately 500 words. This might include, for example, aim, characteristics of participants, the research method used, or the results.

Strategies for answering the questions
- Read the stimulus material carefully. This will give you an idea of what to expect in the questions. Once you have understood what the research is about, read the questions carefully, one by one, so that you get an overall idea of what you are being asked to do.
- Look for command terms—what exactly are you supposed to do?
- Make an outline before you start writing—just a few hints as to what to answer in order to help you remember the facts you need and to structure your answer. You can use mind-mapping for this.
- Answer the questions in a focused way. There is no reason to write more than is necessary.
- Make sure you refer to the stimulus material when you argue, but do not use long quotations from this material. You are supposed to demonstrate your knowledge of qualitative methodology and that you can use this knowledge in relation to the stimulus material.

How to assess paper 3 answers

Read the sample questions and answers set out below. Then read the mark bands and try to place the answers within the mark bands. Explain why you have placed each answer in the mark band you have chosen.

Two researchers carried out a case study of a group of young boys living in a socially deprived area who had problems in relation to educational achievement. Young people in this area are at risk for dropping out of school and becoming unemployed. There is also a substantial risk of criminality and substance misuse. Generally, there are negative expectations and young people are easily drawn into a culture of underachievement. One of the key problems in the community with regard to young people is the lack of facilities and activities, so adolescents often hang around the streets.

A local organization wanted to set up a project to promote positive change. Two researchers joined a group of local community workers doing street work to establish a relationship of trust with the adolescents. This allowed the researchers to conduct some initial observations. They found that the young boys were bored and did not know what to do besides hanging out with their friends. The researchers conducted a focus-group interview with the young boys to find out how they perceived their own situation and what they would be interested in doing. The interview was tape recorded and transcribed verbatim. The researchers read and reread the transcript. The data were coded and the researchers carried out an inductive content analysis on the interview data. An overall theme appeared to be a lack of belief in future possibilities. Subthemes were: no interest in schoolwork, no trust in the school system, conflict with adults, and interest in sport and hanging out with friends. The researchers also found that the boys were interested in participating in sports activities if they had the opportunity and if these were free. The researchers used extensive quotes from the participants to support the conclusions reached, in order to ensure credibility, and they also presented the results of their analysis to five of the participants for the same reason.

Based on the researchers' account, a young sports coach from the area became the peer leader of a basketball group. Two of the researchers undertook participant observations as coaching assistants of all the training sessions during the first year. After two months' training, the group expressed the wish to take part in competitions. They produced field notes after each training session. The sports coach was able to challenge the boys to work hard and persistently towards the common goal, and he found more young people who were willing to invest time and energy in the project. The team started to participate in competitions and achieved some success.

Those who did not meet regularly for training were not allowed to continue on the team. The researchers followed the development and conducted two more focus-group interviews and face-to-face interviews with the coach after 6 and 12 months. They found that participation in the team had positive effects, not only on the boys' levels of fitness and motivation, but also on their attitudes to learning, self-esteem, and social competence.

The researchers concluded that the results of this case study show that there is a choice beyond antisocial behaviour and failure, if the community provides concrete opportunities for individuals to develop and realize personal and educational goals.

Sample questions

Answer **all** three questions.

1 Explain how the case study was used to investigate and find a solution to a social problem.

2 Evaluate the use of focus-group interviews as a data collection method in this case study.

3 Discuss whether the findings from this single case study can be generalized.

Sample answers

1 The case study method was used in the present study to investigate whether it was possible to promote positive change for a group of boys who were in danger of dropping out of school and perhaps developing social problems. The boys had negative expectations about their future, so the aim of the study was to find out whether this could be changed. The case study aimed to explore the participants' own perception of the situation and possible ways to change in order to ensure that they supported the strategies for change that were eventually set up. The researchers used the focus-group interview at the beginning of the study to encourage the participants to explore the issues that were of importance to them. The findings from the focus-group interviews indicated that participating in sport was a way to promote change, and this was used to set up a basketball team, with a young coach from the area who knew what problems the boys were facing. The researchers followed the basketball team for one year, conducting participant observations. They were able to do this as assistants to the sports coach, and this gave them an opportunity to follow the development of the team and the individual boys over a long period.

Furthermore, the two focus-group interviews after 6 and 12 months gave indications as to what positive changes had taken place as the boys saw it themselves. The interviews with the coach suggested ideas of what he found was important in order to motivate the boys. The case study used method triangulation to study how changes in group culture and beliefs influenced the boys' behaviour and self-esteem long-term, not only in sport, but also in other areas (288 words).

2   The focus group is an important way to collect data as the participants are supposed to interact with each other as they would do outside of the research context. This is more likely to happen if participants already know each other, as they did in this group. The researcher acted as a facilitator and, after introducing the topic of the project, ensured that progress was made in the group. This data collection method is particularly useful in a research project like this one, where the goal is to identify a problem and promote social change in a group. The facilitator can monitor the group discussion and bring the group back on track, suggesting things that they can agree on. This is important because the purpose of the research was that the whole group should be empowered, so the same effect could not be achieved in an individual interview with each of the boys. There is, however, the possibility that the presence of other participants could have resulted in group dynamics such as conformity. Overall, the focus group was a quick and convenient way to collect data from the whole group simultaneously in a natural setting. In this particular case study, it was important for the researchers to explore the participants' knowledge and experiences in order to gain insight into *what* they thought and why they thought that way, in order to set up something useful to bring about change in their situation. The researchers used inductive content analysis of the interview transcripts. This allowed them to identify important themes in the way the boys themselves saw their situation (266 words).

3   This single case study uses a small sample that has been carefully selected so it is not statistically representative and this makes it difficult to generalize findings to other populations in traditional (quantitative) ways. However, qualitative researchers argue that if evidence from other studies confirms the findings it may be possible to generalize to other people who are similar to those in the case study. A single case study can also be used for inferential generalization, i.e. the findings may be applicable to similar settings if the researcher has provided a "rich" description of the phenomenon and the context so that other researchers can identify the case and follow the conclusions made based on the documentation, for example quotations from the participants. This is referred to as "transferability". The use of sport as a way to motivate problem children could be used as a hypothesis on a causal link between specific strategies (sport) and specific outcomes (increased motivation in learning and social competence) but it will remain a hypothesis until it is supported or disproved by further evidence. It has been argued that if the patterns found in a single case study can be found in multiple cases, i.e. they "replicate the pattern" found in the single case study—the theory derived from the single case study gains in robustness. This is also considered to be a way of generalizing in qualitative research (234 words).

Assessment details for paper 3

The framework below only provides a general guide to the assessment of responses to paper 3 questions.

Mark band	Level descriptor
0	The answer does not reach a standard described by the descriptors below.
low	There is an attempt to answer the question, but knowledge and understanding are limited, often inaccurate, or of marginal relevance to the question. The response makes no direct reference to the stimulus material or relies too heavily on quotations from the text.
mid	The question is partially answered. Knowledge and understanding are accurate but limited. Either the command term is not effectively addressed or the response is not sufficiently explicit in answering the question. The response makes limited use of the stimulus material.
high	The question is answered in a focused and effective manner and meets the demands of the command term. The answer is supported by appropriate and accurate knowledge and understanding of qualitative research methodology applied to the stimulus material.

Mark bands for paper 3

11 Writing papers in psychology: SAQs and essays

Writing papers in psychology is about showing that you have psychological knowledge and that you can use it sensibly. A good paper will present relevant information and argue in a focused and structured way to answer a question. A good paper will also demonstrate critical thinking skills.

Papers 1 and 2

Paper 1 is the same for SL and HL. It deals with the biological, cognitive, and sociocultural levels of analysis and it consists of two sections: section A, with three short-answer questions (SAQs), and section B, with three essays.

● In section A, you have to answer all the SAQs.
● In section B, you should choose one of the three essays.

You have 20 minutes to write each short-answer question during the exam. For the essay, you have an hour. A typical response to a short-answer should be around 250 words. A typical essay should be around 800 words.

In paper 2, SL candidates choose one essay from three possibilities for each option; HL candidates choose two essays, each from different options. Paper 1 section B and paper 2 are assessed in the same way.

The command terms in section A relate to assessment objectives 1 and 2. The command terms in section B and paper 2 relate to assessment objectives 1–4. Take a look at the assessment objectives. The most important are assessment objectives 1 and 2. In paper 1 they are worth 70 per cent of the marks, and in paper 2 they are worth 60 per cent.

Assessment objectives relevant to SAQs and essays

Having followed the psychology course at SL and HL, students will be expected to demonstrate the following:

1 Knowledge and comprehension of:
   a specified content
   b key terms and concepts
   c psychological research methods
   d a range of appropriately identified psychological theories and research studies
   e the biological, cognitive, and sociocultural level of analysis
   f one option (SL) and two options (HL).

2 Application and analysis:
   a demonstrate an ability to use examples of psychological research and psychological

concepts to formulate an argument in response to a specific question.

3 Synthesis and evaluation:
   a evaluate psychological theories and empirical studies
   b discuss how biological, cognitive, and sociocultural levels of analysis can be used to explain behaviour
   c evaluate research methods used to investigate behaviour.

4 Selection and use of skills appropriate to psychology:
   a write an organized response.

Introduction to writing and arguing

In IB Diploma Programme psychology, the SAQs or essay questions may ask you to explain and evaluate a theoretical explanation of behaviour, question the interpretation of a study, or discuss various approaches to therapy, to mention just a few examples. No matter what the question is, you will need to *focus on the question*. Ask yourself: "what is my position on this particular question?" Then consider what *relevant knowledge* you will use to address the question, as well as your *line of argument*. You need to give your paper a *clear structure*, so that it is easy to follow your argument and the supporting evidence. Any SAQ or essay question will also ask you to apply some *critical thinking skills*.

The best approach to writing is to make an *outline* in order to see whether your answer makes sense. The outline will help you to structure your argument. If your answer does not have a main point, it cannot be arguing for anything. Asking yourself what your point is can help you to avoid writing the first thing that happens to come into your head or engaging in disorganized "information dump". What is stated here is true for the SAQs and the essays, but it is particularly true for the extended essay. Information dump will not give you high marks.

You cannot expect that the reader of your papers will accept anything you say simply as fact. You have to *argue*. This is basically about *persuasion*. In academic papers, arguing follows certain conventions that you need to learn.

When you write a paper in psychology, you write for what is called "an audience". The audience in this case is your teacher or an examiner. Think of your audience as someone you are supposed to convince, who is reasonably knowledgeable, but not necessarily an expert. You should also consider that your audience may not necessarily agree with you. It is your job to convince the audience by presenting good solid arguments and providing evidence. In psychology, empirical research and psychological theories count as evidence. It is not enough to express your opinion or feel very strongly about something in order to make your audience accept your claims.

Finally, you must be aware that your audience cannot read your mind. It is up to you to inform the reader through your explanation and interpretation of the evidence you present in support of your claim. This so-called **meta-text** is the key to good grades. You must spell out and say very clearly what you want the reader to understand after reading your paper. The reader should not be left to guess.

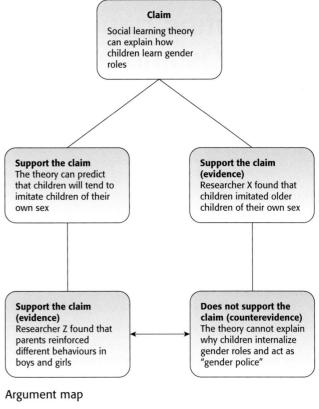

Argument map

Apply your analytical skills

Read the two answers below to the same SAQ and consider the following questions for each one.

1 Do they address the question asked—that is, do they *explain* how physiology and cognition interact?

2 Is there a clear structure?

3 Can you identify the main claim?

4 Can you see a clear argument in favour of the main claim?

5 Which SAQ is the best in your opinion? Support your answer.

SAQ 1: Using one psychological study, explain how physiology and cognition interact

Cortisol is a hormone that impairs memory. Cortisol is released via the adrenal glands and it can also depress the immune response. People become ill if they have too much cortisol in their blood. Newcomer et al. (1999) carried out an experiment with three groups of people. One of them got a tablet with a lot of cortisol and the rest got less cortisol or a placebo. They wanted to see what the reaction was. The study was conducted in a laboratory and there was a lot of control, so this affects the ecological validity. The result of the study was that cortisol caused memory impairment because the participants could not recall some information that they should recall after four days. It was a test of their declarative memory. Declarative memory is memory for facts. There is also something called biographical memory and procedural memory. Newcomer did an experiment where he manipulated an independent variable and measured the effect of that on the dependent variable, so there was a cause-and-effect relationship between levels of cortisol and memory processes.

(word count 179)

SAQ 2: Using one psychological study, explain how physiology and cognition interact

A study by Newcomer et al. (1999) investigated how the hormone cortisol influences memory functioning in a laboratory experiment. Cortisol is a stress hormone, and it is believed that prolonged secretion of cortisol is the cause of the memory impairment, which is one of the symptoms of chronic stress. The researchers used three experimental groups. Group one was given 40mg of cortisol in a tablet per day of the four-day experiment. Group two was given 160mg cortisol in a tablet and group three was given a placebo tablet. After four days, the participants were asked to listen to and recall a prose paragraph that tested their verbal declarative memory.

The results of the experiment clearly indicated that the participants who were given the high level of cortisol showed a significant impairment of memory. This supports the claim that there is a link between physiology and cognition, because it is well known from scanner studies that chronic stress can result in shrinking of the hippocampus, a brain structure which is very important in memory processes. Newcomer's study showed that even short-term increases in cortisol secretion can have a damaging effect on memory. Since it was an experiment, it can be concluded that there is a cause-and-effect relationship between levels of cortisol and memory processes.

(word count 215)

Writing short-answer questions in paper 1 section A

As indicated, the short-answer question is *short*. This means that there is no introduction and no conclusion. You simply answer the question as it is. You do not need to evaluate in the SAQs since this is part of assessment objectives 3 and 4. The following points provide a guide to writing SAQs.

1 Read the question carefully. What are the *command terms*? What *content* are you to address? Make sure that you address the question as it is written.

2 Make a brief outline, with a possible structure and key words according to the question. Divide the answer according to the question. If you have to address two factors, structure the answer so that you first address one and then the other.

3 Start the opening line in the SAQ by repeating the essentials of the question.

4 Write a reasoned argument in relation to each part of the question. This means that you should include relevant evidence (research) to support your answer.

Example: **Outline two principles that define the cognitive level of analysis.**

The command term is *outline*. This means that you have to give a brief account or summary.

You are asked to deal with two principles that define the cognitive level of analysis. You should produce two small paragraphs in the SAQ, each with a relevant principle.

Practise your skills

Here is an example of an SAQ from the cognitive level of analysis, with a sample answer from a student using the model outlined above. Read the answer carefully and then assess it using the mark bands below. Decide where you will place the SAQ and give your reasons for this, using the criteria set out in the mark bands.

Outline two principles that define the cognitive level of analysis.

Two principles that define the cognitive level of analysis are that mental processes guide behaviour and that cognitive processes are influenced by social and cultural factors.

Cognitive psychologists see the mind as a complex machine—or rather, like an intelligent, information-processing machine. According to this line of thinking, the input to the mind comes via bottom-up processing (from the sensory system), and the information is then processed in the mind by an active top-down processing via pre-stored information in the memory (schemas). Humans use these cognitive schemas to make sense of the world. Stereotypes are examples of cognitive schemas. Research has demonstrated that stereotyping can cause discrimination.

The second principle that defines the cognitive level of analysis is that cognitive processes are influenced by social and cultural factors. One of the first to say this was the British psychologist Frederic Bartlett (1932). Bartlett claimed that cognitive schemas are culturally determined. He asked people from a western culture to recall a Native American story. When he asked them to recall the story, they remembered the meaning of the story, but many of the details were changed to fit with their own cultural schemas. This experiment can explain why it is difficult to remember something unfamiliar. Bartlett demonstrated that memory is not like a tape recorder, but rather that people change information so that it makes sense to them.

(word count 227)

Assessment details for paper 1 section A (SL and HL)

Mark band	Level descriptor
zero	The answer does not reach a standard described by the descriptors below.
low	There is an attempt to answer the question, but knowledge and understanding are limited, often inaccurate, or of marginal relevance to the question.
mid	The question is partially answered. Knowledge and understanding are accurate, but limited. Either the command term is not effectively addressed or the response is not sufficiently explicit in answering the question.
high	The question is answered in a focused and effective manner and meets the demands of the command term. The response is supported by appropriate and accurate knowledge, and understanding of research.

Writing essays for paper 1 section A and paper 2

What is said about focus, structure, and argument in the SAQ section is equally relevant for the essay. The purpose of the essay is also for you to show that you have relevant knowledge (criterion A), that you can apply critical thinking skills, such as evaluation and analysis (criterion B), and, finally, that you can structure the essay and build an argument (criterion C).

Introduction to writing essays in papers 1 and 2

Read the essay question very carefully. Identify command terms and content. What exactly are you supposed to do (command terms) and with what (key words in relation to content)? This first step in essay writing is very important, since everything in your answer must relate to the essay question and nothing else.

Before you start writing the essay itself, it is a good idea to make an outline following "the principle of six paragraphs". This model leaves two paragraphs for the introduction and the conclusion, and four for the development. Each paragraph should contain a single argument, backed up by relevant research as a response to the essay question. The question may be parted, but the total marks awarded are given for the whole response to the question according to the assessment criteria.

Making a plan is particularly important, since organization of the essay is one of the skills assessed. If you spend 10 minutes planning, you will still have 50 minutes to write and check the essay at the end. Outline what should be addressed with reference to the essay question. Then write *relevant* theory and empirical studies, and a few key words to indicate how they are included in the argument. This outline could take the form of a mind-map. The most important thing in this exercise is to search for a possible argument and relevant evidence to support it.

Why spend time on this? Provided you have the relevant knowledge, a good plan allows you to write a good quality answer with a coherent argument that is substantiated, as compared to a poor quality answer which is chaotic and disorganized.

The traditional structure of an essay

The accepted convention is that an essay consists of an introduction, a main body, and a conclusion. This is also the structure you learn in theory of knowledge. Here is a brief overview of the content of the different parts.

The **introduction** must introduce the essay question and your line of argument. This could be in the form of a main claim (thesis statement), depending on the essay question. It gives the reader an idea of what to expect in terms of answering the question. Normally, the introduction is a short and focused paragraph. It must deal with the demands of the essay question—for example, what is the issue to be addressed? why is it important? and what line of argument have you chosen?

The **main body** must present information in a clear and logical manner. It should build an argument to answer the essay question. If there are questions divided into parts, be sure to address each part. Each paragraph should contain an argument and include relevant knowledge to support it. Sometimes it is relevant to produce a counter-argument as well, but it depends on the essay question.

The **conclusion** should relate directly to the question raised. It is not just a summary of the whole essay, but rather relates to the argument and follows logically from what you have written in the main body. The conclusion is the ultimate answer, based on your argument.

Practise your writing skills

Here is an example of an essay question from paper 1 section B (the cognitive level of analysis).

Discuss the use of **one** research method in the cognitive level of analysis, with reference to **one** research study.

Eight steps towards a successful essay

Step one: Identify command terms. Discuss, which means: offer a considered and balanced review that includes a range of arguments, factors, or hypotheses. Opinions and conclusions should be presented clearly and supported by appropriate evidence.

Step two: Identify content. One research method in the cognitive level of analysis—for example, the experimental method (variable control).

Step three: Find one relevant research study: Loftus and Palmer (1974) on the role of leading questions on recall (memory).

Step four: What argument? (1) Why the experimental method is often used in the cognitive level of analysis. (2) Possible reasons for using it in Loftus and Palmer (1974). (3) Was it a good choice? (i.e. advantages and disadvantages in general, but specifically in Loftus and Palmer—evaluation)

Step five: Consider the argument. It could be that the cognitive level of analysis uses the experimental method when it is important to establish a cause-and-effect relationship, but that not all research within the cognitive level of analysis uses this method—for example, research into everyday memory.

Step six: Make an outline. Include your main points in the introduction and conclusion.

Step seven: Write according to your outline.

Step eight: Read through your essay and use the following checklist.

1 Does the introduction provide a brief introduction to your line of argument?

2 Did you address the essay question, and only that?

3 Did you include relevant knowledge—and only relevant knowledge (theories and empirical studies)—to support the argument?

4 Does your answer demonstrate critical thinking skills? (e.g. evaluation and analysis)

5 Is your answer clearly organized and focused on the essay question?

6 Is your argument well developed?

7 Does the conclusion follow logically from your argument?

Possible outline

Introduction: Explain why the experimental method is used in the cognitive level of analysis and how this is illustrated in Loftus and Palmer (1974).

Paragraph 1: The cognitive level of analysis—briefly discuss why the experimental method is used in some studies.

Paragraph 2: Characteristics of the experimental method, including strengths and limitations.

Paragraph 3: Why the experimental method was used in Loftus and Palmer (1974) rather than another method.

Paragraph 4: Briefly describe the study, focusing on experimental features (aim, procedure, results, and interpretation of results) to justify the use of the experiment.

Paragraph 5: Evaluation.

Conclusion: The experimental method has proved useful in research studies on memory, but it is important to be aware of the limitations of the method, especially when generalizing to real-life memory.

Assessment details for paper 1 section B and paper 2 (SL and HL)

A. Knowledge and comprehension

Marks	Level description
0	The answer does not reach a standard described by the descriptors below.
1–3	The answer demonstrates limited knowledge and understanding that is of marginal relevance to the question. Little or no psychological research is used in the response.
4–6	The answer demonstrates limited knowledge and understanding relevant to the question, or uses relevant psychological research to limited effect in the response.
7–9	The answer demonstrates detailed, accurate knowledge and understanding relevant to the question, and uses relevant psychological research effectively in support of the response.

B. Evidence of critical thinking: application, analysis, synthesis, evaluation

Marks	Level descriptor
0	The answer does not reach a standard described by the descriptors below.
1–3	The answer goes beyond description, but evidence of critical thinking is not linked to the requirements of the question.
4–6	The answer offers appropriate but limited evidence of critical thinking, or offers evidence of critical thinking that is only implicitly linked to the requirements of the question.
7–9	The answer integrates relevant and explicit evidence of critical thinking in response to the question.

C. Organization

Marks	Level descriptor
0	The answer does not reach a standard described by the descriptors below.
1–2	The answer is organized or focused on the question. However, this is not sustained throughout the response.
3–4	The answer is well organized, well developed, and focused on the question.

12 The internal assessment in psychology

Getting started

The internal assessment (IA) in IB Diploma Programme psychology is a replication of a *simple* experiment. For all candidates the first step is to choose an experiment to replicate. In principle, it can be any experiment, but you should choose one in which it is easy to identify the variables under investigation. The success of your own experiment is to a large extent dependent on finding an appropriate study for your research. It is essential that your research be based on an experiment that has been published: you should not invent something of your own.

Be aware of the following:

- SL candidates are required to carry out a simple replication of a published study.
- HL candidates may carry out a replication of a published study or make modifications to the original study.

What to do

The best advice is to keep your experiment *simple*. Here is a set of guidelines for getting started.

- Find the experiment first. Do not choose a topic and then spend hours looking for an experiment. There are several online sites, as well as studies in textbooks, which are appropriate for IA. Cognitive experiments on memory and perception are often easy to do.
- You must manipulate only *one* independent variable.
- You should measure only *one* dependent variable.
- Make sure that the data you will obtain are appropriate for the application of statistics (descriptive in SL/HL and inferential in HL).
- Experiments must meet ethical standards.
- Make an outline and deadline for the stages of your research, as well as what to do at each stage.

What to avoid

Be aware that there are certain things to avoid. Failure to do so means that your internal assessment will score zero. You must avoid:

- conformity and obedience studies
- animal research
- placebo experiments
- experiments involving ingestion (i.e. food, drink, smoking, drugs)
- experiments involving deprivation (e.g. sleep, food)
- experiments involving young children
- quasi-experiments—that is, studies where you do not manipulate the independent variable because it is naturally occurring (examples of naturally occurring variables are gender, age,

ethnicity, any personal characteristic of the members of the sample, culture, socioeconomic status, left- or right-handedness, native language, education level, or time of the day)

- correlational research that describes a relationship between variables, surveys, and observational studies
- using something that is "pre-packaged", such as a computer program or a pre-designed test, is not allowed—you must design your own materials

Ethical guidelines for IA

- Any experimental study that creates anxiety, stress, pain, or discomfort for participants is not permitted.

- Any experimental study that involves unjustified deception, involuntary participation, or invasion of privacy must be avoided.

- All participants must be informed before commencing the experimental study that they have the right to withdraw at any time. Pressure must not be placed on any individual to participate or to continue with the investigation.

- Each participant must be informed of the aims and objectives of the research and must be shown the results of the research.

- All data collected must be kept confidential.

- Participants must be debriefed and given a chance to withdraw their data.

- All candidates must ensure that all participants who are 16 years or older sign an informed consent statement. For experiments with participants under the age of 16, parental consent must be obtained. A copy of the paper used for obtaining consent must be included in the appendices in the internal assessment report.

Here is a brief overview of the main differences between SL and HL. You only have to consult the information for your own level of research.

SL	HL
Explain the study to be replicated	Review of literature (analysis of relevant background studies and theories) on the topic to be investigated
Study must be replicated	The study may be modified
Statement of the aim of the research	Statement of a null and research hypothesis
Descriptive stats are applied (measures of central tendency and dispersion)	Descriptive and inferential stats are applied; there is a statement of the significance of the data
Comparison of results to the original study	Comparison of results in light of the review of literature
Word limit: 1000–1500 words	Word limit: 1500–2000 words

Differences between HL and SL internal assessment

What should be in the internal assessment report?

The content of the report is on the last page in this chapter. The guidelines here follow the order of appearance of the assessment criteria so it starts with the introduction and then guides you through the different parts of your research and the report to show you how you will be assessed at the end of each part. Be aware that some assessment criteria are different for SL and HL.

Overview of assessment criteria for the IA

Criterion	HL	SL	Content	Max marks HL	Max marks SL
A	+	+	Introduction	5	2
B	+	+	Method: Design	2	2
C	+	+	Method: Participants	2	2
D	+	+	Method: Procedure	2	2
E		+	Results		4
E	+		(HL) Results descriptive	2	
F		+	Discussion		6
F	+		(HL) Results inferential	3	
G		+	Presentation		2
G	+		Discussion	8	
H	+		Citation of sources	2	
I	+		Report format	2	
Total				28	20

Writing your introduction

The introduction provides background information, as well as a rationale for the investigation. It is important that this section of the paper clearly sets out what you are going to investigate, and why the investigation is important. This is one of the sections of the IA which is significantly different for SL and HL students. At SL, the introduction includes the study that is being replicated and the aim of the study at hand. At HL, the introd This section is used to justify the aim of your own study. By reviewing related research studies, you can explain how a previous study relates to their own study, and explain the reason behind their prediction. This section should move from an introduction to the area of research (e.g. cognitive psychology) to more specific studies that are directly related to the current experiment (e.g. Kahneman and Tversky, 1979).

The SL introduction

The SL introduction should focus only on the study that is being replicated. Explain the study—that is, state the *aim, procedure, findings*, and *conclusions* of the original study. You will need this to make comparisons of your results to this study in the discussion.

After explaining the original experiment, you should state *why* you think the study is worth replicating. What value does this research have in our understanding of human behaviour? You should finalize your introduction by clearly stating the aim of your research. The aim should be a clear statement of what you are going to study. For example:

- **Aim:** to investigate the effects of particular adjectives on the formation of impressions.

- **Aim:** to investigate the effect of leading questions on estimation of speed in a car accident.

The HL introduction

The HL introduction must contain relevant previous research and relevant theories. The introduction should develop logically into a statement of the reason for the current experiment, ending with a clear statement of the investigation's aim(s) and hypotheses.

- You should begin with a general introduction to the psychological subject area under investigation.
- Then give a brief summary of the theory and key pieces of research associated with the topic under investigation. You should not include more than three pieces of relevant research. More is not necessarily better. Keep full details of your references while reading. The research you are replicating must be focused on the topic and logically lead to your own investigation.
- The rationale (reasons) behind your investigation: how did your ideas develop from the previous research and why was this considered to be an interesting area of investigation? You should specify the aim of your study and include details about why you chose your hypothesis.
- The introduction should end with a statement of your specific research hypothesis—that is, a clear prediction of what you expect to find through your investigation. The research hypothesis should be clearly justified by previous research. It should be written in an operationalized form, which is precisely testable.
- The null hypothesis (alternative hypothesis) should state that the results found are not due to the manipulation of variables, but rather due to chance.

Research and null hypotheses

In experimental research, psychologists first must state what they predict will happen. To do this, we state a null and a research hypothesis.

The null hypothesis states that there will be no effect of the manipulation of the independent variable on the dependent variable—in other words, the null hypothesis states that any difference found is due to random variables and not the manipulation of the independent variable.

The research hypothesis predicts *how* the independent variable is expected to affect the dependent variable.

The goal of research is not to *prove* the research hypothesis correct, but to *refute* the null hypothesis. In other words, we want to establish that there actually is a relationship between the IV and the DV, and that any results we have obtained were not just due to chance. When we can statistically establish that the results are not due to chance, the data are **significant**. When the data are significant, we *refute the null hypothesis*. When our data are not significant, we *retain the null hypothesis*. This simply means that the IV did not cause changes in the DV.

Examples of experimental hypotheses

H_0 **(null hypothesis):** The level of noise will have no significant effect on the number of words recalled.

H_1 **(research hypothesis):** Participants in the loud noise condition will recall significantly fewer words than people in the no noise condition.

A sample introduction for HL
(From an experiment on memory and schemas)

Cognitive psychology deals with mental processes such as memory. Research indicates that human memory is not just a replica of experience, but is in fact reconstructive. Memory is now largely studied from an information-processing approach, which focuses on encoding, storage, and retrieval. These three components are involved in the process of remembering. One of the most influential theories of information processing is schema theory based on the concept of schema, a concept first used by Bartlett (1932) as part of his theory of reconstructive memory.

Schema is a concept defined as an integrated mental network of knowledge, beliefs, and expectations concerning a particular topic or aspect of the world. It is believed to affect memory processes at many levels. Bartlett developed schema theory in his book *Remembering* (1932). His schema theory suggests that all new information interacts with the old information represented in the schema—that is, what we remember is influenced by our existing knowledge and experience. Our knowledge is stored in memory as a set of schema—simplified, generalized mental representations of everything we understand by a given type of object or event, based on our past experience. According to Bartlett, we reconstruct the past by trying to fit it into our existing schemas, and the more difficult this is to do, the more likely it is that elements are forgotten or distorted. On the basis of this, it could be expected that people will remember information that is consistent with their schema and forget schema-inconsistent information.

Schema theory provides us with ready-made expectations which help to interpret the flow of information reaching the senses, and help to make the world more predictable. Furthermore, schemas allow us to "fill in the gaps" when our memories are incomplete. Although Cohen (1993) criticized the schema theory on the basis that the concept of schema was too vague to be useful, schema theory has proved useful in our understanding of cognitive processing involved in remembering. Loftus and Palmer's (1974) experimental work with eyewitness testimony also demonstrated that human memory may be influenced by leading questions and "reconstructive memory" to fit the schema. This can be used to say that "memory may be influenced by schema processing".

Researchers have discussed when schemas influence information processing. One such study is by Anderson and Pitcher (1978), who found that schemas have some effect at retrieval as well as at encoding. In the same line, Brewer and Treyens (1981) tested memory for objects in a room. Participants were brought into an office room with a number of consistent and some inconsistent objects, and were told to wait. After 35 seconds' waiting in the office, the participants were called into another room and given the unexpected task of writing down what they could recall from the office room. The results showed that schema-consistent objects were more accurately recalled than schema-inconsistent ones. This indicated that memory for the scene was apparently strongly influenced by the pre-existing office schema, and when the participants had to recall details, they supplemented with default values from this schema. We have chosen to replicate Brewer and Treyens (1981) in our research because it is relevant to investigate if schema processing is actually as consistent as they found it to be.

Due to the suggestions of Bartlett, and Brewer and Treyens' (1981) study, the aim of this experiment is to determine if schema processing affects memory for places such as an office room in a school like Nørre Gymnasium. Our experiment will be carried out by presenting the participants with a list of mixed objects normally present in an office room (consistent), as well as objects not normally in an office room (inconsistent).

H_0 null hypothesis: There will be no difference in the recall of schema-consistent objects and schema-inconsistent objects.

H_1 research hypothesis: The mean number of schema-consistent objects recalled will be higher than the mean recall of schema-inconsistent objects.

How you are assessed
The following pages show you how to achieve the highest possible mark under each criterion for SL and HL respectively.

Criterion A: Introduction

SL (2 marks)	HL (5 marks)
The aim of the student's study is clearly stated. The study being replicated is clearly identified and relevant details of the study are explained.	The aim of the study is clearly stated. The background theories and studies are adequately explained and highly relevant to the hypotheses. The experimental and null hypotheses are appropriately stated and operationalized. The prediction made in the experimental hypothesis is justified by the background studies and theories.

The method section
This section is where you describe how your study was designed and carried out. In this section, you demonstrate your understanding of the experiment as a quantitative methodology. The section is subdivided into four parts, each with a label: design (criterion B), participants (criterion C), materials, and procedure (criterion D).

Design
Depending on what you investigate, you can choose between two basic designs: an *independent samples design* or a *repeated measures design*.

The independent samples design. This design makes use of two different groups of participants: one group is given the experimental treatment; the other group receives no treatment. For example, one group is given a list of words to memorize while listening to very loud, rhythmic music; the other group is simply given a list of words to memorize. The group in which the IV is manipulated—for example, music is played—is called the **treatment group**. The group that gets no treatment is called the **control group**. This group allow us to see how the list is memorized under normal circumstances. You may also have two different treatment groups, where one group gets one treatment (e.g. memorizing a list of words using imagery), and the other group gets a different treatment (e.g. memorizing a list of words using rehearsal). In such an experiment, you simply compare which treatment results in the highest recall.

The independent samples design is used when it is not possible to use the same participants in the two experimental conditions. This might be the case if your independent variable is the same sentence but with a slight variation, to test if one particular word influences recall. If you use the same participants, they would learn what to remember in the first trial and this would affect the second trial. This is called the **order effect**.

A strength of an independent samples design is that the participants are less likely to guess the hypothesis of the study. Another strength is that it is less likely that the participants will be bored or tired with the test, or that they will actually improve a skill simply through repetition—an example of order effects. A final strength is that the same materials may be used with both groups. For example, both groups could be given the same list of words to memorize under different conditions.

The limitation of using an independent samples design is that there may be **participant variability**—that is, the participants may differ so much (e.g. in memory ability) that the differences between the two groups may actually be due to this and not simply to the manipulation of the IV.

The repeated measures design. Because of the limitations of the independent measures design, researchers may use a repeated measures design. This design involves using the *same* participants in both the treatment and the control group. For example, the group is asked to memorize and recall a list of words (control group). Then they are asked to memorize and recall a similar list of words while listening to rock music (treatment group). One strength of this design is that it eliminates the problems of participant variability. Another strength is that it requires fewer participants. Ten participants would be enough for your IA.

However, a repeated measures design also has its limitations. First, doing the same task twice may result in order effects. Another potential problem is **demand characteristics**, when participants guess the aim of the study and do not act naturally because they want to be helpful—or the opposite. Lastly, a repeated measures design does not work for all types of experiments. It is best for experiments where the researcher wants to see how an IV may change participants' performance on a specific task—for example, in the Stroop test.

The design section

- Identify the design you have used—either independent samples or repeated measures.
- Explain and justify why you chose the design that you did (e.g. to avoid order effects) and describe the controls you have undertaken to avoid extraneous variables, (e.g. by giving a standardized briefing to the participants).
- Identify the independent and dependent variables.
- Document how ethical guidelines were followed—explain how consent was obtained and how the briefing and debriefing were carried out.

A copy of the letter of informed consent should be included in the appendices. Make sure that the consent form is written in a way that informs the participants of the nature of the experiment.

> - If you choose the independent samples design you need 20 participants (N=20)
> - If you choose the repeated measures design you need 10 participants (N=10)

Sample consent form

Dear Participant,

As part of my IB Psychology Internal Assessment, I am carrying out a study of memory. This study is going to test your ability to memorize a list of words while listening to music. After the briefing, I would ask you to sign the statement below:

- I have been informed about the nature of the experiment.
- I understand that I have the right to withdraw from the experiment at any time, and that any information/data about me will remain confidential.

➡

- My anonymity will be protected as my name will not be identifiable.
- The experiment will be conducted so that I will not be demeaned in any way.
- I will be debriefed at the end and have the opportunity to find out the results.

I give my informed consent to participating in this experiment.

Name and date:

Standardized briefing notes are a copy of the script that you used in the briefing of your participants. These include the aim and instructions regarding the procedure of the study, as well as information about ethical issues. Attach the standardized briefing notes to the appendices.

By using standardized briefing, you ensure that you control extraneous variables that could interfere with the experiment.

Standardized debriefing notes are a copy of the script that you used in the debriefing of your participants when the experimental procedure was over. The notes should include what you expect to find in your study, and that participants can learn about the conclusions drawn from the research when you have completed your analysis of the data. You should remind participants that they have the right to withdraw their data, in keeping with ethical standards. Attach the standardized debriefing notes as an appendix.

How you are assessed

Criterion B: Design

SL (2 marks)	HL (2 marks)
The independent variable and dependent variable are accurately identified and operationalized. The experimental design is appropriate to the aim and its use is appropriately justified. There is clear indication and documentation of how ethical guidelines were followed.	The independent variable and dependent variable are accurately identified and operationalized. The experimental design is appropriate to the aim and its use is appropriately justified. There is clear indication and documentation of how ethical guidelines were followed.

Participants

The *participants* section of the IA describes the sample and how it was obtained. A sample of 20 participants is sufficient. Larger samples are strongly discouraged in an IA experiment.

Sampling procedures should be identified and justified. The sampling method (random, opportunity) must be identified, and you must explain why this sampling method was chosen. It is enough to say that opportunity sampling was the easiest, for example. In addition, the manner in which participants were allocated to the treatment or control group should be explained.

Relevant characteristics of the sample should be identified—for example, in terms of colour-blindness or English proficiency. It is normal procedure to describe the sample in terms of the number of participants, age, and gender distribution.

Example: The 20 participants (N=20) were evenly distributed between males and females; the mean age was 16. Because of the nature of the experiment, it was important that participants were not colour-blind and that they were fluent in English.

HL

HL candidates also need to identify the target population. Remember, the target population is the group you are interested in and the one from which you draw your sample. It is also the one to which you will be able to generalize your results. This means that if your target population is IB students or non-native English-speaking students, you will be able to generalize the results only to IB students or to non-native English-speaking students respectively.

How you are assessed

Criterion C: Participants

SL (2 marks)	HL (2 marks)
Relevant characteristics of the participants are identified. The sample is selected using an appropriate method and the use of this method is explained.	Relevant characteristics of the participants are identified. The sample is selected using an appropriate method and the use of this method is explained. The target population has been identified and is appropriate.

Materials

This section is a list of materials developed for use in the experiment. Basic materials, such as tables, chairs, paper, and pencils should not be listed. Any written materials (e.g. list of words to recall) that were specially developed for the experiment should be listed and referenced to a sample copy included in an appendix. The standardized briefing notes, informed consent letters, and standardized debriefing notes should be included in an appendix.

Procedure

You must carefully and accurately describe how the experiment was carried out, step by step. Enough detail should be provided so that another researcher could replicate the experiment. It must include reference to any ethical issues that were addressed—for example, when briefing and debriefing were carried out.

Procedures may be written either as a paragraph or in bullet-point format. If you are writing in bullet points, make sure that enough detail is there for someone to replicate your procedure.

How you are assessed

Criterion D: Procedure

SL (2 marks)	HL (2 marks)
The procedural information is relevant, clearly described and is easily replicable. Necessary materials have been included and referenced in the appendices. Ethical guidelines were followed.	The procedural information is relevant, clearly described and is easily replicable. Necessary materials have been included and referenced in the appendices. Ethical guidelines were followed.

Results

The results should be stated in (1) a narrative form (i.e. by means of a written statement) and in (2) a graphic form. The reader should be able to understand the results by only reading the text or only looking at the graph and table. The data should be reported in a way that reflects the aim of the research hypothesis.

The data collected in research can represent different levels of detail. The difference in the levels of information that can be carried by numbers is referred to as *levels of measurement of the data*. There are four levels of measurement.

Nominal. Data at the nominal level are the simplest. The data collected are placed in categories and you simply count how many fall into each category, for example smokers and non-smokers.

Data at the nominal level provide the least amount of information of all. Only the mode can be used as a measure of central tendency.

Ordinal. Ordinal data can be put into ranks. For example, women who participate in a judo competition are ranked as number 1, 2 or 3. We cannot say anything about how much better number 1 did compared with numbers 2 and 3—only who came in first, second, and third.

An example of data at the ordinal level could also be Likert scales, such as the following: (1) strongly agree, (2) agree, (3) disagree, (4) strongly disagree.

Interval. Data at the interval level are measured on a scale which has precise and equal intervals. Temperature is a good example. If the temperature today is 24 degrees Celsius, you know accurately what the weather is like. Other examples of interval data could be IQ scores or the number of correctly recalled items in a memory test. Data at the interval level carries much more information than ordinal data.

The mean, median, and mode may be calculated for interval data. If you rank interval data, they become ordinal data—for example, Peter is 179cm tall, and Pierre is 180cm, so Pierre is the tallest and Peter is the smallest.

Ratio. Data at the ratio level have all the characteristics of interval data, plus they have a true zero point—for example, weight in grammes is a ratio scale, as something cannot weigh −600g.

The results section

In this section you need to describe your results in words (narrative) and using tables and graphs which result from calculation of **descriptive statistics**. You should calculate both the central tendency and dispersion if the level of measurement of your data allows it. Depending on your data, you choose either the mean, median, or mode. Raw data should not be included here, but must be in an appendix. Only summarized data should appear in the results section.

Ratio and interval levels of measurement usually lend themselves to more effective statistical analysis. These are particularly useful for

> **Levels of measurement of data**
>
> **N**ominal
> **O**rdinal
> **I**nterval
> **R**atio

analysis using descriptive statistics, as nearly all measures of both central tendency and dispersion can be calculated.

Nominal-level data have fewer appropriate descriptive statistics that may be calculated, and the only appropriate calculation is the mode. It is not recommended for SL students to carry out research that only produces nominal data, since descriptive statistical analysis is limited.

Measures of central tendency	
Mean	Not influenced by outliers (extreme scores) A very imprecise stat; not very useful if there are many modes
Median	Not distorted by outliers Can be distorted by small samples
Mode	The most sensitive measure of central tendency Can by distorted by outliers
Measures of dispersion	
Range	Easy to calculate, but distorted by outliers
Standard deviation	The most sensitive measure of dispersion using all data

Descriptive stats: measures of central tendency and dispersion

All these descriptive statistics may be calculated easily using your calculator. You do not need to include calculation of descriptive statistics in your appendices.

As stated previously, it is important to know the level of measurement of data because this indicates what measures of central tendency and dispersion we can calculate. It is not considered correct to calculate the mean on data that are not at least interval. Level of measurement also affects what types of graphs and tables you can use, and influences choice of statistical tests (HL only).

Level of measurement of data	Possible descriptive stat	Possible tables and charts
Nominal	Percentages; mode	Frequency table; pie chart; bar chart
Ordinal	Percentages; median	Frequency table; frequency polygon; bar chart
Interval and ratio	Mean, median, mode Quartiles Range, standard deviation	Frequency table; box and Whisker plot; bar chart; histogram

Appropriate choice of descriptive stat and graphs according to type of data

Graphs and tables may be drawn using a computer. No matter what graph you choose, it must accurately reflect the data in relation to the prediction of the research hypothesis. One graph is sufficient. Computers can create many nice graphs, but it is not advised to produce irrelevant graphs. The report should not include graphs showing each individual participant's score.

Inferential statistics: HL only

HL students must include inferential statistical analysis of the results in this section. Candidates must justify the use of the inferential statistical test chosen. Any calculations should be in an appendix and not included in your results section.

There are three statistical tests that are generally used for the IA.

You should refer to the design of your experiment and the level of measurement of your data in justification of your choice of the statistical test. Here are the necessary details for the statistical tests that are recommended for the IB internal assessment in psychology.

- The **Chi Square test:** used for nominal data in an independent samples design in an experiment testing a difference between two conditions.
- The **Mann Whitney U test:** used for at least ordinal data in an independent samples design in an experiment testing a difference between two conditions.
- The **Wilcoxon Signed Ranks test:** used for at least ordinal data in a repeated measures design in an experiment testing a difference between two conditions.

Though other statistics may be used in principle, it is recommended that you use these tests in your internal assessment. If, for some reason, you decide to use other tests, be sure to justify their use properly. In principle, parametric tests such as the t-test can be used if they are properly justified—for example saying that although the criteria for a parametric test are not met, these tests are very robust.

You can find good instructions on calculations of statistical tests in books. There are also suitable sites on the Internet where you can insert your own data once you have chosen the appropriate test. You are not required to include calculations in the appendix if you use an online source.

How you are assessed

Criterion E: Results and criterion F: Results inferential stat (HL)

SL (4 marks) (criterion E)	HL (2 marks) Descriptive stats (criterion E)	HL (3 marks) Inferential stats (criterion F)
Results are clearly stated and accurate and reflect the aim of the research. Appropriate descriptive statistics are applied to the data and their use is explained. The graph of the results is accurate, clear and directly relevant to the aim of the study. Results are presented both in words and tabular form.	Results are clearly stated and accurate and reflect the hypotheses of the research. Appropriate descriptive statistics are applied to the data and their use is explained. The graph of the results is accurate, clear and directly relevant to the study. Results are presented both in words and tabular form.	An appropriate inferential statistical test has been chosen and explicitly justified. Results of the inferential statistical test are accurately stated. The null hypothesis has been accepted or rejected appropriately according to the results of the statistical test. A statement of statistical significance is appropriate and clear.

The discussion section

The discussion is the final part of the paper. This is an important part of your report, so make sure you do everything that is set out in the assessment criteria. In this section, you interpret your own results in the light of previous research. You must relate your findings to each of the theories or studies referred to in the introduction, and say how your results differed and where they were in line with the study you replicated. Then you need to say why you think you achieved the results you did. No new studies or citations should be introduced.

You should analyse and evaluate your methodology. Be sure to discuss the limitations that may have affected the outcome of the experiment. The strongest reports will identify possible extraneous variables that may have influenced the study, and will not rely on a simplistic evaluation, such as "the experimental study should have used a larger sample". Suggestions for modifications for future replications should also be included. Ideally, these should address the limitations you have identified in your own study.

It is a convention to finish the discussion with suggestions for further research that may have arisen during an investigation but was not dealt with in the actual study. You are supposed to do the same. You could say that your results showed that noise is an important factor in people's ability to recall information, but that you did not investigate whether people recall better if there is only background noise. This could be a topic for further investigation.

Finally, a brief conclusion should be presented, summarizing the results of the experiment.

How you are assessed

Criterion F: Discussion and criterion G: Discussion (HL)

SL (6 marks) Criterion F	HL (8 marks) Criterion G
Discussion of results is well developed (e.g., differences in the results of calculations of central tendency and/or dispersion may be explained). The findings of the student's experimental study are discussed with reference to the study being replicated. Limitations of the design and procedure are highly relevant and have been rigorously analyzed. Modifications are suggested and ideas for further research may be mentioned. The conclusion is appropriate,	Analysis of results is well developed and complete (e.g., descriptive and inferential statistics are discussed). The findings of the student's experimental study are discussed with reference to relevant background studies and theories. Limitations of the design and procedure are highly relevant and have been rigorously analyzed. Modifications are suggested and ideas for further research may be mentioned. The conclusion is appropriate.

Presentation (SL) and citation of sources and report format (HL)

For SL the final marks for the IA are for presentation of the overall report. The requirements here are valid for both SL and HL. This includes, among other things, that the report is in the correct format, that references are provided, and that the abstract is clearly written. For HL students, this is where marks for citation are also awarded.

Here are some points to consider for a good report.

Title page

The title page provides essential information about both you and your IA. The title should give a clear indication of the experimental method and the specific topic of the study. The hypothesis will determine how the title is constructed. For example, if the operationalized research hypothesis is "The mean number of words correctly recalled by a group using a list with category headings will be greater than the mean number of words correctly recalled by a group not using category headings", then an appropriate title could be, "An experiment to investigate the effect of category headings on the recall of a list of words". A title such as "An experiment on memory" is not specific and is therefore inadequate. The title must include the method used (experiment), the topic under investigation (recall), and the variables (category headings and their impact on word recall).

Abstract (max. 200 words)

The abstract contains a summary of important information about the study. It clearly states the aim, procedure, results, and conclusion. The independent and dependent variables are identified. The abstract should be the last section of the report to be written, and should contain fewer than 200 words.

References

In this section, include a complete set of references to all the works cited in the study. Do not include works that are not cited. An approved reference format should be used, such as that of the American Psychological Association or the British Psychological Society. These formats are freely available on the Internet.

For HL students it is especially important to provide proper references to all in-text citations since this is assessed in criterion H.

Appendices

In this section, include blank copies of any supplementary information, as well as the materials used, such as standardized instructions, debriefing notes, informed consent letters, and calculations. This section provides all the materials necessary to allow the experiment to be replicated. Tables of raw data must be included here. However, it is not necessary to include all participant responses—one blank copy or a sample is sufficient. Make sure that each appendix is numbered and has an appropriate title—for example, Appendix 4: Calculation of the Mann Whitney U.

How you are assessed

Criterion G: Presentation (SL), criterion H: Citation of sources (HL) and criterion I: Report format (HL)

SL (2 marks) Presentation (criterion G)	HL (2 marks) Citation of sources (criterion H)	HL (3 marks) Report format (criterion I)
The report is in the correct format and within the word limit of 1,000–1,500 words. The report is complete and in the required format. The reference for the study being replicated is cited using a standard method of listing references. The abstract is clearly written and includes a summary overview of the student's experimental study, including the results.	All in-text citations and references are provided. A standard documentation style is used consistently throughout the body of the report and references section.	The report is within the word limit of 1500 -2000 words. The report is complete and in the required format. Appendices are labelled appropriately and are referenced in the body of the report. The abstract is clearly written and includes a summary overview of the student's experimental study, including the results.

	Standard Level	Higher Level
Title page	● Title	
	● Candidate name and number	
	● Subject and level	
	● Date of submission	
	● Word count	
Abstract	● Summary of aims	
	● Identify IV and DV	
	● Summary of procedure	
	● Summary of results	
	● Conclusion	
Introduction	● Summary of aims, procedure, and results of study replicated	● Review of background literature (theories and studies)
	● Statement of aim of study	● Aim of study
		● Null and research hypotheses
Method	● Design: type and justification of design; controls; ethical procedures; identification of IV and DV	
	● Participants: relevant characteristics of sample, sampling techniques, and justification; relevant characteristics of target population identified	
	● Materials: list of materials used; reference to copies in appendices	
	● Procedures: itemized in sufficient detail to allow full replication	
Results	● Narrative account of results	● Narrative account of results
	● Calculation and interpretation of descriptive statistics and use explained	● Calculation and interpretation of descriptive statistics, including graph that reflects the aim of the study
	● Graph that reflects the aim of the study	
		● Analysis using inferential statistics and justification for their use
Discussion	● Discussion of results	● Discussion of results
	● Linking of results to study being replicated	● Linking of results to literature review in the introduction
	● Identification of limitations of methodology	● Identification of limitations of the methodology
	● Suggestions for modification and further research	● Suggestions for modification and further research
	● Statement of conclusion	● Statement of conclusion
Presentation	● Word limit 1000–1500 words	● Word limit 1500–2000 words
	● References of works cited	● Works cited within the report
Appendices	● Supplementary information	
	● One copy of the instrument(s)/materials used	
	● Copy of standardized briefing and debriefing notes	

Summary of report format

13 The extended essay in psychology

Psychology is a fascinating subject, so there are probably areas of psychology that you would like to explore further. The extended essay is an excellent chance to do just that. It is not recommended to write an extended essay in psychology unless psychology is part of your diploma programme.

The extended essay is a challenge on many academic levels, since it requires you to apply research and communication skills as well as critical thinking. This last part is linked to psychology's concern with interpreting and evaluating evidence, and building arguments to support claims. Before you start writing, it is important to familiarize yourself with the assessment criteria.

Research involves hard work, but also a lot of pleasure. Conducting independent research—although under supervision—encourages you to experience the same intellectual challenge as researchers. Like them, you must plan the project, select and evaluate knowledge, and, last but not least, communicate the result of your inquiry in a formal way, using psychological concepts and terms relevant to your area of research. You are *not* expected to produce new knowledge in psychology during your research. The purpose of writing the extended essay is mainly to show that you can research a topic that is new to you and show a new angle on the topic you have chosen.

In psychology, the extended essay is **literature based**. This means that you should read scientific journals and books that deal with the topic you are investigating. Based on your reading, you must formulate a *focused research question* and find appropriate material to answer it. The extended essay should be in the form of an argument for its conclusion. An extended essay in psychology cannot be an experiment, and you are not supposed to carry out interviews to collect data.

About the extended essay (EE)

The EE is a compulsory part of the IB Diploma Programme, which should take around 40 hours of work to complete. The EE is an *independent*, in-depth investigation on a topic chosen by the student in cooperation with a supervisor. The result should be presented as a formal piece of scholarship, within a maximum of 4000 words.

Aim of the extended essay

In working on the extended essay in psychology, you are expected to:

1 plan and pursue a research project with intellectual initiative and insight
2 formulate a precise research question
3 gather and interpret material from sources appropriate to the research question
4 structure a reasoned argument in response to the research question, on the basis of the material gathered
5 present your extended essay in a format appropriate to psychology, acknowledging sources in one of the established academic ways
6 use the terminology and language appropriate to psychology with skill and understanding
7 apply analytical and evaluative skills appropriate to psychology, with an understanding of the implications and the context of their research.

The research process

All research takes time. It is not possible to produce a good extended essay in a few days. Ideally, you should plan to spend some time on your extended essay every day over the course of a few months. This gives you time for reading and discussing progress with your supervisor. One of the first things to do is to make a plan for the progress of your writing, as well as an overview of official deadlines. Make a list of internal deadlines and decide what to do when. After some time, you may have to readjust your plan, but try to keep track of the progress of your work as well as the deadlines, in order to avoid stress.

Make sure you make appointments with your supervisor and come prepared for the consultations. Your supervisor can give you advice on how to find resources and how to formulate good research questions, so do not miss out on this opportunity. Regular contact with your supervisor ensures that you are on the right track. The figure below provides an overview of the research process.

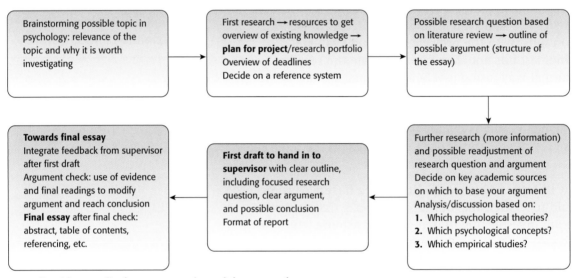

From first ideas to final essay—overview of the research process

Brainstorming possible topics

The most important aspect of research is to find a *topic* that you are interested in, because you have to spend quite a long time on this project. Look around. What psychological problems do you find relevant? You may have noticed that some people smoke and others do not, and you want to find out why this is so. Maybe you wonder why people stereotype and discriminate, or maybe you would like to know if a traumatic childhood will ruin an individual's life. Perhaps you want to know why people become depressed and how they are treated. There are many interesting topics out there for you to explore.

Whatever catches your interest, ask yourself why it is worth investigating and how it could be relevant to people's lives. When you have decided on a topic, you need to find resources so that you can discover how this topic can be approached. Some of the more exotic topics (e.g. serial killers) can be very difficult for students to deal with in an academic manner, so such topics are not recommended.

From topic to first research

The next step is to find a more focused research problem within the topic you have chosen. Now you have to find appropriate sources to deal with it. A general rule is that if you cannot find appropriate academic resources, you should find another topic. Start searching on the Internet or in encyclopedias to get an idea of the knowledge that is available. Talk to your supervisor, who will guide you in your literature search.

Even though you do not know exactly what you are looking for at the beginning of the research process, you can make a preliminary plan once you have assembled some material and done some reading on your topic. You should sketch a rough outline that indicates the direction of your inquiry. This plan may change as you proceed because you find new information. This is perfectly normal in a research process.

Make a research portfolio with summaries of readings and citation of references so that you can keep track of your sources. From the very first day, you should start writing. Whenever you read something useful (e.g. a piece of research), you should summarize the main points and make sure you have the exact reference. Writing helps you to better understand and reflect on what you are reading and how you can use it to deal with the research problem you have identified. Apply critical thinking skills, such as questioning the validity of the information. Add these comments to the draft.

Most students use a computer to keep track of their research. You can create an extended essay folder (research portfolio), with different subfolders so that you have all material in one place. It is also possible to establish an archive based on cards as you go along, or simply use a notebook. Any organized system can help you to have an overview of the research process and to keep track of your sources and your private notes on them.

Decide which reference system to use (e.g. APA) and use it consistently throughout the research process. Proper referencing is the academic way of demonstrating academic honesty.

> **Academic honesty**
> Plagiarism is defined as using the ideas or work of another person and presenting them as one's own. One of the most important rules in the academic world is to avoid plagiarism. It is expected that researchers cite other researchers to give them credit for their work. You should do the same. Citing sources is an important tool in academic writing because it allows you to place your own work in the context of previous research, and to provide an overview of the sources you have used in your work.

Deciding on a research question

The purpose of reading is to deepen your understanding of the topic and to collect evidence and generate ideas for the content of the essay. Reading on a topic means finding out what is already known. You need relevant knowledge in order to formulate a research question yourself. At the beginning, you are just looking for possible topics, but eventually these topics are narrowed down to a few possible research areas. Once you have decided on a topic, you can begin to think about a possible research question. Consult your supervisor to discuss your research question(s), in order to narrow the scope of the question. Now it is time to make a preliminary outline, with a research question and possible ways to answer it. This is the core of your argument.

Further research—structuring the essay and the argument

You should construct preliminary arguments very early in the research process. This will help you to gain clarity of your own thinking. In research, you are supposed to present objective and logical arguments that are faithful to the evidence. You should also be able to see a question from different sides if you are to produce counter-arguments. If you include quotations, be sure to copy them correctly and note the reference.

Once you have made an outline plan for the essay, you can transform it into a structured draft of the essay. Use headings and subheadings. This draft can be used to write single paragraphs, and it helps you to organize the argument. You can always remove or move text later in the process. If you want to make changes to an existing draft, you can create a new version of the draft on the computer after saving it, by using "Save as". Give this new version a new name—for example, EE_version 5_091008.

Structuring the extended essay

The structure of the extended essay in psychology follows a standard for academic writing which includes an introduction, a body (or development), and a conclusion.

The **introduction** is meant to present the problem under investigation and show why it is important and worthy of investigation. Some details related to the background of the problem should be outlined briefly in order to place the problem in a relevant context before the research question itself is presented. It is also the norm to present briefly some of the most important research in the area, in order to justify your own research question. Perhaps you want to question existing findings or interpretations, or maybe you want to show that there are important points that have been overlooked. Make sure that you present your research question very clearly in this part of your essay. It is also a good idea to include your main claim (thesis statement) here.

The **body** is the main part of your extended essay. It contains the different parts of your argument in relation to your main claim(s). This is where you try to convince the reader that your claim is valid—for example, that women are more likely to suffer from anorexia because the cultural body ideal of women in the West is being thin—because you can *document* your argument with valid evidence. It is important that your argument is structured in a logical way. Avoid emotional reasoning and the use of unsupported claims. (See more later on how to construct arguments.)

The reader cannot guess what you are thinking, so you should explain how to interpret empirical studies in the light of your research question. This includes evaluation of the studies—for example, in terms of cultural, ethical, methodological, or gender considerations, which are part of the critical thinking skills referred to in the psychology guide. You need to convince the reader that your claim is correct. The only way to do so is to present solid evidence.

The **conclusion** summarizes the leading facts in the argument. It must be clear, consistent with the thesis statement, and relevant to the evidence that has been presented. It should also include any unresolved questions that have emerged from the research.

Constructing the argument—knowing how to argue in psychology

When you write, think about the reader. The main claim of your essay is a response to the research question. Basically, you should see the essay as an argument where the aim is to convince the reader. You cannot expect the reader to think like you do, and this is why your extended essay must have a clear structure and the arguments must be clearly understandable. Remember that you must explain to the reader what your point is and support this with evidence all the way through. You should expect your reader to question any part of your argument, so you have to anticipate their questions and acknowledge these.

TV violence can have harmful psychological effects on children *claim* because their constant exposure to violent images makes them unable to distinguish fantasy from reality *reason supporting claim*. Smith (1997) found that children aged 5–9 who watched more than three hours of violent television a day were 25% more likely to say that most of what they saw on televison was "really happening" *evidence*.

It is possible, of course, that children who tend to watch greater amounts of violent entertainment already have violent values *counter-claim*, but Jones (1989) found that children with no predisposition to violence were just as attracted to violent entertainment as those with a history of violence *response to counter-claim*.

Reference: Booth, W.C., Colomb, G.G., and Williams, J.M. (2003) *The Craft of Research*, 2nd edn. Chicago and London: University of Chicago Press, pp.114–23.

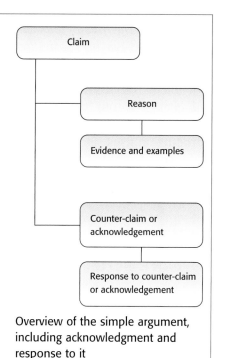

Overview of the simple argument, including acknowledgment and response to it

First draft

The first draft is a paper which probably gives your supervisor an idea of where you are heading and what your argument is. It is a good idea to hand in a first draft that looks much like the final essay, in terms of structure, argument, and possible conclusion. The reference section should be included in the first draft so that your supervisor can help you correct possible errors. You may not be in a position to write the abstract at this point, but if you have more or less completed your research, then include the abstract in the first draft. Make sure you check the required format of the extended essay—for example, word count, table of contents.

Towards the final essay

Use the feedback from your supervisor carefully. You may have a face-to-face meeting where your supervisor can elaborate on comments and you can discuss alterations. This feedback is very important.

Check once again if your paper lives up to the format of an extended essay.

Now it is time to go through your paper carefully to check your argument. You might carry out some final reading and add this to your paper, but avoid adding too much new material at this point. Concentrate on the essentials, such as language, word limit, clarity of argument, use of evidence, and referencing. When you have finished, you should make a final check, based on the assessment criteria, to see if your essay is consistent with each criterion (A to K). After this check, it is time to hand in the final version of your extended essay.

Criterion A: Research question (maximum 2 marks)

Descriptor. *The research question is clearly stated in the introduction and sharply focused, making effective treatment possible within the word limit.*

The most important thing in a successful extended essay in psychology is to formulate a clear and focused research question that enables you to handle it within the 4000 words. The research question should be clearly justified and precisely stated in the introduction itself. Be aware that if the research question is not clear and focused, you will not only lose marks here, but also in criteria C, D, and E.

> ### From topic to research question—some examples
>
> **Topic:** Attachment
>
> **Research question:** To what extent are attachment patterns culturally determined?
>
> **Topic:** Anorexia
>
> **Research question:** To what extent is anorexia a western phenomenon?
>
> **Topic:** Sport psychology
>
> **Research question:** Is it possible to prevent burnout in professional young athletes?
>
> **Topic:** Depression
>
> **Research question:** Why are more women than men diagnosed with depression?

Criterion B: Introduction (maximum 2 marks)

Descriptor. *The context of the research question is clearly demonstrated. The introduction clearly explains the significance of the topic and why it is worthy of investigation.*

The purpose of the introduction is to make it clear how the research question relates to existing knowledge on the topic. This includes explanation of why the topic chosen is significant and worthy of investigation. There must be details on relevant studies or theories to justify the research question—the student's personal experiences or views are not enough. The studies presented in the introduction could introduce controversies or be supportive of one line of

How you are assessed—the assessment criteria

All extended essays are marked according to the same criteria, and each subject has its own interpretation of the criteria. There are 11 criteria (A to K), worth a total of 36 marks. Only the highest achievement level is mentioned for each criterion level.

argument in a debate, but they are unlikely to answer the research question in an entirely satisfactory manner. The student's research question should point to problem areas in past work, and thereby indicate how his or her essay could help to resolve some of the problems that have been identified.

Criterion C: Investigation (maximum 4 marks)

Descriptor. *An imaginative range of appropriate sources has been consulted and relevant material has been carefully selected. The investigation has been well planned.*

The criterion assesses the extent to which the investigation is planned and based on an appropriate range of sources relevant to the research question. If the research question does not lend itself to a systematic investigation in psychology, the maximum level that can be awarded for this criterion is 2.

Most libraries can help you find relevant sources. University libraries have access to international databases, such as PsychINFO or ProQuest, where you can find articles that you can email to yourself. Your school may also subscribe to databases such as Questia, where you can find books and articles on all kinds of psychological topics. Popular scientific magazines like *Scientific American Mind* can also be used. The online version of the journal from the British Psychological Association, *The Psychologist*, has many relevant articles.

It is expected that you will include a number of relevant academic sources. You can find some of these on the Internet, but be certain to make a copy of the articles or download them to your own files, as they may be removed from the original site at any time. In general, you can use information from university websites where the author(s) has been identified. Avoid using non-academic sources from the Internet. If you have downloaded an article from the Internet, note the date you downloaded it for your bibliography. When you have decided which sources you are going to use for your extended essay, you should print a copy of each one and place them in your research portfolio.

Some places to search online

You can search the following site: Diane Hacker, Research and Documentation Online
www.dianahacker.com/resdoc/p03_c06_s11.html

You can find good research summaries on the website Psychology Matters (http://psychologymatters.apa.org) and on the BPS Research Digest (www.bps.org.uk/publications/rd/rd_home.cfm).

Criterion D: Knowledge and understanding of the topic studied (maximum 4 marks)

Descriptor. *The essay demonstrates very good knowledge and understanding of the topic studied. Where appropriate, the essay clearly and precisely locates the investigation in an academic context.*

If the research question does not lend itself to a systematic investigation in psychology, the maximum level that can be awarded for this criterion is 2.

What is meant by "academic context" is the current state of the field of study under investigation, but only on a level that can reasonably be expected of a pre-university student. For example, to obtain a level 4, it would be sufficient to relate the investigation to the principal lines of inquiry in the relevant field; detailed, comprehensive knowledge is not required. Students are simply expected to use relevant evidence and findings from empirical studies and psychological theories in their essay.

Criterion E: reasoned argument (maximum 4 marks)

Descriptor. *Ideas are presented clearly and in a logical manner. The essay succeeds in developing a reasoned and convincing argument in relation to the research question.*

This criterion assesses the extent to which the essay uses the material collected to present ideas in a logical and coherent manner, and develops a reasoned argument in relation to the research question. Where the research question does not lend itself to a systematic investigation in psychology, the maximum level that can be awarded for this criterion is 2.

The research question is the central focus of the argument which is developed throughout the essay. The best way to build an argument is to follow a logical structure where the most important points are gradually presented, and supplemented with evidence as well as counter-arguments.

Criterion F: Application of analytical and evaluative skills in psychology (maximum 4 marks)

Descriptor. *The essay shows effective and sophisticated application of appropriate analytical and evaluative skills.*

In psychology, this refers to how evaluation and analysis are used in regard to empirical studies, theories, and so on, in support of the argument. One way to do this is to critically evaluate the evidence— for example, by referring to methodological considerations or by acknowledging alternative interpretations. This is known as a counter-claim or acknowledgment. You can see an example of this in the diagram on page 408.

Criterion G: Use of language appropriate to psychology (maximum 4 marks)

Descriptor. *The language used communicates clearly and precisely. Terminology appropriate to psychology is used accurately, with skill and understanding.*

Psychology uses its own terminology, such as psychological concepts, and these should be used throughout the extended essay.

Criterion H: Conclusion (maximum 2 marks)

Descriptor. *An effective conclusion is clearly stated; it is relevant to the research question and consistent with the evidence presented in the essay. It should include unresolved questions where appropriate to psychology.*

The criterion assesses the extent to which the essay incorporates a conclusion that is relevant to the research question and is consistent with the evidence presented in the essay. This means that the conclusion should follow logically as a result of the focused presentation of psychological evidence in support of the research question.

Criterion I: Formal presentation (maximum 4 marks)
Descriptor. *The formal presentation is excellent.*

This criterion assesses the extent to which the layout, organization, appearance, and formal elements of the essay consistently follow a standard format. The formal elements are: title page, table of contents, page numbers, illustrative material, quotations, documentation (including references, citations, and bibliography), and appendices (if used).

Academic research papers are presented according to a standard, and criterion I relates to the extent to which your extended essay conforms to these. An essay that does not include all the required elements cannot receive full marks. If the essay exceeds the word limit of 4000 words, it will score a zero in this criterion.

References

Academic papers have rules for using text from other sources. If you copy and paste a passage from a text, if you quote from it, or if you just summarize the main points, you have to state where the ideas come from.

You should cite sources using a consistent citation style, as outlined by the American Psychological Association (APA) or the British Psychological Society. The following examples are according to the APA style. You can learn more on this at www.dianahacker.com/resdoc/p04_c09_o.html

When citing a study in your EE using APA style, you simply include the year after the name of the researchers:

In a study by Bandura et al. (1961), children watched a Bobo doll…

Your list of references (bibliography) should begin on a new page. The list should be organized alphabetically by each author's last name. The reference list is a list of every work cited in the essay and *only* those cited.

Here is an example of a list of references.

References

Anderson, C.A. and Bushman, B.J. (2001) Effects of violent games on aggressive behavior, aggressive cognition, aggressive affect, physiological arousal, and prosocial behavior: a meta-analytic review of the scientific literature. *Psychological Science*, 12, pp.353–9.

Bandura, A., Ross, D., and Ross, S. (1961) Transmission of aggression through imitation of aggressive models. *Journal of Abnormal and Social Psychology*, 63, pp.575–82. Retrieved 22 October 2007 from http://psychclassics.yorku.ca/Bandura/bobo.htm

Brewer, W.F. and Treyens, J.C. (1981) Role of schemata in everyday memory for places. *Cognitive Psychology*, 13, pp.207–30. Also in Cohen, G., Kiss, G., and Le Voi, M. (1993). *Memory. Current Issues*, 2nd edn, pp.33–4. Buckingham: Open University Press.

Cohen, G., Kiss, G., and Le Voi, M. (1993). *Memory. Current Issues*, 2nd edn. Buckingham: Open University Press.

Steele, C. *Thin Ice—Stereotype Threat and Black College Students*. In TheAtlantic.com. Retrieved 22 June 2008 from www.theatlantic.com/doc/199908/student-stereotype

Criterion J: Abstract (maximum 2 marks)

Descriptor. *The abstract clearly states the research question, how the investigation was undertaken, and the conclusion(s) of the essay.*

The abstract should clearly state all the elements listed in the descriptor to gain maximum marks. If one of these is omitted, or if the abstract exceeds 300 words, it will score a zero.

An example of an abstract of 297 words that includes the research question, how the investigation was undertaken, and the conclusion.

Abstract

This essay investigated the research question: To what extent does psychological stress affect the development of cancer after diagnosis?

The relationship between the immune system and progression of cancer was investigated to see what part of the physiological aspects within an individual seems to contribute in the progression of cancer. Researchers such as Cox (1984) and Pross (in Marx 1980) demonstrated that natural killer cells in the immune system have a specific function of finding and killing cancer cells. Hanna and Burton (1981) demonstrated that metastases elicit a strong response from NK-cells, and since studies (e.g. Stoll 1979) have shown that humans with cancer diseases often die of metastases rather than the actual tumour, these results seem to be highly relevant. The different pathways and interactions between the mind and body were studied, and studies (e.g. Kiecolt-Glaser et al. 1984) showed that psychological stress results in a decrease in NK-cell activity, thus making these people more susceptible to acquiring or further developing a disease (e.g. cancer).

In addition to the physiological aspect of stress, *the transactional model of stress and coping* was studied, where the key is the individual perception of the difference between demand and ability which induces stress, thus functioning on the importance of psychological factors. It was found that coping strategies in cancer patients play a large role in survival. Several longitudinal studies (e.g. Hislop et al. 1987) showed that patients who actively cope with stress associated with the disease live longer than cancer patients with a depressive style of living.

In conclusion, it can be said that psychological stress has a large effect on the development of cancer cells, and coping strategies are crucial. However, cancer diseases are a biological phenomenon that needs treatment—coping strategies only deal with the psychological processes.

This abstract was written by Shazleen Rajan, a Danish student from Nørre Gymnasium in Denmark.

Criterion K: Holistic judgment (maximum 4 marks)

Descriptor. *The essay shows considerable evidence of intellectual initiative, breadth and depth of understanding, and insight.*

Ways of showing the qualities that are rewarded under this criterion could include the following.

- Intellectual initiative could be demonstrated in the choice of topic and research question.
- Insight, as well as breadth and depth of understanding, could be demonstrated in the results of detailed research, a focused and well-informed argument that addresses the research question effectively, and evidence of critical thinking.
- Intellectual initiative could be demonstrated by evidence of a personal approach that could include a reflective approach, involving the views and imagination of the student, to make a unique contribution to understanding the topic.

Index